James Riker

Harlem

It's Origin and Early Annals

James Riker

Harlem
It's Origin and Early Annals

ISBN/EAN: 9783742818218

Manufactured in Europe, USA, Canada, Australia, Japa

Cover: Foto ©ninafisch / pixelio.de

Manufactured and distributed by brebook publishing software
(www.brebook.com)

James Riker

Harlem

HARLEM

(City of New York):

ITS ORIGIN AND EARLY ANNALS.

PREFACED BY

Home Scenes in the Fatherlands;

OR,

Notices of its Founders before Emigration.

ALSO,

Sketches of Numerous Families,

AND THE

RECOVERED HISTORY OF THE LAND-TITLES.

WITH ILLUSTRATIONS AND MAPS.

By JAMES RIKER,

Author of The Annals of Newtown; Life Member of the New York Historical Society; Member also of the Massachusetts Historical Society; The New England Historic-Genealogical Society; The New York Genealogical and Biographical Society; The Long Island Historical Society; The Pennsylvania Historical Society, etc.

NEW YORK:
PRINTED FOR THE AUTHOR.
1881.

MY EARLY AND EXCELLENT FRIEND,

EDGAR KETCHUM,

WHOSE HEARTY INTEREST IN THIS WORK HAS CONTRIBUTED

TO RENDER A TOIL A PLEASURE, AND TO BRING

IT TO A HAPPY ISSUE,

THIS VOLUME

IS

Cordially Inscribed.

GENERAL CONTENTS.

CHAPTER I.

§ 1.

DUNKIRK TO ST. MALO. Pen-sketches of the coasts of Holland, Flanders, Picardy, Normandy, and Brittany. Historic memories awakened. Inklings of localities and persons connected with our subject. Picturesque scenery of the Norman Archipelago. Island of Jersey; home of the Carterets and Pipons. St. Malo quaint and suggestive .... Page 3.

§ 2.

HARLEM: SPRINGS OF ITS HISTORY. Special relations to the countries named. Their archives explored; and with good results, touching our first settlers. These of various nationalities, but mostly Hollanders and French Refugees. Their character bears investigation. Their history invites inquiry .... Page 11.

§ 3.

GLIMPSES OF THE FATHERLANDS. Land of the Huguenots. Retained in the sixteenth century the essential features of its ancient state. Noticeable characteristics of the country and people. Amiens; its civil history. Glance at the national annals down to the Reformation .... Page 16.

CHAPTER II.

AVESNES AND ITS EXILES. French Refugees at Harlem: district whence they came. Walslant, or Walloon Country. Principality of Sedan. The Walloons; origin and character. Avesnes. Its lords and people. Spanish tyranny; persecution of the Reformed. They find refuge at Le Câteau. That city taken by Count Mansfield. Huguenots slain and scattered. Netherland patriots rise in arms. Walloons join them, but soon yield the contest. Liberty crushed; Protestants in despair; many leave. The De Forests flee to Sedan .... Page 27.

CHAPTER III.

OUR SETTLERS FROM FRANCE AND WALSLANT. Huguenots; their history to the Edict of Nantes. Rest under the Edict. Troubles after the death of Henry IV. Louis XIII. sacks their towns and fortresses. A doomed people. Era of our Refugees considered. Status of the Huguenot. Many seek exile. West India colonies. Casier family. La Montagne (Muntanye), Vermilye, Delamater, etc. Picardy and Picards. The Amienois and Amiens; trials of the Huguenots. Two pageants. Demarest. De Labadie preaches reform. Antagonisms. An attack and defence; Tourneur forced to flee. France at war with Spain; hostilities carried into Hainault and Artois. Protestant Walloons escape to Holland and England. Du Four, Oblinus, Kortright, Journeay, Tiebout, Cresson, Bertholf, etc., seek other homes .... Page 44.

CHAPTER IV.

HOLLAND: THE DE FORESTS, AND LA MONTAGNE. Leyden the refuge. Its Walloons, and cloth trade. Jesse de Forest and brothers; family items. Life at Leyden. Remonstrant troubles. The University. Jean de La Montagne, student of medicine. University, how located. The Kloksteeg. Pilgrim Fathers leave for America. Walloons propose the same; not encouraged. War with Spain. De Forest goes to Brazil; dies. Dr. Montanye marries his daughter. De Laet's book, "The New World," stimulates emigration. Tobacco raising promises rich returns. Henry de Forest marries Geertruyt Bornstra; and with his brother Isaac sails for Manhattan........Page 78

CHAPTER V.

EMIGRATION. Amsterdam, chief port of departure. Oppression the prime colonizing agent. Good proof of character. Our colonists: Captain Kuyter, Bronck, De Meyer, Slot, Meyer, Dyckman, Bussing, Terbosch, Benson, Dolsen, Waldron, Sneden, Verveelen and Vander Vin. John Montanye visits Holland and marries. Brevoort, Van Tilburgh, Ackerman, Storm, the Kortrights and Bogert emigrate. French and Walloons—Tourneur, Delamater, Dissosway, Genung, Du Four, Lozier, Cousseau, Cresson, etc. Mannheim colonists—Demarest, Casier, Uzille, Journeay, Oblinus, Parmentier, Du Bois, De Voe, Vermilye, etc. Visitors from Manhattan influence colonization........Page 102.

CHAPTER VI.: 1609–1636.

MANHATTAN. Its discovery. Harlem in its aboriginal state. Schorakapok, or Spuyten Duyvel. Whence this name? Steps to colonize Manhattan Island. Rev. John Robinson. French and Walloon colonists arrive. Locality embraced in our history—Yorkville to Kingsbridge. Van Twiller appropriates Ward's Island; gives Van Curler the Otterspoor. Aboriginal Harlem as viewed from McGown's heights. Great Kill, or Harlem River. Papparinamin. The Hellegat. Muscoota, Rechawanes and Schorakin located. Indian names to be cherished. Muscoota, or, as afterwards called, Montanye's Flat, first of these localities to attract the European........Page 121.

CHAPTER VII.: 1636–1640.

SETTLEMENTS. The De Forests arrive; granted Muscoota. Dr. Montanye follows. Progress on the Flat. New and trying experiences. "O solitude! where are the charms?" Van Curler begins improvements. Van Twiller makes Barent Blom his overseer. Great and Little Barent's Islands; why so called. Henry de Forest dies. Montanye looks after the plantation. Daily fare. The widow De Forest marries Hudde. Hans Bergen. Hudde's patent. Hudde and wife visit Holland. The farm sold. Bought by Montanye. Claes Swits leases Van Curler's land. It is sold to Van Keulen of Amsterdam. Account of Swits. Van Keulen's Hook. Arrival of Kuyter and Bronck. Kuyter gets Schorakin; calls it Zegendal. Jochem Pieters' Flat. Montanye's farm named Vredendal. Hudde and wife return. Montanye gets his deed. Bronck at Ranachqua; calls his home Emmaus........Page 139.

CHAPTER VIII.: 1640–1645.

INDIAN TROUBLES. Friendly relations with the natives of mutual benefit. Peace broken. Kieft attacks the Raritans. Bloody retaliation on Staten

Island. A Wickquaskeek kills Claes Swits. His tribe screen him. Kieft wants to chastise them; the Twelve Men advise delay. The tobacco crop. Kuyter unable to ship his; Montanye's crop damaged. The Doctor loses his wife. Swits' murder unatoned for; others follow. Time to act; an expedition. Indians alarmed, sue for peace. Peace-council at Emmans. Farmers keep at work. Kuyter as church-builder. The Mahicans war upon the Wickquaskeeks. These fly for safety to the Dutch. Kieft seizes the chance to slaughter them. The savages avenged upon the settlers. Kieft and the Otterspoor. Peace again patched up. Death of Bronck. Montanye leases his farm. Indians resume hostilities. Settlers fly to Fort Amsterdam. Kuyter depicts their distresses. Cry to Holland for help. Colonists turn soldiers; invade the Indian country. Savages burn Kuyter's house. He and Kieft dispute about it. Peace for the third time; "solid and lasting"....................................Page 152.

CHAPTER IX.: 1645–1650.

LAND PATENTS: KUYTER'S TRIALS. Sibout Claessen secures a title to Hoorn's Hook. Dr. Vander Donck buys Papparinamin Island. Matthys Jansen gets a patent for Papparinamin on Manhattan side. Tobias Teunissen. Jansen-Aertsen patent, since the Dyckman Homestead,—*Inwood*. Montanye marries. Vredendal patent. Isaac de Forest gets a title. Kuyter's opposition to Kieft. He and Melyn arraigned by the ex-Director, before Stuyvesant and Council, for contempt. Are fined and banished. Sent away in the ship with Kieft and Bogardus; are wrecked, and the two latter perish. Kuyter and Melyn reach Holland and appeal to the States-General. Arrest of judgment. Stuyvesant summoned to answer for his severity. Kuyter, on returning to Manhattan, has his property and offices restored. Engages in trade. Dangerous to live on the Flats. Few places occupied. Peter Beeck buys a plantation at Hellgate. De Forest sells his plantation to Beeckman. Kuyter's victory a triumph of popular rights....................................Page 162.

CHAPTER X.: 1651–1656.

NEW EFFORTS, BUT SAD FAILURES. Kuyter resumes his plantation, with Stuyvesant, etc., as co-partners. Their contract. Country yet disturbed; Kuyter, before proceeding, applies for a groundbrief. Public danger imminent. Indians murder Beeck and his workmen. Threaten Kuyter, Beeckman and others. Alarming rumors afloat. Kuyter's popularity. Elected schepen. Is killed by the Indians. Sorrow at his fate. Honors awaited him. Steps to settle his estate. More trouble. Savages on a bloody raid. Slay Tobias Teunissen near Spuyten Duyvel, and Cornelis Swits. Beeckman's successor. All the farms laid waste; the district abandoned by the settlers....................................Page 174.

CHAPTER XI.: 1656–1660.

NEW HAERLEM FOUNDED: ITS COURT AND CHURCH. Plan to settle isolated farms, a failure. Resolved to form a village on the Swits and Kuyter lands. Grounds for this measure. Ordinance thereupon. Work begun; a village plot and farming lots laid out. The latter, why so narrow. Named *Nieuw Haerlem*. Hindrances. Stuyvesant urges on the work. Guarded by soldiers. Indian war at Esopus. Military officers for Harlem. Court of Justice instituted. Church formed. Do. Zyperus engaged to preach. John Montanye is chosen deacon. Zyperus' previous history obscure. Only a licentiate. Harlem people join Selyn's church at the Bouwery. No church built at Harlem yet, nor for years later...Page 185.

CHAPTER XII. : 1661–1662.

REARRANGEMENT OF LANDS: NEW ALLOTMENTS. Grain plenty, but no mill. One projected. The Montanyes wish to form a hamlet at Vredendal. Council refuse; will hinder New Harlem. The latter growing. Settlers' names, etc. Scandinavian element. Calls for more land. Order thereupon. Van Keulen's Hook allotted. Grantees. First "Harlem Land Case." John Montanye is Town Clerk. Gets part of Vredendal (the Point); the Flat to be divided up. Settlers ask Director to modify the terms on which they took up land. Declines. Applicants for lots on Montanye's Flat. First owners. Wm. Montanye a resident. The alienation of the Flat indisputable. Land speculation. Conveyancing; model Deed. Deeds, Wills, etc.; how executed. Cattle-herder employed. The contract. He gets in trouble; is superseded. Sneden dies; and his wife. Property sold. Slot made building master. Fence masters. Some chief men fined. Mr. Muyden....................................Page 201.

CHAPTER XIII. : 1663–1665.

STIRRING EVENTS; END OF THE DUTCH RULE. A wedding; rustic custom; a riot. Death of Dericksen and Casier. Petition again for relief in paying for their land. Granted. Indian massacre at Esopus. Montanye's sister a captive. Harlem stockaded. Military companies organized; arms and ammunition. Guns mounted. A detachment goes to Esopus. Wickquaskecks camp near Harlem; creates alarm, but the Sachem explains; brings tidings good and bad. Asks leave to fish. Powder distributed. News of an armistice. More settlers from Fatherland. Do. Zyperus goes to Virginia. Want a *voorleser*. Montanye willing to serve. Petitioned for; appointed. Le Maire arrives. Patents taken out. Swits' widow surrenders her land. Calves on Little Barent's Island. Slaves. Saw mill. Country menaced by neighboring English. General Assembly. Peace with the Indians. English fleet takes New Amsterdam, etc. Called New York. Conflicting opinions at Harlem. Waldron retires thither. Some leave for Holland. Montanye disaffected. Moesman sells to Capt. Delavall. Hymenial....................................Page 218.

CHAPTER XIV. : 1665–1666.

RELUCTANT YIELDING TO ENGLISH RULE. Local authority suspended. Drunken Indians commit abuses. The Schout's disaffection. Nicolls' order thereupon. Harlem to form part of the City. Town officers discharged. Waldron made constable; to appoint magistrates and hold court. De Meyer's tenant absconds; leads to an issue with the new court. He comes out best. The court carry things imperiously; banish an inhabitant. Waldron accuses Teunissen of stealing a quilt. He resents it; sues for slander. Waldron has the advantage. Comments. Bad feeling engendered. Other cases cited. Demarest buys land; removes here. Monis Staeck assaults the herder; is fined. Litigious times. Move to erect a church. Stuyvesant feasted. More garden plots laid out and sold. The church up and inclosed. A good wife defamed. The Mayor sees her righted. The costs. Her experiences....................................Page 239.

CHAPTER XV. : 1666–1667.

THE NICOLLS PATENT; THE COURT, MILL, CHURCH. Grazing customs. Order to draw a line for more range for horses and cattle. Governor directs a patent to be drafted. THE PATENT. Not satisfactory, and why. Tourneur "pays" Waldron. Both cautioned by the Mayor's Court. Waldron takes his discharge as constable. New officers appointed. Instruc-

tions and oath. Still at work on the church. Order; trespasses by cattle. Sabbath workers arrested. Old story about Tourneur revived. Capt. Delavall. His antecedents. Proposes improvements. The town acts upon it. Verveelen to run the ferry and tavern. Bronck's Land and Little Barent's Island. Col. Morris buys the former. Town builds a mill-dam; Delavall a mill. The Mill Camp. Montanye voted leave to build on his Point. Village expanding; other house lots laid out. Church finished. Burial place located, etc. Meadows granted Tourneur; the *Bussing Meadows*. Montanye gets the church-lot's meadows.....Page 250.

CHAPTER XVI. : 1667–1669.

NEW NICOLLS PATENT; THE FERRY; RUPTURE WITH ARCHER, ETC. Petition for a Patent. Town growing in importance. Dairies. Knoet the herder. Verveelen; his ordinary, ferry and rates. Smuggles beer. Compromised. Ferry lease. Beer drinking. Brewers. Matthys Jansen's heirs and John Archer threaten trouble. THE HARLEM PATENT. Nagel, etc., fined as rebels. Capt. Delavall going to England. Tourneur, as agent, lets land to W. Gerritsen. Archer buys the Jansen-Aertsen patent. Nicolls won't confirm it. Tourneur bargains for Hoorn's Hook patent. Inhabitants protest. Queer conduct of Verveelen's negro. Baignoux misses his *novias*. Harker ignores the ferry. Trouble with Archer. His history. Gets lands at Fordham. His cattle trespass; are seized. The Jansen-Aertsen patent awarded to Harlem. The ferry incommodious. Spuyten Duyvel to be viewed. Tourneur craves Hoorn's Hook. Gets land on Cromwell's Creek. Death of the miller. Vessel built. An *erfje* granted Pelszer. A wagon-road ordered between New York and Harlem. Horses, etc., to be branded. Ferry taken to Spuyten Duyvel. Contract with Verveelen. He to be constable of Fordham. Mill repairs. Delavall returns. Hue and cry after a slave. Montanye's Indian deed. Indians claim other land. De Meyer sells to Kortright and Low ancestors. Calf pasture; its rules. J. Cresson makes his will; sells his farm. Le Roy names Tourneur sole heir.......................................Page 266.

CHAPTER XVII. : 1670–1672.

VILLAGE LIFE; HARLEM TWO CENTURIES AGO. Maturity; accruing responsibilities. Porkers missing; Tippett suspected; an inquiry. Branding, etc. Wolters dies. Waldron buys Dolsen's house. Delamater's will. Waldron and Verveelen divide meadows. W. Gerritsen mulct for poor fences; his *vrouw* scolds Waldron. Payment on the Patent. Freeholders and lands. Vermilye sells; sale void. Wolters' curators. Cresson *vs.* Delamater. Kortright to keep tavern. An *erf* voted J. Demarest. Waldron sells Nagel an *erfje*, etc. Nagel and Vermilye marry his daughters. Jansen-Aertsen patent. Order to pay claimants 300 gl. Richard takes a bond. L. Gerritsen sells Karsten's *erf* and garden. Legacy at Leyden. New *voorleser*, Vander Vin. Martino leases town lands. Cresson denounces the magistrates; is arrested. Disosway *vs.* Archer. Colevelt *vs.* Le Roy. Pound ordered. Town debts; accounts audited. Cupid captures Meyer and others. Pelszer sues Verveelen. Use of an *erfje* granted Carstensen. Road to City impassable. Lease by Lourens Jansen. Bogert buys Montanye's farm. Journeay sells Storm his Brooklyn lands. Bogert makes his will. Mayor's Court, met at Harlem, tries Archer. Fordham petty causes to be heard at Harlem. Archer's leases. Tax for the voorleser fails; people prefer voluntary giving. Fines settled. Archer gets a patent for Fordham. Claessen, Valentine ancestor. Indian deed for De Voe's Point. Tourneur makes his will. Demarest loses a child; makes his will. Leases Moertje Davids' Fly. Montanye's deed for his Point. The "wagon path" to New York..........Page 291.

CHAPTER XVIII. : 1672–1673.

THE DORP OR VILLAGE; INCIDENTS AND INSIGHTS. Demarest *versus* Delamater; assault. Death of Montanye. His estate. Harlem church to have an elder. Deacons' accounts. Church-days observed. *Allerheyligen.* Tippett again, with Hunt and others. Death of Capt. Morris and wife; leave but "one poor blossom." Order; meadows on Fordham side. Vander Vin made secretary. Waldron *vs.* Tourneur; assault. Church lot let to Mrs. Montanye. Monthly-mail; New York to Boston. Town patents; none under Stuyvesant. Houselots to be taxed for town expenses. List. Accounts to be overhauled; Roelofsen sent for. Journeay makes his will. Accounts audited. Creditors. List of freeholders and lands. Owners of Montanye's Flat form a combination. A history connected with this Flat. Cresson and Carbosie make wills. A big row. Tourneur lets land at Cromwell's Creek; his death. Dyckman and Bussing marry. A stroll through New Harlem in 1673. Homes of the chief residents. In what style a magistrate lived....................Page 314.

CHAPTER XIX. : 1673–1674.

REOCCUPATION BY THE DUTCH. Minute by Vander Vin; recapture of New York. Official letter received. Hearty response. Town officers appointed; swear allegiance. Commonalty take the oath. Roll of names. Cut pickets for city defences. Morris and Delavall estates. Barent Waldron, messenger. Carbosie *vs.* Bogert. Delamater fined for striking Adrian Sammis. Plan to alternate crops on the farm lots. Instructions to schout and magistrates. Fordham people *vs.* Archer. Delavall's affairs. Petition for his out-garden. Vander Vin retained. Contributors. Delamater will not give. Some Englishmen threaten to rob and burn. Action taken. A Night Watch; Jansen (Kortright) made captain. The Roll. Seasons for thanksgiving, fasting, and prayer. Proclamation. Death of Gerritsen. Alarms continue. Beado arrested. His offence. Branded and banished. English expected; fears increase. Letter from the Governor. A panic. Kiersen and Michielsen tried for shooting a hog. Curious examination. Search for horses of late English officials. How land sold. Peace. Preparing for it. Litigation. Town officers chosen. Church accounts audited. Fruits of Nieuwenhuysen's ministry. Hot heads from Westchester alarm the villagers. Inquiry. Country reverts to the English....................Page 336.

CHAPTER XX. : 1674–1677.

ENGLISH RULE RESTORED; REFUGEES; CAPT. CARTERET; INDIAN WAR; LAND GRANTS; SPUYTEN DUYVEL OCCUPIED. Accession of French. Schout and schepens superseded. Bastiaensen (Kortright) hires Tourneur farm. Tourneurs still vexed by story of the homicide. Mayor's Court checks it. Voorleser continued. Delamater and Demarest refuse to give. Terbosch to be dunned. Jansens divide their lands. Le Count dies. Capt. James Carteret. His antecedents. Comes to Harlem. On a committee to get the patent confirmed. Palmer assaults Gano, while picking cherries. Indian outbreak at Narraganset. Fear at the news. Precautions; watch, etc. Verveelen cited to the watch. Won't leave his ferry. Vexed by Archer, who abducts his goods. Verveelen sues. New alarms. Our Indians ordered within Hellgate. Some are stopped, passing Harlem. General arming. Night watch; the roll and rules. Indians to plant at Spuyten Duyvel. Watch re-formed. De Voe, from Mannheim. Passes for Hellgate. Indian troubles end. Farming interests; concerning fences. Straitened for land. Report of Andros' grants; inhabitants petition. Persons proper to have land. Van Keulen's Hook surveyed. Coopers

stopped cutting timber; appeal. Town cuts stockades for the City. Clerk's house repaired. Junior David Demarest will not pay toward it; gets into trouble. Senior Demarest and Delamater at issue with the town about clerk's salary. What now ensued. The Demarests sell out. The elder buys land on the Hackensack. Town debts. An assessment. Andros' grants cause anxiety; Carteret, etc., deputed to see the Governor; an episode. Andros very gracious; will send a surveyor. Elphinstone grant, etc. Ryder lays out lots for the Harlem people. Dispute over meadow on Spuyten Duyvel; Meyer in trouble. Dyckman and Nagel secure five lots at Spuyten Duyvel. Lease them. Dyckman Homestead. Large order for palisades............ ....Page 356

CHAPTER XXI.: 1677–1682.

THE FRENCH LEAVING; NEW TOWN HOUSE; LAND QUESTIONS; LABADISTS; CAPT. CARTERET; SALE OF MOERTJE DAVIDS' FLY. Nicholas de Vaux *versus* Cresson. Sieur Dubuisson. De Vaux removes. The French leaving. Magister. Town accounts. Subscribers to clerk's salary. The Demarests depart. Compromise with Vander Vin. House to be rebuilt. Mr. Kip dies; his widow assigns her contract for timber; Tourneur to fill it. Vander Vin mortgages. Suits about lines on Van Keulen's Hook. New officers. Codrington weds Miss Delavall. Robbery at De Voe's. Brevoort and Nagel buy out Cresson, who leaves. Land case; Tourneur, etc., *vs.* Col. Morris. Labadists visit Harlem. Entertained by Waldron. Pick up stories about Carteret. Call at Valentine's house. Object of their visit; make proselytes. Seem to confound Waldron with Vander Vin. A word for Carteret. He goes to England. Carstensen dies. Robinson buys Saw Kill farm. Oblinus *vs.* Bogert; meadows. Du Four *vs.* Bogert. "True Lips." Bear hunt; Rev. Charles Wolley. Robert Wolley and partner buy half of Robinson's farm. Timber for Major Cuyler. Contract for town house given out. Sale of Moertje Davids' Fly. Outside owners. Tourneur, etc., *vs.* Morris; verdict for plaintiffs. Morris ignores it, and holds possession. Mending highway, Barent Waldron, absent; Constable Vermilye refuses to collect the fine. Offended dignity. Work on town house. Proposed to bridge the Papparinamin; but ferry-lease extended. Sieur Dubuisson. Journeay's estate. Five lives lost in Hellgate. Dr. De Forest. Precaution in choosing town officers. Tax to pay for town house, etc. Proprietors and freeholds.. ....Page 369.

CHAPTER XXII.: 1682–1685.

INCIDENTS; DEATH OF DELAVALL, ARCHER, DELAMATER AND VANDER VIN; TOURNEUR *vs.* MORRIS; DONGAN'S ASSEMBLY; TOWN COURT REMODELLED; HALF-WAY HOUSE; GLOUDIE'S POINT OCCUPIED, ETC. Carbosie; given use of land near Bogert's meadows. Bogert scolds the magistrates. Makes the *amende honorable.* Delamater forced to pay up. Barlow *vs.* Loodon. Tourneur, etc., *vs.* Young. Young sells to Holmes. Old pastors dead. Selyns returns. To preach at Harlem once a year. Death of Capt. Delavall; his will, etc. Mrs. Tourneur, sick, makes a will, survives; her sons Daniel and Jaco marry. How the Tourneur lands were finally divided. Brevoort leases Church Farm. Hedding. Balgnoux sells. Ald. Cox buys out Robinson. Capt. KIDD. Gov. Dongan arrives; a General Assembly; Harlem joins in choosing delegates. Tourneur *vs.* Morris; proceedings at large. Local doings. Charter of Liberties; its chief provisions. Counties and courts erected. Common Council include Harlem in the Out Ward. Its court, etc. Viervant. Postmael; the Post ancestor. Commissioners meet. Give Waldron a deed. Deacons visit Carbosie; his will, death. Archer dies suddenly. Nagel's slave fires his barn; hangs himself. His body burned. Patents called for

with reference to quit-rent. Kortright builds the Half-Way House. Tourneur *vs.* Morris; final decision. Meyer again in office. Death of Vander Vin. Succeeded by Tiebout. Barent Waldron settles at the New Lots. Glaudie's Point sold; bought by Resolved Waldron, Barent gets the deed. Theunis Idens's and Jacob De Key's purchases. Grant to Bickley, De Vos's Point...Page 430.

CHAPTER XXIII.: 1685–1687.

Wolves; Delavall estate; tenures; tenths cancelled; new stone church; great maize land; Dongan Patent; quit rent; corporation rights; Indian claim; common lands; French gone; Dutch manners and customs. Woodlands infested by wolves; a general hunt. John Delavall makes an exchange with the town; his father's executor. Land Tenures; their history. The feudal tenure modified. Free and common socage. Quit Rent. The tithes never exacted. Quit Rents compounded for. Levied and paid. The tax list; exhibits the lands occupied. Village regulations; refuse straw, chimney ladders. Losses by fire. Lead to building outside. Taxed for clerk's salary. New arrangement with Do. Selyns. New church. People begin the work. Carpenter's contract. First service. Payments. Dolsen and Kiersen lease Great Maize Land. Improvements; Hoorn's Hook, Great Barent's Island. Harlem Patent to be confirmed. Important saving clause in the New York Charter affecting said patent. Order to stay the waste of timber. Nagel and Dyckman in law about a goose! Agreement; that the common lands be drawn *pro rata*, according to the estates. The Dongan Patent. Paid for. Obvious intent of the patent to confirm rights already granted. Did not the City Charter trench on those rights? Indian claim satisfied. Lands still in commons. Taken up by allotments in 1691 and 1712. History of these divisions important, but hitherto unknown; given in Appendix. Closing remarks. French families nearly all gone; last word about them. Court records negative evidence of good morals. Capable of self-government. Succeeding times eventful, but more easily traced. A staid Dutch society. Style of living, farming, habits, and customs; topics talked about, tales of Fatherland; general thrift; slow to adopt English modes and manners. Their history a legacy of useful lessons..............Page 445.

CHAPTER XXIV.

Notices of the Patentees and their Heirs or Successors. Benson, Bogert, Brevoort, Bussing, Delamater, Dyckman, Haldron, Kiersen, Kortright, Low, Montanye, Myer, Nagel, Oblenis, Parmentier, Tourneur, Vermilye, Verveelen, Waldron....................................Page 480.

*** For notice of other patentees not named here see Index.

See Contents of the Appendix on p. 570.

The Abbreviations used in this work are: *ab.*, for about; *ae.*, for aged; *anc.*, for ancestor; *a. q. r.*, for acres, quarters, rods; *b.*, for born; *br.*, for brother; *brs.*, brothers; *ch.*, for child, *chn.*, for children; *chh.*, for church; *d.*, for died, death; *desc.*, for descendant, descended; *dr.*, for daughter, *drs.*, daughters; *d. y.*, died young; *f.* or *fl.*, for florin; *fa.*, for father; *gd-fa.*, for grandfather; *gt-gd-fa.*, for great-grandfather; *gl.*, for guilder; *hus.*, for husband; *inf.*, for infancy; *m.*, for married, marriage; *mem.*, for member; *mo.*, for mother; *nfa.*, for no further account; *sr.*, for sister, *srs.*, sisters; *st.*, for silver, or street; *unm.*, for unmarried; *w.*, for wife; *wid.*, for widow; *yr.*, for year; *yrs.*, years; *Corn.*, for Cornelius; *Hend.*, for Hendrick; *Joh.*, for Johannes, etc.

ILLUSTRATIONS.

ACKNOWLEDGMENTS.

It is obvious that any work like the following, made up of innumerable details, must take character for credibility largely from the reputation of its author; since it is scarcely possible to cite an authority for each of the multitudinous facts presented, whatever of force and value such a feature might impart to the work. And when it is considered how often statements rest on logical inference, or result from careful comparison and analysis, the difficulty of giving authorities becomes more apparent, though from such processes spring much of the life and spirit of the narrative, which the tame letter of the record fails to evoke.

For a general indication of the sources whence the present author has drawn his facts, the incidental references in the ensuing pages to manuscript and printed works must suffice. And however pleasant it would be to particularise the numerous correspondents who have kindly favored the author with facts in their possession, the mere mention of their names would fill too large a space in these pages. To all such he now tenders his very cordial thanks. Correspondents abroad, who have thus aided him, are noticed at page 14.

Special encouragement in his work, received from Mr. Henry G. De Forest, Mr. S. Whitney Phoenix, and Mr. Samuel Riker, and his estimable kinsmen, demands more than a passing acknowledgment, and lays the author under a lasting debt of gratitude.

HISTORY

OF

HARLEM.

CHAPTER I.

§ 1. DUNKIRK TO ST. MALO.

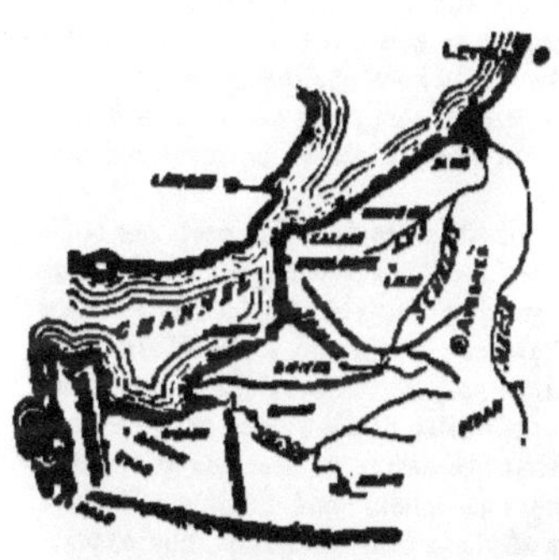

AS the coaster bound for St. Malo leaves the old Flemish port of Dunkirk, now the nor'-most city of France; having passed through the narrow artificial sluice-way which stretches out from the town a mile or more across the broad strand, to the open waters between the inner and outer line of sands forming the harbor or roads of Dunkirk, and cleared the ruined walls of castles *Verd* and *Bonne Espérance*, those trusty sentinels once guarding on either side its mouth; he must still feel his way cautiously, to shun the exterior shoals, the *Braque* and *Tartre* banks, which with others serve as a natural breakwater to shelter the roadstead from the wash of the sea. Safely past these impediments, he spreads his broad canvas to the breeze, and shapes his course. No trip more hazardous than that to St. Malo; an epitome, as it were, of life's voyage in those old lands—ever a struggle, but neither aimless nor fruitless, as shall appear.

How exhilarating the scene now opened to view—this grand sweep of unique landscape and wide waters! On the left the eye takes in the coast—a line of low sand-hills, but half concealing picturesque villages, with their tall spires and busy wind-mills, and in the distant offing snowy sails wafted on their inward or outward mission; while again, sternwise, the blue waters of the German Ocean spread out expansively far northward between the English and the Netherland shores. Unlike the zigzag coast whither our vessel is bound, the latter of these shores stretches north-easterly with a seeming even line; but beyond the vision curves gently to the north, skirting the exterior sides of the islands of Zeeland and the low dykes of Holland, till, at full eighty leagues or more, it reaches that insular pilot station, the Texel, behind whose sheltering heights and hamlets the ships of Amsterdam, Hoorn, and other cities on the Zuyder Zee usually anchor to await a clearance for their destined port.

The land ahead of us trending nearly south-west, our well-laden, clumsy galiot skirts for about twelve leagues the borders of Flanders and Picardy, passing the old Anglo-French town Calais, and the Straits of Dover; while the white chalk cliffs which here line the coast now project to form the capes Blanc and Gris-Nez, the abrupt termini also of a highland range which, penetrating the interior, parts the basins or sections of country drained by the rivers l'Escaut or Scheldt and Somme. Beyond the last-named and bolder of these two headlands, our experienced skipper alters his course to due south, as the coast bends; old Neptune kindly granting a fair breeze down the Channel, for better to scud under bare poles before the brawling tempest, than to encounter fierce head-winds, or the bewildering fog common on this coast, either of which might spoil his adventure.

A few miles bring us off the harbor of Boulogne—to its name often added, for distinction, *sur mer*, or "on the sea." Claiming—though in rivalry to Wissen, an ancient port between the capes just mentioned—to be the *Portus Iccius* whence Julius Cæsar embarked his legions for the conquest of Britain, Boulogne has been the favorite thoroughfare for travel between England and France from remote times. The old walled town is seen back upon the heights, looking from seaward quite as in centuries past; while on the flat nearer the sea has grown up the lower town, a populous suburb, where then were but two or three old monasteries and a few cottages, nestled around the church St. Nicholas. Its once famous light-house, known as the *Tour d'Ordre*, but to seamen as the Old Man of Boulogne, lives only in tradition and the ruins which yet mark its site on the rocks at the entrance of the harbor,—an old graystone octagon tower of Roman origin, which after battling the storms of over a thousand years, was finally undermined and destroyed by the sea in 1644.

The white cliffs, here so noticeable a feature of the French coast, presently give place again to sand downs; while our progress along the tedious stretch of low-lying country which borders Ponthieu is marked successively by the mouths of the rivers Canche and Authie, and the broad estuaries of the Somme. Scarce an object is presented to fix the attention or beguile the weary hours, save now and then a picturesque group of huts, tenanted by hardy Picard fishermen, or distant glimpse of town or spire—perhaps a craft or two leaving the mouth of the Somme, with freights from its little port of St. Valery, or the quaint old town of Abbeville, or from Amiens, the populous capital of Picardy; these two, with their important manufactures, seated far up the valley of the Somme. Imperceptibly steals over one a sense of dreariness, which is only deepened by the splash of waters and creak of cordage, or even the hoarse wild scream of the sea-birds that sail across the vessel's track, bound to either shore.

But hoary History, here dealing with marvellous prodigality, has strown these shores with memories of past centuries far more enduring than their old cities or crumbling cliffs. Under his inspiration the various scenes that meet the eye assume new interest, and become instinct with the heroic forms and deeds which crowd upon the mental vision. Carried back to the bellicose days of the chivalry, now the potent Duke of Normandy, in ambition rivalling a Cæsar, musters his three thousand vessels from the several Norman ports at St. Valery-sur-Somme, and sails to seize the English crown, and win the title of the "Conqueror." Or to the martial times of Edward III. and of Henry V., successors of this same Anglo-Norman king, as with gallant hosts they traverse the region of the Somme, and against great odds gain the brilliant victories of Cressy and Agincourt. The past revivified becomes as the present, while its magic creations impart a new zest to the voyage. E'en our hardy skipper, versed only in nautical science, in winds, clouds, and storms, in bars, reefs, and light-houses, spins from out his store of local yarns something to enliven many a spiritless scene. It's perchance a bold sea-fight 'twixt the rival neighbors so long contesting the mastery of the Channel; or yet some touching story of fleeing victims of persecution or tyranny, of whose heroism and sufferings not the half has been told! How exceeding probable that it was the experience of Huguenot exiles who a little more than two centuries ago found a refuge at Harlem, most of whom came from this section of France we are now skirting! Along the fruitful valley of the Somme were scattered the homes of our Demarest, Tourneur, Cresson, and Disosway, not to enlarge the number; most of them prominent among the Harlem settlers, and heads of well-known families hereafter to be noticed. Others will be brought to light as we extend our voyage.

The eye is now sensibly relieved, as the coast again becomes elevated, and the chalk cliffs reappear, crowned with green waving tufts of forests and orchards. At ten miles beyond the Somme, and eighteen leagues from Gris-Nez, is visible the gap or opening at the river Bresle, which marks the southern limit of Picardy. Now, putting helm aport, we bear south-west along the rock-bound coast of Normandy, its continuity only broken here at intervals by the openings through which the rivers fall into the sea, and which form several secure harbors, as Dieppe, St. Valery-en-Caux, and Fécamp, near the latter of which the bluffs attain an altitude of seven hundred feet. Dieppe is associated with two of our settlers, Lozier and Lemaire.

Bearing westerly from Cape La Heve, near the broad mouth of the Seine—just within which lies Havre, the modern and handsome seaport of Paris, and on the opposite shore the antiquated town of Honfleur, its harbor choked with great sandbanks—we now skirt the flat, rich grazing district of Normandy, with its numerous villages, and fine old cities Caen and Bayeux. We must give the coast a wide margin to avoid the dreaded "Black Cows," and the yet more dangerous rocky reef that lines it for some eighteen miles, full half a league from shore, and which, proving fatal to a vessel of the Spanish Armada, took its name, the "Calvados."

The peninsula of Cotentin, running northerly twenty miles beyond the shore line of the Norman meadows, ends, on the side we are approaching, in the picturesque *falaise* or cliffs of Barfleur, which stand boldly forth, as if to greet our vessel in its track. But passing this cape, and the harbor of Cherbourg, noted as the last town abandoned by the English, when finally driven from Normandy in 1451, and now a famous naval station, we reach, after a run of a hundred and fifty miles from the Bresle, where we first struck the line of Normandy, the western limit of this large province, at Cape La Hague. Bearing to larboard under favoring winds, we double the cape, and stand again due south, up the boisterous race between the island of Alderney and the main, in rough weather extremely dangerous from its conflicting currents, and run inside Guernsey and the other channel islands—those ancient appendages of Normandy, and now more Norman even than the mother province, though held by the English. The rocky headlands on the main serve to mark our progress—the stately Jobourg, Gros-Nez and Nez-de-Carteret, respectively five, ten, and twenty miles south of Cape La Hague. Leaving to the left the last of these, sheltering within its projecting arm the village and small haven of Carteret, distinguishable by its line of yellow sands, we pass on the right the low rocky islets of Ecrehou, and some miles farther, "old" Jersey, in area only equal to our Staten Island, but the largest island of the Norman Archipelago, and the home, formerly, of the Carterets and the Pipons, not unknown in Harlem story. Difficult of approach on account of its cordon of rocks, reefs, and shoals, we pass near its massive but ruined castle of Mont Orgueil, so picturesque in its mantle of ivy, and crowning a high and craggy spur that juts into the sea.

A more than panoramic beauty captivates the eye at each stage in this passage, enhanced by that which so multiplies the perils of the navigation. Huge rocky *débris*, environing these islands, abound on every hand, now a solitary rock, now a confused cluster, but oft taking most fantastic forms. Some tower majestically, like the Caskets, off Alderney, above the highest reach of the billows, when, storm-driven, they break upon them in such grandeur and fury. Others with black heads but just visible amid silvery foam and spray, or lying in fatal ambush beneath the surface, prove the grave of many a hapless bark, especially when enshrouded in sea fog, and the helmsman unable to discern the friendly buoys.

Fitting resort for the old Druids was Jersey, with its interior of umbrageous groves and silent vales, where now are rural villages and farm seats; and its exterior, on the north side of bold ragged cliffs, rising in places over three hundred feet, and on its southern of deep sandy bays, within the largest of which is seated its chief town, St. Helier. Everywhere intersected by winding lanes, nearly hidden by bordering hedges; banks of mosses and ferns, rich shrubbery, and vine-embowered, cottage-like houses, add new beauty at every turn among its highly rustic walks. Toward the western side yet stands the venerable parish church of St. Brelade, now in its eighth century, and to the north of this, the church of St. Ouen; in the first of which the Pipons, in the last the De Carterets, Lords of St. Ouen, worshipped, and were entombed. And hard by St. Ouen's Church, the old granite manor-house, till late the home of the De Carterets, still lifts its quaint double gables, an object of curious legends with the islanders.* Remarkable not only for its scenery, but for its unique government and society, remains of an old feudal aristocracy modelled in the twelfth century by King John of England, its industrious people, busied with their dairies, cider-making, oyster beds, shipbuilding and maritime pursuits, are more of a study. Mostly Protestants, of simple manners, very frugal, living quite after the French mode, and speaking only the harsh unwritten *patois* known as Norman French, except in town, where modern French—used in all local court pro-

* This ancient seat of the *De Carterets* (we condense from "Scenic Beauties of the Island of Jersey," by Philip J. Ouless, Esq., of St. Helier) is situated in the parish of St. Ouen, from which it takes its name, about six miles from St. Helier, and a short furlong from the parish church, on the military road from that town to St. Ouen's Bay. To the old castellated mansion, believed to have been built about the reign of Edward I., are annexed the more modern wings, which project in front, and are not older than the time of Charles II. Entering its low oaken door, which seems to have remained unchanged for ages, a fact is recalled, not least among its pleasing reminiscences, that here the last-named monarch found refuge when, a proscribed exile, he arrived in Jersey in 1649, and was proclaimed king, sharing the hospitality of his brave and faithful subject, and which he afterwards so well repaid. But for this (strange as it may seem), some episodes in Harlem history could not be written!

ceedings—is more popular than English, they resemble an old Huguenot community; and not without cause, as many of that worthy class took refuge here during the series of persecutions in France which culminated at the Revocation of the Edict of Nantes.

Our course from Jersey lying southward, we descry in the distance, upon the charming heights of the Cotentin, another landmark welcome to the coaster—the tall spire of the cathedral at Coutances. Little else can be seen of this much-admired structure, though its huge symmetrical form so towers above the town—and anon its receding figure falls far astern. On crossing the Bight of La Manche, formed by the sudden deflection of the coast to the westward, and between the rocky isles the Chausseys and the more terrible Minquières, Brittany's rugged border lifts to view its bald cliffs, so wild and desolate in their grandeur; most conspicuous the headland of Cancale, forming a bay in the depth of the Bight, in which lies the islet of Mont St. Michel, with its famous old abbey high up on the precipitous rock. We must forego a visit to the grand abbey hall, where the knights of St. Michel (the creation of Louis XI. in 1469) long held their banquets, and pass untasted those delectable bivalves, here abounding, and so toothsome when taken from the half-shell! We soon reach the St. Malo roads, and the insulated town of the same name, our place of destination, with its fleet of traders and its fishing craft. Bars and reefs obstruct the entrance; but now at the mooring, we leave our matter-of-fact skipper to sell his lading, and the jolly tar to rest his sea-legs at his usual resort in the town, while we proceed to explore this quaintly primitive place, which seems to carry one

St. Ouen or De Carteret Manor-House, Jersey.

back into some by-gone century. We are not now in Jersey, as is apparent! Hidden within strong walls black with age, and seated on a rocky peninsula, which becomes an islet at every flood-tide—here rising forty feet—and at the ebb girt about by broad sands, the rank sedge growing there haunted by sea-fowl, and under a hot sun emitting no pleasant odors, St. Malo does not agreeably impress the approaching visitor. A turn through its streets may not better those impressions; but his curiosity is deeply enlisted, not only in the place, a small, sombre marine town, with its dingy, oddly-fashioned old houses, and its array of shipping stores, cordage, cables and anchors, but in its people, true to the national instincts, so polite and deferential, yet surcharged with good feeling, so very chatty and free! Wealthy, but none too moral, yet (contradiction easy in this land of anomalies) they yield to none in keeping the Sabbath! Once no other French port throve as this upon its lucrative foreign trade, its cod and whale fisheries, and not less upon rich harvests gathered in war times by its bold privateersmen, ever as vigilant as their trusty night-watch—not the present patrolling coast-guard, but when, a century ago, it consisted of a pack of dogs! These, let loose outside the walls, in charge of a soldier, served both as a protection to the ship-yards on the strand, where timber and cordage lay exposed to pillage by the neighboring peasantry, and to raise the cry of warning should an armed foe attempt to steal in, either from seaward or *via* the Sillon—the long causey, so called, that led from the main to the town gate, and where it was and still is guarded by a drawbridge and huge round towers that flank the gateway. Truly suggestive was the old night guard at St. Malo of that *dogged* watchfulness of their rights common to this people at large, the violation of which rights by despotic rulers had caused such effusions of blood and wholesale expatriations. But in the centuries since flown, like as the night-watch has changed from the canine to the human, so to the credit of that fatherland has public sentiment there made great advance in all that is humane and fraternal. Yet the story of former wrongs which it devolves upon us to tell is fraught with lessons too important to be forgotten.*

* Oh for a full toleration in that land with reason endeared to the American heart, when no such despotism shall tarnish the public character as the

§ 2. HARLEM—SPRINGS OF ITS HISTORY.

WITHIN these far-stretching leagues of sea-washed dykes, downs, and cliffs, remote from Harlem ocean-wide, lie the opening scenes of its history! They carry us not only to the great marts, but to obscure interior homes of Holland, Belgium, and Northern France. Vouched for by records freshly gleaned from this richly historic field, involving no small amount of careful research, they at once possess the merit of authenticity, and present us pictures of former times which are now in every essential of outline and detail.

Admired and revered world-wide, as are those old continental countries, for the peculiar fascination which invests all that pertains to them—their remarkable peoples, venerable institutions, and annals almost unparalleled for soul-stirring vicissitudes; their antique remains and rare works of art, the standing wonder of tourists—how strong their claim upon *our* remembrance and veneration, in their intimate relation of fatherlands, the source largely of our brave and virtuous ancestry, and per sequence a national prosperity that is unexampled!—fact which scarce needs an appeal to written history, because attested, as well by the characteristics and traditions of our people as by our family nomenclature, and the names of our towns, districts, and States. Should not these ties of affinity which bind us so strongly to the fatherlands lend an additional charm to the study of their institutions and epochs?

Let credit be given to those primary agencies which paved the way for the colonization of our country—those hazardous but eventful voyages which began very early in the sixteenth century, when a new field for maritime adventure had but just been opened to Europe by the astounding discoveries of Columbus.

imprisonment of a Christian minister on the trivial charge of exceeding his parish limits in the exercise of his functions! We refer to the recent case of M. Larberet (by report, not from him, but others), the excellent pastor of Maubeuge, on the Sambre, and a contributor of materials for this work. Quite too analogous, both as to spirit and locality, is this act of intolerance to others of past times recited in these pages. But we trust this enlightened nineteenth century will see that old and hideous blot upon the nation's honor effectually wiped out!

It was the heroic enterprise of the merchants and mariners of the French seaports Dieppe, Honfleur, St. Malo, Nantes, Rochelle, and others, which, favored by the national prosperity under Louis XII., first thoroughly explored the North American coast, to find in the Newfoundland fisheries an exhaustless mine of wealth, and to ravish the popular mind with glowing fancies as to the character and resources of the New World! Highly conducive to this were the several voyages of the Florentine Verrazzano, and Cartier of St. Malo, both sailing under the royal auspices of Francis I.: the former, after a visit to our coast and harbors in 1524, returning to Dieppe with report of his success; and the other, ten years later, the pioneer explorer of the bay and river St. Lawrence. And many a hapless expedition, as that of the Picard, Sieur de Roberval, and those growing out of the exigencies of the Huguenots prior to their first civil war, which, with the aid of Coligny and Calvin, undertook to plant colonies in Brazil and Florida, e'en by their misfortunes pointed most impressively to this remote land as the ultimate refuge for the oppressed of Europe. This idea of colonizing America, which in France slumbered during the civil wars, was revived in the time of Henry IV., and with greater promise under his enlightened patronage; when the names of such daring spirits as De Vaux, Pontgrave, and Champlain fill the page of maritime discovery, the last of whom in 1608 founded Quebec, the first permanent European colony in North America! The cotemporary efforts of the Spaniards and English, in the same line of exploration, concern us less.

But Holland now appears, a rival in the field of discovery. Rife with the spirit of commerce, already enriched by her East India trade in spices, silks, and gems, and just concluding a favorable truce with Spain, which as the fruit of a glorious struggle was to virtually secure her independence, with the monopoly of this lucrative trade—she opportunely joins in the arduous search for that long-sought passage to the Indies by a western route, quicker, as was believed, than by the Cape of Good Hope. To this end was the voyage of Hudson from Amsterdam in 1609, which, though futile as to its specific object, startled the merchants and capitalists of Holland, alive to every new scheme of aggrandizement, with reports of the noble river explored by their bold English skipper and thereafter to bear his name; promising, in the affluence of its natural products, its forests of ship-timber, and its more valuable furs, to eclipse the fame of Newfoundland, and rival the wealth of the Indies. The importance of this discovery, confirmed by sundry trading voyages to Hudson's river, covering a series of years, led to the formation of the Dutch West India Company, under whose direction the first colonists proceeded thither in 1623, composed chiefly of French or Walloons, who, driven from their own countries by war and persecution, had taken refuge in the free states of Holland.

From this small beginning, as we know, grew the flourishing States of New York and New Jersey, respecting whose origin the zeal and industry of the historian has left but little to be added, save in a knowledge of the pioneer colonists themselves. Of but few of the large number who came from the continental parts of Europe have we any personal account prior to their advent upon the American soil. Thrown upon these shores, as are the delicate sea-shells cast up by restless waves, whose alternate ebb and flow efface their tiny furrows in the sand, our French and Belgic sires had emerged from rude billows of peril and conflict in their native lands, enough, in human view, to have swept away all trace of them there. We may follow them in their subsequent career, with rarely a failure, by means of scanty records; but this opening chapter of their history, how difficult to recover it, especially where is missing the connecting link between the exile and his former home in the fatherland!*

To regain this lost link, this unknown page in the story of

* Tradition is rarely of much service in this connection. The extravagant stories that the worthy Demarest "purchased the whole of Harlem," and that the Benson ancestor on coming here "had the choice of the whole island," on which were "only five houses," are amusing specimens of the vague and unreliable utterances of tradition! Demarest was a recently arrived Huguenot exile, and as for Benson, he did not come to Harlem till sixty odd years after its settlement began.

It is quite natural to give credence to such traditions as are flattering to our ancestry. But few comparatively of our early colonists, on coming here, brought much wealth, and fewer, perhaps, had enjoyed rank and position in their own lands. Still, our colonists rise in the social scale with later investigations, and it becomes more apparent that wealth, rank, and culture were not such rare endowments with them as has been supposed.

the colonist, so important a prelude to his after-life, and almost of necessity eventful and touching, became a prime object with the author. It was to trace these wanderers amid the scenes of their native lands and homes, where were their firesides, their altars, their fields of conflict, and to study them in the face of such circumstances as must have influenced their character and destiny. In resolving the causes that led them to abandon their native for a foreign soil, we should acquire the means wherewith to better apprehend them in their new sphere, which, however different, yet involved great sacrifice, danger, and hardship to themselves and families; insomuch that the problem of their strange exile could be clearly solved only by a knowledge of the rugged experiences, which had impelled them thereto. Their antecedents must aid in forming an estimate of their personal worth, and in accounting for their peculiar tastes, habits, and attachments. Placing their simple virtues in bolder relief, even their foibles would seem more excusable, when viewed in contact with the sterner age in which they lived, the conflicts they had to wage, and the circumscribed light and advantages which fell to their lot.

So judging, the author was led to make such inquiries abroad as have resulted in the recovery of many interesting details touching the first settlers at Harlem prior to their emigration; facts which, buried for centuries in the musty archives of the fatherlands, now come to us with all the novelty of an original narrative.*

* Baron *W. J. C. Rammelman Elsevier*, Archivist at *Leyden*, Holland, to whom I here express my thanks, has furnished materials of the utmost value, extracted, with much painstaking, from the ancient archives of the city, the University, and the Dutch and Walloon churches there. Mr. *Frederik Muller*, of Amsterdam, also heartily interested himself in causing similar searches to be made at *Amsterdam*, *Slooterdyk*, and *Haarlem*, by Mr. Magnin, Brother of the Order of the Netherland Lion, and former Archivist of Drenthe. Mr. *Osgood Field*, of London, who, in hours spared from mercantile duties, has proven his love for the historic *field*, also has my warm acknowledgments for aid in procuring, through Mr. H. G. Somerby, since deceased, important extracts from the registers of the Walloon churches of *London* and *Canterbury*; as also other data from parish registers at *Newcastle-on-Tyne*, copied by Rev. R. Gould, of Earsdon Vicarage. Also Mr. *W. Noel Sainsbury*, of *Her Majesty's State Paper Office*, for materials in his custody. Thanks are due to Rev. *N. Weiss* late of *Paris*, for the hearty interest he manifested in my labors, and who supplied some useful items from the records at *Avesnes*, obtained through the agency of M. Larberet, pastor at Maubeuge; and also a valuable *brochure* upon the church of *Le Cateau*, besides many facts and

Traced to many parts of Western Europe, from the sunny plains of France to the bleak, fir-clad hills of old Scandinavia, these founders of Harlem were neither exclusively nor mainly Hollanders, as has been the common opinion. From the last-named section came sturdy Danes, Swedes, and Norwegians, in faith Lutherans, and inured to toil, with manners betraying the blood of the brusk Norsemen, once the scourge of France and the British Isles; but as the native asperity had been softened under ages of culture, so had hard fortune, in the case of these exiles, added its chastening effects. They were few in number, yet included several of undoubted worth and superior attainments.

Other exceptions there were; but the community was made up mainly and in about even proportion of Hollanders and French Huguenots: names than which none suggest a truer ideal of sterling character, of patriotism, exalted faith, and heroic suffering! Nor do our settlers cast discredit upon this general estimate of these classes. They and their families had sacrificed much in behalf of liberty and the reformed religion. They were men of probity, equal to those of their times in intel-

suggestions pertaining to the general subject of the Huguenot refugees and the specific names submitted to him—he also having the kindness, unsolicited, to lay one of my letters before the *Société de l'Histoire du Protestantisme français*, a member of which, M. Bordier, an able historian, politely lent his efforts to further its object. Also to Hon. *Edward M. Smith*, U. S. Consul at *Mannheim*, for instituting searches in that city; and to the gentlemen who engaged in them: Mr. Eduard Lemp, custodian of the city archives; Herr von Feder, Deputy of the Second Chamber and Historian of Mannheim; and M. Ruckhaber, pastor of the Concordia, late Walloon church. Also to M. *Gerlach*, pastor of the Walloon church, *Middelburg*, Zeeland, who sought to satisfy my inquiries, but found nothing in his registers. M. *Louis Bardy*, Mayor of *Sedan*, also politely attentive to my inquiry, assures me with regret that they have no registers for the period I had indicated. An article concerning the Carterets and Pipons, inserted in the *British Press*, island of *Jersey*, brought a response from a lineal descendant of Capt. James Carteret, Mrs. *Braithwaite*, of Terrace House, St. Helier, daughter of the late Gen. James Pipon, of Noirmont, in that island, and whom I have to thank for several communications. And I am also happy to acknowledge the valuable aid given me in the *spécialité* to which this note refers by the late lamented Professor *Pierre Blot*, and the artist, Mr. Ed. *Kalshoven*, of New York, but till recently of Amsterdam; as also by Mr. *John Callanan*, of Binghamton, N. Y., deserving to be better known, and who loves to roam amid the florid scenes of his native isle, Jersey. His kindness has procured us the view of the St. Ouen, or De Carteret Manor-House, obligingly furnished at his request by his friend *Philip J. Ouless*, Esq., of St. Helier, artist, and author of "Scenic Beauties of the Island of Jersey."

ligence, education, and enterprise. Highly industrious, they scorned, even in poverty, any dependence upon the charitable, while they could practise an honest trade or handicraft, such as each invariably possessed. In a word, their record, though not faultless, well sustains this general good character. Tried men, used to conquering difficulties, undaunted by the exposure and peril incident to a wild, a hostile land, theirs was the arduous work of constructing a new society, a civilization, to which despotic Europe was then a stranger, or which it could not tolerate! Its safeguards, invaluable even for the security of life and estate—the church, the school, the civil magistracy—they were careful to bring with them, to plant and nurture as on a more congenial soil; and which, deeply rooted, and with broad spreading branches, still yield for us their golden fruits. How, and under what circumstances, they acquired these valuable ideas which possessed them, this peculiar fitness for their high destiny as colonists and founders of empire, is surely a most inviting subject of inquiry.

§ 3. GLIMPSES OF THE FATHERLANDS.

To catch the spirit and genius of the times under review, is to ignore such changes, political, moral, and physical, as three centuries have wrought; for Europe of to-day is not the Europe of the sixteenth century. By the light of the historic past, its wealth of significant fact and incident is more clearly revealed. In the land of the Huguenots the remote eras of the Gaul, the Roman, and the Frank yet lived in piquant story, and might be traced in existing monuments as well as in musty tomes. Still in popular use were the old provincial names, time-honored and interwoven with all the history of the country; for not yet had revolution stripped the French provinces of these means of identity, in its well-conceived but too radical onslaught upon feudal rights and institutions. An exhaustless theme, with our Huguenot refugee, was his dear old Picardie, or Artois, or Normandie; the talisman which in his remotest wanderings, e'en till death closed his exile, recalled all that was endearing in the word home. In church and state the ancient *régime* was intact. The old provincial dynasties which had grown up and flourished under the feudal system, but whose lines of puissant counts and dukes were long since extinct, lived even yet in important senses, not only in monumental stones and structures, and in the local annals and traditions, but in countless charters, privileges, laws, and usages, still prized and cherished by the people. History, as if to deepen its impress upon the popular heart, had scattered its monuments over the soil with lavish hand; and around these, time—which in the annals of Gaul meant a score of centuries—had woven its weird and marvellous legends, often a tax upon credulity, but perchance too real: some tale of gallant heroism, of gentle piety, or dark superstition, touching the heart or quickening the blood, but, whether true or otherwise, a telling paraphrase upon the national traits or instincts. The old baronial castle proudly rearing its towers was rich in reminiscences of warlike feudal times. The razing its ponderous walls as material for the mason?—sacrilegious thought! Dingy cloisters, over whose turrets crept venerable ivy, still swarmed with pious monks, yet had come to be symbolic of that moral darkness which in the early ages first drove the gentle handmaids religion and learning to the covert of such strong and friendly walls. Held by the masses in profound veneration, they evidenced the singular religious fervor of the race. But here's a touching emblem, the cross—it is coarsely fashioned in stone—which surprises one in some rural solitude, but near the highway, so none may fail to see it, and, kneeling, offer up a *paternoster*. Mute; yet it tells, maybe, the affecting tale of some early martyrdom, or of the gallant brave slain in battle, on this now sacred spot! How suggestive of that strong, unnatural alliance between war and religion; whence bloody crusades against Turks, Albigenses, and Vaudois, and, we may add, the Huguenot wars!

Between the cities or villages all is forest, or heath, or tilled lands, but alike a solitude, unbroken by cheery farm-houses or villas; no fences even, but rows of ancient yews, or hedge of flowering holly or thorn, or yet the natural streams, to mark the limits of estates. The farmer, however distant his acres, lives in town or hamlet. The wealth, industry, and social life concentre in teeming cities or towns. These are mostly seated on the rivers—the latter almost the only medium of domestic trade and travel—or upon the old Roman ways; cross-roads were few and neglected. Treasuries of all that was venerable and curious were these cities. Many had sprung from rude towns of the Gauls, and owed their first significance to Roman civilization and law, and the architectural and other improvements then introduced; still attested by noble ruins, found everywhere, of fine structures, besides immense stretches of paved military roads, bringing the chief places into easier communication. Shut up in massive walls, the city, each within itself, was a little world, sparing, beyond the necessities of trade, of any intercourse or sympathy with others around it. The older portions were easily told, the houses so antique, the streets narrow and crooked, with a gutter running down the *centre*. Through others ran canals, lined with vessels receiving or discharging merchandise, and where stood the tiled houses, two or three stories high, occupied by merchants or traders, who mainly composed the burghery, the enterprising and well-to-do middle class. More pretentious were the mansions of the lords and gentry, the upper strata of society; the lower, the toiling artisans and work-people, tenanting squatty cottage-like houses, their low eaves overhanging the humble doorway; and windows, or little lookouts, not the best for admitting air or sunlight, but quite large enough in cold or stormy weather, since window-glass was too great a luxury for the poor. But the clergy often surpassed even the nobility in the richness and comfort of their abodes, which with monasteries and other houses of the religious orders, usually well endowed, engrossed a large area within the cities. Above the clustering gables arose the turrets and crosses of parish churches not a few, and the lofty spire and pinnacles of the stately cathedral; witnesses alike to the devotion and taste of their votaries, but the latter the crowning glory of the city, whether for the grandeur of its design, or for its wealth of sculptures, frescoes, and paintings. Within, its lofty solemn arches inspired the worshipper with reverence and awe; its very plan, a *cruciform*, told where his faith should rest; and even the dumb *effigies* of the noble dead, recumbent on their costly tombs in the silent transept, read him a lesson upon his own mortality. Still, in aid of his devotions, were images, tapers, and clouds of incense; with "sacred relics" in profusion, accredited with healing power and other miraculous virtues, and rarely excepting either a piece of "the true cross," or the denuded bones of the city's ancient patron, and still guardian saint. The citadel afforded secure quarters to the royal governor, who need fear no disaster incident to those times, as insurrection, or those more dreaded from want of skill to cope with them, fire, famine, and pestilence, which often caused fearful ravages. But what recuperative energy had these cities, and to what unwonted prosperity they attained, especially in the wool and flax working districts of the Netherlands and Northern France! Grand displays characterized the periodical fairs and the frequent religious festivals. Tournament and feats of arms were the high sport of the nobility; their pastime hunting or hawking. Tennis or ball playing was the great popular game, and dancing the universal amusement for both sexes. Ancient and often grotesque customs were kept up with great spirit. *Crowning the rosière* was a usage not only very ancient (instituted by St. Medard of Noyon, in Picardy, in the fifth century), but pretty and touching. It was the public presentation of a hat bedecked with roses to the most exemplary maiden of the town or village. The entire family of the recipient share the honor. "The crown of roses," says the Countess De Genlis, "is expected with emotion, awarded with justice, and establishes goodness, rectitude, and virtue in every family."

One of the cities most closely identified with our refugees was Amiens. Within its encircling moat and high massive walls, strengthened at short distances by round abutments and towers, it was not then the open, airy town it now is, since its sombre walls have given place to a handsome boulevard; but it was noted "for the beauty of its buildings, and for the quality, industry, and number of its inhabitants." The city lay south of the Somme, whose main channel formed a bend around its northern part known as the Old or Lower Town, where three branches also entered it under arches in the wall, and which, diffusing into canals, threaded its narrow streets, here lined by low and antiquated dwellings and shops, and uniting again on the western side, escaped by a single outlet at St. Michel's

Bridge. To this portion, which had led Louis XI. to call Amiens his Little Venice, lay joining southerly a larger part known as the Upper Town, having broad and quite regular streets, fine houses, mainly two stories high and of uniform style; with two spacious squares "where seven fair streets centred." Henry IV. had built its city hall and citadel, the latter in the form of a star, with five sharp angles, commanding the northern approach to the city, and though still incomplete, deemed impregnable. But all its fine edifices, the bishop's palace not excepted, paled before its grand cathedral, Notre Dame, pronounced at that time "the fairest and most lovely structure in the West of Europe." In plan the usual cruciform, it dated from 1220, when its foundations were laid; excepting as to its western front, which was of later construction, very rich in Gothic decorations, and flanked by two massive unfinished square towers of unequal height. From over the transept arose a light and airy spire three hundred and seventy feet high. It would consume too much space to describe its interior magnificence. Among its treasured relics was the decapitated head of John the Baptist, alleged to have been brought by a Picard crusader from Constantinople, after its capture in 1204. Its great value consisted in its entire *genuineness*, though this was not quite demonstrated till 1665, when done in a learned treatise prepared at the request of the chapter by the great savant of Amiens, Sieur du Cange! Another relic they had, equally real, and hardly less valuable—the finger of "doubting Thomas," which had restored his faltering faith by a touch of the Saviour's wounds! If aught could better show how strong a grasp old superstitions had upon the popular mind at Amiens, it needed but a stroll among its numerous abbeys and parish churches, or through its great cemetery of St. Denis, hard by the cathedral, where monumental crosses, antique and moss-grown, told the faith in which slept its dead of many centuries.

Amiens was the city of the brave Ambiani, who having sent a strong force to oppose the victorious Cæsar, were at last obliged to open their gates to this mighty conqueror. Galling as was the yoke, it was alleviated by the benefits of the Roman municipal government, with its magistracy and senate, having a share in enacting the laws and dispensing justice. Upon the introduction of Christianity the people chose their own bishops —a right they had ever since exercised, save when obstructed by violence or arbitrary rulers. After the Frank conquest near the end of the fifth century, the powers of the magistrates were extended, the senate was opened to all citizens, *including the clergy;* and the bishop, whose functions before were scarcely more than spiritual, became, by the elective vote of the people, president of the municipal body, and thus was invested with a temporal authority, and a chief influence in all the affairs of the city. The Frankish kings also established in this, as in other principal cities, a civil and military governor, called a *count*, who exercised the powers of judge. Charlemagne, among other beneficial changes, created judges called *scabini*, who were elected conjointly by the count, the imperial officers, and the people, by which the citizen acquired a new and valued right; the political and administrative power being now shared by the bishop, the count, and these judges. It was the suspension by the counts in feudal times of this important franchise, with other abuses of power, that led the burghers of Amiens to form that compact for their protection called the *commune*. This was effected at the beginning of the twelfth century (1113), when, revolting against the encroachments of the count and the exactions of the viscounts which he had arbitrarily substituted for the judges, the people, excited thereto by the bishop, and sustained by the king, Louis VI., constituted themselves an incorporation, adopting a charter which served as a model for many other communes in the North of France. "The commune," says Thierry, "was sovereign, because it had the right of self-government by its proper laws, and the right of life and of death over all its members; it had, following the language of the ancient jurisprudence, high, middle, and low justice. Its power, legislative, administrative, and judicial, was delegated by it to a corps of elective magistrates, renewed each year, and whereof the head bore the title of mayor (*maire*), and the members that of *échevin*, or the joint titles of échevin and *prévôt*." King Philip Augustus confirmed these rights by a charter in 1190, and this ancient form of government still subsisted at Amiens. Now it had become a great commercial city, the struggles of its citizens in all the centuries past to preserve their privileges against domestic and foreign enemies, and countless other incidents of its history, are not essential to our present design.

The national history counted its centuries before the Christian era; its first known epoch was a barbaric age, devoted to war and the bloody rites of the Druids, or the religious mysteries of the Gauls, who, to propitiate their gods, immolated human captives. The Gauls were then divided into three nations—the Belgæ, Celtæ, and Aquitani; the first being of German extraction, and superior in *physique*, energy, and courage to the others. The Gauls told Cæsar that the ancestors of the Belgæ had crossed the Rhine at an early date and appropriated the fertile country north of the Seine and Marne, after driving out the Celtæ. These three nations were subdivided into independent tribes, as the Nervii, the Ambiani, the Veromandui, the Bellovaci, and the Suessiones, all of the Belgæ, and all tribes of Picardy, except the Nervii, which lay next northward.

Five centuries of Roman subjugation formed the second epoch, during which Gaul was civilized, through the influence of Roman law, letters, and arts, and of Christianity. Clovis, king of the Franks, overthrew the Roman power in 486, and founded the monarchy, which, despite many convulsions, had subsisted for twelve centuries. A dismal period of anarchy ensued after the death of Clovis, and ended in the dethronement of his race. It was marked by the corruption of the church, which had allied itself to the civil power, and by the rise of monasticism, which spread over Northern Gaul in the seventh century.

The monarchy rose to great splendor and the dignity of an empire under the ambitious but wise Charlemagne, who added two kingdoms to France. But all this greatness vanished under his weak successors. Rent by internal dissensions, a general revolt of the nobles, and the inroads of the piratical Normans, the mushroom empire soon fell asunder; its two acquisitions, Italy and Germany, resuming their separate existence, while France proper was resolved into numerous petty governments, which, ruled by hereditary dukes and counts under what was styled the Feudal System, subsisted for centuries independent of each other, and so far of the crown as to pay it scarcely a nominal homage. Thus arose among others, in the ninth and tenth centuries, the proud earldoms or counties of Flanders (from which

Artois was subsequently taken), Hainault, Holland, and those which afterwards united formed Picardy; besides the duchy of Normandy, founded by Rollo and his Norsemen out of their rich conquests.

This localization of power causing many domestic wars, with the utter humiliation of the monarchy, was for a time fatal to social order and progress. But this state of things ultimately found its remedy in the perfecting of the feudal system, the restraining power of the church, the rise of the spirit of chivalry, and above all in the famous Crusades, whose object was to wrest the land of Palestine from the Mohammedan power. Conceived in a desire to end the cruelties inflicted by the Turks upon Christians going on pilgrimage to the Holy Sepulchre, and first set on foot in 1095 by a Picard called Peter the Hermit, these remarkable expeditions were repeated at intervals during two centuries. Monarchs took the field, and the chivalry of France and the Netherlands, including many from Normandy, Picardy, Hainault, Artois, and Flanders, bore a distinguished part. Directly productive only of disaster—a prodigious waste of life and treasure, and naught in return of which to boast, beside valorous deeds, but a brief occupation of Jerusalem by the crusaders—the Crusades, strange as it may seem, ultimately wrought out results highly beneficial to society. By impairing the strength and resources of the feudal chiefs, great and small, who had alike squandered all they had on these costly expeditions, the way was opened to the monarchy to regain by degrees its control; and to the cities to cast off their allegiance to the counts or seigniors, feudal masters, who had long oppressed them, and to accept the protection of the king: nor did the latter relax their efforts to aggrandize their power (a policy begun by Louis VI., crowned in 1108), till, by the use of diplomacy and force, they had regained their supremacy over all the French territory which had revolted in the ninth century, excepting only the Netherland provinces lying north of Picardy. These by a train of favoring causes had fallen to the dukes of Burgundy, and through them to the crown of Spain; thus exposing to this rival power another and more accessible frontier, where no lofty Pyrenees opposed a difficult barrier, and which in subsequent wars between them became a principal theatre of hostilities.

But the elevation of the sovereign consequent upon the crusades was no more marked than that of the subject. Everywhere the bands which held the vassal to his lord were sundered, and the bondman went out free. The dissipated wealth of the feudal aristocracy had found its way largely into the coffers of the merchants, shipwrights, mechanics, and manufacturers. With the development of their energies and resources the cities rapidly advanced toward that high state of prosperity which they long enjoyed, until arrested by the persecutions and civil wars of the sixteenth and seventeenth centuries. The church temporal flourished, or at least the clergy, who became rich and more arrogant; the churches, with the monasteries or abbeys, already enjoying princely endowments, had added largely to their estates from those of the crusaders, who had mortgaged or sold them to the bishops, etc., and all this augmented by the recovery of property alleged to have been stolen by the feudal lords. From this profusion of wealth at the church's command, supplemented by generous donations from the noble or affluent, and innumerable offerings by the common people, were built the magnificent cathedrals of the twelfth and thirteenth centuries; also countless new monasteries and cloisters. Out of all this again came benefits other than the spiritual, which latter we would not undervalue—masses of mechanics and workmen had bread, while the large demand for skilled architects and artisans became a powerful stimulus to many important branches of art. To the various home industries thus created or quickened were added at this period many useful arts —not to speak of luxuries—through the opening of commercial intercourse with the Oriental countries by means of the crusades.

Yet there ensued results of far greater magnitude—least anticipated, though essential in the chain of progressive events—when a nation, till then but little given to foreign commerce and strangers to distant sea voyages, having become a thoroughly maritime people, through the acquired arts of shipbuilding, and of navigating the ocean, found in the opportune discovery of a new western continent so grand a field for exploration and conquest, and such alluring prospects of wealth, that, joining in the eager strife to seize and possess these advantages, they became unwittingly the advanced heralds of our American colonization!

The feudal system, under which during the crusades and the many wars of the Middle Ages the military art had acquired such brilliancy, had crumbled to decay. The chivalry had long since passed its palmy days; though still having the shadow of an existence in the famous semi-religious order of *St. John of Jerusalem*, instituted in the Holy City during the crusades, or as afterwards called from the island made their retreat and headquarters, the *Knights of Malta;* as also in others of more modern creation—in France, the *Chevaliers des Ordres du Roi*, and in the Netherlands the *Knights of the Golden Fleece.** But the spirit of chivalry, born of generous impulses, yet perverted when the ardent soul of the knight-errant, aglow with martial fire and thirsting for bold adventure, could be moved to court any peril in cause noble or trivial, merely to win an approving smile from his fair lady-love, had lost its former prestige, but had developed a more general and enlightened philanthropy. Time had stripped feudalism of its essential feature—the fascinating but onerous military service. The weakened nobility were no longer to be depended upon by the crown, and the *feudal* had given place to a *paid* soldiery. But while this hard condition of the feudal compact, as regarded the vassal, was thus annulled, much of the martial spirit, and even some of the grosser features of that system, survived. As the villages had generally sprung up either upon the estates and about the castles of the nobility whose descendants still occupied them and were the lords of the soil, or about ancient monasteries, which held the fee of the ample domains on which they were seated, the inhabitants of these villages, mainly tillers of the ground, were largely tenants either of the nobility or clergy, and many of these peasants, "to the manor born," were still under the old vassalage. In such case the poor ploughman or hedger sighed in vain for other employment or better wages; virtually tied to the soil, he was as much a fixture as his humble cottage, or the old village church where he had been christened, at whose altar he had so often bowed, and beneath whose shadow, with the forgotten of ages, his weary frame would rest at last. So oppressive were

* Chevaliers des Ordres du Roi, or *Knights of the King's Orders*, was the general designation for the two orders, that of *St. Michel*, before noticed, and that of the *Holy Spirit*, the latter instituted by Henry III., in 1578.

these bands, even in Picardy and Normandy, that, waiving the claim which birth and service gave him upon his lord for protection and support, the bondman would often abandon his home to carve out a fortune elsewhere. And though at this time the relation of modern landlord had been widely substituted for that of the feudal superior, yet so slow was this process, and so strong a hold had the old system of servitude, that it survived till the French Revolution, when it was wholly abolished.

The more favored freemen within the cities and towns, imbued with a spirit of progress as yet unfelt by the agricultural population, and engaged in lucrative pursuits, bore more easily the heavy imposts levied by their sovereigns than had their predecessors the severer exactions of feudalism, though not indeed without many a protest. Society at large also felt their influence, and mainly through their agency had been consummated the *renaissance*, as is called that remarkable and universal development, the expansion of industries, the diffusion of knowledge, the revival of letters and arts; all accelerated by that crowning invention, the printing-press. The common mind, liberated and awakened to higher impulses, ventured to roam in new channels of thought, touching even the intricate subjects of science religion, and human rights. Thus was society ripened for the great moral reform of the sixteenth century, which as respects France and the Netherlands was not more remarkable for the ability and piety of its advocates, for the breadth and power of its manifestation, than for the fiery ordeal to which its adherents were subjected, and the ultimate effects of this severity upon the welfare of other countries.

Momentous as was this struggle both in character and consequences, we must confine us to two distinct passages in its history which bear directly on our subject. The one will show by what remote causes and influences were gradually developed and put in motion the first efforts to plant the seeds of civilization upon the Harlem soil; the other, the circumstances under which the mass of the Harlem refugees were impelled to leave France and the Netherlands, involving one of the most affecting eras in the history of the Huguenots, but which, in view of its bearing upon our early colonization, has not been given its due prominence by our local annalists.

CHAPTER II.

AVESNES AND ITS EXILES.

THE old province of Picardy took in a strip of the coast from Calais to the river Canche. But its major portion between the Canche and the Bresle, and through which flowed the Somme, stretched eastward, wedge-like, from the Channel to Champagne, having on the north the Walloon provinces of Artois, Cambresis, and Hainault, and on the south Normandy and Isle of France. Its easterly sections, Thiérache and Vermandois, were charmingly diversified by wooded heights, which however told of an earlier age when the adjacent Forest of Ardennes, the "Noar Pai," or "Black Country," of the Walloons, spread its sombre shades westward over this region. About these heights four noted streams took their rise—the Scheldt and Sambre, watering the Netherlands, the Somme and Oise, rivers of Picardy; while the hills here diverged in four several chains or ridges which parted the respective valleys or basins of these rivers. Altogether, these formed a most remarkable feature in the topography of the country. Often sinking to slight elevations, rarely did these ranges exceed an altitude which in our land of grander proportions would mark them as but ordinary hills; yet with gentle slopes and summits mantled in woods or vineyards, and here and there rising to view some old *château* or castle, they gave a charming variety and beauty to these miniature countries. One range, crossing the eastern borders of the Cambresis, where it formed the large and venerable forest of Mourmal, linked with stirring events soon to be noticed, skirted for some miles the valley of the Sambre, then from northeast wound about to north-west, cutting in halves the Duchy of Brabant, and parting the basins of the Scheldt and Meuse. Another chain diverging westerly, then northward, till ending at Cape Gris-Nez, on the Straits of Dover, formed the bounds between Picardy and Artois. A third ran south-west, crossing Picardy obliquely, then westerly through Upper Normandy, to Cape La Heve, at the mouth of the Seine; while the fourth, stretching westward through Thiérache to Champagne, formed in part the series of hills which environed that province and Isle of France—the basin of the Seine—then followed the southern borders of Normandy to Brittany. Within the shadows, so to speak, of these several hill-ranges—in Normandy, along the borders of the Somme, in the basin of the Scheldt, and the valley of the Sambre—were the homes of nearly all the French refugees, mostly Picards and Walloons, who came to Harlem.

Much in advance of the districts further south were these, in most of the externals of a genuine civilization and prosperity. It was due jointly to their greater natural resources, and to the superior organism and spirit of the people. Artois and Picardy both abounded in grains, grasses, and fruits; the one significantly called the "Granary of the Netherlands," the other, the "Storehouse of Paris." Flanders was renowned world-wide for the products of her looms. Hainault, the "Saltus Carbonarius" of the Romans (the Coal Forest), was rich, not only in coal, but in iron, lead, and marble; while the grazing lands, cornfields, and orchards of Normandy were in unrivalled repute. More densely populated than the south, this northern section exhibited in its people a more manly development, both physical and mental; in stature above the average height, and more intelligent, logical, inventive, and industrious, better fed, housed, and educated. While plodding husbandry tamely drove the plough through the mellow soils of La Beuce and Toureine, gathered her vintages from Burgundy to Languedoc, and fed her flocks on the green meadows of Berry and the sterile heaths of Brittany and Les Landes; in the north busy trade and manufactures, enlisting all the energies and resources of people and country, brought to most a competence and to many affluence. And even husbandry, better rewarded for its toil, was more ambitious and successful.

No class of Gallic blood was more remarkable than the Walloons, a people at the present day numbering nearly two millions, and mainly included within France and Belgium. Time has wrought but slight change among them, but we needs must describe them as they were. Theirs was a belt of country extending eastward from the river Lys, beyond both Scheldt and Meuse, and embracing French or Walloon Flanders, most of Artois, the Cambresis, Hainault, Namur, Southern Brabant, and parts of Liege and Luxemburg. Within the last lay the principality of Sedan, stretched along the east side of the Meuse, on which the city of Sedan, its strong capital, was seated. A fruitful region, and in the sixteenth century an independent Protestant state, it attracted many of the persecuted Walloons during the religious troubles of that period. The northern limits of the Walloon country would have been nearly defined by a line drawn from the city of Liege, on the Meuse, to Calais. On the south it was bounded by Picardy, Champagne, and Lorraine, provinces which in the times referred to composed the French frontier.*

The Walloons were a hardy, long-lived race, tall, stout, and muscular; in which respects, quite unlike the ordinary French, they compared better with their neighbors the Flemings, but again were readily distinguished from the latter both by their physiognomy and their speech, which last was a crude French patois, spoken by them unchanged for centuries, and still in common use among them. Of strong intellects, manly bear-

* The term *Walloon* is derived from the word *Gaul*, which the Germans, by an etymological substitution of W for the Latin G, changed into *Wahl*, and in the plural *Wahlen*; the Low Dutch making it *Waal* and *Waalen*. But we observe that both German and Dutch, in speaking of the Walloons, more commonly used the adjective form, saying the *Walsche*—that is, the Walsche people. The old Germans applied this term indiscriminately to all the Romanized people along their western and southern borders, not the Gauls only, but the Romans; giving their several countries the name of *Walschland*, as the Germans designate Italy even to this day; and which term is also traceable in the Swiss canton of Vallais, in the old canton of Bern, north of Lake Leman, or Geneva (embracing the Pays, now canton, of Vaud), and (skipping the two provinces of Alsace and Lorraine, early overrun by German tribes) as far to the north as Walloon Brabant. The French themselves used the term Walloon (by them written Wallon, or Ouallon) only with reference to the French-speaking people of Belgic descent, occupying their northern frontiers, within the Walloon country. The term Walsche was so restricted by the Hollanders; and by Walschland, or Walslant, as they wrote it, they meant the Walloon country, and not the more distant Pays de Vaud, as was wrongly held by Mr. Vanderkemp, who should have been better informed, in making his translation of the Dutch records at Albany. Almost any of the old Dutch histories will show the correct usage, but one will suffice, *Van Meteren*, Amsterdam, 1652, fol. 40, etc.

ing, a sagacious, practical, and laborious people, they were also noted for the plainness of their tastes, manners, and dress. These several traits were clearly traceable to their ancestors, the old Belgæ, their descent from whom was also unmistakable in their coolness and pertinacity, so in contrast with the excitability and fickleness characterizing the French of proper Celtic blood. It was these qualities, combined with a natural love of arms, and the courage inherited from their ancestors, whom Cæsar describes as the bravest of all the Gauls, that made the Walloons such famous soldiers. Ever tenacious of their rights, and thus excessively litigant, they were yet hospitable and social, possessing much of the French vivacity. In domestic life they lacked no element of solid, homespun comfort: the plain, substantial domicile, roofed with tile or thatch; a bare floor, but genial hearth-stone, with ample pile of blazing wood, or turf, as it suited; the oaken board, set with brown ware or pewter, with goodly supply of simple, wholesome food—this satisfied the Walloon ambition in the line of living. Song, or instrumental music, of which they were excessively fond, commonly enlivened the social hour. They were very devout, and as a people intensely attached to the Roman ritual.

The Walloon emigrations of the sixteenth century, already referred to, went largely by way of the Scheldt, the Meuse, and their affluents, to Holland. Skirting interiorwise the districts which were the homes of our refugees, the Meuse flowed northerly, then swept westward around Brabant, reaching the sea by several outlets between the insular parts of South Holland. It is unsurpassed for bold and grand scenery, which beginning near Sedan, is heightened to the sublime as it reaches Namur, where the Sambre enters it. Towering walls of rock, now bare, now clad in rich foliage, rise on either side; while here and there huge cleft or ravine opens to view some far-reaching and romantic vale, or dark unfathomed dell—fitting retreat either for fabled sprites or fairies, or stern feudal chiefs, who once took tribute of each passing vessel. Weird stories are woven around its fantastic forms and crumbling castles; for example, the popular legend of the Fox and Wolf, drawn seemingly from that fierce rencounter of the year 900, when the shrewd Renard, Count of Hainault, with his compatriots, slew the tyrant Zwendibold, King of Lorraine. But stranger tales were those of the sixteenth century—of crafts richly freighted, but not with merchandise, stealing down its favoring current, bearing the victims of persecution, Protestant Walloons from the adjacent districts, to a land of safety. One such family of exiles will claim our notice and enlist our sympathies.

The famed and picturesque Sambre was a principal branch of the Meuse, and had its sources in that wild corner of Picardy called Thiérache, which joined upon Hainault. Flowing northerly, it entered the province just named, near the border of the Cambresis, soon passing the city of Landrecy; whence taking its course north-easterly through a rugged, wooded country, it left again the confines of Hainault before joining the Meuse. A league below Landrecy it received the Petit Hepre, and, several miles beyond, the Grand Hepre; those sister streams gently coursing their way, in nearly parallel currents, down from the principality of Chimay, a few leagues eastward. Between these two streams lay the *Land of Avesnes*, an ancient baronial estate, whose chief town, seated on the Grand Hepre, six miles from its mouth and eight leagues directly south of Mons, is one with the present Avesnes, capital of an *arrondissement* of the same name in the *departement* Du Nord, France. Paris is 123 miles to the south-west.

The town lay mainly upon the left or south bank of the river, which was not navigable, and within an uneven, but here quite open country, save that to the north of the town the view was intercepted by the Hedge of Avesnes, as was popularly called a line of pretty heights studded with forest trees, a spur of the historic Ardennes, and which followed the course of the stream westward to the Sambre.

This old town dated from the eleventh century, when Werric, surnamed *with the beard*, a bold feudal chieftain, lord of Leuze, near the Haine, and who had inherited the lands between the two Hepres, given to his ancestor by the Count of Hainault, erected a castle upon the most northerly of these streams, midway between its outlet and the even then venerable abbey of Liessies, which was seated on the same stream six miles above the castle. About this castle the town had grown up. As a "key of Hainault," it was guarded with jealous care by the later counts, its lords paramount; but cut off in a manner by the "Hedge," was much exposed to aggression from the French border, which was less than two leagues distant. Nor was it spared, during a long period in which its ownership was vested in titled subjects of France, from too often becoming common plunder ground; since among these warlike proprietors were some of the most renowned knights of the chivalric ages, whose varied and often stern fortunes it had largely shared. But at the period of which we write it had withstood the rude blasts of five centuries; trusting to the old Latin chronicle left by Baudouin of Avesnes, who laid him to rest in 1289.

The old clock in the belfry that so faithfully struck the hour was not all that was striking about the town: equally so to the eye was the prevailing architecture, plain, durable, betraying its Walloon character, if not a high antiquity. Solid as the old stone houses at our Kingston or Hurley, built by the Walloon settlers, few of the buildings were grand or even ornamental; and the streets were ill-arranged—only one, near and parallel with the river, running its whole length, crossed midway by another at right angles, while most of the other angles were any thing but right; and around the venerable cathedral St. Nicholas, in the eastern and plainly the oldest section of the town, some of its "squares" took the most eccentric and original forms—circular, wedge-like, and awry! Yet, "*oppidum elegans admodum et celeber,*" says a learned monk of 1655; "*a very handsome and celebrated town.*"

Many things at Avesnes, surviving its partial ruin by Louis XI. in 1477, still wore both a militant and a religious aspect. The remains of the old feudal castle hoary with age; the smithy of the armorer, whose forge and skill could fit you a trusty blade or battle-axe, a helmet or a coat of mail; the significant sign-board, on which the Walloon youth, ambitious of arms, read in *rouchi français*, his own rude patois, SWORD AND HALBERD TAUGHT HERE. It had its sacred crosses, its religious houses, and its collegiate church, or cathedral already named, the latter endowed in 1534 with a chapter—or dean, provost, and dozen canons—through the benevolence and piety of the Lady of Avesnes, Louise d'Albret, widow of its former proprietor, Lord de Croy. Here were convents of the Franciscans, both of monks and nuns, mendicants whose austere life and vow of poverty gave them great favor with the people; and here also was a *congrégation séculière*, or society of Beguines, a less strict order, composed of worthy matrons passing their waning years in partial seclusion from the world, in teaching the young, and in works of charity. Devout indeed were its people, Catholics of a loyal type, as was apparent from the number and reputed wealth of the clergy, and the many abbeys and chapters supported by the country at large, from which their superior, the ducal archbishop of Cambray, drew a liberal stipend.

Traces of a former vassalage were yet visible among this people; but the innumerable wars that had marked their history had served to foster the martial spirit and love of liberty derived from their ancestors. Yet how cramped the ideas of liberty among a people so intolerant of opinions opposed to the teachings of the church, so submissive to lords and masters not of their own choosing, but holding by inheritance, or marriage, or even by purchase! But now they were drawn to worthier pursuits than the shedding of blood—to productive industry, and mainly to those solid and useful branches of labor in a degree peculiar to the Hainaulters, and well suited to develop their large and sinewy frames, and to make the positive characters the Walloons were. They wrought in timber, iron, and stone, and the fine white, sculptor's marble found in their quarries. Others worked the collieries, tanneries, and potteries scattered over the district, or in mills for expressing vegetable oils from flax and rape seed and beech mast. The abundant forests supplied building timber, firewood, and charcoal for a large traffic. The pastures nourished some flocks and herds. Sheep-rearing and flax-growing gave activity to the woollen and linen workers, whose loom or spinning-wheel in its accustomed niche in the owner's dwelling rarely ceased its hum or clatter in working hours.

The well-preserved annals of Avesnes gave witness to the warlike proclivities of its feudal lords, around whom as its centre and soul all its history clustered. Their brilliant exploits, rehearsed by admiring vassals, and transmitted down from age to age in legend and song—what a stimulus to that courage and martial spirit to which we have alluded! A famous roll it was of these lords and dames of eighteen generations, who had ruled Avesnes since *Werric with the beard* reared his castle there, and all of whom could boast his Belgic blood.

It told of bold Thierry, son of Werric, whose *hache*, or axe, subdued (and whence its name) the adjoining district, Thiérache; of his nephew and successor, Goswin d'Oisy, proud castellan of Cambray, who essayed to strengthen Avesnes and bid defiance to his liege lord of Hainault, only submitting after a fierce battle of three days on the banks of the Sambre; of the equally stern warrior Gautier Plukellus, who had succeeded his uncle Goswin, and was slain, 1147, in an attack on the castle at Mons; also of his son Nicholas, who built the castle at Landrecy, and *his* son Jacques d'Avesnes, "the most renowned, wealthy, and daring knight of this country," and a famous crusader, who in 1191 fell in battle in the Holy Land, fighting the Saracens under Saladin. Among the succeeding lords were two Hughs, counts of St. Paul, also Louis Count of Blois, who was slain at the disastrous battle of Cressy, whither he went to oppose the invading English, with his wife's father, the gallant Sir John de Hainault, whose fame is sung by Froissart. Sad the story which was related of a son of Louis, the brave and generous Guy, one of the most affluent of the lords of Avesnes, who, forced to sell his inheritance of Soissons to effect his release when a dreary captive in England and later his earldom of Blois to satisfy luxurious living, died in 1397, in comparative penury, at Avesnes; this estate passing to his cousin John of Brittany, son of the unlucky Charles of Blois, who, in a famous contest to establish his right to Brittany had lost both his duchy and his life at the battle of Auray. A granddaughter of John of Brittany, Frances, Dame or Lady of Avesnes, gave this estate with her hand to Alain d'Albret, one of the most puissant nobles of France, and after her death the unsuccessful suitor of the much-wooed duchess, Anne of Brittany, subsequently the wife of two kings. It was Louise, Lady of Avesnes, Lord Alain's daughter, who in 1495, by wedding Charles de Croy, Prince of Chimay, placed the Land of Avesnes in possession of the Croys. The latter was an old Picard family; but when Picardy was under Philip Duke of Burgundy, Jean de Croy, grandsire of Charles, attached himself to that potent duke, who made him a knight of the Golden Fleece, when he first instituted that order at Bruges in 1430. Charles took his title from the estate of Chimay, to which he fell heir in 1482 on the death of his father Philip, and which was erected into a principality four years later by the Emperor Maximilian, whose son Philip, King of Spain, conferred on the new prince the additional honors of the Golden Fleece. It was a singular pride, a result of their training under the feudal relation, felt by the subjects in such marks of distinction bestowed on their chief; and how often told and retold as household stories, and further that the prince had held the infant Charles V. at the baptismal font, and given him his name, and subsequently received from that emperor and king a costly helmet wrought in silver and gold, and how after him his family enjoyed substantial proofs of that monarch's favor! Frances, Lady of Avesnes, eldest daughter and heiress of the prince, marrying her kinsman Philip de Croy—for their parents were cousins—the latter took the estates on the death of his father-in-law in 1527, the next year further securing the land of Avesnes to his house by a release obtained from Henry d'Albret, King of Navarre, cousin to his wife, and grandfather of Henry IV. of France.

Since Avesnes fell to the house of Croy no less than five wars between France and Spain had successively convulsed these exposed borders. In the earlier of these contests Philip de Croy, now Prince of Chimay and Knight of the Fleece, rendered important service with his Walloon troop; and Charles V. in 1533 showed his love for his "nephew" by giving him the title of Duke of Arschot, from an estate he held in Brabant. In the destructive war of 1543, armies of Francis I. overran this part of Hainault, holding Landrecy against a siege of six months, conducted by Charles in person; but peace ensuing the next year, France restored to Spain its several conquests, soon after which Landrecy was detached from Avesnes, and ceded to the crown by the Duke of Arschot, who meanwhile had been created a grandee of Spain. After his decease in 1549, leaving his heirs such rich possessions and dignities, the family of Croy became "of greatest revenue and authority of any in Belgium." Philip, second duke, now enjoying his father's titles and estates, including Avesnes, had great influence in governmental affairs, as had also his brother, Charles Croy, Marquis of Havre, in Hainault; in which province their no less proud and aspiring cousins, the Counts Lalain, seemed born to the gubernatorial seat. Great destinies were in the grasp of this influential family. Time was to eliminate, as one of the results, an humble transatlantic enterprise, to which some of their born subjects were to contribute.

Hainault was to have its share in that bloody struggle with despotism which rent the Netherlands in the sixteenth century. Spain now ruled these provinces as with a rod of iron. This policy began with Charles V., and culminated under his son, Philip II. One oppressive measure after another, subversive of their civil rights, had reduced the inhabitants to a subjection well nigh absolute.

The religious reform which was rife in France and Germany had also spread through the Netherlands, but met with deadly opposition from the ruling powers, civil and ecclesiastical, being subjected to every cruel means for its suppression that these could exert, among which was the infamous system of espionage and torture known as the Spanish Inquisition. The Walloons were of all others most inveterate in their religious attachments. But being essentially French, and living in close proximity to France, the Calvinistic views had found early entrance among them and many warm adherents. As a people, their loyalty to the crown had been much shaken by the grave inroads upon their ancient rights and form of government. The Walloon, ever impatient of subjection—whence the boastful proverb, that "Hainault is subject only to God and the sun"—beheld with the utmost jealousy his country brought under the dominion of foreign tyrants, every part of it swarming with Spanish soldiers, whose presence and arrogance so spirited a people could ill brook; while the vile Inquisition thrust upon them, and working dismay and death among those indulging the new doctrines, was repulsive and terrible, even to many of the Catholics themselves.

At Avesnes, which since the year 1559 had had a Spanish garrison, the new religion found no toleration; yet nevertheless some of its worthy people, members of its old family *De Forest* included, had embraced the new faith, though this exposed them to imminent peril; for woe to him who dared avow that heresy or quit the old church.

Beyond the Sambre, within the borders of the Cambresis, was the handsome forest of Mourmal, consisting of heights covered with oaks. With a breadth of six miles it stretched northward as many leagues, from the bounds of Vermandois in Picardy, to near Bavay, the ancient capital of the Nervii. At its western edge, on the Selle, an affluent of the Scheldt, five leagues from Cambray and two west of Landrecy, stood the small city of Le Câteau, or *The Castle*, so called from its very old tower built by Bishop Erlnin. The Cambresis being a fief of the German Empire, Le Câteau, through the favor of the emperors, had long enjoyed immunities and privileges of which its citizens were justly proud.

For the space of some years many of its good burghers and their families had talked together freely and earnestly about the holy Scriptures; but with great secrecy, fearing persecution if it were known to any not in sympathy with them. Unobserved they made visits to the neighborhood of Bohain, a city up the Selle, in Vermandois, to hear the evangelical preaching; also to Tupigny, in Thiérache, and even as far as Crespy, near Laon, and Chauny, on the Oise; only to return with stronger faith in the gospel plan as found in the Scriptures, and utterly dissatisfied with their old belief. The new doctrines thus spread quietly but surely, and the whole town was leavened with them.

So it stood when Archbishop de Berghes, who was lord temporal as well as spiritual of the Cambresis, in order to check the growing disaffection to the church, fulminated an edict against the practice of attending the so-called Reformed preaching, reading heretical books, or chanting the psalms of Marot and Beza. To this little regard was paid, and two years passed by. Then it was repeated, and its execution enjoined upon all magistrates. A case was soon found. Certain burghers, who with their wives and children had attended the preaching of Rev. Pinchesrt, at Honnechy, a village south of Le Câteau, near Premont, on the line of Picardy, were tried and sentenced to be banished. This, and other attacks by the archbishop's officers upon the rights of the people of Le Câteau, led to popular meetings and strong remonstrances on the part of the latter. The numbers of the Reformed meanwhile had rapidly increased, and Rev. Philippe, minister of the church of Tupigny, by invitation preached for them many times in the faubourgs of the city, and organized a church, with a consistory of ten members. On August 16th, 1566, a deputation from the archbishop visited the town, and held grand mass in the Church of St. Martin, when Dr. Gemelli harangued the people, threatening them, should they not at once return to the Roman Church and make peace with the archbishop, with a ruin as dire as that which overwhelmed Jerusalem. Then a conference was held in the town-hall; but the appeals of the learned doctor fell powerless upon men who valued God's truth more than an archbishop's favor. Two days after this, the Dean of Avesnes, anxious for some of his own flock who had left his fold, visited Le Câteau on his return from an interview with the archbishop, and reiterated in the ears of the burghers what dangers hung over them all, the good with the evil; but to all his arguments they gave so brave a response from the Scriptures that he accomplished nothing.

In the midst of many trials of patience, from the repeated interference of the castellan and magistrates with the exercise of their religion, the news reached Le Câteau August 25th, from Valenciennes, a large Walloon town fifteen miles northward, that the people there had cast out all the images, relics, and other symbols of Romanism from their churches, and that the same had also been done in many other cities. This startling intelligence brought together that evening a large concourse of people with torches in the cemetery of St. Martin, to discuss this new posture of affairs. Very early the next morning Rev. Philippe arrived, and meeting with the consistory at the house of Claude Raverdy, it was resolved after discussion to follow the example of those of Valenciennes, and clear the churches of the objects deemed offensive, beginning at St. Martin's. So to St. Martin's they went, Philippe and a few others, pulled down the images and altars, and burnt them, with all their ornaments, and the missals, anthem books and others relating to the mass; the like being done in all the other churches, both in the city and faubourgs. This ebullition of iconoclastic zeal has been much condemned; but if the Reformed, where largely in the majority as at Le Câteau, claimed the right to order their worship as best pleased them, who may question it?

After this work of expurgation, a large number of the citizens gathered in the Church of St. Martin to hear a sermon from Rev. Philippe; many others also from the neighboring villages being present, who had come to the grain market. He also baptized three infants, and in the afternoon another.

Though the citizens, Reformed and Catholics, had wisely agreed not to harm each other on account of religion, the succeeding months were those of great public excitement. Two Huguenots being held prisoners in the neighboring village of Troisville by the castellan and échevins of Le Câteau, David du Four and others went with arms and liberated them. These magistrates finding themselves powerless retired to Cambray, leaving the field to the Reformed. The latter chose new municipal officers, and put the city in a better state of defence. Pastor Philippe continued his services at St. Martin's. Three couples were joined in marriage December 15th, one of the brides being the daughter of Jean de Forest, then living at Le Câteau. On Christmas the church, to their joy, celebrated the Lord's Supper in the city; whereas hitherto they had gone to Valenciennes, or to Premont or Tupigny, and even as far as St. Quentin and Laon.

The next spring a terrible stroke, planned by the archbishop, fell upon Le Câteau. On March 24th, 1567, two hundred cavaliers, led by the noted Count of Mansfield, soon after made Governor of Avesnes, surrounded the city. The gates being secured, the people made a good defence from the ramparts, pastor Philippe going from gate to gate to encourage them. But an entrance being gained through treachery, the city was taken. Philippe and his deacon were the first victims: the one, after a cruel beating, was hung; the other beheaded. The pastor's wife was subjected to gross treatment. Many executions followed during the ensuing month. One was that of David du Four, before named. He was a tailor at Le Câteau, and only twenty-two years of age. But on his examination he with firmness declared that "he paid more regard to his salvation and to God, than to men." He and four others were hung on April 9th. The Reformed who saved their lives were now in great affliction. An oath of fidelity to the archbishop and the Roman Church being imposed on the citizens, such as could not take it were expelled from the city. The Reformed Church, if it survived there, existed only in secret.

Hope was awakened the following year. The persecutions under the royal governor, the bloody Duke of Alva, had become so insufferable, that in 1568 the more northerly provinces broke out in revolt, and took up arms under the lead of that noble patriot, William of Orange. Fortune at first did not favor, and the prince, with a depleted but heroic band, concluded to join the Huguenot army in France. Passing Le Cateau, he "obtained a slight and easy victory" over the Spaniards at that place. But the city being well defended by the archbishop's soldiers, and Alva pressing hard on his rear, the great patriot, whose triumph yet lay in the future, was constrained to pass on.

Brighter were the prospects when, eight years later, the Walloons struck for their liberties. Unable longer to bear the outrages heaped upon them, these at length appealed to arms, joining the Flemings and Hollanders in the effort to drive the Spaniards from the country; for which a formal league was made at Ghent, November 8th, 1576. Sustained by "almost all the nobility of Hainault and Artois," the Walloon people, Catholic and Reformed, joined heartily in the common cause. With the latter class, now numerous, especially in the cities and towns on and near the Scheldt, this struggle was of highest import, not only appealing to their patriotism, but holding out the promise of religious toleration in case victory crowned their arms. But this gleam of hope, bright as a passing meteor, was equally transient. The struggle was maintained but two short years, when the Walloon leaders, cajoled by royal emissaries, and excited to jealousy of their compatriots the Dutch, first refused to contribute further of men or means; then renounced the confederacy, and privately formed a separate league, January 6th, 1579, in which Walloon Flanders, Artois, and Hainault uniting, promised to stand by the king and adhere to holy church. In a reconciliation with the king and renewal of their allegiance which followed on September 4th ensuing, the heads of the provinces aforesaid, pledged themselves to extirpate heresy.

Thus a death-blow was given to Walloon liberty, while the

Spanish cause secured the active support of the Catholic Walloons, both nobles and people; turning their weapons against their deserted friends, the Hollanders and Flemings, in their life and death struggle. Indeed, the king found no readier recruits nor better soldiers than the Walloons; "a people," says a contemporary writer, "taking delight in war, and whom the Spaniards might safely make use of in all dangers."

As a sequence, Holland, Zeeland, Gelderland, and other provinces, by a union published at Utrecht, January 29th, 1579, formed the free republic known as the Seven United Provinces; achieving their independence after a long and obstinate struggle. But the remaining Netherlands, part unwilling, part unable to shake off their fetters, relapsed into a more servile bondage to Spain and the Papacy. By the king's great clemency, the Protestant Walloons were allowed two years in which either to return to the bosom of the church or leave the country. Shut up to this alternative, thousands sought safety in exile.

Arschot, and the Croys and Lalains, all deeply implicated in the late revolt against the Spaniards, whom at heart they devoutly hated, were yet among the most active in promoting the submission of 1579, and now the Spanish cause had nowhere more zealous partisans. And they were pledged to root out the new religion, toward which they had only waxed more bitter since their cousin Antoine de Croy had embraced it and attached himself to the fortunes of Admiral Coligny; and another kinsman, William Robert, Prince of Sedan, had generously opened his gates to their persecuted and fleeing subjects, with whose faith and trials he was in sympathy. How opposite a character the Duke of Arschot, the ambitious, selfish courtier, whose frown was to be dreaded by the Huguenots, more especially those who, living on his own domains, were directly subject to his imperious will!

In the keeping of such were the destinies of Avesnes. The region round had indeed felt the blighting effects of the late war. It was invaded in the spring of 1578 by Don John, Alva's successor, who, advancing from eastward up the valley of the Sambre with his destroying army, captured the chief places in revolt, as far as Berlaimont, eight miles north-west of Avesnes, with many small towns "commodious for quartering the army;"

then again moving eastward, he took Beaumont, a seat of the Duke of Arschot, six miles south of the Sambre; also Chimay, in which was the young prince, the duke's son, and his troop of horse, these, by courtesy, being allowed to march out with their carbines. Then storming Philipville, the Don departed, leaving his general, Gonzaga, with horse and infantry to guard these frontiers; a duty he well performed, dispersing several parties from France coming to the aid of the Belgian patriots, while he also scoured and wasted the country to the very corn-crops in the field.

But this was as nothing to a people inured to the chances of war, or the general impoverishment to which they were now reduced; while there was hope of deliverance. But upon the ignominious submission of the Walloon nobles to the Spanish yoke, with the crushing blow thus given to the cause of patriotism and religious liberty; and the successes of the Spanish arms in the Cambresis, which reduced the few places still held by the malcontents, to whom no mercy was shown—the Reformed realized their desperate situation, and hastened to act upon the proffered alternative, abjuration or flight!

Deeply involved in these trying scenes were some of the De Forests already noticed, and of whom much remains to be said. The family, judging from its numbers, had been some time seated at Avesnes, where members of it still resided many years later. So much is well attested, though there is no redundance of details. Of Avesnes we have drawn the sketch as it had been and now was; the little world beyond which, probably, they had never far roamed, till forced to it by the untoward circumstances here related. Past are those blithe and budding years, spent in childish gambols along its rippling streams and through its oaken groves, or in listening to those winning tales of olden times about the lordly tenants of the castle, whose gray, dilapidated walls still linked so closely the present with the past, till its martial annals were as household words. Maturer life, with its stern realities, has also brought more tender attachments and domestic cheer as Heaven's kind gifts and the fruit of arduous but welcome toil—and which, despite life's corroding cares, have multiplied the ties of home, kindred, and friendships, which now can grow neither stronger nor dearer. But what a change in the times and in their prospects? They have heard, have embraced those soul-saving truths, revealed as they believe from heaven; and leaving the confessional and the mass, altars at which they had so blindly knelt, have cast in their lot with the devout but despised Huguenots. Their kindred adhering only more closely to the old church, there is a wide breach, and would it were only in sentiment! Dangers surround the Huguenot portion, and the safety of themselves and little ones of tender years depends upon an immediate flight. In the face of grave difficulties, they have renounced the altars and faith of their fathers, and what heart-struggles it cost them none may know but those who are led to relinquish a belief in which they have been trained and educated from youth to manhood. Now they lack not courage to accept the issue, to follow the utmost mandate of duty, though home endearments must give place to a painful exile. Noble proof of their faith and piety!

Sedan, on the Meuse, whither many were going, offered the nearest retreat; and thither also went the De Forests, some sixty miles south-eastward by way of the French border. Though the exact date of their exode has not been found, collateral circumstances assign it to the period directly succeeding the Walloon submission. Not to anticipate the important *rôle* reserved for this exiled family when they shall again come to our notice under better auspices, we dare venture an opinion that it will justify this effort, imperfect though it be, to illustrate the more obscure portion of their history.

CHAPTER III.

OUR SETTLERS FROM FRANCE AND WALSLANT.

AN eventful century in the affairs of France had rolled its round since the collegiate halls of the Sorbonne at Paris echoed the first notes of the Reformation uttered by the learned and inspired Le Fevre. That period, radiant with hope and promise, which directly followed the accession of Francis I., and in which the Reformed doctrines, joyfully embraced by the sober, thinking classes, were rapidly disseminated over all France, had been succeeded (1525) by terrible persecutions, when at times the whole land seemed fairly to reek with the blood of martyrs. Forced thereto in self-defence, the Huguenots took up arms in 1562, whence ensued a ruthless civil war, which raged with only brief intervals for over thirty years, during the reigns of Charles IX., Henry III., and, in part, of Henry IV. Assuming, as then and there was unavoidable, the double character of a politico-religious conflict, which involved in its toils king and clergy, noblesse and people, these long-protracted and bloody wars exhausted the country and reduced it to the verge of ruin. Only by this heroic stand, however, were the Huguenots able to maintain even a recognized existence in the land; but when the King of Navarre, their old leader, distinguished on many a battle-field, had fought his way to the throne as Henry IV., he issued in 1598 that famous decree for the pacification of his kingdom, called the Edict of Nantes, which threw its protecting ægis over the Huguenots, and gave them a season of peace and prosperity such as they enjoyed at no other period. A knowledge of what this Edict pledged, and how its pledges were violated in the succeeding reigns, will help us to understand the proper status of the Huguenots in the time of our refugees.

The Edict was based on a limited toleration, but was "the best that the state of the times allowed." It declared a full amnesty, conceded to the Huguenots liberty of conscience, made them eligible to all public offices and dignities, and for their protection provided special chambers within the local parliaments, the chief being the "Chamber of the Edict," in the Parliament of Paris. They were allowed to build and maintain churches and schools in all places where these had been permitted by former edicts. But this did not apply to episcopal or any walled cities, saving only La Rochelle and a few other strongly Huguenot towns, which for their security they were suffered to hold under the Edict. Further, *all lords, nobles, and other persons of the pretended Reformed religion*, holding a tenure by knight's service, or having the powers of a civil and criminal magistrate within their seigniory or manor, might, after due notice to the king's officers, and having the place registered, hold religious services at their principal residence, or cause it to be held for *their families, subjects, and all who shall wish to attend.*

The last was a most important concession. The places otherwise assigned the Reformed in which to erect churches and schools were but few and scattered, and to multitudes in distant localities proved of no benefit; but under the friendly shelter of private castles and manor-houses many suspended churches could be regathered and new ones organized, as was done; though often only by persistent effort and in the face of violent opposition, because the Reformed worship was seldom tolerated nearer any sizable town than from three to five miles, and for its peaceful enjoyment the faithful were often obliged to journey as many leagues. Laboring under the same disabilities in regard to schools, it was creditable to their parental fidelity that the secular education of their children was cared for equally with their religious training; and hence we notice that nearly all of our refugees had enjoyed advantages and were good penmen. Under the Edict the Reformed were not exempt from such burdens and annoyances as the payment of tithes to the parish priest, and the closing of their business places and suspension of all out-door and noisy labor on the oft-recurring festival days, when they must join in decorating the fronts of their houses in honor of the occasion, or permit it to be done by the official persons—and to all which it was dangerous to object.

Briefly, these were the advantages enjoyed by the Huguenot population under the Edict, during the halcyon days of Henry the Great. But trouble began with his assassination in 1610; an event which excited the utmost alarm among the Reformed, who in the change of rulers saw reason to apprehend a change of policy fatal to their interests. In vain the queen-mother, as regent, in the name of the young Louis XIII., as also that king himself, on assuming the reins of power in 1614, tried to allay these fears by professing a purpose to maintain the Edict of Nantes. Concini, an Italian favorite, being elevated to the position of prime-minister, the government from the first was wholly under Jesuit influence, which was regaining itself in the country; while the king, in 1615, by the arbitrary dissolution of the old States-General or national parliament, that "guardian of the public liberty," for which he substituted an assembly composed of more pliant materials, plainly foreshadowed the imperious policy which he had marked out, and by which he sought to centre all power in himself; thus giving cast to an administration characterized by a French writer of that day as "the most scandalous and dangerous tyranny that perhaps ever enslaved a state."

Soon followed the predicted change of policy touching the Huguenots, which first planned by the Archbishop of Paris, was now seconded by the ambitious Charles d'Albert, Duke de Luynes, who, with the blood of Concini fresh upon his hands, had supplanted the latter in the favor of the king, and also as prime-minister. It was to humble the Huguenots and take away their power of self-protection, by wresting from them their fortified towns and their political organization, which latter Henry IV. had sanctioned as a means of conserving their interests, through their general assemblies. The new government looked with jealousy upon these assemblies, some of whose acts at this feverish juncture were dictated rather by passion than cool judgment, and these indiscretions were made a ground for the high-handed course to which the government now resorted.

At the bare mention of the new policy, which the Catholic pulpits everywhere zealously lauded, all the old animosity against the Reformed again burst forth, bearing fruit in numerous acts of violence, both in the towns and rural districts. The first aggressive step taken by the king was in 1620, when he ordered the Catholic worship to be restored in Bearn, a part of Southern France, where for sixty years the Reformed had been the only religion. Being opposed as a flagrant breach of the Edict, the king invaded Bearn to enforce his decree by the bayonet. The Huguenots flew to arms, the cautionary cities acting with great spirit; and war desolated the Protestant communities of Bearn, Guienne, and Languedoc. The royal arms were only too successful. But Montpellier, chief city of Languedoc, having been taken by siege, and the regiments of Picardy and Normandy set at work to level its defences, here a peace was proposed, and concluded October 19th, 1622. Only La Rochelle and Montauban, of all their strong places, now remained to the Huguenots.

Deeply interested were the Reformed at the north in the struggles of their co-religionists in arms, and scarce dissembling their sympathies they fared as accomplices, being "given over to the hatred of the governors, the military commandants, the priests, and the populace." Mob outrage was common; the fine temple at Charenton, near Paris, was pillaged and burnt, though rebuilt at the public charge after the peace. The government disarmed the Huguenots of St. Quentin and others in Picardy, many of whom in 1621 retired to Geneva, Sedan, and England.

The hollow peace, as it proved, was ignored by Cardinal Richelieu, who became prime-minister in 1624. His grand idea, the unity of France and the supremacy of the church and monarchy, involved the prosecution of the war against the Huguenots, and the restless state of that people became the pretext. La Rochelle must be reduced, and was at length invested by powerful armies. The resistance was heroic, lasting a year and three months, while half its population died of famine and disease. Then it was forced to capitulate, October 28th, 1628.

Great excitement prevailed during this siege among the Huguenots at the north, who, under the guise of visiting, attending weddings, etc., often met to confer together about their affairs. Hence exaggerated rumors which reached the king's camp of conspiracies in Lower Normandy (about Caen and the Bessin), and in Picardy and Champagne. The king had demanded of the people of Amiens to send to his camp five hundred cloth suits and as many pairs of shoes; but the serge-makers, indignant at this demand, threatened the king's officer, who fled by night from his lodgings while the mob threw his coach into the Somme.

But Richelieu followed up his successes. Montauban, in the heart of Southern France, was also reduced early in 1629, and its defences razed. All the Huguenot strongholds were now in the king's hands, and the last civil war was at an end. The "Edict of Grace," so called, issued the same year, fixed the condition of the Protestants. *Submission and loyalty* were the specious terms on which they should continue to enjoy their religious privileges. But well they knew that this meant nothing less than an absolute subjection to the royal will, with no ability to ward off any further aggression upon their rights, since they were robbed of their only safeguard—that material power on which had depended the security of their persons, property, and religion.

Alarmed and grieved as were the Protestants at seeing their cause thus utterly ruined, their trials were only beginning, for they were now to be subjected to a course of proscription, which, growing more and more oppressive, was at length to become insupportable. Deserted by nearly all the nobility, and gradually ousted from government service and from most of the civil offices, there was still this gain—that they were freed from the temptations and snares of political life, which rendered so many idle and dissolute; while restricted in their pursuits to agriculture, to trade, and the industrial arts, they were repaid by a new development of their industry, and additions to their wealth. Even the infertile soils of the south, by dint of their toil, were made to wave with bounteous harvests. As merchants and manufacturers their integrity and proficiency was known and recognized in other lands. Nevertheless they were ill at ease.

Anachronisms in regard to the Huguenots easily occur from inattention to the order of events, or to the many diverse phases of their history. The period to which we have now arrived—the era proper of our refugees—was to them and their compeers fraught with no such promise as that which ushered in the reformation; nor yet a reign of persecutions dire, as that which immediately succeeded. In the past the few bright years of Henry IV. came up in the memories of long and dismal civil wars as a little oasis in the almost boundless desert waste. These wars being ended, they were now entered upon a term of thirty years, having the semblance of rest, but with its deep undercurrents of unrest. Even then was foreshadowed (but our refugees did not wait to see it) that final, doleful epoch, opening about 1661 with the destruction of temples or churches, with *arrêts du conseil*, for excluding the Reformed from trades and professions, etc., and closing with the Revocation of the Edict of Nantes in 1685, with dragoons, dungeons, and galleys; causing multitudes of these purest and noblest of the land—artisans, tradesmen, professors, and divines—to escape to other countries, which were thus enriched by their industries, their talents, and their piety.

Hence *our* refugees lived in times of but semi-repose, in which painful memories of the past gave ghastly form and reality to the graver presentiments of the future. True, it was an age of more enlightenment and less fanaticism than those preceding, but the popular aversion to the Huguenots had not essentially lessened. It had only in a degree transferred itself from their creed to their position as a social class. They were an unpopular minority, having peculiarities repulsive to the habits and tastes of the people at large. Their views, feelings, and mode of life, their strict discipline, the simplicity of their worship, and scrupulous observance of the Sabbath, afforded nothing in common with those within the pale of the dominant church. To them the Huguenot appeared reserved, rigid, and even haughty. His very gravity was thought to betoken a felt superiority. He claimed to be controlled by a purer faith, a better code of morals. Intelligence, discrimination, and independence, as well as piety, were essential supports to the religious tenets he avowed and maintained. He valued and improved his freedom to inquire and interchange opinions upon matters of church polity, and questions of doctrine and discipline, as well as those affecting his civil rights. Keeping within the limited circle of his home and people, and wont to deny himself, the Huguenot yielded but sparingly to the luxury in which others indulged. Thus order and economy ruled both his house and business, and brought him thrift. In his frugality of living, and in the time saved from useless festivals for needful toil, he found a temporal gain. His industry and business assiduity seemed ever to reproach his neighbors with their slackness and improvidence; and envy of his superior intelligence, advantages, and prosperity too commonly showed itself, after the loss of his military and political significance, in an air of triumph over his humbled condition. He still trusted for protection to his legal charter, the Edict of Nantes; but this soon lost its prestige with the courts. His greatest fear was from the covert designs of government and clergy to effect his ruin; the latter over and anon reiterating their demands for new restraints upon the Reformed. In 1630 began systematic efforts to reclaim them to the church by means of *convertisseurs*, who were paid a definite sum for every proselyte; and in 1635 Richelieu created in each province a Royal Intendant, "to promote a stronger national unity," but which meant the use of all means for suppressing the religion. These officials, chosen with special reference to their fitness, dispensed their authority with rigor, and first instigated those severe and effective measures eventually employed to complete the ruin of the Huguenots. The decisions of the Intendant were invariably adverse to the Huguenot. And it was usually so in questions which came before the local parliaments; the rule obtaining in the various tribunals, that the Reformed had no rights except by sufferance. Law and fact were wrested against them; every severe sentence became a precedent; and so by one restriction after another nearly all of value that the Edict of Nantes had pledged was taken away long before the Edict was formally rescinded. With a painful sense of insecurity, it became an ever-present, momentous question with this afflicted people, how to avert the greater calamities which passing events so plainly foreshadowed, except by quitting their country.

What this question involved we may not apprehend. The bitter conflict going on within, as the stricken man pursued his daily avocation, was often known only to his family and his God. Thrice dear to him was his country, so venerable in antiquities, heroic in deeds, romantic in legends; all that was charming in stream and landscape, genial in the air, and generous in the soil; all that was prized in institutions and customs, in social and home endearments. His religious ideas had not weakened, but only in one direction changed his attachments. With a sort of aristocratic pride he cherished the hereditary records of the virtue, constancy, or piety of his ancestors who had suffered for the faith. These were the letters of his nobility. They were links binding him only the more closely to his native soil, which had grown dearer with every trial or loss he had been called to endure, and each act of arbitrary power designed to force him from its bosom. But the very act of leaving was hedged with difficulties: business, property, and personal effects were more easily sacrificed, than converted into available means. The younger class, with few such entanglements, found a change much easier than did their seniors; and hence the emigrations at this era consisted very largely of the former.

Those spasmodic flights of the Huguenots under some great and sudden terror—of which there had been many in the course of their history, when multitudes by families, and of every age and class, left hastily for foreign lands, had ceased with that which took place on the fall of La Rochelle and Montauban, when the final blow was dealt to the civil power of the Huguenots. For the thirty years ensuing, and during which most of the Harlem refugees sought other lands, the emigration was not large, but of a valuable character. The removals were usually undertaken thoughtfully and heroically—in general, as just said, by a young and enterprising class—in the belief that the time had come to leave a country, where, surrounded by so many hostile elements, it was especially difficult for them to live, and which threatened to become worse instead of better. Their eyes naturally turned toward Holland, England, and America, as more hospitable lands, and the chief emigration was to those countries from the marine provinces, Picardy, Normandy, and those south of them, for which their numerous seaports afforded every facility.

The West Indies, inviting both for climate and fruitfulness, were becoming the resort of many for whom the cold region of Canada had no attractions. Removals to these islands had been going on under the direction of a company formed at Paris in 1626, at the instance of M. d'Enambuc, who the year before had visited the island of St. Christopher, in a brigantine from Dieppe. There he planted the first colony in 1627, and which became the nursery of others afterwards formed on the adjacent islands. In 1635, Martinique was occupied by a hundred old and experienced settlers from St. Christopher. But D'Enambuc died; in 1640 Jesuit missionaries arrived at Martinique (where were then near a thousand French, "without mass, without priest,") and reluctantly admitted by the governor and people, heightened the public dissensions which broke out in the islands, and which grew so violent five years later, especially in Martinique, that many of the Huguenots were glad to get back to Europe; these going mostly to Holland, and some of them, as the Casier family, of Calais, eventually finding a more tranquil abode at Harlem. We shall allude to these again before concluding our account of the homes and wanderings of our refugees.*

Home!—fancy is ever swifter than pen or pencil to draw the picture. The old familiar spot around which the heartstrings entwine, endeared by many tender associations, perchance made sacred by its sanctified sorrows. And how bitter the moment when the refugee, gazing upon it for the last time, turned his steps toward a foreign soil; like the great patriarch departing from Haran, knowing not his destiny, but trusting his covenant God! But alas! to too many of our refugees, forced to changes as they were by a regard for their personal safety or to secure a livelihood, or both, home, as restricted to the place of their birth and early life, must have lost much of its significance. To these pilgrims home was often less the locality and society of which they bore the type, than the circle or community of like faith in which for the time being their lot was cast. Difficult ofttimes as this makes it to trace the refugee to his original home, we shall leave the reader to note how far our efforts in that regard have succeeded.

* Inquiry can but partially break the silence which hangs over these wanderings. And here starts a query: was our David Demarest a sharer with Philip Casier in his West India, as he was in some of his subsequent travels? Did he sustain toward Sieur *des Marets*, (an old captain of St. Christopher who was beheaded Sept. 7, 1641, by the governor, De Poincy, for joining the populace in opposing his tyranny,) such relations as made him one most deeply affected by his tragic fate? Oisemont, in Picardy, the seat of the Demarests, had a Commandery of Malta, of which De Poincy was commander. Strange coincidences if merely accidental!

SAINTONGE was one of the provinces lying within the Bay of Biscay, and which, owing to the tendency of the Huguenots during their protracted troubles to remove from the interior into the marine districts and towns, became crowded with refugees, and were a principal theatre of the bloody civil wars. Saintonge was the birthplace of our "very learned" Dr. Johannes de La Montagne, whose history will contribute much of interest to these pages. *La Montagne* was not his family name, but an adjunct which finally took the place of the former, and was originally derived, as correlative facts seem to indicate, from La Montagne, a district of Burgundy. But Dr. La Montagne was called a *Santo*, which is the provincial designation for a native of Saintonge—akin to that of Norman, Picard, etc. His birth happening in 1595, but three years before the Edict of Nantes restored order to the realm and peace to the Huguenots, and under which emigration mostly ceased up to the death of Henry IV., it is highly probable that La Montagne left France somewhere within the ten years of public unrest succeeding the murder of the king, and culminating in the last civil wars under Louis XIII., which opened in 1620, prior to which date, however, La Montagne and others of his family were enjoying peace and security in Holland. He therefore knew as little personally of these latter wars as he did of the earlier troubles which preceded the Edict of Nantes. Among our French refugee families, his was the first to become exiles. We speak irrespective of the Walloon families, of whom the first to flee their country were those of De Forest and Vermeille or Vermilye, the latter in the troubles of the sixteenth century taking refuge in England. Not till after the last civil wars, as before said, and which occurred quite too early for them to have borne arms, did the body of our refugees leave their native France.

Saintonge counted among its cities La Rochelle with its heroic memories, and which gave us Jacques Cousseau and Paul Richard, both sterling characters and identified with Harlem. We know not if either was old enough at the time of the final siege and reduction of Rochelle in 1628 to have shared its terrors and miseries; but both probably left on account of the severe measures pursued by Louis XIV. for restoring Catholicism in that old Protestant stronghold, and which occasioned many removals.

Northerly from La Rochelle, the rugged peninsula of Bretagne, or Brittany, jutting far into the Atlantic, is as remarkable for its strange vicissitudes as for its dreary forests, barren heaths, pent-up valleys, vast fields of Druid remains, and lone hillocks crowned by the ruins of castles; or yet its brawny peasantry in grotesque garb, and (in Lower Brittany) still speaking the harsh Celtic tongue. Long a distinct sovereignty, it was conquered by the Norman dukes; later an affluent duchy, for which Charles of Blois and his race valiantly but vainly battled with the house of Montfort, it was finally engrossed by the crown. But not feudal nor royal tyranny could ever crush the native independence and hauteur of the Breton, which so cropped out in the case of our Glaude le Maistre (Delamater), whose ancestors were the lords of Garlaye, in the diocese of Nantes, though he happened not to be born in Brittany. Near La Moussaye, in the interior of Lower Brittany, southward from St. Malo, was the original seat of the family of our David Uzille. The Reformed churches at Nantes and La Moussaye found in the Le Maistres and Uzilles warm supporters.

One of the three districts forming the great Norman meadows, whose fine horses and cattle were so celebrated, was the Bessin, from a forest largely converted into tillable lands and orchards by the patient industry of its peculiar people; French indeed, but unlike their neighbors and more like the English, being descendants of the Otlings (or Osterlings), a Saxon tribe which overran this district in the fourth century. Their small town, St. Lô, occupied a rocky eminence, girt on three sides by a ravine through which ran the river Vire, parting the low-lying Bessin from the mountainous Cotentin. Its streets, lined with antiquated houses, ascended steeply to the crown, whereon stood its old sombre cathedral. Full a century earlier it had its Huguenot church, which sent delegates to the first synod at Paris in 1559. From this secluded Norman town—strange transition truly!—a worthy refugee, "Letelier," as with some claim to rank he signs himself, found his way to Harlem, to woo and wed a Picard's daughter!

Beyond the Seine in Upper Normandy we next find traces of

our refugees. Dieppe, capital of the high and mainly level region called the Land of Caux,* the land of grain and grass, of cider and perry, embracing the coast country from the Seine to the Bresle, was seated at the foot of hills through which flowed the river Arques, passing under the great stone bridge that united the town to its suburb Le Pollet, the fishermen's quarter, where under the Edict of Nantes the Huguenots had their church and enjoyed the ministrations of Montdenis and others. Dieppe also had an immense commerce, its mariners famous of old for distant voyages. Hence sailed D'Esnambuc in 1625 to St. Christopher, paving the way for French colonies in the West Indies, in which, as before intimated, Harlem settlers first tried their fortunes. And from this port many of the refugees took ship for other countries, as we presume did François le Sueur and Robert le Maire, who came thence to Harlem. How it was with these we know not, but may conclude that some left Dieppe and other French ports destined for New Netherland, since its invitations to such colonists had already reached these ports through intercourse with Holland. Le Sueur was born at Challe-Mesnil or Colmenil, a small borough or market town three miles south of Dieppe. His name—taking such forms with his descendants as *Leseur*, *Lesier*, *Lasier*, and *Losier*—was well established in Caux, and a century previous had figured among the cloth makers of Rouen.

Very interesting is Picardy, whence came so many of the French exiles who made their homes at Harlem for longer or shorter periods; in all some thirty families, of which a full third were Picards or of Picard descent. Of this class were our Tourneur, Cresson, Demarest, Casier, and Disosway, all of whom, except the last, served as magistrates.

But who were the Picards? A quite superior people to the average French; being of a mixed origin, descendants of both Belgæ and Celtæ, and occupying the border between these two ancient nations, or rather the district which parted the Celtæ from the Nervii, the most invincible of the Belgic tribes. Thus, sanguine and choleric like the Celts, they approached the Belgæ in their moral and physical stamina. In stature above the

* Pronounced *Ko*. It is highly probable that our well-known family of *Coe* derive their name from Caux.

medium, with usually a well-developed frame, they betrayed their affinity to the Walloons, whose patois, rough and disagreeable, theirs resembled; yet, proud and spirited, they held those neighbors and all others in secret disdain. The love of independence was not so strong within them as the love of equality; it was here their vanity showed itself, but it tempered the popular homage to wealth or titles. Though hasty, blunt, and obstinate, yet without the effrontery of the Normans or the superstition of the Champenois, and more religious than either, the Picards were withal lively, generous, honest, and discreet. Their conversation sparkled with wit, mirth, and sarcasm. Necessity rather than inclination made them industrious, yet they yielded their full share of workers and proficients in the arts and sciences; as also of able physicians and divines, some of the latter as much distinguished in the controversial history of the Reformation as others had been who were its earliest champions. With intelligence, and a manly aim to excel in what they undertook, even though it were but agriculture, in which by far the greater number were engaged, the Picards could not but add a valuable element to any society so fortunate as to attract them.*

The narrow strip of the seaboard, in breadth twenty miles or less, which stretched southerly from Calais to the Canche, embraced the districts of Guines and Boulonnais, two subdivisions of Picardy. Of its larger part lying on either side of the Somme, but extending a hundred miles inland to the borders of Champagne, the coast section called Ponthieu reached some thirty miles up the Somme, Abbeville being the chief town. Easterly lay in succession the Amienois, Santerre, Vermandois, and Thiérache, their southerly sides forming a line sufficiently

* *Picard*, though a term of disputed origin, is admitted to have been first local and restricted to the people of the Amienois, the district in which Amiens, the provincial capital, is seated; but it early spread to the whole, supplanting all the tribal designations. It probably came from the *pique*, an ancient war weapon, with the German affix *ard*, meaning *species* or *race*; adhering to this people as inventors of that weapon, or from the renown they had acquired in handling it. So they became known as the Picards, or *pikemen*. Gibbon, who dates the name not earlier than the year 1200, says, "It was an academical joke, an epithet first applied to the quarrelsome humor of those students in the University of Paris who came from the frontier of France and Flanders." But its occurrence early in the eleventh century refutes this statement.

winding, but in general east and west. These seven districts composed modern Picardy; but five others lying southerly of these—to wit, the Beauvoisis, Noyonnois, Soissonnois, Laonnois, and Valois—were equally Picard territory, as proven by the characteristics of the people, although these districts had been annexed to the Isle of France.

These several sections of Picardy, save Guines and Boulonnais, were watered by one or more of its three principal rivers, the Somme, the Oise, and the Aisne; and seated on these were most of those fine old cities with strange histories for which Picardy was noted. Two streamlets, engrossing many little rills from Champagne and Hainault, united in the centre of Thiérache to form the Oise, which now stretched westward to Guise in the same district, but soon took its course in general south-westerly, nearly parallel with the coast, till it entered the Seine at *fin d'Oise*, below Paris, distant from Guise ninety odd miles. Scattered along its charming banks from Guise downward, at intervals of some ten miles lay in delightful seclusion other antiquated towns as Ribemont, La Fère, Chauny, Noyon, Compiègne, Verberie, Creil, Beaumont, and Pontois; the last six adorned with royal palaces, exclusive of Noyon; a pretty town and a bishop's seat, but of more interest to the Huguenots as the great Calvin's birthplace. Just above Compiègne, the Aisne, a large tributary, entered the Oise from the eastward, and on it lay the stately city of Soissons. Below Creil a smaller branch, the Thérain, entered from the westward, on its upper waters seated, within a cordon of charming hills, the venerable town of Beauvais. The Somme, rising near the borders of Thiérache, on passing St. Quentin in Vermandois curved southward to Ham, then again to the north to Péronne, when it resumed its course westerly past Corbie to Amiens, and thence north-west through the Amienois and Ponthieu plains to its outlet. The region around its head-waters about Vermandois was rendered very picturesque by the wooded hills which here crossed Picardy; the broad plains below, just referred to, were less attractive to the eye, though varied by a succession of pretty intervales which bordered the tributary streams, and whose green pastures, trees, and shrubbery agreeably relieved the general nakedness of the country and the apparent hardness of the whitish soil, the latter composed one third of chalk, but productive, and yielding fine crops of wheat. The sub-district of Ponthieu called the Marquenterre, embracing extensive pastures adjoining the coast, on the north of the Somme, had been recovered from the wash of the sea by a line of downs and dykes; to the south of the river's mouth the land had a gentle rise toward Normandy, till it formed the table-lands of Caux and the chain of cliffs that there bound the coast.

Picardy was originally composed of many small counties or earldoms, instead of forming but one under a single count. Never so united and ruled, it was in this respect an anomaly among the French provinces. Its ancient tribal divisions determined mainly its modern districts, and eight of the dozen composing it took name from their chief city. Its history, says Michelet, "seems to embrace the whole of the ancient history of France." Its plains and hills had been trodden by the great Cæsar and his legions, and it was on the banks of the Sambre near Maubeuge that he encountered the warlike Nervii, whose intrepidity almost wrested victory out of that fatal defeat which broke their power and gave Gaul to the conqueror. Near Soissons, five centuries later, the warrior Clovis in an equally decisive battle extinguished the Roman power and established that of the Franks. Here also had the Austrasian and Neustrian factions found a battle-ground, till the defeat of the latter in 687 at Testry, in Vermandois, initiated the varied fortunes of the race of Charlemagne. Up the Somme had often rolled that fearful tide of Vandal and Norman invasion, which left no river unvisited from the Meuse to the Loire, desolating their banks and sacking towns, churches, and monasteries, at last contributing with other causes to the fall of the monarchical power in the ninth century and the disintegration of the kingdom. Picardy, or rather its several sections, had come within the grasp of haughty chieftains, mostly of the family of the defunct Charlemagne, and who, as refractory as their compeers ruling the larger provinces and equally greedy of dominion, played a no less conspicuous part in the turbulent drama of the times. The early annals of these small earldoms superabound with deeds of rapine and blood. Not content with the conquest of neighboring towns or territory, they made kings or humbled them at will; and in fact these imperious Picard lords for a long time ruled the destinies of the kingdom. But what strange freaks had fortune played with these old titled dynasties! Once scarce recognizing any sovereign and with all the advantage of a hereditary entail, yet one by one they had shared the fate of the great provinces, Champagne, Normandy, and others: the old counts, with all the dazzling splendor of their houses, had passed away, and their possessions by a studied policy of the kings had been mostly engrossed as crown domains. True, it had taken from the twelfth century to the sixteenth to consummate these changes. More favored, however, were some of those districts which took the form of bishoprics. Descending by the elective process from one prelate to another in regular succession, these had withstood the feudal powers of the Middle Ages and the civil convulsions of many centuries. Nor restricted to the exercise of spiritual power in their bishoprics, some of these bishops had come to enjoy great temporal dignity, even the high position of peers of the realm, as were those of Laon, Noyon, and Beauvais; to the first of whom also pertained the title of duke, and to the other two that of count. Herein may be seen the superior advantages of the existing hierarchy to hold and transmit or even to augment its power. All this while the sturdy burghery, their rights ever being trampled on, figure in many a sharp struggle with their tyrannical rulers; but appealing for help to royalty only to be ultimately betrayed, vanquished, and despoiled of their choicest franchises, as the power ecclesiastic and kingly came to acquire that supreme ascendency which it held in the reigns of Louis XIII. and Louis XIV., the times of our refugees.

Of the chief dignitaries then ruling parts of Picardy was the Duke de Chaulnes, in whom was the temporal, and Bishop Le Fevre who held the spiritual, power in the Amienois: but more of these presently. Augustine Potier was supreme in the Beauvoisis, which was the most wealthy bishopric in Picardy. Holding the fee of the soil as had his predecessors since the year 1015, when Bishop Roger got the county by deed from his brother Eudes, the Count of Champagne, Potier gloried in the titles of "Bishop and Count of Beauvais, Peer of France and Vidame of Gerberoy." He was also Grand Chaplain to the

Queen, and intensely zealous for the church and monarchy, though it was hinted that his capacity did not equal his ambition. The Noyonnois was under the rule of Henri de Barradat, to whose titles of Bishop and Count of Noyon was added that of Peer of France. The Marquise de Hocquincourt, Charles de Mouchy, had succeeded his father as royal governor in Santerre, for which he was held fitted by his valor and his devotion to Louis XIII. This district had been taken from ancient Vermandois in 1215 by King Philip Augustus, who had annexed Vermandois to the crown, upon the old counts, the most affluent and potent in Picardy, and whose sway lasted over three centuries, becoming extinct. It included the cities of Péronne, Montdidier, and Roye, the first, the old seat and stronghold of the counts, being now the residence of the governor, and deemed the key of France on these frontiers. De Mouchy distinguished himself in the war in the Low Countries, etc., and in 1651 was made a Marshal of France; but taking offence at Louis XIV. he joined the Spanish cause, and was killed at Dunkirk in 1658. Vermandois proper now formed a bailiwick, subject to the Bishop and Duke of Laon, Philibert de Brichanteau. Thiérache was mainly engrossed by the Duchy of Guise, of which the town and castle so called was the seat, being still the domain of the House of Guise, those infamous and deadly foes of the Huguenots, and one of whose ancestors, a Duke of Lorraine, had gotten this estate by marriage with a grandchild of the great crusader, Jacques d'Avesnes. But retributive justice seems to have visited the later Duke of Guise, Charles de Lorraine, who as admiral of a fleet had served against the Huguenots at La Rochelle in 1622. Ambitious and intriguing like his predecessors, he quarrelled with Richelieu, and retiring in 1631 with his family to Florence, died in exile in 1640. Ponthieu, much to the disgust of its people, and in violation of pledges given them by Henry IV., had been conferred by Louis XIII. upon one who had little merit, unless it consisted in his two plots to dethrone Henry IV., for which he lay long in the Bastile; this was Charles de Valois, natural son of Charles IX. of St. Bartholomew infamy. But as he was a good soldier and zealous for the king, he ruled till his death in 1650. Boulonnais and Guines, held directly by the crown, had long been ruled by royal governors.

Louis XI., on recovering the former from the House of Burgundy in 1477, had ceded it to the Virgin Mary, by an act of homage in the church at Boulogne, and consenting to hold it of her as a fief; by which curious stroke of policy he thought to preserve it to France. Now what enemy would dare touch it; what inhabitant would not die in its defence? And it had succeeded admirably!

The Amienois, as the seat of the provincial capital, was the most important division of Picardy. Spreading across the fertile valley of the Somme in the form of a not very regular quadrangle, it was ten leagues broad and twenty in length north and south, reaching from the bounds of Artois, and in part the earldom of St. Paul, to the hills anticlinal of the basins of the Somme and Oise, which separated it from the Beauvoisis. It took name from its ancient possessors, the Ambiani, whose jurisdiction, extending west to the Channel, included Ponthieu, which even now was within the diocese of the Bishop of Amiens. Many thrifty villages, with broad, well-tilled fields irrigated by brooks and streams, which from distant hill sources gently coursed their way to the Somme, gave it the aspect of a rich country. From a peculiar feature of its government it was styled the *Vidamate of Amiens.* The office of vidame, once common, was now almost peculiar to this district of Picardy. From some powerful chieftain called in ancient times by the bishop to aid him in protecting his domains against the invasions of the Normans and the rapacity of native seigniors, had originated the office of *vice dominus*, or vidame. And from the reluctance of the proud baron to yield the advantage thus gained, and the inability of the bishop to dispense with his services, the office became fixed and hereditary. It was now one of chief dignity and influence in the Amienois, the present vidame, Honore d'Albert, being a duke and peer of France. As brother to the prime-minister, Duke de Luynes, he also had ingratiated himself with the king, and through his favor obtained in 1619 the hand of the daughter and heiress of Philip-Emanuel, Lord de Picquigny, the last of the vidames of the House d'Ailly; and with her, beside the vidamate, the seigniory and castle of Picquigny, on the Somme, with an annuity in rents of £9000. The king at the same time made him his lieutenant-general in the Government of Picardy;* the next year he was dubbed a knight of the King's Orders, and raised to the dignity of Duke de Chaulnes and Peer of France. The important post of Governor of Picardy, Henry IV. had conferred with his name upon Henry of Orleans, Duke de Longueville, at his baptism in 1595; his uncle, the Count of St. Paul, acting during his minority. Longueville's father and *his* father had held the same post. But in 1619 the Duke de Luynes aforesaid superseded De Longueville, and to him was also given the government of the city and citadel of Amiens. But he being killed in 1621, while absent prosecuting the war against the Huguenots, the particular government of the city and citadel was transferred to his brother, the vidame. The Government of Picardy in the next few years passed through several hands, including the Dukes of Elbœuf and Chevreuse, both of the noted House of Guise and knights of the King's Orders; but Chevreuse retiring in 1633, this position also was conferred on the Duke de Chaulnes, and to it soon after added the powers of Royal Intendant, an office, as before said, created to keep a watch over the Huguenots, and which could not have been better bestowed than on the duke, bound as he was by every obligation to the king, and also true to the mandates of the church.†

The Bishops of Amiens claimed a succession from St. Firmin, first on the prelatical roll, and held to have suffered martyrdom in 287, with many of his flock, by order of the Roman magistrate. The present bishop, François le Fevre, son of Sieur de Caumartin, of Ponthieu, having become coadjutor to Bishop la Marthonie in 1617, the next year succeeded him in the See, and though some of the people violently resisted his induction, he had sustained the character of an amiable and good man, meas-

* The *Government* of Picardy, as distinguished from the old province, embraced only the Amienois, Santerre, Ponthieu, Boulonnais, and Guines; the latter also called "Calais and Pais-reconquis," because it had been recovered from the English in 1558.

† The Duke de Chaulnes died October 31, 1649, in his 69th year, and was succeeded in his titles by his son Henry Louis, born 1621; but he dying May 21, 1653, without issue, the vidamate passed to a collateral branch of the family. In naming this son after the king and his late father, the duke showed his attachment to his royal patron; and at his baptism by the bishop, June 13, 1625, during a festive season at Amiens, hereafter noticed, the widow of Henry IV., and the king, represented by the Duke of Chevreuse, stood as god-parents.

ured by a standard which then and there was not the highest. Upon 30,000 livres of income yielded by his eight hundred parishes, he lived elegantly in his palace at Amiens. This city, described in former pages, with allusions to its early and heroic history, was the capital of the Amienois, as indeed of all Picardy. It had a brave 50,000 people, more or less. Abbeville, twenty-five miles down the Somme, its nearest rival in population, then boasted 35,000 or upward; but after Boulogne-sur-mer and St. Quentin, each about half the size of Amiens, the Picard cities rapidly dwindled to a paltry three thousand or less. The chief spiritual and ecclesiastical authority thus reposing in the bishop, and the secular in the duke with his numerous functions and dignities, while the *provosts* and other officials of the king came in for a share in the local jurisdiction, it is obvious the people of the Amienois had quite enough of rule. Without need to further define their respective powers, we know they made a unit against the Huguenots and their interests.*

Picardy's part in the great moral struggle of the sixteenth century was peculiar. Etaples, a little seaport on the Canche, sent its Le Fevre to herald the Reformation; Noyon a Calvin, to vindicate it by voice and pen, and give a system of faith to the Huguenot churches; and Cuthe, in Vermandois, the no less excellent Ramus, slain in the St. Bartholomew—worthy representative of its noble martyrs. And humble peasants, back from their harvest labors at Meaux, had borne to Thiérache a richer harvest of precious truth, and planted at Landuzy-la-ville one of the earliest of the Reformed churches. Thus nowhere had arisen stronger moral forces in support of the religion. On the other hand, does not Guise, in Thiérache, recall its hereditary foes, those sanguinary dukes, and Péronne one of their foulest plots, the "Holy League," impiously so called, which, sworn to extirpate the Huguenots, soon plunged the country into the bloodiest of its civil wars? But mark a fact: among the two hundred "subjects and inhabitants of the country of Picardy," embracing "princes, lords, gentlemen, and others, as well of the state ecclesiastic as of the noblesse and third estate," who subscribed this infamous League and took the oath in the town-hall

* Bishop Le Fevre died of apoplexy, November 17, 1652, probably after all our refugees had left Picardy.

at Péronne, February 13th, 1577, we find but one of the family names afterwards appearing at Harlem; so nicely drawn were the family lines between the friends and foes of the religion! Zealously did the League pursue its nefarious object of "crushing out heresy;" till, at the close of the ensuing civil wars, in which Picardy, if not often the scene of actual hostilities, had helped to swell the ranks of the respective armies (and its regiment a fixed part of the royal forces), the Huguenot churches within its bounds, once numerous and flourishing, were reduced to a few scattered and timid flocks.

Dark pictures of the times preceding loomed up to the Huguenot mind at Amiens, where the Reformed opinions had early been received with great favor. Of Louis de Berguin, a Walloon from Artois, who, first to maintain those doctrines here in 1527, was burnt for it at Paris. Of mob violence; of fines and imprisonments for refusing to decorate their houses at Corpus Christi. Of that fell day in 1568, when one hundred and twenty Huguenots were slain in the streets of Amiens; and the terror caused by the Paris St. Bartholomew, which was only averted here by strict orders from the Duke de Longueville, Governor of Picardy. And of the dismal era of the League, in which plot were implicated some of the most powerful lords of the Amienois; the vidame, Louis d'Ailly, a noble exception, having with his family embraced the religion. He encouraged the faithful, who for a time met at his house for worship; though his successor, Philip Emmanuel, last vidame of that house, was forced in 1588 by the violence of the people to pronounce for the League. Only when Henry IV. turned Catholic did the citizens of Amiens acknowledge him as king, and expel their late governor, Count d'Aumale, who was a Guise. But they carefully "stipulated in making their submission that the Huguenot preaching should be prohibited in their precincts and suburbs." This was on August 10th, 1594. Not long after occurred the Spanish occupation of the city, which they entered by an ingenious artifice, and its deliverance by the armies of Henry IV. Peace with Spain soon followed, with another event more felicitous—the passage of the Edict of Nantes, arresting the civil wars and restoring order to the realm. Then Amiens, especially for the rest of that happy reign, became the mart of a flourishing trade and commerce, of which its looms furnished the staples; but a half century later and the Huguenot emigrations had reduced these industries to the verge of ruin—so alarming in 1665 as to lead the general government to interpose a remedy. In no wise exempt from the grievances common to the Reformed, under the Edict, those at Amiens and vicinity also had their own.

On June 7th, 1625, Amiens witnessed a brilliant pageant. It was the city's generous welcome to a young queen, the beautiful Henrietta Maria, of scarce sixteen years, sister of the king and child of Henry the Great, who was on her way from Paris to Boulogne to meet her spouse, already wedded though but once seen, Charles I. of England, then but two months a king. A letter from King Louis, bespeaking for the youthful queen "une joyeuse entrée," had led to ample preparations; so on the set morning the city was all excitement, in every quarter heard the sound of trumpets and drums to muster the military bands, with the noblesse, who were present from all the country round to take part in the grand reception.

The Duke de Chaulnes, with three hundred well-mounted cavaliers, rode out two leagues to meet the bride and her retinue (which last included the queen-mother and queen-regnant, besides dukes, earls, and lords, English and French, with many noble dames and damsels, and withal a guard of soldiers), and escorted them to the city. Their approach thereto, entrance through the Beauvais gate, and march to the cathedral, where they were met and greeted by Bishop le Fevre and the Chapter, was one grand ovation; many complimentary addresses and the thunder of musket and arquebuse bidding the young queen welcome. Just outside the city gate was first passed a magnificent triumphal arch with a beautiful tableau and other devices, all intended to please the queen and courtly party. Six other principal pieces, replete with designs drawn from classic and French history, surprised them along the way to the cathedral; one representing Jason and the Golden Fleece, a motto affixed declaring "Maria is the Fleece and Charles the Jason." In another, three belles personified the goddesses Juno, Minerva, and Venus contending before Paris as judge for the prize of beauty, the golden apple. But Paris, disallowing all their claims, turned and presented the apple to Queen Henrietta as "the real beauty." At the cathedral *Te Deum* was chanted, the grand organ pealing forth eloquent music, followed by prayers. Then her majesty was escorted to apartments in the episcopal palace, where were presentations and addresses to the queen, with gifts of some dozens of superb hypocras, besides a large variety of living birds and game of choice kinds, all in handsome cages. The queen-regnant and others of the royal party were sumptuously entertained at the citadel by the Duke and Duchess of Chaulnes for the nine days they were at Amiens, and then they departed with many rich presents and kind wishes.

Amiens looked but coldly on another pageant, more significant if less imposing. The two were probably among the recollections of some later at Harlem, as we are assured was this to be described, leaving deeper and more enduring traces upon the heart. Betimes on Sunday morning from that same Beauvais gate, called also the Gate of Paradise—from a legend that here our Saviour in the garb of a beggar once appeared to St. Martin—a human stream began to issue, representing both sexes and all ages, sires and matrons, blooming youths and happy-faced children, all in best attire. With decorum suited to holy time, but enlivening the journey by cheerful and pious conversation, to the looker-on it needed not to be told the all-important errand upon which these devout people were going along that well-trodden way to the pleasant village of Salouel, on the Celle, two or three miles to the southward of Amiens.

The Huguenot worship had been long banished beyond the gates of the city. Prohibited in express terms, as already seen, by the decree which restored Amiens with Péronne and Abbeville to obedience to Henry IV., this was also confirmed by the Edict of Nantes.

Taught also by experience that they could not meet for worship within the city walls except at the risk of being molested, perhaps broken up by a mob; it in some measure reconciled the Reformed to what was felt to be a harsh and burdensome requirement. The privilege of meeting at Salouel had not been gotten without effort. By the Edict two towns only in the entire Government of Picardy were allotted the Huguenots, at which to build churches. These were Desvres, in the Boulonnais, and Hautcourt, near St. Quentin; of what advantage this to those of Amiens? At first, these were wont to hold their worship within the castle of the Seigneur d'Hencourt, at Havernas, five miles northerly from Amiens; but the distance was so far, and in inclement seasons very trying and often fatal, especially to infants taken thither for baptism, as well as to the infirm and the aged, that M. de Hencourt in the year 1600 notified the lieutenant-general at Amiens of his intention to have public worship for himself, his family, and the inhabitants of the city, within his fief of Hem, a village or suburb of Amiens, and where thirty-six years previous the Protestants had built a temple. This privilege, to which he claimed a right under the Edict, being denied him, an appeal was made to the king, who gave his sanction, but the opposition of the clergy and the civil authorities was so violent as to nullify it. However, through the favor of the Lord of Guignemicourt, his château was also opened to the Reformed, being to the south-west of Amiens, and only half as far as Havernas. It was an important gain for those of Amiens, and this became for some years their principal resort. As the Count of St. Paul positively refused his consent to their meeting in Hem, they obtained permission in 1611 to remove their worship to Salouel, and there to build a temple. This, as already stated, was a small village on the Celle. It was within a fief appertaining to the widow of M. de Hencourt before named; and there was nothing remarkable about it but a subterranean cavern, used as a refuge, it was said, as early as the ninth century. Strange enough the bishop and clergy assented to this measure, and on February 24th, 1612, half an acre of land was ceded to the Huguenots, upon which they erected their temple. Here they long met for worship, under the pastorates of Le Hucher, La Cloche, Lauberan, and Pinette; and to this day the by-road leading to it is known as the "Chemin du prêche." These pastors also labored at Havernas. There was another large and flourishing church gathered at Oisemont, a market town twelve miles south of Abbeville, where the Huguenots were strong. It was some eighteen miles west of Amiens, to which its royal provost was subordinate. In the time of our refugees this church enjoyed the labors of Rev. Jacques de Vaux, a native of Compiègne. One of its elders living at Oisemont at the date of the passage of the Edict of Nantes was David des Marêts, Sieur du Ferets. In 1625 he represented the church in the Provincial Synod held at Charenton, near Paris. Beyond question our David des Marest, who came from Picardy, was of this family; but we cannot say how related.

Would we truly estimate the character of such men as Demarest, and Disosway, and Casier, and Cresson, and their real value to the community at Harlem, we should follow up the pageant last introduced, and admit the moral sublimity of that primitive worship, with its power to mould the life—the fervid invocation, the holy song, set to the metrical psalms of Clement Marot, the simple Gospel clothed in the warm, persuasive eloquence of the times, which raised the soul heavenward. Also note the activity and zeal which pervaded the Huguenot churches, and the watchfulness over the walk of the members, which so contributed to soundness of faith and purity of life.

We might show, were it needful, how this active moral element was effectual for good upon the very society by which it was scorned and derided; how the trammels upon thought and speech had to a great degree been thrown off, in regard especially to politics and religion—subjects once tenderly touched upon, but now handled with an astonishing boldness. What latitude was taken in the doctrinal disputes between the Huguenot pastors and Catholic prelates, so rife at this period. How the popular mind was awakening to the necessity of *religious reform*, and even showing itself among the old clergy, as in the earlier days of the Reformation. But alas! it now went little beyond efforts to render external rites more impressive, or to make the rules of monastic life more austere. A step in the right direction was taken at Amiens by Jean de Labadie, later an avowed Protestant and founder of the Labadists, of Wieward, in Friesland, some of whom visited Harlem five years after his death, which took place in 1674. In 1640, Labadie, by invitation, preached at Paris. Among the crowds drawn to hear him was Bishop le Fevre, who, charmed with his zeal and eloquence, made him a canon in the cathedral. Here Labadie, imbued with the evangelical spirit, urged upon his parishioners to read the Scriptures, and caused many copies of the New Testament in French to be distributed; while his sermons upon repentance, grace, and predestination awakened profound interest. But his views were severely censured by the clergy and by the Sorbonne; so after a few years' service at Amiens, in which also he had not been sparing of the Jesuits, the clamors against him forced him to leave. The excitement stirred up by Labadie in the end reacted upon the reformed, to whose "pernicious teachings" his "heresy" was imputed.

Picard society was always exceedingly impressible and excitable. But at Amiens its good and bad elements assumed the most positive forms. It was a centre of political factions and sinister plots; and it was this spirit, long fostered among the nobility, that arrayed itself against the ministry of Concini; only just failed in 1636 to assassinate Richelieu during the siege of Corbie, and in 1649 plunged his successor, Mazarin, in the war of the Fronde: a war, by the way, in which the Huguenots won praise from this minister by keeping neutral.

But with a people or society so irascible, it made an element in the dangers which beset the Reformed; dangers which were now daily thickening by reason of the cruel proscription designed to crush them. And religious antagonisms needed but slight incentive to leap forth into activity. If the Huguenots when assailed by brute force dared stand and defend themselves, it often led to a bloody collision such as that which obliged one of our refugees to escape for his life. Daniel Tourneur, with other Reformed (according to Tourneur's version of it, which we see no reason to question), had been attending a burial at Amiens, when some of the Catholics made a wanton attack upon them. The pretext we know not; but Huguenots were debarred using the common cemeteries. However, Tourneur, young and spirited, in his veins the blood of the old Picard lords *de Tourneur*, one of whom had fought under William the Conqueror at Hastings, drew his sword as did others in self-defence, when some of the assailants were slain. Tourneur being charged with the death of one Tilie Maire, he found it best to take a sudden leave. Marc Disosway, who seems to have known of this affair at its occurrence, made quite a stir about it at Harlem in after years, when he and Tourneur happened to be at variance.

The breaking out of war between France and Spain in 1635 caused a considerable influx of Protestant refugees into England, from Picardy, Artois, Hainault, and Flanders. Involving these provinces in all the perils and disasters of a pitiless border warfare, and lasting nearly the fourth of a century, it resulted in the conquest of Artois, and parts of Flanders and Hainault, and their annexation to France. Begun by Louis XIII., jointly with the Dutch, (these agreeing to divide the Spanish Netherlands between them), this war opened adversely to the French,

Cathedral and Cemetery of St. Denis, at Amiens.

for the enemy at once invaded Picardy, overran Thiérache, and captured Corbie, on the Somme, only nine miles above Amiens. In terror the inhabitants of the villages fled with their goods into the cities, while the Spaniards, marking their course by burnings and massacres, stopped only at the Oise, which they could not pass as the bridges had been broken down. But the energy of Richelieu soon turned the tables; for, retaking Corbie, he drove the enemy back across the border, and began those aggressive movements which, followed up by Louis XIV., after the disasters of the Fronde were repaired, added, as before said, a large domain to France, secured to her in 1659 by the treaty of the Pyrenees, and which she has ever since held.

Although hostilities were so soon transferred to the enemy's soil, Picardy was now called upon to maintain garrisons for the defence of her extended frontier, and to marshal her forces for the seat of war, whence came almost daily some new and alarming rumor; a state of things especially disheartening to the Huguenots, whose trials before were great enough. With no incentive to enter the army in a war waged only for conquest, and to add strength to the despotic arm which was crushing them, it naturally proved a turning point with those who now left the country. Their nearness to the Low Country border offered the Huguenots of Picardy every facility for escape, as also their several seaports and the long range of coast, only frequented by fishermen, whose boats often aided fugitives to get away when obliged to shun the publicity of the town. Numbers for sufficient reasons took the weary and hazardous journey through Belgium to Holland, many going by way of the Vermandois forests, and resting at Bohain, a little city of wool-workers twelve miles north-east of St. Quentin, where were many Huguenots; so fleeing across the Cambresis, or Hainault.* Our Demarest, and Cresson, Disosway, Tourneur, Le Roy, and others from the Amienois and Ponthieu, had the choice of these routes, but which they took is left to conjecture. Calais, then the extreme northern outlet of the kingdom, at an inviting proximity to the shores of England, and its people partly of that nation, which had ruled it for over two centuries till it was recovered in 1558 by the French under the Duke of Guise, was also strongly Protestant, and hence a great resort for escaping refugees. Our Philip Casier was from this place, as also his son-in-law, David Uzille.

While many left Picardy, the French advance and successes

* JEAN COTTIN, of New York, merchant, who died quite aged in 1721, was a fugitive from Bohain, where he left a brother Daniel, and sister Susannah, married to Louis Libot. He intrusted by his will £30 to Peter van Oblinus and Samuel Waldron, of the town of Harlem; "the income thereof to be yearly employed for and towards the maintaining of their minister of the Dutch Protestant church there."

in Hainault and Artois was causing a larger migration of the Protestant Walloons; and among these also a number whose destiny led them to Harlem. We can barely allude to such events, military or otherwise, in their respective localities, as seemingly influenced their removal.

Landrecy, on the Sambre, was the first place invested and taken by the French on beginning the invasion of the enemy's territory in 1637, and which they held with adjacent places for ten years. It was during this domination, so odious to the Walloons, that *Simon de Ruine*, living near Landrecy, removed with his family to Holland, whence fifteen years later he found his way to America. Through daughters married to Demarests, he has many living descendants. *Jean Gervoe*, another of the Harlem settlers, was from Beaumont, to the east of Avesnes, then a country seat of the Duke of Arschot, but an old appanage of the princes of Hainault. From Mons, the rich capital of this province, seated to the north of Avesnes, and within the coal region called the Borinage, came *David du Four*, of the same name and not improbably the same blood as the martyr of Le Câteau, but whose posterity, which became numerous in this country, changed the form of their name to Devoor and Devoe.

Passing to the west of the Scheldt we find the homes of other of our refugees along the banks of the river Lys. The noble Scheldt, the boast and pride of Belgium, rising in the edge of Picardy behind the abbey of Mont St. Martin, and flowing to the north or rather to the north-east, but upon several zigzag reaches or courses, waters the western parts of the Cambresis and Hainault, and then eastern Flanders, forming for some distance the barrier between the latter and Brabant. It has passed in the mean time Cambray, at the head of navigation; Valenciennes, Condé, Tournay, all Walloon cities, Ghent, and Antwerp. At the latter, a hundred and twenty-five miles from its head—swollen by many tributaries, chief of which is the Lys—the now puissant Scheldt turns north-west for fourteen miles, when it divides into two mighty arms, each of which rolls on still forty miles to the German Sea. These two broad estuaries taking the names of the East and West Scheldt—the latter also termed the Hond—form, in conjunction with the left arm of the Meuse, here called the Maas, the fertile Dutch islands of

Schouwen and Walcheren, in Zeeland, both of interest to us as the home or place of sojourn of some of the Harlem colonists.

Running parallel with the coast, and uniformly thirty miles or so therefrom, in a course very direct, the Lys parted Flemish from French or Walloon Flanders. It was navigated by light vessels all the way from Aire, in Artois, to Ghent. About centrally of the fertile plains between it and the Scheldt lay the city of Lille, with its teeming and busy population, the capital of French Flanders, and the great city and centre of the Walloons. Owing its origin to Lideric du Buc, the first Grand Forester or Count of Flanders, who in 640 here built a castle, only the shapeless ruins of which remained, but growing into significance as a town in the eleventh century, when enlarged and walled by other of these counts, Lille had become to the Walloons what Ypres, its great rival, which lay but fifteen miles north-west, was to the Fleminge—the chief emporium of their cloth manufacture. Round about it and all in Walloon Flanders were the large and handsome cities of Douay and Tournay, the small cities of Orchies, Armentières, La Bassée, St. Amand, etc., besides 193 boroughs and villages. Old towns and famed for their industries, they formed the heart of the great woollen and linen country of preceding centuries; enjoying a prosperity almost fabulous, till Spanish tyranny and French conquest brought blight and ruin. The cruel expatriations thus caused gave to Harlem at least four families, who came from neighboring places on and near the Lys.* Richebourg, a small city scarce noticed by gazetteers or maps, but seated fourteen miles west of Lille, on a small branch of the Lys and in the district of Bethune, within Artois, was the birthplace of our *Glaude le Maistre*, or *Delamater*. Delamater's family was from France, his immediate ancestor probably from Picardy, whence many families seem to have worked up into Artois; and it is pretty cer-

* It is said ("Du Bois Reunion," pp. 32, 33) that the Peace of Westphalia, 1648, by maintaining the Catholic religion in the Austrian dominions, caused the emigration from Artois. But this emigration began years before, and at the date of that treaty, which did not restore peace between France and Spain, the former was in military possession of Artois. Nor could this province be affected by the pacification of 1648, in which the Spanish Netherlands were not included. It is plain that the emigrations referred to were not due to that treaty, but to the French invasion. See "Burn's Refugees, London," 1846, p. 42.

tain that Glaude, on leaving Richebourg, took the course of the Walloon migration to England, before referred to. We doubt if many of these Walloons from Artois went to Holland at that time, for which there was poor inducement for these Spanish subjects, seeing the Dutch were then in league with their enemy the French, while the English held a neutrality, but leaned strongly to the Spanish side. In fact, by the threats of England the Flemish ports were left unmolested till 1644, and from these that country was much nearer and more accessible than Holland. Naturally enough some of these fugitive Walloons retired at first into Flanders, hesitating perhaps to quit the country, as the state of the Protestants was somewhat improved under the more humane rule of Philip IV. The family of *Oblinus*, one well known in the early history of Harlem, fled from Houplines, two leagues north-west of Lille; and that of *De Pre*, from Comines, a few miles below Houplines. Kortryk was a Flemish town yet farther down the Lys, which within the previous century had witnessed cruel persecutions, and during the existing war (how great its calamities!) had changed hands four times in five years. But one of its families had escaped these last troubles by leaving some years before: we refer to the ancestors of the *Kortright*, or *Courtright*, family, in its day one of the most wealthy in landed possessions in Harlem.*

* FAMILY NAMES were the exception and not the rule among our early Dutch colonists. The mass of people in Fatherland used only a patronymic, formed by adding to the child's Christian name that of the father, with the affix *sen*, or son; by which originated all names so terminating, as, for example, *Jan Jacobsen* (meaning *Jan, son of Jacob*), or *Pieter Jansen* (*Pieter, son of Jan*), and the like. In correct usage in writing, the affix was often shortened to *se* or *s*, and always in the case of females to *s*. This custom necessarily produced among the male descendants of the same progenitor a great diversity of surnames, if we may, for convenience, so call them. Thus *Pieter*, *Willem*, and *Hendrick* being sons of *Jan Jacobsen*, would be known as *Pieter Jansen*, *Willem Jansen*, etc., while their children would be named respectively, *Pietersen*, *Willemsen*, and *Hendricksen*, and these names in turn each afford other varieties in the next generation. On the other hand, this use of the patronymic caused a frequent recurrence of the same name where no family connection whatever existed. The inconvenience thus arising, and particularly the liability of confounding persons of similar name, was partially obviated by the practice in vogue in Fatherland, and kept up by our colonists, both in familiar speech and in formal writings, of distinguishing persons by their *birthplace* (not, as is now the usage, by the *residence*, except the one and the other were the same); as, for example, *Jan Jacobsen van Amsterdam*, that is, J. J. *from* Amsterdam. This valued link connecting the colonist with his former home, it was in many cases di-

On the Flemish seaboard between Calais and the Hond, lay, distant a few miles apart, the several old strongly intrenched towns of Gravelines, Dunkirk, Furnes, Nieuport, Ostend, and Sluis, the latter seated ten miles south of the Hond, within a harbor on the German Sea called the Paerdt-markt (Horse-market), from the noise of the elements during a storm sounding very like the neighing of horses. To hold these seaports it cost the kings of Spain dearly within this century. Ostend, in particular, was taken by the Spaniards from the Hollanders September 14th, 1604, after a terrible siege of over three years, in which there perished 80,000 of the former and 50,000 of the latter. A few days previous (August 19th), Sluis surrendered to Prince Maurice, after an investment of four months, the Spaniards having made vain efforts to relieve it. Peace reigned from 1609 to 1621; when Spain and Holland resumed hostilities. In 1635, as we have seen, France took part with Holland; but England interposed to keep these ports, of so much benefit to her trade, open for some years. However, the French, aided by the Holland fleet under Admiral Tromp, took Gravelines in 1644, and Dunkirk and Furnes in 1646. Mardyk was a rural hamlet midway between the first two places, three miles from either, where once stood a city claiming too to be the famous *Portus Iccius*, but, sacked and burned by the Normans, and in 1383 by the English, now consisted only of a church and a few cottages which could hardly excite envy, looking out so unpretendingly upon the sand dunes and the sea. But in common with all that border region, it was to suffer much from the con-

rarily to his interest to preserve. In Holland, as with us, the name of the place thus used often became the permanent family name, of which instances abound. But it sometimes resulted that two or more brothers, *born in different places, and from these deriving their respective surnames*, gave rise to as many families, whose common origin, after a few generations, none would ever suspect. In many cases the *van* has been dropped; and often the name so changed as to disguise its origin, as those of *Oblinus* and *Kortright*. The first of these, derived from Houplines; after emigration, probably in conformity to English utterance, became Oblinus, and by the usage before mentioned, was then, if not before, written *van* Oblinus. The Kortrights at first also used the *van*.

The subject of our Dutch family names is a curious one, as will be abundantly verified in the coming pages; and should be first well studied by those who undertake to compile Dutch genealogy. See other remarks, and a list of Dutch baptismal names, with their English equivalent, in "*Annals of Newtown*," page 265.

tending forces. Fort Mardyk, in the vicinity, was seized by the French on their taking Dunkirk. After six years they were driven out of the fort and both towns by the Archduke Leopold, Governor of the Low Countries; but the French again became masters of all in 1658, conferring Mardyk with Dunkirk upon the English, now their allies, who in 1662 restored both to the French, whence Mardyk fell under the iron rule of Louis XIV. *Meynard Journee*, a young man born here, withdrew during these troublous times, and after wandering up and down the Rhine appears at Harlem, and finally on Staten Island, founding there the reputable family of *Journeay*.

Bruges was the last Flemish town as one approached the Dutch border, distant eight miles from the coast and ten south of Sluis. Very ancient too, it was the veritable godfather of Flanders, to which it had given a name, originally *Vlonderen*, a Flemish term equivalent to Bruges (or *Brugge*, that is *Bridges*, as its Dutch people called it), and which it early took from the many bridges in the town and environs. Once among the most commercial and opulent of the Netherland cities, it dared defy the Emperor Maximilian, whose vials of wrath vented upon it, and its troubles under Alva, with the rivalry of its neighbors Ghent and Antwerp, had ruined its industries. It was six years under Protestant rule, but on May 22d, 1584, submitted to the King of Spain. By degrees its Protestant population forsook it; and so did the good *Jan Tibout*, the *Tiebout* ancestor, for a dozen years town-clerk and *voorleser* at Harlem, and also *Joost Jansen Kockuyt*, who belongs to its history.

Sluis was made very secure by the Dutch, after being wrested from the Spaniards in 1604, the latter trying in vain to retake it in 1621 on the renewal of the war at the end of the twelve years' truce. Its large gardens and bleaching grounds told the useful occupations of its people; but its air was so malarious, as in all that flat country, that strangers could not well abide there, even its garrison having to be changed every year. But it was the nearest Dutch town within reach of refugees from France and Flanders, and its strong walls offered them safety, so that many such, and among them our *Cuvier* and *Cresson*, found a temporary home here. Sluis castle had a reminiscence affecting to the refugees, for here the

Admiral Coligny, taken by the Spaniards at the battle of St. Quentin in 1557, was confined, and alone with his Bible in his cell, became a Protestant, going hence indeed to meet a cruel death in the St. Bartholomew, but not till he had nobly served the Huguenot cause, both in council and in the field. One who could wield with equal skill the sword of the Spirit came from Sluis at a later day: we refer to *Guiliaem Bertholf*, parish clerk at Harlem, before he entered the ministry to become the "itinerating apostle of New Jersey." *

* GUILIAEM BERTHOLF and his w. Martina Hendricks Verwey, with letters from Sluis, joined the church at Bergen, N. J., Oct. 6, 1684. He lived at Ackquackneck. In 1690 he removed to H., continued there about a year and a half, and soon after went to Holland for ministerial ordination. On his return he became pastor at Hackensack, in which service he ended his days in 1724. Indefatigable in his work, he labored extensively among the surrounding churches, several of which he was instrumental in forming. Mr. Bertholf had three children when he came to this country, viz.: Sarah, Maria and Elizabeth, all b. at Sluis; and afterwards Hendrick, Coryous, Jacobus, Martha and Anna. All were church members at Hackensack. *Sarah* m., 1698, David D. Demarest; *Maria* m., 1699, John Bogart; *Elizabeth* m., 1699, John Terhune, in 1718, Roelof Bogart; *Hendrick* m., 1707, Mary Terhune; *Coryaus* m., 1718, Anna Reyersen; *Martha* m., 1713, Albert Bogart; *Jacobus* m. Elizabeth van Imburgh; and *Anna* m., 1718, Abraham Varick, and in 1734, Peter Post. Some of this name we have known but to respect; an honor to an excellent ancestor.

CHAPTER IV.

HOLLAND: THE DE FORESTS, AND LA MONTAGNE.

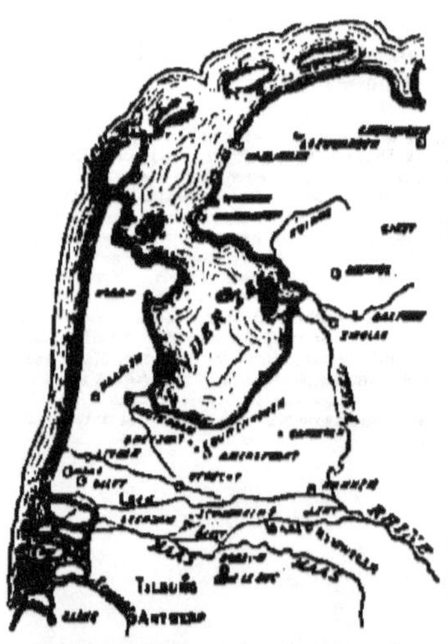

THE final adieu to Europe marked a crisis of no trifling import, a grand turning-point in the life and the destiny of our colonists. Cherished hopes of a return were seldom realized. That they were led to this decisive step by a wonderful series of providences, we have sought to show. So far as signal and of general bearing, these are matters of common history; if less fortunate in our search for special causes, limited to precise times, places, and individuals, we must plead the difficulties attending such minute inquiry. But while the craving for such details of personal experience can be but partially satisfied, our gleanings of this description, reserved for the present chapter and the next following, will include some touching passages of refugee life in Holland and elsewhere.

Holland, in natural features simply, had little that was winning: a boundless stretch of low pastures, which, walled in by lines of dykes both from the sea and the internal net-work of sluggish rivers and artificial watercourses, formed the tame surroundings of the Zuyder Zee. The latter, the delight of the Hollander, of whose imperturbable nature its broad glassy bosom in its unruffled repose presented a fit emblem, was changed from a lake to an inland sea by an inundation in 1282, which, breaking through the narrow barrier on the north, united it with the German Ocean, but leaving to guard its entrance small patches of land forming the Texel and several lesser islands. The Zuyder Zee had on the west the peninsula of North Holland. On the opposite side, which swept in a half circle from north to south, it washed the shores of Friesland, Overyssel, Gelderland, and Utrecht; the latter reaching westerly to South Holland, which with North Holland composed but one province. In the last-named was Amsterdam, the rich commercial emporium of the Dutch, seated in the mouth of the Y, an arm or inlet of the Zuyder Zee. With these five districts, which nearly encircled this inland sea, the Seven United Provinces also numbered Groningen, to the east of Friesland; and Zeeland, lying between South Holland and Flanders, but broken into several islands by the outlets of the Maas and Scheldt. Groningen, with Drenthe next southerly, and then Overyssel (of which Drenthe was usually reckoned a part), formed in conjunction with Zutphen, a section of Gelderland to the south of Overyssel, the great eastern boundary of the United Provinces along the German circle of Westphalia.

With all its monotony of landscape, Holland, even in the time of our colonists, bore witness to the indefatigable industry of its people, in its vast system of canals, extensive dykes and drainage, and thorough cultivation; the neatness and thrift of its towns and villages, and its incessant activities, domestic and maritime. Scarce enough of resemblance was found to ally it to the parent country we have so fully described, so striking was the difference, both in the temper of its people and in the matters of government and religion; for in all that was essential to render its people both free and prosperous, the happy release from the double yoke of Spain and the Papacy had wrought here a marvellous transformation. Its antique cloisters were now applied to secular uses, its venerable churches and cathedrals devoted to the Reformed service, its dingy castles the merest relics of an expiring feudalism. And if the scarred walls of its

Leyden, from the Tower of the City Hall.

cities told the tragic story of a recent desperate struggle, innumerable crafts plying upon its canals and rivers, and shipping crowding every seaport, as plainly witnessed to its present prosperity. Its glory now was in being free; the recognized home of civil and religious liberty!

But however worthy our study, Holland will now engage us only with reference to the homes or the movements of the particular persons whose checkered story forms a part of the history we are writing. Every one of the United Provinces was represented in the original community at Harlem, though the settlers from those provinces hailed chiefly from cities or villages on or near the German Ocean and the Zuyder Zee. Naturally, the great cities Amsterdam and Leyden gave the largest number, the last-named place being situated but twenty-two miles southwest of the former, and at that day communicating with it by means of the Leyden Canal, the Harlem Lake, and the Y.

LEYDEN was unexcelled for the beauty of its surroundings, as Dutch beauty went. It stood in the midst of the Rhineland, a fertile flat, aptly called the Garden of Holland. On these broad meadows grazed numerous herds, the district being famous for its superior butter and cheese dairies. Directly environed by pretty villas and gardens, the city was inclosed by ramparts (since removed), around which ran a moat, crossed by seven drawbridges leading to the city gates; the approaches to these, arched with the foliage of overhanging trees, most agreeably impressing the visitor entering for the first time. The city was intersected by the river Rhine, which rolling down from the classic Alps through two hundred leagues of grandest highland scenery, but reft of force and volume by diversion in the lowlands, flowed placidly into the city in two branches, which uniting in one near the centre, slid on six miles farther, to the German Ocean. It fed canals which traversed the town in all directions between lines of shade-trees, and under numerous bridges. The thoroughfares were broad and cleanly, and the dwellings and shops, built mainly of brick and standing with gables to the street, exhibited the true Holland style. The Dutch burghers and their *vrouws* were wont to resort for recreation to the shady walks upon the city walls; or to the battlements of the Burg, an old castle or fortress rising from a mound central of the town, at the point where the Old and New Rhine joined; and which afforded a picturesque view—rows of curious notched gables, belfries and church steeples, with a wide and charming outlook over the country beyond. With the advantage of a clear atmosphere (an unusual condition in that moist climate) the eye might roam westerly to the ocean, see southerly the masts of Rotterdam, easterly follow up the tortuous course of the Rhine, descry to the north-east the shipping of Amsterdam, and catch glimpses of that great inland ocean, the Zuyder Zee.

Leyden had early become a principal refuge for the persecuted. Its brave and effectual resistance during the Spanish siege in 1574 gave it pre-eminence as a place of strength and security, and attracted to its gates the flying multitudes driven by oppression from other lands. Of these the Walloon refugees were by far the most numerous, and being welcomed by the magistrates and people, they formed a church in 1584, the burgomasters at their request giving them the permanent use of an old edifice erected in the fourteenth century on the Haerlem-straat, in the northern section of the city called Marendorp, and still styled as by its Catholic founders, the Lieve Vrouw Kerk, or the Church of the Virgin Mary. It was thence known as the French or Walloon Church. On a later influx of refugees, this building being found too small for the large increase of communicants, they were permitted to celebrate the Lord's Supper in the Gasthuys (or Almshouse) Kerk, which stood convenient to the other, on the north side of the Breedestraat (the main thoroughfare running east and west through the city), and attached to the St. Catharine Gasthuys, which occupied grounds in its rear. In 1606 the Walloons founded a college, for the better training of their youth in their favorite Calvinistic theology; as the

Walloon Church at Leyden.

divinity school connected with the Leyden University, though now enjoying great patronage, had become much distracted by the doctrinal controversy between its professors Gomarus and Arminius. Daniel Colonius, pastor of the Walloon Church, was made regent of the new college. The Walloons, nurtured, as we have seen, in the iron cradle of trial, bore with them into exile less wealth than virtue, but with the latter a remarkable degree of common-sense and business energy. At Leyden their skill and industry soon told upon the commercial interests of the city, especially through the medium of the cloth trade, for which Leyden was now justly famed above all the other towns in Holland. Given its first impetus by Flemish artisans from Ypres, in the fourteenth century, the woollen manufacture had grown to such magnitude as to engross a large share of the activities of the citizens; by more than three hundred busy hand-looms turning out per annum fifty thousand pieces of cloth—not to include flannels, carpets, baize, etc., amounting in addition to over nine thousand pieces a year!

The Zaay Hall.

The older part of Leyden contained four "vierendeels," or quarters; which districts, surrounded by the several enlargements of the city made from time to time, formed the central part of the town, and stretched along the Breedestraat, two upon the north side and two on the south. One of the latter, called the Woolhouse Quarter, was so named because within its limits, on the north side of the Steenschuur Canal, a little east of where it crossed the Voldersgraft, stood the Zaay Hall, the great cloth emporium of the city of Leyden. This building, formerly, in popish times, a chapel of the St. Jacob brotherhood, had been vacated by this order, sold to the city, and for some time used for the storage of wool, whence it was called the Woolhouse. About the year 1500, it was refitted and appropriated to the cloth trade. Here, before they could be sold, must be brought all the serges and camlets, broadcloths, single cloths and gentry cloths, with some coarser sorts, which were made within the town, to be inspected and appraised, and have attached the indispensable "vent loot," or official leaden stamp. And here resorted the cloth manufacturers and drapers of Leyden—the one to display and sell his goods, the other to buy. From the "saays," or serges, the building took its name, the Saay Hall. On every weekday in this great mart for trading was presented an animated scene: the inspectors, as required by law, busily examining the white, black, or colored goods, to determine both quality and quantity; the noisy *klopper*, with a blow affixing the proper stamp; and the vociferous salesman, crying his price to the buyers who thronged the place; while interrupting the buzz of voices, the two clocks overhead faithfully struck the hour and half hour, and anon the chime of small bells which also adorned the tower, to each its name, as the *Weaver*, the *Dyer*, etc., rung out a pleasing melody.

Another district, called the Gasthuys Vierendeel (Almshouse Quarter), had on the north side the Rhine below the junction of its two branches, upon the south the Breedestraat, and to the east the Wanthuys Quarter. It took its name from the St. Catharine Gasthuys, which with its kerk, before spoken of, stood within its limits, a little to the west of that antique and massive pile, the Stadt Huys, or City Hall. Through this quarter, along the west side of the Gasthuys kerk yard, a little street called the Vrouwsteeg (woman's lane) led northward across the Rhine to the Walloon Church, and was often devoutly trodden by the feet of the refugees.

In the Gasthuys Quarter lived a Walloon named Jesse de Forest. He was one of the exiles from Avesnes, in the province of Hainault, as already noticed, driven by the perils of the times to take refuge at Sedan; and whence the De Forests, after a sojourn there apparently of some years, had removed down the Maas to Holland.

Jesse, Jean, Michel, and Gerard, recognized as brothers, are found at Leyden, with a sister Jeanne, whose husband was one Cartier, from Colombier, France. The De Forests stood prominent among the French refugees. Jesse and Gerard, of whom only we shall need to speak further, were by occupation dyers. It was their subtile art which imparted beauty and value to those useful fabrics displayed and sold at the Zaay Hall. Gerard, whose birthplace was Avesnes, married at Leyden, on August 12th, 1611, a young lady of French parentage, but born here, Hester, daughter of Crispin and Agnes de la Grange, the latter now a widow. Surviving his marriage forty-five years, he was blessed with a goodly competence, and in seeing his children respectably married at Leyden. His brother Jesse had brought a wife with him to Holland, Marie du Cloux, whom he probably married at Sedan, as his eldest son was born there. Five children that reached maturity came of this union, namely, Jean, Henry, Rachel, Jesse, and Isaac. More than once, however, had death invaded their circle, taking little Israel and Philippe from their fond embrace. Yet having for love to God forsaken country and kindred, they could accept these painful visitations as the salutary chastenings of an All-wise Father, teaching them the lesson of resignation to His will, and inspiring a faith to look upward and beyond. Diligent also in his avocation, which had long ranked among the "Greater Arts," Jesse de Forest, in the easy position of a master artisan, was one of a limited number having license from the magistrates "to dye serges and camlets in colors." It was a tribute to his skill; for only the most expert and approved dyers were thus preferred, as on the beauty and permanence of the colors so largely depended the reputation and success of the cloth trade of Leyden. Plying his useful art, De Forest mixed his delicate tints, and among his steaming vats daily earned an honest living. His home was near the Walloon church, at which he and his Marie loved to offer up their devotions, and where from time to time they dedicated their offspring to God in baptism.

But Jesse de Forest had again fallen upon perilous times. Leyden was at this date rent by popular discords, which affected the whole country, but "this city in particular." While the people of Holland were crushed and humbled by the Spanish war, and had to struggle for existence, they showed, as we have seen, the deepest sympathy for the victims of oppression who fled to their country for refuge. But once in the flush enjoyment of peace and prosperity, and forgetful of their former trials, feelings of national pride prompted them to draw lines of social distinction, especially between themselves and the foreign population, insomuch that the refugees now began to be eyed with contempt, treated as inferiors, and often refused employment. This intolerant spirit was also fostered by the parties and feuds which had sprung up in church and state. The old dispute about *predestination*, which had arisen among the professors at the University, had "proceeded from the schools into the pulpits," and the people readily took sides. Hence the controversy spread far and wide. The pastors of the various churches, as well as their flocks, became sorely at issue, many of both classes embracing the Arminian views; those holding these opinions being called Remonstrants. The famous Synod of Dort, convened November 13th, 1618, on account of these dissensions, remained in session for over six months, and handled the Arminian preachers with great severity. Its action being sustained by the government, initiated a general crusade against the Remonstrants, and a large number of their ministers, men of undoubted talent and piety, were deposed and driven from the country. The Synod of South Holland, which met at Leyden in July following, though numbering but thirty ministers and ten elders, expelled about sixty Remonstrant preachers, who refused to subscribe to the canons adopted by the Synod of Dort. Many of this proscribed sect left the country, a part of whom retired to Denmark, and by favor of the Duke of Holstein, founded the town of Frederickstadt in 1621, though, the troubles over, "most of them returned to their native country."

At Leyden, where prior to the Synod of Dort the new sect had gained a multitude of adherents, including some of the city magistrates, every thing was now done to suppress them. Ejected from their churches, they met for worship in a private house, only to be driven out by a mob. In vain they prayed the magistrates to allow them the public exercise of their religion, urging that the Lutherans, English Puritans, and even the Jews, enjoyed that right unmolested! A burgher at whose dwelling they assembled upon a night in August was heavily fined, and expelled the town for a year. Two months later a saay-weaver for having a meeting at his house was mulct two hundred and twenty-five florins, stripped of his rights as a freeman, and banished from Leyden and the Rhineland. Some of the citizens were fined and imprisoned for collecting money in aid of the exiled pastors.

At the University a change was made in the faculty, by the removal of all the professors who were Remonstrants, and the appointment of approved Calvinists. Even after their ejectment they were followed with a malevolence which is in strange contrast with our ideas of toleration. And it was but the culmination of this same politico-religious persecution that brought to the block that venerable and pure-minded patriot Oldenbarneveldt, May 13th, 1619, while the Synod was yet in session at Dort; a cruel episode of the war upon the Remonstrants, and which thrilled the nation with horror. The severity toward that sect did not cease for some years after; several executions took place at Leyden, and this town was the last to grant them toleration. These party strifes and public tumults having a tendency to unhinge society, to fetter speech and conscience, to check the industries of the people and make a livelihood more difficult, greatly disquieted all classes, but more especially the foreign refugees.

While these things were transpiring, there attended the Walloon church a young Frenchman, who was a boarder in the family of one Robert Botack, a shoemaker on the Voldersgraft, and was studying medicine under the learned Heurnius at the University, where he had been registered as a student November 19th, 1619, in the Latin style, *Johannes Monerius Montanus*, or as in French, *Jean Mousnier de La Montagne*. His surname might betoken social rank, or as already suggested point to a family origin in La Montagne, or both; yet without doubt connects him with the talented family of that name which became so distinguished in the fields of theology, medicine, and literature during the sixteenth century. Himself, as before seen, a refugee from Saintonge, he was twenty-four years of age on entering the University. It was directly after the aforesaid

University. St. Peter's Church.

View on the Kloksteeg.

change in the faculty had taken place, a change much approved by the French families, who as Calvinists were opposed to the former *régime*; and which may have had its weight with Montagne in going thither, but more the better facilities afforded by a new edifice, with the other and peculiar advantages which a membership conferred.*

The University building stood in the south-western part of the city, upon the west side of the street and canal called the Rapenburg, where it was crossed by the Nun's Bridge upon the lane running east and west known as the Kloksteeg. The building being nearly consumed by fire November 11th, 1616 (a very plain structure, formerly a cloister of the White Nuns), it had been rebuilt with more elegance and better accommodations, and adorned with a spire and clock.

From the eastern windows of the University looking down the Kloksteeg, could often be seen a company of English dissenters assembling for worship at the dwelling of their pastor, John Robinson, on the south side of the street, opposite St. Peter's Church. Here were wont to gather the pious Carver, and Brewster, and Brewer, and Bradford, Winslow and Standish, and many others of the "Pilgrim Fathers," to receive the word of life, "enjoying," says one of them, "much sweet and delightful society and spiritual comfort together, in the ways of God." Many of these persons working at honest employments connected with the staple manufacture of the city, such as weavers, carders, dyers, etc., were almost as well known as was their pastor Robinson, who was a constant visitor at the University and a reader at the library, and who being "versed in the Dutch language," had "procured him much honor and respect," in the pulpit of St. Peter, by his defence of Calvinism in the recent discussions. And at the time Montagne entered the University, the affair of Brewer and his associate Brewster was in every one's mouth. These worthy men, in a room near

* Montagne's age warrants the belief that he had finished a course of study elsewhere before coming to Leyden, and now attached himself to the University, as was a common practice, for professional improvement, as well as to secure other benefits and immunities which such connection conferred. All thus entering were termed *students*; and so Montagne was always enrolled "student of medicine," though his membership was three times severed and as often renewed in a space of seventeen years.

Robinson's house, were engaged in printing religious books for the English dissenters. Being complained of by Sir Dudley Carleton, the English ambassador at the Hague, it devolved upon the University of which Brewer was a member to investigate the matter. The accused persons being exonerated, the affair was eclipsed by the graver agitations of the times; yet the fears which it excited gave spur to a movement now contemplated by the English congregation.

Robinson and his flock feeling ill at ease in Leyden, had been led "both deeply to apprehend their present dangers, and wisely to foresee the future, and think of timely remedy." Having resolved upon a "removal to some other place," they were looking toward America as their future home. But several years were spent in fruitless negotiation for aid with "The Virginia Company of London," and "The New Netherland Company" at Amsterdam. At length obtaining the needed assistance from private sources, a good portion of the church, "the youngest and strongest part," after a farewell meeting at Robinson's house, departed from "that goodly and pleasant citie," July 21st, 1620, to embark at Delft Haven. "They that stayed at Leyden," says Winslow, "feasted us that were to go, at our pastor's house, being large, where we refreshed ourselves after tears with singing of psalms, making joyful melody in our hearts, as well as with the voice. . . . After this they accompanied us to Delft Haven."

So remarkable an exodus, its preparation, object, and destination, being generally known throughout the city, had its influence upon others, who like the former, "pilgrims," wearied and alarmed by the prevailing disorders, were casting about for a better home. It especially affected the French and Belgian refugees, to whom another cause of apprehension now presented itself. This was a threatened war with Spain, which reviving gloomy recollections of former trials, set many to planning some way of escape from the dreaded atrocities of war, to which they were likely to be again exposed. Hence the subject of a removal to America began to be agitated also among the Walloons at Leyden, whose numbers were now daily and largely increasing by the arrival of other refugees, impelled by their fears to leave the southern provinces; and many needed only the necessary means or guarantees of protection, etc., to induce them to emigrate. Of the number pledged to do so, were Jesse de Forest and his family; with two named Mousnier, or La Montagne, kinsmen, one of whom was our Jean, "student of medicine," and the other an "apothecary and surgeon," like the former single, and probably his brother.

For many years efforts had been making in Holland, by the more wealthy Walloon and other Belgian residents, to organize a "West India Company," to open up a trade with America. During the truce with Spain this project had slumbered, but was revived on the prospect of a renewal of the war; the States-General being now ready to encourage the formation of the company, whose reprisals upon the settlements and commerce of the common enemy, by means of its armed vessels, would help to weaken his power.

But the company met with various hindrances even after obtaining its charter in 1621, not the least of which was the want of sufficient capital. Tracts "for the instruction of the public," with which the press literally teemed, many from the forms of Elzevier, the University printer, set forth the grand undertaking in glowing terms, and urged the people to invest. But still subscriptions came in slowly; great doubt and uncertainty hung over "the long-expected West India Company;" insomuch that when in 1621 the Walloons began in imitation of Robinson's people to make plans for their contemplated emigration, the hope of aid from this source, especially in the same work of planting a colony, was too faint to be seriously entertained. Therefore they resolved to apply to the English ambassador at the Hague in regard to emigrating to Virginia.

Jesse de Forest, whose standing among the Walloons and interest in the enterprise marked him as a suitable person to present a letter of inquiry in their behalf, had been full twenty years in Holland, and well understood the condition and needs of his countrymen, as also their peculiar views and aims in respect to this movement, upon which so much was depending. In an ably drawn communication to Sir Dudley Carleton about the first of August, 1621, he asks whether His Majesty of England will permit fifty or sixty families, Walloons and French, all of the Reformed Religion, to settle in Virginia; will aid them with an armed vessel to make the voyage; will guarantee them protection in their persons and religion; grant them land to cultivate, and allow them to form a town and enjoy various specified rights and privileges pertaining to the soil and to a free community.*

These inquiries being forwarded to England were referred by the king to the directors of the Virginia Company, who on August 11th, 1621, gave "so fine an answer"—in the words of a letter conveying the news to their agent in Virginia—"as we consider they will resolve to go." But the Walloons thought otherwise, for as the company "were contented to receive them upon certain conditions," and these quite different from their own, and could promise no aid in the way of providing ships, it virtually amounted to a refusal.

Jesse de forest

Autograph of Jesse de Forest.

From an original of 1621, in the State Paper Office, London.

Jesse de Forest continued his calling, and when the people of Leyden were registered for a poll-tax in the autumn of 1622, the dyer with his family, numbering his wife and five children, and their maid-servant, Margariete Du Can, still lived on the Breedestraat, within the Almshouse Quarter. The great theme

* De Forest's letter, translated by Dr. O'Callaghan from the French copy in the Broadhead papers, is printed in "*Documents Relating to the Colonial History of the State of New York*," vol. iii., p. 9. The signature, as in the copy, is there erroneously printed *Jose* de Forest; see above, facsimile of the original autograph, from a tracing obligingly sent me by Mr. W. Noel Sainsbury, of Her Majesty's State Paper Office, London. The closing paragraph of this letter, in the original, reads thus:

"Sur ce que dessus mondict Seigneur l'Ambassadeur donnera avis s'il luy plaist comme aussi, si son plaisir servit de faire expedier le dict privilege en forme beur le plustost que faire se pourra a cause du peu de temps qui reste d'icy au Mars (temps commode pour l'embarquement) pour faire l'acceuil de tout ce qui est requis ce faisant obligera ses serviteurs a prier Dieu pour l'accomplissement de ses saincts desoins et pour la sante et longe vie.

"JESSE DE FOREST."

which had absorbed his mind—America—was nevertheless not forgotten. Anon this wish of his heart was to be realized, but in an unexpected way.

The West India Company had so far succeeded in its organization, and in raising the necessary amount of capital, as to begin operations through its board of managers chosen September 17th, 1622. Under its patronage and bound to a term of service, a company of Walloons with their families sailed for New Netherland early in the succeeding March; but De Forest and the Montagnes declined to accompany them, as did most of those who had subscribed to the Virginia project. This was not the inviting plan of free colonization which De Forest had proposed; and though the adventure was attractive for its very novelty, nothing probably but their necessities would have induced any of the Walloons to accept so tame a servitude, considering their natural aversion to restraint and love of personal freedom. A new purpose soon usurped his mind—perhaps it had already—and the fortunes of Jesse de Forest were to take a sudden turn.

The lone ship dispatched with the Walloons, and other vessels sent out by the company soon after to the West Indies, were designed merely to secure possession of the country and to forestall the trade. The grand business in hand was the conquest of Brazil. Invested with the control of the Dutch possessions in Africa and America, with ample powers to trade with and colonize those countries, expel the Spaniards, and prey upon their commerce, the company now began the most extensive preparations to this end. The dockyards of Holland resounded with the noise of busy workmen, and loud was the call for seamen and soldiers to man the fleet. At length a powerful armament was ready to sail. On December 21st and 22d, 1623, nineteen ships of war left the Texel and the Ems, with the Admiral Jacob Willekens, joined the next day by three more from the Maas, making twenty-two vessels of war destined to operate against the Spanish settlements in the West Indies and Brazil. This expedition, designed also to cripple the maritime power of Spain, and ultimately compel her, if not to yield her control of the Low Countries, at least to grant civil and religious rights to the inhabitants and the restoration of their sequestered estates to the refugees, was in high favor with the Walloons, whose patriotism and martial spirit were aroused by this stirring call to arms. For some time Leyden had witnessed "nothing but beating of drums and preparings for war." Even the excellent Colonius, pastor of the Walloon Church, had taken the field with Prince Maurice, the Stadtholder, against the Spaniards. And so Jesse de Forest, giving up his old occupation, enlisted in this grand naval expedition to Brazil. He had latterly occupied a house with his brother Gerard, on the Maro, a canal running north from the Rhine to the city gate called the Mare Port. Gerard was to continue the business, but was licensed only to dye in black. Appearing before the burgomasters January 4th, 1624, and stating that his brother Jesse had "lately departed with the vessels for the West Indies," he requested to be appointed in his stead to dye serges and camlets *in colors*, as the number of dyers engaged in this specialty would not thereby be increased; and his request was granted.

But here the veil drops over the career of our De Forest. The summer was not quite ended when the yacht De Vos brought news of Willekens' success in Brazil, but no good news of De Forest. He seems either to have fallen at the siege of St. Salvador, or to have otherwise perished during that arduous service, for the fact of his decease soon became known to his family in Holland. The sad tidings as it reached Leyden that Jesse de Forest, the dyer, was dead, must have caused many an honest regret; but a deeper sorrow within that small circle of bereaved hearts, the desolate widow and orphans, whose wants could no longer be met by his provident care. But the breach in the social circle caused by the departure of even so good and useful a man—what was it in the grievous mortality which visited Leyden in the years 1624 and 1625? Years roll on, and those whom he left enjoy the fruits of his patient labor; but the voice of the lost husband and father comes back no more. Time buries alike his virtues and his foibles, and oblivion claims the memory of Jesse de Forest. Ah! not so; he still lives in his last ambitious adventure, to mould other destinies which are yet in the unrevealed future.

Near the time De Forest went abroad, our Jean La Montagne, latterly a boarder, with other "students," in the family of

Thomas Cornelisz, on the Breedestraat, in Meat Market Row, is found to have quit the University. The coincidence, and at a juncture when physicians were needed for the fleet, almost forces the conviction that he too had joined the expedition.* But perhaps he had merely retired from Leyden to avoid the plague, which, as intimated, made fearful ravages in that city in the two ensuing years. Leaving this to conjecture as we must, it at least appears that after having been gone for some time, Montagne returned to Leyden, and in order that he might continue his favorite studies, which had been interrupted by his absence, and also enjoy the various privileges of the University, which he seems to have valued very highly, was enrolled anew at that institution as a "student of medicine," July 7th, 1626. He had taken convenient lodgings with the widow De Forest—now living on the Voldersgraft, the second street east of St. Peter's Church—whose only daughter, the fair Rachel, had already stolen his heart, and to whom, with the approval of the family, as signified by her uncle Gerard, who was present, Montagne was united in wedlock by the pastor of the Walloon Church, December 12th, 1626. Living so near to St. Peter's, one of the principal churches in the city, it was here during the following year that they had the joy to present for baptism their little son, Jolant, their precious first-born, but, alas! destined soon to be taken from them.

Holland was now overflowing with people, all intent on making a livelihood, but "where one stiver was to be gained there were ten hands ready to receive it." Many on that account were leaving that country in search of other homes, where they might find better opportunities, and obtain a living more easily. The possessions of the Dutch in America, known as New Netherland, presented to such persons special advantages, and very alluring was the offer of the West India Company to grant each colonist as much land as he should be able to cultivate. So, while many of the sturdy sons of Holland were turning their faces thitherward, the subject was daily becoming of wider and more practical interest.

Often might have been noticed, poring over the musty tomes

* One *La Montagne*, captain in the Dutch service in Brazil, was killed in the Portuguese assault upon Fort Hinderson, 1646.

at the University library, a person of studious mien, known as Johannes de Laet, one of the several directors of the West India Company who resided at Leyden. An elder of the church, and distinguished for learning, moderation, and probity, De Laet enjoyed the public confidence; and the two Synods of North and South Holland, by selecting him to write an ecclesiastical history, paid a high tribute to his judgment and impartiality. His prolific pen had done much to familiarize the public mind with the discoveries of the Dutch in America. One of his works published at Leyden, entitled "The New World; or a Description of the West Indies," having been five years in print, appeared in an improved form in 1630, and gave the first full and authoritative account of New Netherland, awaking a lively interest not only in the circles of Leyden, but throughout Holland.

While De Laet's first edition was yet in press, sundry letters had been received from the Walloons who had gone out in 1623 to Manhattan and Fort Orange (Albany), in which they spoke in glowing terms of their new home, extolling its "beautiful rivers and babbling fountains," the excellence of its soil, and the abundance of its timber, fruits, game, and fish; then urging their friends to come out with their families and enjoy the benefits of a country which fairly rivalled "the paradiso of Holland."

The natural effect of these letters* was to induce not a few persons here and there forthwith to emigrate, while in many others was awakened a keen desire for fuller information, such as the work of De Laet was designed to gratify. The demand for the book became so great as only to be met by repeated editions. With the original journals of Hudson and succeeding explorers before him, many of the details presented were exceedingly entertaining.

Opening De Laet's vellum-bound, attractive folio, fresh from the press of the Elzeviers, the reader presently found his attention drawn to the extraordinary advantages and resources of the

* Quoted in the "*Gedenkwaardige Geschiedenissen, so Kerkelyke als Wereldlyke*," or "Remarkable Events, as well Ecclesiastical as Secular, from 1603 to 1624," by Rev. WILHELMUS BAUDARTIUS, of Zutphen; printed at Arnhem, 1624, in 2 vols. folio. See *Doc. Hist. N. Y.*, iv. 131. Baudartius was grandfather of our Wilhelmus Beekman.

country around the Island of Manhattan, and bordering the Great River of the Mountains. "The land is excellent and beautiful to the eye, full of noble forest trees and grape-vines; and wanting nothing but the labor and industry of man to render it one of the finest and most fruitful regions in that part of the world."

He then condenses the accounts given by "our countrymen who first explored this river, and those who afterwards made frequent voyages thither." The trees are "of wonderful size," fit for buildings and vessels of the largest class. Wild grape-vines and walnut trees are abundant. Maize or Indian corn, when cultivated, yields a prolific return; and so with several kinds of pulse, as beans of various colors, pumpkins—the finest possible, melons, and similar fruits. The soil is also found well adapted to wheat and several kinds of grain, as also flax, hemp, and other European seeds. Herbaceous plants grow in great variety, bearing splendid flowers, or valuable for their medicinal properties. The forests abound in wild animals, especially the deer kind; with other quadrupeds indigenous to this part of the country. Quantities of birds, large and small, frequent the rivers, lakes, and forests, with plumage of great elegance and variety of colors. Superior turkey-cocks are taken in winter, very fat, and the flesh of fine quality. Salmon, sturgeon, and many other kinds of excellent fish are caught in the rivers. The climate differs little in temperature from our own, though the country lies many degrees nearer the equator than the Netherlands. In winter the cold is intense, and snow falls frequent and deep, covering the ground for a long time. In summer it is subject to much thunder and lightning, with copious and refreshing showers. Scarcely any part of America is better adapted for colonists from this quarter; nothing is wanting necessary to sustain life, except cattle, which can be easily taken there, and as easily kept, on account of the abundance of fodder growing naturally and luxuriantly.

The Indians are indolent, and some crafty and wicked, having slain several of our people. The *Manhattans*, a fierce nation, occupy the eastern bank of the river near its mouth. Though hostile to our people, they have sold them the island or point of land which is separated from the main by Hellegat, and where they have laid the foundations of a city called New Amsterdam. The barbarians are divided into many nations and languages, but differ little in manners. They dress in the skins of animals. Their food is maize, crushed fine and baked in cakes; with fish, birds, and wild game. Their weapons are bows and arrows; their boats made from the trunks of trees, hollowed out by fire. Some lead a wandering life, others live in bark houses, their furniture mainly mats and wooden dishes, stone hatchets, and stone pipes for smoking tobacco. They worship a being called *Manetto*, are governed by chiefs called *Sagamos*, are suspicious, timid, revengeful, and fickle; but hospitable when well treated, ready to serve the white man for little compensation, and susceptible of being imbued with religion and good manners, "especially if colonies of well-ordered people should be planted among them, who would make use of their services without rudeness or abuse, and by degrees teach them the worship of the true God, and the habits of civilized life."

These accounts, here epitomized, were published in French as well as in the vernacular tongue, and being eagerly sought for and read, proved a powerful incentive to emigration; turning the scale with many desiring a change in favor of that new country, whose superior advantages had been depicted with so graphic a pen.

The same year in which the Walloon college was founded, a child was born in the city of Leyden, of Walloon parents, who being well-to-do no doubt educated him in that school of learning. This was Henry de Forest, the son of Jesse and the brother of Rachel. Bereft of his father while yet under age, he had looked to his uncle Gerard for needed counsel; and there is pleasing evidence that the relations of the uncle and nephew were intimate and confiding. Time, with rapid flight and many a change, had ushered in the year 1636. Henry was now of the mature age of thirty years; his brother Isaac—an infant of four months when the bells rung for the great fire at the University—had grown to be a young man of twenty; Jean, the eldest brother, a dyer by occupation, had recently taken a wife, and was living at the Hoogewoert in Leyden; while Jesse, the other brother, was spoken of tenderly—he was dead.

Since that memorable day when the elder De Forest left the shores of Holland never to return, his family had felt no common interest in all that related to America. The favorite theme of the social hour, it lent a fascination to their dreams. As seated around their smouldering turf fire they talked of the eventful past, and now of the flattering advantages to be enjoyed in New Netherland—thought of the unwholesome air and prevalent agues of Leyden, and of the appalling scenes of the preceding year, when pestilence again raged around them, and many thousands of their neighbors and townsmen were swept off by the plague—the two brothers Henry and Isaac de Forest resolved to turn their backs upon Holland, for a venture in New Netherland. There the tobacco culture now assumed new importance, and promised large profits to those who should engage in it, owing to the late failure of that crop in Virginia, as reported by vessels which had returned the preceding fall from James River, mostly without cargoes. This then was their opportunity. Aided in their plans and preparations by their uncle Gerard, whose son Crispin, it would seem, intended to make one of the emigrating party, their project doubtless had all the encouragement and support to be given it by their influential cousin, Mr. Johannes Panhuysen, of Leyden—married to a daughter of Gerard de Forest—who was then a director of the West India Company, and represented Leyden in the Chamber at Amsterdam, in which office he had succeeded Johannes de Laet. The plan seemed complete when their only sister Rachel, and her husband, Dr. La Montagne, agreed to go; the doctor, under assurances of some preferment there, deciding to give up his practice, and his associations and membership at the University, which but lately—that is on March 3d, 1630—he had renewed, as also his old home on the Kloksteeg, where he had for some years lived, at the sign of the *Queen of Bohemia.**

* The Queen of Bohemia, a noble Christian woman, was long an exile in Holland, the object of profound respect and sympathy among all Protestants; hence her effigy upon Montagne's signboard. She was Elizabeth Stuart, daughter of James I. of England, and wife of Frederick V., Elector Palatine of the Rhine and King of Bohemia, who had been driven from his dominions by the Catholic powers in 1621. He died in 1632, leaving the Queen with a large family. Neal says they "were always the delight of the Puritans," the hope of Protestantism in England resting on their expected succession to that throne; an event which happened not till 1714, when a grandson of the Queen of *Bohemia* was crowned as George I.

But all things were not yet ready; others who were deeply interested in these plans were to be consulted. Across the Zuyder Zee, on the west coast of Friesland, and between and extending nearly to the towns of Workum and Hindelopen, lies a pleasant grazing district called Nieuwlant. Here dwelt the respectable Dutch family of Bornstra, to one of whose members, a maiden of two and twenty years, named Gertrude, Henry de Forest was affianced. The same pleasing relations subsisted between her sister Margareta and Henry's cousin Crispin. To marry; to leave the kindly covert of the parental roof, and go across the sea to a far country—it was a bold adventure, to which the familiar passage of the Zuyder Zee, though that was often dangerous, was a trifling matter. But what confiding young bride ever refused to follow her Henry, wherever he might lead, and to feel safe under his protection? And so it was agreed that the nuptials in both cases should take place at the same time, and in the seat of Dutch fashion, Amsterdam. Accordingly, on Saturday, June 7th, 1636, the two happy pair were there, and attended by Gerard de Forest, as voucher for his son and nephew, and having the written consent of the father of the brides, attested by Secretary Van Neck, of Nieuwlant, presented themselves in the chamber of the eminent regent and physician, Dr. Claes Tulp, and Jacob Bicker, both schepens or magistrates of the city, and also the "Commissaries of Marriages," to have their bans registered as required by law, and to request the usual publication of the same. Names, residence, age, etc., being then recorded, and the record signed by the parties, this first public step toward their union, one so trying to bashful lovers, was taken. The next was to send notice to Leyden to have the bans published in the church on three succeeding Sundays; and this also having been done "without delay," the two couple, on Tuesday, July 1st, again attended by the father and uncle, Gerard, and by other friends, met in Amsterdam, and were married by Domine Baudius; probably at the New Church, in the public place called the Dam, on whose register the event stands recorded.

The social festivities, few and simple at that day, the parting visits to the dear old homes at Leyden and Nieuwlant, and busy, thoughtful preparation at both places for their coming departure, could not but wear a tinge of sadness in view of their long and perilous voyage, and uncertain absence from kin and country. The kind uncle Gerard engaged two persons to accompany them in the capacity of farmer and farmer's boy, each of whom entered into a formal contract to "serve said De Forest or his agent three successive years after arriving in New Netherland." The circumstances of Crispin de Forest's marriage, and the active part taken by his father in the preparations for the voyage, are reasons for the belief before expressed, that he also intended to be of the party. If so, something changed his purpose during the long delay before the others sailed, and Crispin stayed at Leyden.

The company yet consisted of Dr. La Montagne and his wife, and three children, Jesse, Jean, and Rachel; Henry de Forest and his bride, and Isaac de Forest, with the assistants Tobias Teunissen and Willem Fredericks Bont, both natives of Leyden. The last was a sturdy lad of sixteen years, perhaps an orphan, for his education had been neglected, but of a surname common there, and even distinguished. Teunissen, by trade a wool-washer, had reached middle life, having married in 1618. An attendant of St. Peter's Church, where he had several children baptized, and being known to the Curators of the University as a trustworthy person, he was employed in 1622 as a night-watchman at that institution, for which he received six florins a week. But time had brought him sad changes, and having been bereft of his family he now resolved to leave behind his native land and kindred, *and*, as he vainly hoped, also his adversities.

Now arrived the long-expected day of embarkation, when hopes and fears, congratulations and farewells, smiles and tears, strangely commingled! The party (except the Montagne family, who for some reason deferred their going) set sail from the Texel for New Amsterdam, October 1st, 1636, in the yacht Rensselaerswyck, of which Jan Tiebkins was skipper, and carrying colonists to Fort Orange, in the service of the Patroon, Kilian Van Rensselaer, of Amsterdam.

Interrupting for a space the story of these pioneers, let us note the movements of others in whom we are interested, who were led to follow upon the same adventurous voyage across the ocean.

CHAPTER V.

EMIGRATION.

AMSTERDAM, as the great commercial mart of Holland, and the seat of the principal business chamber of the Dutch West India Company, had become the great point of embarkation for colonists going to New Netherland. They came from all parts of the country: not only the native Dutch, and fugitives from France and the Catholic Netherlands, but also refugees from the German and Scandinavian countries, multitudes of whom, rendered miserable by the Thirty Years' War, were seeking a home and employment in the United Provinces. Of these refugees the historian of Holland has drawn the character in happy terms. Says Davies: "Nor was it more in the *numbers* than in the *sort* of population that Holland found her advantage. The fugitives were not criminals escaped from justice, speculators lured by the hope of plunder, nor idlers coming thither to enjoy the luxuries which their own country did not afford: they were generally men persecuted on account of their love of civil liberty, or their devotion to their religious tenets; had they been content to sacrifice the one or the other to their present ease and interest, they had remained unmolested where they were; it was by their activity, integrity, and resolution that they rendered themselves obnoxious to the tyrannical and bigoted governments which drove them from their native land; and these virtues they carried with them to their adopted country, peopling it, not with vagabonds or indolent voluptuaries, but with brave, intelligent, and useful citizens."

Thus our Captain Jochiem Pietersen Kuyter, who had formerly commanded in the East Indies for the King of Denmark, and who with his friend Jonas Bronck came out in 1630 by way of Amsterdam, was from Holstein; as were also our Nicholas de Meyer and Jan Pietersen Slot, who arrived a few years later: all these being sterling men, and, except the last, well educated. The small county of Bentheim—a part of Westphalia bordering on Overyssel, diversified with mountain ranges, forests, and fertile plains, and yielding to a laborious people more than they needed of cattle, wool, linen, honey, etc., all which found in Holland a ready market, and whence had arisen a free intercourse between the two peoples—furnished three colonists whose well-known surnames yet survive with us, to wit, Adolph Meyer, Jan Dyckman, and Arent Harmans Bussing, the last-named of a family not unknown to fame in that country; and two bore prenomens popular in their part of Germany, as among the rulers of Bentheim none were such favorites as the late counts Adolph and Arent. Other Westphalians found their way to Harlem, as Hendrick Karstens, from Oldenburg, whose sons were called Boch, or Boeck; Jan Terbosch, from *Tellust*, or Delmenhorst, whose descendants are numerous; and Jan Meynderts, from Jever, in Oldenburg, and the father-in-law of Barent Waldron. Kier Wolters, the Kiersen ancestor, who had lived at Gees and at Aernhout, two obscure villages in the "Groot Veenen," or desert-like fens of Drenthe, came out *vià* Amsterdam; as did also our Benson ancestor, who was originally from Groningen. From Workum, on the coast of Friesland, came Captain Jan Gerritsen de Vries, or Van Dalsen, progenitor of the Dolsen family, of Orange County, whose blood may also be traced in those of Waldron, Kiersen, and Myer.

Amsterdam itself gave us of its resident families those of Waldron, Sneden, and Verveelen, familiar names yet found in this State and others, and to which the Slots and Bensons may be added. Direk Benson, the ancestor, though himself from Groningen, as stated, had lived at Amsterdam, where he married Catalina, daughter of Samson Berck and Tryntie van Rechteren; whence the name *Samson*, so common in the Benson family. Benson came out about 1648.

Also from Amsterdam was Hendrick Jansen Vander Vin. Well educated, and a good accountant, he was commended to the notice of the West India Company, and went under their auspices to Pernambuco, in Brazil, where he acted as clerk to the High Council of Justice at Maurits Stadt, a town built by the Dutch near the Reciff. Some fragments of his minutes kept at that place in 1646 are yet extant. He was there during the dismal period of the Portuguese conspiracy to extirpate the Dutch, happily discovered and thwarted, but which was followed by many reverses to the Dutch arms, and then by the surrender of Brazil to the rival power in 1654. Vander Vin had left some years prior to the final catastrophe, and returned to Amsterdam, resuming his business as a notary. But in 1651 he went out to Manhattan Island to see the country. It pleased him so well that returning for a stock of goods to set up trading in New Amsterdam, he again repaired thither in 1653, taking his *good vrouw* Wyntie to share with him the blessings and privations of his new home. He subsequently served fourteen years at Harlem as *voorleser*, and twelve of these as town-clerk.

Joseph and Resolved Waldron, sons of Resolved Waldron, of Amsterdam, were book-printers. The family was English; the name, of repute in England from the time of the Conqueror, had spread through nearly all its southern tier of counties. But born and raised at Amsterdam, these brothers had acquired all the characteristics of Hollanders, having also married Dutch wives, the sisters Aeltie and Rebecca Hendricks, whose father, Hendrick Koch, was a respectable Amsterdam burgher. It is stated on pretty good authority that Resolved had made the voyage to Brazil, but of this we will not speak further here. Having the misfortune to lose his wife, he married again, on May 10th, 1654, a lady of thirty years, living near the West India House, Tanneke Nagel, daughter of Barent Nagel, deceased, of Groningen. Resolved was living at this time in the Teerketelsteeg, a short street just north of the Dam; but the same year sailed with his family for America. His brother, Joseph Waldron, had preceded him to this country by two years, according to his son's reckoning. He also was accompanied by a second wife, Annetie Daniels, but twenty-five when he married her at Amsterdam April 4th, 1649, she and Resolved's wife being of even age.

Near the time Resolved Waldron left for the Manhattans, the young John La Montagne, who had spent seventeen years at the latter place, indeed had grown up there, where he was highly esteemed and was now in business with Vincent Pikes, "both free traders in company," arrived at Amsterdam in the ship King Solomon. Not only to visit his native land and kindred, alike as strange and new to his eye as though he were an alien: he came to buy a stock of merchandise, and also to sell a lot of tobacco, of which he was consignee, and invest the proceeds in goods for his uncle, Isaac de Forest; but what more deeply concerned him, to choose a wife, the fair one selected being Peternella, sister of his business partner, and daughter of Jan Pikes, of Amsterdam. The nuptial knot being tied by Pastor Meursius, at Slooterdyk, a village a mile from Amsterdam, on March 14th following (1655), La Montagne sailed very soon on his return, his wife remaining till after the birth and baptism of her son John, which occurred late in the same year.

Jan Pietersen Slot, before named as from Holstein, and ancestor of the respectable family of Slott or Sloat, of Orange County, and of Rockland, and the Ramapo Valley, came out with his children, born and reared in Amsterdam, about the same time with Resolved Waldron; and Johannes Verveelen and Jan Sneden followed them in 1657. Sneden was descended from a family long at Amsterdam, and was accompanied to America by his wife Grietie Jans, two children, and brother Claes Sneden. They sailed in the St. Jan Baptist, December 23d of the last-named year, one which witnessed the departure of many colonists for New Amstel, on the Delaware, under the patronage of the City of Amsterdam, and among whom was Kier Wolters, father of the Kiersens, as before stated.

Verveelen was born in 1616 at Amsterdam, but of German stock with an infusion of French, being a son of Daniel Verveelen, who with his parents Hans Verveelen and Catharina, daughter of John Oliviers, had some five years prior to the birth of Johannes removed to that city from Cologne, on the Rhine. Religious intolerance, which culminated in 1618 in the expulsion of all the Protestants from that town, had doubtless driven the Verveelens to Amsterdam. Here the son Daniel, born at Cologne in 1594, married in 1615, and became a "shopkeeper;" and here also his son Johannes, the eldest of six children, was reared and educated, and in 1637 married Anna Jaarsvelt, by whom he had, all born in that city, three children, Daniel, Anna, and Maria. The first of these when a mere boy preceded his father to New Netherland, under the care, we believe, of Domine Gideon Schaets, one of whose daughters he married. After several years his father followed, bringing his wife and daughters, and widowed mother, Anna Elkhout, aged about sixty-six years.

Utrecht and Arnhem, cities on the Rhine, the latter within Gelderland, supplied settlers to Harlem. A hamlet near Amersfoort, in the province or diocese of Utrecht, gave us Jan Hendricks van Brevoort, coming to this country in boyhood with his father, and from whom have sprung the reputable family of Brevoort. At much the same time (about 1655) emigrated the head of the Van Tilburg family, Jan Teunissen, from Tilburg, in the Mayory of Bosch (or Bois le Duc), in Dutch Brabant; and from the same district afterward came two other colonists whose progeny are numerous and respectable, to wit, David Ackerman and Dirck Storm, names not unknown at Harlem. Ackerman was from Berlikum. These, with their families, sailed from Amsterdam, September 2d, 1662, in the ship Fox, Captain Jacob Huys, which also brought Jan Terbosch and Robert le Maire, already named, and identified with Harlem.

The large emigration to New Netherland from the exposed borders nearest the Spanish possessions, and especially the insular district having on the south the river Waal, and on the north the Rhine and Leck, furnished Harlem with several substantial families. Central of the district mentioned, upon the small river Linge, which empties into the Waal, stood the city of Leerdam, giving name to a county in which it was seated—a level, grazing country, otherwise called the Prince's Land, because inherited by a son of William of Orange, from his mother, Anne of Egmont. To Leerdam had retired from the religious troubles in Flanders, as before noticed, the family of Sebastian, or Bastiaen van Kortryk—about all we know of this Kortright progenitor with his royal Spanish name. Two sons of Bastiaen, of whom we must speak, Jan and Michiel, were born at Leerdam; but the first married and settled some farther up the Linge, at a busy little village within sight of Wolfswaert Castle, as also of the ruined abbey of Marienwaert, and called Beest, its bailiwick of the same name joining westerly to the Prince's Land, but within the Gelderland border. The spirit of emigration reaching this locality, many of its people began to pack up and leave for New Netherland, in which they had a safe precedent in no less a personage than the village pedagogue—much reverenced was he and looked up to in those days—for, in the spirit of his deceased senior, Mathias Bartholomeus Schaets, late pastor at Leerdam, who died four years before Gideon was born, the latter, good *Master* Schaets, after a course in theology, had gone thither with his family in 1652, to preach the Gospel, under license from the Classis of Amsterdam, and also, as before, to fill "the office of schoolmaster for old and young." Among those, accordingly, who at length set their faces to follow their old preceptor to the New World were two brothers, of Beest, sons of Peter Buys. Aert, the elder, with wife and son Cornelis, joining some families from that place, and single persons of both sexes, his friends and neighbors, set sail from Amsterdam May 9th, 1661, in the ship Beaver, reaching Manhattan July 29th.* Two years later Johannes Buys joined his brother at Harlem.

Michiel, or, as often called, 'Chiel Kortright, the other son of Bastiaen, had also married and been living in "the Prince's Land, near Schoonrewoerd;" the latter a pretty village two miles northerly from Leerdam, whence there had been some emigrating to the Colonie of Rensselaerswyck, at the instance of the Patroon, who had a seat and estates at Vianen, but four miles from Schoonrewoerd. Foremost in this service were Rutger Jacobsen, who went out in the vessel with the De Forests,

* PETER MARSELIS, his wife, 4 chn. and 2 servants; *Frans Jacobsen*, w. and 2 chn.; *Goosen Jansen van Noort*, and *Hendrick Bries*, were among those referred to from Beest. The first two went to Bergen, N. J.; the others, I believe, to Albany. See *Pearson's Albany Settlers*. Bries must not be taken for *Hendrick Volkertsen Bries*, from Jever, in Oldenburg, who m. at New Amsterdam in 1655, and whence came the *Breese* family of Long Island, Staten Island, and New Jersey. Marselis d. Sept. 4, 1681, leaving desc. Jacobsen, having a son Jacob Franssen, b. in 1664, d. about that time, and in 1665, *Cornelis Abrahams*, from Deyl, near Beest, m. his wid., Geertie Gerrits. She d. a wid., at Pemrepogh, in 1680, having the year before lost her eldest son Gerrit Franssen, and m. her dr., Marritie Frans, to Johannes Spier, son of *Hendrick Jansen Spier*, from Ascheward, in Bremen, common anc. of the Spier or *Speer* family of N. J.

The same ship, the Beaver, took over *Hugh Barents de Kleyn*, from Buren; *Aert Teunis Middagh*, from Heykoop (settled in Brooklyn); and *Evert Pietersen Keteltas*, returning to New Amsterdam as "consoler of the sick, chorister, and schoolmaster;" also *Etienne Genoan*, a Huguenot from La Rochelle, his w. Lydia Meteren, and 3 chn. He lived at Harlem, I believe, in 1675, but went to Staten Island, and was the *Gano* anc.

SCHOONREWOERD.

and also his brother Teunis Jacobsen, the ancestors of families since well known.* To the Colonie afterward Do. Schaets had also gone. Each bit of news wafted home from time to time in friendly letters served to quicken interest in the new country which had caused so many vacant tenements and broken families about Beest and Schoonrewoerd. Yet 'Chiel Kortright tarried some years at the latter place, till blest with three or four children; when he and his elder brother, Jan Bastiaensen, whose three sons, born at Beest, his humble home in a bend of the Linge, were now fast approaching manhood, yielded to the flattering offers held out to colonists, and agreed to leave together for that distant land. The contagion had also seized some of the neighbors at Schoonrewoerd, one of whom was Jan Louwe Bogert, a young man with wife and two children, and whose kinsman, Theunis Gysberts Bogert, of Heykoop, two miles northwest of Schoonrewoerd, had been already ten years in America.

* RUTGER JACOBSEN was the ancestor of the *Rutgers* family of New York, and also, through his dr. Margaret, who m. 1667, *Jan Jansen Bleecker*, from Meppel, a progenitor of the highly respectable family of this name. Teunis Jacobsen's descendants, who have been numerous in Albany County, took name from his birthplace, but shortened to *Van Woert*. See *Holgate's Am. Gen.*, *Pearson's Albany Settlers*, and *O'Callaghan's N. Neth.*, i. 436, 439.

Proceeding to Amsterdam, they all embarked, April 16th, 1663, in the Brindled Cow, Jan Bergen, master, in which ship there also sailed several French refugees from Mannheim, in the Palatinate, who will command further notice.

For years the streams of Huguenot emigration, setting out of France and the Low Countries, had been bearing to Holland now a solitary wanderer, now a stricken family, some to abide here for a time, others seeking a passage to the New World, but destined ultimately to find at Harlem a resting-place. Coming by no general or concerted action, but only as a crisis in the affairs of each had indicated the time and the mode, it is not easy to fix the exact date of their flight, though the era has been sufficiently shown. We shall name them, as we have the Dutch colonists, in the order of their departure for New Netherland.

DANIEL DE TOURNEUR (so his name was sometimes written), leaving Picardy by a sudden necessity, as already related, and coming to Leyden, had here followed the business of a draper; and on September 5th, 1650, married Jacqueline Parisis, of a Walloon refugee family from Hesdin, in Artois, and a sister to Rev. Eustacius Parisis, then of Amsterdam. Near two years later, Tourneur sailed, with his wife and infant son Daniel, for New Netherland, probably in the ship with Do. Samuel Drisius, of Leyden, which left Holland April 4th, 1652. *Jean le Roy*, a kinsman of Tourneur, appears to have accompanied him with his wife Louise de Lancastre, whose name implies an English birth.

GLAUDE LE MAISTRE, or Delamater, as usually written by his descendants, had sprung from an ancient house of Brittany, the Lords of Garlaye, whose château and estates lay in the parish of Derval, in the diocese of Nantes. It was eminent in the civil and military service, the church, and the law. Its members had held commands in Picardy, where one of its now scattered branches in which the name Claude first appears, became allied early in the sixteenth century to the lords of Caumartin. Claude le Maistre, Sieur de Hédicourt, becoming a Protestant, was with others imprisoned and fined at Amiens in 1588, at the instance of the League. He was a man of talent and spirit, and showed great valor in opposing the entrance of the Spaniards into that city in 1597, when soldiers in the garb of peasants, selling apples and nuts, had gained admission. Our Glaude le Maistre was no doubt of this family, some of whom removing into Artois, there he was born, as before said, in the town of Richebourg. After escaping the country he comes to notice at Amsterdam in 1652, an exile and a widower, living in the Tanners' cross-street, having lost his wife, Jeanne de Lannoy. But on April 24th of that year he married Hester, daughter of Pierre du Bois, of Amsterdam, though late of Canterbury, England, where Hester was born. Some of the Le Maistres had also taken refuge at Canterbury, and circumstances make it nearly certain that Glaude was among them, and with the Du Boises had left England because of the civil wars then raging or the threatened rupture with Holland; and perhaps in his case to take ship for New Netherland, as he soon did so, appearing simultaneously with Tourneur at Flatbush, and both subsequently at Harlem.

Marc du Sauchoy, whose name will hardly be recognized by his worthy posterity the Disosway family, was a native of Picardy, and probably from Amiens. The lords Du Sauchoy came from the house of Clermont, in the Beauvoisis, and one of them went to the conquest of Britain with the Duke of Normandy; perhaps our Marc, a man of worth and enterprise, was of that blood, but we know not. In his exile he worked as a wool-carder, but in search of something better made a voyage from Holland to New Netherland in 1655. Sufficiently pleased with the country to make it his future home, he returned to Leyden, married March 11th, 1657, Elizabeth, daughter of Guillaume Rossignol, and with his bride again sailed from Amsterdam for Manhattan, on April 2d ensuing, in the ship Draetvat, Captain Bestevaer, taking also to aid him in farming, two workmen, and two boys over twelve years of age. One of the adults was Johannes Smedes, from Harderwyck, in Gelderland, and one of the lads, Jean Gnenon (now Genung), of Leyden, both of whom have many descendants.*

* Teunis Kray (or Gray), from Venlo, on the Maas, returned in this ship to New Netherland, where he had already lived several years. He was now accompanied by his wife and chn., one of the latter afterwards the wife of Capt. *Jan van Dalsen*, of Harlem, already noticed.

DAVID DU FOUR, a native of Mons, in Hainault, upon this place being threatened by the successes of the French in the Walloon districts, retired with others of his family to Sedan, and afterwards to Amsterdam, where Du Four, though fitted by education for a better position, became an "opperman," or drayman. Left by the death of his wife, Marie Boulen, with a young child, Jean, born during their stay at Sedan, he found another companion in Joanne Frances, a lady of mature thirty-two years, from Queivrain, a little east of Mons, to whom he was married July 10th, 1657. That same year, with his new wife and his little son aforesaid, he sailed for Manhattan Island.

JEAN GERVOE and FRANCOIS LE SUEUR went out at near the same date, the first being a young man from Beaumont in Hainault, and who, choosing the congenial calling of the Walloon, afterwards served the West India Company as a soldier at Harlem. Le Sueur, the *Lozier* ancestor, was from Colménil, in Normandy, and was attended by his young sister Jeanne, neither being married.

JACQUES COUSSEAU, merchant at La Rochelle in 1653, and for four years later when he retired to Amsterdam, took his departure soon after, with his wife Madeleine du Tulliere, for America, evidently per ship Gilded Beaver, which sailed May 17th, 1658. This need hardly be doubted; Cousseau paid the fare of Simon Bouche, who went in that vessel, and directly on its arrival at New Amsterdam, several of the passengers, and with them Cousseau, on July 18th, applied for and were granted the small burgher right.

SIMON DE RUINE, another refugee, familiarly known among the Dutch at Harlem as *de Waal*, and with the French as *le Ouallon*, that is, *the Walloon*, bore a name found at Valenciennes, but had himself lived near Landrecy, whence escaping to Holland and there tarrying for some years, he went out with his wife Magdalena Vanderstraaten, and several children, in the ship Faith, "a private trader going to the Manhattans," which sailed February 13th, 1659, with nearly an hundred passengers, but no French except De Ruine.*

* GILLIS JANSEN DE MANDEVILLE, from Garderen, in the Veluwe, Gelderland, and anc. of the American family of Mandeville, came out in this vessel; as did his neighbor, also a farmer, *Wouter Gerritsen*, from Koetwych,

PIERRE CRESSON was another worthy refugee, and whose family seat, as is believed, was at Ménil la Cresson, or Cresson Manor, a little north-east of Abbeville, in Picardy, though he was no doubt allied to the Cressons of Burgundy, of whom were several Reformed ministers. Such change of residence was common during the long Burgundian rule in Picardy. Pierre, whose character for piety is well attested, fled with some of his kin to the noted refuge, Sluis, in Flanders, but soon moved farther north, and in 1640 is found (with Nicolas and Venant Cresson, both married) among the refugees at Leyden. The many of these emigrating to New Netherland had doubtless an effect upon Pierre, though, with a vigor and activity, which indeed he retained till old age, but at this date scarce more than thirty, he supported himself in Holland for yet some seventeen years, living parts of that time at Ryswyk and Delft. Employed as gardener to the Prince of Orange, he was ever after known as *Pierre le Gardinier*. But Cresson was at last taken with the favorable offers of the City of Amsterdam to those who would go to their new colony on the Delaware; and it seeming a good opportunity for him and his growing family, he gathered up his little means, and with wife Rachel Cloos and children, embarked in 1657, at Amsterdam, for New Amstel. The next year Governor Stuyvesant visiting the Delaware, engaged Cresson "for his service" at the Manhattans, "with the proposition that what he owed the city (Amsterdam) should be settled." Soon after Cresson made a trip to Holland, returning in company with several other French agriculturists in the ship Beaver, which sailed April 25th, 1659, reaching its destination after a quick passage of six weeks. Each passing year thus added to the roll of worthy fugitives, who led by an unseen

some three miles from Garderen; and likewise *Jan Meyndertz*, already named. The last two will appear at Harlem.

Gillis (often written Yellis) or Giles de Mandeville was accompanied by his w. Elsie Hendricks, and four chn., having two born afterward, one being David. Yellis bought a farm at Flatbush, which he finally gave to his eldest son Hendrick, and got the grant of another, of 30 acres, at Greenwich, on Manhattan Island, laid out to him Dec. 5, 1679, and patented Dec. 30, 1680. Here he d. between 1696 and 1701. All of his chn. m. He had but the two sons, both of whom left desc. David remained on the farm at Greenwich. Hendrick removed from L. I., to Pequannock, N. J. These have given several pastors to the Reformed Church, including Rev. Giles Henry Mandeville, D.D.

but mighty hand out of oppression into the atmosphere of freedom, were perforce of their common nationality and sympathies to find a common home beyond the Atlantic.*

But this roll is not yet complete. England, as already hinted, first became an asylum for some of our settlers. Many persecuted refugees from France and Flanders took that direction, embarking usually in regularly plying vessels, but often, if hard pressed, venturing to cross the Channel in any sort of craft, even at the peril of their lives, while making for the most accessible port on the opposite shore. They landed principally at Dover, Sandwich, and Rye, within the counties of Kent and Sussex. Meeting a uniform welcome and sympathy, they formed colonies and churches at these places, and set up various manufactures, mainly those of cloth and linen, in which they were encouraged by the general and local authorities. The seaports named and others becoming crowded with these exiles, many by invitation went inland to Canterbury, Norwich, etc., and still more up the Thames to London, at all which places they founded similar communities and industries. These colonies were greatly multiplied after the time of which we are writing. The story of the refugees in England is very touching; while their patient toil, the skill and ingenuity they exhibited in the production of various useful articles, evoked the admiration of the English, their devotion to their religion, their care to maintain its ordinances wherever they went, was highly creditable. Kept well informed of affairs in their native lands, the sympathy they manifested for their still suffering brethren sets them in a most amiable light. Bound to their fellow-refugees in Holland by common interests as well as by many family ties, there was a free intercourse, and removals from one country to the other often took place due to these affinities or the simple desire to better their state; but sometimes prompted by dangers which threatened them as a people, or those countries at large. Ever keenly alive to passing events in anywise bearing on their cause or that of Protestant-

* MARTEN VAN WEERT, a hatter from Utrecht, who had visited this country five years before, came out in the ship with Cresson in 1659. He m. Dec. 4, 1660, Susanna, dr. of Abraham Verplanck. The Van Weerts, his chn., were prominent in the church at Sleepy Hollow, Westchester Co. Isaac Van Wart, one of the captors of Major André, the spy, was a desc. See *Bolton's Westchester*, i. 197, 235.

ism in general, one which greatly affected the refugees was the Peace of Westphalia, in 1648, ending the Thirty Years' War, and opening to them a new asylum up the Rhine, unto which many resorted, as we shall see.

The family DES MARÊTS was of the old Picard gentry, and was also prominent in the church at Oisemont, of which David des Marêts, the Sieur du Ferets, was an elder. His son Samuel, born at Oisemont in 1599, and taught at the great schools of Paris, Saumur, and Geneva, became in 1619 pastor of the church of Laon. But forced to leave in 1623 by an attempt upon his life which nearly proved fatal, he accepted a new charge at Falaise in Normandy, but after a year went to Sedan, and thence in 1642 to Groningen, in Holland, as professor of theology. Our *David des Marest*, who wrote his name thus, was born in Picardy, and, as is strongly indicated, was of the same lineage. For dignity of character and fidelity to his religion worthy so excellent a kinship; the clerical tendency among his descendants is also very significant. He went to Holland and joined the French colony in the island of Walcheren, at which place his eldest son Jean Demarest was born in 1645. Here David probably married his wife Marie Sohier, as a family of this name from Hainault had taken refuge at Middelburg in the first Walloon emigrations.

In 1651 Demarest is found at Mannheim, on the Rhine, within the German Palatinate; to which were going many French and Walloon refugees from England, and also from the Dutch seaboard, partly in view of an expected war between the English and Hollanders, but especially drawn thither by the assurance of freedom and protection under the government of the Protestant Elector Charles Lewis, who, invested by the Treaty of Westphalia (1648) with the Lower Palatinate, from which his father, Frederick V., had been driven in 1621 by the Catholic powers after the battle of Prague, held out strong inducements to the refugees, especially Calvinists, to settle at Mannheim, and which found a ready response through the lively interest always cherished by the refugees, in common with the English Puritans, in the strange vicissitudes of his late father, and his excellent and yet surviving mother, named in a former note as the "Queen of Bohemia." By 1652 Demarest and others among the numbers gathered there joined in forming a French church; the elector himself building them an edifice, which he called the *Temple of Concord*, because the Lutherans were also allowed to worship there.

PHILIPPE CASIER and family, originally of Calais, also found this inviting refuge, as did *Simeon Cornier*, "from France," *Meynard Journee* (the Journeay ancestor), from Mardyk, Flanders, *Joost van Oblinus* (now O'Blenis), his son Joost and family, from Walloon Flanders, and *Pierre Parmentier*, also from "Walslant," that is, the Walloon country—all these afterwards at Harlem. Here Peter van Oblinus, son of Joost, Jr. and his wife Marie Sammis, was born in 1662, and who afterwards at Harlem was distinguished. Among the Walloons from Artois found here, were *Matthieu Blanchan*, *Louis du Bois*, and *Antoine Crispel;* Blanchan having sojourned in England, as perhaps had the other two, who became his sons-in-law. Others joining this Mannheim colony, and to be hereafter noticed, were the families of *Le Conte*, from Picardy, and *De Vaux*, from Walslant, whose descendants are called De Voe. De Vaux and Parmentier were clearly names derived from Picardy.

Philippe Casier was a husbandman and something of a traveller, having lived several years in the island of Martinique, to which he had gone with other colonists under the auspices of the French West India Company. But weary of rough pioneer life among wild Caribs, and more weary of the civil anarchy then reigning in the islands, he returned with his family to Europe, and tarried awhile at Sluis before removing up the Rhine. While at Mannheim, a son, Peter, was born (1659) to his eldest daughter Marie, the wife of *David Uzille*, the latter also mentioned as from Calais, but no doubt of the Brittany family. But neither was Casier contented at Mannheim, still indulging, as it would seem, visions of a better fortune for him in America. His wife's brother, *Isaac Taine*, called also *la Père*, "the Father," had gone out some years previous, and had been made a burgher of New Amsterdam; and thither the Casier family, Uzilles included, resolved to go.* Returning to Holland, they

* ISAAC TAYNE, as he wrote his name, obtained a grant of land, June 24, 1666, at New Castle, Del., where he was living ten years later.—*Penn. Archives*, I. 35. His wife was Sarah Reson. This name, ending with the French nasal sound *ng*, is sometimes written *Ting*.

sailed directly for the Manhattans in the ship Gilded Otter, which left the Texel April 27th, 1660, carrying also Blanchan and others from Mannheim, beside a band of soldiers, among whom were Jacob Leisler, famous in our colonial story, and Joost Kockuyt, heretofore mentioned, afterward part owner of the land since forming the "Dyckman Homestead." Later, Simeon Cornier, with his wife Nicole Petit, left Mannheim and returned to Holland, whence they sailed in the ship Faith, March 24th, 1662, from the Texel for the Manhattans, arriving June 13th.

Isaac Vermeille, one of the Harlem settlers and head of the well-known family of *Vermilye*, was the son of Jean Vermeille and Marie Roubley, who are found among the Walloon refugees at London toward the close of the sixteenth century.* They were members of the Walloon church, and had several children born in that city, among these Isaac, in 1601. The last child was Rebecca, born 1609, and three years later we lose sight of the father. Some of the family soon removed to Leyden, where Isaac's elder sister Rachel, who had been admitted to the church in London July 15th, 1613, was married April 25th, 1615, to Jacques Bordelo, a Walloon from Valenciennes. Jean Vermeille, to whom a child was born in 1633 at London, and who married a second wife at Leyden in 1647, was probably brother to Isaac. Marie Vermeille (mother or sister?), with her husband Jean Dimanche, stood as godparents for Isaac's daughter Marie (afterward Mrs. Montanye), at her baptism at Leyden, August 2d, 1629. Then Isaac first attracts our notice here, with his Dutch *vrouw*, Jacomina Jacobs, but later has two other children baptized, the last in 1637. Thence not finding his name at Leyden for full twenty-five years, it seems to imply his absence; and

* We nowhere find it stated that our Vermilyes were Walloons, but think it a safe assumption, for several reasons. The congregation at London of which they were members was then composed quite exclusively of that people. Then their Christian names favor it. And one of the Walloon towns bears the name *Vermelle*; being in Artois, south-east of Bethune, near a lake at the source of the Papegay, which latter runs northward, entering the Lys near Armentieres. Traced to its origin, the surname was doubtless the same as the Italian *Vermigli*. "Its birthplace," says Rev. A. G. Vermilye, "was probably Peruggia." Peter Vermigli (or Martyr), the reformer, was born at Florence. Like many others, the name had evidently worked upward to Northern France, but how early we know not. *Vermeille* is the French for vermilion.

he probably went to Mannheim, as the name Isaac *Wurmel*, found on its civil records, is thought by a good authority there to refer to him. However, again at Leyden in the company of other French, who "by advice of some gentlemen, and reading the New Netherland conditions, were allured and persuaded to emigrate with their families," we meet with Vermeille, about to leave with them for that much-mooted country, whither during his time so many Leyden refugees, back to the De Forests and Montagne, had already gone. With wife, his two sons and as many daughters, Vermeille embarked October 12th, 1662, in the ship Purmerland Church, Captain Barentsen, which on the 14th weighed anchor and "passed the last village on the Texel," bound with supplies to New Amstel.*

Soon after this the Palatinate was threatened with hostile invasion by the Duke of Lorraine and other neighboring Catholic princes. The refugees having every thing to fear from such enemies to their kind and religion, many more of these hastily quit Mannheim. The Demarest, Oblinus, and Parmentier families, with Journee, returned to Holland, apparently with purpose formed of going to New Netherland, for making short stay at Amsterdam they all embarked for that country in the Brindled Cow, April 16th, 1663; having in company Jean Mesurolle, a Picard, but then from Mannheim, Jerome Boquet (Boker) and Pierre Noue, both originally from Walslant; beside our several Dutch colonists before noticed, the Bogerts and Kortrights, from Schoonrewoerd and vicinity. Men, women, and children, there were ninety odd passengers, the French composing a third. Each adult was charged for passage and board thirty-nine florins; children of ten years and under, except infants, half price. It cost Jan Bastiaensen (Kortright) for himself and family 204 fl. 10 st., and David Demarest, 175 fl.

* The charges for their passage stand thus in the accounts of the West India Co.:

"ISAACQ VERMIELH debet

Voor vracht en costgelt dat by A°. 1662, 12 Octob^r. pr: 't Schip de *Purmerlander Kerck*, Schipp^r. Benjamin Barentsen, is herwaerts gecomen	*f.* 39
Voor syn vrou	39
En 4 kinderen, alle boven de 10^e Jaeren	156
	f. 234"

10 st.* These refugees from Mannheim nearly all took certificates of membership from the French church there. Some others who followed them ten years later, will be noticed hereafter.

Holland had now lost the special attractions it presented to the first refugees. These finding sympathy and employment, were generally content to remain as permanent residents. But the disturbances of later years had unsettled many, while trade had steadily and greatly declined, with no hope of any revival. Moreover, other unfortunate fugitives were flocking in "from Germany, Westphalia, and those countries which within two years had been ruined by hard times, but mainly by persecutions, to which the faithful all through France (as also the Waldenses) had been subjected." Under these circumstances many were easily drawn into the current of emigration to New Netherland, which was extolled as "beyond question the finest country in the world, where every thing can be produced that is grown in France or the Baltic," and whose virgin soil and settlements, free from the tyranny of kings and the contagion of European society, offered a most inviting abode and ample scope for enterprise. The most flattering reports of that country were rife, as given by those visiting Holland in search of farm-laborers, and by merchants whose business took them over to Amsterdam. Among those by whom the section of Manhattan Island since known as Harlem was first brought to the favorable notice of colonists, was Andries Hudde, late counsellor in New Netherland, who spent the winter of 1658–9 in Holland, and part of whose errand was to send out hands to work his tobacco plantation, afterwards known as Montanye's Flat. It was plainly his representations regarding that locality that took Captain Knyter and others thither, and induced Van Keulen, of Amsterdam, to secure the two-hundred-acre tract thence called Van Keulen's Hook; the purchase of which was effected directly upon Hudde's return. And Sibout Claessen, an energetic burgher of New Amsterdam, going to Fatherland in the autumn

* The Dutch *florin* or *guilder* is usually valued at forty cents, the *stiver* at two cents; but taking into account that, in the times we are treating of, money in Holland, as compared with labor, commodities, or whatever else it purchased, had *about four times its present value*, certainly these emigrants paid well for their passage.

of 1649, spent nearly two years between Hoorn, his native place, and Amsterdam and Leyden, while prosecuting charges against Stuyvesant. Bad as, in his view, was the administration, none had a higher opinion of the country, Manhattan especially, where Claesen had a fine property opposite Hellgate, which he called Hoorn's Hook. And Jean La Montagne, who revisited Holland in 1654. With his many years' experience in the new country, glowing, we dare assert, were the pictures he drew of it—when tenderly pressing his suit with the fair Peternella, who was to share his home and fortunes! And Nicholas De Meyer, the clear-headed and thrifty trader at New Amsterdam, making a trip to Holland in 1662, to remain over winter, no doubt astonished his auditors as he told of lands on Manhattan at one dollar sixty cents an acre, and his recent purchase of two farms in the young settlement, New Harlem. What interest must have attached to these accounts by visitants from the New World, as every listener caught up the story of its almost fabulous advantages and resources! To the young and ambitious, the far-off America had all the dazzling attractions of a fairyland, when so often even the tender sex were led as by an irresistible charm, in the face of many perils, to venture its wild solitudes. But again, with more caution, one of a family first goes to the New World, as if to report from personal knowledge upon the expediency of the change before others should follow; so with the Verveelens, the brothers Waldron, Buys, etc. The colonists were wont to revisit Fatherland to obtain wives; whence its records show many nuptials consummated on the eve of embarkation. And timid maidens, in not a few cases, drawn by ties of kinship or some more tender impulse, stopped not to count the hazards of the voyage: instance young Barentie Dircks, of Meppel (her sister Geertie then some years in New Netherland as wife of Jan Metselaer),* going over with other colonists from Drenthe in 1660; lo! scarce a year passing, when she and a sister Egbertie found their daring re-

* JAN ADAMS METSELAER was b. at Worms in 1626; was in service as corporal on the Delaware, and returned to New Amsterdam in 1654. He d. in N. Y. in 1696 or 1697. His sons who reached maturity were Jacobus, b. 1668; Abraham, b. 1671; Hendrick, b. 1676. Desc. of Abraham early settled on the Raritan, and whence the respectable family of which is Rev. Abraham Messler, D.D.

warded and the highest aspiration of their womanly hearts realized, in Nelis Matthyssen and Hage Bruynsen, honest Swedes, the one called to the magistracy at Harlem, the other to become its first miller. All most natural truly; yet we mistake if these glimpses of simple life among our colonist ancestors are wholly devoid of interest.*

Such moral courage as they exhibited, especially the refugees, commands admiration; such trials as they endured when called to resist or flee oppression, appeal to our sympathies! Clinging to their faith or principles though at the cost of their peace and safety, and all the endearments of home, country, and kindred; choosing rather to venture the treacherous ocean and the dangers of an untried wilderness where still was sovereign the savage and the beast of prey—and all to secure the sacred boon of liberty denied them in their native lands; do they not deserve the first place in history, and in the grateful remembrance of those who are reaping the benefits of their labors and sacrifices?

* THE FRENCH REFUGEES were sometimes designated, not by a proper surname, but by the name of some place, evidently that of their nativity or former abode, appended to their Christian name. The effect, no other clew to their identity appearing, is confusion like that liable to occur in Dutch nomenclature. Cases in point are Etienne *Rochelle* (his proper name Geneau), Pierre *Grand Pré*, Jean *Belin*, Etienne *Bulton*, etc., all names of French towns; and Jean *Paris*, also written *de Parisis*, but no other than Jean Lequiere, from Paris, afterwards of Bushwick. Some retained these as family names; Button or Baton was perpetuated on Staten Island and in N. J. Belin, written *a Belin*, became Ablin. (See also note on Jean Haignous.) That this designation by place (as well without as with the prefix *de* or *du*) was a usage prevalent in France (not to trace it further), any one who examines the subject will see; and it starts the question whether it is always safe to take such prefix as proof of nobility, when it may serve only to show the birthplace, or residence, or perhaps the place of the family origin; as *le* or *la* often indicates names derived from a trade, calling, office, etc. (See Index, *Chaudronnier*.) The children of some of our refugees, ambitious to assume these prefixes, sometimes made bad work of it; thus the name *le Maistre* (*the Master*), taking on the *de* (and whence Delamater), came to signify *of* the Master!—a use of the prefix wholly inappropriate. On the contrary, the sons of Dr. La Montagne very properly prefixed the *de*, and the fact adds strength to our hypothesis as to the source of that name. Very few old names among us at present, whether of French, Dutch, or other descent, preserve their original form; a result to be deprecated, though a return to the early orthography may now be neither practicable nor desirable.

CHAPTER VI.

1609–1636.

MANHATTAN.

IN the year 1609 a Dutch ship was feeling its way along the then wild and unfrequented coast of North America. Her intrepid commander, as in former fruitless voyages made for the same object under English patronage, was still eagerly seeking a western route to China, the golden Cathay of the ancients. Dispatched in this instance by the East India Company of Holland, the HALF MOON left Amsterdam the 4th of April, and after gaining the American waters had explored each principal bay and inlet from north to south, and now again northward, five weary months, but with no results. To one of less resolution than Henry Hudson the case might well have seemed hopeless, but still the undaunted mariner continues the search.

The 3d of September dawns upon the vessel enshrouded in a dense sea-fog which at the hour of ten, lifting its vapory mantle, leaves upon her spars and rigging myriads of watery jewels which sparkle in the sunbeams, bright harbinger of a coming success, while the ship, quitting her moorings, spreads her "mainsail and spritsail," and under a clear sky and with a balmy breeze from the south-south-east resumes her northerly course. Five hours pass, when Hudson makes the headlands of Neversink, "very pleasant, and high, and bold to fall, withal;" and "at three of the clock in the afternoon" approaches "a very good harbor," into which flow "three great rivers." These at once arrest his attention; their sources wrapped in mystery naturally invite the boldest speculation. Has he not been told "there was a sea leading into the Western Ocean by the north of Virginia?" Curiosity and hope receive a new impulse; surely he has found at last the long-desired passage!

Hudson at first stands for the northernmost river, but repelled by a very shoal bar before its mouth changes his course and bears away southward across the bay, where another passage seems to open, casts his anchor, and prudently sends in the yawl to sound. On a favorable report he again weighs, runs farther in with the ship, and finally drops his kedge on the soft oozy bottom at a depth of five fathoms. Hudson takes the latitude—forty degrees and thirty minutes—and enters it in his log. As the vessel rides at ease upon the bosom of these expansive waters, no fellow-craft greets the eye of the brave mariner; not so much as a tiny sail breaks the monotony of the scene. The undulating land is beautiful in varied shades of green, but, as far as the eye can scan, bare of human habitation, even to a rustic cabin; all yet appears lone, wild, charming in its very air of desolation. The fish seem surprisingly tame as they swarm about the vessel, and the white sea-gull disports itself familiarly, soars upon its broad pinions, or stoops to kiss the wave.

But the arrival had not passed unnoticed. Some of the tawny natives engaged in fishing—for the salmon and mullets and rays were plenty—espied, far out on the ocean (so the red man handed down the story), a large and strange-looking object.* Hastening back to land, they break the news to some of their countrymen, who also go out, in order to discover what it may be. They view with astonishment the strange phenomenon, now so near as to be plainly visible, but are quite disagreed as to what it is; some take it to be an enormous fish or animal, others a very big wigwam floating on the sea. As the curious object comes nearer and nearer to the land their apprehensions increase; they conclude that it possesses life, and resolve without further delay to put all the neighboring Indians on their guard. Messengers depart to carry the news to the scattered chiefs and braves, and to urge their immediate presence. Many of these soon arrive in breathless haste, and, viewing the queer object which has now gained the very entrance of the river or bay, finally conclude that it is nothing less than the

* The Indian tradition of Hudson's visit is taken from *Heckewelder*; otherwise the facts have been drawn from original statements by *De Laet*, *Juet*, *Vander Donck*, and others, every circumstance and intimation being duly weighed. We believe these will warrant all the amplification here given, the traditionary part finding strong confirmation in these authors.

wigwam of the great *Manitto* or Supreme Being himself, who has evidently come to pay them a visit. This opinion prevailing, they begin preparations to give him a suitable reception. The women must cook the most savory food, and a grand *kintekoy* or dance be given, measured to their best music, as "an agreeable entertainment for the Great Being."

Early the next morning Hudson, after sending the boat to take soundings farther up the bay, finds a better anchorage; and remaining there all day, some of the crew go ashore to draw a net for fish, returning with ten big mullets, a foot and a half long, and a great ray, taking four men to haul it into the ship. By this time the Indians, having carefully watched the movements of their strange visitor, are so well assured of his supernatural character and friendly mission that they resolve to venture out to the ship and extend him a welcome. Two of them, clad in loose deer-skins and taking a bundle of green tobacco as a present for the Manitto, launch forth in their canoe, and being admitted on board the vessel manifest their pleasure at seeing the pale-faced strangers by every sign and exclamation at their command expressive of wonder and delight. Making their offerings, they receive in return a few knives and beads. Admiring the dress worn by the Europeans, they signify a wish to have the same for themselves; but so far from showing any rudeness, their decorum is such that the officers notice it and declare them "very civil."

On the succeeding day Hudson and others from the ship make a formal visit to the land, when the assembled Indians, "men, women, and children," receive and entertain them in their best manner. "The swarthy natives all stood around and sung in their fashion," says Hudson; the ceremony without doubt indicated more of fear and reverence than of confidence, and was designed to propitiate his favor. The usual present of green tobacco is given, and refreshments served, including bread made of maize or Indian corn, of which Hudson partook and found it "excellent eating." Then the ship's party strolled "up into the woods, and saw great store of very goodly oaks and some currants." Many Indians of both sexes also visit the ship during the day, "in their canoes made of a single hollow tree," says Hudson. They are dressed, "some in mantles of feathers, and some in skins of divers sorts of good furs." About their necks are ornaments of copper. They bring offerings of dried currants, "sweet and good," and Indian hemp. These expressions of good-will do not throw the shrewd navigator off his guard. From common prudence he "durst not trust them," yet his keen eye can detect no lurking evil intent, and he frankly admits that "they appear to be a friendly people." Such his testimony of "the people that he found dwelling within the bay." Their entire deportment thus far had betrayed only profound respect and veneration for their mysterious visitors.

But, strange, pleasing hallucination of the untutored son of the forest, how quickly did one untoward circumstance dispel it forever, reduce his supposed divinity to the level of a mortal, and place him in the attitude of an enemy! On the morning of the 6th, the weather being fair, Hudson, with more accurate conclusions as to the best direction in which to continue his search, ordered John Coleman and four others to proceed with the yawl "over to the north side, to sound the other river," yet little dreaming that all that was to impart fame to his voyage hung upon its undisclosed mysteries. Rowing twelve miles to its mouth (the Narrows) they ascended and entered a spacious harbor, "with very good riding for ships," whence extending their search two leagues up "a narrow river to the westward between two islands"* and reaching "an open sea,"† they were returning filled with admiration of the country, "as pleasant with grass and flowers and goodly trees as ever they had seen," when suddenly, in a manner unexplained, they came in fatal conflict with the natives, twenty-six in number, in two canoes. Coleman was slain by an arrow, and two others of the crew wounded, but strange to say the savages did not follow up their advantage. A rain set in which, extinguishing their match, made their guns useless, and after toiling all night "to and fro on their oars" the party reached the ship. They declared "they were set upon" by the Indians; the latter have not left us their story! Why, so superior in force, did they spare any of the whites to tell their

* *Kill van Kull.* † *Newark Bay.*

tale? Why the sudden change which Hudson observed in the temper of the savages? Peradventure in this affray the Indians were "more sinned against than sinning;" then the case becomes clearer. If, smarting under a deep sense of unprovoked injury, they retired to dress their wounds and bury their dead, then the news, which spread rapidly, at once stamped the new-comers as enemies.

Suspicious of the savages from the first, Hudson now had great reason to fear an attack. He thereupon ordered a strict watch to be kept day and night to prevent a surprise, which indeed the Indians were plotting, and only seeking an opportunity to execute, as was apparent from the many canoes filled with armed men which prowled around the ship. Admitting but few of the savages into the vessel, he seized two, who came on board with a treacherous design, and held them as hostages. Passing the Narrows September 11th, Hudson entered the harbor with his ship. The morning of the 13th found him skirting "that side of the river that is called Mannahata," having "fair weather, the wind northerly." With the full of the tide he casts anchor opposite a gorge in the hills from which a stream, meandering through verdant meadows, empties into a small cove or bay (Manhattanville).

News of his coming has preceded him. From one Indian village to another and from wigwam to wigwam runners have carried the startling tidings; delegations from the Flats and parts contiguous have poured in through the ravine till the multitudes crowd the beach and crown the acclivities, eager to catch a sight of the big canoe, about which and its inmates such strange rumors have spread far and wide, exciting "great surprise and astonishment among the Indians." Hudson and his officers greet with civility the natives, who here approach the ship in four canoes, bringing "great store of very good oysters." He accepts the present and gives them some trinkets in return; but the menacing attitude of the savages only the day previous indisposes Hudson to any intimacy, or to admit any of them on board—a wise precaution, as events will show.

Barred from intercourse, and withal ignorant of their language, Hudson could as yet have acquired but scant knowledge of the country from the natives. But this was in a measure supplied by his own habit of close observation, noting objects so trivial as the ornaments and tobacco-pipes of the natives, whence he inferred the existence of copper. And on this bright September morning, while cooling breezes from the north amble through the rigging of the ship as it lies idly at anchor for several hours waiting for the tide to set in, and the practiced eye of the great navigator surveys on the one hand the pure watery expanse, on the other the charming wooded bluffs which here adorn the Island of Manhattan, doubtless it penetrates the notable cleft in the heights, opening to him a distant vista of the broad and beautiful plains upon which our interest centres, as yet, save only to the aborigines, a very *terra incognita!* We may read his emotions as, turning from this scene, he records in his journal the admiration of a sailor: "It is as pleasant a land as one need tread upon; very abundant in all kinds of timber suitable for shipbuilding." *

Hudson ascends the river. A fortnight spent in its further exploration and he has realized, not the prime object of his ambition, but results in the highest degree important; the best indeed of all his voyages. Since he first entered Sandy Hook he had been delighted with the country. He had penetrated nearly to its source the noble river which was thereafter to take his name, finding at every stage in his progress something new to admire in its extended reaches, its majestic highlands, its fruitful vales, and its grand and diversified scenery. Now, elated with his valuable discoveries, inspirited by the bracing air and gorgeous appearance of the highlands, clad in the richest hues of autumn, he is on the downward passage. At break of day October 2d the ship leaves its moorings at "Sleeper's Haven," near the jutting *Senasqua*, or Teller's Point, at the mouth of the Croton, and with canvas bending under a stiff breeze from the north-west, runs down twenty-one miles till, the tide setting in too strongly, it again casts anchor at the

* *Hudson's Journal*, as quoted by *De Laet* (see *Coll. N. Y. Hist. Soc.*, 2d series, vol. I. p. 300), places this incident in latitude 40° 48′, which agrees well with the locality given. *Juet's Journal* (ibid. p. 325) gives the date and other particulars, and when closely studied aids in fixing the locality beyond a reasonable doubt. See also the subject of Hudson's voyage carefully treated in *Yates and Moulton's Hist. of N. Y.*, which unhesitatingly gives this incident as happening when the ship was "anchored off Manhattanville."

upper end of Manhattan Island, near the beautiful inlet *Schorakkapok*, since "by the Dutch" called the *Spuyten Duyvel.*

But unlooked-for danger was lurking in its track. An incident of the upward voyage, already alluded to, now had a most painful sequel. The two natives whom Hudson kept on board as hostages were carried up the river. But the haughty captives were not to be beguiled by a voyage in the big canoe of the great Manitto, nor long amused by the red coats with which they were bedecked. In the highlands these restless spirits escaped through a port-hole and swam off, hurling back from a safe distance cries and gestures of scorn and defiance. Making their way down the river, and thirsting to avenge the indignities offered them, they sounded the war-whoop to rouse their people to arms, and at the head of Manhattan Island collected a force, with the evident purpose of seizing the ship and appropriating the rich booty which it contained.

No sooner does the returning vessel heave to near their place of ambush than several canoes dart out filled with armed warriors, led on, as is observed, by one of the savages who had escaped from the ship. Hudson, seeing their hostile design, warns them to keep off. Hereupon two of the canoes fall back near the stern and let fly a volley of arrows. Six muskets return the assault, and two or three Indians are killed. Meantime the ship having gotten under way, the main body of warriors, about a hundred, collect at a point of land (now Fort Washington) to get a fair chance at her as she slowly moves along. But a falcon-shot from the vessel kills two of them, and the rest flee into the woods. They are now quite discomfited; yet about ten of the boldest, still firm in their purpose, jump into a canoe and paddle to meet the ship. Another cannon-shot kills one of their number and pierces the canoe. A volley of musketry slays three or four more, and puts an end to the fight. The savages are left to mourn the loss of nine of their braves, while Hudson pursues his way to the ocean. Ah, hapless fate! which at this first interview thus sealed in blood an enmity between the two races, destined for half a century to redden the soil of Manhattan Island with Christian blood to glut the Indian's vengeance. The inlet where began this fatal encounter soon took the name of Spuyten Duyvel, but for what reason has not been explained. True, that veritable author Diedrich Knickerbocker makes it the presumptuous boast of Petrus Stuyvesant's valiant trumpeter, who essayed to swim the stream in a storm, *spyt den duyvel*, but was seized and carried under by his satanic majesty in the form of a huge mossbunker! But for those to whom this story may wear a tinge of incredibility we give another possible derivation. By what more fitting term could the savages, so apt in the choice of their names, have designated Hudson's ship, recalled as an uncouth monster vomiting streams of deadly fire, than by that which (from the object adhering to the locality) found its Dutch equivalent in Spuyten Duyvel, that is, *Spouting Devil?* But if this also will not bear criticism, we ask the reader to soberly weigh a fact which seems to indicate the true source of the queer designation in question. From the large spring which spouts or bubbles out near the foot of Cock Hill and flows into the creek, "The Spring" became but another name, with the early settlers, both Dutch and English, for the locality known as Spuyten Duyvel; and an ancient record of 1672 expressly calls it *Spuyten Duyvel, alias the Fresh Spring!*

Hudson's discoveries so aroused the enterprise of the merchants and shipmasters of Holland that for a series of years vessels were annually dispatched to New Netherland to prosecute discovery and the fur trade, for which purpose they were sometimes "ordered to remain there the whole year." / That section of Manhattan Island in which our interest centers could not long elude these enterprising Dutch traders, though this seat of the hostile Manhattans remained inaccessible for years after they had gained a foothold on the upper Hudson. Wrapt in that normal state which for untold ages had known no change, its weird charms must have strangely impressed such daring spirits as were foremost to navigate its untried waters or first to penetrate its slumbering solitudes. The Hollander—his eye accustomed only to a flat country, to dykes and polders—beheld with admiration this majestic display and picturesque blending of heights and low land, of wood and meadow and meandering brooks. But no hum of busy industry caught his ear, no familiar sight yet met his eye; the waters' gentle ripple, the winds moaning through the tall pines, the cry of startled beast or bird was his greeting. The group of rustic cabins and the moving forms of dusky savages clad, if at all, in skins or furs and feathers but enhanced the weirdness of the scene. Lucky too was he if his first welcome was not conveyed by the swift-winged arrow from behind the thicket, as was the case with Captain Dermor, ten years after Hudson's visit, but before the Dutch had yet occupied Manhattan Island. Coming from the eastward, and passing "a most dangerous cataract among small rocky islands," he soon found greater perils than those of Hellgate in the hostility of the natives; for, says he, "the savages had great advantage of us, in a strait not above a bow-shot, and where a multitude of Indians let fly at us from the bank; but it pleased God to make us victors." Only escaping, as his words seem to imply, and as had Hudson, by making his assailants feel the superiority of firearms, it seems hardly credible that such was ever the rude and perilous state of our beautiful Island, the now secure abode of peace and refinement.

As introductory to the history of the section in which we are most interested, we must notice the advent and progress of settlement upon the southern point of the Island, which antedated by some thirteen years the first known attempt to locate at Harlem. The idea of a permanent occupation of the country naturally followed upon the more intimate knowledge of its resources acquired through the frequent visits of the Holland traders. But the first move in that direction must be accredited as before mentioned, to Rev. John Robinson, pastor of an English congregation at Leyden, and to the directors of the company engaged in trading to New Netherland. In negotiating with said directors, Robinson had informed them that upon condition of the government protection, etc., he was "well inclined to proceed thither to live," and also "had the means of inducing over four hundred families to accompany him thither, both out of this country (Holland) and England," who would "plant there a new commonwealth." But the company's charter meanwhile expiring, the directors, on February 12th, 1620, laid their case before the States General and besought them to take these colonists under their protection and detail two ships of war to convey them to that country, in order to keep out other nations and make it "secure to the State."

But this application failed, as did another of similar import made the next year to the London Company by the French and Walloons of Leyden, as heretofore noticed. Nevertheless the States General were not indifferent to the benefits likely to accrue from such colonies being planted in New Netherland. Hence in their charter to the West India Company, in view of "the great abundance of their people, as well as their desire to plant other lands," they enjoined upon the company, as one among the important objects contemplated, "to advance the peopling of those fruitful and unsettled parts." * Accordingly a first act of the company was to equip and send out (March, 1623) a vessel of 130 lasts, the New Netherland, in command of one familiar with the voyage, Captain Cornelis Mey, and which carried about thirty families, "mostly Walloons," with a few single men, all engaged to the company for a term of service, and who were to occupy and garrison several new points along the coast, besides forming a settlement up the Hudson. Captain Mey was to be the director or governor in New Netherland, with Captain Adrian Tienpont, who accompanied him, as deputy. Arriving at Hudson's River about the beginning of May, they lay at anchor for several weeks at Manhattan, where eight men were set ashore "to take possession" for the com-

* No credit is due to the statement that *colonies* were planted in New Netherland, on Manhattan Island or elsewhere, prior to 1623. Sir Dudley Carleton, English ambassador at the Hague, no doubt makes a true representation when, in a letter of Feb. 5, 1621 (Feb. 15, 1622 N. S.), to the Lords of the Council in England, he says: "About four or five years since, two particular companies of Amsterdam merchants, began a trade into those parts betwixt 40 and 45 degrees, to which after their manner they gave their own names of New Netherlands and the like; whither they have ever since continued to send ships of 30 and 40 lasts, at the most, to fetch furs, which is all their trade; for the providing of which they have certain factors there continually resident trading with savages, and at this present there is a ship at Amsterdam bound for those parts; *but I cannot learn of any colony either already planted there by these people, or so much as intended*; and I have this further reason to believe there is none, because within these few months divers inhabitants of this country to a considerable number of families have been suitors unto me, to procure them a place of habitation amongst his Majesty's subjects in those parts; which by his Majesty's order was made known to the Directors of the Plantation; and if these countrymen were in any such way themselves, there is small appearance they would desire to mingle with strangers, and be subject to their government." (*Col. Hist. of N. Y.* 3:7. Stuyvesant does not claim for the Dutch any earlier possession of Manhattan Island. *Ibid*, 2:412. See also *ibid*, 1:149, and *Doc. Hist. N. Y.*, 4to, 3:31, 32.)

pany, and others dispatched for a like object to the rivers Connecticut and Delaware. Some eighteen families proceeded with the vessel up the river to Castle Island, at or near which the Dutch had for nine years maintained a trading-post. Choosing a spot for a settlement still higher up (within the present city of Albany), there they "made a small fort," calling it Fort Orange, "built themselves some huts of bark," and entered into "covenants of friendship" with the Mahicans or River Indians, the Maquas, and other neighboring tribes, who "desired that they might come and have a constant free trade with them, which was concluded upon." Such a beginning had the now wealthy capital of our State.

Those left to form a trading-post at Manhattan intrenched themselves at Capsee, on the southern end of the island, and built them houses "of the bark of trees." Three years later and Governor Peter Minuit came out, Manhattan Island was purchased from the Indians "for the value of sixty guilders," and with a view of making this "the principal colony," the settlement, which had already received important accessions from Holland, with a supply of live stock and farming tools, was further increased by the families from Fort Orange, who, disquieted by a recent affray with the savages in which some of their number were slain, gladly accepted this change; and as the *Manhattes* "were becoming more and more accustomed to the strangers." * New Amsterdam, as now called, and containing two hundred and seventy souls, was permitted, April 7th, 1628, to welcome its first minister, Rev. Jonas Michaelius, from Holland. This devoted man, educated at Leyden, preached a dozen years, then went out to Brazil with the great expedition in 1624. After a short term of service at St. Salvador he labored a year or two in Guinea before coming to New Amsterdam. Here at once he "established the form of a church," but as the Walloons and

* *Harlem was settled before New Amsterdam*, if we may credit the tradition current among our old New Yorkers half a century ago; the first colonists, after living here a while, for some cause removing to the lower end. Such, then and even later, was the popular belief, as we have had it from the lips of several aged persons long since deceased. But finding no mention of this either in Wassenaer or De Laet, or in any contemporary or early record, we suspect the tradition is due to the removal from Fort Orange or to the abandonment of Harlem for a time by its first settlers because of the Indians, as hereafter related, or perhaps to the confused and faded memories of both.

French knew very little Dutch, he preached to them in their own language. Hither resorted the Indian hunters, bringing quantities of furs, of which from year to year valuable cargoes were taken to Holland in the company's ships. Their agents also used every means to increase this trade by exploring in their yachts all the adjoining coasts, while others scoured the woods and sought the Indian villages for friendly traffic. But it was not only the fur trader, the hunter tracking the game, or the amateur drawn hither by curiosity to see the country; others were already intent upon finding out its varied resources—the husbandman noting the quality of the soil, the mechanic and artisan whatever for each had a practical business value, the scientist or naturalist in quest of mineral and other treasures—some new wonder in every stone, tree, shrub, and flower, every beast that starts at his approach, or bird that warbles from the bough. Much of this useful information was presently transmitted to fatherland, both in private letters from the colonists to their kindred and in official reports to the West India Company. Isaac de Rasieres, who came out in 1626 and served some two years as chief commissary and secretary at New Amsterdam, has left us, in an account written after his return to Holland, the earliest known description of Manhattan Island by an eye-witness. It is, he says, "full of trees, and in the middle rocky," but the north end "has good land in two places, where two farmers, each with four horses, would at first have enough to do without much clearing." So early had the attention of the Hollanders, instinctively attached to rich bottom lands, been drawn to these fertile plains, then known to the colonists as the *Flats of the Island of Manhatta*.

In tracing the history of this section of the Island, the territorial limits will be those given in the patent or charter granted the inhabitants of Harlem by the colonial governor Nicolls in 1666, which embraced all the upper portion, from Kingsbridge south, as far as Manhattanville on the west side and Seventy Fourth Street on the east.

Of those who early manifested an interest in this particular section were Wouter van Twiller, now Director-General of the colony, and his friend Jacobus van Curler, who bore the title of Jonkheer. They were both young men, from the same place,

Nieukerck, and Van Curler had accompanied the new director hither in 1633. A residence of three years giving them the opportunity to spy out the land, Van Twiller had improved it by selecting for himself several choice tracts in the vicinity of New Amsterdam, among which was the island lying "over against" the Flats, and known to us as Ward's Island. The Jonkheer, in his rambles, had fixed his covetous eye upon these rich Flats, and, with leave of the director, had pre-empted a goodly section bordering upon the river, opposite the island referred to, and which obtained the name of the Otter-spoor, or the Otter-track. It is scarcely a departure from the literal facts to picture these two dignitaries upon one of their tours of observation up the island; and in fancy we may accompany them. Van Curler well knows the lay of the land, for he loves to scour the woods in quest of game; but one of his feats, which he took some pride in relating, was the killing an hundred and seventy blackbirds at a single shot!

Quitting the drowsy little town of New Amsterdam, its thatched roofs and its fortress with low turf wall receding from view, we follow the Indian trail leading to *Wickquaskeek*, or "the birch bark country," which lies beyond the quiet waters of the *Papparinamin*, as that part of the Spuyten Duyvel was called where it turns the extreme northerly point of Manhattan. Spring is in her loveliest attire. Around and along our pathway she displays in rich profusion her grandest works. Plains scarce trodden by human kind save by the red man are clothed in all the beauty of their pristine verdure, while the rock-capped hills and the resonant forest echo back and forth the sounds of wild and savage life. Plumed songsters fill the woods and enliven our journey with their music. Perchance the shrill cry of the eagle, startled from its eyrie, or the plaintive note of the cuckoo or the busy hammer of the woodpecker in turn arrests our attention.

> "And playful squirrel on his nut-grown tree:
> And every sound of life was full of glee, . . .
> While hearkening—fearing nought their revelry—
> The wild deer arched his neck from glades, and then,
> Unhunted, sought his woods and wilderness again."

Treading that "central" part of Manhattan, in our day rescued from mercenary uses and restored again to nature and art, to resume under their culture more than its original beauty, we emerge upon the bluff near that romantic spot since known as McGown's Pass, and before us lie the "Flats of Manhattan." Let us survey the charming panorama which opens to our view, note its more striking features, and point out the several sections of the land, as it is subdivided by the aborigines, under distinctive names. At our left a chain of high land extends away to the northward till lost to the eye, but broken at one point by a ravine, beyond which are dimly visible through the entangled foliage the silvery waters of the majestic Muhican-ittuck, or Hudson. In the distance a lesser stream, which flows from the Papparinamin, and is known simply as the *Great Kill* (its Indian name is undiscovered), comes gently coursing toward the troubled waters of the Hellegat.* Familiar to us as the Harlem River, it has been fitly designated as "one of the sweetest streams that ever gave a charm to landscape." Along the heights through which flow its upper waters the scenery, though less imposing, still rivals that of the classic Hudson in all that is picturesque and pleasing. On the hither side the banks, rising boldly from a rocky base and clothed with lofty forest-trees, present by their very abruptness a fine contrast to the eastern shore, where undulating hills, woodland, and meadows form a gradual descent to the water's edge. Here, aforetime, till its quiet was invaded by the snort of the iron horse, the visitor loved to tarry, wrapt in the contemplation of a scene sublime, and quite forgetful of the outer world, till his reverie was broken by the wild cry of the heron, or the plunge of the kingfisher as it darted from an overhanging bough—"most celebrated and besung of all other birds"—species which had ever haunted these waters and nested in the lofty pines. Lingering tenant of these solitudes, the heron was seen at early dawn assiduous at his piscatory work. Taking his gloomy stand in the

* MUSCOOTA, says the *History of Westchester County*, was the aboriginal name for Harlem River, but various original authorities agree in making it the common Indian term for *flats* or *flatland*! After diligent but vain search among our early records to discover some warrant for applying it to the river, we gave it up, when an inquiry addressed to Mr. Bolton, and answered with his usual courtesy, failed to elicit his authority on this point.

water's edge, and motionless, as if meditating mischief, he kept his head turned on one side, and eyed the pool intently for an opportunity to strike his prey. If undisturbed, he spent the day, resting when gorged, with his long neck sunk between his shoulders, but retiring long before night to his retreat in the woods. The scene is better depicted by M'Lellan, in "The Notes of the Birds."

"Far up some brook's still course whose current mines
The forest's blackened roots, and whose green marge
Is seldom visited by human foot,
The lonely *heron* sits, and harshly breaks
The sabbath silence of the wilderness:
And you might find her by some reedy pool,
Or brooding gloomily on the time-stained rock,
Beside some misty and far-reaching lake.
Most awful is thy deep and heavy boom,
Gray watcher of the waters! Thou art king
Of the blue lake; and all the wing'd kind
Do fear the echo of thine angry cry.
How bright thy savage eye! Thou lookest down
And seest the shining fishes as they glide;
And poising thy gray wing, thy glossy beak
Swift as an arrow strikes its roving prey.
Ofttimes I see thee, through the curling mist,
Dart like a spectre of the night, and hear
Thy strange, bewildering call, like the wild scream
Of one whose life is perishing in the sea."

Hellgate, or *Hellegat*, as the name was given by the Dutch, after an inlet of the West Scheldt, lies in full view at our right, the terror of ancient voyagers, and whose conception of it is well given in these words of an early writer: "Being a narrow passage, there runneth a violent stream both upon flood and ebb, and in the middle lieth some islands of rocks, which the current sets so violently upon that it threatens present shipwreck; and upon the flood is a large whirlpool, which continually sends forth a hideous roaring, enough to affright a stranger from passing further, and to wait for some Charon to conduct him through." The Indians, in the last century, had a tradition "that at some distant period in former times their ancestors could step from rock to rock, and cross this arm of the sea on foot."

Beneath us spreads out, as a royal tapestry of velvety green, a section of rich bottom land, known to the Indians by the euphonic term *Muscoota*, that is, *The Flat*, as the whites, who adopted the name, rendered it. The hills form its southern limit, with a fresh water run long known as the *Fountain*, from its spring upon the hillside, and which, passing out to the Great Kill, skirts northerly a point or neck of land opposite Hellegat, its surface slightly elevated, and which the natives call *Rechawanes*, or, as interpreted, the *Great Sands*; since the Benson or McGown property. It is bounded southerly by a creek and broad marshes which stretch from the Bay of Hellegat even to *Konaande Kongh*.*

Beyond the creek of Rechawanes lies Van Curler's grant, reaching away to the Great Kill, a broad and level tract, called in the language of the natives *Conykeekst*, but by the Dutch the *Otter-spoor*, from the little amphibious animal which sports hereabout, burrows, and leaves its foot-tracks (*spoor*) on the margins of its streamlets and river, and whose furs are so coveted by the Dutch trader. Northerly still lies *Schorakin*, with a mostly level surface, and stretching along the Great Kill upward toward the hills. It is partly separated from the Otter-spoor by a creek and meadows, and partially hidden from view by the *Ronde Gebergte*, or Round Hills. One is an abrupt wooded eminence, by modern innovation styled Mount Morris, but which the Dutch called the *Slang Berg*, or Snake Hill, from the reptile tribes that infested its cleft rocks and underbrush even within the memory of the living. Southerly from it the gneiss rock crops out in huge, disordered masses. A little way to the right is the other, a lesser height or ridge, and which to the inhabitants came to be known as *The Little Hill*, when was built opposite to it (Kingsbridge road only parting them) the goodly Dutch farm-house of Johannes Sickels, still

* An *Indian term* which occurs in a Dutch document of 1669 (see under that year), but misread, apparently, by the late Do. Westbrook, who rendered it *King's Highway*, the proper Dutch for which is *Koning's Hooge Weg*. It may come from *ko*, a fall or cascade, and *ononda*, a hill; *kong* signifying elevated place or locality. Hence probably refers to the spring aforesaid, but possibly to a village site (an Indian village, or perhaps the one contemplated in 1661), *nunda* being the term for village. It approaches in sound nearly to the Iroquois *Canunda*, or *Kannata*, Village on the Hill, and from which, says Charlevoux, the name Canada is derived.

standing in 123d Street. Strewed over the plain, and here and there conspicuous, are rounded boulders of gray, red, and ferruginous sandstone, unlike any rock found here *in situ*, and whose presence is ascribed to some mighty action of nature in times far remote, by which they had been drifted and deposited here. The hugest of these weather-beaten boulders, which lay behind the Sickel's house, still lives in memory and in the written romance of the Child of the Singing Rock.*

O'er all this fair domain still roams the haughty Manhattan or Wickquaskeek, as properly called, making forest and waters alike contribute to his subsistence, as though he yet held rights in the soil, notwithstanding the sale, ten years previous, to the West India Company. So the sachems of Mareckaweek, or Brooklyn—a fact quite remarkable if they were not a band of the Manhattans—claim the two islands, one before referred to, lying opposite the Otter-spoor and called *Tenkenas*, since named Ward's Island, and the other called *Minnahanonck*, now Blackwell's Island. But cast the vision across the intervening centuries, and it strips this virgin landscape of its almost bewitching charms; its every feature changes like a dissolving view, and the congregated homes of a cultivated people engross these several tracts of many hundred broad acres, forming one of the fairest sections of our great metropolis! Gone is every memento of the aborigine, save a few uncouth names or unearthed relics.† The former, as applied to places within Harlem, we have endeavored to rescue, because, however unintelligible or difficult of rendering are such Indian terms, they are, as

* *The Bachelor's Ward, or the Child of the Singing Rock: a Legend of Harlem*, was begun in the *New York Sun* of Sept. 24, 1860, and extended through twenty-two chapters. It was written by Mr. William E. Pabor, then of Harlem, son of the late Alexander Pabor, whose father, Martin Pabor, by birth a Swiss, came to this country *via* Bordeaux about 1803, and died at Bloomingdale May 16, 1816, aged 48 years.

† A deposit of *Indian arrow-heads* was found at Harlem in 1855, in excavating for a cellar on avenue A, between 120th and 121st streets, a spot nearly central of the old Bogert or Morris Randell farm, and on the ancient Otter-spoor. Being in considerable number, of various sizes, and in all stages of manufacture, it shows that here had been the red man's workshop, where with wondrous patience and skill he chipped out those little implements, of equal use to him in peace and war. They were made of a buff-colored flint, resembling the yellow semi-opal of India, but, what is remarkable, unlike any stone to be met with on or about Manhattan Island. Some of these arrow-heads, obtained by him at the time, are in the author's cabinet.

admitted, usually found to be aptly significant, generally descriptive of the locality, or of some signal event in its Indian legends.*

Here, lying as it were at our feet, is Muscoota—The Flat—stretching northward from the elevation we occupy, a fine level plain, shut in westerly by bold heights dressed in the primeval forest, the substratum of gray gneiss, like artificial grass-grown bulwarks, bare and exposed to view along their entire face; its eastern limit a tiny creek that glistens in the sunlight from between its bushy banks as a thread of limpid silver, and which meeting at flood tide the flow into the ravine through the heights, or the "Clove of the Kil," as afterward called, serves to bisect the island and to bear the canoes of the natives from the Hellegat to the Hudson. Rejoicing in its primitive integrity and beauty, no farm lines, no Harlem Lane or Avenue St. Nicholas yet intersect it, nor ever a furrow has upturned its deep, rich vegetable mould, though partially cleared, and tilled by the Indian women with the hoe, in their rude way, for raising scanty crops of maize, pumpkins, beans, and tobacco. This inviting spot has also been appropriated. Its repose must now be broken by the ring of woodman's axe, the noise of saw and hammer, for the first European settlers have arrived, to rear their isolated dwelling. Their story in the Old World has already been told, and will now be continued, with its checkered experiences in the New.

* Hon. J. Hammond Trumbull, of Hartford, the eminent Indian philologist, in a letter of February 3, 1880, with which he has had the kindness to favor me, remarks:

"Nothing disguises an Indian name so effectually as a Dutch pen; and few of the names of Northern New Jersey or Southern New York are easily recognized in the shape they come to us in the Dutch records or under Dutch corruptions. The Indian dialect differed very slightly from that of Massachusetts or Eastern Connecticut, but the Dutch spelling transforms them to an unknown tongue, and it is only by comparison of all the various ways of writing a name, and by a careful study of the locality to which it is appropriated—and probably wrongfully appropriated—that one can guess at the original sound, and so, at the meaning."

CHAPTER VII.

1636–1640.

SETTLEMENTS.

UNDER most flattering auspices, and well supplied with needed stores and house and farm utensils, including arms and ammunition, Henry and Isaac de Forest have at length the satisfaction of treading the strange country, so long the object of mingled hope and solicitude. Equally cheering was this unexpected arrival to the denizens of New Amsterdam, who for some months had seen no new faces from fatherland; their isolation the more keenly felt since the departure together, August 13th, of the ship King David, Captain David de Vries, and a company's ship, the Seven Stars, the first having brought a small accession to the settlers.* The merry salvo from the fort, the grasp of welcome which greeted the new-comers, only betokened the general gladness; while to the old Walloons, who spake but broken Dutch, it gave an opportunity, not often enjoyed, for free inquiry in their native *patois* about friends and events in Europe.

It did not take long to fix upon a location, and fully inform themselves of the nature of and best mode of doing the work to be entered upon. But buildings and fences were to be erected, trees felled, and the land prepared to receive the crop. Having come so late in the year instead of in the spring, the usual time

* JACOB WALINGS VAN WINCKEL, from Hoorn, and *Peter Cæsar Albertus*, an Italian, from Venice, were of the number, and we believe *Claes Cornelise*, who certainly came out this year. The first was the anc. of the *Van Winkle* family, of Bergen, N. J., the second of those of *Alburtis* and *Burtis*. From Claes Cornelise, the emigrant of 1636, two well-known families have sprung, viz., that of *Wyckoff*, through his son Pieter Claessen Wyckoff, a child when his father came over, and that of *Van Arsdale*, his dr. Pietertie, b. here in 1640, marrying the common anc. Simon Jansen van Arsdalen.

for sailing, they needed to be diligent in order to accomplish this preparatory work in season for the spring planting. Choosing as his future home the rich flats at Muscoota, promising to rival in productiveness the fertile meadows around his native Leyden, and, as memory ran backward, perchance recalling his father's description of the old home in Hainault, the plains, skirted on the one side by the heights of Avesnes, on the other by the gentle Hepre, Henry de Forest at once obtained from director Van Twiller the grant of Muscoota, then roughly estimated at one hundred morgen, or two hundred acres, and offering no impediment to its immediate occupation, as sometimes occurred where the Indian title had first to be acquired. Here, as the weather favored, De Forest and his assistants began their toilsome work.

The winter had scarcely closed when their hearts were cheered by the arrival of Dr. La Montagne and his family. The voyage, as was not uncommon, had been long and tedious, occasioned by their taking a circuitous course by way of the Canary Islands, in order to reach the trade winds. They introduced a little stranger, Marie Montagne, born at sea off the Island of Madeira, January 26th, 1637, and called after its grandmother De Forest.* Montagne was a welcome and valuable addition to the colonists. Reputed skilful in his profession, he so soon rose in public favor that Governor Kieft, on his arrival, called him to a seat in his council, and which appointment, if not by positive instructions from the directors, met with their approval.

Winter and spring had not passed in idleness, as is manifest from the amount of work which had been accomplished in clearing land and getting ready for the season of planting. A farmhouse was being built, in the Dutch rural style, having an ample ground floor "forty-two feet long by eighteen feet wide, with two doors." The roof was thatched, and as a protection against the Indians the house was surrounded by a high close fence of heavy round palisades or pickets. The inclosure, which was entered by a well-secured gate or gates, was ample for out-buildings, including a house for curing tobacco; this article,

* This date, with that of Montagne's coming, rests upon a note in *Holgate's Am. Genealogy*, p. 112, the original authority for which I have inquired for in vain, but I see no reason to doubt its accuracy, while collateral facts are in harmony with it.

as before hinted, intended to form the principal crop, one to which the soil, "on account of its great fertility, was considered well adapted," and yielding the best returns. It was also "well suited to prepare the land for other agricultural purposes." Fixed in their new home, with the requisite means of defence afforded by their strong stockade and four guns kept ready for use, and with humble trust in a kind Providence, who had hitherto so favored them, the De Forests, with their helpers Tobias and Willem, addressed themselves industriously to the work of tilling the virgin soil. With no neighbors but the roving Indians, those who had been reared amid the activities of a great city, with its busy, crowded marts, must have been strangely impressed by this scene of wild solitude and this lone isolation. The dusky savage, whose trail lay near them, leading from the forests of Wickquaskeek to New Amsterdam, as he passed to and fro on his trading errands and eyed with ill-disguised suspicion this inroad upon his ancient hunting-grounds, must doubtless have excited, by his uncouth dress and demeanor, his very coyness, a corresponding suspicion and dread in the minds of the toilers.* And when weariness invited repose, perchance sweet dreams of home and kindred; how oft were these disturbed by the dismal howl of the wolf or the terrifying scream of the panther suddenly breaking the death-like stillness of the night!

However, Jonkheer van Curler now set about improving his fine tract of two hundred acres, called the Otter-spoor, lying next to De Forest's plantation; but, to describe it in terms now familiar, situated north of the Mill Creek, at 108th Street, and extending from Harlem River to near Fifth Avenue. He erected

* "THE INDIANS about here," says Capt. David de Vries, who had been a great deal among the Wickquaskeeks and other tribes living around New Amsterdam, "are tolerably stout, have black hair, with a long lock which they let hang on one side of the head. The hair is shorn on the top of the head like a cock's comb. Their clothing is a coat of beaver skins over the body, with the fur inside in winter and outside in summer; they have also sometimes a bear's skin, or a coat made of the furs of wild cats or raccoons. They also wear coats of turkey feathers, which they know how to put together; but since our Netherlanders have traded here, they barter their beavers for duffels-cloth, which they find more suitable than the beavers, and better for the rain. Their pride is to paint their faces hideously with red or black lead, so that they look like fiends. Then are they valiant; yea, they say they are *Manetto*—the devil himself."

"a dwelling-house and out-buildings," and procured all things necessary for a well-regulated plantation—domestic animals and farming tools, with the no less needful "boat and fixtures" for passing to and from New Amsterdam. Van Twiller also built upon the larger island, opposite the Otter-spoor, the Indian *Tenkenas*, now called Ward's Island, and put there some choice Holland stock, all in charge of Barent Jansen Blom, a stalwart Dane, as his overseer or farmer; after which, on July 16th, 1637, the director purchased the Indian title to this island, and also the lesser one "lying westward," called *Minnahanonck* (Blackwell's Island), from the sachems, Heyseys and Numers, who took in payment "certain parcels of goods." From Barent Blom, whose huge proportions had gained him the nickname of "Groot Barent," the island whereon he lived received the name of Great Barent's Island. Years later, when Blom had removed to Brooklyn and Van Twiller been dispossessed by the government, the term *groot*, or great, losing its proper reference to Barent, was applied to the island itself, to distinguish it from the smaller one adjacent (now Randell's Island), which latter from mere proximity was called Little Barent's Island!*

* BARENT JANSEN BLOM, whose desc. write their name *Bloom*, was b. in 1611, at Ockholm, a town of Sleswick in Denmark. After quitting Van Twiller's service he settled in Brooklyn, bought in 1652 a farm near the Wallabout, and there lived till his d., June 5, 1665, caused by a stab in the side given him by Albert Corn. Wantenaer, and at once fatal. As Albert set up the plea of self-defense, the Court of Assize, at his trial Oct. 2, convicted him only of manslaughter. He "was then and there burnt in the hand, according to law;" the further penalties, which were the loss of his property and a year's imprisonment, being remitted by the governor.

By his wife, Styntie Pieters, whom he m. in 1641, Barent left two sons, Jan, b. 1644, and Claes, b. 1650. His dr. Engeltie, b. 1652, m. Adam Vrooman, of Schenectady, and another dr., named Tytie, b. 1654, m. Lambert Jansen, van Dyck. JAN BARENTSEN BLOM became a farmer in Flatbush, m. Mary, dr. of Simon Hansen, and had issue *Barent*, of Flushing, (d. ab. 1735, having by w. Femmetie, sons Garret, b. 1695, John, 1697, Abraham, 1703, George, 1706, and Isaac, 1709); *Simon*, of Jamaica (d. 1722, having by w. Gertrude, sons John, b. 1706, Isaac, 1708, Bernardus, 1710, Abraham, 1713, Jacob, 1715, and George, 1716, of whom Bernardus, of Newtown, blacksmith, 1731–'84, was fa. of Simon and gd-fa. of Capt. Bernardus Bloom, see *Annals of Newtown*), and *George*, of Flatbush, who d. without ch. ab. 1737. CLAES BARENTSE BLOM m. 1685, Elizabeth, dr. of Paulus Dericksen and wid. of Paulus Michielse Vandervoort. He remained in his native town, Brooklyn, and was still living in 1737. He had several chn., of whom was *Barent*, of Bedford, also *Jannetie*, who m. Jacobus Lefferts and Peter Luyster, the first the gd-fa. of the late Judge Leffert Lefferts, of Brooklyn. Barent of Bedford, whose w. was also named Femmetie, d. in 1756, having chn. Nicholas, Jacob, Phebe, Elizabeth, Jane, Barbara, and Maria. Nicholas d. at Bedford

Illusory is the dream of worldly aggrandizement; how often, alas, the fondest hope of the heart only buds to be blighted! Such was a frequent experience of our early colonists. Suddenly a gloom black as night overshadowed that lone dwelling on the plain; death had reaped the first harvest. "Henry de Forest died on the 26th July, A° 1637." Painfully brief the record. Had exposure in a new and variable climate proved too much for one reared amid the comforts and protecting influences of a city; or had the over-zealous toiler suddenly fallen under the burden and heat of the day? Was it due to disease or violence? Vain are all surmises. We only know that, far from his native land, from the endeared forms and scenes of other days, saving the presence of some he most loved, the first European settler on these Flats met his fate! He was borne to his last resting-place—doubtless at New Amsterdam—with fitting tokens of respect, and the sympathizing pastor Bogardus, who but six months agone had greeted and welcomed him on his arrival, performed the last sad ritual, presenting each pall-bearer a silver spoon as a memento of the departed. These tokens were furnished the domine by direction of Dr. Montagne, and at his own cost. Then—it was the approved custom—when the assembled burghers had gravely lit their pipes and spent some honest regrets, over their wine and beer, at the untimely exit of one thus snatched away at the manly age of thirty-one years, the scene closed over Henry de Forest.

As De Forest was childless, his estate fell to the widow and next of kin. Dr. Montagne took charge of the plantation, and saw the ripening crops properly harvested. He also finished the house and barn, till which he boarded at the house of Van

ab. 1782, leaving Jacob and Mattie. Consult *Bloom* wills, Surrogate's office, New York. For other facts touching this lineage we refer with pleasure to the *Bergen Genealogy*, in its new and improved form, a perfect *thesaurus* of our Dutch family history, yet, to our regret, must take issue with it upon the Bloom ancestry.

FREDERICK ARENTS BLOEM, anc. of the Bloom family of New York City, distinct from the former, was from Swarte Sluis, between Zwolle and Meppel, in Overyssel, and came over *via* Amsterdam in 1654, with and under engagement to *Laurens Andriess van Buskerk*, turner, and common anc. of the Van Buskirk family. Bloom, also a turner, and hence often called "De Drayer," m. at New Amsterdam, in 1656, Grietie Pieters, from Breda; issue nine chn., four being sons, viz., Arent, b. 1657, Pieter, 1661, Johannes, 1671, and Jacob, 1676, of whom at least the first and last m. and had chn.

Curler. An account of his expenses while in charge of the farm affords us a bill of fare which might challenge the luxuries of a European table. Items "powder, shot, and balls" suggest not only a care for their personal security, but as well the means of supplying their larder with savory venison, deer being so plentiful in the island as often to stroll within gun-shot of the farm-house. Besides a variety of game, with fish, and "salted eels," pea soup, wheat and rye bread, butter, eggs, and poultry, they adopted the wholesome native dish called *supaan*, a mush made of Indian corn.

The year following, Andries Hudde, an ex-member of Van Twiller's council, won the heart and hand of the young widow De Forest, and they were married. Preparing to visit Holland with his bride, Hudde engaged Hans Hanson, from Bergen in Norway, by trade a shipwright, but with some knowledge of farming, and who during eleven years' residence had "borne a respectable character," to cultivate tobacco, upon shares, on the De Forest farm, Hudde pledging to send him six or eight farm laborers, with suitable tools, "by the first opportunity of any vessel leaving a port of Holland." Lastly, prior to leaving, Hudde made good his title by a "groundbrief," or patent, from Director Kieft, dated July 20th, 1638, none having been taken out before; in fact, no such deeds had yet been issued to any of the settlers. Only on June 24th preceding had the governor and council, upon a petition from "the free people," resolved to give titles for the farms in course of improvement. This conveyance to Hudde, here given entire, is the earliest of its kind known relating to Harlem lands, if not the very first, in point of date, issued by the government.

WE, the DIRECTOR and COUNCIL of NEW NETHERLAND, residing on the ISLAND of MANHATAS and in Fort Amsterdam, under the authority of the HIGH and MIGHTY LORDS, the STATES GENERAL of the UNITED NETHERLANDS, and the GENERAL INCORPORATED WEST INDIA COMPANY, at their Chambers at Amsterdam; By these presents do publish and declare, that pursuant to the *Liberties and Exemptions* allowed on the 7th day of June A.D. 1629, to Lords Patroons, of a lawful, real, and free proprietorship; WE have granted, transported, ceded, given over and conveyed; and by these presents We do grant, give over and convey, to and for the behoof of ANDRIES HUDDE, *a piece of land containing one hundred morgen, situated on the North East end of the Island of Manhatas, behind Curler's land*; on condition that he and his successors shall acknowledge their High Mightinesses, the Managers aforesaid, as their Sovereign Lords and Patroons, and *shall render at the end of ten years* after the actual settlement and cultivation of the land, *the just tenth part of the products with which God may bless the soil*, and *from this time forth annually for the House and Lot, deliver a pair of capons to the Director for the Holidays;* constituting and substituting the aforesaid HUDDE in our stead and state, the real and actual possessor thereof, and at the same time giving to him or to his successors full and irrevocable might, authority and special license, *tanquam actor et procurator in rem suam ac propriam*, the aforesaid land to enter, peaceably to possess, inhabit, cultivate, occupy and use, and also therewith and thereof to do, bargain and dispose, in like manner as he might do with his own lands honestly and lawfully obtained, without they the grantors, in their said quality, thereto having, reserving, or saving in the least, any part, action, or ownership, other than heretofore specified: Now and forever, finally desisting, abstaining, withdrawing and renouncing, by these presents; promising moreover, this their transport, and what may be done by virtue thereof, firmly, inviolably and irrevocably to maintain, fulfil and execute, as in equity they are bound to; in all good faith, without fraud or deceit. In Witness whereof, these presents are confirmed with our usual signature and with our Seal. Done in Fort Amsterdam the 20th of July, 1638.

WILLEM KIEFT, DR.

All their arrangements made, including authority to Do. Bogardus to administer the De Forest estate in their absence, Hudde and his Gertrude sailed for Holland, we believe in the company's ship the Herring, of twenty guns, which had brought out Director Kieft. Naturally after a nine years' absence, Hudde longed to see his native city Amsterdam and his widowed mother, Aeltie Schinckels; his father, Rutger Hudde, was dead. Besides the business of his wife's estate, certain sums due him from his guardians at Amsterdam and deposited in the Orphan Chamber required to be looked after, as well as moneys coming from his deceased brother, Claes Hudde, and a legacy at Campen, left him by his old aunt Scurbeeck, who had lately died; amounting in all to nearly 8000 fl. 1

Since Montagne took charge of the plantation he had expended over a thousand guilders, in paying claims against it, in completing the improvements, and for current expenses, as per his statement rendered to Do. Bogardus July 23d, and which had been approved and taken to Holland. Wishing a settlement, he petitioned the council, September 16th, that Bogardus as administrator be required to assume the care of the farm and refund him the amount which he had advanced upon account of it. As Bogardus was not prepared to do this except by a sale of the property, the court at their next meeting thought best and so decreed, that the plantation should be put up at public vendue in Fort Amsterdam, October 7th, "for the benefit of the widow," and that from the proceeds of the sale Bogardus should pay Montagne "such moneys as he hath disbursed for the improvement of the bouwery." The sale taking place, the farm, with its fixtures, was struck off to Montagne for the sum of 1700 gl. Included were portions of the recent crops of tobacco and grain, two milch cows and other cattle, two goats, domestic fowls, farming tools, and a "wey schuyt" or boat used by the farmers to bring salt hay from their meadow.

But Montagne had now to meet a new vexation, for no sooner had the farm changed owners than Tobias and Willem, refusing to work, applied to the council, October 14th, to be released from their engagement, "as they were not hired by the defendant but by his uncle." Montagne, however, "produces the contracts made between the plaintiffs and Gerard de Forest, from which it clearly appears that the plaintiffs are bound to serve said De Forest or his agent for three successive years after their arrival in New Netherland, and the defendant further exhibiting power and authority from the said De Forest to employ the plaintiffs in his service till the expiration of their bounden time; all this being considered, the plaintiffs are condemned to serve out their term with La Montagne without further objection, he promising to pay them the wages which shall be due them at the expiration of the said term." The secret of the dissatisfaction with Tobias, and which had caused him to vent a little Dutch spleen against his employer, would appear in his complaint to others that he had been stinted in his allowance of meat at Montagne's house. But when put to the proof of this also before the court, he confessed to having wronged Montagne in what he had said, admitting "that he had his share of the beef as well as the plaintiff." Thus this trouble ended.

Jonkheer Van Curler, constantly in the public service, and now engrossed with the duties of inspector of merchandise under the new director, found it expedient, May 18th, 1638, to lease the Otter-spoor farm, which he had improved at great expense, to Claes Cornelissen Swits, for a term of three years, the lessee engaging to employ a good plowman, and Van Curler an active boy to assist him. The rent was to be paid in produce, and the land, when vacated, to be left well sowed. But some months later the Otter-spoor changed owners, Cornelis van Tienhoven, provincial secretary, becoming its purchaser, "at the request and on behalf of Mr. Coenraet van Keulen, merchant, residing in Amsterdam," for the sum of 2000 gl. The Van Keulens of that city were much interested in New Netherland, one of them, Matthys van Keulen, being a principal partner director of the West India Company in the Amsterdam Chamber. Coenraet, a kinsman of Matthys, we presume, with his friend Elias de Raet, also a prominent director of the company, and who had befriended Kieft in getting the directorship here, both invested in lands on Manhattan Island, and subsequently Kieft became their agent to manage this property, including the Otter-spoor after Van Tienhoven's charge of it ceased. On January 25th, 1639, Van Tienhoven gave a new lease to Swits, and with him as a partner, Jan Claessen Alteras, late planter on Verken, or Blackwell's Island. Two span of horses, three cows, farming utensils, and "twelve schepels of grain in the ground" were included in the lease, which now was to run for six years, the rent payable in live stock and butter and "one eighth of all the grain with which God shall bless the field."

Claes Cornelissen Swits' earlier history is little known. Captain de Vries, in noting the circumstances of his death, styles him a *Duytsman*, by which term the Hollanders of that day meant a *German*. But his true nationality is clearly indicated by the adjunct to his name, which when used is commonly written *Swits* or *Switser*, and so we may accept the tradition held by his descendants that he was a Swiss. He and his family had sojourned in the Island of Schouwen, and thence came to Amsterdam, boarding with other Germans at Peter de Winter's inn before embarking for this country. He had been here now some five years, being advanced in life, and on a chosen spot at Turtle Bay, on the East River, "had built a small house and set up the trade of a wheelwright." With a still vigorous manhood, some education and means, and a fair business tact, Claes Rademaker, or Claes the Wheelmaker, as from his occupation he was familiarly called, proved "a very useful man," given to enterprises outside of his regular calling, assisted probably by his sons Cornelis and Adrian, as he was by Alteras at the Otter-spoor. All this made his tragic death some years later the more regretted. He was killed by an Indian, and, strangely enough, his son Cornelis, from whom the present Swits family are descended, met with a similar fate at Harlem, as will be further noticed.

Van Tienhoven had obtained his deed for the Otter-spoor from Jacobus van Curler* only the previous May, and having now "been fully satisfied and paid" by Van Keulen of Amsterdam, he executed a conveyance to the latter for that valuable property, August 22d, 1639, subject only to the lease to Swits. From its new owner this large section became known in all the subsequent history of the town as VAN KEULEN'S HOOK.

A most valuable accession was now made to the settlers, resulting from the more liberal measures recently adopted by the States General and the West India Company to promote colonisation to New Netherland. *Captain* Jochiem Pietersen Kuyter, a Danish gentleman, born in the district of Ditmarsen in Holstein, and liberally educated, had arisen to position, having held a command in the East Indies under commission of King Christian IV. He was now in his prime, forty-two years of age, and had acquired considerable means. Resolving to come to this country, he made his plans known to the directors of the company at Amsterdam, who showed him marked attention, not only giving him every assurance, but instructing Director Kieft to afford him all needed facilities, in order the better to encourage others. Engaging the Fire of Troy, a private armed vessel at Hoorn, he shipped "a large cargo of cattle," perhaps of

* JACOBUS VAN CURLER remained many years in this country. He took an active part, in 1657, in the settlement of New Utrecht, where he built one of the first houses, and served as town clerk and magistrate. At the age of sixty years he returned to Holland, sailing from New York May 29, 1669, in the ship Duke of York.

On losing his first wife, Adriana, Van Curler had m. in 1652 a worthy but much-injured maiden, Lysbet van Hoogvelt, whom the false-hearted Van Tienhoven, when in Amsterdam in 1650, had cruelly deceived by a promise of m., and induced to accompany him to this country, though he had a w. and chn. living here. Exposing him publicly in court, Lysbet found great sympathy, and Tienhoven's baseness being proved by testimony sent for to Holland, it came near going hard with him, but he escaped punishment only to become a few years later a public swindler, a fugitive from justice, and, as was believed, a suicide!

the fine breed for which his native Ditmarsen was famous, and sailed for New Netherland, accompanied by his friend and countryman, *Seignior* Jonas Bronck. Each was attended by his family and a number of farmers or herdsmen, and with them came several laborers sent out by Andries Hudde, from which person, it is highly probable, Kuyter had received such information respecting the grazing lands upon Manhattan Island as served to direct him in his choice of location. Early in July, 1639, the ship, with its valuable cargo, reached New Amsterdam, where its arrival was hailed as a great public good.* In the joy of his honest heart, Captain de Vries, who returned to Manhattan on July 16th, but a few days after Kuyter had arrived, wrote in his journal, "It were to be wished that one to three hundred such families, with laborers, had come, for then this would soon be made a prosperous country."

So warmly commended to the favor of Kieft, Kuyter immediately obtained from him a grant of that extensive and beautiful tract before noticed, called *Schorakin*. On these rich lands was found ample pasturage for his stock, and here Kuyter built his thatch-roofed dwelling and out-buildings, inclosing the whole with a high palisade fence, with proper gates. In due time fruit-trees and various improvements adorned his home. This plantation, which embraced about four hundred acres, may now be located in general terms as that section of Harlem bordering on the Harlem River north of what composed the old village lots, and referred to in title deeds, even till a modern date, as JOCHEM PIETERSEN'S FLAT; though Kuyter, in the gratitude of his pious heart, named it *Zegendal*, or *Vale of Blessing*.

Montagne had chosen for his bouwery—its air of sweet repose so in contrast with the turbulent scenes of his early life—the name *Vredendal*, or *Quiet Dale*. Alas, he was to realize but little of the happiness which he anticipated in its possession and use! Tobias and Willem, his two farmers, having served out their time, were now to leave him, the former to occupy a bouwery near Papparinamin. A question arising as to some extra pay due them, under an agreement made before Montagne came,

* DE VRIES, in the journal of his voyages, places Kuyter's arrival under *June*, but it is shown by other data that the journal is here at fault as regards the month.

and to which Jacob Stoffelsen was privy, he being at that time "werkbaas" over the company's negroes, who usually assisted in the heavy work on new bouweries, such as cutting palisades, clearing the land, etc., Stoffelsen testified "that in the year 1636 Henry de Forest promised to pay the said persons twenty florins annually for their improvements." Parties came to a settlement March 5th, 1640, when Tennissen and Bont gave a receipt in full, acknowledging themselves to have been well treated and paid to their satisfaction by Mr. La Montagne during and for their three years' service on the farm Vredendal.

After a year's absence Mr. and Mrs. Hudde returned to New Netherland, apparently in the Herring, which arrived here again July 7th, 1639, bringing goods and supplies purchased by Hudde in Amsterdam, where before sailing he had been obliged to borrow two hundred carolus guilders from Mr. Jonas Bronck, to be paid when they should arrive in New Netherland. But Hudde now learned of the sale of the farm Vredendal and the defeat of his plans as a tobacco-planter. Some questions arose, as was natural, and for a full year the legal transfer of the property from Hudde to Montagne was delayed, though the latter had made the former a payment upon it of 200 gl. July 18th, soon after he arrived from Holland. But the parties finally came to terms July 12th, 1640, and on August 28th ensuing Dr. Montagne received his deed.*

This plantation and those at Zegendal, the Otter-spoor, and Great Barent's Island were the only places yet occupied in this vicinity, with one exception. When Kuyter set him down at Schorakin, his friend Bronck located at *Ranachqua*, on the other side of the Great Kill, directly opposite to Kuyter's land. Bronck was of a family long distinguished in Sweden, though

* ANDRIES HUDDE, as before said, was the son of Rutger Hudde of Amsterdam, and was b. in 1608. He arrived in New Netherland in 1629, and in 1633 became a permanent member of Van Twiller's council; in 1642 was appointed the public surveyor, and in 1644 was sent as chief commissary to the Delaware, where he subsequently held other offices, and also officiated as *voorleser* in the church, under the ministry of Do. Lock. Here he lost his w., she that had been Mrs. De Forest, but he m. again in 1657. Dismissed at his own request from the public service, he left for Maryland, intending to set up a brewery there, but d. at Appoquinimy Nov. 4, 1663. On April 19, 1667, Isaac de Forest, "representing Andries Hudde, deceased," sold his house and lot on the Heere-weg.

probably himself from Copenhagen, where some of his kindred lived. He had last resided at Amsterdam, and had there married his wife, Antonia, daughter of Juriaen Slagboom. His interviews there with Hudde and Kuyter upon the subject of New Netherland having quickened if they did not originate his purpose to emigrate, he at once applied his ample means to securing a proper outfit, and with his family, farmers, female servants, and cattle, arrived here in the Fire of Troy, as before stated. Immediately, with consent of the government, he purchased from the Indian sachem Tackamack and his associates the large tract of land called by them Ranachqua, lying between the Great Kill and the river *Ah-qua-hung*, now the *Bronx*, comprising over five hundred acres, and since included in the Manor of Morrisania. Here Bronck began at once to make substantial improvements, including "a stone house, covered with tiles, a barn, tobacco house, two barricks," etc. Pieter Andriesen and Laurens Duyts also leased portions of his land, July 21st, 1639, for three years, for raising tobacco and maize, from the proceeds of which they were to reimburse Bronck for their passage-money in the Fire of Troy, which he had paid. Upon the same "stipulations," Cornelis Jacobsen Stille (later of Harlem) and his brother Jan took, August 15th, part of Bronck's land, with a good dwelling and some stock, for six years. With his house neatly if not richly furnished for those times, and his *vrouw* pronounced "a good housekeeper," Bronck was pleasantly situated.

North of Bronck's land, only separated from it by the kill *Mannepies* (the Indian name of Cromwell's Creek) was the hilly tract or district of *Kaxkeek*, "lying over against the flats of the Island of Manhatas, extending in its length along the kill" from "opposite the high hill of the flat land" till it reached "the source of the said kill." On August 3d, 1639, just about the time of Bronck's purchase, Kaxkeek was also bought for the company, from Tackamack aforesaid and others. Now a populous district of Westchester—in fact forming a part of New York City—then it had yet to welcome its first white occupant, and Bronck and his farmers had only for neighbors the native tenants of the forest, the prowling beast and savage. But the devout Bronck had an arm whereon to lean; a Lutheran in faith, he had brought with him Luther's catechism and other devotional books, with his most prized folio Danish Bible. And as he drew therefrom a name for his new home, *Emmaus*, it carried with it the sweet assurance that even in this secluded wilderness his risen Lord would reveal himself, if not visibly, as to the two disciples of old, yet with tokens of his presence no less comforting because no less real to his eye of faith.

CHAPTER VIII.

1640–1645.

INDIAN TROUBLES.

THRICE happy was the colonist in the friendship of the Indian; for he coveted his furs, to be had for a trifle, but worth at New Amsterdam a good price in cash or its equivalent; he ate of his maize when his bread failed, and often stood in need of his labor or other service. And the advantage was mutual. The red man was quick to see that various articles in use among the Dutch would be of equal use to him. He admitted the superiority of the Holland *duffels*—a thick-napped woolen cloth, blue or red—by adopting it for his own wear. No longer prostrating himself through fear on the discharge of a musket, he could now handle this firearm, and would give a pile of beavers for an old gun and some ammunition. But of worse consequence, he acquired a taste for the Dutch *fire-water*, and for a draught of the exhilarating beverage would strip the last fur covering from his body!

His visit to the bouweries or farms upon peaceful errands, usually for something which he needed and to barter a little game or peltry, was no longer a novelty, and the sight of these savages in their canoes, daily passing and repassing on the streams and rivers, or engaged in their favorite employment of fishing, excited no apprehensions. The farmers, writes Kuyter, "pursue their out-door labor without interruption, in the woods as well as in the field, and dwell safely, with their wives and children, in their houses, free from any fear of the Indians."

> "The drowsy herdsman now reviews his charge,
> Unbars his stalls and sets his flocks at large;
> The ploughboy next comes trudging o'er the plain,
> With merry heart to yoke his team again;
> He slowly goads along the lounging pair,
> As whistling on he goes for want of care.
> Unconscious of his happier lot below,
> In thought confined he wields his steady plow;
> And all the joyful train with sickles bright,
> Now join the harvest fields in gay delight;
> And as the rustic jest goes jocund round,
> The rural hour in guileless mirth is crowned;
> While health does o'er each cheerful visage play,
> Content and joy beguile their hours away."

Sweet dream of security, it was past!; a mortal enmity was brewing between the white and the red man, in the face of their every interest which should have bound them in friendship. Though the responsibility lay not with the colonist, but with the authorities, the effects fell heavily on the former. In 1639 Director Kieft was guilty of a most impolitic act, in attempting to levy a tax upon the several Indian tribes, sending his wily agent Tienhoven to demand their corn, furs, and sewant.* The demand was indignantly spurned, and served only to arouse a hostile feeling toward the Dutch. Montagne's prediction was well made when, seeing the folly of this measure, he said, "a

* SEWANT, also called *wampum*, was the Indian money, consisting of tubular beads made from the conch-shell, perforated lengthwise and fastened with thread upon strips of cloth or canvas. For many years it was almost the only *money* in circulation among the settlers, and for trading with the Indians was preferable to coin. Even the contributions at church were made in sewant. The color of the beads, whether white or black, and the finish determined its value. For an exhaustive article upon its manufacture, etc., see Munsell's *Annals of Albany*, vol. ii. pp. 1-8, second edition.

bridge has been built, over which war will soon stalk through the land." Some petty depredations being committed soon after, which were, in part falsely, charged upon the Raritan Indians, the hot-headed Kieft dispatched a body of soldiers to demand satisfaction. They too well executed their mission by a wanton attack on the Indians, July 16th, 1640, killing several, and burning their maize.

The next year, 1641, brought retaliation from the Raritans, who, on September 1st, swept off the settlers upon Staten Island, while Manhattan Island was already smarting under the first stroke of savage vengeance. A Wickquaskeek who from boyhood had harbored a grudge against the Dutch, because at that time three of Director Minuit's men had slain his uncle and stolen his beavers, could no longer restrain his thirst for revenge. On a day in midsummer he entered the house of Claes Swits, at Turtle Bay, "on the road over which the Indians from Wickquaskeek passed daily." Assuming a friendly air, and being known to Swits, for whose son he had worked, he was "well received and supplied with food." Then he wanted to trade some furs for duffels; but while the unsuspecting old man was bending over the chest in which his cloth was kept, the savage, with an axe that lay near, struck him upon the neck, when "he fell down dead by the chest." He "then stole all the goods" and fled into the forest. This cruel murder, at their very doors, aroused the authorities, and a yacht was sent to Wickquaskeek to demand satisfaction from the sachem. He not only refused, but justified the act. "He wished twenty Swannekins (*i.e.*, Dutchmen) had been murdered."

Burning to scourge the savages, but fearing to assume the responsibility, Kieft referred it to the citizens, who at his request came together and chose twelve of their number to decide upon the grave question of making war to avenge the murder of Swits. The twelve men, Kuyter being one, reported their conclusions on the 29th of August. They counselled delay. A better opportunity should be chosen to inflict the blow, for their cattle were now pasturing in the woods, and the settlers were living isolated from each other, east, west, north, and south. Meanwhile another demand should be made for the murderer, and repeated, if necessary, "twice or three times." Then, his surrender being still refused, let war begin "at once." "The attack should be made in the harvest, when the Indians were hunting," or deferred "till the maize trade be over, and until an opportunity and God's will be made manifest." These reasonable counsels prevailed; peace was maintained, and Kuyter and his neighbors pursued their farming work unobstructed, though not without more or less of apprehension.

Vredendal and the Otter-spoor, in the year which inaugurated these troubles, had yielded profitable returns for the "great expenses" put upon those bouweries, while Kuyter, after "a heavy outlay, much pains, and immense labor" upon his buildings and lands at Zegendal, to complete the one and bring the other under good cultivation, had also realized a valuable crop of tobacco, which being wintered and well cured he was intending to ship during the summer of 1641 to Coenraet van Keulen, at Amsterdam, who had already made him advances thereon. But his purpose was defeated by the sudden departure of the Oak Tree for Virginia, the vessel in which he had designed to make his shipment, adding to his disappointment and loss the necessity of refunding to his consignee the sum advanced by him. Montagne was hardly as fortunate, for while his crop was being sweated and cured, his tobacco-house, too slightly built, blew down, by which accident the tobacco was injured. He prosecuted John Morris, the carpenter, for damages, which ended in a compromise. And so, notwithstanding a malicious report which reached Holland, that Montagne "daily filled his pockets with *ducatoons* and *jacobuses*," his pecuniary affairs really began to wear a discouraging aspect, his domestic horizon being also clouded just at this time by the loss of his wife.

Meanwhile satisfaction for the murder of Swits had been "several times sought for, but in vain." Indeed it was reported that the savage tribes were combining for a general war upon the colonists, and the killing of two other persons at Staten Island and Hackensack was proof of the hostile spirit animating the savages. All this was very alarming to the inhabitants, especially those upon exposed bouweries, who lived in constant fear, "and not without reason, as the Indians were daily in their houses."

Persuasion having failed, Kieft now felt justified in using

force with the savages. He summoned the twelve men, November 1st, and asked their opinion. "Mr. Jochem" (Kuyter) advised "to be patient, and to lull the Indians into security;" and most agreed with him. On January 21st, 1642, the twelve men gave their assent to an expedition against the Wickquaskeeks, but (knowing his cowardice) suggested that the director himself should lead the forces! The latter declined the honor, but began warlike preparations. All being ready, and spies sent to reconnoitre reporting that the Indians "lay in their village suspecting nothing," Ensign Hendrick van Dyck with eighty men left Fort Amsterdam early in the month of March for Wickquaskeek. Arriving at the *Annepperah*, or the Saw Mill Creek, at Yonkers, Willem Hont, who held a subordinate command, bravely passed over with his men and "marched on with the advanced troops," expecting the ensign to follow.* But Van Dyck halted at the creek for more than an hour before he crossed with his command and came up; but now darkness had set in, Tobias Teunissen, the guide, lost his way, and the ensign, perplexed and out of temper, ordered a return. The result was more happy, probably, than if they had met the savages, for the latter, noticing by the tracks of the soldiers near their wigwams "that they had narrowly escaped discovery," dreaded another visit and sent messengers to sue for peace. Kieft accordingly sent delegates, including Van Tienhoven, who understood Indian, to meet the chiefs of Wickquaskeek in council at the house of Jonas Bronck, at Emmaus, and here was made a formal treaty, in which, among other things, the sachems engaged to deliver Swits' murderer to the Dutch.

Under this pledge of peace the spring and summer witnessed considerable labor on the several plantations on the Flats. At the same time Montagne, as a member of the council, was much occupied with official duties, and Kuyter made his *début* into public life as a "kerkmeester," one of those chosen to oversee

* WILLEM FREDRICKS BONT the same year removed to Fort Orange, and being a "free carpenter" took part in constructing the first church there. Later he was for several years a magistrate, kept tavern, farmed the excise, and acquired property. He m. ab. 1650 Geertie Nanningks, as her fourth hus.; in 1683 both were members of Do. Delius' church. Whether he left chn. is not known.

the erection of a church at New Amsterdam, because Knyter was "a devout person of the reformed religion, and had good workmen who would quickly prepare the timber." The church was begun forthwith, its walls "laid up with quarry stone," and "built in the fort, to guard against any surprise by the Indians."

Illusory indeed was the hope of living in peace with the natives, now that the old ties of friendship had been ruptured. It so happened that in midwinter following, the Mahicans, who lived below Fort Orange, came down and made war upon the Tappans and Wickquaskecks, it was said to force those tribes, whom they had once subjugated, to render them tribute. Numerous as were these tribes, they were easily overpowered by the Mahicans, who were well armed with guns, many of the men being slain, the women and children made captives, and a crowd of terror-stricken fugitives forced to take to flight through a deep snow to find shelter in the Dutch settlements. Half dead of cold and hunger, they were kindly received by the people and fed for two weeks, till, gathering courage, they returned to their castles. But soon, another panic seizing them, they again sought the protection of the Dutch. Now Kieft, with no commiseration for these wretched beings, thought it his chance to avenge the death of Claes Swits and others. "God hath wholly delivered them into our hands," impiously said Van Tienhoven and other restless spirits, who, simply echoing the sentiments of Kieft, made a formal request for leave to destroy them.

Knyter and other considerate persons opposed this stoutly, insisting that it would only recoil upon their own heads, bring disaster upon the country, and especially expose the out-plantations to the rage of a vindictive and cruel foe. Montagne, having just arrived from Quiet Dale, its stalls of cattle and full garners all endangered, urged his objections with unusual warmth. "We ought first to consider well," he insisted, "whether we shall be able to give protection to those who are living at a distance." But this pertinent suggestion was unheeded, evil counsels prevailed, and Kieft, set in his mad purpose, rashly issued his orders. On the night of February 25th, 1643, a party of Dutch soldiers sallied forth from the streets of New Amsterdam and made a savage onslaught upon the sleeping Wickquaskeeks at Corlear's Hook, forty of whom were massacred "in cold blood." Another party, crossing the Hudson, slaughtered a band which had sought refuge at Pavonia. Nor did it stop here, for a day or two after several of the friendly Mareckawecks were basely murdered.

The enraged savages were not slow to resent such treatment, and several tribes joining hands made common cause against the Dutch. Issuing from the woods and thickets, they boldly attacked and slew the farmers, both in their dwellings and in the open field, put the firebrand to houses, haystacks, and grain, killed or drove away the stock, and carried off women and children into a painful captivity. Happy they who had the means of defence or timely notice to flee. "The winter passed in confusion and terror." No out-door labor could be safely done. Kieft, as agent of Van Keulen, had contracted on December 6th for the erection of a fine substantial stone residence on the Otter-spoor, fifty by an hundred feet on the ground, with porticos front and rear, and all very complete; for whose occupancy we cannot tell, unless for Van Keulen or some of his family, but certainly not for the chicken-hearted director, who kept himself "safely protected in the fort, out of which he had never slept for all the years he had been there." But this work was probably arrested.

At length "the season came for driving out the cattle, which caused many to desire peace; the Indians, on their part, seeing that it was time to plant maize, were not less solicitous for a cessation of hostilities; so, after some negotiation, peace was concluded." It was ratified April 22d, 1643, though many doubted of its lasting. But the colonists, and especially Kuyter, had met with a sad loss in the recent death of Jonas Bronck. Was it at the hands of the Indians? We judge not, as his property was spared. On May 6th Kuyter and Do. Bogardus visited Emmaus, and, aided by the widow * and Peter Jonassen Bronck, took an inventory of the estate, of which Kuyter and

* BRONCK's widow afterward m. Arent van Curler, of Rensselaerswyck, whom she also survived. She d. at Schenectady Dec. 19, 1676, as per a letter written from Kingston, twelve days after, by her nephew, Wilhelmus Beeckman, whom for want of chn. she named as one of her heirs. Her will was made Nov. 11, 1676; the date of probate being inadvertently given in *Pearson's Schenectady Settlers* as the date of her death.

the domine had been appointed guardians. *Seignior* Bronck, as he was styled, must be rated quite above the ordinary colonists, his Danish and Latin library, stored with law and history as also divinity, being indicative of his tastes and culture as well as of his piety.

The bouweries of Montagne and Kuyter were also intact. Buildings and stock well intrenched within palisades had escaped the general devastation. Montagne had already put twenty-six acres in rye, barley and peas, when, willing to be relieved of a charge so fraught with danger, he leased his bouwery, with the "farm-house," kitchen, out-houses, orchard, stock, and all as it stood, June 14th, to Bout Fransen, from Naerden, for the term of three years. In three months (September 22d), Franssen gave it up, for the Indians, having harvested their maize, began again their bloody work. Terrible scenes ensued. The settlers, compelled to fly, took refuge at Fort Amsterdam, to within sight of which the brutal savages tracked their victims. Montagne "was driven off his land," involving the loss of all he could not carry away; and scarcely a settler remained on the bouweries of Manhattan Island. "Almost every place is abandoned," wrote Kuyter and others, of the popular board of Eight Men, in a letter of November 3d, 1643, imploring aid from the directors in Holland. "We wretched people," say they, "with our wives and little ones that still survive, must in our destitution find refuge together in and around the fort at Manhattan, where we are not safe even for an hour, as the Indians daily threaten to overwhelm us. Very little can be planted this autumn, and much less in the spring; so it must come to pass that those of us who may yet save our lives will necessarily perish next year by hunger and grief, as also our wives and children, unless our God have pity on us."

But relief from Holland could not be immediate. The question of self-preservation now pressed upon the colonists; to remain inactive was but to die. Their courage rising to the emergency, it was resolved to muster in every man able to bear arms, and to take the field with all their available force against the wily and powerful foe. Montagne and Kuyter, however opposed at first to the war, had now no alternative but to second the effort to conquer a peace. The former, appointed to the chief military command, led several expeditions sent out in various directions during the succeeding winter and spring, and in which Kuyter held the captaincy of a burgher company. These forces scoured the Indian country, driving the foe from his rude castles and villages with sword and firebrand.

Thus far Captain Kuyter, by means of a guard of soldiers stationed at Zegendal under Sergeant Ael, had protected his house and farmers. But on the night of March 5th, when he was absent, the Indians stealthily surrounded his inclosure. The guard was sleeping in a cellar or underground hut;* but two young men in Kuyter's employ, apprehensive of danger, were patrolling around the farm-house. Near two o'clock in the morning these were startled by a blazing arrow, "the flame having the appearance of brimstone," which darted through the air and fell on the roof of the dwelling. The wind blowing strongly, the thatch at once took fire, and soon the house and contents were burned to the ground. During and after the conflagration the savages made the night hideous by whooping and discharge of guns, to the terror of the two maid-servants, while the sergeant, with the caution of years, kept within the cellar, refusing to expose either himself or his men, though the other persons, and especially the young men, in face of a double danger, saved what they could from the flames.

The Wickquaskeeks were set down as the authors of this villainy. But this was denied by Ponkes, a Marechaweek, to two Dutchmen who understood his language, and whom he met but two days after the fire. "It was their way to boast," he said, "whenever they committed any mischief." But not one had he heard boast of this; besides, "it was well known among the Indians that the Swannekins themselves burned the house, and removed through dread of being killed there!" This piece of Indian logic, evidently invented by the artful savage to shield his tribe from retribution, was too transparent. Kuyter censured "the English soldiers" for not assisting. Kieft, on the other hand, took occasion to throw the blame on Kuyter, charging him

* UNDERGROUND HUTS were made use of by those who at first had no means to build farm-houses, and in which they could live "dry and warm for two, three, or four years." The method of making them is described by Van Tienhoven, *Doc. Hist. N. Y.*, iv: 31.

with rashly sending away part of his guard just before the fire, leaving to protect the property only "four soldiers and five laborers." * This dispute between Kieft and Kuyter betrays a state of feeling which afterward led to very serious results.

Overcome by dread of the savages, neither the planters nor their laborers had courage longer to engage in work upon the Flats; and thus things continued till at length a brighter day dawned upon the colonists. Wearied with "a two years' war," the Indians themselves manifested a wish to bury the hatchet. The sachems of the adjacent tribes upon Long Island and the banks of the Hudson were accordingly invited to a grand council, held in Fort Amsterdam August 30th, 1645, when was happily concluded, "a solid and durable peace." Some of the powerful Mohawks, with their interpreter Cornelis van Slyck, also attended and assisted in the negotiations. Little Ape, chief of the Mahicans, spoke in behalf of their tributaries, the Wickquaskeeks, pledging them to the observance of the treaty, by the terms of which the Indians were "not to come with weapons on Manhattan Island, nor in the vicinity of Christian dwellings." The treaty was signed, in the presence of many citizens, by several of the more distinguished, and by the sachems, among the former being La Montagne; and also by the two interpreters, in which capacity the worthy Norman, Claes Carstensen, who later ended his days at Harlem, acted for the colonists.

* Sergt. Martin Abl and three English soldiers, Thomas Foster, William Gilford, and Abraham Newman, with Cornelis van Houten, Jan Hegeman, Pieter Jansen, Jacob Lambertsen, and Derick Gerritsen, and the two dairy-maids, made eleven persons within the palisades. Three soldiers had left only a few days before the attack.

CHAPTER IX.

1645–1650.

LAND PATENTS—KUYTER'S TRIALS.

PEACE thus assured, the planters whom the Indians had driven from the Flats and parts adjacent again took heart and ventured to return to their desolated bouweries. But, grown wiser since their late expulsion, they had come to realize by how uncertain a tenure they held their lands, having as yet received no patent or groundbrief. By a neglect to secure such patents there was imminent risk of losing whatever they invested, as well as the land itself; and how soon some new contingency might arise, to wrest all from them and their heirs, who could tell? Moreover, in so unsettled a state of the country the legal seizin by documentary title was a needed stimulus to exertion, an inducement to bear the toil, hazard, and hardship involved in a residence upon one of those exposed bouweries. The settlers were led to expect a groundbrief after having held and improved their lands for two years; in most of the cases to be named where such patents were received there had evidently been a much longer occupancy. But meanwhile some new farms had been begun, not as yet noticed, and as will further appear by a brief survey of the progress of settlement at this date.

Sibout Claessen, one of the burghers of New Amsterdam, was from Hoorn, on the Zuyder Zee. He was respected, and as a builder of practical consequence to the community, insomuch that Director Kieft granted him fifty morgen of land "on the Island of Manhattas, beginning at the hook at the Hellegat where *Verken Island* ends." With filial affection for his native place, where rested the bones of his father, Claes Sibouts, and still lived his brother Hendrick and other kinsfolk, Claessen called his new possession *Hoorn's Hook.* It was patented to him June 5th, 1646.*

The narrow kill called by the Indians *Papparinamin*, which, winding around the neck of land forming the extreme northerly part of Manhattan, connected the Spuyten Duyvel with the Great Kill, or Harlem River, gave its name as well to the land lying contiguous to it on either side. Papparinamin, as interpreted, *Place where the stream is shut*, was thus confined neither to the land nor stream, but to the locality, and was certainly well given, as it has ever been the great bar to navigation around Manhattan Island. The noted Dr. Adrian vander Donck, who owned "a saw-mill, bouwery, and plantation" some distance above on the Annepperah, had selected the island on the northerly side of the Papparinamin Creek, "containing some thirty or forty morgen, with a convenient meadow about it," intending, as he himself states, "to go and dwell on the said spot, or to make gradual preparations therefor, by building upon and tilling it, since both his inclination and judgment led him to that place." Having, with Kieft's consent, bought the land from the sachem Tackamack and other Indians, Vander Donck, with his newly-married wife, the daughter of Rev. Francis Doughty, visited Holland, expecting on his return to bring over his "mother, sister, brother, servants, and other members of his family," to make their home at Papparinamin. But, offending the directors by acting as a representative of the commonalty of New Netherland in certain charges against Stuyvesant, Vander Donck was restrained for several years from again leaving fatherland, and then returned to his possessions only to die a year or two later.

* Jan Aertsen van Putten and his two sisters, whose mo. Susannah had recently m. this first proprietor of Hoorn's Hook, were chn. of Aert Teunissen van Putten, who in 1643 was massacred (but not his family, as some say) by Indians at Pavonia. Jan Aertsen chose the trade of a blacksmith and settled at Esopus, where he joined the church April 15, 1661, and soon after was made an elder. Having been of the party who attacked the Indians there in 1659, this was too well remembered, for in the vengeful onslaught made by the savages upon that place June 7, 1663, he was killed in his house. Only a few days before this, his w. Grietie Hendricks, and little dr. Annetie had reached their home from a visit to Wie by Swolle, in Holland, Grietie's birthplace. The dr. and only ch., Annetie, b. 1659, afterward m. Hendrick Kip., son of Isaac of H., by whom she had sons John, Hendrick, etc. See *Du Mont.*

But the opposite section of Papparinamin, forming the upper extremity of Manhattan Island, was not less inviting for its arable lands, meadows, and circumambient creeks, and, if we do not mistake De Rasieres, was one of the two places he found at the north end—the other Harlem Flats—where was "good land," ready, with little or no clearing, for tillage. Here another Hollander, Matthys Jansen van Keulen, had obtained a grant of fifty morgen of land from Director Kieft, probably in advance of Vander Donck. His patent was issued August 18th, 1646, and in after years was confirmed to his children, from whom are descended two families of Ulster County—*Jansen* and *Van Keuren*, the last name corrupted from *Keulen*.* It does not appear that Matthys himself ever occupied this land; at the date of the patent he was living at Fort Orange. His hundred acres must have reached quite down to the Jansen and Aertsen grant, hereafter noticed. The latter, according to the patent, as certainly reached northward to "Tobias's Bouwery." Tobias Teunissen, late farmer for Dr. La Montagne, is here referred to, and the facts stated warrant the conclusion that Teunissen now occupied Matthys Jansen's land either under a lease or an agreement to purchase. To his sequestered home, beside the Great Kill, Tobias had taken a new *vrouw*, in hope of happier years, though the spirit and activity he had shown

* MATTHYS JANSEN became a trader on the Hudson, removed to Fort Orange, and thence to Esopus, where he d. prior to 1663. That year, Feb. 15, the deacons loaned 1000 gl. from his estate. His wid., Margaret Hendricks, m. Thomas Chambers, Lord of the Manor of Fox Hall. Jansen had four chn., viz., Jan, Matthys, Catharine, m. 1660, Jan Jansen, from Amersfoort, and Anneke, who m. 1668 *Sergt.* Jan Hendricks Buur, alias Pearsen.

Jan Matthyssen, b. at Fort Orange, m. in 1667, Madelaine, dr. of Matthew Blanchan, was an elder of the Kingston church, and d. between 1719 and 1721. He had *Matthys*, *Thomas*, *Jan*, *Hendrick*, *David*, *Margaret*, who m. Harent Burhans; *Magdalene*, m. Richard Brodhead; *Sarah*, m. Elias Bunschoten; *Catharine*, m. John Crook, Jr., and *Mary*, who d. early. These bore the name of *Jansen*, in English *Johnson*. Jan took to the sea, went to England, and in 1690 was thought to be dead. From the other sons were the respectable Jansens of Ulster County, some of whom bore a conspicuous part in the Revolution.

Matthys Matthyssen was made a captain in 1685, and later served against the French on the northern frontier. He m. Tietie, dr. of Tjerck De Witt, and had issue *Matthys*, *Tjerck*, *Nicholas*, *Thomas*, *Gerardus*, *Hasuelt*, *Sarah*, m. Matthew Du Bois; *Leah*, who with Hasuelt removed to New York, and *Barbara*, m. Peter Tappen. (See *Annals of Newtown*, p. 303.) It was these six sons of Matthys who, says an old manuscript, "changed their name of Matthyssen to *Van Keuren*," and whence the numerous family so called.

in the late Indian war made his situation not without peril. But, courageous of heart, he did not anticipate the fate which awaited him.

Pieter Jansen, in company with Mr. Huyck Aertsen, then a schepen at Brooklyn, had taken up a tract of land lying between Tobias's bounds and what is now known as Sherman's Creek, and for which a groundbrief was given them March 11th, 1647. Jansen was a hardy Norwegian of twenty-seven years, had been in the employ of Kuyter, and was present on that fearful night when his house was burned by the savages. The next summer after the patent was secured, Pieter the Norman, as he was usually called, took to his heart and home a young wife, Lysbet Jansen, from Amsterdam, and near the same time, by the death of Aertsen, was left in sole care of the bouwery, though between the widow and the next of kin (for Aertsen left no children) his share did not want for claimants. Aertsen was born at Rossum, a village of the Bommellerwoert, an island formed by the Waal and Maas; but he had a brother, a burgher at Utrecht, who, on having notice of his death, and taking proof thereof December 30th, 1647, was declared his only heir. For reasons similar to those for which other patents within Harlem were afterward held to be vacated or void, the validity of this title was subsequently called in question, and by a decision of the governor and council and a compromise with the successors of Jansen and Aertsen, became vested in the freeholders of Harlem. It has additional interest as covering the identical tract known in our time as the "Dyckman Homestead." *

These bouweries, forming the outposts of settlement on the

* THE JANSEN AND AERTSEN PATENT, or rather the descriptive part, reads as follows: "A piece of land lying between Montagne's bay meadow and Tobias's bouwery, stretching from the north corner of said meadow south-south-east to the hook, two hundred and seventy-five rods. It goes * to a spring [*fontyn*] against the high land, and from there to the end of a creek coming out of the North river, north-east by north along the high hills an hundred and seventy-five rods, and from there,† to the kill which runs around the Island of Manhattans, an hundred and twenty rods south-south-east, seventy rods south-east, and thirty south-south-east; and along the before-named kill to the aforesaid hook, two hundred rods; the same amounting to seventy-four morgen, one hundred and six rods." Dated March 11, 1647.

* *i.e.* On the west side. † Being its northern boundary.

north end, were evidently laid out by actual survey, whence the courses and distances and the uneven quantity, seventy-four morgen, one hundred and six rods, in that to Jansen and Aertsen. The stretch of alternate heights and hollows, reaching from Sherman's Creek down to the Flats, had not yet a solitary white settler. Through its forests and thickets red men hunted the deer and beaver, and rudely tilled other portions, one of which was known as the "Great Maize Land." Indeed the Indian title to this part of Manhattan Island was not fully extinguished till 1715.

Coming to the settlements on the Flats, the Otter-spoor farm, which Van Tienhoven had "long since conveyed" to Van Keulen of Amsterdam, and whence, as before said, it took the name Van Keulen's Hook, was only made sure to the latter the month before the new Indian treaty was ratified, by a patent from Kieft to Van Tienhoven, the object and effect of which was to give him power to sell, and to perfect the title in Van Keulen, no patent having been issued before. With so firm a tenure it is remarkable that no evidence appears of any further attempts on the part of Van Keulen to improve this valuable tract, nor is his ownership again distinctly recognized. While the evidence we have bearing upon it is far from satisfactory, our solution is that Matthys Jansen van Keulen, being authorized by the Amsterdam merchant, received from Kieft the grant of Papparinamin in exchange for Van Keulen's Hook.

Dr. Montagne, with brightened prospects, and about to wed the widow of Arent Corssen Stam, who two years previous, sailing for Holland on the public service, had perished at sea, took occasion, May 9th, 1647, only two days before his friend Kieft closed his directorship, to secure a patent for the farm Vredendal, to which was now joined what was not included in the original grant to Hendrick de Forest, namely, the point or neck of land called Rechawanes, extending out to the East River, and since known as the Benson or McGown farm. As belonging to the oldest title in the township, and one to which an unusual interest attaches, we feel warranted in giving a translation of the patent entire.

We, WILLEM KIEFT, DIRECTOR GENERAL, and the COUNCIL, residing in NEW NETHERLAND, on behalf of the HIGH and MIGHTY LORDS the

States General of the United Netherlands, his Highness of Orange, and the Honorable Messieurs, the Managers of the Incorporated West India Company, do, by these presents, acknowledge and declare, that we on this day, the date underwritten, have given and granted unto *Sieur* Johannes La Montagne, counsellor of New Netherland, a piece of land situate on the Island of Manhattans, known by a name in the Indian language which in the Nether Dutch signifies the *Flat Land*, containing one hundred morgen in the flat, lying between the hills and kill; and a point named *Rechawanes*, stretching betwixt two hills, till to the East River; (which above described land was occupied by Hendrick Forest deceased, and has been purchased by the said La Montagne at public auction in the Fort, for seventeen hundred guilders;) with express conditions and terms that he Johannes La Montagne, or whoever by virtue hereof may accept his action, shall acknowledge the Honorable Managers aforesaid as his Lords and Patroons, under the sovereignty of their High Mightinesses the Lords States General, and obey their Director and Council here in all things, as good inhabitants are in duty bound to do; provided further that they subject themselves to all such burdens and imposts as are already enacted, or may hereafter be enacted by their Honors; constituting therefore the said *Sieur* La Montagne, or whoever may hereafter obtain his action, in our stead in real and actual possession of the aforesaid lot and land, giving him by these presents, full power, authority, and special order, the aforesaid parcel of land to enter upon, cultivate, inhabit, and use, as he would lawfully do with other his patrimonial lands and effects, without we the grantors in the quality aforesaid, thereunto having, reserving, or saving any, even the slightest part, action, or control whatever, but to the behoof as aforesaid, from all desisting, from now henceforth and forever. Promising moreover, this transport firm, inviolable and irrevocable to keep, respect and fulfil, all under the penalty provided therefor by law. In witness, these presents are by us signed, and confirmed with our seal in red wax hereto appended. Done in Fort Amsterdam, in New Netherland, the 9th day of May, 1647.

Willem Kieft.

Six days afterward Dr. Montagne's brother-in-law, Isaac de Forest, obtained from the new director, Stuyvesant, the ground-brief for a bouwery previously granted him, consisting of fifty morgen of surplus land which had been found to lie between the Kuyter and Van Keulen tracts. It bordered on the Harlem River, opposite the mouth of "Bronck's Kill"—the passage, still called "The Kills," parting Randell's Island from the Westchester shore. Upon this fifty-morgen tract the village of New Harlem was subsequently laid out and run its humble career, but "the lawn where scattered hamlets rose" has so changed before the rise of modern structures that but barely one of its ancient dwellings remains.*

The boweries mentioned, with Zegendal, or Kuyter's farm,

* See De Forest Family, Appendix A.

were the only ones, so far as known, yet begun within the territorial limits to which our history refers. Kuyter, though one of the most energetic of the settlers, had been strangely baffled in his efforts to improve his lands. Yet to his various disappointments and losses other trials, and more severe, were to be added. But the indomitable spirit of the man, rising superior to misfortune, exhibits Kuyter throughout in a character to be admired, and in which we cannot but be interested. The ill-feeling which had sprung up between him and Kieft, as already alluded to in connection with the burning of Kuyter's house, grew out of Kieft's culpable rashness in bringing on the Indian war. The good Domine Bogardus, sorely grieved by the director's course in authorizing the cruel massacre of the Indians, and thus provoking the fearful retaliation which had followed, had expressed himself freely in regard to these things, "many times in his sermons," while also rebuking the prevalent immorality, avarice and other gross indulgences. This pungent preaching so offended the director that he forsook the church, absenting himself for more than three years, his example also leading off nearly every officer of the church and government, not excepting the usually discreet counsellor Montagne, who had formerly been an elder. Kuyter himself had once felt hard toward the domine for refusing him a favor which Kieft had asked in his behalf; but he was not vindictive, and this was a bygone. As a ruling elder, and controlled by his religion and strong sense of justice, he did not hesitate now to sustain the minister and his utterances, although not another member of the consistory stood by him. In consequence he brought upon his own head the maledictions of the director, which were in no wise appeased by Kuyter's official action as one of the Eight Men, a body which, representing the people, had felt it a duty to address the directors in Holland, exposing Kieft's misrule in New Netherland and the ruinous condition to which, as a consequence, the colony had been reduced. As to the differences between Bogardus and Kieft, these, after a sharp paper warfare, had ended in a reconciliation. But not so with Kieft and Kuyter, whose mutual animosity another year did not quench, while Cornelis Melyn, also an active member of the Eight Men, came in for a share of Kieft's hot displeasure. These two honest men were as thorns in the side of the director. Nor could they easily bear either the insults which he had heaped upon them, or the heavy losses they had sustained through his maladministration; and thus the case stood when Kieft was superseded in office by General Petrus Stuyvesant, who arrived May 11th, 1647. In some remarks made on the occasion of formally resigning the government to his successor, Kieft thanked the people for their fidelity, evidently expecting to be complimented in return. But on the contrary, Kuyter, Melyn, and one or two more had the frankness to speak out and tell him that they would not thank him, as they had no reason for doing so!

The existing quarrel, brought thus directly to the notice of Stuyvesant, now took the form of a complaint preferred by Kieft against Kuyter and Melyn, whom he charged with having sent "some letters to Holland, to the directors, in the name of the Eight Men; among others, one dated 28th October, 1644, containing nothing but libels and lies." He demanded justice and the punishment of the accused. This was on June 18th, and next day a copy of the complaint, containing the points of objection to the obnoxious letter, was handed to the accused by the court messenger, with a summons to answer within forty-eight hours. Kuyter and Melyn replied at length on the 22d, and in a telling statement, and invited an inquiry into the truth of what they had written. This defense had little weight with the arbitrary Stuyvesant, himself a great stickler for the divine right of rulers, and the tables were turned against Kuyter and his associate, who, after further preliminaries, were placed under arrest, and on July 16th brought before the director and council for trial. It was plainly to be seen that the court held the attitude of both prosecutor and judge. The charges, in brief, were that they had slandered and threatened Director Kieft. The prosecution relied mainly on the letter before referred to, written to the directors in Holland, and pronounced by Kieft to be "full of libels and lies;" of which letter, though it purported to be a memorial from the Eight Men, the accused were declared the authors, and to which, as was charged, they had fraudulently obtained the signatures of their associates. Kuyter, it was further alleged, had, at a meeting of the Eight Men, raised his finger to Kieft in a threatening manner, and said to him that when he should doff his robe of office then he would have him! Melyn, as was charged, in speaking of the orders for destroying the Indians in the winter of 1643, had dared to say, "They who gave such orders should look well to themselves, lest they come either to the gallows or the wheel." Words almost prophetic, considering the manner of Kieft's death. Kuyter explained his remark as quite different from that imputed to him. He and Melyn, standing to their former answer, in which they had fully and ably met the several points of objection to the obnoxious letter,* now offered certain memorials, proofs, and witnesses, "in order to establish the truth of what was written." But these were either rejected or allowed to have no weight, and thus, the evidence being unjustly set aside, the case was carried against the accused, who were pronounced guilty of high contempt of authority. Stuyvesant, in his judgment in Kuyter's case, hinged it on sacred and civil law. "He who slanders God, the magistrate, or his parents," says Bernard de Muscatel, "must be stoned to death." Then he quoted the Scriptures: "Thou shalt not speak evil of the ruler of thy people." On July 25th they were sentenced—Kuyter to a fine of 150 gl. and three years' banishment from New Netherland; Melyn to a heavier fine and longer exile.

Elated with his success, Kieft soon after took passage for Holland in the ship Princess, carrying with him a fortune which he had amassed here. In the same ship Do. Bogardus and others embarked, while Kuyter and Melyn, "publicly banished the country," were "brought on board as exiles, torn away from their goods, wives and children," while, as if to mock their misery, the bells in the church were made to ring a merry peal. The vessel sailed August 16th, 1647, but never reached its destination. On September 27th, having mistaken their course, they were wrecked upon a rock on the coast of Wales. The wretched Kieft, with death before his eyes, sighed deeply as he said to Kuyter and Melyn, "Friends, I have done you wrong; can you forgive me?" All night the ship rocked in the sea,

* This letter may be found and its character judged of by reference to the Col. Hist. of N. Y., i. 209–213. Kieft's points of exception to it are given at p. 203, and the able rejoinder of Kuyter and Melyn at p. 205.

and toward morning went to pieces, a large number of persons perishing, including Kieft and Bogardus. Kuyter and Melyn providentially escaped with their lives, though the latter lost a son. "Kuyter remained alone on the after part of the ship, on which stood a cannon, which he, observing in the gray of the morning, took for a man; but speaking to it and getting no answer, he supposed him dead. He was at last thrown on land, together with the cannon, to the great amazement of the English, who crowded the strand by thousands, and who set up the piece of ordnance as a lasting memorial. Melyn, floating back to sea, fell in with others who had remained on a part of the wreck on a sand-bank which became dry with the ebb. They then took some planks and pieces of wood, fastened them together, and having made sails of their shirts and other garments, they at last reached the main land of England. As these persons were more concerned for their papers than for any thing else, they caused them to be dragged for, and on the third day Jochem Pieterss recovered a box containing a part of them."*

The resolute Kuyter and Melyn passed over to Holland, and appealed to the States General from the sentence rendered by Stuyvesant. Upon a hearing of their case, this body granted a suspension of the judgment, with permission for them to return to New Netherland, and summoned Stuyvesant to appear at the Hague, in person or by attorney, either to sustain his decision "or to renounce the same."

Armed with a mandamus and passports from their High Mightinesses, and also bearing a letter from his Highness the Prince of Orange to Stuyvesant, dated May 19th, 1648, admonishing him "duly to respect and obey those commands," Kuyter and Melyn were now prepared to return to this country and face

* EVERARDUS BOGARDUS, the pastor, counsellor and friend of our De Forests, La Montagne, Kuyter, Bronck, and their fellow-colonists, who cheered them amid their toils and adversities and in dark hours of peril, joined many in marriage, baptized their offspring, oft performed in their stricken homes the last sad rites of sepulture, and frequently acted as guardian of their estates; full justice is yet to be done his memory. His advice often sought for in many affairs affecting individuals or the community, the amount of important business with which he was intrusted on his final departure for Holland evinced the continued respect and confidence of his people. In the record of a useful life, as we apprehend, Do. Bogardus has left his numerous heirs a better inheritance than they will ever realize from his landed possessions. See *Valentine's Manual* for 1863, p. 595; also *Corwin's Manual.*

their accusers. But detained for some months longer by other engagements, Melyn sailed at the close of the year, leaving Kuyter behind, probably to manage the case should Stuyvesant attempt to prosecute it further. Reaching New Amsterdam about January 1st, 1649, Melyn presented his letters to Stuyvesant, who was in great wrath over the mandamus, declaring with much bluster his purpose to answer it. Melyn was inclined to push his advantage, but joining the citizens in other complaints against the director, affairs became rather involved; while Kuyter, remaining abroad for a year longer, more or less, found on his return no obstacle interposed to his resuming his property, and, contenting himself with his own business, he was reinstated in his several offices by Stuyvesant, the breach of friendship between them being soon healed.

Kuyter was not in circumstances to restore his ruined plantation at Schorakin; indeed there was little encouragement for any to prosecute labor on the north part of the island, owing to the hostile temper of the Indians, who during these several years waylaid and murdered a number of the settlers dwelling in exposed places. Some still kept up their bouweries; others disposed of theirs. Pieter Cornelissen Beeck, an old and respected citizen of New Amsterdam, had come to own one "on this island near Hellgate," apparently the Hoorn's Hook patent; while De Forest, expending his means in building several fine houses in New Amsterdam, sold his plantation, November 10th, 1650, to the distinguished burgher Wilhelmus Beeckman. But both Beeck and Beeckman resided in town,*

* PIETER CORNELISE BEECK, whose tragical fate remains to be noticed, was master carpenter to the West India Co., in New Netherland, and was b. in 1607, at Rotterdam. He came out early *via* Amsterdam, where he had resided, with him coming his w. Aeltie Willems, and a young dr. Marritie, who in 1635 m. Pieter Jacobsen Marius, a prominent merchant at N. Y. who emigrated in 1644 from Hoogwoudt, his desc. now writing their name Morris. See *Bergen Gen.* Pieter Beech had other chn. b. here, viz., *William*, Deborah, who m. 1667 Warner Wessels; Elizabeth, who m. Capt. Silvester Salisbury, Dr. Corn. van Dyck and Capt. Geo. Bradshaw; Cornelia, who m. 1672 Jacobus de Haert, and *Cornelius*, who m. 1677 Marritie Claessen, and had sons Peter, Nicholas, John, Isaac, William, Henry. From these we presume all the Beecks of this stock have sprung. *William Beeck*, b. 1640, son of Pieter, m. Anna, dr. of Tielman van Vleeck (notary public and first sheriff of Bergen), and d. at Esopus in 1684, leaving issue Peter, Tielman, Aeltie, and Deborah, who all d. chless. The wid., Anna, m. 1686 *Capt. Jacob Phenix*, a son of whom by this union, Capt. Alex. Phenix, was fa. to Hon. Daniel Phoenix, fa. of the late Rev. Alexander Phoenix, of H.

and there Kuyter had entered upon trade, on the Heere Graft, now Broad Street, enjoying a respite from the ills which had hitherto beset his pathway, and retaining a warm regard for his compatriot Melyn. We have dwelt the more fully on Kuyter's case, not only as an interesting passage in Harlem's infantile history, but because it shows how the old struggle with arbitrary power, which had long convulsed European countries, was thus early renewed on this free soil. Kuyter was a representative man. Many like him held that the people had rights as well as their rulers, and that one of these, of vital importance to the colonists, was that of appeal to higher courts in fatherland from verdicts rendered here, the denial of which right was a cause of much public clamor against both Kieft and Stuyvesant. Kuyter had proved the fallacy of that assumption, and had achieved a victory, not for himself alone, but for the community, for which he was held in highest respect.*

* ISAAC ADRIANCE, gone but not forgotten, was in many respects and in the best sense another Kuyter. "In his life were exhibited Dutch courage and firmness, along with New England enterprise and activity. A true benevolence marked his character, and a high sense of justice. He hated robbery and wrong, and set himself especially against abuses under municipal law. He sought to reform that law and its administration, and had a powerful influence in doing so. He honored the schoolhouse and the church, and was ever ready to aid them; and many a public work, now deemed noble and valuable, owed its origin in part to his sagacity and labor. Many a young man owed to his kind interest in his welfare the course of his after life, and his success in it. Hundreds of shade-trees now adorn the streets and avenues of Harlem, planted by him." Fond of such matters, he had gathered a mass of information relative to that section, and especially to its land titles, both in MSS., and in the storehouse of his retentive memory; and which, with an enlightened liberality that so distinguished him, he permitted the author to make free use of for the compilation of this work. Mr. Adriance was b. Feb. 13, 1794, in the old Sickels house spoken of on page 136, was educated at Yale, and devoted his life to the law. He d. Aug. 26, 1863. He was a lineal desc. of *Adriaen Reyerse*, an early settler at Flatbush, L. I., the son probably of Reyer Elberts, from Utrecht, whose w. by a former hus. was mo. of Goosen Gerritse van Schaick, anc. of the Albany Van Schaicks. See *Pearson*. Adriaen Reyerse came to this country, as he stated, in 1646. He m. July 24, 1659, Anna, dr. of Martin Schenck, a name of celebrity in Holland; was a leading man and an elder at Flatbush, and d. Nov. 24, 1710. One of his chn., Elbert, b. 1663, settled in Flushing, m. 1689, Catalina, dr. of Rem Vanderbeeck, anc. of the Remsens, and by her had Rem, Elbert, and Anneke; these retaining the patronymic (whence Adriance), as their surname. Rem m. Sarah, dr. of George Brinckerhoff; and d., æ. 40 yrs., in 1730. His sons were, Elbert, b. 1715; George, 1716; Abraham, 1720; Isaac, 1723; Jacob, 1727; Rem, 1729. George, Abraham, and Isaac went to Dutchess Co.; Isaac m. Letetia van Wyck and Ida Schenck, and was fa. of Rem, Theodore, Isaac, John, and Caroline, who m. Charles Platt, of Plattsburgh. John came to Harlem after the Revolution, m. Mary, dr. of John S. Sickels, and d. Oct. 23, 1849, æ. 87 yrs., being the father of Isaac, first named.

CHAPTER X.

1651–1656.

NEW EFFORTS, BUT SAD FAILURES.

KUYTER'S thoughts now turned wistfully toward his deserted bouwery at Zegendal, which stood in danger of forfeiture for non-improvement. He longed to make one more attempt to occupy his broad acres, if by the favor of Heaven he might retrieve the misfortunes of the dozen checkered years that had passed since his eye first rested with delight upon that lovely spot. But his unaided means were inadequate to the effort. His house and barns must be rebuilt, the soil again brought under the plow. The course he took to effect it is explained in the following instrument.

THIS DAY, the 23d of September 1651, a friendly agreement was made between Mr. JOCHEM PIETERSEN KUYTER, a free merchant on one side; and the Hon. PETRUS STUYVESANT, Director General of New Netherland, Curaçao, and its dependencies, LUCAS RODENBURG, Governor of Curaçao, and CORNELIS DE POTTER, free merchant, of the other side, concerning a piece of land lying on Manhattan Island, and belonging to said Jochem Pietersen Kuyter, named *Zegendal*, or by the Indians called *Schorrakin*, bounded on the south by land of William Beeckman, Lieutenant of the Burgher Company at this place, and westward by the bounds of the Hon. Johannes La Montagne, so on in a north course to the first rock, and on the east to the Great Kill; having to the west toward the North River, a meadow of three or four morgen; the aforesaid land containing about two hundred morgen, yet not precisely known, but remaining to be ascertained with more accuracy; on the following conditions, viz:

That said Kuyter shall cede, transport and convey to the said Stuyvesant, Rodenburg and De Potter the three fourth parts of said land, being one fourth part for each, while the said Kuyter retains one fourth part for himself, and to his own behoof, upon condition that the said Kuyter shall receive from the aforesaid gentlemen the sum of One Thousand Carolus Guilders, of which sum each of said gentlemen is to pay a third part, with the understanding that the said money is to be employed at once in the cultivation of the said land; which land is to remain undivided, until it is agreed by a majority of those interested, to make a partition of the shares.

During which time said Jochem Pietersen Kuyter is to remain the cultivator and superintendent of all the land, to the greatest profit and best advantage of all interested, among whom he is to distribute the profits in equal shares, whether such profits come from grain, stock, or otherwise. It being understood, however, that the wife of Jochem Pietersen Kuyter may keep for her family some hens and ducks. The said Kuyter shall receive for his services, as cultivator, one hundred and fifty guilders (per annum), that is to say, each of the three co-partners shall pay fifty guilders.

And in order to make a good beginning, with God's assistance, there shall be built at the expense of said partners, on the land aforesaid, a suitable dwelling house to accommodate the said Kuyter. But this dwelling house shall be the property of all the partners in common; and Kuyter shall keep a correct account of all expenses connected therewith, and of other expenses, and communicate it to the partners.

And it is further stipulated that as soon as any distribution of grain is made, or that the land shall be divided by the partners aforesaid, the said Kuyter shall previously receive his thousand guilders for the transfer and cession of said land, and when such division shall take place, it shall be done by lot, without allowing any preference to any of the parties. Further stipulated that in case of the absence of one of the partners, another must be put in his place, and secondly that in case the said cultivator should die, another may be placed in his stead, though all the partners be not consulted. Further, that in case of such decease, the widow of the deceased shall succeed in his share, or may transfer it to one of the partners.

And therefore that this contract may have full effect, said Jochem Pietersen Kuyter transfers his lands to the partners aforesaid, as if he had actually received the stipulated sum; while they on their part, for his security, submit their persons and property, real and personal, present and future, to the control of any court of justice. In witness whereof it is signed at New Amsterdam.

Jochiem Pr. Kuyter.
P. Stuyvesant.
L. Rodenburg.
Cornelis De Potter.

Witness, Nicholas Blank.

In presence of me,
Jacob Kip, *Clerk*.

But the state of the country was becoming "more and more disquieted." Under such circumstances, no wonder that Kuyter hesitated about proceeding to restore his ruined buildings and fences, more especially as he could show no deed for his lands, which had either never been executed or had been lost in some one of his disasters. This left his boundaries if not his title in uncertainty. But, applying for a groundbrief and receiving a favorable answer (Montagne and Van Tienhoven stating to the council their knowledge of the original grant by

Kieft, and its limits), Kuyter was reassured on this point, and led to prosecute his work, though with no slight misgivings as to the result.* The farmers on the Flats had no heart to make improvements which in an evil hour might be laid in ruins by the savages, who, on pretext of not having been paid for their lands, did not hesitate, as a chance offered, still to attack and murder the settlers on the scattered bouweries. Thus it soon after happened to Pieter Beeck, before noticed, formerly deacon and now one of the selectmen, to which office he and Kuyter had recently been appointed. He and three workmen, while engaged at his bouwery near Hellgate, May 17th, 1652, were surprised by savages and all cruelly murdered.

Kuyter, Beeckman and others were threatened to have their bouweries burned, should no satisfaction be given. Montagne was otherwise embarrassed. Heavily indebted to the company and burdened with a large family, he was dependent upon the director or government for a meagre support, and had no means to expend on his deserted plantation. Many persons who would have undertaken new bouweries were kept from doing so "through dread of the Indians and their threats." The public disquietude was greatly enhanced during this year and the next by absurd rumors that the Dutch authorities were plotting with the Indians to cut off the English residents in and near Manhattan; reports which had well nigh caused a rupture with the New England colonies, and so wrought upon some of the neighboring English settlers upon Long Island that they left hastily and took refuge in Connecticut. As the natural effect of this state of things, no new bouweries had thus far "been formed on the Island of Manhattan during Director Stuyvesant's administration," though "some had been abandoned."

Kuyter in the mean time won for himself a large share of

* "JOCHEM KUYTER, by petition, requested a groundbrief for his lands which the Hon. Dr. W. Kieft, deceased, gave him in the year 1639, in July; and which were pointed out by Mr. Montagne and the Secretary.

"*The Director and Council answer:* The applicant is directed to take a copy of his groundbrief from the register book of the groundbriefs, where the Director and Council think the same is recorded. If it is not, he shall be preferred before others, and a new groundbrief of his lands be executed; in case the petitioner remains inclined, according to promise, again to improve and cultivate his lands. Done in meeting of the Director and Council, the 29th January 1652." Extract from *Council Minutes*.

the public favor as one foremost in the church, and since he was chosen, January 30th, 1652, an efficient member of the board of selectmen. After this, on an important occasion, Stuyvesant honored him with a request to sit with the council. Indeed it excited surprise that one "whom the director formerly, for the affair of the selectmen, did publicly banish the country with ringing of the bell," should have been reinstated in the same office, and also in the eldership. But a new honor was now conferred upon him, a seat among the schepens of New Amsterdam, on the first institution of that office here in 1653. Usually present at their sittings, so valued were his counsels that on some special occasions a messenger was sent to Zegendal to solicit his attendance. But on March 2d, 1654, he met with the city council for the last time. The threats of the Indians were now to be put in execution. Only a few days after, the savages murdered him in his house on his bouwery. Secure in their city home, his family were spared his fate.*

Kuyter's death caused a profound sensation. The community had lost a good and useful member, and with unfeigned sorrow Stuyvesant announced the sad event to the directors in Holland, who responded with expressions of regret at his untimely death. Labor on the bouwery was necessarily interrupted for a time. On April 22d following, Kuyter's widow, Leentie Martens, empowered two of her friends, Govert Loockermans and the notary Dirck Schelluyne, "to proceed to the liquidating, taking and fairly closing to the final account and *reliquia*, with Director General Petrus Stuyvesant, Hon. Lucas Rodenburg, and Mr. Cornelis De Potter, regarding the

* THE INDIANS were resolved upon expelling the whites from this end of the Island, upon the ground that they had not been duly paid for their lands. True the Indians had sold the Island to the company in 1626, and by virtue of this purchase the government had made the land grants to the settlers. Of course the latter deemed their title good and valid. But it is certain that the Indians did not recognise the sale aforesaid as a surrender of all their rights and privileges on this part of the Island. Perhaps, grown wiser in a generation, they saw that the trivial price then paid them ($24) was no equivalent for their rich maize land and hunting-grounds. But they probably claimed to have reserved (as they often did in their sales) the right of hunting and planting, because in after years the Harlem people so far admitted their pretensions as to make them further compensation. Well had it been for the colonists had they earlier given heed to the dissatisfaction of the Indians and done something to remove it.

lands named Zegendal, belonging to her deceased husband, with the effects, as they were farmed and cultivated by her said husband in company with the above named gentleman, pursuant to contract dated the 23d September, 1651."

These managed to keep the farm under tillage, while the widow, in the persons of other friends, gave bonds for the delivery of the grain which should be raised, in satisfaction of the claims of the several partners. For two summers the farm work went on, the sowing, reaping, and gathering the ripened harvest; not, however, without much distrust of the wily savages and fears for their personal safety. So insecure was it considered that the sureties for Mrs. Kuyter required of the other owners indemnity bonds "for all losses and interests which should occur through fire, robbery, or other unexpected accident, either to the lands of the late Kuyter or to the crops." These apprehensions of further trouble from the Indians were well grounded. This island and its vicinity now of a sudden became the scene of ruthless massacre.

Very early one morning, September 15th, 1655, sixty-four canoes of armed savages landed on the beach at New Amsterdam, and before scarcely any one had risen scattered about the town and began to break into the houses for plunder. All was alarm and confusion, and to make matters worse, Stuyvesant was absent, having departed on an expedition to the Delaware a few days before, taking with him most of the garrison. The members of the council finally prevailed with the chiefs and their people to withdraw from the city, but at evening they returned, and a skirmish took place between them and the Dutch soldiers, blood flowing on both sides. The now enraged Indians departed, but on that doleful night began a horrible slaughter of the settlers, full fifty of whom fell within three days, while over an hundred, mostly women and children, were carried into captivity.

Hordes of armed savages, thirsting for blood, swept over these Flats, slaying the settlers, plundering and burning their houses, and devastating their bouweries. Cornelis Claessen Swits, whose father, as we have seen, had been killed by an Indian, now owned the farm on the Flats originally granted to Isaac de Forest, but which Swits had purchased from Beeckman,

March 10th, 1653, selling the latter in exchange his plantation near Corler's Hook, later known as the "Delancey Farms." * Since his good *vrouw* Adriana had lost her father, Cornelis Trommels, of Rengerskerk, a quiet hamlet in the Island of Schouwen, what changes she had experienced! Left an orphan to the care of a guardian at Brouwershaven, she had, after other vicissitudes, found a home on those beautiful but solitary plains, having since her arrival here inherited some property

* WILHELMUS BEECKMAN, whose desc., numerous and highly respectable, have usually written their name *Beekman*, was a son of Hendrick Beeckman, by his w. Mary, dr. of the excellent Wilhelmus Baudartius, annalist, and pastor at Zutphen, in Gelderland, at which place our Beeckman was b. April 28, 1623. Holgate (*Am. Genealogy*) says he was b. at Hasselt, in Overyssel, but Beeckman's marriage entry in the N. Y. Coll. Chh. Rec., more reliable as indited by himself, says at Zutphen. Coming out to Manhattan, in 1647, to serve as a clerk for the W. I. Comp., the next year he exchanged this for a mercantile life, and the year following m. a young lady from Amsterdam, Catharine, dr. of Hendrick de Boog. Being "an honest and polite man," he was elected schepen in 1653, and began a long and honorable public service. His "ability, piety, and experience" gained him the position of Vice Director on the Delaware, which he held from 1658 to 1663. Then recalled and made sheriff at Esopus, he served as such till the close of Gov. Lovelace's rule, when he engaged in the brewing business at the Smith's Fly, in N. Y. Filling an alderman's seat much of the time, till his final retirement in 1696, and having also served as an elder both at Kingston and at N. Y., he d. in this city in his 85th year, Sept. 21, 1707. He had nine chn., viz., Maria, b. 1650, m. Nicholas William Stuyvesant, son of the governor; Hendrick, b. 1652, Gerardus, b. 1653, Cornelia, b. 1655, m. Capt. Isaac van Vleck; Johannes, b. 1656, Jacobus, b. 1658, d. 1679, William, b. 1661, Martinus, b. 1663, and Catharine, b. 1668, who m. Gerard Duyckinck, as per Holgate, p. 75. Of these, *Martinus* is not again named, unless he that joined the military force sent by Leisler to Albany in 1690. *William*, who united with the N. Y. church in 1681, became a Labadist. *Johannes*, "a mariner," m. in 1685 Aeltie, dr. of Thomas Popinga, from Groningen, and in 1699 removed to Kingston, N. Y.; issue William, Thomas, Johannes, Hendrick, Mary, Catharine, Rachel. *Hendrick*, who also settled in Kingston, m. 1681 Johanna, wid. of Joris Davidsen and dr. of Capt. Jacob Loper; issue William, Catharine, Hendrick, and Cornelia. *Gerardus*, M.D., of Flatbush and N. Y., m. Oct. 25, 1677, Magdalena, dr. of Stoffel Janse Abeel, of Albany. He d. Oct. 10, 1723. His chn. were William, b. Jan. 25, 1679, d. young; Christopher, b. Jan. 4, 1681, m. Mary, dr. of Abram Delanoy; Adrian, b. Aug. 22, 1682, m. Aletta Lispenard and Lucretia De Key; William, M.D., b. Aug. 8, 1684, m. Catharine, dr. of Peter Delanoy; Jacobus, M.D., b. Aug. 7, 1687, m. Elizabeth, dr. of Johannes de Peyster; Catharine, b. May 25, 1689, m. Charles Le Roux; Gerardus, b. June 9, 1693, m. Anna Maria Van Horne and Catharine Provoost; Cornelia, b. May 25, 1698, m. Richard Van Dam; Hendrick, of N. Y., merchant, b. Dec. 11, 1701, d. unm. Sept. 4, 1743; and Maria, b. Jan. 10, 1704, m. Jacob Walton. Our distinguished New York Beekmans have been chiefly of this branch. For fuller details consult Holgate's mainly accurate account before cited, and also *Our Home*, which contains a valuable but not faultless article upon the Beekman family.

from an aunt in Zeeland. She was now the mother of five children between the ages of three and fifteen years. Swits had built him a house, and labored hard upon his farm of fifty morgen, in clearing the land, etc., hoping by patient industry to cancel a debt of seven hundred guilders due the West India Company for commodities advanced to him. His good friend Tobias Teunissen was equally busy on the bouwery near Spuyten Duyvel. His present wife, whom he had married in 1649, was a daughter of Claes Boone, of Amsterdam, at which place her mother, Beatrice Hermans, was still living, on the Boomstraat. Jannetie also had had her trials, having lost a former husband, Urbano Leursen, with whom she had come to New Netherland (we think he perished in the Princess, on board which he had served), and who left her with three children, other three being added after she married Tobias, though but one was surviving, namely Teunis, now between four and five years of age.

These two households felt the full force of the Indian raid. Being "miserably surprised by the cruel, barbarous savages," both Swits and Teunissen were massacred, their goods plundered or burned, and their terrified wives and little ones captured and hurried away to their haunts in the forest. The crops on the bouweries were destroyed, and the cattle either killed, driven off, or left to wander in the woods. The same scene was enacted at the Kuyter bouwery. The grain, etc., was burned, but, sadder still, the widow Kuyter, now the wife of Willem Jansen, from Heerde, in Gelderland, also fell a victim to savage fury, though the husband by some means escaped.*

The Indians had threatened "to root out the Dutch," and well they kept their word; nor did they spare the English

* JOCHEM PIETERSEN KUYTER was no ordinary man. His career was one of those not so rare in human history, which seem a failure in the light of worldly ambition, but when viewed from a higher standpoint, both a success and a triumph. Not in his laudable efforts to subdue the wilderness, but by his bold defense of popular rights, he conferred invaluable benefits upon his fellow-colonists and those succeeding them, and which entitles him to a place on the roll of public benefactors. Kuyter should have a memorial in Central Park. It is an interesting query whether his desc. do not compose the highly respectable family of Keator, seated very early in Marbletown, Ulster Co., most patriotic "associators" in behalf of Independence in 1775, though now widely scattered, some having Anglicised their name into *Cator*. These are traced back to *Meindert Claes Keeter*, b. at Amsterdam, who m., in 1674, wid. Susanna Richards, from Oxford, and settled in Marbletown.

either. All the neighboring settlements were also swept off. The lands of Vander Donck, "bordering on our island, and only parted from it by a small creek, in some places passable at low water," had been "divided and settled by his children and associates, in various plantations and farms, but which in the massacre were abandoned." The occupants of Jonas Bronck's land met with no better fate. Adjoining to Bronck's land lay Cornell's Neck; its patentee, Thomas Cornell, an Englishman from Herefordshire, who had served the company as a soldier, "was driven off his lands by the barbarous violence of the Indians, who burned his house and goods and destroyed his cattle." On Long Island side the house and plantation of William Hallett, another Englishman, opposite Hoorn's Hook, "were laid waste by the Indians." Their canoes kept prowling about Hellgate, and on October 13th about thirty savages stealthily approached the house of Hallett's neighbor, Pieter Andriessen, living at the present Ravenswood, and the same who came over with Bronck. He and five other persons who chanced that day to be at his house were attacked, four of the six wounded, and all captured; the savages then having the effrontery to send two of them to New Amsterdam, with an offer to release the others on receiving some guns, ammunition, etc., which they demanded.

In a few days the Indians, having glutted their revenge, and willing to get the captives off their hands, made overtures, which resulted in the ransom, during the month of October, of a large number, but the families of Teunissen and Swits were not included. Meanwhile Stuyvesant having returned from the "conquest" of the Swedish colony on the Delaware, his soldiers were ready for an exterminating war upon the Indians, and which some strongly advised. But this was opposed by Montagne in the council, on the ground of their weakness. "If," he urged with a convincing logic, "we have no power to prosecute a war, then it becomes necessary that we remain quiet till we shall obtain it, and meanwhile not to place too much confidence in the Indians. As for the great damage we have suffered from the savages, I know of no remedy, because reparation seems not to be had from them either by war or peace; and with respect to the captives, experience has taught us that they cannot be recovered without a ransom." This moderate and discreet advice met the approval of the director himself, who also expressed his opinion that the first attack upon the Dutch was not premeditated, but was provoked by a "too hasty rashness on the part of a few hot-headed spirits."

Parties were sent out to bury the dead and collect the stray stock. Such a scene was presented of poor slaughtered remains, blackened ruins, and general devastation as appalled the hearts even of brave soldiers. Some of the cattle belonging to the murdered Swits were found in the woods, brought in and cared for. And toward the close of November his widow and children, with those of Tennissen, were happily restored to their friends at New Amsterdam.* The hostile attitude of the Indians and the fear "of being again as suddenly surprised" were an effectual bar to any present attempt at rebuilding the ruined habitations on the Flats. Indeed, such of the settlers as survived were impoverished; "dispossessed of their properties, and not left wherewith to provide food and clothing." And though others, having courage and means, would venture upon these lands and run the hazard, they were now wholly prevented from so doing by an ordinance of the director and council, passed January 18th, 1656, which prohibited all persons from dwelling in exposed situations, and required the farmers upon isolated bouweries to forthwith remove, with their families, into the nearest village, where they could abide more safely, be able to act in concert in case of danger, and go out in armed parties to till their lands and gather their crops.

Such an ordinance was a necessity. The history of settlement on these Flats, up to this period, presented but a series of adversities, and it was time to arrest these single-handed attempts to plant bouweries, costing as they had so many valuable lives. Need we recount the gloomy roll of the dead?—De Forest, the

* TOBIAS TEUNISSEN, with no such culture as shone forth in Kuyter, yet possessed measurably those sterling qualities needed to battle manfully with adversities, and he deserves honorable mention among those pioneer settlers by whose toils and sacrifices the way was paved for the ultimate success of the settlement. His wid. m. Thomas Verdon, of Brooklyn, where both joined the chh. in 1661. Her son *Teunis Tobias*, b. in 1651, was living in 1692, on his farm at Gowanus (*Deeds*, Brooklyn, vol. 1 : 313), but search and inquiry fail to trace him farther. Perhaps his desc. compose the Tobias family, found from an early date in the States of N. J. and N. Y.

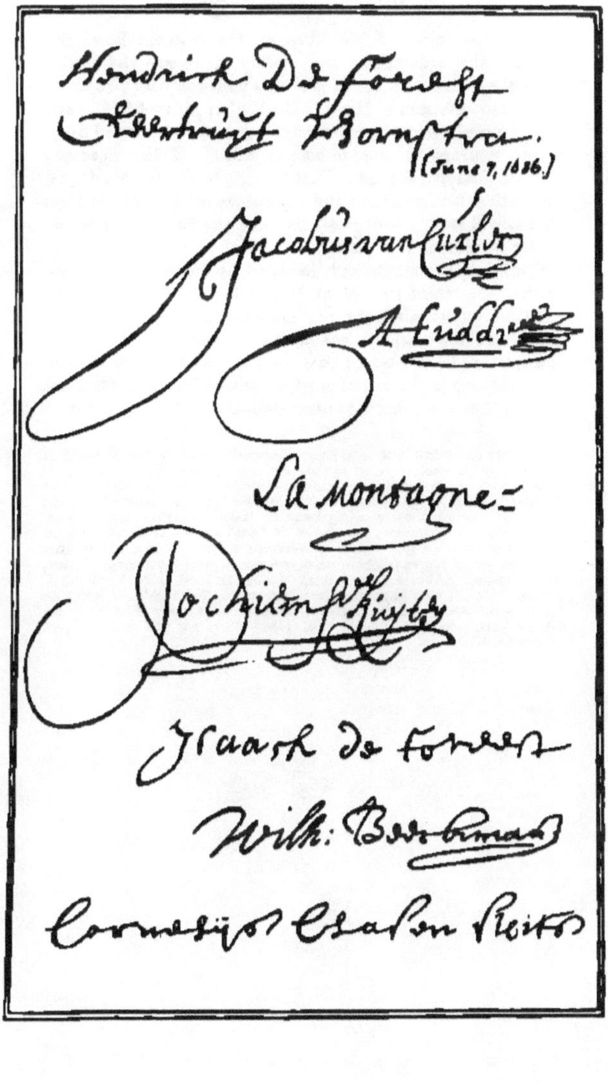

Hendrick De foreest

Aldertruyt Bornstra.

(June 7, 1636.)

Jacobus van Curler

A. Hudde

La Montagne

Jochiem Kuyter

Isaack de foreest

Wilh: Beeckman

Cornelis Claesen Sleits

pioneer, the respected Van Rossum, the excellent Beeck and Kuyter, the industrious and worthy Tennisen and Swits! Governor Rodenburg, one of Kuyter's partners, also died about this time. Claessen of Hoorn's Hook, after his visit to Holland for redress of personal grievances charged upon Kieft and Stuyvesant, returned no more to his plantation. Willem Bont and Matthys Jansen had gone to Fort Orange, as also Dr. Montagne, who with exhausted means and no prospect of any returns from his wasted bouwery had gladly accepted the honorable position of vice-director at that place.*

Bereft of inhabitants and desolated by firebrand and tomahawk; the current rumors of Indian threats which still agitated the public mind, the prohibition against isolated settlements, and the complications arising in regard to the interests and estates of the persons slain in the late massacres were so many barriers in the way of any immediate effort to rescue these fertile plains and primeval forests from the wildness of nature.

* SIBOUT CLAESSEN, first proprietor of Hoorn's Hook, showed strength of character by his resolute stand against the assumptions of Stuyvesant. It accords with the belief that his parents were Friesans—most stalwart and strong-minded of Netherlanders—and had removed to Hoorn before his birth: for Sibout was no doubt cousin-german to Harck Siboutsen, from Langedyk, on the river Kuinre, in the district of Zevenwolden, or Seven Forests. See "Cronkhite Family," *Annals of Newtown*, p. 316. Claessen m. in 1645 Susannah, dr. of Jan van Schoonenburg and wid. of Aert Teunisz van Putten, before noticed. After returning from Holland he lived in N. Y. till his d. in 1680. He left 1000 gl., wampum value, to the Dutch chh., of which he and w. were mem., and his remaining estate on the decease of his w. to her drs. by Teunissen, viz., Wyntie, w. of *Simon Barentsen*, and Susannah, w. of *Reynier Willemsen*.

CHAPTER XI.

1656–1660.

NEW HAARLEM FOUNDED; ITS COURT AND CHURCH.

AN interesting period in our history is that which gave origin to the village of Harlem. This inviting section of Manhattan was to be peopled and cultivated; but by some new and more efficient mode than that already tried, fruitful only in unrequited labor, the waste of property, and the loss of precious lives. It could only be done by the direct aid of government. The farm owners were nearly all dead; their estates insolvent. La Montagne and Swits, having had large advances from the public stores to supply the wants of their families, were deeply indebted to the company: Swits in the sum of seven hundred guilders, to satisfy which, with "other debts," he left nothing but his ruined bouwery. Dr. La Montagne, as early as 1652, was reputed to be owing the company "several thousand guilders." As Vice-Director, his salary of six hundred florins, with an extra allowance for board of two hundred florins per annum (increased in 1659 to three hundred), proving inadequate to his support, things had gone from bad to worse, and were fast tending to that crisis in his affairs which, in 1662, wrung from him the touching admission to Stuyvesant, that he had not the means of providing bread for his family, and being sixty-eight years of age, was reduced to penury and want.

The Kuyter heirs were in no better case, and "divers persons interested in the estate" began to clamor for its settlement. Proceedings to this end were begun soon after Mrs. Kuyter's death; when, on a petition from Gov. Stuyvesant, "relative to certain share belonging to him," the burgomasters ordered "that an inventory be taken of the lands, houses, and other effects of the deceased Jochem Pieterson Kuyter, and of his widow, she having remarried, and being now dead; so that his Honor, as well as the other private creditors, may obtain justice." Next came a claim, preferred against one of Mrs. Kuyter's sureties by Cornelis De Potter, for a balance due him, which was to have been paid in grain from the farm; but the court rejected the demand, upon the ground that "the grain had been destroyed in the troubles with the Indians," and De Potter had covenanted not to hold the bail responsible for any default arising from such losses.

Two years passed, when the plans having matured for closing up the estate of "Jochem Pietersen Kuyter and Leentie Martens his wife, killed by the Indians," their city residence on the Heere Graft was put up at public sale by the administrators, January 12th, 1658, and struck off to one of the schepens, Hendrick Jansen Vander Vin, later a resident of Harlem, to whom, on February 14th, the burgomasters gave a deed.

As to the Zegendal lands and others adjacent, the Director and Council, with a just regard for all the interests involved, both of a public and private nature, resolved upon forming a village there, by laying out suitable building and farming lots, to be sold to settlers at a fixed price per morgen, and to apply the moneys so derived for the benefit of the late proprietors, their heirs or creditors. The Van Keulen tract, besides the Kuyter lands, was to be disposed of, with the Swits bouwery lying between them; and the cleared portion of the latter was fixed upon as the village site.* As Stuyvesant owned a fourth part of

* CORNELIS CLAESSEN SWITS, whose history, with that of his fa., as before related, challenges romance, had 10 chn.; of whom reached maturity only Claes, b. 1640, Isaac, b. 1642, Jacob, b. 1645, Apollonia, b. 1648, and Cornelis, b. 1651. His wid. had one or more chn. by her second hus.; Albert Leenderts. Apollonia Swits m. Jan Thomase Aken, and their dr. m. Vincent Delamontagne. Claes Swits was accidentally killed at Albany in 1663. Cornelis joined the church at Kingston, Ulster Co., in 1678, was afterwards an elder, and d. 1734, in the town of Rochester, leaving only his wid., Jannetie, dr. of Tjerck De Witt.

Isaac Corneliassen Swits, the only son, as far as is known, who left desc., was familiarly called "Kleyn Isaac," or Little Isaac. He settled at Schenectady, where his posterity have been among the most respectable residents. By his w., Susanna, dr. of Simon Groot, he had 8 chn., of whom need be named only *Cornelius*, *Simon*, and *Jacob*; all of whom left desc. At the sack of Schenectady by the French and Indians, Feb. 8, 1690, Isaac, for the second time, became a captive, he and his eldest son Cornelius, æ. ab. 12 yrs., being taken with other prisoners to Canada; but after five months' captivity Isaac escaped, reaching Albany, July 9, and was soon followed by his

the Kuytor tract, he reserved his share, probably to avoid unpleasant complications; so that only 150 morgen of this tract were to be laid out into lots. These lands being deemed ample for the wants of the proposed village for some time to come, the Vredendal or Montagne farm was not as yet included; in fact, it was held that "it could not be from thence conveniently cultivated, being over a kill."

The government had another important object in view besides that of obtaining its dues, or promoting the settlement of this district. This was to enhance the safety of the city of New Amsterdam, as would naturally result from planting a strong village, with a garrison, on this frontier end of the island. But in carrying out this design, as already hinted, neither the honest efforts of the late owners to comply with the terms of their grants by improving their lands, neither their misfortunes and heavy losses, were lost sight of. True, these lands had been granted subject to the imperative condition that the soil should be brought under tillage. By such means were the resources of the country to be developed, its growth promoted. Not to comply with this condition was ordinarily to forfeit the grant, even though a patent had issued; in which case the government felt

son. Gov. Leisler shortly after gave Swits a commission as lieut. of militia. While he was in Canada a fort was built on his lot in Schenectady, in lieu of which he was granted 1000 acres along the east side of the Mohawk, for which he also got a deed from the Indians Aug. 16, 1707. He survived this only about a month, but this purchase was confirmed to his son Cornelius, as his heir at law, by patent of Apl. 14, 1708. *Cornelius*, in 1702. m. Hester Fisher, and lived in Albany. *Simon* m. Geslna Beekman in 1711, and resided at Schenectady. The other br., *Jacob Swits*, of Schenectady, b. 1695, m. 1719, Helena De Witt, of Esopus, by whom he had issue, Isaac, b. 1720, Andries, 1723, Susanna, 1726, Jannetie, 1727, Abraham, 1730, Cornelius, 1733, and Maria, 1737. Abraham, known as Major Swits, at eighteen yrs. distinguished himself for his courage on the day of the Beckendal battle, when the Indians killed 32 of the best men of Schenectady. In the Revolutionary war he held a commission as "First Major of the Regiment of Militia, of which Abraham Wemple is Colonel," dated June 20, 1778. Two of his sons bore arms in that struggle, viz., Walter and Jacob, the latter afterwards Major General of the state militia. After the war Major Swits resided in a brick house on the north corner of Maiden Lane and State Street. In this house was b. his gd-son, the late F. N. Clute, of Herkimer, who always spoke with interest of his gd-fa. Swits. Major Swits d. Aug. 17, 1814, having had thirteen chn., nine by his last w. Margaret, dr. of John Delamont, whom he m. Nov. 22, 1760. Their son Jacob, b. Nov. 3, 1762, was fa. of the late Rev. Abraham J. Swits, of Schenectady; and their dr. Susanna, b. June 12, 1766, became w. of Nicholas F. Clute, and mo. of Mr. Frederick N. Clute aforesaid, who was b. at Schenectady, March 12, 1797 and d. Dec. 15, 1879 See *Pearson's Schenectady Settlers.*

warranted, and usually did not hesitate, to reclaim the land and give it to others as it pleased. But as manifest injustice would result from applying the above rule of forfeiture to the specific cases under consideration, where the unfortunate proprietors had done what they could and had failed through no fault of their own, it behooved the government, in whatever action it might take touching these lands, to have a proper regard for the interests of the said proprietors, while exercising the usual prerogative of the civil power, the right of *eminent domain*, or that of judging how far private interests and convenience must yield to the public necessities; and, under the Dutch rule, it had always been held "that a private farm or plantation ought never to be prejudicial to a village." How far this measure was agreed to by the parties interested, does not appear; but it certainly commended itself as the readiest way to make these otherwise useless lands yield them some returns, whereby to relieve their indebtedness to the government and others. It was this conjunction of circumstances that called forth the following ordinance:

The DIRECTOR GENERAL AND COUNCIL OF NEW NETHERLAND hereby give notice, that for the further promotion of agriculture, for the security of this Island and the cattle pasturing thereon, as well as for the further relief and expansion of this City Amsterdam,* in New Netherland, they have resolved to form a new Village or Settlement at the end of the Island, and about the land of Jochem Pietersen, deceased, and those which are adjoining to it. In order that the lovers of agriculture may be encouraged thereto, the proposed new Village aforesaid is favored by the Director-General and Council with the following Privileges:

First: Each of the Inhabitants thereof shall receive by lot in full ownership, 18, 20, to 24, morgen of arable Land; 6 to 8 morgen of Meadow; and be exempt from Tenths for fifteen years commencing next May; on condition that he pay within the course of three years, in instalments, Eight guilders for each morgen of tillable land for the behoof of the interested, or their creditors, who are now or formerly were driven from the aforesaid Lands, and have suffered great loss thereon.

Secondly: In order to prevent similar damage from calamities or expulsions, the Director-General and Council promise the Inhabitants of the aforesaid Village to protect and maintain them with all their power, and, when notified and required, to assist them with 12 to 15 Soldiers on the monthly pay of the Company, the Village providing quarters and rations; This whenever the Inhabitants may petition therefor.

Thirdly: When the aforesaid Village has 20 to 25 Families, the Director-General and Council will favor it with an Inferior Court of Jus-

* The words in the original are, "tot meerder *recreatie* en *uytspanninge* van dese Stede Amsterdam," etc.

tice; and for that purpose, a double number is to be nominated out of the most discreet and proper persons, for the first time by the Inhabitants, and afterward by the Magistrates thereof, and presented annually to the Director-General and Council, to elect a single number therefrom.

Fourthly: The Director-General and Council promise to employ all possible means that the Inhabitants of the aforesaid Village, when it has the above-mentioned number of Families, will be accommodated with a good, pious, orthodox Minister, toward whose maintenance the Director-General and Council promise to pay half the Salary, the other half to be supplied by the Inhabitants in the best and easiest manner, with the advice of the Magistrates of the aforesaid Village, at the most convenient time.

Fifthly: The Director-General and Council will assist the Inhabitants of the aforesaid Village, whenever it will best suit their convenience, to construct, with the Company's Negroes, a good wagon road from this place to the village aforesaid, so that people can travel hither and thither on horseback and with a wagon.

Sixthly: In order that the advancement of the aforesaid Village may be the sooner and better promoted, the Director-General and Council have resolved and determined not to establish, or allow to be established, any new villages or settlements, before and until the aforesaid Village be brought into existence; certainly not until the aforesaid number of Inhabitants is completed.

Seventhly: For the better and greater promotion of neighborly correspondence with the English of the North, the Director-General and Council will at a more convenient time authorize a Ferry and a suitable Scow near the aforesaid Village, in order to convey over Cattle and Horses; and will favor the aforesaid Village with a Cattle and Horse Market.

Eighthly: Whoever are inclined to settle themselves there or to take up Bouweries by their servants, shall be bound to enter their names at once, or within a short time, at the office of the Secretary of the Director-General and Council, and to begin immediately with others to place on the land one able-bodied person, provided with proper arms, or in default thereof, to be deprived of his right.

Thus done in the meeting of the Director and Council, held in Fort Amsterdam, in New Netherland, on the 4th of March, A° 1658.

The number of applicants for the land being sufficient to warrant a beginning, ground was broken for the new settlement August 14th ensuing; between which date and September 10th was completed the preliminary work of surveying and staking out the lands and village plot, etc. Hilarity and good-cheer marked the occasion, for one of those present was Johan Verveelen, not till five years later a resident, but who acted as tapster, regaling the company with generous potions of his New Amsterdam beer.

The village was laid out adjoining the Great Kill or Harlem river, taking for the principal street what had apparently been used before as a road by the ill-fated Swits and others, or at least an Indian trail. Touching the river (about 125th Street) just north of a small cove, where a ferry to *Bronckside*, or Morrisania, was soon established, it lay "about east and west," continuing beyond the village, on much the same course, till it reached the north branch of *Montagne's Kill*. A second street, north of the former (distant at the river end fifteen Dutch rods), was laid out in the same direction, as far as found necessary. Being broader than the other, it was called the "Great Way," but since that day has been better known as the Church Lane, with its old homesteads, and rows of stately elms; of all which, however, there now remains scarce a trace, save upon the maps. Between these two streets were located the *erven*, or house lots, lying in two ranges, a central line dividing those facing one street from those facing the other, as in modern fashion; but the lots were nearly square, and measured about ninety-three English feet in depth, with a frontage somewhat less; while cross-streets formed these into blocks containing four lots each. It should be said that the erven toward the west end exceeded considerably the depth stated, owing to the fact that the two main streets did not preserve their parallel, the southern, at a point between the second and third cross-streets, suddenly diverging about eight degrees from a direct line. Larger plots laid out on the north side of the Great Way, though some were subsequently built upon, were designed only as *tuynen*, or gardens, one for each of the *erven*. They were described as five by twenty Dutch rods, or one sixth of a morgen, but were meted out by liberal measure (the case also with the erven), and being soon extended in the rear and otherwise enlarged, came to be reduced to half the original number, and to contain one morgen or two acres.*

* The CHURCH LANE, like a faded picture almost reft of power to recall the lovely reality, still lives, with its air of rural repose, in the memories of a few who in their juvenile days trod its grassy paths to the old Dutch church, which stood near the Harlem river, on the south side of the Lane, in a corner of the old cemetery removed in 1868. Extending from the river, where on its north side stood the Judah house, on its south the Benson house, this ancient road, cutting the modern blocks diagonally, struck 3d ave. at 121st st., then crossing where was since the Park to Sylvan Place and 120th st., turned south-west just beyond that point, and joined the original Harlem and N. Y. Road, or continuation of the lower village street, which in early times extended west to the little Mill Creek, (north branch of Montagne's Kill,) and across to Harlem Lane, now Avenue St. Nicholas.

To each *erf*, or house lot, was laid out upon Jochem Pieters Flat a lot of *bouwland*, or farming land. These were simply staked off and numbered, the lots running from the river into the woods westerly; No. 1 lying against the rear of the tuynen, at the south end of the range, and No. 25 at the north end. These lots were laid out for six morgen, but were soon after enlarged a little, and the number reduced, as we shall see. These twenty-five lots were the only farming lands taken up at first. In form like all those subsequently laid out for the same purpose, they were made narrow and long, and butted either on the river or creeks—a favorite mode of dividing up land, borrowed from Holland, but here having its peculiar advantages. The

The church, the second which had occupied that spot, was taken down in 1825, a new one being built on the present site, then part of the Church Farm. The old vane, bearing the date 1788, when the former house was erected, was taken care of, and may still be seen on Judge Ingraham's barn in 2d ave. See note on *The Reformed Church*. The Benson house, aforesaid, yet in good repair, standing cornerwise to the upper side of 125th st., and occupied by Mr. J. K. Cowperthwait, but early in this century the home of Lawrence Benson, then of Capt. Bailey, and later of Judge Morrell, marks the situation of a much more ancient house—that of the original settler David Demarest. The Judah house, which stood opposite, on the north side of the Lane, was a deserted ruin long before it was pulled down in 1867, but had been a tasteful structure for the times, and was owned prior to the Revolution by Peter R. Livingston. Kept as a tavern just after the war for some years by the noted patriot, of whaleboat fame, Capt. William Marriner, who also ran the ferry to Morrisania, it was also known as the Ferry House. It was bought in 1822 by Mr. John Moore, and became his residence. Both the above were originally stone houses, of one story, but had been raised to two. Before the present century, the *erven*, or ancient village house lots (on one of which is the Benson house; the church and graveyard having occupied two others), had nearly all lost their buildings, and become pasture-lots, or been thrown into the adjoining fields, by closing up the lower street before named, the river end only being kept open; while the *tuynen*, or one morgen lots, on the north side of the Church Lane, being joined two or more in a plot, and built upon, had come to form the best part of the village, the homes a century ago of the Bussing, Waldron, Livingston, and Myer families, succeeded later by those of Sickels, Chesterman, Brady, etc. The Myer house, of stone, one story and very old, was removed by Judge Ingraham when 125th st. was opened, on which it stood. The Brady house, a frame building, erected by John Livingston some years before the Revolution, was torn down in 1863. The stately frame house with heavy columns, yet standing at 2d ave. and 124th st., was built by the late James Chesterman in 1821 on the site of the old stone Waldron house. The old Bussing house, occupying the plot next the Church Farm, was destroyed in the Revolution, and on the same spot after the war John S. Sickels built the house still standing on 123d st., north side, just west of 2d ave., it having been turned to line with the street. This property descended in 1804 from Sickels to his gd-son John S. Adriance, who sold it, June 7th, 1820, to Christopher Heiser.

farmers liked this water privilege, as they were long in the habit of removing their produce from the field to their barns in the village by means of canoes and scows, until suitable roads were made. Again, the laborers had less fear of the Indians, when working near each other, in a common field (for it was a full half century before they built division fences,) as, always having their guns with them, there was a better chance, if attacked, to unite in defending themselves. And tradition adds that they used the ingenious precaution of planting each particular crop in a continuous row across their several lots, that the workers need not be very far apart while engaged in cultivating or harvesting their crops.

Salt hay was thought indispensable for the cattle; hence a small parcel of marsh or meadow, usually about three morgen, was set off to each lot of bouwland. That all might be supplied, these had to be taken wherever found—on Little Barent's and Stony Islands; on the other side of Harlem River; about Spuyten Duyvel, and in the Great Meadow, upon Sherman's Creek. The meadows in the Bay of Hellgate were reserved to the church, to be used or rented for its benefit, with the bouwland in the village, set apart to the same use.

With its first advent into life and activity, the infant settlement received its name; fitly taken from a famous old city of North Holland. It was called Nieuw Haerlem; conferred no doubt by Stuyvesant, who seems always to have exercised that right, though usually a formal request coming from the people gave it the look of a courtesy paid to their chief ruler. Its selection was such as could neither flatter any one settler, nor excite the jealousy of others, as none of them were from Haerlem. Perhaps the semblance in the two localities first suggested it. New Haerlem and New Amsterdam, like the two great cities after which they were named, lay apart "about three hours' journey;" or so thought two observing tourists of that century. Old Haerlem, watered on its eastern side by the gentle Sparen, and girt about landwise by groves "of shadowy elms," for beauty and extent unrivalled in Holland, where are few forests, might well have dictated a name for a situation so similar. But more suggestive was its history. To the Hollander the word Haerlem was the synonym for all that was virtuous and heroic.

During the memorable siege sustained by that fated town, when for seven long months the choicest troops in the Spanish army were foiled by the intrepidity of its citizens, women vieing with the men in bearing arms, was displayed a patriotism worthy the loftiest flights of the poetic muse. And though Haerlem fell, there went up from the merciless slaughter of its brave but vanquished people such a piercing cry as palsied the weakened arm of the invader, and nerved the patriots to an uncompromising resistance—freedom was virtually achieved for the United Provinces! Noble Haerlem! illustrious example of courage, endurance, and sacrifice, ever to live thy memory, and tenderly to be cherished, among the proudest and dearest of Fatherland!

Thus the name New Haerlem was aptly chosen. Like its great exemplar, it might be called upon to withstand the onslaught of a savage and relentless foe. In such dark and trying hour—and who could tell, after the gloomy experience of past years, but it might come—the inspiration of a glorious name was something to incite its people to noblest proofs of fortitude and heroism. Peril was in the new enterprise, equally with labor and hardship; and those entering upon it had clearer apprehensions than we can well understand of what they might be called to do or suffer to maintain and defend their new home.*

The beginning was not auspicious. Summer in 1658 brought "an unusually distempered atmosphere," and "many persons died." Others were prostrated for weeks and months "with sickness and debility." Then "flooding rains which came about

* HAERLEM, in writing which we now drop a letter for brevity, is derived by Dutch writers from *Heer Lem* (Lord Willem, or William), an early prince of Friesland, in Holland, the reputed founder of Haerlem, from him called the stadt (town) of Heer Lem; whence the easy transition into Haerlem, or Haarlem, as the Hollanders now write it.

Among the oldest of our historic names, significant for reference, and entering into the corporate titles of our churches, our railway and navigation companies, etc., how preposterous the suggestion that this time-honored designation is become useless, and should be ignored! Rather cherish it, together with the more local names within Harlem, many of which it has been our good fortune to rescue. *Apropos* to this—has justice been done the worthy pioneers of Harlem, in selecting names for the streets, avenues, and places? Mount Morris, from its former owners, would surely find a more significant name in *Mount Benson*. And *Kortright Avenue*, for a like reason, more happily apply to Harlem Lane than Avenue St. Nicholas! Since "God's Acre" has been desecrated, and the forefathers' gravestones uprooted as things obsolete and useless, what more proper tribute to their memory than that here suggested?

the time of harvesting" so damaged the fruits and crops as to cause "a scarcity of bread." Many feared it would "be impossible to get in winter forage for the cattle." With so serious a check upon labor and enterprise, but slow progress was made at New Harlem.

With a view to urge the work forward, the Director and Council, on November 27th, issued a peremptory order in these words: "All persons whom it may concern are hereby forewarned and notified, that all those who have obtained lots or plantations in the newly begun village of Haerlem shall take possession, or cause possession thereof to be taken, and commence preparations for fencing and planting the same, within the space of six weeks from the date hereof, on pain of having the lots and plantations which are not entered upon within that time given and granted to others who may be disposed to improve them."

This premonition was not without its effect, but the winter setting in early and with severity must have retarded the work. However, in place of those who abandoned their lots came other settlers, who put up buildings and undertook to cultivate the soil. The number of landholders thus augmented, during the ensuing spring and summer building after building began to adorn the new village, among the earliest to take up a permanent residence there being the Slots, Cressons, Tourneur, and Montagne junior, who all bore an active part in its affairs. For the security of the settlers, all of whom were required to be well armed, the government furnished eight or ten regular soldiers from Fort Amsterdam, in the pay of the company, whose presence were a necessity in the "newly begun village," as the Indians were yet a source of anxiety, especially to the wives and families of the colonists; the recent murder of a Swedish family at Mespat Kills serving to heighten this feeling among their fellow Swedes, of whom there were several in the new community at Harlem.*

* Elbert Engelberts, one of the murdered Swedes (see *Annals of Newtown*, 46, 51), m. in 1656 Sarah Walker from Boston; issue Anna-Maria, b. the same year at Maspeth Kills, and who m., 1680, Clement Elsworth, of N. Y. He and three brs. (sons of Stoffel Elsworth) all left families, whence those of this name. Capt. Verdine Elsworth, of Orange Co., a desc. of Clement, m. Dorothy Gale, in N. Y. 1759, and took an active part in the old French war.

This public disquietude arose to an actual panic when, on September 23d, the startling news arrived at the Manhattans, that a fierce and bloody war had broken out between the Esopus savages and the settlers there. A general consternation seized the inhabitants upon Manhattan Island and in the neighboring settlements, many of whom forsaking their boweries, crops, and cattle, fled hastily to New Amsterdam. Operations at New Harlem were wholly suspended for a time, especially as every soldier and public servant had to leave and accompany Stuyvesant on an expedition to Esopus. These soon returned, but things continued in a very threatening attitude the whole winter; and until the renewal of peace with the Wickquaskeeks and other tribes about Manhattan, early in the spring, brought some quiet to the public mind in this quarter. But the Director-General, on a second visit to Esopus, finding the savages there still hostile, resolved to give them their fill of war. He sent a message to the secretary, Van Ruyven, that the entire country was in danger, and directed him to warn the out settlements around Manhattan to carefully guard against a surprise. This having been done; the next day, being March 23d, 1660, the people at New Harlem were further notified that since it was "highly necessary to keep a good watch in the newly settled village," the Council had appointed as its military officers, Jan Pietersen Slot, as *sergeant;* Daniel Tourneur, as *corporal;* and Jaques Cresson, as *lancepesade.* They called upon all the inhabitants to obey the commands of Sergeant Slot, till other orders should be given by the Director and Council. This was the first step taken for the establishment of local authority at Harlem. Furnished with a supply of powder from the public magazine by Derick Looten, the commissary, the inhabitants were prepared for defense. This state of unrest lasted for several months, when it was relieved by news that a peace had been ratified with the Esopus Indians, and approved by the river tribes.

Meanwhile the settlers, having steadily increased in numbers, now deemed themselves entitled to a Court of Justice, agreeably with the original conditions under which they had settled here. They met therefore and nominated a double number of the best qualified persons among them, to bear rule as "commissaries"

was yet no church to receive him. But before the letter bespeaking a minister for this place could have reached Holland, the faithful here had joined themselves in church fellowship, and secured Zyperus' services; apparently, late in November. His purchase of a house and lot here, with the usual bouwland, etc., shows a purpose of remaining.

Unhappily, but few particulars can be given, as to the origin of the church, from the paucity of records at this period. Patterned after the Reformed Church of Holland, it was to be under the care of the Consistory at New Amsterdam, having at the first no officers from its own membership, except a single deacon, to which place Jan La Montagne, Jr., was now chosen. Thus its organization was quite informal and incomplete. Another deacon was added after some years, whence ensued a regular succession of these officers, intrusted with the financial and eleemosynary work of the church. Their resources were the Sunday collections, fines levied in the town court for the benefit of the poor, rent from the church lands, and burial fees, with the usual legacy left by testators of from ten to fifty guilders. Thus were met the wants of needy members and other worthy poor, as also the domine's salary and sexton hire. And after Zyperus left, till they secured a resident pastor, which was a long period, the deacons provided a horse and wagon to bring the domine and return him to his house in the city.*

We know little of Do. Zyperus' services here. Obviously he was never installed as pastor over this church; and as a mere licentiate, he could preach and teach, but not administer the ordinances. Still more obscure is his previous history. His name, in its unlatinized form, was probably the French Cipierre, an honored one in Huguenot story; his knowledge of both the Dutch and English languages, and, as will appear, his evident predilection for episcopacy, seem to warrant the belief that he had resided in Holland, but had acquired his theology in an

* No proper record of the organization of this church has been found; but of the date we may be reasonably assured. Montagne's term as deacon (which agreeably to usage in the Dutch establishment must have covered two years) expired Nov. 30, 1662. It began then in 1660, the earliest date consistent with the existence of a church here, as it was just after the magistracy was instituted; prior to which there could have been no church organization. The same date is given in *Corwin's Manual*.

English divinity school; the latter opinion strengthened by the fact that the records of the Leyden University, and of that city and Amsterdam, are silent as to his name. Nor is his former service in a Dutch colony any proof that he went thither under Holland licensure, since the Church of England was quite ready to both license and ordain the Dutch ministers, though Zyperus, as is plain, had not been ordained.

His disability to administer the sacraments, to admit to church membership, or perform the marriage rite, constrained the flock at Harlem, for these several objects, to resort to Stuyvesant's Bowery, where Rev. Henry Selyns, pastor of the church of Brooklyn, over which he had been installed September 7th, 1660, had, at the governor's desire, instituted a Sunday afternoon and evening service, in his private chapel, on the site of the present St. Mark's Church. Only *five miles* to enjoy these valued privileges, and Do. Selyns an able and attractive preacher, it naturally resulted that many of those living at Harlem sought and were received into membership at the Bowery, during the four years that Selyns officiated, and who were wont to attend there, especially to celebrate the Lord's Supper, and present their infants for baptism. Most of the marriages among them, from that of Sigismund Lucas, October 31st, 1660, were also performed by Do. Selyns. The practice was to first publish the bans in the church at Fort Amsterdam; and this being formally certified to the domine, he tied the nuptial knot. These Harlem marriages still stand upon the church register at Brooklyn. A few of the Harlem members not enrolled by Do. Selyns at the Bowery retained a connection with the lower church in the Fort. At one or the other place their children's baptisms were performed and recorded; save in only two cases, where the parties went to Brooklyn for that purpose.

No mention of a church edifice, or any effort to erect one here, occurs till four years later, and it but shows the general struggle with poverty, in the origin of the settlement. As in the older community at Brooklyn, where they still held public worship in a barn; so the infant church at New Harlem during this time had no better sanctuary than a private house or outbuilding; as happened once again, for a like term of years, at the close of the Revolutionary War.

CHAPTER XII.

1661-1662.

REARRANGEMENT OF LANDS: NEW ALLOTMENTS.

TOBACCO, though still cultivated, had been supplanted as a leading crop by others needed for home consumption, mainly wheat, maize, rye, buckwheat, peas, flax, etc. But what if full garners of *corn*—which term then stood for all the grains,—were rewarding the toil of these husbandmen; as yet they had no mill to grind it. This was now the felt need. If, with their grist in the canoe, they rowed some miles to Burger Joris' mill at the Dutch Kills, being the nearest; this at best could only grind three schepels per day, or two and a quarter bushels, on the word of Mark Disosway, who had lately run it under a lease! To the distance, the dangers of Hellgate added an objection. It had been contemplated to build a tide mill and dam upon Montagne's Kill, and many thought the time come to act upon it. But needing no demonstration, while backed by those convincing Dutch arguments, capacious stomachs and good appetites, yet the effort spent itself in fluent talk and foaming beakers; and it was not undertaken till done by the energy and capital of a distinguished stranger.

But out of the mill question while yet rife, and the demand for additional homes and bouweries to supply the newly-arriving colonists, grew another plausible project. The farm Vredendal, stretching along the stream aforesaid, and still owned by Dr. Montagne, had lain for some years unused, except as cattle and goats browsed in its deserted clearings and woodlands. The Montagne family now proposed to occupy it, as is set forth in the following petition to the Director and Council, July 4th. 1661:

To the Noble, Great and Worshipful, the DIRECTOR GENERAL and HIGH COUNCIL in New Netherland: Represent with due respect, *John de La Montagne, Junior, Jacob Kip*, who married the daughter of La Montagne, Senior, and *William de La Montagne*, for themselves and in behalf of the absent heirs, the true proprietors, pursuant to the letters patent, of the land lying back of New Haerlem, called Vredendal, or commonly, Montagne's Land, to your Honors well known; how that they the petitioners are willing and inclined to take possession of their land, which is situated nearly a mile (*een quartier verganns*,) from New Haerlem. And whereas from there it cannot be conveniently cultivated, lying beyond a kill, whereon in time a water-mill for the use of the said village can, and as they are now informed, is actually to be made; and whereas they the petitioners—for whose greater convenience it will not only serve, in the cultivation of their lands there, but will be for the better protection of the village of New Haerlem, as for the benefit of the said mill, and also afford a resting place for strangers, whether they have lost their way, or be looking for their cattle, or any others,—are inclined to form there a concentration of six, eight or ten families, to remain under the jurisdiction of New Haerlem, in a similar manner as this has been granted by your Honors to others; they therefore with all respect petition that they may be allowed to establish such concentration there, either on the point of the flat land, opposite the place where the mill is to be built, on the heights near the spring, (*fonteyn*,)* or otherwise wherever your Honors may deem most proper, within the jurisdiction of New Haerlem; which, if your Honors are pleased to permit, they promise to settle there before the next winter, six, eight or ten families. Praying your Honors' favorable consideration of this request, we remain your Honors' servants,

LA MONTAGNE, Junior.
JACOB KIP,
WILLEM DE LA MONTAGNE.

To this came the following negative: "The request is dismissed, because it is tending to the great prejudice and retarding of the village of Haerlem; and is also contrary to the privileges granted said village some years ago." Though he does not expressly say it, we doubt not the Director, even then, had his own purpose in regard to the Montagne lands; to be made manifest in due time, and that not far distant.

The decision was highly satisfactory to the people of Harlem, for several reasons. A rival settlement so near them, indeed

* MONTAGNE'S SPRING.—Perennially flowing, as in the virgin days of the settlement, this spring is still to be found in Central Park. Its source is on a hillside, at a point (were the ways mentioned extended into the Park) on the line of 105th Street, some 200 feet west of the 6th Avenue. But this natural basin is now covered over, the water being led by a subterranean conduit to the foot of the hill, were, in a secluded, romantic nook in the rocks, it again leaps forth as playfully as of old, when it was known among the Dutch inhabitants as the "fonteyn;" whence, in following its ancient outlet or run, it is soon lost in the modern Harlem Lake. Should it not be called *Montagne's Spring!*

within their very limits, was not to be thought of! Not only would it tend to weaken them by drawing away some whom they could ill afford to spare, but would naturally attract persons who otherwise would come hither to settle. Thus it would greatly obstruct and hinder their present growth; and, looking to the future, the very lands proposed to be settled, would be required for the proper subsistence and development of their own village. For three years this had been steadily growing, and at the close of 1661 contained over thirty adult male residents, mostly heads of families and freeholders. The following are the names of these pioneers, who first succeeded in planting the seeds of civilization and religion in this vicinity.

Michel Zyperus,	*French.*	Jan Sneden,	*Hollander.*
Jan La Montagne, Jr.,	"	Michiel Janse Muyden,	"
Daniel Tourneur,	"	Lubbert Gerritsen,	"
Jean le Roy,	"	Meyndert Coerten,	"
Pierre Cresson,	"	Aert Pietersen Buys,	"
Jaques Cresson,	"	Sigismundus Lucas,	"
Philippe Casier,	"	Jan Pietersen Slot,	*Dane.*
David Uzille,	"	Nicolaes De Meyer,	"
Jacques Cousseau,	"	Jan Laurens Duyts,	"
Philippe Presto,	"	Jacob Elderts Brouwer,	"
François le Sueur,	"	Nelis Matthyssen,	*Swede.*
Simon de Ruine,	*Walloon.*	Monis Peterson Staeck,	"
David du Four,	"	Jan Cogu,	"
Jean Gervoe,	"	Adolph Meyer,	*German.*
Jan de Pré,	"	Adam Dericksen,	"
Dirck Claessen,	*Hollander.*	Hendrick Karstens,	"

La Montagne, of all these, had been longest in the country, namely, twenty-five years; and Duyts was the only one born here, being twenty years of age, and the son of Laurens Duyts, who came out with Bronck, the good Kuyter having stood as godfather for Jan at his baptism. Karstens, Gerritsen, and Claessen had had a dozen or more years' experience in the New World, Tourneur and Le Roy nearly ten, but the others less. Casier, Uzille, and Meyer had come to Harlem only the last year. Casier and family arrived here from Mannheim in June, 1660, having in company Matthew Blanchan, and his son-in-law, Antoine Crêpel; these two going to Esopus, while Casier, at New Amsterdam, engaged, "with his three beside," in timber sawing. Here De Meyer and Cousseau were in trade, as had been Montagne, and Tourneur was a "sworn butcher." Slot and

Matthyssen were carpenters, Muyden a soap-boiler, De Pré a cooper, Claessen a pot-baker, Elderts a brewersman, Lucas a shoemaker, Gervoe and Coerten soldiers, Karstens, before a seaman, now worked as a mason, and Cogu had a lime-kiln, and soon took in Staeck as partner. Most of these also took up land. Possibly one or more, who appear a little later, should be added. Several had already gone, after a short stay, as Matthys Boon and Simon Lane, of whom we know little but their names.*

From what has heretofore been said of these colonists, of their rough and checkered experiences before quitting the shores of Europe, we cannot but regard their future with special interest, while better facilities will be found to study their individual character. Little remains to be said of them in generalities. Though the Dutch and French elements were dominant

* BLANCHAN and Crêpel (now written Crispell) were originally from Artois, as before stated; and the first of some note in his native town of Nouville le-Comte. With him came his w. Madeleine Goore, and (beside *Marie*, Mrs. Crêpel), three other chn., viz., *Madeleine*, æ. 12 yrs., *Elizabeth*, 9, and *Matthew*, 5, the last b. at Mannheim. Stuyvesant welcomed them, and gave Blanchan a letter to Sergt. Romp, at Esopus, directing him to provide them accommodations. Arrived there, and Do. Blom having also come, it was a solace to the pious Blanchan, for all he had suffered, and the loss of property in his native place, and at Armentières, (Flanders) and elsewhere, to sit down with his w., and son and dr. Crêpel, at the Lord's Supper, on Dec. 25, ensuing. Louis Du Bois, m. to Blanchan's dr. *Catharine*, probably came out with his br.-in-law Pierre Billiou, also from Artois, in the ship St. Jan Baptist, which arrived here Aug. 6, 1661—reasons, Du Bois and w. were not present at the communion season referred to, but with letters joined the chh. there not till Oct. 1, 1661, having a ch. baptized nine days after. Blanchan, Du Bois, and Crêpel all got land in Hurley, near Kingston, and received groundbriefs Apl. 25, 1663. Du Bois d. at Kingston in 1696, and his wid. m. Jean Cottin, named page 71. On May 18, 1679, Blanchan, "lying sick in bed," made his will. Later that year Matthew Blanchan, Jr., m. Margaret van Schoonhoven, and succeeding to his fa.'s farm in Hurley, left beside 4 drs., a son Nicholas, whence all of the name in Ulster Co. desc. His sr. Madeleine, b. in England, m. Jan Matthyss, anc. of the *Jansen* family, as before noticed. His other sr., Elizabeth Blanchan, m. Pieter Cornelise Low, of Kingston, whose progeny have been numerous and widespread. Cornelius Low, of New Jersey, b. 1670, was eldest son of Pieter, and fa. of Cornelius, fa. of Isaac and Nicholas Low, leading merchants of N. Y. in their day. The first was President of the Chamber of Commerce, but when Independence was declared forsook the "Liberty Boys" and adhered to the Royal cause; while his br. Nicholas continued an active patriot, and was a member of the Convention of N. Y. for adopting the Const. of the U. S. See *Stevens' Chamber of Com.* Honored names in various sections of our country have been and still are those of Blanchan, Du Bois, Crispell, Jansen, and Low.

in giving tone to the community, the Scandinavians and Germans, few in number as seen, were second to none for sterling common-sense, while foremost to breast danger and hardship, to wield the axe whose ring first startled the slumbering forest, or turn the first furrow in the virgin soil! Hardy sons of toil, bred to habits of untiring industry, none were more fitted for the task of converting the rude wilds into an abode for civilization. Frank and outspoken, but of honest aim and dealing, with essentially the same language, which was closely allied to that of the Dutch, toward whom, as Protestants, they were drawn in sympathy, they readily assimilated to the latter; and if less indebted than these to the schoolmaster, being in great part unable to read or write, this was in a degree supplied by their native good sense and equanimity, which contributed not a little to harmonize the diverse elements composing the settlement, and to mould them into a well-ordered society.

> "Oft did the harvest to their sickle yield,
> Their furrow oft the stubborn glebe has broke;
> How jocund did they drive their team afield,
> How bow'd the woods beneath their sturdy stroke!
> "Let not ambition mock their useful toil,
> Their homely joys and destiny obscure;
> Nor grandeur hear with a disdainful smile,
> The short and simple annals of the poor."

By the large influx of settlers, who with scarcely an exception gave their attention to farming, either as proprietors or tenants, the original allotments of land had all been taken up, causing the demand, before noticed, for additional erven and bouwlots. It was a want now equally felt by other villages, and as a first step toward meeting it the government resolved to inform itself as to what lands were available (tracts lying unimproved, and not needed as pasturage or woodland), that these might be distributed to settlers and brought under tillage. With this view the Director and Council issued a general order, of which the people of Harlem received a copy as follows:

ALL Inhabitants of New Netherland, and especially those of the Village of *New Harlem*, with all others who have or claim any Lands thereabouts, are ordered and commanded that within the space of three months from the date hereof, or at least before the first of January next, they shall have all the cultivated and uncultivated Lands which they claim, surveyed by the sworn Surveyor, and set off and designated by proper marks; and on the exhibition of the Return of Survey thereof, apply for and obtain a regular Patent as proof of property, on pain of being deprived of their right; To the end that the Director General and Council may dispose, as they deem proper, of the remaining Lands, which after the survey, may happen to fall outside of the Patents, for the accommodation of others. All are hereby warned against loss and after complaints. Thus done, in Fort Amsterdam, in New Netherland, the 13th of September, 1661.

This order moved the community to give immediate attention to the whole subject of their lands, it being necessary for each inhabitant to consider and decide what quantity he further needed and could pay for. The idea largely prevailed, and very naturally, that the ordinance for planting the village secured to all able to purchase and improve that quantity, as high as 24 morgen of bouw-land. The magistrates and freeholders having canvassed the matter and laid it before Gov. Stuyvesant, he gave his assent to the following measures, looking to a further distribution of land, and in connection therewith, to some convenient changes in the old lots. Discarding the former ground-briefs, Van Keulen's Hook and Montagne's Flat were to be laid off into lots and distributed among the freeholders. It was agreed that John La Montagne should hold the Point, as having belonged to his father, and take his full allotment there, by throwing up his lot No. 1 on Jochem Pieters; and as a special immunity should enjoy the Point free from any future demands in the way of town tax. He was to conform to the town regulation against building upon the bouwlots, and was not to build or live upon the Point till the town saw fit to allow it. Jan Pieters Slot and Simon de Ruine, owning two lots apiece on Jochem Pieters, also consented to give up one each, lying toward the further end; instead of which Slot was to draw 9 morgen together on Van Keulen's Hook, and De Ruine to draw a lot, 3 morgen, on said tract, and enough more on Montagne's Flat to make good his quantity. Moreover both were to retain their two erven.

All this being arranged, the lots on Jochem Pieters,* now numbering but 22, were staked out anew, and to each lot (be-

* Jochem Pieters' Flat, with the history of the several lots, showing the origin of the titles in this section, is treated of in Appendix E.

fore 6 morgen) was added 400 Dutch rods, or two thirds of a morgen; a remnant of 8½ morgen, left of No. 1, being taken to enlarge the gardens. The owner next adjoining to No. 1, Daniel Tourneur, to whom fell part of that lot with part of No. 2, now became No. 1; a similar change occurring to the next owner, and so on.

Van Keulen's Hook, the large plain directly south of the village, and lying mostly in woods, was laid off into lots, narrow and long, and these, for convenience of ingress and ultimate building upon, were, excepting the first three, butted on the main street, from which they ran south to the river and Mill Creek; being each twelve Dutch rods in breadth, and containing three morgen, or about six acres. Twenty-two lots were laid out, as on Jochem Pieters, and numbered from the river westward. Nos. 1 to 8, instead of reaching up, as did the others, to the village street, ended at the marsh or meadows, some acres in extent, which lay intervening, and through which a creek, forked and winding, overflowed its banks or lapsed to its muddy channel with the tidal flood and ebb. The upland between street and meadows was reserved for the common use of the village, and to allow free access to the creek-side and small cove at its outlet, which was the usual landing-place for the villagers and others, as it afforded a safe mooring for canoes and skiffs.

The Van Keulen Hook lots were drawn in the beginning of 1662, the original owners being as follows:

No. 1. David du Four.
" 2. Jan Cogu.
" 3. Lubbert Gerritsen.
" 4. Michiel Zyperus.
" 5. Daniel Tourneur.
" 6. Sigismund Lucas.
" 7. Jan Pietersen Slot.
" 8. " " "
" 9. " " "
" 10. Philippe Casier.
" 11. Jean Gervoe.
No. 12. Simon de Ruine.
" 13. Adam Dericksen.
" 14. Jaques Cresson.
" 15. Nicolaes De Meyer.
" 16. David Uziele.
" 17. Dirck Claessen.
" 18. Jan Sneden.
" 19. Jan de Pré.
" 20. Pierre Cresson.
" 21. Jacques Cousseau.
" 22. Jean le Roy.*

An episode of these land operations here claims a notice—the first "Harlem Land Case," not reported, we believe, either in *Wheaton* or *Wendell!* Sigismundus Lucas, as his autograph

* See the subsequent history of the Van Keulen Hook lots in Appendix F.

in working long and lustily on his cobbler's bench, had gotten him "a house, barn, and plantation, at New Haerlem." But early in January, 1662, he agreed to sell out to Nicholas De Meyer, then a Harlem freeholder, for 400 gl. in sewant. Going home from New Amsterdam, where the bargain had been made, cobbler Lucas considered the many *stitches* that property had cost him, sorely repented his act, and tried to back out, on the ground that De Meyer had given him till morning to decide if he would sell. De Meyer began to smell *leather*, and forthwith took written statements from two witnesses to the bargain, and also that of Evert Duyckinck, whom Lucas had told of having sold his farm to De Meyer, but did not think "the costs would run so high." Coming in court at Harlem, January 13th, De Meyer claimed the property, showing his papers, and offering also the testimony of Meyndert Coerten, who had heard defendant admit the sale. Lucas, who was present, demurred, pleading that the sale was not peremptory; that Coerten, having hired land of De Meyer, was an interested witness, and that the affidavits were not sworn to. The last objection was sustained, and the case was adjourned, to give plaintiff time to remedy this defect. This was done the next day before the Heer Tonneman, schout of New Amsterdam. On the 16th the town court again examined the papers and heard the pleas of both parties; then ordered Lucas to give up the farm on receiving the price, and to pay the costs of suit. But in vain did De Meyer send once, twice, thrice, to tender the money and demand the delivery of the premises; the resolute cobbler, maintaining his *ends*, only *waxed* firmer in his refusal, so that on a further complaint, February 2d, the court authorized De Meyer to take possession. Now Lucas, still showing his *bristles*, appealed to the Director and Council, praying "to be relieved of the sale to De Meyer, and the sentence of the court at Harlem, in whose jurisdiction said houses and lands are situated, as he loses by that sale *more than half of their value.*" He was directed to give De Meyer a copy of the petition, and notify him when to appear and answer. On February 16th both parties presented themselves, when the Director and Council, after reviewing the case, confirmed the action of the local court, and held Lucas to his bargain. The poor shoemaker had held on to the *last*, but must now yield up his *all* (indeed his awl was now everything to him !), and in disgust he soon left the town.*

It may be added that, two years later, or January 29th, 1664, De Meyer obtained a patent from Gov. Stuyvesant for his several lands in Harlem, then including twelve morgen upon Montagne's Flat ; which tract, as proposed, had been divided up among the people of Harlem, and to the particular history of which we now return.

John La Montagne, after the project to form a new settlement on the farm Vredendal had failed, continued at Harlem, one of the most useful and honored of its inhabitants. The Director and Council, November 3d, 1661, appointed him schepen, with Slot and Tourneur as associates ; and when Slot retired a year later, he succeeded as schout, which office he retained till the Dutch rule ended. He was the first Town Clerk, so far as appears from the earliest protocol or register, but which commences only with January 13, 1662, leaving the preceding sixteen months a blank ; an unfortunate vacuum at the introduction of the town history, though partially filled by other records. But from this date Montagne's minutes (save another hiatus of fifteen months) are quite complete for ten years, up to his death.

* SIGISMUND LUCAS, on quitting H., bought him a house in Pearl Street. He was sued in the Court of Burgomasters, Jan. 15, 1664, for a pair of shoes left to be mended "during the Indian troubles" of the previous year. They were "stuffed into the straw bed," for safe keeping, as he had "neither kist nor chest in which to lock them." The case was dismissed upon Simon making oath "that he knew not what became of them." He now threw aside his cobbler tools to become a carman, and on the Dutch reoccupation, 1673, good loyal Dutchman, he worked gratis at the city defenses, only taking pay for horse and cart. But the English succeeding, the sheriff wished Simon to "cart down a cable," by order of Gov. Andros ; but now in other mood he refused, saying "he would not cart for the Governor, nor nobody else." Hereupon the Mayor's Court, Dec. 22, 1674, "Ordered that he shall cart noe more until ye Court think meete to admit him thereto." He and w. made a joint will "Sunday evening about eight o'clock," Sept. 17, 1673, which he survived four years at least, but both were d. when the will was proved in court Apl. 26, 1681. The Court, Oct. 11 ensuing, authorised his effects to be "sold at an outcry for payment of debts." He left by his first w. Engeltie Jans, a dr. *Maria*, who m. André Lauran, of the French Church, and by his second w. Gertrude Bulderen, a son, who wrote his name *Johannes Simonsis*, also a cordwainer, later a carman, in N. Y., and admitted a freeman July 19, 1726. He m., 1692, Phebe, dr. of Capt. Titus Syrachs de Vries, of Flatbush. Her brs. bore the name of *Titus* (see *Annals of Newtown*), one of whom, Syrach Titus, removed to Bensalem, Bucks Co., Penn., d. 1761, and left desc. there. *Hazard's Reg.*, 7 : 30.

However thwarted were the Montagnes in their plans respecting Vredendal, they yielded gracefully to the alternative which secured to John La Montagne, the doctor's eldest son, that part of the property called the Point, of which his father was the original grantee, but surrendered the Flat to the government, to be parcelled out to such of the people of Harlem as still wanted more land, and upon terms which, though not stated, probably did not differ from those of the previous allotments, but without doubt looking to a liquidation of the large debt due from Dr. Montagne to the company. While John La Montagne was to remain the possessor of the Point, which was rated at 16 morgen, it was open to his brother William (we think then engaged to succeed Zyperus as schoolmaster, and hence usually styled by his brother "*Meester* Willem"), if he should become a freeholder, in same manner as others, by the purchase of the usual allotment, to draw with them his proportionate share of the Flat, enough to give him likewise 16 morgen. It was clearly a compromise regarding Vredendal, arranged, as it could only be, with the sanction and by order of the Director and Council; and the correspondence which at this time these were having with Dr. Montagne respecting his long-standing indebtedness to the company, and for which they strongly censured him, shows that their action as aforesaid was a stern necessity.*

The question of the disposal of the Flat was intimately connected with another of vital interest to the community. The three years allowed them in which to pay for their lands had nearly expired, and with not a few it became a difficult problem how they should provide the 8 gl. per morgen which the government must have. In this dilemma the schepens represented to the Director and Council, March 9th, 1662, what embarrassment several of the inhabitants must experience if compelled at once to pay the purchase money for their lands, eight guilders per morgen, and praying to be relieved of this payment; in lieu of which they proposed that the term of fifteen years' exemption from tithes should be shortened to ten years.

To this the Director and Council would not assent, but in their answer "insist upon the conditions on which the village

* See a letter from Montagne upon this subject, with touching allusion to his needy circumstances and frugality of living, in Appendix D.

of Harlem has been laid out." But they added: "No person is obliged to accept more land than it is convenient for him to pay for."

It was plainly owing to the difficulty of raising this morgen-money, or *morgen-gelt*, as called (a term also denoting any tax assessed according to the morgen), that a number of persons quit the town during this year, to try their fortunes elsewhere; as well landholders as others designing to become such. Of these were Coerten, De Pré, Du Four, Gervoe, and Le Sueur.* Du Four sold out his allotment to Jacob Eldertsen, a sturdy Dane from Lubeck, and late a brewersman, who resold it, June 1st, 1662, to Jean le Roy for 350 gl. But these few withdrawals only making place for others, it was soon apparent that all the land now to be distributed would be eagerly taken. The following list was made out by Montagne, at a meeting of the resident proprietors, called to ascertain how much land they wanted:

List of Lands at N. Haerlem, according to each one's request, 14*th March*, 1662.

Jan Pietersen Slot,	24	*morgen*.
Daniel Tourneur,	24	"
Michiel Zyperus,	18	"
Lubbert Gerritsen,	24	"
Adam Dericksen,	6	"
David du Four,	10	"
Simon de Ruine,	12	"
Jan Cogu and Monis Petersen,	10	"
Jean Gervoe,	10	"
Hendrick Karstens,	6	"
Widow of Jan Snedes,	4	"
Philip Casier,	24	"
Jan de Pré, *absent*.		
Jaques Cresson,	12	"
Simon Lucas,	10	"
Peter Cresson,	8	"

These bids were made with obvious reference to the offers in the ordinance of 1658, as the quantities indicate. But to meet

* Meyndert Coerten, from Arnhem, came out as a soldier of the West India Co. He m. in 1660 a girl of Picard parentage, Maria, dr. of Pierre, Pia, and visited Holland, returning the next year in the ship with Muyden, who probably drew him to H. Here he leased land of De Meyer, and kept stock. In his brief residence he won respect, and the court honored his abilities in naming him with Do. Zyperus, Feb. 16, 1662, to settle a financial dispute between Cogu and Tourneur. Coerten soon went to Flushing, and thence to New Utrecht, where he arose to position and served as an elder.

these demands, as was apparent, must exhaust the allotments proposed to be made on Montagne's Flat, to the exclusion of some of the ablest proprietors, living in the city and not now present, as De Meyer, Cousseau, Claessen, and Muyden. In such case the government could only use its discretion in revising the list. It decided that 10 morgen must at present be the maximum of a single allotment. Slot was therefore dropped; others raised to said number of morgen, except asking for less. But of course we cannot know all the reasons which weighed in making up the list.

Under such circumstances was the Flat now laid out into parcels of from four to six morgen each, by an actual survey; running in narrow strips from the little creek due west to the hills, originally some twelve lots, and numbered from south to north. As near as can be told, the first owners were Nicholas De Meyer, Lubbert Gerritsen, William de La Montagne, Simon de Ruine, Derick Claessen, Do. Zyperus, Jean le Roy, Jacques Cousseau, and Daniel Tourneur. De Meyer, as owning two allotments, obtained two lots on the Flat; and so of Cousseau. Montagne had lot No. 4, being six and a half morgen, he having met the required conditions by purchasing, April 7th, 1662, from Jan de Pré,* who had advertised to sell the same at auction, his "house, house-lot (erf), garden, and land"—the land being No. 7 Jochem Pieters. Lot 19 Van

He was high sheriff under Leisler, and one of his council; but his devotion to that party cost him a long imprisonment. In 1698 he represented Kings Co. in the Gen. Assembly. He d. on his farm, *Bruynsburg*, ab. 1706, in a good old age. For his chn. see the *Bergen Gen.*, 1st edition; not in 2d edition, as later evidence changed the opinion that he was of the Van Voorhees family.

* JAN DE PRÉ, born at Commines in 1635—a Fleming, but of Walloon or French descent, judging from his surname—was a cooper, and before coming to H. lived several years as a "small burgher" in New Amsterdam, where he m. in 1655 a Scotch lassie, Margaret, dr. of John Cromartie. His present w. was Jannetie, dr. of Simon de Ruine, m. in 1659. De Pré finally went to New Utrecht, and thence to Staten Island. By his first w. he had *Andries*, b. 1656 (but one ch. called a dr. is referred to in his m. settlement of Dec. 31, 1659), and by his second w., *Jannetie*, b. 1662, *Francina*, 1665, *Maria*, 1667, *John*, 1671, *Simon*, 1676. Jannetie m. Cornelius Banta, of Hackensack, where her uncles, the Demarests, resided. She d., and Banta m. her cousin Magdalena Demarest. Banta was a son of *Epke Jacobs Banta*, farmer, from Harlingen, common anc. of the prolific family bearing that name, and who with his w. and 5 chn. emigrated in the same ship with Simon de Ruine. How often the acquaintance thus formed proved a link uniting the fortunes of the children!

Keulen's Hook also made part of this allotment. But after a temporary residence, Montagne sold out to his brother John, and returned to Albany, whence he removed to Esopus, married, and was long the parish clerk. Had we no other evidence of this alienation of Montagne's Flat, the bare fact that while Dr. Montagne and his sons were yet living these lands are found divided up, and in the possession of several other of the Harlem people, nearly all holding under special patents from the Governors Stuyvesant, Nicolls, and Lovelace, is evidence *prima facie* that the title had passed from the original owners; a conclusion which none may now gainsay without ignoring the official acts of the government in the issuing of these patents.*

The spirit of land speculation, infecting few places as it has Harlem, is in no wise peculiar to our century. In the days under review, and mainly for the cause we have stated, many transfers of land took place, the buyers the more thrifty class, with usually a keen eye to a bargain. Very informal was the legal act of transfer. The earliest deeds, most simple and brief, seem especially defective in *describing the property*. But this information was supplied by the original surveys and allotment lists on file with the town clerk, while no complex chain of title embarrassed the question either of location or propriety. That of boundary came up occasionally. Payment was made, not by bank check, but either in sewant, in beaver-skins, in cattle, grain, or tobacco; and property was often sold subject, because not previously paid, to the *morgen-gelt* (before explained), the *meet-gelt*, or survey money, the cost of *groundbrief*, and, in sales by vendue, the *stuyver-gelt*, or auctioneer's fees. A curious sample is the deed to Montagne, before mentioned, the earliest save one to be found of date subsequent to the planting of the village. It was drawn up by Do. Zyperus, as the clerk was an interested party, being brother of the grantee, and otherwise involved in the transaction of which this purchase was a part. The morgen money being unpaid, the consideration named was only for the improvements and improved value of the land. As the scribe forgets to tell us where the contract was signed and sealed, and where on this mun-

* See further remarks upon Montagne's Flat under the year 1673, and in Appendix G.

dant sphere the land was situated, we judge he was not an experienced clerk. In the Domine's neat Dutch penmanship it still stands in the protocol.

ON THIS DATE, the 7th of April A°. 1662, have agreed and bargained, *Jan de Pré*, on the one side, and *Wilhelm Montagnie* on the other, in relation to, and over the sale of his allotment bought of Simon Lane,* on the following conditions: Jan de Pre acknowledges to have sold his house and house lot, land and garden, all that is fast by earth and nail, to Wilhelm Montagnie, for one Cow, and Fifteen Guilders in sewant, the which he acknowledges to have received. The purchaser shall be held to pay the morgen money and the survey money. This all so done, and have with our hands subscribed. Dated as above.

Witness, JAN DE PRÉ,
M. ZYPERUS. WILLEM DE LA MONTAGNE.
A°. 1662.

In executing a deed, bill of sale, lease, or other contract, custom required the parties to appear with two witnesses before the town secretary, who, after hearing their statement, wrote out the instrument in his register, receiving for such service a fee of thirty stivers. When signed by all the parties, this remained as the original; but if desired, an attested copy was furnished by the secretary, for an additional fee of twenty stivers. Wills, in the making of which the wife commonly joined with her husband (thus it was mutually fair and mutually binding) were executed in a similar way. A will in the usual form gave to "the longest liver" the use of the property for life or till a remarriage, after which it went equally to the children or other heirs. Sometimes in default of heirs it fell to the deacons for the benefit of the church or poor.

The grant of the commons west of the village for grazing purposes, of which we soon find the inhabitants in the peaceable enjoyment, must have dated from the very origin of the settlement; for while such grant unfortunately does not remain of record, it logically follows from the necessities of the case, the

* As first written it read "his lot No. 7," but Zyperus erased "No. 7," and inserted instead "gecocht van Symen Leen," *i.e., bought of Simon Lane*. It was to save misapprehension, as Lane had held and was registered for No. 8, though changing with the rest when Jan Montagne vacated No. 1, he now held No. 7; and further the allotment carried with it No. 19, Van Keulen's Hook, just drawn by De Pré. Hence "No. 7" fell short of the proper description; yet without this number we could hardly identify the lot conveyed.

keeping and increase of cattle promising the facilities for doing it, and to which the settlers were directly encouraged in the ordinance of 1658, by the promise of "a cattle and horse fair." The extent of the first grant for the range of their cattle was probably left indefinite, to be determined by the future needs of the place, but it seems at least to have embraced the entire flats to the westward. The kine of the village, now much increased, were liable, if not carefully looked after, and with no fences to hinder them, to stray off and become lost in the woods and swamps. So, to save the time of many, it was resolved to employ a common herder, who should collect the cows after milking in the morning, drive them with the oxen out to pasture, and watch over them till brought in again toward evening. Hence was made the following:

Agreement with the Cow Herder.

I, David du Four do acknowledge to have taken the cows to herd, belonging to the Town of New Haerlem, at my own expense, and also from each house one pair of oxen; for the sum of three hundred guilders in sewant, and one half pound of butter for every cow; provided I pay for the cattle that may be lost through my neglect. The time shall commence on the 23d of April, and end a fortnight after All-Saints Day, at the option of the Inhabitants. It is also stipulated that the butter shall be paid in May, and the further payment as the Herder shall perform his work. Also the Herder grants power of *parata executie*. The above obligation we on both sides engage to hold to and fulfill. In N. Haerlem, 20th April, Anno 1662.

DAVIT DU FOUR,
I P [*mark of* JAN P. SLOT],
D. TOURNEUR,
M. J. MUYDEN,
J. LA MONTAGNE, Junior.
* *mark of* LUBBERT GERRITS,
MEYNDERT COERTEN,
PHILIPPE CASIER,
H H. KARSTENS,
SIMON + DE RUINE,
JE *mark of* JACOB ELDERTS,
Moy PIER CRESSON.

Daniel Tourneur and Lubbert Gerritsen promise to collect and pay the Herder money at the appointed time. Dated as above.
D. TOURNEUR,
*

Du Four, the Amsterdam drayman, better at driving a team than stupid cows, was soon disgusted with his new occupation, and turned it over to Jean Gervoe, the soldier. But now the cattle were not well looked after, as was alleged; in fact, some of the oxen, when needed for the yoke, were missing. As things went, it was necessary to engage another herder, and on April

29th Jan Cogu and Monis Peterson, who were partners in a lime-kiln, etc., undertook the herding for 350 gl. being 50 gl. more than Du Four was to have. The collectors, Tourneur and Gerritsen, sued Du Four to recover the difference, and the town court decided he must pay it, the defendant only making the flimsy plea that he "was led by artful talk" to undertake the herding.*

Meanwhile occurred the first case of mortality brought to our notice in the little community, and soon another. The persons were Jan Sneden and his wife, who died in quick succession early in the year. Descended of an Amsterdam family, as before stated, Sneden came to Harlem in 1000, where he occupied Monis Peterson's house and bouwery, but soon secured an allotment of his own, being No. 14 Jochem Pieters, with the *erf* and garden belonging to it. The Snedens were probably interred in the ground used later for the negroes, and lying at the rear of the Judah plot, as interments were made there many years before "the old graveyard," removed a dozen years since, was taken for that use. The magistrates proceeded to settle Sneden's estate, as he was indebted to Isaac de Forest and others. His property was sold at vendue on three separate days, beginning March 25th. First the house and lands, with the grain on the latter sown by Sneden the previous fall, were, pursuant to notice, set up, and struck off at 135 gl. to Jacques Cousseau, who bid 25 gl. over his highest competitor, Tourneur. Jan La Montagne bid 100 gl., perhaps for his brother, who had not then purchased. At the two subsequent sales the household articles were disposed of, bringing 189 gl. But a mere pittance, 42 gl., was left to the orphans, Carsten and Grietie, over whom, on April 28th, Philip

* JEAN GERVOE, who apparently came out under an engagement as a soldier, had done such duty for several years at H., but was free when not required to bear his musket, to till the land which he had taken up, or engage in other honest labor. But on leaving, in 1662, he sold his allotment, being Nos. 13 Jochem Pieters and 11 Van Keulen's Hook, with house and lot and meadows, to Philip Casier. He served as *adelborst*, cadet or corporal, under Lieut. Stilwell, in the Esopus war, for which, on his petition, Jan. 10, 1664, he was allowed extra pay. He m. in 1659, but his only ch. mentioned was Hillegond, at whose baptism, Mar. 5, 1664, Jaques Tuynier (Cresson) stood as godfather. When the English took the country, Gervoe probably left with the Dutch forces.

Casier and Lubbert Gerritsen were appointed guardians, with directions "to act according to law." Grietie soon chose another protector, being married, August 13th following, to Jean Guenon, of Flushing, from which union have sprung the now widely scattered *Genung* family.*

On November 16th new magistrates were appointed by the Director and Council, from a double number nominated by the old board. The new board consisted of Jan La Montagne, Philip Casier, and Derick Claessen. One of their first acts was to provide for the more careful placing of houses and fences; which some seem to have disregarded, to the damage of particular and general interests. It was to check this abuse, and also to prevent any houses being put up outside the proper limits, that the magistrates, November 25th, passed the following:

"The Hon. Heere Schepens find it good to appoint and authorize Jan P. Slot, former schepen, as *Rooy-meester* (surveyor of buildings), for the improvement and sightliness of the village; and the builders shall every one be charged, after this time, to set no fences nor houses in the absence of the Hon. Heer *Rooy-meester*."

Upon November 30th, Montagne's term as deacon having expired, Daniel Tourneur was chosen in his place, and also as *brandt-meester*, or fire-warden. Simon de Ruine and Monis Peterson were appointed *keur-meesters van de heyningen*, or inspectors of fences, in place of Hendrick Karstens and Adam Dericksen; and a fine of 3 guilders was ordered against the owners every time their fences should be found defective. The court also directed "the fences at the north side of the village to be set within fourteen days, under a penalty of two pounds Flemish" for each failure—equivalent to 12 gl. A

* CARSTEN JANSEN SNEDEN, still at H., entered Daniel Tourneur's service, Jan. 15, 1668, for a year, and at its expiration was to have 300 gl. and "a pair of shoes and stockings." His uncle, Claes Sneden, lived in N. Y., where his chn. by his w. Maria were bapt. between 1663 and 1667. He or Carsten was no doubt the anc. of the Snedens of Rockland Co.

JEAN GUENON d. at Flushing, L. I., in 1714. His will, made when he was in perfect health, dates Nov. 24, 1703; that of his wid. Margaret, Feb. 21, 1721-2. At the latter date their sons, John, b. 1669, and Jeremiah, b. 1671, were living; as also their drs., Hannah, w. of Joseph Hedger, and Susannah, w. of Loucreer. John and Jeremiah Genung shared their fa.'s farm in Flushing; their desc. are now to be found in many parts, especially of the State of N. Y.

placard to that effect was posted up. This was called for by the great damage done the past summer to the crops of peas and buckwheat upon the land of Jochem Pieters, from the cattle getting in; and which the schout, Slot, had taken no means to remedy, though the fence-masters and others had gone to him with loud complaints. The new officers going to view the fences, December 18th, found that Michiel Muyden, Hendrick J. Vander Vin, Daniel Tourneur, and Jean le Roy had not complied with the placard. They were all complained of December 27th, by the new schout, who demanded the fines, viz., from Muyden 24 gl. for his two lots, and 12 gl. from each of the others. Tourneur pleaded sickness and other excuses, but the court exacted the fine from him and from Le Roy, with costs of suit. Muyden and Vander Vin, after being thrice in default, were also sentenced, January 25th, 1663, with order to pay inside of eight days.

It showed admirable pluck on the part of the magistracy to thus deal with persons of the first standing; for Vander Vin and Muyden were both great burghers of New Amsterdam, and the first an ex-schepen. On several occasions, by invitation, Muyden had occupied the bench at Harlem, as "an extraordinary schepen," his intelligence and fitness for the office leading to a regular appointment soon after to fill a vacancy. He had visited Holland in 1661, bringing out on his return a number of hardy Norwegian workmen, and was now prosecuting the business of soap-making. And thus closed 1662, with its various measures of public utility and impartial dispensing of justice, alike necessary to protect and promote the common interests of the villagers.*

* François le Sueur, who left the town early in 1663, was the anc. of the families of Leseur and Losier, now mostly seated in N. Y. City and Bergen Co., N. J. François first lived in Flatbush after coming to Manhattan, and in 1659 m. Jannetie, dr. of Hillebrand Pietersen, of Amsterdam: in which year Jannetie's br., Pieter Hillebrands, was captured by Indians at Esopus, but this did not deter her from removing there with her hus. Before going from H. he sold some of his effects, and his w. bought "a little bed," etc., at Sneden's sale. Le Sueur's sr. Jeanne went with them to Esopus, and there m. Cornelis Viervant, with whom she returned to H. Le Sueur was living in 1669, but on Nov. 30, 1671, his wid. bound out her son Hillebrand, eight years old. He was engaged by the deacons in 1673 to ring the bell at 5 gl. a year. Afterward the wid. m. Antoine Tilba, and by him had chn. also. Those by Le Sueur, all but the first, b. at Esopus, were

CHAPTER XIII.

1663–1665.

STIRRING EVENTS: END OF THE DUTCH RULE.

IT happened that Pieter Jansen Slot, son of the ex-schepen, was to wed a fair damsel of Ahasimus, by name Marritie van Winckel. The young roysters of the village hearing, on Friday, February 2d, 1663, that the bans had that day been registered, were jubilant over the news, and set to work—it was an ancient rustic custom of fatherland—to honor the happy Pieter by planting a "May-tree" before his door. Now some workmen in the employ of Mr. Muyden and others, in far ruder sport, not only raised "a horrible noise in the village, by shouting, blowing horns, etc., while others were asleep," but proceeded to deck the May-tree with ragged stockings; at which, when discovered by Pieter, he was very worth, taking it as "a mockery and insult." He at once cut the tree down, but the young men brought another to take its place; when, as it lay before the

Jannetie, b. 1660, who m. Jan Postma (now Post) and Thomas Innis; Hillebrand, b. 1663, John and Jacob, b. 1665, and Nicholas, b. 1668. *Hillebrand* m. 1688 Elsie, dr. of Jurian Tappen, but soon d., leaving apparently but one ch., Jannetie, b. 1689, who m. William Ekling. Hillebrand's wid. m. Abraham Delamater, previously of H. *John*, of Kingston, m. Rachel Smedes, in 1686, was an elder of the chh., and quite distinguished. He had Jannetie, b. 1687, John, b. 1689, Catharine, b. 1692, etc., of whom the first m. Abm. Low. *Nicholas*, whose branch of the family write their name *Lozier*, m. at N. Y., May 8, 1691, Tryntie, dr. of Peter Slot. He afterward left Kingston and settled near Hackensack, where he m., in Jan., 1709, Antie, dr. of Derick Banta. His chn. were Hillebrand, b. 1695, Peter, b. 1697, John, b. 1699, Mary, b. 1701, Antie, b. 1703, Lucas, b. 1705, Jacobus, b. 1707, Benjamin, b. 1708, Tryntie, b. 1710, Hester, b. 1711, Rachel, b. 1714, Jacob, b. 1719, Abraham, b. 1721, Leah, b. 1723, and Margaret, b. 1726. These intermarried with the Demarests and others, but we must here leave them. In Ulster Co. the French pronunciation of this name was, for a time, tolerably preserved in the form *Lashier*, but it is now extinct there, though the blood runs in the Post family and others.

house, along came Mnyden's men and hewed it in pieces. Not to be baffled, the young folks the same night procured and raised a third tree, which, however, shared the same fate.

On Sunday morning, February 4th, Jan Pietersen, at whose house Pieter was staying and all this happened, made his complaint to Montagne, the schout; the masters also informing him that their men were plotting other mischief, but they had no power to prevent it. The schout, now going thither, ordered the rioters to disperse; but they only defied him, and even threatened him with their guns and axes. Only more enraged, they gave the Sabbath to cutting down and burning the palisades around Jaques Cresson's barn. Next morning Jacob Elderts, who had lately bought a lot on Van Keulen's Hook, was engaged bringing thatch from Bronck's meadow. Before he had spoken "a single word," they caught and beat him, also wounding him on the head. In vain "Meester Willem," who witnessed the assault, commanded them to desist. Perhaps it was to pay off Elderts for the death of their countrymen, Bruyn Barents, a cooper, five years before; perhaps not. The two were then working in a brewery at Brooklyn, and Bruyn made at Elderts with a knife, when the latter, in self-defense, knocked him down with a sledge. Bruyn lingered six months, and died February 12th, 1658. As the case stood Jacob was arrested, but let off by the court with a fine of 100 gl. for the wounding. But be this the explanation or not, the schout seeing the rioters heeded not his authority, and apprehending further trouble, hastened, the same day, to inform the Director, who with the Council referred the matter to the Attorney General, "to take further information about it."

Here ended, or is lost sight of, this almost tragedy; the public attention at Harlem being absorbed by the death, in quick succession, of two worthy inhabitants, Adam Dericksen and Philip Casier. Dericksen was from Cologne, owned an allotment of land and had served as inspector of fences with Hendrick Karstens in 1661–2. In the first of these years he married Magdalena, daughter of Lambert van Tcekhuys. Left with an infant Grietie, his widow, a few months later, became the wife of Monis Peterson. In the death of Casier the community lost one of its sterling men, a skillful farmer, and valued for his experience and judgment. His place in the magistracy was filled, April 23d, by the appointment of Michiel J. Muyden.*

The old question touching the payment for their lands now came up in a somewhat different shape, and with better success. The following memorial, explaining it, was drawn up by Heer Vander Vin; the clerk, Montagne, having now no personal interest in this matter apparently:

TO THE NOBLE, GREAT AND HONORABLE, THE DIRECTOR GENERAL AND COUNCIL IN NEW NETHERLAND.

The undersigned, owners and occupants of the lands within the village and jurisdiction of *New Harlem*, respectfully represent, that to their great surprise and solicitude, they have been informed that the *eight guilders* which your Honors required said proprietors to pay for each morgen of land taken by them, should be paid in *beavers*, or their value; whereas this was not the understanding of your petitioners, who, in regard to the announcement made by your Honors, on the 4th of March, 1658, as to the privileges with which this village was to be favored, did not otherwise conceive respecting the price set upon said land, but that payment thereof was to be made in *sewant* currency, according to the

* PHILIPPE CASIER, had he lived, must have proved a most useful inhabitant. His adventurous voyage from France to the West Indies, back to Holland, thence up the Rhine, and finally to this country, with his eight in family, are events in his life already noticed. Another ch., Sarah, was added in 1662, when Casier had become a resident and landholder at H. He and w. Marie Taine united with the chh. Oct. 2, of that year, and on Nov. 16, he was made a magistrate. But near the close of the ensuing winter, 1663, death arrested his usefulness. He had but just sold, Jan. 11, 1663, a lot on Van Keulen's Hook to Jacob Eldertsen, also called Brouwer (Brewer), from his former occupation. Selling her lands to Joost van Oblinus, the wid. bought a house in the Markvelt-steegie, in N. Y., and lived there for some years, with her sons Jean and Jacques, who were bakers. In 1671 she m. Jean le Roy, of H., and afterward went with him to Staten Island. Her dr. Hester, b. at Sluis, in Flanders, m. in 1677 Jean Belleville, who was living in 1703. They had sons Jean, b. 1677, Philip, b. 1679, etc. See *Martine*. The younger dr., Sarah Casier, m. 1680 Jacques Guion, merchant, from St. Martin, France, she being much his junior. His will, made May 3, 1680, was proved Dec. 1, 1694, and his wid. admitted executrix. Guion visited Europe in 1678. He owned 200 acres of land on Staten Island, granted him Oct. 13, 1664, on which some of his desc. still reside. Philip Casier's two sons, in 1673, were members of Capt. Steenwyck's troop; but Jacques appears to have soon d. unm. Jean accompanied his mo. to Staten Island in 1676, obtaining that year a grant of 80 acres of land on Long Neck. He m. in 1680 Elizabeth, dr. of John Damen, of Brooklyn. In 1701 he, and his br.-in-law, Jean Belleville, owning an adjoining farm, with other neighbors like themselves, born French subjects (Casier had his birth in the French island of Martinique), sent their names to England, and were naturalized by act of Parliament. Casier made his will Dec. 26, 1709, which was proved the next month, Jan. 24, 1710. Susannah, a second w., survived him. His chn. then living were Philip and Peter, who shared his farm, and drs. Sophia and Elizabeth. Has not this name become *Cary*?

customary usage. Had they understood differently, they would never have agreed, nor could have been persuaded, to burden themselves with so hard an undertaking as that of bringing those lands under cultivation, besides paying thus heavily for them; and even yet the petitioners, instead of finding themselves eased in their labors, have great difficulty in making these lands fit for tillage, so they are now wholly discouraged, as they did not apprehend that they should encounter the present difficulty. Wherefore, addressing themselves to your Honors, they pray that your Honors may be pleased to declare, by a favorable answer on the margin, that the petitioners may pay the eight guilders per morgen, in *sewant*, in the usual course between man and man.*

JAN PIETERSEN, *his mark* IP	DIRCK CLAESSEN.
HENDR. J. VANDR. VIN	D. TOURNEUR.
JEAN LE ROY, *his mark* +	*Moy* PIER CRESSON.
MORRIS PETERSON, *his mark* 9	N. D'MEYER.
JAN LOUBESE, *his mark* N	SIMON DE RUINE, *his mark* +
COURSEAU.	M. MUYDEN.
HENDRICK KARSTENS, *his mark* II	JAQUES CRESSON.

As the effect of their former decision upon this subject had been to force some worthy persons to sell out their improvements and quit the town, the Director and Council now conceded more than the petition asked for. Their answer was as follows:

This 19th March, 1663. The foregoing petition being presented and read, and besides this, the proposals of the schepens of the village of New Haerlem, made in the name of the inhabitants of that village, having been heard and considered; the Director-General and Council, after some debate *pro* and *con*, have resolved to relieve the inhabitants from the payment of the eight guilders per morgen, which they agreed to and were held to pay, by the terms upon which the lands were distributed: *Provided*, that the said inhabitants, in lieu of an exemption from tithes for fifteen years, shall enjoy the same but eight years; so that they shall be obliged to satisfy the tithes promptly in the year 1666, which said tithes, from 1666 to 1672, both years inclusive, shall, in place of the eight guilders per morgen, be for the benefit of the parties (or their creditors), who were formerly expelled from said lands.

* BEAVER and other furs, with sewant (see note p. 153), together formed the common currency among the settlers. Beaver was convenient for large payments, especially for remittances to Holland, as was sewant for small payments and for making change, and this was the currency mainly used in all ordinary trading. But beaver, which was as gold, always commanding its fixed price, had become so scarce as often not to be had for the payment of a debt, without going a long distance for it, even to Fort Orange or the Delaware River; while sewant was plenty, and its value fluctuating. Therefore this distinction; a *guilder beaver*, that is, a guilder payable in beaver, was counted 40 cents, at the standard value of the guilder, but a *guilder sewant* was worth only one third of the former, or 13⅓ cents, and depreciated still more. Hence a wide difference how the bargain was, whether to pay the stipulated number of guilders in beaver or in sewant.

Thus was put to rest, to the great relief of the inhabitants, a question which had been a long-standing source of anxiety with them; and the history of which is important, first, as showing on what terms the lands were finally held, and second, to what labor and trouble the settlers were put, in felling the forests and subduing the soil, to make themselves a home; a struggle truly, with their scanty means. But they had come to a point when their courage, energy, and faith in God were to be put to a more severe test.*

Astounding news reached the villagers of an Indian onslaught and massacre at Esopus, on June 7th, in which some of their friends and kinsfolk were sufferers, and witnessed by Jacob Elderts, who had lately gone thither. The schout, Montagne, in the flush of nuptial greetings on his union with Maria Vermeille, a lady from his native place, was shocked to hear that his sister Van Imbroch and her little Lysbet were in captivity with the savages. Harlem was all alarm. The town people assembled June 12th, by orders from below, and with the advice of the magistrates, Montagne, Claessen, Tourneur and Muyden, and clear-headed Slot, asked to sit with them as extraordinary schepen, proceeded to take the necessary steps for inclosing the village with a line of stockades, and putting it in a complete state of

* DAVID UZILLE, the Huguenot, m. to Maria, dr. of Philip Casier, had now left the town, and, as did the Casiers afterward, probably went to Staten Island, because his son, Peter Uzille, was living there Apl. 6, 1686, when he m. Cornelia Damen, of the Wallabout, a sr. of Mrs. Jean Casier. Peter went thence to Bushwick, near his br.-in-law, Michael Parmentier, but both ultimately removed to Poughkeepsie, Duchess Co., where Uzille was living in 1714. His sr. Maria-Magdalen Uzille, b. at H. in 1663, m., I believe, Jonas Le Roy, of Esopus. Peter Uzille's chn. were John, b. 1688, of whom n/a.; Sophia, b. 1691, m. 1712 Storm Bratt, of Albany; Cornelia, b. 1693, m. 1714 Joh. Becker; Helena, b. 1696, m. 1716 William Hooghteeling; Elizabeth, b. 1701, Peter, b. 1703, and David, b. 1708. David, living at Albany, had by w. Engeltie Vrooman, the following chn., viz.: Peter, b. 1733, Cornelia, b. 1734, Gertrude, b. 1736, and Adam, b. 1738. Peter Uzille, b. 1703, m. Anna Ackerson 1724, and settled at Schoharie. In his will, made on a sick-bed, Feb. 9, 1747, he provided that if his w. should have a son, he was to take half his farm; otherwise to go to his drs., after his w.'s d. To these, viz., Cornelia, Elizabeth, Engeltie, Maria, Annetie, Janneke, and Catharine, the pious fa. gives this touching counsel: "My loving children, this is the last I shall recommend to you; divide my estate peaceably amongst you all, according to the intent and meaning of my last will and testament, and look upon the poor and help them, love your neighbor, and keep the peace among you and with all men, honor your mother and your king, and fear God and keep his commandments." Some of these drs. m. Vroomans. This name took the form of *Zielle* and *Seely*

defense. Ten persons were designated to cut palisades, and four others to draw them to the village; while Tourneur and Jaques Cresson were deputed to procure a supply of arms and ammunition promised from the Manhattans. At the same time the dozen or more soldiers stationed here, together with the settlers (exclusive of the presiding magistrates), forty persons in all, were formed into military companies, which after some time spent in changing and rearranging the ranks, were duly organized. For officers the eldest and most capable persons were selected. In the first company, Pierre Cresson, in the ripe manhood of fifty-odd years and still very active, was assigned the chief and responsible command of *corporal;* with Isaac Vermeille, aged sixty-two, as his *lancepesade;* and Glaude le Maistre, turned of fifty years, and Lubbert Gerritsen, about forty, as *adelborsts* or *cadets.* Of the second company Willem Jansen was made *lancepesade,* and the *cadets* were Jan de Weever (the weaver) and Arent Snyder (or the tailor), by the last probably meant Arent Harmans Busing. Of the third company, Simon de Ruine, "the Walloon," was chosen *corporal;* Nelis Matthyssen, *lancepesade,* and Pieter Jansen Slot and Barent Acker, *cadets.**

Two days after the munitions of war were received from Heer Van Ruyven, the government officer, to wit: 3 *steen stucken* (cannons carrying a seven or eight pound ball); 5 *snaphaanen,* or firelocks; 3 *musquets,* or matchlocks; 36 *steen* balls (for the *steen stucken*); 50 pounds of cannon powder; 10 pounds of fine

* The privates were as follows:

1st Company.

Abram Vermeille,
Jean le Roy,
Joost van Oblinus,
Aert Pietersen Buys,
Johannes Piet'n Buys,
Jaques Cresson,
Jan Teunissen,
Hendrick Karstens,
Jan Jansen Slot,
Thomas Ottosen.

2d Company.

Jan Schoenmaker,
Hans Litson,
Abram Litsou,
Michiel Litson,
Ambrosius de Weerham,
Jacob Droogscheerder,
Arent J. Moesman,
Jan Noorman,
Arie Noorman.

3d Company.

Mouis Peterson,
Jan Cogu,
Roelof Noorman,
Jacob Noorman,
Govert Noorman,
Hans Deen,
Derick de Vries,
Adolph Meyer,
Cornelis Aertse Buys,
Jean Casier.

powder, and 15 bars of lead for running bullets. At once the small arms were distributed to such as needed them. On the 16th six more matchlocks were obtained, together with a bundle of match for touching off the matchlocks and cannon. The former were placed in the hands of those still unsupplied. The persons to whom the small arms were given, one to each, were Daniel Tourneur, Jan La Montagne, Michiel J. Muyden, Jaques Cresson, and Jan P. Slot, supplied with *firelocks*; and Isaac Vermeille, Abram Vermeille, Pierre Cresson, Jean le Roy, Claude le Maistre, and Aert P. Buys, with *musquets*. Mr. Muyden also took musquets for two of his workmen. The "steen stucken" were properly mounted. Thus prepared to repel an attack, the villagers awaited the course of events, keeping up a strict watch.

New Harlem now became in fact a garrisoned outpost to New Amsterdam, and a barrier against Indian raids; with Stuyvesant, a cherished object, as before seen, in his anxiety to protect the metropolis. In view of the public danger the Director and Council invited delegates from all the villages to a conference at New Amsterdam, on July 6th. Harlem found it safest to keep every man at his post, but answered by letter, promising to detail a force of eight soldiers "whenever the necessity might require it." Troops being needed soon after for an expedition to Esopus, to subdue the Indians and give relief to the settlers there, a part of the regular force at Harlem departed upon that service, accompanied by others who went in response to the urgent call for volunteers which was made through all the villages about New Amsterdam.

The savages at Esopus were soon made to flee before the advance of the resolute Dutch soldiers; but armed parties still kept the war-path, threatening vengeance on the whites and whoever should aid them. It happened during the month of July that the now friendly Wickquaskeeks, apprehending a hostile visit from such, left their usual haunts and removed for safety over into the woods near Harlem. The sudden appearance of so large a body of Indians, including some eighty warriors, in the vicinity of the village, caused much excitement there, till the sachem Sauwenárack, with his brother, came to the magistrates and gave the reason of their visit. They brought the pleasing intelligence that the sister of Mr. Montagne had been released from captivity through the intervention of the friendly Mohawks, and conveyed to her home; but they also gave this piece of disagreeable news, that the Indians of the Wappinger tribe had warned them that the Esopus Indians were intending, within five or six days, to descend the river, forty or fifty strong, in order to surprise and murder them, the Wickquaskecks, and also destroy New Harlem and other settlements about Manhattan. Their message delivered, the chiefs hastened "of their own accord" to New Amsterdam, and repeated it to the Director General, with the offer of their services, in the common peril to which all were exposed.

No little anxiety was felt at Harlem for a time, but the talked-of visit was not made, and the movements of the Wickquaskecks came to excite no apprehension. The sachem and his people—a thing they once would have scorned to ask of the white man—sought permission to fish near the village, which was granted on condition that they should never approach that place with their weapons; and for the purpose of ready identification, in their intercourse with the settlers, they were given copies of the official seal of the West India Company, "printed in wax upon small billets," to be shown upon occasion. Still the magistrates relaxed none of their vigilance. Another thirty pounds of powder, obtained of the commissary, was distributed, September 2d, to the following persons, a pound to each:

Monis Peterson,	Barent Acker,
Simon de Ruine,	Pierre Cresson,
Hendrick Karstens,	Jaques Cresson,
Jan Janson Slot,	Jean le Roy,
Jan Tounissen,	Jan Cogu,
Jan Schoenmaker,	Michiel Litton,
Arent Snyder,	Joh. Pietersen Buys,
Nelis Matthyssen,	Glande le Maistre,
Adolph Meyer,	Lubbert Gerritsen,
Aert Pietersen Buys,	Jean Frenchman,
Cornelis Aertsen Buys,	Jan La Montagne,
Hans Dean,	Jan Pietersen Slot,

Govert Noorman,	Daniel Tourneur,
Jacob Droogscheerder,	Pieter Janson Slot,
Jan Noorman,	Mr. Willem.*

The public apprehensions were gradually removed by a series of victories over the Esopus Indians, which forced them to submit. But the people of the province were ill at ease. Delegates from the villages, met to consider their common dangers, signed, November 2d, an urgent appeal to the West India Company, praying for protection both against the Indians and the neighboring New England colonies, which latter were now preparing to end a long diplomatic warfare with the Dutch authorities touching their boundaries, by boldly asserting a claim to the whole of New Netherland.

Notwithstanding the ruffled state of public affairs, there was a growing activity at Harlem, as may be judged from the valuable accession to the number of inhabitants which the current year (1663) had brought. With most of these, already incidentally mentioned in the transactions of the year, we have been made acquainted in former pages. Glaude le Maistre (or Delamater) had removed here, after living about ten years at Flatbush, where he owned a farm and two village lots, which he sold July 31st, 1662. He bought two allotments of land at Harlem from Daniel Tourneur, who had purchased them of Jacques Cousseau, and subsequently got a patent for them. Johannes Verveelen, previously for several years an innkeeper in New Amsterdam, had come to resume his old business, and to enter immediately upon public life.

But the new arrivals were mostly direct from fatherland. The Vermeille or Vermilye family, six in number, had reached Manhattan early in 1663, *via* the Delaware River; the family of Oblinus arriving during the ensuing spring, after a quick pas-

* Jan Schoonmaker and Arent Snyder may have been Dyckman and Bussing; but we have no sufficient proof. By "Mr. Willem," and "Willem Jansen," Jan La Montagne, who makes the record, no doubt means his brother. Fourteen of those enrolled June 12 are not in the above list, viz., Isaac Vermeille, Abram Vermeille, Jean Casier, Arent Moseman, Hans and Abram Lubbertsen, Ambrose de Weerham, Jan de Weever, Thomas Ottosen, Dirck de Vries, Arie Noorman, Roelof Noorman, and Jacob Noorman. Gone, we presume, with the forces to Esopus; Moseman certainly had, and he, Casier, and Isaac Vermeille are the only ones known to have returned to Harlem.

age, and coming direct to Harlem; as did Johannes Buys (though by another vessel, the Rosetree, which left Amsterdam March 15th, 1663), joining his brother, who had preceded him hither some two years.* The younger Oblinus at once entered the employ of Delamater, but before the year closed his father became a proprietor by the purchase of the allotment of Philip Casier, deceased. Of Oblinus' companions on board the Spotted Cow, Demarest went to Staten Island, Journee and Bogert to Brooklyn, and the Bastiaensen brothers to Stuyvesant's Bowery, though they all soon after came to Harlem. The Bastiaensens, it may be observed, were the ancestors of the entire Kortright or Courtright family, in the States of New York and New Jersey, and also through other branches, of the families of Ryer and Michiel (now Mekeel and McKeel—a Dutch metamorphosed into a Hibernian name!) of Westchester and other counties of our State, and that of Low, in Somerset County, New Jersey, but distinct from the Lows of Ulster County, named in a preceding note. Arent Jansen Moesman—first met with at

* ISAAC VERMILYE had as companions on the voyage, Jacque Cossart, Nicolas du Puis, Gideon Merlett, Jean le Conseillie, Louis Lacqueman, Jacob Kolver, and Jan Boeckhoolts, as also Arnout du Toict (these now written *Casbow*, *Depew*, *Marlett*, *Conselyea*, *Lakeman* or *Lackman*, *Culver*, *Buckhout*, etc.), all having lived at Leyden, we presume, as we know had Buckhout, Culver, and Vermilye; and probably all Walloons except Buckhout. Vermilye, with his w. and dr. Maria (later Mrs. Montanye), and all his fellow-passengers above named, save Culver and Buckhout, joined the chh. at New Amsterdam Apl. 1, 1663, no doubt by letter. The wives of Cossart, Du Puis, and Lacqueman also united. Vermilye came directly to H. Buckhout became "koeherder van de gemeente desen stede." The rest made an application, Mar. 19, 1663, for land and seed grain, and victuals for six months, showing their necessities. Buckhout later owned a farm at Mespat, and left two sons, Capt. Matthias, who sailed a coaster, and Peter, a farmer; and whence come the families of this name. Du Toict was from Lille, and probably related to David du Toict, of Leyden, son-in-law of Gerard de Forest. By his w. Madeleine Arnaud she had a son Abraham, b. 1649, lessee of Pierre Cresson's meadows at H. in 1668; who m. Jannetie, dr. of Jerome Boquet (Bokee), and had a family. He went to New Utrecht and bought a farm, served during the second Dutch rule as a soldier, under Capt. Knyf, in N. Y., afterward lived at Bedford, but with his w. joined the Bergen chh. July 21, 1681. Lakeman brought a w., Anna du Sauchoy, and 3 chn., b. 1656, 1658, 1660, but had also a Jacob, b. 1664, besides other chn. by a second w., Maria Walters. Two of the chn. that came over with him were Abraham and Peter, who afterward got grants upon Staten Island, but Peter Lakeman removed to N. Y. in 1698, when he m. wid. Jannetie Stavast. Marlett brought his w. and sons Joshua, b. 1647, Paul, b. 1654, John, b. 1656, and Abraham, b. 1658, and settled on S. I. The name has now left the Island, but is found in other sections of N. Y. and in N. J.

Amsterdam in 1662, acting as purveyor to the passengers about to leave, March 11th, in the merchant ship Golden Eagle, for New Amstel on the Delaware, and in which he also took passage, arriving at the Manhattans May 2d—had found his way to Harlem, as before seen. Now returned from the Esopus war, with the credit and profits of some special service rendered, he became the purchaser of a bouwery upon Jochem Pieters and Van Keulen's Hook, the history of which derives interest from its subsequent owners, Delavall, Carteret, and others. Indeed the village was fast filling up, and already showed a disposition to exceed the limits of the protecting palisades. At a court held on December 4th, Derick Claessen, who after quitting the town had again returned, applied for "the house lot lying without the gate;" and Johannes Vermilye also made a similar application. Many, with the returning sense of security, were laying plans for the future.

By a recent choice of magistrates, confirmed November 17th, the new board consisted of Jan La Montagne, "who for certain reasons," say the Council, "shall yet be continued for one

Cosart brought his w. Lydia Williams and 2 chn. of 18 months and 5 yrs. They had also Jacob, b. 1668, David, 1671, Anthony, 1673. Jacob m. 1695 Anna Maria, dr. of Joh. Caspars Springsteen. He, and Anthony who m. 1696 Elizabeth, dr. of Jan Tymensen Valentine, of Schenectady, were residents of Brooklyn; their posterity bearing the name Casbow or Carshow. Jacob *Cosart*, b. at Brooklyn 1701, a son of Anthony, d. at Bound Brook, N. J., Apl. 19, 1772. David Cosart, m. 1696, Seyntie, b. 1677, dr. of Joris Jansen van Hoorn, and had with other chn. b. in N. Y. city, sons George, Jacob, David, John, Francis. He d. between 1736 and 1740, in Somerset co., N. J., leaving farms there to his sons George, David and Francis. Conselyea m. Phebe Schut, and lived in Bushwick, where his old farm-house till late remained. He had sons, John, b. 1679, Peter, 1688, and a dr., Margaret, who m. Joh. van Tilburg and Claes Bogert. Culver, whose w. was Sarah, dr. of Peter Hasbrouck, d. soon after the birth of his dr. Sarah, and the next year, 1664, his wid. m. Jacob Jansen Blaeck, from Amsterdam, by whom she had other chn. The dr., Sarah Culver, b. 1663, m. Peter Lowee, of Bushwick; her sr. Geertie Culver, b. 1657, m. Cornelis Jansen Zeeuw, and their br. Jacob Culver (b. 1659, at Leyden, d. 1694, in N. Y.) m. 1684 Jannetie, dr. of Joh. Caspars Springsteen, of Brooklyn. Their dr. Sarah, b. 1686, m. David L. Ackerman, of Hackensack; their dr. Maria m. Joost Springsteen, of Newtown, and their son Johannes Culver, b. 1689, m. Sarah, dr. of James Way, and Mary, dr. of John Gancel, served as an elder at Newtown, and there d., June 12, 1760, leaving several sons. Depew, who was from Artois, was sworn as "beer and weigh-house porter," at N. Y., June 19, 1663. Here he d. in 1693, leaving issue by his w. Catalina Renard, Jean, b. 1656, Moses, 1657, Aaron, 1664, Susannah, 1667, and Nicholas, 1670. From these spring the numerous Depew families of Ulster and Orange counties and of the Minisink Flats.

year;" besides Daniel Tourneur, Johannes Verveelen, and Jan Pietersen Slot. The religious interests of the village were suffering, and called for their first care. Do. Zyperus had recently taken his leave, probably early in 1663, when his wife transferred her church connection from New Amsterdam to Brooklyn. Chosen at different times as an arbiter between parties in litigation, Mr. Zyperus had made himself useful outside of his office or special sphere of duty, and had acquired the respect of the community. Disposing of his lands to Sergeant Juriaen Hanel, of Bergen, he removed with his family to Virginia, where he afterward preached many years, in North River Precinct, now Kingston Parish, in Mathews County; having conformed to the Church of England.*

The experiment had evidently proven the inability of the congregation to support a minister, and since the departure of Zyperus, not without much effort had the Sabbath services been sustained. Hence at the meeting referred to, on December 4th, 1663, one of the magistrates, Mr. Verveelen was "chosen by a popular vote to inquire for a *Voorleser*," or, in other words, a parish clerk. This office, though akin to that of *precentor* or chorister in the Romish cathedral service and in the Scotch kirk, was in its range of duties quite peculiar to the Reformed

* Do. ZYPERUS' w. was the dr. of Claes Duurkoop; her br., Jan Duurkoop, and st. Jannetie, w. of Hendrick Jansen Heen, were living at Brooklyn in 1662 whence, probably on their account, Mrs. Zyperus took her church letter Mar. 25, 1663. With the departure of herself and husband soon after disappear also her kindred above named. While here Do. Z. had two chn. baptized, viz., Cornelius, Dec. 21, 1659, and Hillegond, Aug. 14, 1661; the last named for Mrs. Cornelis Van Ruyven. He is noticed as rector of Kingston Parish in a list of the Virginia clergy, dated June 30, 1680. But this is verified by his old vestry-book, now in the custody of the Episcopal Theological Seminary near Alexandria, extracts from which were kindly furnished me by the late principal, Rev. William Sparrow, D.D., since deceased, and containing all additional that I know of Zyperus in Virginia. The record begins only with Nov. 15, 1679, but the last mention of him, as follows, is suggestive:

"The 27th of June, 1687. The day abovesaid Mr. Mychaell Zyperus, Minister, did promise to give fitt and convenient Glasses for ye Window at ye Gable End of ye New Chappell to be built for ye North River precinct. In witness whereof he hath hereunto sett his hand. M. ZYPERUS."

Interesting thus to take leave of him actively at work rearing the walls of Zion, in that field which he had chosen, and where he probably ended his labors. I strongly suspect that Do. Zyperus' descendants compose the respectable family of *Sypher*, of Pennsylvania, whose early Michaels—a fact, with others, made known to me by Mr. J. R. Sypher, of Philadelphia—seem to favor it.

Dutch Church. Its incumbent, acting either in place of or as an assistant to the domine, must needs be a person not only of suitable gifts and culture, but of exemplary life and approved piety. Standing before the pulpit, he read the Scriptures at the opening of public worship, whence came his title, *voorleser*, or *forereader*. He led the congregation in singing David's Psalms in metre, lining off the verses one by one, as they proceeded, with melodies long drawn out, but stately and solemn.* In the absence of a preacher his duties were augmented. He then read a sermon from the works of some orthodox Dutch divine, and in a word conducted the entire service so far as belonged to a layman to do. He visited and administered comfort to the sick, and those nigh to death, and when desired performed the burial service. He instructed the children in the Heidelberg catechism, filled the office of schoolmaster, and in addition kept the records and accounts of the church and town. In fact, except the administration of holy ordinances, he performed all the functions of pastor, besides those of chorister, schoolmaster, and secretary. To these were usually added the duties of vendue-master, or public auctioneer.

Jan La Montagne, already acting as secretary, being conferred with and found willing to assume the full office of voorleser, the schepens, after advising with Governor Stuyvesant, prepared the

* Imagine our devout fathers thus gravely singing, in the following words, their favorite 23d Psalm:

1. Myn Godt voed my als myn Herder gepresen;
   Dies sal ik geenes dings behoeftik wesen.
   In't groene gras seellestik hy my weydet;
   En aen dat soet water hy my geleydet;
   Hy verquickt myn siel, die was in verslegen;
   Om syns naems wil leyt hy my in syn wegen.

2. Alwaer't schoon dat ick in't dal des doots ginge,
   En dat my des doots schaduwe omvinge,
   Ik vreese niet, gy syt by my gestadig,
   En gy troost my met uwen staf genadigh,
   Gy maeckt ryk met goede seer velerhanden
   Myn tafel voor d'oogen myner vyanden.

3. Gy salst myn hooft met riekend'oly goedigh,
   En schenkt my den beker vol overvloedigh.
   Gy sult doen dat uwe gunst, O Heer krachtigh,
   Myn leven langh by my steedsvlyft eendrachtig:
   Soo dat ick hoop eeuwighlick vast te wounen
   In Godes Huys, 't welk niet is om verschoonen.

following interesting petition, which was presented through Mr. Verveelen :

To the Noble, Very Worshipful, their Honors the Director General and Council of New Netherland.

Gentlemen : Your Noble Worships' petitioners, residents of New Haerlem, show with due reverence and submission, that by their saving faith, obtained through hearing the gospel preached and taught, they too find themselves for the sake of their salvation compelled, conscientiously to promote with increased diligence and zeal whatever your Noble Worships' petitioners and Commissaries of this village have determined upon and undertaken for the maintaining of public worship and the outward means of grace, to the magnifying of God's Name, the observance of his day of holy rest, and the upbuilding of the body of Jesus Christ. But having seen from Sabbath day to Sabbath day the small and insignificant success of the public gatherings, and believing confidently, that everything relating to public worship may be brought in better train and all be more properly ordered, by the services of a salaried *voorlezer* and schoolmaster, to read God's word and edifying sermons, keep school, catechise and visit the sick, your Noble Worships' petitioners, appointed to attend to the public welfare and advantage of the said village, thought it proper, very timely and only their duty, to speak to the community about this matter, that they persuade Jean de la Montagne, a resident of the said place, to undertake such services provisionally for the least possible salary, and then present themselves before your Noble Worships as patrons of the church of Jesus Christ with this humble and Christian petition, that your Noble Worships may please to consent both to the office and person before named, for the benefit of God's church and not less necessary teaching of the children. But perceiving their present inability and incapacity to give in the aforesaid case a full and proper salary, and not having been able to collect for his support more than 24 schepels of grain,* they respectfully request your Noble Worships, that in their usual noble discretion your Noble Worships contribute something towards a decent salary and the greater encouragement of your Noble Worships' very humble petitioners and God's subjects.

Your Noble Worships' most dutiful petitioners and humble subjects,

Done New Haerlem, Dec. 25, 1663.

D. Tourneur.
Johannes Verveelen,
I P *mark of* Jan Pietersen.

To this the following reply was given, January 10th, 1664 :

Received and read the foregoing request of the Commissaries of New Haerlem, and therewith heard the verbal statement of Sieur Johannes Verveelen, at present commissary there, that it is highly necessary that a person be appointed there as *voorlezer* and schoolmaster ; therefore the Director General and Council accept and appoint thereto the proposed person Johannes La Montagne, Junior ; and in order that he may attend

* The *schepel*, a Dutch measure, was commonly rated in this country at three English pecks. *Woolley's Journal*, p. 34.

to these officers with greater diligence, to him shall be paid annually on account of the Company the sum of fifty guilders, according to the state of the treasury.

Thereafter the church had a regular succession of voorlesers, to perform the varied and responsible duties before specified; except when partially relieved by the visits of the city ministers, who officiated here by occasional appointment, or under engagements made with them from time to time, as will further appear.

New arrivals in the village were still occurring. One was that of a French refugee heretofore mentioned, and who is first alluded to in the minutes of January 23rd, 1664, thus: "*Robert le Maire* requested an" . . . . the record left unfinished; but probably explained by the fact that he soon obtained *an erf* from the town. A few of the larger landholders, as Slot and De Meyer, now took occasion to obtain patents or groundbriefs for their lands, though the two named and that of Hanel, dated May 16th ensuing, are the only patents found, issued by Governor Stuyvesant, for the allotments under the ordinance of 1658. This accords with what the inhabitants afterward told Governor Nicolls, namely, that most of them "never had a groundbrief." An event of interest to the villagers was the surrender by the widow of Cornelis Claessen Swits, to the Director and Council (pursuant to an offer which she made to them February 7th, 1664, and by them accepted), of all her claim to the farm occupied by her late husband, but "purchased and cultivated by her," in lieu of the debt due from Swits to the West India Company. The title thus reverted to the government, and the lands on which was the village plot were thereby relieved of any mediate claim which could possibly be set up under the old patent of 1647.*

* This petition and answer are of sufficient interest to be given entire.

To the Noble, Right Honorable, the DIRECTOR GENERAL and COUNCIL in New Netherland: Shows with all humility, Ariaentie Cornelis, late widow of Cornelis Claessen Swits, now married to Albert Leendertz; how that the supplicant with her now deceased husband, and their children, occupied for several years and actually built upon, a parcel of land whereon has since been laid out the village of Haerlem; upon which farm, after much labor there expended, she, with her said deceased husband, was in September 1655, miserably surprised by the cruel barbarous savages, who at once murdered her husband, plundered or burnt all their goods, and carried her off

The opening spring brought its share of work for the farmers. A shelter was needed for the young calves turned out to feed on Barent's Island, and at a meeting held March 13th it

with her six children captives. From whose cruel hands, by the aid of her good friends, being delivered, with her six naked children, she remained bereft of all that she had possessed, her husband and all means of subsistence, except only the aforesaid farm, on which she hoped, sooner or later, by the assistance of others, to be able to maintain herself in an honest manner; but in this she was disappointed, as well by the continued troubles, and the want of means, as by the orders issued against having any isolated habitations, and so was compelled for a time to abandon that farm. When at last it was resolved by the Director and Council to lay out the village of Haerlem, and the supplicant was inclined, with her present husband, Albert Leenderts, to again occupy the said farm, this could not be done, because her cleared land had been distributed among others, and the only offer then made her, was, to draw lots with the rest; to which she could not agree, as it was to her great prejudice, and thus was her whole *farm*, bought and cultivated by her, given to others, and the supplicant deprived of the means by which, with God's help, she could have maintained herself, instead of which she is now, with her children, reduced to poverty. The land being so distributed by the Director General and Council, it was provided that those interested, who had been driven off their land, should be paid by the actual possessors, *ten* guilders (*sic*) per morgen, but it was afterwards granted that in lieu of ten gl. per morgen the said occupants should, 5 years (*sic*) earlier than had been before determined, pay tithes of the produce, in behalf of those interested, but this cannot be collected but slowly. Our humble petition, therefore is, that it may please your Honors, either to return again the said parcel of land to the supplicant, or that its value, that for which it was before sold, may be reimbursed to her,—or otherwise, (as the supplicant's deceased husband remained indebted to the Hon. Company about seven hundred guilders, for commodities, for whose liquidation with that of other debts, he left her nothing besides the said land), that your Honors may be pleased to accept that farm, or what shall be paid for it by its actual possessors, in place of the aforesaid debt, and then to favor her with a receipt for it in full—which proposal the supplicant humbly requests your Honors may be pleased to seriously consider, with her present situation, and may through compassion let her enjoy a favorable answer, which doing she will remain

Your Honors' obedient
her
ARIAENTIE X CORNELIS.
mark

This *petition* being read, and the supplicant's poor condition considered, the following order is thereupon made:

Although the debt incurred by the supplicant's deceased husband, should long since have been paid, and ought now to be paid without any further delay, yet, considering the scanty means which were left to the supplicant by the barbarians, as is explained more at large in her petition, and furthermore, her present situation; therefore resolved that we accept in payment of what her deceased husband Cornelis Claessen Swits remained indebted to the Company, whatever shall in time be collected from her land, as mentioned in her petition, *giving her by this a receipt in full*, so that neither she nor her posterity shall ever be troubled about it in future, provided that she deliver to the Noble Company, her deed, transfer, etc., which she may have for the aforesaid land. Done in Fort Amsterdam, in New Netherland, the 7 Feb., 1664.

was agreed to build one on April 1st. They also resolved to fence the gardens. Some of the inhabitants, in want of servants and laborers, seized the opportunity to buy a number of negro slaves, sold at auction in Fort Amsterdam, May 29th, by order of the Director and Council. They had arrived on the 24th instant, in the company's ship Sparrow, from Curacao. At that sale were eager bidders, Johannes Verveelen, Daniel Tourneur, Nicholas de Meyer, Jacques Cousseau, Isaac de Forest, and even Jacob Leisler, himself, in 1678, enslaved by the Turks, and years later the champion of liberty! Verveelen bought a negro at 445 fl., De Meyer one at 460 fl., and Tourneur another at 465 fl. These were probably the first slaves owned at New Harlem, and, strange as it may seem, the recollections of the living run back to the time when negro slavery still existed here.

Of much advantage to the whole neighborhood was the new saw-mill constructed soon after by Jan van Bommel, a thrifty citizen of New Amsterdam, on the run of water emptying into the East River near the foot of 74th Street, and known ever after as the Saw Kill, which stream the people of Harlem claimed as their southern limit. The right to run this mill, granted May 26th, expired in three years, when it was discontinued; but its site became a noted landmark in connection with the Harlem Patent line.

While the inhabitants were thus busied with their own domestic affairs, the general interests of the country were in greatest peril; the government, assailed by enemies within and without, was rapidly approaching its fall. The seizure of the Dutch possessions on the Connecticut River, the successful revolt of the English towns upon Long Island and in Westchester, and their alliance with New England, too plainly told the impotency of the powers at New Amsterdam to resist any further aggressions which enemies might choose to make. Added to these were the yet existing Indian troubles. Alarmed for the safety of the state, Stuyvesant, before slow to recognize the principle of popular representation, at last was constrained to yield, and call a general assembly of delegates from the several Dutch towns, *chosen by the people*, and which met at New Amsterdam on April 10th; Harlem sending two of her most active men, Daniel Tourneur and Johannes Verveelen. But with an humbling sense of their weakness or want of resources, they did little more than to send an urgent appeal to the States General of Holland for aid in defending their homes and firesides. However, a new treaty being concluded on the 16th of May with the Indian tribes on the Hudson, the harrowing fears from that quarter were quieted; and the families at Harlem found relief in the fact that the neighboring chief Sauwenárack, head sachem of the Wickquaskeeks, renewed his pledge of friendship by signing the treaty.

Some months of mingled hope and fear now lulled both government and people into a false security, when an English fleet, under Colonel Richard Nicolls, suddenly appeared before New Amsterdam, and made a short and easy conquest of the province. The fort was surrendered on September 8th to the invaders, who named the city, as also the province, New York. Surprised into a change of rulers, the staid old settlers at New Harlem accepted the condition with a mixed sentiment. Tired of the late administration, some welcomed a change which in any respect could hardly prove for the worse, but a majority, with the attachments of native or adopted citizens, would have preferred the old government with all its faults. Nor could the wise and conciliatory course taken by the new governor, Nicolls, at once allay the feeling of indignation which found expression among the Harlem people, or repair the injury inflicted on the whole colony by a nation professedly at peace with the mother country.

The withdrawal of the Dutch soldiers from Harlem—most of these at the surrender returning to Holland,—and the abrupt departure of others, gave an air of desertion to the village. But new residents soon took their places, prominent among whom was Resolved Waldron, late deputy schout of New Amsterdam, an efficient officer, to whom Stuyvesant had been much attached. Now finding his vocation gone, he retired with his family to Harlem, to spend his remaining years, but not to be released from public service.

Among the persons leaving was Jurisen Hanel, who ten years before first came to this country as a soldier of the company, and, raised to be a sergeant, had been rewarded for faithful service by an increase of pay. He was a native of Poland and a man of no little consequence at Harlem, to which place he had removed from Bergen only within a few months, having, as before said, purchased Do. Zyperus' lands, but which before leaving he sold to Johannes Verveelen. Jan La Montagne was much disaffected by the change of government, and while his father and brother William, both living at Albany, accepted the issue and took the oath of allegiance, he with the tie of a native-born Hollander, which neither of the former could boast, made haste to dispose of his property, with a view no doubt of quitting the town or country, as many were doing. On October 22d, 1664, he sold to the partners Jan Myndertsen and Johannes Smedes, his "piece of land, and meadow belonging thereunto, called by the name of Montagne's Point, paled in betwixt two creeks, according as the bill of sale doth mention," for 800 gl., wampum, to be paid by installments.*

Another inhabitant, Arent Moesman, respected in the church and community, though he took the oath of fidelity to the English, prepared, with his brother Jacob, to visit fatherland. Conveying his property lying in this town to Captain Thomas De Lavall, an Englishman who had lately arrived here with Governor Nicolls, he bought instead a house and lot in Broadway, offered for sale by Meyndertsbefore named, after contracting for Montagne's Point. For this he gave a deed, or power of sale, to Dirck Vandercliff, taking from him a mortgage on the premises for 700 gl. Thus secured, Moesman, December 10th, 1664, obtained a pass for Holland in the ship Unity, Captain Jan Bergen. Michiel Muyden, the late proprietor, after holding a prominent standing in the town and contributing no little to its welfare, had sold his two erven, and indeed his whole allotment, to Jaques Cresson in 1663. He too returned to Holland, and like a true Dutchman warmly advocated the forcible

* MEYNDERTS and Smedes were in business together in N. Y. The former is noticed at pp. 103, 112; the latter at p. 110. Meynderts m. 1660, Beltje Plettenborg, by whom he had several drs. besides Mrs. Barent Waldron.

SMEDES is called *Smith* in the contract with Montagne, a render of his name into English, which never prevailed, at least with the earlier generations of his desc. He m., Jan. 3, 1665, Lysbeth, dr. of Michiel Verschuur, and on Feb. 2, 1676, Machtelt, dr. of Jan Willems van Iselsteyn. He had sons b. in N. Y., *Johannes*, *Benjamin*, and *Abraham*, the last by his second w. I believe he removed to Ulster co., but the name has spread to many localities.

M. Zyperus Courreau Tourneur

J Lamontagne Jurgen Dirck Claessen

Hogu David Uselle marc du Sauchoy

Resolvert Waldron Philippe Fraher

David Desmarest M Muyden

recovery of New Netherland from the English. Subsequently his city residence in the Winckel Street, left in care of Jacob Kip, was confiscated.

These removals, causing painful breaks in families, as in the case of Verveelen, whose eldest daughter, Anna, went to Holland with her husband Derick Looten, late military commissary, were the least disastrous consequences, as affecting New Harlem, of the political change which had happened the country. Months were required to restore order and check abuses which had suddenly sprung up to disturb the peace of the community. Yet these disquieting circumstances were not allowed to hinder several genial gatherings at the hymenial altar during the winter and spring of 1665. The old schepen Jan Slot ended his widowerhood by choosing another wife, and provident Pierre Cresson, whose son Jaques had married since coming to Harlem, found a worthy companion for his daughter Christina in a young man from St. Lô, in Normandy, named Letelier, now a magistrate at Bushwick.*

* JEAN LETELIER was one of "fourteen Frenchmen" by whom Bushwick was settled in 1660, and was made one of its first schepens, Mar. 23, 1661. He always signed his name simply "Letelier," the usual mode among the French gentry. In 1663 he gave 3 gl. toward the ransom of Teunis Cray's son Jacob, in captivity with the Turks. Removing to New Utrecht, he there d. Sept. 4, 1671. In his will (to which Abraham du Toict is a witness) he speaks of his chn., but does not name them. His wid. m. Jacob Gerrits De Haes, by whom she had issue Jacob, b. 1678, John, b. 1680, etc. Letelier was usually called by the Dutch Tilje (*Tilya*), and whence perhaps the family of *Tillou* or *Tilyou*, whose anc. *Pierre* (see N. Y. Gen. and Biog. Rec., 1874, p. 144), if the son of Jean, took the name of his gd. fa. Cresson.

CHAPTER XIV.

1665–1666.

RELUCTANT YIELDING TO ENGLISH RULE.

UPON the late surrender of the country by the Dutch it was conceded that "all inferior civil officers and magistrates shall continue as they now are, if they please, till the customary time of new elections." But "the customary time" arriving, no new election took place at Harlem; while the old officers, either from indifference, or from doubts as to their power to act without the schout, who positively declined, utterly failed in their duties. Sundry violations of law and order naturally followed upon this suspension of authority, and at the bottom of which was that ever prolific cause of evil—rum! Who the offenders, or what the offences, is not further specified than in the following missive, addressed "To the Schout and present Magistrates of Harlem:"

A WARRANT to the Magistrates of Harlem for the Prohibition of the sale of Strong Liquors to Indians.

Whereas I am informed of several abuses that are done and committed by the Indians, occasioned much through the liberty some persons take of selling Strong Liquors unto them; *These are to require you*, that you take special care that none of your Town presume to sell any sort of Strong Liquors, or Strong Beer, unto any Indian, and if you shall find any person offending therein, that you seize upon such Liquor and bring such person before me, to make answer for the offence. Given under my hand, at Fort James in New York, this 18th of March 1664 [1665 N.S.].

RICHARD NICOLLS.

These infractions of law were largely due to the disaffection of Jan La Montagne, to which reference has been made. For some cause failing in the sale of his Point, he remained here, but threw up his office as schout, refusing to arrest and prosecute offenders, by which means law-breakers went unrebuked, and the course of justice was obstructed. A state of things so abhorrent to the law-abiding Waldron and others could not long be endured; and the result was another order, more explicit than the previous one, and in this form.

To the Magistrates of Harlem:

Whereas complaint hath been made to me, that the Schout of Harlem doth not execute his office, and that several disorders are committed and the Inhabitants hindered of their accustomed rights; *I do therefore order*, that the Magistrates now in being do act, as formerly; and in case the Schout will not execute his office, that the Magistrates do Justice in his place, for the good of the Town, and to decide all matters that doth or shall happen there, not exceeding the value of One Hundred Guilders in Wampum: and this to continue till further order. Given under my hand at Fort James in New York, this 20th of April, 1665.

RICHARD NICOLLS.

In the reconstruction of the city government after the English form, which now took place, the want of a better administration of authority at Harlem operated as a reason for bringing that district within the jurisdiction and control of the city. Hence, Gov. Nicolls' proclamation of June 12th, 1665, constituting the new municipal government, declared "that the inhabitants of New York, New Harlem, with all other His Majesty's subjects, inhabitants upon this island, are, and shall be forever accounted nominated and established, as one body politic and corporate, under the government of a Mayor, Aldermen and Sheriff." In these was vested "*full power and authority to rule and govern, as well all the Inhabitants of this corporation, as any Strangers, according to the general laws of this Government, and such peculiar laws as are or shall be thought convenient and necessary for the good and welfare of this His Majesty's corporation, as also to appoint such under officers as they shall judge necessary for the orderly execution of justice.*" One of the aldermen therein appointed was Mr. Thomas De Lavall, whose relations to Harlem were to form an important chapter in its history.

One of the first acts of the new Common Council was to adopt the following, June 15th: "*Resolved*, to send for the Court of Harlem, and the constable, Resolved Waldron, by letter, to come hither by Saturday next." What was brewing was hardly hinted at in the polite billet thereupon addressed: "To the Honorable, the Court of New Harlem." It ran in these words:

HONORABLE and affectionate Friends:

These serve only that your Honors hold yourselves ready to appear here in this city, on Saturday next, being 17th June, old style, with Resolved Waldron, and to receive all such orders as shall be communicated. Whereunto confiding, we commend your Honors, after cordial salutation, unto God's protection, and remain

Your affectionate friends,

The MAYOR, ALDERMEN and SHERIFF of the City of New York.

By order of the same, JOHANNES NEVIUS, *Secretary.*

Done, N. York, the 15th June, 1665.

Punctually those sent for appeared, and the record reads thus: "Resolved Waldron entering, is notified that he is elected Constable of New Harlem, which accepting, he hath taken the proper oath; and the Magistrates who accompanied him are informed that they *are discharged from their office.* The aforesaid Constable is authorized to select three or four persons, who shall have power to decide any differences or dispute to the extent of Five Pounds Sterling, in Sewant, and no higher; and the party who shall not be satisfied with the decision of those elected as aforesaid, shall be bound to pay to him the Constable, the sum of Six Stivers, and further to bear the costs of proceeding before this bench of Justice." *

* JAN PIETERSEN SLOT, the old magistrate, had just before left the town with his family. Himself from Holstein, as before noticed, his sons Pieter and Jan were b. at Amsterdam. Pieter sold his property at H., gotten from his fa., to Resolved Waldron, and removed to Bergen, where he owned 25 morgen of land, bought May 14, 1657, and where, on Apl. 1, 1665, he joined the chh. with his w., who was the dr. of Jacob Wallings van Winckel, of that place, dec. His fa. sold his lands at H., named in his patent of Jan. 4, 1664, to Johannes Verveelen, and on Apl. 20, 1665, bought other property at the Bouwery, from Gov. Stuyvesant. But he again sold out here Feb. 12, 1669, having on Aug. 24 preceding sold to Capt. Delavall for £10 a parcel of meadow on "the north side of Barent's Island," which he held by ground-brief from Stuyvesant. In 1686 he and w. resided in Wall street; in 1703, in the South Ward. His chn. were by his first w. Aeltie Jans; his second, Claertie Dominicus, he m. while at H.

Jan Jansen Slot m. 1672, Judith, dr. of Stoffel Elsworth, took a house in the Smith's Fly, and that year joined Capt. Steenwyck's new troop of horse. A warm partisan of Leisler in 1689, he was made an ensign. He is named Oct. 7, 1695, as selling his city property. His chn., so far as known, were *Hester*, b. 1672, who m. Capt. Zebulon Carter; *Johannes*, b. 1674; *Stoffel*, b. 1677; *Annetie*, b. 1681, m. David Demarest 3d, and Jonathan Hart; *Hendrick*, b. 1684; and *Judith*, b. 1687, who m. John van Horn.

Pieter Jansen Slot sold out at Pemberpogh on Bergen Neck, Jan. 30, 1671, and on March 23 ensuing, bought a place in N. Y., to which he removed, but in 1673 his house, with others, was taken down to enlarge the grounds about the fort. In 1677 Slot hired a farm at Esopus, to which place he had

Waldron, clothed with these unusual powers, called Daniel Tourneur, and who else we know not, to the magistracy. Johannes Vermilye was given the place of *gerechtsbode*, or court messenger; and Tourneur, the now deacon and magistrate, was soon after, by the appointment of the governor, made "under sheriff" at New Harlem, and "president of the court there." Thus was abolished the Court of Schout and Schepens.

Entering zealously upon their duties, the very first act of the new magistrates had nearly got them into trouble. While Nicholas de Meyer was busied with his merchandise at New York—having lately taken out, March 21st, "a certificate of denization, with liberty to traffic to Fort Albany"—his farm tenant at Harlem, Aert Pietersz Buys, took occasion to abscond, being in arrears for rent, and in debt to the town. By authority of the Mayor's Court, De Meyer, June 19th, proceeded to "attach all his goods." This the new magistrates opposed, asserting their own claim as paramount. De Meyer at once appealed to the Mayor's Court, which set the matter right by declaring the attachment valid, and citing Waldron and his colleagues "to show cause, on the next court day, why they claim to be preferred, in the disposal of said property, before the prosecutor of the attachment." The silence of the record makes it evident that the magistrates declined to press their claim.

But, abating none of his vigilance, the zealous Waldron soon found more work at hand. A quilt had been stolen from Jan Dircksen, usually called, from his former occupation, "Jan the Soldier." Waldron searched in all the houses without finding it. He then called the townfolks together in the square, and

gone to follow his trade as builder. Returning in 1683, he and w., to Bergen, with letters to the church there, they were soon back to N. Y., living for years on property which they owned "at Crommesshe, near Stuyvesant's Bouwery." Selling this Apl. 10, 1688, Peter d. soon after. In 1692 his wid., still of N. Y., m. John Demarest, Esq., of Hackensack. Pieter's chn. were *John*, b. 1665, *Jacobus*, b. 1669, both at Bergen; *Tryntie*, b. 1671, in N. Y., m. Nicholas Losier, of Hackensack; *Aeltie*, b. 1678, at Esopus, m. Adam van Norden and Cornelius Banta; and *Jonas*, b. 1681, at Esopus, and who m. 1713, Jannetie Ostrum of Po'keepsie, where he was living in 1738. John Slot, b. 1665, was residing in N. Y. in 1703, with his w. Jannetie Andries and chn. Jacobus Slot settled at Hackensack, m. Mary, dr. of John Demarest, aforesaid, and was fa. of Petrus, b. 1696; John, 1699; Eve, 1701; Leah, 1706; Jonathan, 1712; Sarah, 1715; Tryntie, 1718; Benjamin, 1721. These have many descendants in Bergen, Rockland, and Orange counties, including the *Sloats* of the Ramapo Valley.

reminding them that no stranger had been in the village, declared that some one of them must have taken the quilt. Hereupon it occurred to Pierre Cresson that Jan Teunissen, the brother-in-law of Dircksen, had told him, one day before the quilt was missed, that Jan the Soldier *had only an empty chest in the house.* Suspicion at once fastened upon Teunissen; and the more readily as during the previous winter Verveelen's negro had been caught by his master taking a schepel of grain from his barn toward Teunissen's house, and had laid it upon Teunissen; albeit the integrity of the negro, as will be seen by and by, was not above suspicion. Waldron therefore asked Teunissen "how he knew that there was nothing in Jan the soldier's chest." Getting a curt answer, Waldron retorted, "You may as well be guilty of stealing the quilt, as of Sieur Verveelen's corn!" This roused Teunissen to defend his injured reputation, and forthwith he summoned Waldron before the Mayor's Court, to answer for having "accused him of being a thief."

But when the case came up, August 22d, Waldron rehearsed with such effect all the suspicious circumstances, backed up by written testimony, as to completely turn the tables against Teunissen, who was not only made to pay for defendant's lost time, with the costs of suit, but was sharply reprimanded in these terms: "And if further complaints of your improper conduct come before the court, you shall be punished as the merits of the case may require, for an example to others!"

This case perhaps was clearer to the court than the record makes it, but it should be viewed in the light of certain collateral facts. The conflicting views and feelings which had divided society at Harlem into the English and anti-English parties, had brought various individuals and families into most unfriendly and even hostile relations. It plainly crops out both in the nature and increased amount of the business which occupied the two courts. This ill-will, added to the spirit of lawlessness before noticed, while it lent eagle eyes to suspicion, disposed the courts to be strict; their decisions, especially when based upon circumstantial evidence, to which in those early times undue weight was often attached, were very liable to be partial, if not to wholly ignore such mitigating or rebutting circumstances as might even warrant an acquittal. Then Waldron, his official training akin to that of a modern detective, intent only on finding the evidence leading to conviction, and with ideas of the rigid Stuyvesant stripe, whose severity often met a rebuke from superiors in Holland, was prone as magistrate to administer justice sternly, and law to the letter. Add to this Teunissen's uniform good standing, and there is room to question whether he was fairly treated. The same may apply to the case of another person, most respectably connected, who the same year was accused of theft, declared guilty, and forbidden a residence in the town.*

* JAN TEUNISSEN, better appreciated by a later court held Dec. 14, 1666, was appointed with Lubbert Gerritsen and Jeremias Jansen Hagenaer, to arbitrate in a difference between Nelis Matthyssen and Cornelis Jansen, concerning timber; and again at another court Oct. 24, 1667, when the high-sheriff Manning presided, was named with Valentine Claessen as referee *in re* Johannes Buys *vs.* Jan Duyts and Lubbert Gerritsen. He was rarely referred to while living at Harlem, otherwise than as Jan Teunissen, but from his birthplace, Tilburg, as before noticed, he ultimately took the name *Van Tilburg.* Jan Teunissen m. at New Amsterdam, 1655, Tryntie Pieters Cronenberg, an orphan, though 23 years of age, who had been sent out that year at the charge of the city of Amsterdam. They settled at Fort Orange, Teunissen getting a house and lot; but for selling liquor to Indians he fell under severe penalties. He thence went to the Delaware to follow his trade as a carpenter, found times hard, and applied to be a soldier. Returning in 1659, he worked some time on Long Island, and then came to H. Engaging in farming, he bought Dirck Claessen's place, but was unable to keep it, though he took it again in 1661, on a lease from Tourneur, then the owner. The next year he hired one of Archer's farms at Fordham, but finally removed to N. Y. Here his w. joined the ch. in 1674, and he the year after. In their will, made Jan. 24, 1686, they name their chn. Peter, Barent, Johannes, Jacob, Isaac, and Abraham, who are to share equally their real and personal estate. Teunissen outlived Tryntie, m. again in 1691, and in 1703 had his third w.

Peter van Tilburg, b. 1648, at Albany, became a bolter in N. Y., m. 1685, Lysbeth, dr. of Frans van Hooghten, and had chn. (with [illegible] named Frans who d. in inf.), *Johannes*, b. 1686; *Abraham*, 1694; *Frans*, 1699; *Catharine*, 1700; *Petrus*, 1703. The Negro Plot of 1712 was begun by a slave of Mr. van Tilburg's, who at midnight, Apl. 6, set his master's outbuildings on fire, when the citizens running thither, the negroes killed several. Peter d. at Newark, N. J., in 1734, aged 76 yrs. Barent van Tilburg, b. at Flatbush, m. 1686, Marritie, dr. of Adam Brower, and wid. of Jacob Pietersen. He had chn. *Gerrit*, b. 1691, and *Jan*, 1697, and was a widower in 1703, living in N. Y. Johannes van Tilburg was b. at New Utrecht. He and his br. Isaac served Leisler as soldiers in 1690. He m. 1686, Anna-Maria van Giesen, and, 1698, Margaret, dr. of John Conselyea, who survived him, and m. Claes Bogert, 1703. Chn., *Teunis*, b. 1693, *Peter*, 1694; *John*, 1702; and *Catharine*, 1703, who m. Cornelius Turk, Jr. Jacob van Tilburg, b. at H., m. 1688, Grietie, dr. of Abm. Kermer, and wid. of Hend. de Boog; was a mariner, and had chn., *Metje*, b. 1692; *Catharine*, 1698; *Abraham*, 1700. His wid. m. Derick Benson, of N. Y. Isaac van Tilburg, b. 1670, at Fordham, m. 1693, Aeltie, dr. of Hendrick Barents Smith, of Bushwick. He survived but four yrs.; his wid. in 1698, m. Pierre Chaigneux, of N. Y.

Soon after this, Montagne, the Vermilyes, and some others fell into a sore wrangle with Tourneur, and all because Tourneur's dog had bitten one of Montagne's hogs. It went so far that Tourneur cited Montagne and two others before Waldron's court, Sept. 28th, when each of the three was fined a pound flemish, "for the benefit of the poor." They appealed, but the Mayor's Court sustained the sentence. The natural effect was to still more sour the parties. Montagne, cherishing the purpose to sell out and leave (arrangements for which he completed only just before his death), now disposed of his village property and bouw-land, recently his brother's, with the crop he had just sown thereon, to David Demarest, late of Staten Island, who became a resident of the town, where he at once took a prominent position.

One of the three individuals fined as aforesaid was Monis Peterson, who was also complained of at the same session of the town court for an assault upon Jacques, "the herdsman of said village," with whom he had a dispute about his oxen. For this he was fined 100 gl. The burly Swede not only refused to pay the fine, but threatened the constable, to *serve him as he had Jacques!* This, even from the belligerent Monis, was insufferable; Waldron arraigned the offender before the Mayor's Court, which, approving the former sentence, directed Slaeck to be kept in custody till he gave security for his good behavior. But enough. These cases, which illustrate the times, and possess interest as showing the then procedure, are but samples of the many which engaged the courts, and supplied topics for the village coteries, during the latter half of 1665.

But the signal event of that year, in the town's history, awakens more agreeable reflections, and deserves a particular notice. Do. Selyns had received into his spiritual fold at the Bouwery, up to his leaving for Holland, July 23d, 1664, seventeen of the Harlem residents of both sexes, whose names, after he left, were transferred to the register of the church at Fort Amsterdam, to which several of them had previously belonged. Other communicants living at Harlem (Vermeille, Waldron and Slot, and their wives) still held their original connection with that church. This seems indicative of two facts—the yet imperfect organization of the church at Harlem, and its dependence, by mutual agreement, upon the city pastors and consistory.*

The ensuing winter the congregation, though not strong in numbers, undertook to build a house of worship. A pleasant little episode growing out of it was "a feast" given to General Stuyvesant by the three magistrates Tourneur, Montagne, and Verveelen, but probably acting as well in their specialties of deacon, voorleser, and innkeeper. It came off January 23d, 1665, costing the deacons' fund 21 gl. 19 st., and so was plainly identified with the building movement, as to which, and probably other matters affecting their interests, they naturally sought counsel of their honored guest before he should leave on his intended voyage to Holland; he whose advice they had hitherto so greatly leaned upon and valued, both as their governor and an old elder and father in Israel. In order to provide the ways and means it was resolved to lay out additional *tuynen*, or gardens, suitable also for building lots, to be sold to actual freeholders or residents at 25 gl. each, "for the benefit of the town." This was at once carried into effect. The gardens, twenty in number, and containing about half an acre each, lay at the west end of the village plot, and ran north and south from street to street. To distinguish them from the others they were called

* The CHURCH-MEMBERS referred to were the following

Jan La Montagne, Jr., and *Maria Vermeille*, his wife.
Daniel Tourneur and *Jacqueline Parisis*, his wife.
Johannes Verveelen and *Anna Jaarsvelt*, his wife.
Joost van Oblinus, Sr., and *Martina Westin*, his wife.
Joost van Oblinus, Jr., and *Marie Sammis*, his wife.
Claude le Maistre and *Hester du Bois*, his wife.
Pierre Cresson and *Rachel Cloos*, his wife.
Jaques Cresson and *Marie Renard*, his wife.
Jean le Roy.
Isaac Vermeille and *Jacomina Jacobs*, his wife.
Resolved Waldron and *Tanneke Nagel*, his wife.
Pieter Jansen Slot and *Marritie van Winckel*, his wife.

Of former residents or landholders here the following had been church-members; De Meyer, though a non-resident, being still a proprietor.

Nicholas de Meyer and *Lydia van Dyck*, his wife.
Hendrick J. Vander Vin and *Wyntie*, his wife.
Jacques Cousseau and *Madeleine du Tullier*, his wife.
Philip Casier and *Marie Taine*, his wife.
Willem de La Montagne.
Anna Verveelen.
Arent Jansen Moesman.
Juriaen Hanel.

the *Buyten Tuynen*, or Out Gardens, as they lay outside the palisade. Dirck Claessen bought No. 1, next to the town plot; Daniel Tourneur, No. 2; Claude le Maistre, No. 3, and Nicholas de Meyer, No. 4. Captain Delavall engaged the next four numbers, but the rest went off slowly. For the history of the church erection, at best obscure, yet its every detail interesting, we are largely indebted to Montagne's accounts as treasurer, showing what the deacons expended for materials, labor, etc.*

* The *Deacon's Accounts* covering the time the church was building are sufficiently curious to be given entire. The charges are in florins and stivers.

THE WORTHY DEACONRY, Credit:

1665,	23	Jan.	By feast given *Stuyvesant* by *D. Tourneur*, *J. Verveelen* and *J. Montagne*	*f.* 21	19
			" a book by *J. Montagne*		
"	26	"	" 5 planks for benches at the Church	7	10
"	"	"	" labor making the benches	8	0
			" ½ lb. nails for ditto		12
			" to *Wessels* for bringing the *Domine*	7	0
			" to the *Sexton* (*Koster*)	6	0
			" ditto	1	0
			" ditto	6	0
"	20	Dec.	" nails for the house on the Church lot	15	0
			" nails for the Church	49	2
			" wages for labor at the Church	36	13
			" a piece of gold to the *Preacher*	50	0
			" nails for the Church	16	5
			" wages for labor at the Church to *Jan Gulcke* and *Nelis*	24	0
1666,	27	Jan.	" ditto to ditto	40	0
"	3	Feb.	" to the *Sexton*	6	0
"	25	Mar.	" ditto	6	0
"	25	Apl.	" nails for the Church	17	18
			" planks for the Church	90	0
			" *Hendrick Karstens* for raising up the Church and making the foundation (*stander*)	30	0
			" ditto for plastering of the same	6	0
"	1	Dec.	" to the *Sexton*	18	0
1667,	30	Jan.	" at allotment of the seats	4	0
			" *Jan Teunissen* for a plank for the Church	1	10
"	7	Mar.	" to the *Sexton*	6	0
			" *Nelis* for making the table	3	0
			" 1 lb. nails	3	0
			" 3 planks for the table and benches	4	10
"	27	"	" *Bart* the mason	40	0
"		Sept.	" to the *Sexton*	6	0
			" 2 schepels rye to sow upon the Church lot	9	0
1668,		Jan.	" to the *Sexton*	6	0
			" a town book	4	0
			" *Matys* for taking away the *Domine*		19
			" to the masons and lime by *Verveelen*	19	0
				f. 569	18

Doubtless, as is usual in new settlements, the people undertook the incipient labor of preparing the timber, etc., as a voluntary offering. This work, of which no record remains, had evidently been completed and the building inclosed and ready for seats at the date of the "feast" aforesaid, as the deacons' accounts indicate.

The church was built on the north side of the Great Way (since the Church Lane), on a vacant lot between the east end of the old gardens and the river, seemingly reserved for this purpose. The work, suspended during the farming season, was resumed on the approach of winter by the mechanics Jan Gulick and Nelis Matthyssen, in order to make the house more comfortable before cold weather should set in. And some special, genial occasion it must have been, most likely a dedicatory service, which in midwinter brought the domine, and drew forth the generous acknowledgment of *twenty dollars in gold!* Do. Samuel Megapolensis had now taken Selyns' charge, his father being senior pastor at New York, and Samuel Drisius his colleague. To one of these, doubtless, Harlem was indebted then, as at stated times thereafter, for ministerial visits and services—always notable occasions, and welcome interruptions to the ordinary routine of the voorleser.

Better for the peace of the village had Madam Gossip never made her *début* there; but, alas! the unfriendly prejudices which had crept into the community gave a tempting opportunity to employ her insinuating but venomed tongue to the injury of a worthy church-member; for "slander loves a shining mark." To speak plainly, three Dutch matrons, Sarah Tennis, Tryntie Pieters, and Mayke Oblinus, with no fear of law or husbands before their eyes, had "falsely accused of theft" a French woman, and neighbor, none other than the wife of Jaques Cresson. The first two being the wives of Jan the soldier and Jan Teunissen; may be it was a retort upon the Cressons, for the affair of the stolen quilt. Upon the injured lady's complaint, Mayor Delavall, March 27th, 1666, directed the under sheriff and constable at Harlem to interrogate the fair transgressors, "regarding the matter at issue," and advise him by the hand of Mrs. Cresson. So much for her advantage did the investigation prove, that the Mayor required the trio to make a public confession before the court at New Harlem, and also sign a writing to that effect, that they knew nothing of her whom they had defamed, "except what is honorable and virtuous." But mark the inevitable costs of justice in these neat little bills which the clerk at Harlem presented to the amiable litigant.

MARIE RENARD, DR.

To an extra court	*f.*	23 :	0
" *seven citations*		4 :	4
" *a copy of examination*		2 :	0
" *a copy of the appeal (nullatis)*		3 :	0
" *a copy of the account*			12
	f.	33 :	16
To after signing		1 :	9
" *signing the certificate*		1 :	3
" *copy of the certificate*		2 :	6
" *notice of extra court*		3 :	0
" *copy of the appeal*		3 :	0
	f.	11 :	0

Marie, thus injured in her good fame and purse, was of Huguenot parentage and of unquestioned piety, her husband also being one of the "real Reformed of France." Once having "some remarkable experiences, of a light shining upon her, while she was reading in the New Testament about the sufferings of the Lord Jesus," it greatly startled her, yet "left such a joy and testimony in her heart as she could not describe." Constrained, as she was, to speak to others about "this glory," her brother-in-law, Nicholas de la Plain, rashly told her, "You must not go to church any more; you are wise enough." These words, the tempter's prompting to spiritual pride, impressed and grieved her, "for not to go to church, and to leave the Lord's Supper, she could not in her heart consent." So, seeking higher counsel, she remained steadfast in her religion, whose support she so much needed in the peculiar trials which fell to her lot.

CHAPTER XV.

1660–1667.

THE NICOLLS PATENT; THE COURT, MILL, CHURCH.

HARLEM was now a well-ordered rural hamlet, owning some eighty head of neat cattle. These, from April till November, were to be seen grazing on the commons west of the village, usually in care of a herder, hired by those who kept stock, on terms such as were at first made with Du Four and Peterson.* For the same season the young horses, cattle, and swine, after being branded or marked, with the initials of the owner's name or otherwise, were turned out to feed in the common woods, free as the native deer, till necessary to look them

* MANS STAECK was from Abo, in Finland, and was best known as Monis Peterson, bearing a prenomen common among the Swedes. Being at New Amsterdam when the order issued for laying out the village of Harlem, he took part in that enterprise by securing a house and bouwery, but which he first rented and then disposed of, entering into a three years' partnership, Jan. 17, 1662, with Jan Cogu, a fellow Swede, but better educated, from whom Peterson received the half of his allotment of land, with house, barn, etc., for 125 gl., giving Cogu in exchange a half interest in a lime-kiln, with a canoe valued at 15 gl., and a balance in cash. With farm and lime-kiln and the herding to attend to, they also engaged Aug. 22, 1662, to work Tourneur's land, "already under the plough;" but Cogu d. near the time the partnership expired, which was on Feb. 1, 1665. Peterson held minor offices in the town, and here m. in 1663, as before noticed. Unlettered, but by nature gifted, much reliance was placed upon his judgment; yet strong drink often made him abusive and violent, and this failing marred his whole life. The heavy penalties put upon him in 1665 may have led him to quit H., and he soon removed to Elizabeth Town, N. J., taking his lumber thither in a canoe, aided by Gillis Boudewyns; and there Monis took the oath of allegiance Feb. 19, 1666. By a previous appointment by the court as a referee to fix the damages in a case of trespass, he reported at H., July 3, ensuing. Within ten years he went to the Swedish colony at Upland, Penn., and got land at Calkoen Hook, where he was yet living in 1693. Too often mastered by his bad habit, once for scolding a magistrate he was fined 1000 gl., but the fine was remitted at the request of the injured party, upon Monis asking pardon for his abuse, and pleading that he said it "in his drink." His native frankness and good sense disarmed resentment, and despite his weakness won respect. His sons, Peter, Matthew, and Israel, are understood to have been the anc. of the *Stack* family.

up and stall them from autumn rains and winter's snows. The growing need of enlarged commonage and of having the limits thereof fixed naturally brought up the subject of applying for a general patent, which should confirm the community in these and their other rights and privileges, and also secure to them the large outlays made in building their houses, as well as what it had cost them to clear, fertilize, and fence their lands. Governor Nicolls, on knowing their case, sent to Cortilleau, the surveyor who had first laid out the village, "a warrant directing a line to be drawn for the range of Harlem cattle." It read:

WHEREAS, you have formerly received order to draw a line from the River near the Town of Harlem, upon this Island, one mile into the woods, somewhat in relation as it stands from this place, some particular point of the compass; These are to authorize you to draw the said line from the River against the middle of the said Town, one mile directly into the woods, for the greatest conveniency of range of cattle belonging to the said Town, not considering so exactly how it lies from hence, whether southerly, or westerly, or otherwise. For so doing, this shall be your warrant. Given under my hand, at Fort James, in New York, the 20th day of March, 1665–6.

RICHARD NICOLLS.

To Mr. JAQUES CORTILLEAU.

The lines being run out pursuant to this order, and a return of the survey made to the governor, he thereupon gave written directions for drafting a patent, in which he specified three things to be observed, namely:

"There is one condition, which is, that that town is to be forever thereafter called by the name of *Lancaster*."

"To build one or more boats fit for a ferry."

"There is also liberty of going further west into the woods with their horses and cattle, for range, as they shall have occasion."

In due time the patent was received, and read as follows:*

* "A PATENT granted unto the Freeholders and Inhabitants of *Harlem*, alias *Lancaster*, upon the Island of Manhattan."

Such is the title or heading given to the patent as recorded in the Secretary of State's office, Albany, in the original book of Patents, Liber 1, p. 57; but which stands disconnected from and forms no part of the instrument, although so appearing in the copies printed by Mr. Adriance. In the date the day is left blank. By a careful collation with the original records, we are enabled to present exact copies of the several Harlem patents; only conforming to modern orthography.

Richard Nicolls, Esqr., Governor under His Royal Highness James, Duke of York, &c., of all his Territories in America; To all to whom these Presents shall come, *sendeth Greeting*. Whereas there is a certain Town or Village, commonly called and known by the name of New Harlem, situate and being on the east part of this Island, now in the tenure or occupation of several freeholders and inhabitants, who have been at considerable charge in building, as well as manuring, planting and fencing the said Town and lands thereunto belonging; Now for a confirmation unto the said freeholders and inhabitants, in their enjoyment and possession of their particular lots and estates in the said Town, as also for an encouragement to them in the further improvement of the said lands, Know ye that, by virtue of the commission and authority unto me given by His Royal Highness the Duke of York, I have thought fit to ratify, confirm and grant, and by these Presents do ratify, confirm and grant unto the said freeholders and inhabitants, their heirs, successors and assigns, and to each and every of them, their particular lots and estates in the said Town, or any part thereof. And I do likewise confirm and grant unto the freeholders and inhabitants in general, their heirs, successors and assigns, the privileges of a Town, but immediately depending on this City, as being within the liberties thereof; Moreover for the better ascertaining of the limits of the lands to the said Town belonging, the extent of their bounds shall be as followeth, viz., That from the west side of the fence of the said Town, a line be run due West four hundred English poles, without variation of the compass, At the end whereof another line being drawn to run North and South, with the variation, that is to say, North to the very end of a certain piece of meadow ground commonly called the Round Meadow, near or adjoining to Hudson's River, and South to the Saw Mills over against Hog Island, commonly called Perkins Island;* It shall be the West bounds of their lands. And all the lands lying and being within the said line, so drawn North and South as aforesaid, eastward to the Town and Harlem River, as also to the North and East Rivers, shall belong to the Town; Together with all the soils, creeks, quarries, woods, meadows, pastures, marshes, waters, fishings, hunting and fowling, And all other profits, commodities, emoluments and hereditaments to the said lands and premises within the said line belonging, or in anywise appertaining, with their and every of their appurtenances; To have and to hold all and singular the said lands, hereditaments and premises, with their and every of their appurtenances, and of every part and parcel thereof, to the said freeholders and inhabitants, their heirs, successors and assigns, to the proper use and behoof of the said freeholders and inhabitants, their heirs, successors and assigns forever. It is likewise further confirmed and granted, that the inhabitants of said Town shall have liberty, for the conveniency of more range of their horses and cat-

* From *varken* the Dutch word for hog, and so called because the neighboring settlers allowed their hogs to run there. Now *Blackwell's Island*.

tle, to go farther west into the woods, beyond the aforesaid bounds, as they shall have occasion, the lands lying within being intended for plowing, home pastures and meadow grounds only; AND no person shall be permitted to build any manner of house or houses within two miles of the aforesaid limits or bounds of the said Town, without the consent of the inhabitants thereof. AND the freeholders and inhabitants of the said Town are to observe and keep the terms and conditions hereafter expressed; that is to say: That from and after the date of these Presents the said Town shall no longer be called New Harlem, but shall be known and called by the name of LANCASTER; and in all deeds, bargains and sales, records or writings, shall be so deemed, observed and written. Moreover the said Town lying very commodious for a Ferry to and from the Main, which may redound to their particular benefit as well as to a general good, the freeholders and inhabitants shall be obliged, at their charge, to build or provide one or more boats for that purpose, fit for the transportation of men, horses and cattle, for which there will be such a certain allowance given as shall be adjudged reasonable. And the freeholders and inhabitants, their heirs, successors and assigns, are likewise to render and pay all such acknowledgments and duties as already are, or hereafter shall be, constituted and ordained by His Royal Highness the Duke of York, and his heirs, or such Governor and Governors as shall from time to time be appointed and set over them. GIVEN under my hand and seal, at Fort James, in New York, on Manhatans Island, the day of May, in the eighteenth year of the reign of our sovereign lord Charles the Second, by the grace of God King of England, Scotland, France and Ireland, Defender of the Faith, &c., and in the year of our Lord God, 1666.

RICHARD NICOLLS.

It is putting it in mild terms to say that this patent was not approved by the Harlem people, whose wishes, as is obvious, were little regarded in preparing it. The change in the name of the town, with the governor's pet idea, and tried elsewhere but not always successfully, was a most offensive feature, and was never adopted.* The bench of justice or local court, and, in general, such rights as they had enjoyed in common with the other villages, were indeed comprehended under "the privileges of a town," but as it made all, without limitation, "depending on this city,"—this condition might impose untold burdens. In the vital matter of taxation, it left them quite at the mercy of the Duke, his heirs and governors, and not to the safer operation of the laws. Nor did it fully cover their landed interests,

* LANCASTER, as a name applying to Harlem, is not once found on its records; nor has it been met with as so used in any other record or document of that period, saving the instances above noticed.

as it omitted to name the meadows appertaining to their farms, but separated by the Harlem River. These were grave objections to the patent in its present form, and though it remained of record, and was not "recalled" as were some others, the inhabitants only abided the time when they could secure a better, obviating these defects.

Two positive characters, such as Tourneur and Waldron, the one Under Sheriff and President of the Court, the other Constable, could hardly be expected always to work in harmony, and so it happened that the former took a grudge against the latter for something said or done. Now, Waldron, being requested by the inhabitants, went officially to see Tourneur, who was at his bouwery, "to speak to him about the fences," when the latter, losing temper, caught up a stick, and saying to Waldron, "Now, nobody is looking, I'll pay you!" fell to beating him. Waldron entered a complaint to the Mayor's Court, May 1st, demanding to be sustained in his official acts, or *relieved from his office*. Tourneur being cited, appeared on the 8th, the next court day. On hearing his version of the story the case seemed to wear a different look, and was dismissed, with a charge "that both parties for the future live together in good friendship," he who should first offend to pay a penalty of 50 gl. Tourneur was better satisfied than Waldron, who immediately asked the Court to give him his discharge as constable, which they did. Of Waldron's official acts but one remains to be mentioned—the contract with Nelis Matthyssen to cut and remove the timber from the town lot, and to keep the fences in repair. This work he completed early in 1668.

On May 15th, Johannes Vervelen was confirmed as Waldron's successor, from a nomination (of two persons) *made by the inhabitants*, per order; and in presence of the Court took the oath of fidelity. This was followed, June 12th, by an appointment of four persons as Overseers, *from a double nomination by the people;* those elected being Joost Van Oblinus, Isaac Vermilye, Glaude Delamater and Nelis Matthyssen; while Jan La Montagne was again made Secretary, in which office he had not acted since 1664. The letter communicating the result contained the following instructions:

"The which persons are hereby authorized, together with the

Under Sheriff and Constable,—or three of them, whereof the Under Sheriff or his Deputy shall always make one,—in all questions and suits that between man and man in their village may happen and be brought before them, without respect of persons, to do justice and to determine absolutely, to the sum of Two Hundred Guilders in Sewant, following the laws here in this land established; and all the Inhabitants of the Village of New Harlem are by these ordered and charged to respect the before named persons in all that belongs to them as their Overseers. Done at New York, the 12th of June, 1666."

On June 19th the members elect presenting themselves in the Mayor's Court, were tendered and took the following oath:

WHEREAS you, Daniel Tourneur, as Under Sheriff, and you, Joost Oblinus, Isaac Vermilye, Glaude Delamater and Nelis Matthyssen, by the Honorable Mayor's Court are chosen as Overseers of the Village of New Harlem, for the term of one succeeding year beginning upon this date: you Men swear in the presence of Almighty God, that you will to your best knowledge and with a good conscience, maintain the laws of this government without respect of persons, in all suits that shall be brought before you, to the sum of Two Hundred Guilders; You Men, so far as able, will execute the laws for the benefit of your town and the inhabitants of the same. *So truly help you Almighty God.*

Thus was constituted the first local court at Harlem, in which (save at the first choice of schepens, under the Dutch) the people enjoyed the right of nominating their magistrates.*

* NELIS MATTHYSSEN was from Stockholm. His name (the prenomen usually abbreviated in the Dutch records, though sometimes written in full, *Cornelis*) was, in proper Swedish, Nils Mattson; but he had a countryman and cotemporary of this name who lived on the Delaware, for whom he is not to be taken. He and Barentie Dircks were m. at New Amsterdam in 1661. At Harlem he was well esteemed, his good common-sense going far to supply a lack of early advantages. By occupation a carpenter and timber-hewer, he was the first tenant of the land since known as the "Church Farm," from which he cut and cleared the primeval forest trees. On his lease expiring in 1668, he left the town and bought a small place at Hellgate Neck, Newtown, being also an applicant in 1673, for Pelham's Hook, "lying between Col. Morris and the Two Brothers." He sold out at Hellgate to Thomas Lawrence, and obtained a grant of 60 acres at Turtle Bay in 1676. This he sold to Joh. Pietersen—date not given—and perhaps went to Hackensack (as did his family) after 1681, when he is last named in N. Y. He had chn. Matthys, Hendrick, Anna, Maria, Catharine, Sarah, and Rachel. Sarah m. Jacob Matthews, and Maria m. Samuel Hendricksen, both of Hackensack. *Matthys Cornelissen*, b. 1665, at Harlem, m. Tryntie Hendricks, 1692, and d. at Hackensack 1743-8, his desc. retaining the name *Cornelison*, and of whom, we believe, was the late Rev. John Cornelison, b. 1769, at Nyack, N. Y., d. 1828, at Bergen, N. J.

A first business of the new board was to provide for the completion of the Church. Work upon it had been continued by the two carpenters, off and on, during the past winter, but it was not finished, and money was wanted. Little had been paid in for the out-gardens sold, and some of these gardens were yet undisposed of.* At the motion of Tourneur, the magistrates, on June 27th, resolved that as it was necessary to finish the church, a tax for that purpose should be laid upon the lands, "by the morgen from each lot," but "for the present to borrow it from the poor money with the approval of the ministers and the deacons." Accordingly lumber was procured, and Hendrick Karstens was employed to raise up and underpin the building with a proper foundation, and also to plaster it, that the next winter should find it more comfortable for the worshippers than had the last.

This object secured, the overseers found other business—to stay the damage being done by cattle foddered on the cultivated lands, and hogs daily rooting in the vegetable gardens, causing "manifold complaints." As a remedy, they issued an order, July 25th, prohibiting all persons letting their hogs run at large without being yoked; and providing that for every hog without a yoke found within the fenced lands, the owner should pay, besides the damages sustained, "*six guilders* for each hog for the first offence; *two pounds of powder* for the second, and for the third offence *forfeit the hog or hogs.*" A like penalty was declared against keeping cattle or calves within the general fencing.

On September 2d, being Sunday, the quiet of the village was disturbed, by Jan Tennissen and Phillip Presto bringing in a canoe load of hay from Daniel Tourneur's meadow. The next

* The *Buyten Tuynen*, or Out-Gardens, were in some instances given by the first purchasers to their chn., at their m., to build on, and begin wedded life. At a later date four of these small plots were occupied by Joost Van Oblinus as his homestead, then by his son Peter, who added a fifth garden, and who owned a farm on Van Keulen's Hook to which these adjoined. His nephew and successor Petrus Waldron buying up the remaining ones (two excepted), the whole descended to his son John P. Waldron, forming the north part of his farm where it came to the Church Lane. The two westerly gardens, Nos. 19, 20, were retained in the Bussing family, whose anc., received them from his fa. in law Glaude Delamater, the original purchaser. They finally came to a dr. of Aaron Bussing, Mrs. Catharine Storm, forming the small piece attached to the north end of her farm, on which was her residence, the old family mansion, till late seen standing cornerwise to 119th street, at the north side, between 3d and 4th avenues.

day they and Tourneur also were arraigned by the town court, for working on the Sabbath. Teunissen admitted the charge, but said that Tourneur had ordered it done. Tourneur refused to appear, but said that he had given them no orders to fetch it on Sunday. The Court thereupon directed the constable to take the hay and canoe in charge, till they were redeemed. Tourneur gave bail for Presto, and proceeded to appeal from this action to the Mayor's Court.

But once up for public criticism, Tourneur, whose late affair with Waldron, yet fresh in people's mouths, was no help to him, had now to meet and contend with another damaging report. An act of his youth, long past and buried, suddenly sprang forth to assail his character. Elizabeth Rossignol,* the wife of Marc du Sauchoy, under strong provocation as appears, abused Tourneur roundly with her tongue, calling him "a villain of villains," and tauntingly added, that he durst not call her to account for it either! Tourneur complained to the magistrates September 27th, Elizabeth being present, and prayed that she be put to the proof. The defendant said that she held the plaintiff for a villain, while he did not restrain his children from giving her a vile name in his presence; and furthermore, that the plaintiff in France had intentionally taken the life of a man with a sword. Tourneur declaring that he knew not that his children had railed at her, prayed that the defendant should prove that he had killed a man, or taken his life. Thereupon, Glaude Delamater and Barentien Matthyssen testified, at the request of Elizabeth, that they heard Tourneur say, at the house of Nelis Matthyssen, that "his sword was the cause that he durst not go to France." Tourneur explaining said, that attending a funeral in the city of Amiens, the Papists fell upon the Reformed, and some of them being slain he was obliged to leave. He asked that the defendant be interrogated, whether she had known the plaintiff in France. The defendant said that she had not known him in France, but that the affair was well known to those who had known him there. The Court having heard both sides, referred the parties to the Honorable Mayor's Court.

* In the record she is called Lysbeth *Nachtegaal*, a mere change of her French name into Dutch; and Nachtegaal finding its English equivalent in *Nightingale*.

But Tourneur, at the next meeting of the magistrates, still pressed his suit, praying that the defendant be imprisoned till she prove her words, and held to bail for the costs. Elizabeth was equally urgent that Tourneur should give bail for the costs, and reiterated that *he had given the death to Tilie Meer.* But the magistrates again referred the parties to the higher court, so there the persistent Tourneur went.

His two suits came to trial October 9th. In the "hay case," the Court upheld the magistrates in seizing his hay, etc., on the ground that Tourneur was accountable for the acts of his servants, and disregarding his plea that his orders were to bring the hay early on Monday morning. They fined him 25 gl., but put the costs on the magistrates; instructing them, since Tourneur was President of their board, to apply to the higher Court, "in case plaintiff shall forget himself hereafter, while holding said position." In the matter of Elizabeth Rossignol, the defendant frankly admitted all she had said, and offered to prove it, "if the Hon. Court please to grant her a delay to obtain the proof thereof from France." But the Court declining such an investigation, and keeping itself to the charge of slander, condemned the defendant to acknowledge her fault in open court at Harlem, and pay the costs. This checked, but did not wholly stop, this malicious story, which even after Tourneur's death was circulated by Du Sauchoy, as the widow alleged, "to the great damage of herself and children."

Capt. Thomas De Lavall was an English gentleman, his surname derived from Normandy, but the family of great antiquity at Seaton-Delavall, in Northumberland, where it held large possessions. Members of it were active partisans of King Charles II., by whom Sir Ralph Delavall was knighted in 1660, and made surveyor of the port of Seaton-Sluice; while others in the collateral branches were as noted for their commercial spirit and wealth. Circumstances connect Capt. Delavall with this family, whose tastes, pursuits, and loyalty he so largely shared, but further it is quite well ascertained that he was son of Thomas, a son of Sir Ralph Delavall. The official favor he enjoyed was the fruit of meritorious service for his king and country, before his arrival here in the suite of Gov. Nicolls. During the late war in Flanders he was Deputy Treasurer of the port of Dunkirk, and handling public funds exceeding an hundred thousand pounds, so well discharged his trust, that he was assigned to a similar one at New York, and had entered upon its duties directly after his arrival.

Capt. Delavall, now owning lands at Harlem, including lot No. 22 on Van Keulen's Hook, which extended down to Montagne's Kill, designed to build a grist-mill upon this lot and stream, with a substantial stone dwelling-house near it, in case he could secure the co-operation of the Harlem people, and the patronage of the surrounding districts; though the latter much depended upon the opening of a proper highway between the Bouwery and Harlem, to give the inhabitants easy access to the mill with their grain. It would further insure the success of the undertaking, to draw travel as much as possible toward Harlem, by establishing a ferry there, and to divert it from Spuyten Duyvel, by closing up the passage-way then used as a fording-place for horses and cattle to and from the main. Mr. Delavall now having authority as mayor of the city, resolved to undertake these enterprises, which with his usual sagacity he judged would prove a good investment for him, while also conducing to the public convenience. He therefore made the following propositions to the authorities of Harlem:

On this date, 3d January, A°. 1667, the Honorable Heer Delavall* proposed and requested that the magistrates of this town do consider the following points:

1st. That they make one half of the road from here to the Manhatans or New York; and that Spuyten Duyvel be stopped up.

2d. That like care be taken for a suitable Ordinary (*i.e.* tavern), for the convenience of persons coming and going, as also of the village; and he promises the nails and the making of a scow, provided the ferryman be holden to repay him for the same when required.

3d. That it may be firmly settled, that the inhabitants of the town will make the dam, because other towns promise to make a dam, if so be that he please to build the mill near them.

4th. Requests leave to erect a stone house at the rear of his land near the mill, and to fortify it as a refuge for the village in time of need.

5th. Requests leave to run a fence straight from the fence now standing to the stone bridge, upon Van Keulen's Hook, and to use the land and meadow so inclosed.

6th. Requests that the inhabitants of the town shall set off (fence)

* The word *Heer*, though properly translated Lord, often, as in this instance, had simply the sense of *Mr.* as used at that early day; this latter term being then applied with discrimination, and only as denoting great respect. See *Annals of Newtown*, p. 38, note.

the meadow at Little Barent's Island, in case they wish to keep the same, as said Island belongs to him; or otherwise, not to put the town to inconvenience, he will present them the Island, if they will free the meadows.

7th. Whereas the Bronck's Land has been sold for two thousand guilders in beavers; and as he thought that it should more properly fall to the town—offers for that price to let the town have it.

Upon all which, after consideration given, to notify and inform him.

On this matter being talked over among the magistrates, Johannes Verveelen agreed to take the ferry and ordinary for six years. He was then formally sworn to provide proper entertainment for travellers, as victuals and drink, lodgings, etc., and further, not to tap liquor to the Indians who should resort to the village. On his request for an addition of six feet to his house lot, next the street, "as he was cramped for room, and must make convenience for his ordinary," the Court granted him "six feet into the street, to extend right out at the south side; that is, the line stretching as the street now runs, nearly east and west."

The next day the inhabitants were called together to act upon Mr. Delavall's proposals, and with the following result:

On the 4th of January; Advice of the Inhabitants of the town upon the propositions of the Honorable Heer Delavall.

1st Point. Offer, together with their neighbors, to stop up Spuyten Duyvel, as it was formerly; are also resolved to make a road so far as practicable.

2d. Have provided for this, and settled Johannes Verveelen as ferryman and keeper of the Ordinary for six years.

3d. Agree to make the dam for the mill, provided they may enjoy its benefits according to custom.

4th. Agree that a house be built for the bouwery, to set near the mill, or where is most convenient for him.

5th. Agree that the mill use the land and meadow lying from the fence now standing to the stone bridge on Van Keulen's Hook.

6th. Require further opportunity to consider how this point shall be settled.

7th. They are parties: Hon. Heer Delavall, Nicholas De Meyer, Johannes Verveelen, Daniel Tourneur, Glaude Delamater, Lubbert Gerritsen, Joost van Oblinus, David Demarest, Valentine Claessen and Derick Claessen.

Bronck's Land, referred to under the seventh point, and embracing some five hundred acres, opposite Harlem on the Westchester side, had passed from Bronck's heirs, through several hands, to Samuel Edsall. The answer to the seventh point appears to mean that the "parties" named were the ones most interested, as they were those whose salt meadows lay on that side of the river. With a view of buying the Bronck tract, some of these persons met the next day, and "constituted and authorized Daniel Tourneur, Nicholas De Meyer, and Johannes Verveelen, in their name to agree respecting the payment and redemption of the land called Bronck's Land; to do and execute as would they themselves if present, promising to maintain firm and inviolate whatever these their attorneys may do in the premises." *

As to Little Barent's Island, the case stood thus: Stuyvesant had granted the meadows lying around it to some of the Harlem people, and had allowed all of them to use the island for pasturing their young stock. Later this and Great Barent's Island, as being the property of the West India Company (Van Twiller's title to the latter island under his Indian purchase having been disallowed by the company and annulled by the Director and Council, July 1st, 1652), fell to the English by the general act of confiscation of Oct. 10th, 1665; and were soon after sold to Capt. Delavall, though his patent did not issue till Feb. 3d, 1668, when he was about to visit Europe. Upon Delavall's offer of the lesser island to the inhabitants of Harlem no

* DIRCK CLAESSEN, son of Claes Jacobsen and Pietertie Heertgers, was b. at Leeuwarden, in Friesland; emigrating, I believe, with his w. and wid. mo. in 1653. He was a potter, several of whom came out that year. In 1657, when he became a small burgher, he bought a house and lot in New Amsterdam, and set up a pottery, known afterwards as "Pot-baker Corner, situated near the outlet of the Fresh Water into the East River, and next to Henry Brasier." Leasing this property, Aug. 10, 1662, for three years, he came to H. to manage his bouwery here, and that fall was chosen magistrate. On Nov. 5, 1663, he sold his bouwery to Jan Teunissen, but was obliged to take it back under a mortgage of that date, and finally sold it to Daniel Tourneur, Feb. 1, 1667. He now resumed his pottery in N. Y., where he d. in 1686. He m. Wyntie Roelofs, Annetie Dircks, wid., and Metje Elberts. By the first he had Claesie, b. 1654, who m. John Ray and Gustavus Adophus Horne; Jannetie, b. 1656, m. Cornelis Dyckman; and Geertie, b. 1662, m. Barent Christiaens. By his second w. he had a dr. Gisberta, to whom, and his stepson John Everts (son of said w. Annetie by Evert Jansen), he deeded his pottery property Sept. 10, 1680. Who Gisberta m., if at all, has not been observed. When a miss of sweet fifteen one Wm. Phillips visited her, but on a Sunday morning, Oct. 26, 1679, being caught acting rather free to suit the fa., he indignantly drove Phillips out of the house, nearly cutting his nose off with a knife. Ray was from Berkshire, England, had served here as a soldier in the English garrison, but became a pipemaker. His desc. have been of firm respectability in this State. His dr. Wyntie m. Hendrick Meyer.

immediate action was taken, and on May 3d, ensuing, Daniel Tournour, in Delavall's behalf, urged that Jaques Cresson, who had meadow on the south side of that island, might be removed therefrom, by having other meadow given him instead; and that the Heer Delavall's meadow should be fenced in by the town-folks who had calves pastured there. Delavall's meadow, gotten with the land of Simon de Ruine, lay in common with Cresson's, and Cresson was willing to give up his part, provided he could have "the meadow west of the hills, along Montagne's Kill, at the north side of the Kill," *and if* "the persons using Barent's Island would help him a day in making fence." But this was not agreed to, and no step being taken to "free the meadows," Delavall afterwards purchased them, excepting Cresson's, which he never owned.

Nor was the attempt to buy Bronck's Land more successful; even Delavall did not take it, and that valuable tract was conveyed by Edsall, June 4th, 1668, to "Col. Lewis Morris, of the Island of Barbadoes, merchant," whose brother, Capt. Richard Morris, under a mutual contract of Aug. 10th, 1670, came to reside on the plantation. His death within two years led to a visit from Col. Morris in 1673. But being dispossessed that year by the Dutch, he did not make it his permanent residence till after he had secured a large addition to it by royal grant; the whole of which estate, embracing 1920 acres, upon his death, Feb. 14th, 1691, fell to his nephew Lewis Morris, son of Richard, and in 1697 was erected into the *Manor of Morrisania.*

After much labor the mill-dam was finished (crossing the creek a little west of the present 3d avenue), and near its northern end Delavall built his mill; employing as his miller Hage Bruynsen, a Swede, but for twenty odd years a resident in this country.* The land adjoining his own, of which Delavall had

* HAGE BRUYNSEN was b. at Weisch, in Smallant, and may have been the son of Bruyn Barents, named on page 219. Hage entered the service of Burger Joris, a blacksmith at the Smith's Fly—he who owned a grist-mill at Dutch Kills. Seven years later, 1653, Hage bought a house and lot in Smith's Fly, was enrolled in the city burgher corps, and also m. Anneke Jans, from Holstein, by whom he had a son Bruyn, b. 1654. In 1661 he m. Egbertie Dircks, sr. to Neils Matthyssen's w., and by her had a son Hermanus, b. 1662. His term as miller at H. was cut short by his d. in 1668. His city property was sold in 1670 to Jacob Helliker. Hage's wid. m. Hendrick Bosch, sword cutler, the Hush anc., who afterward owned land near H. *Bruyn Hage* spent his youth with his uncle Dirck Jansen, was

the use for mill purposes, took the name of the "Mill Camp." John La Montagne thought the time favorable for removing to his farm, or at least for asking permission of the town to do so; and on his application the inhabitants, Jan. 4th, 1667, voted him "authority to build and live upon his Point." But Delavall's plan to build a substantial house and fortify it was frustrated by an urgent call soon after to go to England, and whither he went the next year, leaving his property at Harlem in care of Daniel Tourneur, as his agent.

But the village plot was expanding and undergoing material changes. On their petition several of the inhabitants were allowed to extend their erven or house-lots, by taking in portions of the streets. For this they were charged from 10 to 15 gl. Two new erven were also laid out on the north side of the "Great Way," and since forming the Judah place. The one adjoining the river was sold to *Johannes Vermilye*, and that lying next to it, to *Robert le Maire*, each for 25 gl. The vacant land to the south of the village, north of lots 1, 2, 3, Van Keulen's Hook, and reserved to the town uses, was also encroached upon; and a triangular piece in the north-west corner, opposite the erven of Karstens and Cresson (taking its form from the course of the creek), was sold at the above price to *Jan Gerritsen de Vries*, who built upon and fenced it.*

The work upon the church having been prosecuted at intervals, as opportunity and the finances warranted, the building was so far completed by Jan. 30th, 1667, that an allotment of the seats then took place. With the finishing of his work by "Bart the mason," and "the table" which Nelis Matthysen had been employed to make in its place, the modest structure was now assigned to its double use as the church and school-house; having a convenient loft or second story, from

taught his trade by his step-fa., and became a "master blacksmith." He m. in 1681, Geesie, dr. of Frederick Schureman, moved to Esopus, bought land in 1683, but d. the next year. Two years later, his wid. returned with a chh. letter to N. Y., where her dr. Annetie, b. 1683, m. 1699, Robert Jacobsen, from Rotterdam.

* This was he later known as Capt. Jan Gerritsen van Dalsen, anc. of the *Delsens* of Orange Co. The family was from Dallsen, or Dalsen, a village near Zwolle, in Overyssel, but Jan, by chance born in Friesland, was distinguished as *de Vries*, the Friesan or Frieslander; the child's pet name having clung to him up to manhood. The Dutch were much addicted to this mode of designation, and to the use of nicknames of all sorts.

which—O primitive economy!—income was sometimes derived by renting it. But, unpretentious as it was, it suited none the less for the acceptable worship of Him who "dwelleth not in temples made with hands." There was on the church lot (*kerk lot*) an older house belonging to the town (noticed in 1665), and probably was rented with the latter.

The question had come up of some change in the burial-place, so as to have it extend out from the rear of the *kerk-erf*, across the back ends of the Le Maire and Vermilye lots to the river; and the inhabitants being consulted, the following vote was passed on Jan. 5th, when the action was taken for the enlargement of the house-lots: "The worthy court, with the approval of most of the inhabitants, have ordered, that the grave-yard (*kerkhof*) now shall be behind the erven of Jean le Roy and Johannes Vermilye."

The only person to object was Le Roy, who, holding the lot here referred to, as agent for Le Maire, and on which was a small tenement that had belonged to the late Jan Cogu, but had been bought and placed there—came in court, Jan. 25th, and requested that the deacons, Daniel Tourneur and Johannes Verveelen, would be pleased to move his house for him, or that the erf might remain his. But in place of this, Tourneur offered to give him timber sufficient for making a house as large as Cogu's, and Verveelen promised to add 30 gl.; with which Le Roy declared himself satisfied. On May 1st, ensuing, Le Roy sold the lot, "as at present fenced in, excepting the street," to Jan Terbosch, whose wife was sister of Vermilye, the adjoining owner.* On June 14th, ensuing, the town, by agreement with Tourneur, resolved to further enlarge the church-yard (kerk-erf) at the rear, by extending it westerly into his erf or house-lot, "four rods in length, and five in breadth." This left a passage from Tourneur's erf to his lot No. 1, Jochem Pieters. As a

* TERBOSCH and Le Maire, as also the Ackerman and Storm ancestors, emigrated in the same ship in 1662. See pp. 103, 106. Terbosch m. Rachel, dr. of Isaac Vermilye, June 10, 1663. They had issue Johannes, b. 1665, Catharine, b. 1668, Isaac, b. 1669, Maria, b. 1672, Sarah, b. 1674, Johanna, b. 1675, and Jacobus, b. 1677. Terbosch d. soon after, and his wid. m. Dirck Wessels, May 25, 1679. This family removed up the Hudson. Johannes m. at Kingston in 1688. Among the desc., in Dutchess co. and elsewhere, this name, like many others, has suffered some change in the mode of spelling it, as *Terbos* and *Terbush*.

consideration they granted Tourneur "the meadows lying along Montagne's Kill, west of *the hills*, from the rocky point till to the end of the creek on the north side of the said Kill." The hills were Mount Morris, etc.; and the meadows, which lay opposite Tourneur's land on Montagne's Flat (since of David Wood, the Bussings, and others), were those known later as the Bussing Meadows, in part conveyed, as claimed, to Samson Benson, prior to 1800, and added to his farm.

On the same date, June 14th, 1667, "John Montagne was permitted to have, in case of exchange, the church-lot's meadows, lying in the bend of the Hellegat; provided he leave instead a piece of meadow, lying south of the Great Meadow, belonging to *Number* 1." The Great Meadow was that upon the north side of Sherman's Creek; No. 1 referred to the lot on Jochem Pieters' Flat which Montagne gave up to the town in 1661. With that nice economy before observed, the deacons, the ensuing fall, sowed upon the church lot (kerk lot) "two schepels of rye." *

* The land thus early designated the *Kerck lot* was that since known as the Church Farm, a part of which is occupied by the present Reformed Church. It lay at the west end of the old gardens, several of which came to be included in it. The *Kerck erf*, which was distinct from the former, lay at the east end of the old gardens, and was then occupied by the church edifice, being the easterly half of the plot afterward of the Myers, and which Samuel Myer sold to Alexander Phœnix, Mar. 27, 1806, but later known as the Eliphalet Williams plot. The *Kerck hof* was the more ancient burying-place, lying in the rear of the Judah plot, and still remembered as the "Negro Burying Ground." The last contained about a quarter of an acre, as conveyed by John De Wit and Catharine his w. to John B. Coles, April 7, 1794.

CHAPTER XVI.

1667–1669.

NEW NICOLLS PATENT; THE FERRY; RUPTURE WITH ARCHER, ETC.

THE chief event of 1667 was the solving of the knotty question of their patent. The subject was again thrust upon the freeholders, early in the year, by an order from the governor, directing them to take out confirmations of their Dutch groundbriefs, under his hand and seal. But how comply with this order, when very few of them had groundbriefs? On the other hand, the general patent granted by Gov. Nicolls the preceding year was so deficient, that it seemed to some of little more value than so much blank parchment. Out of this dilemma appeared no opening, but in the way of another application to the governor for a general patent which should include *all* their lands and meadows; and this had the additional advantage, that it would give an opportunity to supply what else was wanting in the former patent. To this proposal the following persons gave their assent, at a meeting held on March 15th:

Daniel Tourneur,	Jean Le Roy,
Nicholas De Meyer,	Valentine Claessen,
Resolved Waldron,	Jaques Cresson,
Lubbert Gerritsen,	Pierre Cresson,
Johannes Verveelen,	Hendrick Karstens,
Joost van Oblinus,	Jan La Montagne, Jr.
David Demarest.	

A suitable petition was also prepared, and Waldron and Gerritsen were chosen to present it, and manage the business. It read:

To His Excellency, Col. Richard Nicolls, Deputy Governor.

The Inhabitants of the Town of *New Haerlem*, your Excellency's petitioners, would most respectfully represent, that they are informed that a placard has been issued, that each Inhabitant must get his groundbrief renewed within fourteen days, expiring April 1st of this year; and whereas the most of your Excellency's petitioners even till now have no groundbriefs, they therefore pray that your Excellency may please to grant them a general groundbrief or patent, in accordance with the last survey made by your Excellency's land surveyor Mr. Hubbard,* or otherwise, as your Excellency and wise Council shall find good and proper; as also that therein may be included the meadows which are lying at the other side, and belonging to their land.

Your Excellency; Whereas through ignorance of your Excellency's placards, some faults might be committed by your Excellency's petitioners, they pray that his Honor, the Sheriff, may be charged to send a copy of every proclamation affecting your Excellency's petitioners, so that they may not transgress your Excellency's orders. Herein we await your favorable answer; and meanwhile shall pray God for your Excellency's welfare. Dated New Haerlem, 15th March, 1667.

That this matter, which vitally affected their landed rights, should be determined and settled, was also demanded by the rapidly increasing value of the soil and the growing importance of the settlement. It now had some considerable dairies. Fifty-eight cows, besides other cattle, daily went forth from the village in care of the new herder, Knoet Mourisse van Hoesem, who entered upon this service April 15th, and was to continue "till All-Saints Day, either fourteen days earlier or later, as the winter might set in, or the pasture fail." †

The establishment of the ferry gave a new spur and energy to the village, by the increase of travel this way. Verveelen

* Capt. James Hubbard, of Gravesend, who was a surveyor. We may infer that he had been employed to re-survey for the new patent.

† *List of the Cattle that went with the Herder April 15th, 1667.*

Mr. Delavall	2 oxen,	6 cows.
Daniel Tourneur	2 "	8 "
Nelli Matthyssen		3 "
David Demarest	2 "	4 "
Lubbert Gerritsen	2 "	5 "
Valentine Claessen	2 "	3 "
Johannes Verveelen	2 "	5 "
Joost Van Oblinus	2 "	4 "
Johannes Pietersz Buys	2 "	7 "
Resolved Waldron	2 "	7 "
Jan Teunisz v: Tilburg	2 "	3 "
Isaac Vermilye		1 "
Jan La Montagne	2 "	2 "

having fitted up his "ordinary," and provided boats for transportation, of which his lusty negro Matthys was put in charge, found a congenial employment and plenty to do to wait upon such as frequented his tavern for entertainment or wanted to be ferried across to or from the Broncksside, or bring over their droves of cattle. On his application, Jan. 25th, the town court had provisionally fixed the following rates of ferriage, but subject to the approval of the Mayor's Court:

For one person, 4 stivers, silver money; for two, three, or four, each 3 stivers, silver money; for one beast, 1 *shilling; and for more than one, each* 10 *stivers, silver.*

At the corner of the lower street and third crossway, Verveelen's tavern hung out its sign-board, its site now on the north line of 123d street, 300 feet west of 1st avenue. Well patronized, too, by the lovers of good-cheer and *goed bier*, this is shown by the frequency with which he supplied his vault with *goed bier* and *kleyn bier*, *Spanish wine* and *rum*; but it would occur sometimes that a cask found its way into the cellar, on which no excise had been paid or charged. This had happened before. On Oct. 5th, 1666, Daniel Verveelen sent his father at Harlem two half vats of good beer. Allard Anthony, sheriff, hearing of it, visited Harlem the next day, and found the beer at Verveelen's house, the excise neither paid nor entered with the collector. Verveelen told Anthony he did not know him. Anthony complained to the Mayor's Court. Verveelen plead ignorance, and was found not guilty in regard to the beer. He excused his remark made to Anthony, by saying that he did not know him as *schout*, but well as *sheriff!* For this quibble the court fined him 20 gl. sewant, and costs. In the present case the vigilant Tourneur discovered something wrong, and accused Verveelen of smuggling. Vain were denials or explanations, the sheriff's deputy at once took proceedings as follows:

Most Honorable Heeren, Overseers of this Town:

Whereas Johannes Verveelen, ordinary-keeper in this town, did on the 6th February wickedly smuggle one half vat of good beer; on the 18th April, one vat of good beer, and one anker of rum; on the 27th of April, one half vat of good beer; on the 8th May, one half vat of good beer; on the 27th May, one half vat of good beer, and one anker of rum; all which is contrary to the existing placards on the subject of smuggling, and by the high magistracy approved. Therefore the plaintiff, ex-officio the preserver of the peace, demands that the defendant be condemned in the penalty of twenty-one hundred guilders, according to the placards, together with the costs of prosecution. The 14th June, 1667, in N. Haerlem. Yours, Honorable Heeren,

DANIEL TOURNEUR,
Deputy Sheriff.

The court ordered this placed in the hands of the defendant, who was given till the 17th to answer it. But two days after it was amicably arranged, Tourneur so far abating his demand as to accept Verveelen's note for 125 gl. in sewant, in settlement of "the beer transaction."

Verveelen seems to have gotten the idea that the costs he had incurred as ferryman and innkeeper entitled him to some exemption from the payment of excise; because the following lease which he presently secured gave him such exemption for a year and silenced all cavil regarding his rights:

AT the request of *Johannes Verveelen* of Haerlem, We the MAYOR AND ALDERMAN OF NEW YORK have sold the Ferry there as followeth:

It is agreed he shall have the Ferry for five years, provided he keep a convenient house and lodging for passengers at Haerlem, and he shall have a small piece of land on Bronck-side, about an acre, and a place to build a house on, which he must clear, and not spoil the meadow, which shall be laid out by the Town, which must be a morgan of land;—and at the end of five years it is to be farmed out, and during the five years he shall pay nothing for it, and in case it shall be let to another, the house shall be valued as it stands, and he must be paid for it; provided he may have the preference of the hiring of it at the time expired. Here followeth what he shall ask for every man passenger or horse or cattle. For every passenger, two pence silver, or six pence wampum. For every ox or cow that shall be brought into his ferry boat, eight pence or twenty-four stivers; and cattle under a year old, six pence or eighteen stivers wampum. All cattle that are swum over pay but half price. He is to take for diet, every man for his meal, eight pence, or twenty-four stivers wampum; every man for his lodging, two pence a man, or six stivers in wampum; every man for his horse shall pay four pence for his night's hay, or grass, or twelve stivers wampum provided the grass be in fence. All men going or coming with a packet from our Governor of New York or coming from the Governor of Connecticut, shall be ferried free. Also in regard the said Verveelen must be at the charge of building a house on each side of the Ferry, the Governor hath freed him from paying any excise for what wine or beer he shall retail in his house for one year after the date hereof. Dated at New York, this 3d day of July, 1667.

THO: DE LAVALL, *Mayor.*

Beer was the common beverage. At vendues, or in making contracts or settlements, its presence was deemed indispensable to the proper transaction of the business. The magistrates when occupying the bench always had beer brought in, running up a score with the tapster at the public charge. Nor did the ordination of elders and deacons or funeral solemnities form an exception. At such times wine and other liquors, with pipes and tobacco, were also freely distributed. Families commonly laid in their beer by the quarter and half *vat*, or barrel. Such the social habits and customs prevailing among our ancestors, all oblivious as to the evils of the indulgence. Surely time has wrought a good departure from former usage. Much of the beer consumed here was brewed by Johannes Vermilye, while the breweries of Daniel Verveelen, Isaac de Forest, and Jacob Kip, at New York, were also patronized.*

Events soon demonstrated the wisdom of the steps taken for securing a general patent. The heirs of the late Matthys Jansen, of Esopus, had obtained from Gov. Nicolls, May 23d, 1667, a confirmation of the Papparinamin grant at Spuyten Duyvel. And the summer brought bodings of trouble with John Archer, of Westchester, touching the meadows on that side of the river, opposite Papparinamin, belonging to several

* The *Excise Accounts* from Jan. 16 to July 22, 1667, charge the following persons, the number of times here noted, with excise on beer, obtained usually by the half or quarter vat: Tourneur and Vermilye always for *klyn bier* (small beer), the rest mostly for *good bier*, (i.e., strong beer); Hans Lourens, once for *one ton of strong beer*. The farm-hands were good consumers. We omit Verveelen's invoices.

Daniel Tourneur, Isaac Vermilye, David Demarest, each 6 charges; Jan La Montagne, Lubbert Gerritsen, Joh. Pietersen Buys, each 4; Nelis Matthyssen, Jean Leroy, and "the Indian," each 3; Jan Teunisz van Tilburg, Jan Lourens Duyts, Hans Lourens, Resolved Waldron, Claes Carstern Norman, each 2; and a single charge against John Archer, Claude Delamater, Hendrick Karstens, Mark Disosway, Johannes Pelzer, Jaques Cresson, Arent Harmans Bussing, Valentine Claessen, Jan van Gulck, and Michiel Bastiaensen. It is well that entries such as follow, which occur often in the public accounts, belong to the past:

"June 15, *1667*, To 4½ pints Rum, and 15 cans measured Beer, used at the agreement with Verveelen..... *f.* 20.
Feb. 18, 1678, To one anker Good Beer, dispensed when Do. Nieuwenhuysen was here to ordain the deacon .... *f.* 7 : 10.
Sept. 9, 1688, To Rum at his funeral....................... *f.* 7

The last one is among the charges "for the burial of a stranger who died at Cornelis Jansen's." Jan Tibout (*voorleser*) is allowed *f.* 12, "for an address to his credit."

inhabitants of Harlem; and on their complaint the following order was issued:

A Warrant to the Constable of Westchester, about some Meadow Ground claimed by Harlem:

WHEREAS I am informed that the Inhabitants of Harlem have for divers years mowed their hay in the Meadows on the other side of Harlem River, where *John Archer* of your town pretends an Interest, by virtue of a patent granted for the Yonker's Land to Hugh O'Neale and Mary his wife; THESE are to require you to warn the said John Archer, that he forbear cutting hay in those Meadows this present season, and likewise that he do not presume to molest those of Harlem, untill I shall be fully satisfied of the Titles on both parts, and give my judgment thereupon, to whom of right these Meadows do belong. Given under my hand at Fort James, in New York, this 16th day of August, 1667.

R. NICOLLS.

Shortly after this threatened encroachment by the avaricious Archer, which however did not end here, the Harlem freeholders received their town patent, drawn in the following ample terms.*

Richard Nicolls, Esq., Governor General under His ROYAL HIGHNESS JAMES DUKE OF YORK AND ALBANY, &c., of all his Territories in America; To ALL to whom these Presents shall come, *sendeth Greeting.* WHEREAS there is a certain Town or Village upon this Island Manhatans, commonly called and known by the name of NEW HARLEM, situate, lying and being on the East part of the Island, now in the tenure or occupation of several of the freeholders and inhabitants, who being seated there by authority have improved a considerable proportion of the lands thereunto belonging, and also settled a competent number of families thereupon, capable to make a Township; NOW *for a confirmation* to the said freeholders and inhabitants in their possession and enjoyment of the premises, as also for an encouragement to them in their further improvement of the said lands; KNOW YE, That by virtue of the commission and authority unto me given by His Royal Highness, I HAVE GIVEN, ratified, confirmed *and granted*, and by these Presents DO GIVE, ratify, confirm *and grant* unto THOMAS DELAVALL, Esq., JOHN VERVELEN, DANIEL TOURNEUR, JOOST OBLINUS and RESOLVED WALDRON, as

* RECORDED in original book of Patents, Sec. of State's Office, Albany, in Liber 4, p. 60. The date is there given as 1666, but a palpable error; since Oct. 11, in the 19th year of Charles II., was 1667, and moreover the date is correctly recited in several later documents including Dongan's Patent. From a scrutiny of the record it would appear that the date was omitted when the patent was recorded, and carelessly entered afterward. The names of three of the patentees are also written *Vervelen, Turner, Oblent*; but we count these in with other clerical blunders, and correct them from their own autographs.

Patentees for and on the behalf of themselves and their associates the freeholders and inhabitants of the said Town, their heirs, successors and assigns, ALL THAT TRACT, *together with the several parcels of land which already have or hereafter shall be purchased or procured* for and on the behalf of the said Town within the bounds and limits hereafter set forth and expressed, viz., That is to say, from the West side of the fence of the said Town a line being run due West four hundred English poles, without variation of the compass, and at the end thereof another line being drawn across the Island North and South, with the variation, That is to say, North from the end of a certain piece of meadow ground commonly called the Round Meadow,* near or adjoining unto Hudson's or North River, and South to the place where formerly stood the Saw Mills, over against Verkens or Hog Island in the Sound or East River, shall be the Western bounds of their lands; And *all the lands lying and being within the said line* to draw North and South as aforesaid Eastward to the end of the Town and Harlem River, or any part of the said River on which this Island doth abut, and likewise on the North and East Rivers within the limits aforementioned described, *doth and shall belong to the said Town*, As also *four lots of meadow ground* upon the Main, marked with Number 1, 2, 3, 4, lying over against the Spring,† where a passage hath been used to ford over from this Island to the Main, and from thence hither, With *a small island*, commonly called *Stoney Island* lying to the East of the Town and Harlem River, going through Bronck's Kill by the Little and Great Barne's Islands, upon which there are also *four other lots of meadow ground*, marked with No. 1, 2, 3, 4, TOGETHER *with all the soils*, creeks, quarries, woods, meadows, pastures, marshes, waters, lakes, fishing, hawking, hunting and fowling, and all other profits, commodities, emoluments and hereditaments to the said lands and premises within the said bounds and limits set forth belonging or in anywise appertaining.

* MOERTJE DAVIDS' VLY, or Mother Davids' Meadow, was the name by which this meadow was known ten years later; the word *Vly* (now usually written *Fly*, which gives its English sound) being a contraction of *valley*, the Dutch term for *meadow*. It was the identical meadow named in Kuyter's grant, and lay just within the bay or clove at Manhattanville; and it was to distinguish it from another Round Meadow (that at Sherman's Creek, called in the original allotments the Great Meadow) that it received the name Moertje Davids' Meadow. This name was singularly derived from the larger meadows so called lying upon the opposite side of the Hudson, in Bergen County, and annexed to "Moertje Davids' Plantation." Often referred to in the history of the town, our Moertje Davids' Fly has notoriety as a landmark, not only in connection with the Harlem patent line, but with the Battle of Harlem Plains. The perversion to *Murdanies*, *Mordanis*, etc. (see *N. Y. Cal. of Land Papers*, 16, and *Winfield's Land Titles*, 129), has obviously come by clipping the first word, and mistaking the *v* (often formed as *u*, in old writings) for an *n*.

† THE SPRING: that is, Spuyten Duyvel. See page 128. *Verkens Island*, before noticed, was soon after called Manning's Island, from its owner Capt. John Manning, and later Blackwell's Island. *Stony Island* has hardly yet yielded to the modern name of Port Morris.

AND ALSO *freedom of commonage* for range and feed of cattle and horses further West into the woods upon this Island as well without as within their bounds and limits. TO HAVE AND TO HOLD all and singular the said lands, island, commonage, hereditaments and premises, with their and every of their appurtenances, and of every part or parcel thereof, unto the said Patentees and their associates, their heirs, successors and assigns, to the proper use and behoof of the said Patentees and their associates, their heirs, successors and assigns forever. AND I DO hereby likewise ratify, confirm and *grant* unto the said Patentees and their associates, their heirs, successors and assigns, *all the rights and privileges belonging to a Town* within this Government; *with this proviso* or exception, That in all matters of debt or trespass of or above the value of Five Pounds they shall have relation to and dependence upon the Courts of this City as the other Towns have upon the several Courts of Sessions to which they do belong; MOREOVER the place of their present habitation shall continue and retain the name of NEW HARLEM, by which name and style it shall be distinguished and known in all bargains and sales, deeds, writings and records, *And no person whatsoever* shall be suffered or permitted *to erect* any manner of *house* or *building* upon this Island, *within two miles* of the limits and bounds aforementioned, *without the consent* and approbation of the major part of the inhabitants of the said Town. AND WHEREAS the *said town lies very commodious for a Ferry*, to pass to and from the Main, which may redound to the particular benefit of the inhabitants as well as to a general good, the freeholders and inhabitants of the said Town shall in consideration of the benefits and privileges herein granted, as also for what advantage they may receive thereby, be enjoined and obliged at their own proper costs and charge to build or provide one or more boats, fit for the transportation of men, horses and cattle, for which there shall be a certain allowance given by each particular person as shall be ordered and adjudged fit and reasonable. THEY the said Patentees and their associates, their heirs, successors and assigns, *rendering and paying* such duties and acknowledgments as now are or hereafter shall be constituted and established by the laws of this Government, under the obedience of His Royal Highness, his heirs and successors. GIVEN under my hand and seal, at Fort James, in New York, on the Island Manhatans, the 11th day October, in the 19th year of His Majesty's reign, *Annoq. Domini*, 1667.

RICHARD NICOLLS.

While the proceedings relating to the patent were pending, much ill-feeling had found vent at certain "orders of the new government." One of the most outspoken was Jan Nagel, late soldier in the Dutch service, who, on being notified of the order by the constable Verveelen, returned him the following answer, wherein his sentiments are not disguised:

April ye 13, 1667.

I TAKE this opportunity to send you word that I will see you to-morrow to comply with ye orders of ye new government, as such a course seems now necessary, and leaving no other alternative; but not without very strongly protesting against ye injustice which has long been heaped upon us. Not finding satisfaction in ye confiscation of very valuable property, they are now compelling us to submit to an illegal and tyrannical foreign government. If God has designed in his providence that ye Dutch people should become victims to ye treachery and rapacity of ye English, then all they can do is to submit.

JAN NAGEL.

But, on May 3d, Verveelen complains to the magistrates that Nagel "has not obeyed his order." Nagel replies, saying "he has conveyed the order, but they would not go." On motion of the under-sheriff Tourneur, that the defendant "be bound over to the Mayor's Court as a *rebel*, on the charge of having refused to obey the order of the constable," the Overseers so referred the case. Others were also implicated, for on Sept. 6th, Nelis Matthyssen, ex-magistrate, taking by invitation a seat on the bench, Tourneur (not in love with Nelis, whose wife had appeared against him in the manslaughter case) stoutly protested, charging Nelis with being a rebel; but the court rejected the charge. So it rested till another sitting on Oct. 24th, when affairs had become so grave that Capt. John Manning, the High Sheriff, presided, and before whom Jan Nagel and Hans Lourens, in the same category, were also cited to appear. Matthyssen had summoned Tourneur to prove "that he is a rebel." Tourneur now "proves it by the order of the Mayor's Court, that the plaintiff should not continue as one of the bench." Nelis being cast, and put to an amende of 6 gl. and costs of suit, with becoming nonchalance promised 25 gl. to the poor. The two other cases were then taken up, when Nagel was fined 60 gl., and Lourens 40 gl., each with costs.

Capt. Delavall had become by far the largest landed proprietor in the town, and hence was entitled to be named as first patentee. He now owned (not to specify further) several of the uppermost lots on Jochem Pieters Flat, besides those of Simon de Ruine and the late Jan Cogu, in the same tract. On March 14th, 1668, Tourneur as agent for Delavall, who was arranging his business preparatory to going to England, leased these several lots, with the De Ruine house and garden in the village, for a term of four years, to a respectable settler named Wouter Gerritsen, whose emigration in 1659 has been already noticed.*

In the mean time other old groundbriefs of Gov. Kieft's time were being hunted up by heirs or successors of the grantees for official confirmation. That to Pieter Jansen and Huyck Aertsen for land at Sherman's Creek was now claimed in partnership by Joost Kockuyt, of Bushwick, who had married Jansen's widow, and Thomas Lamberts, of Brooklyn, Aertsen's successor. These parties sold the groundbrief to Archer, of Westchester, for 600 guilders. But when presented to Gov. Nicolls he refused to confirm it, both because he considered it as forfeited by the neglect of the owners to improve the land, and "in regard it might be injurious to the town of Harlem."

The old Hoorn's Hook patent, granted to Sibout Claessen, was also offered for sale to Daniel Tourneur, who, consulting his own interests rather than those of the town, agreed to buy it. This being known, caused great dissatisfaction, and gave rise to the following petition :

* SIMON DE RUINE, otherwise called *de Waal*, i.e. the Walloon, was originally from Landrecy, in Hainault, as before noticed. Having sold his lands at Harlem in 1666, he bought a few acres in Flushing, near Jean Genung, and is named on the rate list of 1675, *Doc. Hist. N. Y.*, ii. 461. On April 27, 1678, the Sieur Dubuisson drew up his will; a copy is here given. It was proved June 13, 1678. Simon was sick, and perhaps *in extremis*, as he did not put his hand to the will, and thus its date may be that of his d. As he always made his mark, and his name takes many forms in contemporary records, we follow Dubuisson as probably correct. The following forms prevail: *Druue, Dreuue, Druwen.* John Montagne varies it thus in a dozen times: *Daruy, Daruyn, Druwen.* Simon had, with other chn., *Jacomina*, b. near Landrecy, who m. John Demarest; *Jannetie*, b. at Amsterdam, who m. John De Pre; and *Maria*, b. at H., who m. Samuel Demarest.

A Jourd huy 27me avril 1678, faict en prensence de *Jean Guenon* et de *Marguerite* sa femme, et *Jean des Conseiller*, et de *Jean Baptiste* de Poictier, *Sieur Dubuisson*, et du libre consentement de SIMON DE RUINE, *le Oualon*, se croiant malade, a recongnu pour le repos de sa consiense, par un libre et s'. jugement, a tesmoigne etre sa volonte ainsy quy seulmt qu apres les despt pales desclare et a les claré *Madlaine* sa femme heritier des les bien et eu disposer sa vie durante, sans toutes fois le pouvoir vendre gra ny engager en quelque facon, que le soit tant meuble et inmeuble demeurant au mesme point qu il sont. C etait et concluet a resté dans la maison du dict Simon de Ruine, dit le Oualon, en presence des tesmoin cy desure nomme l on desclaré ne savoir siner faute de quoy mestre on leur marque.

de *Jean* ## *Guenon*
marque ## *Jean des Conseiller*.

fait par moy

Jean Baptiste de Poictier, Sieur Dubuisson

To his Excellency Gov. RICHARD NICOLLS :

The Magistrates of the Town of New Harlem, with all becoming respect and submission, do represent ; That your Excellency's petitioners have been informed that some persons have bought the lands commonly called *Hoorn's Hook* ; which conflicts with the privileges wherewith this Town was laid out, and is to the great prejudice of the town, the more so as the said privileges have been confirmed by your Excellency, and the lands are situated within our jurisdiction. Your Excellency's petitioners do not desire the same for nothing, but offer to pay what they have been sold for.* Hoping your Excellency will give the preference to your petitioners of having the same, with the redemption thereof, by paying what they have been sold for ; they await your Excellency's favorable answer. In the mean time they will not cease to pray God to grant your Excellency enduring health and salvation. Amen. New Harlem, 15th March, 1668.

In the name of your Excellency's faithful subjects,

J. LA MONTAGNE, Junior,
Secretary.

This paper had scarcely gone on its errand when another excitement arose in the village. The 22d of the same month, Jean Baignoux, a worthy French refugee, and subsequent owner of a farm on Hoorn's Hook, having occasion to cross the river to Morris's, forty pounds of tobacco, with a *noolas* † and other articles, all valued at 76 florins, were stolen out of his canoe while it lay at the landing-place. He charged the theft upon Matthys, the ferry negro, who was arrested, but released on his master, Verveelen, becoming his bail. The case, more serious for that Matthys was *de facto* a public servant, demanded, as thought, an extra court, which was held April 2d, when beside the usual magistrates, his honor, High Sheriff Manning, was present. Pierre Grandpre, another refugee, with Knoet Mourisse, had occasion to go over together just after Baignoux, and described the strange actions of the negro, who "with a sword in one hand and fire in the other," forbade their landing. They also

* In margin ; "*To wit, Seven or eight hundred sticks of firewood.*"

† *Noolas*, a bag made of Indian hemp, in which the natives carried their sewant, tobacco, etc., and measured their corn. They came into common use with the settlers, and are often named in inventories and vendue lists. The court minutes of July 12, 1663, contain the following :

"Lubbert Gerritsen and Marie Taine declare, by request of Nelis Matthyssen, that they heard Madalena Lodewycks say, at said Madalena's house, that Barentien Dircks had stolen the pork of Jacob Brouwer, which was in a *noolas* by the oven door. The court condemn defendant to pay, for the needs of the poor, 6 gl. and the costs of suit." She was w. of Simon de Ruine.

See *Warley's Journal*, p. 58, and *N. Y. Col. Doc.* 1, 282.

saw that Matthys had a *sootas*, but could not say whose it was. The testimony left little doubt of his guilt, but the court thought best to postpone the case for further evidence; Verveelen promising Capt. Manning to make good Baiguoux's loss should the latter be able to clearly fix the theft upon the negro. No more appears.

But new trouble awaited the ferryman. It was found no such easy matter to close up the passage at Spuyten Duyvel, long "used to ford over from this Island to the Main." Fences were rudely thrown down, and the grazing kine strayed across at will. Further, it became known that John Barker, of Westchester, had presumptuously, and to the great damage and loss of the ferry at Harlem, taken over a great number of horses and cattle, toll free. Verveelen and the magistrates hastened to make complaint. The Mayor's Court gave both sides a hearing on June 2d, when some neglect on the part of the ferryman appearing, it was "Ordered that said Barker shall pay the ferry money for all horses and cattle conveyed by him over the Spuyten Duyvel whilst the ferry has been at Harlem, which money the petitioners shall employ to repair the fences at Spuyten Duyvel; and the ferryman is in like manner expressly ordered and charged to finish the house and pen, on the opposite side of the ferry at Harlem, at the earliest opportunity; under such penalty as the Hon. Court shall impose." Verveelen made out a bill for £5 sterling against Barker, but recovered it only by an attachment, issued Sept. 5th, by the Town Court.

A series of troubles now began between the inhabitants and John Archer, respecting their lands and meadows near Spuyten Duyvel. This noted person is first introduced to us as "Jan Arcer, alias *Neuswys*, from Amsterdam." His affix, literally rendered *nosewise*, when coupled with his more familiar nickname, "koop-al," or "buy-all," suggested—that Archer was a shrewd fellow and had an eye to business! One alias, indeed, he got from his father, who in 1658 is called "*Jan Aarsen*, from *Nieuwhoff*, commonly called Jan Koopal," the son in 1662 being styled "Jan Arcer, alias Koopal, *the younger*." He had been in Westchester a dozen years or more, and in its affairs borne an active part. It was an English community, and he, taking to wife in 1659 an English girl from

Cambridge, his name thus came to take the English form of Archer, which has descended to a numerous posterity.* By his assiduity acquiring a large tract of land between the Harlem River and the Bronx, he had "at his own charge and with good success begun a township; in a convenient place for the relief of strangers—it being the road for passengers to go to and fro from the main—as well as for mutual intercourse with the neighboring colony." Archer began by leasing his land in parcels of 20 to 24 acres, to such persons as would undertake to clear and cultivate it (and with each a house and lot in the village), all upon easy terms; so that in the years 1668 and 1669 a good number of the Harlem people were led to go there. The "new plantation" was given the name of Fordham.†

Already, as we have seen, there was a dispute between Archer and the Harlem people about the line parting his lands from their meadows upon that side. It so happened that four of Archer's cattle trespassed on the meadows. They were seized by order of the Harlem magistrates, who entered a complaint against Archer to the new governor, Lovelace. Both parties appeared before his Excellency in Council, at a special session held Nov. 6th, and were heard at length; the Harlem people having deputed Tourneur, Verveelen, Waldron, and the constable Roelofsen to answer for them.

Two charges were preferred against Archer:

* THE ARCHERS, we may hence conclude, are not of English, but of Holland descent, although the contrary is assumed in the *Hist. of Westchester Co.* The anc. was b. at Nieuwhoff, his son at Amsterdam, and the latter has left us his autograph, invariably written *Jan Arcer*, as only a Hollander would write it. This seems pretty conclusive.

† The annexed list of leases executed by Archer at Harlem show who took up farms in Fordham. Nearly all subsequently left and got land of their own elsewhere. The leases with stars affixed are not signed in the record.

Date		Lessee						
Feb. 12,	1669.	Kier Wolters and Pieter Roelofsen, ...	Term	7	years	from	Sept. 20,	1668.
"	"	Marc du Sauchoy..........	"	4	"	"	April 1,	1669.
May 1,	"	Jan Pietersen Buys*.......	"	5	"	"	Aug. 31,	1668.
"	"	Cornelis A. Viervant.......	"	5	"	"	"	"
"	"	Jan Teunias v. Tilburg....	"	5	"	"	"	"
"	"	Jan Hendricks Boch*.....	"	5	"	"	"	"
"	"	Hendrick Kiersen..........	"	5	"	"	"	"
"	"	Louwerens Ackerman.....	"	5	"	"	"	"
"	"	Michiel Bastiaensen.......	"	5	"	"	"	"
Dec. 5,	"	Kier Wolters..............	"	5	"	"	"	"
"	"	Marc du Sauchoy........	"	5	"	"	"	"

1st. "That upon pretence of a certain purchase, he lays claim to a parcel of land upon this Island, near Spuyten Duyvel, which is within the limits and bounds of their Patent, and of right belongeth to their Town."

2d. "That having seated himself very near unto some lots of meadow ground upon the Main, belonging unto their Town, he is a daily trespasser upon them with his cattle, and that the said ground, lying in length alongst the Creek or Kill, cannot without very great charge be fenced in."

Upon the first point Archer replied that he owned the land in question, on this Island, by virtue of a groundbrief granted by the Dutch governor Kieft, which he had purchased from Thomas Lamberts and Joost Kockuyt for 600 guilders. But the court decided, that owing to "the long time since the first groundbrief was given, and no settlement since," the title had "lapsed;" or, in other words, was "of no validity, it being forfeited by several acts of the government." Further, because "it might be injurious to the Town of Harlem," Gov. Nicolls had refused to confirm it. It was therefore "adjudged that the land in controversy doth belong to the Town of Harlem, by virtue of their Patent." But it was recommended, "in regard the owners thereof have sustained loss upon the said land," to find means to pay them "so much as the first agreement for the sale thereof."

Upon the second count, Archer "denies any claim to the lots upon the Main, Nos. 1, 2, 3, 4, with which he is charged; but hath purchased land near adjoining, that was the Yonker Vander Donck's." Thereupon, "it was ordered that the defendant do bring in the patent for the Yonker's land in fifteen days' time, with what right he hath to the land where he hath built; at which time some persons shall be appointed to view the meadow belonging to Harlem, upon the Main, and to make report how it may be preserved from the defendant's trespassing on it. Which persons shall also be ordered to view the passage at Spuyten Duyvel, how it may be made convenient for travellers and drift of cattle; the ferry at Harlem being found incommodious, and not answering the ends formerly proposed." The latter announcement foreshadowed a change which was to plant a lifelong thorn in Archer's side.

On Nov. 15th, Archer attempted "to make out his title." But the court remained of the opinion, that he had "not clearly made it out, he having no bill of sale, nor bonds setting forth his purchase." They gave him till Feb. 14th to "clear his title"—and meanwhile he was to give "no disturbance to his neighbors." An order was then issued for the release of his cattle. The receipt to the magistrates for the "four attached cattle," dated Dec. 13th, and signed "Jan Arcer," shows compliance with the order.

No answer has been found to the application respecting Hoorn's Hook; the decision upon the Jansen and Aertsen patent seems to have answered it. Certainly Harlem held the land, and the upshot of the matter was that Tourneur asked the freeholders to grant him this fifty morgen "as a recompense for his services to the town," or to indorse the purchase which he had made. But when it came up for action, Nov. 20th, some were in favor, others opposed, or said they would have no more to do with it, and so it dropped. Howbeit, Tourneur had already secured, June 15th, a valuable grant from Gov. Nicolls of eighty-one acres on the other side of Harlem River, between Archer's and Bronck's land, and watered by the gentle Mannepies, now Cromwell's Creek; which property, by the marriage of his daughter Esther, became vested in the De Voe ancestor, afterward owner of the adjoining tract known as *De Voe's Point.*

On Sept. 17th, the magistrates Tourneur and the senior Vermilye had been summoned to Delavall's mill to appraise the effects of the miller, Hage Bruynsen, just deceased; and ere the year closed, death claimed another settler, Hendrick Karstens, late a nominee for the office of overseer. The village had been the scene of unusual activity through the working season now closing. The first vessel of size put upon the stocks here, of which any notice is taken, was a sloop built this year, under a contract, by Jan Gerritsen de Vries, for Capt. Thomas Bradley, who before this had sailed a market yacht between New York and "Stafford." On Nov. 27th, the parties discharged each other of their contract, Bradley giving De Vries a bond for the balance due him, 122 gl. in sewant, to which Verveelen and William Sandford were witnesses. As indicative of growth in the village, the magistrates, on Dec. 17th, 1668, granted Johannes Pelszer "a little house-lot, lying south of the house-lot of Glaude le Maistre." *

The following year, 1669, witnessed several important measures for the improvement of the town. On Feb. 22d, Gov. Lovelace and his Council, with "others of the bench at New York," held a court at Harlem to consider two or three matters affecting the town and neighborhood. First and principal was that of laying out a wagon road between New York and Harlem, "which hath heretofore been ordered and appointed, but never as yet was prosecuted to effect," though "very necessary for mutual commerce with one another." The following action was taken:

"IT *is this day ordered* that a convenient wagon way be made between the city of New York and this place, to which end four commissioners shall be appointed, who are to view and consider of the most convenient passage to be made.

"That these four commissioners meet to view the said way on Thursday next, being the 25th of this instant month; and after having concluded upon it, that immediately they fall upon laying out the way, according to their former agreement thereupon; that is to say, the neighbors of the Bowery and parts adjacent to clear the way to be fit for the passage of wagons, *from New York to the Saw Kill;* and the Town of Harlem, *from thence to their town.* That this way be laid out and cleared, according to the intent of this order, by the first of May next.

"That the appointed Commissioners, upon their conclusion of the best way, do immediately give the Governor an account of

* HENDRICK KARSTENS was b. in 1610, in Oldenbourg, Westphalia, but directly after that event, his fa., Karsten Hendricks, removed to Amsterdam. The family were Lutherans. Hendrick took to the sea, but finally m. in 1644, Femmetie Coenraets, from Groningen. Soon after the birth of a dr., whom they called Wybrecht, they left Amsterdam for New Netherland. Karstens took up land at H., but also worked as a mason. Unschooled, but industrious and worthy, he bore his humble part in the building up of the town, holding at times several minor offices. In 1667 he visited the Delaware. The year after his d., his wid. m. Lubbert Gerritsen. Karsten's chn. were *Wybrecht*, b. 1646, at Amsterdam, who m. Hermanus van Borsum; *Coenraet*, b. 1648, in this country; and *Jan*, b. 1650. The name Bosch, assumed by the two sons, was probably derived from Bourg, used familiarly for Oldenbourg, their fa.'s birthplace. After some years they both removed from the town, but whither is not certain; possibly to Kinderhook. Consult *Munsell's Albany Hist. Coll.*, iv. 106.

their agreement, who thereupon will give order for the putting the same in execution.

"That the Commissioners of either party have hereby liberty to make inspection on the sufficiency or defect of each other, to the intent that there prove no failing in either of them."*

The two commissioners appointed for the Harlem district were Daniel Tourneur and Resolved Waldron.

This court "also ordered that all horses and cattle belonging to New York and New Harlem which shall be turned into the woods upon this Island, shall have a mark of distinction upon them; That is to say, those belonging to New York, the Bowery, and parts adjacent, are to have a brand mark with *N. Y.* upon them, and those of New Harlem with *N. H.* And, that there be a person appointed and sworn in each place to mark such horses and cattle as really do belong to the inhabitants, and none others."

The question of the transfer of the ferry from Harlem to Spuyten Duyvel had been for some time mooted. Proceedings in regard to it were opened by the following communication from Gov. Lovelace to the Mayor and Aldermen of the city, dated Feb. 27th, 1669.

"WHEREAS Johannes Verveelen, of New Harlem, hath preferred a petition unto me, in regard the ferry at Harlem is to be removed, and that the passage at Spuyten Duyvel is to be fitted and kept for passengers going to and from this Island to the Main, as also for a drift for cattle and horses, that he may be admitted to keep the said passage; the Petitioner alleging, that having a promise from the late Governor, my predecessor, as also a confirmation from the Mayor and Aldermen of this city, that he should enjoy the benefit of the ferry at Harlem

* HARLEM LANE, as we have reason to believe, was at first an Indian trail. Such forest paths, conveniently marked out by savage instinct, were often adopted by the white settlers as the best routes for highways. In travelling from New Amsterdam to Spuyten Duyvel, at McGown's Pass was the natural descent to the plain, the path striking its northern end, where it would as naturally fork to the left and right, for the equal convenience of the pedestrian passing through the "Clove of the Kill" to the North River, or along the base of the height to and up Break Neck Hill. It is not possible to tell when this path over the Flats became a road, but the indications are that it was very early, many years before it was formally laid out as such, which was done pursuant to an Act of Assembly of June 19, 1703. See Hoffman, ii, 249.

for five years, conditionally that he should provide boats and other necessary accommodation for strangers, which accordingly he hath performed, but there is not as yet above two years of the time expired; I have thought fit to refer the whole case of the Petitioner to the Mayor and Aldermen of this city, who are to return back to me their judgment and resolution therein. Whereupon I shall give order for the laying out of a piece of land near Spuyten Duyvel fit for the accommodation of the person that shall be appointed to keep the ferry and passage there, as also for the relief of passengers and strangers."

The Mayor and Aldermen, by resolution, March 2d, concurred in a change of the ferry from Harlem "to the wading place," and recommended that Verveelen be settled there for the remaining three years, provided he "deliver up annually an account of the income of said ferry." Hereupon the Governor, June 2d, granted Verveelen a warrant which after informing "all officers or other persons whom it may concern," of the purpose to remove the ferry from New Harlem to Spuyten Duyvel, "a nearer and more convenient passage to and from this Island and the Main," and that Johannes Verveelen was found "the fittest person to be employed therein that will undertake it, both in regard to the charge he hath been already at, and his experience that way;" proceeds thus

"THESE are to authorize and empower him, the said Johannes Verveelen, to repair to the said place at Spuyten Duyvel, and to cause a fence to be made for keeping all manner of cattle from going or coming to or fro the said passage without leave or paying therefor, and at his best conveniency to lay out a place upon that piece of land called Papparinamin on the Main side, near unto the said passage, for his habitation and accommodation of travellers, for the which he shall have a patent and articles of confirmation. And for so doing this shall be his warrant."

"Instructions for ye Ferryman at Spuyten Duyvel" were drawn up July 15th, and incorporated in the following curious lease:

ARTICLES OF AGREEMENT INDENTED, consented unto and concluded upon, the 15th day of July, in the 21st year of his Majesty's reign, Annoq' Domini, 1669, Between the R^t^ Honble FRANCIS LOVELACE, Esq',

Governor Gen[l] under His Royal Highness, James Duke of York and Albany, &c., of all his Territories in America, on the one part; and JOHANNES VERVEELEN, of New Harlem, on the Island Manhatans, Ferryman, on the other part, for and concerning the settling of a Ferry at the place commonly called Spuyten Duyvel, between this Island Manhatans and the new village called Fordham, as followeth, viz., that is to say.

IMPRIMIS, It is agreed, concluded upon, and mutually consented unto, by and between the parties to these presents, That the said Johannes Verveelen as Ferryman shall erect and provide a good and sufficient dwelling-house upon the Island or Neck of Land known by the name of Papparinamin, where he shall be furnished with three or four good beds for the entertainment of strangers, as also with provisions at all seasons, for them, their horses and cattle, together with stabling and stalling.

THAT the Ferryman have a sufficient and able boat for the transportation of passengers, horses and cattle, upon all occasions.

THAT the said Ferryman cause the Pass upon the said Island near unto Spuyten Duyvel, to be sufficiently fenced in, with a gate to be kept locked, that no person may pass in or out without his permission.

THAT the Ferryman do bear one third part of the charge of making the bridge over the meadow ground to the Town of Fordham, who are to be at the remainder of the charge themselves.

THAT the said Ferryman do give his due attendance at the said Ferry, either himself in person, or by one sufficiently deputed by him, so that nobody be interrupted in their passage to and fro, about their occasions, at seasonable hours. Except in case of emergency, where the public affairs are concerned, when the said Ferryman is to be ready at all seasons that he shall be called upon.

AND in case of neglect of the Ferryman's duty, upon complaint of the party wronged to the Court of Mayor and Aldermen of this City, the said Ferryman shall incur such a Penalty as the Court shall adjudge, according to the merits of the case.

IN consideration of what is herein required to be done and performed by the said Johannes Verveelen as Ferryman, he the said Johannes Verveelen shall, for the well execution of his office, have and receive as followeth, viz.:

THAT the whole Island or Neck of Land called Papparinamin, whether encompassed with water or meadow ground, shall be allotted to the said Ferryman, together with the piece of meadow ground adjoining to it, lately laid out by Jacques Cortilyou, Surveyor, towards the accommodation of strangers, and the defraying of his charges.

THAT the said Island or Neck of Land and meadow ground, together with the housing, or whatever else he shall erect or build thereupon, together with the Ferry, and the benefits, privileges and profits thereunto belonging, shall be and remain to the proper use and behoof of the said Johannes Verveelen and his assigns, for and during the term and space of eleven years, to commence from and after the 1st day of November, 1669.

THAT for the first year, he the said Johannes Verveelen be Constable of the new Town of Fordham, which said Town or Village is to have its dependence upon the Mayor's Court of this City, in like manner as the Town of New Harlem hath; They having liberty to try all small causes under five pounds amongst themselves, as is allowed in other Town Courts.

That after the expiration of the said term and time of eleven years, he the said Johannes Verveelen, if he so long shall live, and desire the same, shall have the first proffer to continue Ferryman; or in case of his decease, his nearest relation or assign shall have preference before another, in being admitted to take the said Ferry to farm. But if it shall happen that another person shall be invested in the employment, the person so invested shall pay unto him the said Johannes Verveelen or his assigns, and make such satisfaction for his buildings, boats and other accommodations remaining thereupon, as shall be adjudged by two indifferent persons to be chosen between both parties.

That at the expiration of the term of eleven years, the said Johannes Verveelen or his assignee who shall exercise the employment of Ferryman, shall be obliged to have the house tenantable, with a sufficient boat, and the fences and gates kept in repair, as they ought to be continued all the time, so that no discouragement be given to passengers, nor the Ferry through any neglect be discontinued.

That the Ferryman shall take and receive of all passengers, whether alone or whether on horseback, drift of horses or cattle, for lodging, diet, feeding, passage, or ferrying, according to the rates in a Table to that end directed and set forth.*

Provided always that all persons employed by special warrant from the Governor, or any Magistrate upon the public account, shall be exempted from paying either ferriage or passage for themselves or horses, as also such person or persons as shall at any time be summoned to appear in Arms, upon any emergent or extraordinary occasion, who are likewise to be free.

Moreover if the Governor shall at any time within the term aforesaid think it convenient that a Fair shall be kept either in the City or any other part of the Island, it is also agreed upon, that all droves of cattle and horses passing over the said Ferry shall be free from payment, either in going thither or returning back, which privilege shall continue during the time of keeping the Fair, as also a day before and a day after its expiration.

And lastly, the said Johannes Verveelen, or whosoever on his behalf shall keep the Ferry aforesaid, shall pay yearly and every year as a Quit Rent to His Royal Highness, the sum of Ten Shillings.

In Testimony hereof the Parties to these present Articles Indented have interchangeably put to their hands and Seals the day and year first above written.

Francis Lovelace.
Johannes Verveelen.

*Ye Ferryman his Rates.

For Lodging any person, 8 Pence *per night, in case they have a bed with sheets, and without sheets*, 2 Pence in silver.
For transportation of any person, 1 Penny silver.
For transportation of a man and horse, 7 Pence in silver.
For a single horse, 6 Pence.
For a turn with his boat, for 2 *horses*, 10 Pence, *and for any more*, 4 Pence *apiece; and if they be driven over, half as much.*
For single cattle, as much as a horse.
For a boat loading of cattle, as he hath for horses.
For droves of cattle to be driven over, and opening ye gates, 2 Pence *p. piece.*
For feeding of cattle, 3 Pence in silver.
For feeding a horse one day or night with hay or grasse, 6 Pence.

Verveelen was soon settled at Papparinamin, where as ferry-master he kept the key of Manhattan Island. Being constable of Fordham, here he held court after William Betts, sen., and Kier Wolters had been appointed by the governor, Dec. 24th, 1669, as "Overseers and Assistants." The next year he superintended the "making a bridge over the marsh between Papparinamin and Fordham." He was the ferryman here for many years, under renewals of his lease and by the favor of successive governors; but he and Archer were ever at swords' points on the subject of Papparinamin, the latter claiming it to the day of his death as successor to Vander Donck, and "by virtue of his purchase and patent."

Other events of 1669 remain to be noticed.* The mill-dam, "lately impaired by a breach of water," needed prompt attention, but as Capt. Delavall was then abroad, Gov. Lovelace was informed of the accident, June 8th, and ordered John Askew and Peter van Nest, of Flatlands, to go to Harlem, forthwith, with their workmen, and "use the best skill and endeavor in repairing the dam," and "what else is requisite about the mill." Capt. Delavall returned toward the close of the year, to his estates and his honors, and in full favor with the Duke of York; having been acquitted of certain charges on account of which he had gone to England.

* JAN LAURENS DUYTS, who left the town this year, was the son of Laurens Duyts, nicknamed *great shoe*, a Dane, b. in Holstein, in 1610. See pp. 151, 202. The father was banished by Stuyvesant—an easy thing for him to do, and seldom wisely done, but Duyts' case would seem to have been an exception. He d. at Bergen, Jan. 14, 1668, leaving two sons, Jan and Hans. Kuyter stood as godfather for both at their baptism. Hans was b. in 1644, and lived at H. in 1667. His dr. *Catharine* b. 1674, m. 1688, Joost Paulding, from Cassant, Holland, who went to Westchester, and was the anc. of John Paulding, one of André's captors; also of Gen. William Paulding, formerly Mayor of N. Y.

Jan Duyts bore a good name at H., and did not deserve the taunt uttered one day by Jeanne de Ruine, in presence of Monis Peterson. *You schelm, loop by you vaar Deen.* "You villain, run to your father Dane." Monis testified that Jan said nothing to provoke it. He was then twenty years old, and the same year, Nov. 22, 1662, bought of Lubbert Gerritsen the house and bouwery formerly of Matthys Boon, engaging to pay for it 300 gl. He sold out the next year, and Resolved Waldron soon after got this property. In 1667 Duyts was working for Gerritsen aforesaid, and m. that year; but on Jan. 8, 1669, he leased a farm at Dutch Kills from John Parcell, and lived there, when he m. a second time in 1673. His w. were Jannetie Jeurlaens, from Bois le Duc, and Neeltie Adriaens, from Breda; the last m. 1679 Hendrick van Dyck, of New Utrecht. Duyts left some property to his two chn. *Laurens* and *Annetie*.

Tourneur's negro now absconded; inevitable contingency of a state of bondage—African slavery even then existing in all the colonies. So to Westchester went the following warrant, directing the constable to pursue the runaway with "hue and cry."

WHEREAS there is lately a *Negro Servant* run away from his Master's service, and supposed to be gone your way toward *New England*. These are to require all persons within this government and to desire all others, if the said Negro can be found within your liberties or precincts, that you forthwith seize upon and secure him, and cause him to be safely conveyed to this place, or to his Master, DANIEL TOURNEUR, at *Harlem*, upon this Island. The Negro is big and tall, about 25 or 26 years old, and went away from his Master four or five days since. Given under my hand at Fort James, in New York, this 28th day of June, 1669.

FRANCIS LOVELACE.

The Indians still laid claim to portions of the Harlem lands—perhaps reserved rights—one of the tracts being their old and favorite haunt, Rechewanis, or Montagne's Point. The chief claimant was Rechewack, the old sachem and proprietor of Wickquaskeek, who, as far back as 1639, had been a party to the sale of Ranachqua and Kaxkeek. Though he and his tribe had lately been "beaten off by the Maquas," or Mohawks, who were at war with them, and forced to retreat over the Hudson to the deep eloves and forests of Tappan, their enemies, as they affirmed, made war only on their persons and goods, but not on their lands, so that their title still held. Montagne proceeded to satisfy the old Wickquaskeek and his chiefs, and thereby to secure the Indian title—in those times a desideratum. Obtaining a release of the Point, he has left us the following record of it:

Ay 20 Augusty oude steyl hebben de ondergen: Willden myn Jan La Montagne verkocht de punt genaampt Rechewanis, bepaalt tusschen twee killen en bergen, en achter een fonteyn die aen Montangen Vlachte uitleyt; met de Valeyen van de bochte van't Hellegat tot Konsande Kongh.

Verkoopers van de Punt. { Rechkewackan, Achwaaroewes, Sacharoch, Pasachkeeginc, Niepenohau, Kouhamweu, Kottareu } Tappan.

[*Translation.*]

On this date, 20th August, old style, the underwritten Indians have sold to me, Jan La Montagne, the Point named Rechewanis, bounded between two creeks, and hills, and behind, a stream* which runs to Montagne's Flat; with the meadows from the bend of the Hellegat to Konaande Kongh.

Sellers of the Point. } names as above. } Tappan.

Upon the heel of this came another claim. On April 9th, 1670, when certain chiefs met Gov. Lovelace to make sale of Staten Island, "some of the Indians present laid claim to the land by Harlem." But this was answered by producing the Indian deed of 1626, for the whole island, and they were told, "the record shows it was bought and paid for forty-four years ago." But in no wise satisfied, the sachems still held to their pretensions, which later were more successful. The deed to Montagne is especially interesting, as tending to show the identity of the Wickquaskeeks with the Manhattans, so called, a name meaning simply the *Islanders.*

A notable transaction was Nicholas de Meyer's sale, September 25th, 1669, of the two farms embraced in his patent, to the brothers Cornelis and Laurens Jansen; the first of whom was the ancestor of the Kortright family, or that branch afterwards known for its large landed possessions, of which this purchase formed the nucleus.† The town now proceeded to inclose a por-

* The Dutch word *fonteyn*, though usually rendered *spring*, here means as well the brook issuing from a spring, I believe that spoken of on page 201. This brook or run became a recognised boundary, and is several times referred to in connection with this and the adjoining property, and always, in the original, called the *fonteyn*.

† JAN BASTIAENSEN, the fa. of Cornelis and Laurens Jansen, came to this country, as we have seen, in 1663, from the co. of Leerdam, or the Prince's Land, in South Holland; accompanied by his br. Michael Bastiaensen, who afterwards lived in H., and whose family will be noticed elsewhere. Jan may have been the "Kortryck" who owned a bouwery on Staten Island, in 1674. *N. Y. Col. Mss.*, xxiii. 403. He seems to have spent part of his time at H., but is last mentioned here Jan. 8, 1677, when he is witness to a power of attorney, given by his old Schoonrewoerd friend, with whom he came out, Jan Louwe Bogert, to Hendrick Jansen Baker, to collect money due Bogert on Brooklyn property sold to Thos. Lamberts, etc. His chn. were Cornelis, b. 1645, and noticed on a future page; Hendrick, b. 1648; Laurens, b. 1651, also noticed hereafter; and Belitie, b. 1659, who was, as were the others, "uit Holland," and who m. in 1678 Jacob Jansen Decker, of Esopus, whither her br. Hendrick had gone to live.

tion of the commons lying about "the hills" (Mount Morris, etc.) as a calf pasture, probably on being interdicted the further use of Little Barent's Island for that purpose by Capt. Delavall, whose proposition respecting the Island they had declined. The following regulations were passed Nov. 25th, 1669:

ORDINANCE made concerning the *Common Calf Pasture* lying north of the village.

It is first ordered that no one of the inhabitants shall be allowed to pasture therein any beasts except calves, upon the forfeit of *three guilders* for each beast, and for a flock of sheep *three guilders*. Moreover, every one leaving the gate open shall forfeit *three guilders*; also for every beast found in said pasture shall *three guilders* be forfeited; provided that the owner of the beast or beasts may seek his remedy upon those who shall have opened, or left open, the gate or fence. It is also ordered that each one shall duly make his part of the bridges in both meadows within the common calf pasture between this and the last of March next ensuing, upon penalty of *five and twenty guilders*.

Hendrick Jansen van Reest, as he at first styled himself, but later in life, from his fa.'s birthplace, called Hendrick Jansen van Kortright, bought land near Stuyvesant's Bouwery, Feb. 12, 1669, but did not long hold it. He and his br. Laurens, going to Esopus, both m. there; Hendrick, on Dec. 14, 1672, to Catharine Hansen, "born in New York," and Laurens on or ab. the same date, to Mary, dr. of Albert Heymans Roosa. Probably Hendrick's w. was the dr. of Hans Weber, "master at arms," who d. in 1649, and whose wid. m. Matthys Capito, removed to Esopus, and was killed by the Indians in 1663. Hendrick's first ch. being "born at Harlem," in 1674, we presume he was then living here; but as before said he settled in Ulster co., buying land at Mombackus, town of Rochester, where he raised a large family, who bore the name of Kortright, or Cortright, and whose desc. have become numerous and widely scattered. Hendrick lost his w. in 1740, and he d. in 1741, æ 93. His chn. so far as shown, were *John*, b. 1674, who m. Maria, dr. of Wm. van Vredenburgh, of N. Y.; *Hendrick*, b. 1677, who m. 1700 Mary De Witt, and in 1704, Catharine Crom, wid. of Arie van Etten; *Cornelius*, b. 1680, who m. 1701, Christina Rosecrans; Geertie, b. 1682; *Arie*, b. 1684; Antie, b. 1686, m. Jacob Decker; *Lawrence*, b. 1688, who m. 1715 Sarah Ten Eyck; *Jacob*, b. 1692; *Peter*, b. 1696, m. 1717 Marritie van Garden; and Catharine, b. 1699. John, Cornelius, Lawrence, and Peter Kortright subscribe, 1717, for the minister at Rochester, and were leading men there. Peter d. in 1744. Cornelius removed to Marbletown. John and Maria had issue, Hendrick, William, Adrian, etc., two at least of these straying down into Orange co., where William had a family, and in 1740 was justice of the peace. His br. Hendrick, b. 1704, m. 1730 Grietie Van Bunschoten, left Rochester and settled in Minisink. Being very sick, he made his will Dec. 3, 1753, providing for his wid., but naming no ch., and giving his homestead and Great and Little Minisink Islands to his "cousin" (nephew), Hendrick W. Cortright, son of William, dec. His will was proved June 26, 1760. This Hendrick, 'tis said, has many desc. within the old town of Minisink. Friendly intercourse was kept up for many years between the Kortrights of H. and those of Ulster Co.

Jaques Cresson, who in a ten-years' residence had proved himself a worthy inhabitant, made his will before the secretary, Oct. 1st, preceding, his wife joining with him, and Tourneur and Waldron being witnesses. The survivor was to use the property, and "bring up the children reputably, and in the fear of the Lord." Soon after this, Cresson was made constable, but subsequently resolving to remove in the spring to New York, where his brothers-in-law, Nicholas de la Plaine and Nicholas du Puis (Depew) were living, he sold his house, bouwery, etc., Dec. 4th, 1669, to Meynard Journee, of Bedford, Brooklyn, for 1600 gl., sewant. Du Puis, whose wife was Mrs. Cresson's sister, was present, with David Demarest.

The day following Montagne was sent for to the house and sick-bed of Jean le Roy, who wished to make his will; Oblinus, Isaac Vermilye, and Constable Roelofsen being desired to witness it. He had been bereft of his wife, Louise de Lancaster, and his only child, Stephen, baptized at Brooklyn, on April 3d, 1661. Bestowing 50 gl. upon the poor, he named Daniel Tourneur, senior, as his sole heir and *testamenteur*. But Le Roy recovered, to marry again, and to see his kinsman Tourneur buried. Jean was probably related to Marc le Roy, who stood as godfather for young Daniel Tourneur, at his baptism at Leyden.*

* PIETER ROELOFSEN was from Utrecht, as was his first w., Willemtie Jans, m. in this country in 1653. He, with others, started the town of New Utrecht in 1657, put up a house, etc., but after three years sold out, and moved to Flatlands. In 1664 he m. a second w., Elizabeth, dr. of Jan Pater, she having been b. in Brasil. Pieter served two terms as constable at H.; tilled one of Archer's farms, and, in 1671, some of Delavall's land. In 1672 he went to Mespat Kills, and there bought a farm. He and wife sustained a good name here, as certified by the magistrates after his d., which happened in 1679. They made their will in N. Y., Mar. 20, 1678, Jochem Beeckman and Dirck Jansen, burghers, being present. A funny incident is related of the wid. and Dr. John Greenleaf, of Newtown. The latter, by way of a joke, offered to waive his bill for services, for a *kiss*! The wid. took him up, the kiss was duly given, and they shook hands over it. Afterwards, the doctor was so ungallant as to sue for payment. But the magistrates holding the settlement binding, found for the amiable defendant. She subsequently m. Peter Buckhout. See p. 227. Roelofsen had issue by his first w., Roelof and Maria, and by his second, Johannes, Jacobus, Hendrickje, Abraham and Susannah. The sons retained the patronymic *Peterson*.

CHAPTER XVII.

1670–1672.

VILLAGE LIFE; HARLEM TWO CENTURIES AGO.

BUSY yeomen, drawn into such intimacy at home and in the field—from the very proximity of their dwellings and narrow bouwlots, and their modes of tillage in common—theirs was more than a monotonous round of dull rural life.* Hence the variety of transactions and incidents which crowd the years next ensuing, none remarkably signal or startling, but affording nevertheless a curious study touching the ways and customs prevailing among them. A new generation has grown up, taxing the energies of provident sires to give them land, homes, and outfits. The seniors admonished by advancing years that they must pass away, full oft the parish clerk is called in to draw up a last will and testament. Yet following the pioneer work of organization, these are years of maturing and progress. Multiplying interests naturally bring new duties and burdens to both town officers and the community, and to which they seldom prove unequal. It was to engross much of their united effort, wisdom, and vigilance to support the institutions and maintain

* PLAN of the Village in 1670, on page 292. *Explanations:*

Plots *a* to *v* embrace the original *erven* or house lots, to which 5 erven, (*w*, *x*, *y*, *aa*, *bb*,) and 3 half erven, (*z*, *cc*, *dd*,) had since been added. For some cause *v* was also rated as a half erf. On it stands the only remaining house of the old dorp or village proper, being that occupied by Mr. Cowperthwait. The old Ferry House, pulled down in 1867, stood on plot *x*.

A. Site of Reformed Church and Harlem Library.
B. " Chesterman House.
C. " Congregational Church.
D. " Judge Ingraham House.
E. " Derick Benson's House, removed before 1766.
F. " Lewis Morris Coach House, built ab. 1724.

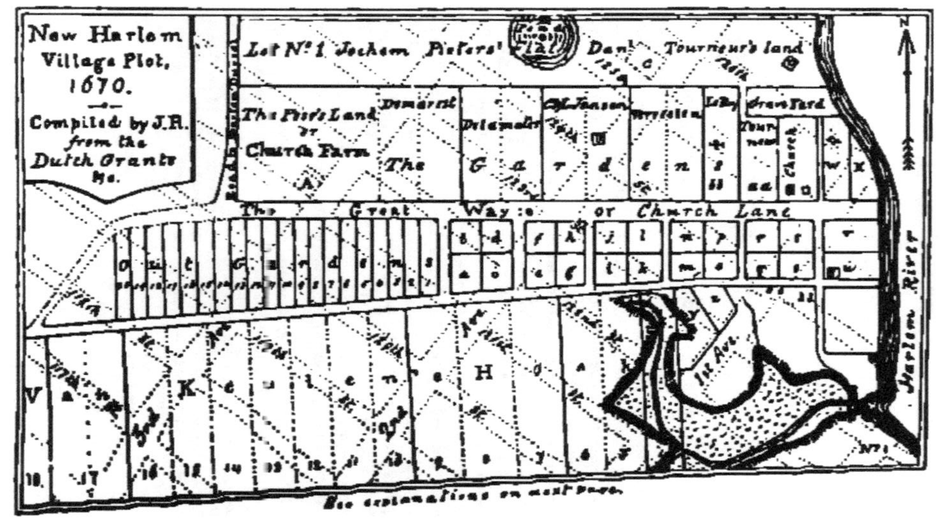
New Harlem
Village Plot,
1670.
Compiled by J.R.
from the
Dutch Grants
&c.
Lot No. 1 Jochem Pieters' Flat
Dan'l. Tourneur's land
The Poor's Land
or
Church Farm
Demarest
Delamater
Grave Yard
Church
The Gardens
The Great Way: or Church Lane
Out Gardens
1st Ave.
Harlem River
Van Keulen's Hoek
See explanations on next page.

the wholesome regulations they had introduced, as well as to guard and utilize the long stretch of territory comprehended in their patent. It greatly enhanced these responsibilities when Fordham was added to their jurisdiction.

The stock, allowed to run at large in the woodlands, was very liable, especially if unmarked, to be embezzled by persons not over-scrupulous. The case of George Tippett, near Spuyten Duyvel, had recently been reported to the Governor. By his Excellency's order of Feb. 10th, 1670, the Constable and Overseers of Harlem met with the court at Fordham, on the last day of that month, to inquire whether certain unmarked hogs which Tippett had slaughtered, belonged to him; the same being "claimed by John Archer, on the behalf of His Royal Highness," under the Governor's warrant. Tippett had once been reproved by the Governor for "the unlawful mark he hath, of cutting the ears of cattle so close that any other marks may be cut off by it;" but the evidence now given at Fordham by Elizabeth Heddy, Benjamin Palmer, and Jan Hendricks, established the weighty fact that Tippett had owned a litter of pigs, "the which were gray, red, spotted and white." Archer protested, and, coming to Harlem March 3d, took the testimony of the magistrates and Daniel Tourneur, as to what Tippett and his witnesses had admitted and said. Nothing seems to have come of it; but, two days after, the Mayor's Court issued new instructions, "that no horses or cattle be fed in the commons of this Island but those that are branded with the Town's mark." They ordered a record to be kept of the color and marks of the creatures, and of the owners' names; and that two days in the week should be designated for branding, etc. The fees were to be 3 gl. sewant for a horse, and 2 gl. for an ox, steer, or heifer. Resolved Waldron and Daniel Tourneur were appointed branders "for the town of New Harlem and adjacent farms," to act from May 1st ensuing, when the above rules were to go into effect.

The removal of Kier Wolters to Fordham early in the winter caused a vacancy in the board of overseers, to fill which Joost van Oblinus was appointed on January 25th. Wolters was present with Archer at Harlem March 3d, aiding him in the Tippett affair; but he died shortly after, having been much respected for character and abilities, notwithstanding Tippett had said "he acknowledged him for no magistrate."* Jan Gerritsen de Vries obtained from the overseers on March 2d a formal grant of the house lot set off to him some years before at the south side of the village, on condition of his "paying as other such small house lots (*erfjes*), and also the same servitudes." He is charged for it in the town book, under 1667, 25 gl. De Vries had sold this lot, with its house and improvements, to Resolved Waldron, to whom he conveyed it the next day, March 3d. Here Waldron took up his residence.

Glaude Delamater and Hester du Bois his wife joined in making their will, April 15th, though he survived a dozen years, and she forty. It shows the then form of such instruments.

IN the year of our Lord and Saviour Jesus Christ, 1670, the 15th April, appeared before me Jan La Montagne, Junior, admitted Secretary of this Town by the Honorable Mayor's Court, residing within the jurisdiction of New Haerlem, *Glaude le Maistre* and *Hester du Bois*, husband and wife, of sound memory and understanding as externally appears; and of mind to make a disposition of their temporal estate. First, on resting in the Lord, they commit their souls into the hands of the Most High God, and their bodies to decent burial, and fifty guilders in sewant to the poor in this place. Secondly, they annul all testaments and codicils that before this were made, and declare this mutual testament to be their final will. One of them having deceased, the survivor is to continue in full possession till again married, when the marrying party shall place into the hands of two guardians thereto appointed by the Court, a full account of all; remaining in possession until

* KIER WOLTERS, the anc. of the *Kiersen* and *Kier* family, arrived here in 1657, as before noticed, from the Dutch county of Drenthe; coming *via* Amsterdam, to New Amstel, on the Delaware, where he was reputed to be one of their ablest and best farmers. Two years later, flattering offers being made him, he came to New Amsterdam, and had the charge of Gov. Stuyvesant's bouwery. He took De Meyer's farm at H., in the fall of 1667 I believe, at 500 gl. rent per annum, and half the increase of the stock; and worked it two seasons. Losing his w. Jannetie Jans, he m. early in 1668 Lysbet, dr. of David Ackerman, removing the next year to Fordham, and there d. in 1670, as above stated. While at H. he was twice chosen an overseer. His chn., so far as known, were Walter, Hendrick, Jan, and Grietie, all b. in Drenthe; Jannetie, b. in N. Y.; and Tjerck, of whom we only know that he joined the chh. at N. Y. in 1674. Jannetie m. in 1672 Claes Jansen van Heyningen, and Grietie m. in 1680 Willem Peersen, of N. Y. Hendrick Kiersen was b. in 1648 at Giest, in Drenthe, and in 1673 m. Metje Michiels, dr. of Michiel Bastiaensen. He finally settled in Fordham; his chn. being *Kier*, b. 1674; *Michiel*, b. 1676; *Jannetie*, b. 1680; *Sarah*, b. 1682; Peter, b. 1684 (see p. 548); Maria, b. 1687; Rachel, b. 1693; Hendrick, b. 1696. Desc. have been called *Kiers*, and, we believe, *Keese*. Jan Kiersen, who remained at Harlem, will be named in treating of the Patentees.

the children arrive at age, or are married with the consent of father or mother: on condition of placing in the hands of the guardians a mortgage upon the real estate, so the same be not alienated. Excluding or renouncing herewith all Orphan Courts, or laws which may conflict with these provisions. In presence of David des Marest, Joost van Oblinus and Marcus du Sauchoy, as witnesses hereto requested, and who beside the testators, have subscribed these presents. Dated as above.

CLAUDE LE MAISTRE.
D. D.
This is the mark of
HESTER DU BOIS.

David des Marest,
J. van Oblinus,
Marc du Sauchoy

With my knowledge.
J. Lamontagne, Junior, *Sec'y.*

Resolved Waldron and Johannes Verveelen, on the same date as above, made a partition of their meadows at Sherman's Creek and Spuyten Duyvel, which they had gotten with the lots bought of Jan Dyts and Jurisen Hanel.

Jaques Cresson, the constable, in view of removing to New York after the first of May, appeared in court April 21st, and gave an account of the fines due from several parties for defective fences. Those of Wouter Gerritsen, lessee of Delavall's land, amounted to 43 gl. 10 st. Much vexed at this heavy loss, Wouter's wife had scolded the magistrates, and called Waldron an *uytsuyper*, a drunkard. Arraigned for it by Waldron and Tourneur at the same court, the afflicted Mary still persisted that the magistrates *were killing her*, but owned she was hasty in abusing them. She was fined for her rashness 6 gl. for the poor, and costs of suit.

The month of May brought a demand from Capt. Matthias Nicolls, colonial secretary, for the first payment on the town patent, his entire bill for which was 332 gl. To meet this call an assessment was authorized and made out, at the rate of 2 fl. 7 st. for each *erf*, or house lot, and 12 st. for each *morgen* (2 acres of land, the assessed lands embracing only Jochem Pieters Flat and Van Keulen's Hook. The following is the list, and which is interesting as an exhibit of all the landholders within the town at that date, and the number of erven, farming lots, and morgen held by each. From reliable data we have added the numbers of the lots, and shown in which tract they lay. This, to those in any way interested in locating the original plots, will give the table greater value, as the title to these lots may in most cases be traced down to a modern date.

"LIST OF THE FIRST PAYMENT OF THE CHARGES FOR WRITING THE PATENT BY CAPT. NICOLLS."

LAND OWNERS. May 1st, 1670.	ERVEN.	FARM LOTS.	MORGEN IN THE LOTS.	AMOUNT OF TAX.	NO. OF LOTS OR JOCH. PIETERS.	NO. OF LOTS VAN KEULEN'S H'K.	LOT NUMBERS: J. P. Flat.	LOT NUMBERS: V. K. Hook.
Thomas Delavall	5	10	48	*f.* 40:11	6	4	3, 13, 19, 20, 21, 22	12, 13, 16, 22
Glaude le Maistre	2	3	13	13:14	2	1	14, 15	21
Cornelis Jansen	2	4	18	15:10	2	2	2, 16	6, 15
Jean le Roy	1	2	9	7:15	1	1	11	1
Daniel Tourneur	3	5	21	19:13	2	3	1, 17	17, 18, 19
Lubbert Gerritsen	1	2	12	9:11	2	0	4, 9	....
Johannes Verveelen	2	4	15	18:14	1	3	10	7, 8, ½ of 4, ½ of 9
David des Marest	1½	1½	8	7:15	1	½	7	½ of 5
Johannes Vermelje	1	0	0	2: 7	0	0	....	....
Joost van Oblinus	2	3	12	11:16	1	2	18	10, 11
Conrad Hendricksen	1	0	0	2: 7	0	0	....	....
Pierre Cresson	1	2	9	7:15	1	1	5	20
Resolved Waldron	2	4	15	18:14	1	3	8	2, 3, ½ of 4, ½ of 9
Jan Nagel	½	1	6	3:12	1	0	16	....
Jean des Marest	½	0	0	1:3½	0	0	....	....
Isaac Vermeille	0	½	1	12	0	½	....	½ of 5
Jaques Cresson	1	2	9	7:15	1	1	6	14
Jan La Montagne*	....	....	....	....	....	....	....	....

* The half-erven in the list are not taxed where the owner holds other land. Montagne having no property here, except his farm at the Point, which was then exempt from town tax, he contributed "in plaats van de Kalver Wey," that is, *on account of the Calf Pasture*; but the amount is illegible in the record.

On May 4th Isaac Vermilye sold his house and house lot on Van Keulen's Hook (part of lot No. 6, and not reckoned among the erven), with the fruit-trees thereon—the buyer, Evert Dircksen, agreeing to pay 600 gl.; but the bargain was not closed, and Vermilye remained in possession till his death in 1676.

On May 19th, the magistrates, pursuant to directions from the Mayor, appointed David Demarest and Arent Evertsen Keteltas curators over the estate of Kier Wolters, late of Fordham, deceased. To these, on a subsequent recommendation of the Mayor, was added, May 23d, "Michiel Bastiaensen, residing at Fordham," who was "reasonably conversant with the estate of the deceased." *

* MICHIEL BASTIAENSEN, of whose history up to his emigration in 1663 we have before spoken, had, so far as known, five chn., viz.: Reyer, b. 1653; Metje, b. 1655, who m. Hendrick Kiersen; Annetie, b. 1658, who m. John Odell (ancestor of the Fordham Odells); Bastiaen, b. 1663; and Aefie, b. 1665, in N. Y., who m. Jacques Tourneur. Reyer Michielsen, named in some curious proceedings, under 1674, m. in 1686 Jacomina, dr. of Jan Tibout, and settled in the town of Fordham. He took part in building the church there in 1706, and a stone bearing his initials may now be seen in the carriage-house wall of Mr. Moses De Voe, who took it from the foundation of the old church, which stood upon Mr. D.'s farm. Reyer d. in 1733, æ. 80 yrs., having had eight chn. to wit: Michiel, Reyer, Hendrick, Teunis; Hannah, who m. Leonard Vincent; Mary, who m. Benjamin Haviland; Sarah, who m. Joseph Haviland; and Jane, who m. Benjamin Corsa. The sons of his son Michiel (being Reyer and Michael) retained the name of *Michaels*, but other of Reyer's sons took the patronymic *Reyers*. Hence have descended the two families of Westchester co., and other sections of this State, named Ryer, and Michael, or as also written McKeel or Mekeel. The name Reyer is said to come from *ridder*, a knight.

Bastiaen Michielsen, always so styled in the town books, though in the church records usually called Bastiaen Kortright, remained in H., where he m. in 1689 Jolante, dr. of John La Montagne, dec. On Sept. 19, 1701, he bought from Peter van Oblienis, a tract of land at Sherman's Creek, laid out to Oblienis in 1691, as lot No. 20. This became the well-known Kortright farm, which continued in the family till 1786. It was originally ten morgen, or twenty acres, and is so rated on the town books for the next half century; but this was exclusive (for meadows were never taxed) of the adjoining marsh, or the *morasse creupelbos*, of the original description. And then, be it remembered, the allotments of 1691 generally overran the estimate, and this lot lying isolated was not likely to be an exception. This brought it up to 45 acres, 27 perches. Here Bastiaen Michielsen built and lived till very aged; at least, his name in the tax lists runs down to 1753. He also owned two pieces of meadow at Kingsbridge, bought of the town by Joh. Vermilye, Apl. 1, 1693, and on the same date transferred to Bastiaen, to whom the town gave a deed Jan. 4, 1700. Bastiaen Michielsen Kortright had issue, as far as appears, Michael, b. 1697; Johannes, b. 1702; Aefie, who m. John Devoor; and Rachel, who m. Isaac Delamontagne. Johannes *Bastiaens*, as he is properly styled in certain deeds, but calling himself (after his fa.'s patronymic) "Johannes *Michielsen* Kortright," m. Aeltie, dr. of

precedent for any other pretense to lands within the Patent of the said Town of Harlem, by virtue of such old claims or groundbriefs. Given under my hand at Fort James, in New York, this 22d day of June, 1670.

FRANCIS LOVELACE.

The matter was arranged thus: Richard bought out Lamberts' share, and took a bond from the Harlem folks for the full amount of 300 guilders.

On Aug. 4th ensuing, Lubbert Gerritsen, who the last year had married the widow of Hendrick Karstens, sold Karstens' erf and out-garden to Joost van Oblinus for 400 gl., to be paid to Coenraet and Jan Hendricks, sons of Karstens, when of lawful age. These afterward took the name of Boch.

A little later (Oct. 23d) Lubbert Gerritsen executed a power of attorney to his brother-in-law, Philip Weckman (Wukeman), of Leyden, to enable him to collect from the orphan masters or others in that city a legacy of 600 gl. left to his wife Femmetie Coenraets, by her mother's sister, Tryntie Gerrits, who had died at Leyden, Oct. 7th, 1669. It is probable that this was sent to Holland by Nicholas de Meyer, who went thither the next spring, having several such collections to make for persons at Esopus.

Jan La Montagne, who had recently lost his father,* now resigned the duties of voorleser and school-master, but retained the secretaryship. To fill the vacant position, the town officers engaged Hendrick Jansen Vander Vin, the former freeholder, for the term of three years, "at *f.* 400 yearly in sewant, or in grain at sewant price," and also a dwelling-house, with 60 loads of firewood, which latter the following persons agreed to cut and deliver, annually, viz.: Resolved Waldron, Glaude Delamater, and Joost van Oblinus, each 12 loads; David Demarest, Pieter Roelofsen, Jan Nagel, and Lubbert Gerritsen, each 6 loads. This contract was entered into October 23d. The change was amicably made as regarded Montagne, who agreed to pay the new voorleser yearly 10 florins 7 stivers. To aid in making up the salary, the town lot, garden, and meadow were, on the same date, leased for a term of six years to Francois Martino, a newly-arrived French refugee, who was to pay an annual rent of 120 gl. in sewant, or grain at sewant price. The land had just been cleared of timber by Nelis Matthysen, and was new; so Wal-

* See MONTANYE FAMILY; Appendix B.

dron. Delamater, Tourneur, Roelofsen, L. Gerritsen, W. Gerritsen, Demarest, and Oblinus together agreed to give the lessee 63 loads of manure, "once for all." For reasons best known to himself, Martino soon turned over his lease to Jean le Roy, and settled on Staten Island, where many of his descendants may still be found.*

The ill-feeling between Cresson and Delamater again showed itself when the term of three years, during which the latter had worked Cresson's farm, was closing. The court had ordered payment for the lost ox, but one of the farm tools was found broken. On Sept. 1st Pierre in open court demanded his tools of Delamater, who was seated on the bench with his brother magistrates. Glaude answered that the broken tool was at the smith's, being mended. The court, hearing what passed between the parties, referred them to their agreement of Sept. 5th, 1667, but put the court charges upon Cresson. Shortly after Glaude sent Pierre word by the constable to come and examine his tools. Cresson would do no such thing, but again went to the court-room, Oct. 6th, and repeated his demand for the tools. Delamater now promised to send them by his son; but the court, to vindicate its injured dignity, directed Pierre to fetch

* FRANCOIS MARTINO, and his friend Jean Belleville, joined the church at N. Y., July 28, 1670; being the first mention of them. The latter was from St. Martin, near La Rochelle; perhaps Martino was—this early association and their later intimacy seeming to favor it. Whether Belleville was he who was also called *le Chaudronnier*, or, by the English, *the Tinker*, as the first signifies, I am not able to determine, but Jan Tincker was enrolled in the night watch at H., Nov. 7, 1673, and went to Staten Island, where he held property, as did Belleville. See note on *Casier*. Martino had 96 acres of land on Staten Island, laid out to him Apl. 24, 1676, near the "Iron Mountain." To this Gov. Dongan added 35 acres in 1685. He m. Hester Dominees, wid. of Walraven Lutin, or Lutine; issue, Stephen, b. 1679; and a dr., who m. Vincent Fontaine. Martino, in 1683, was foremost among the French and Walloon residents in sustaining the French worship. His will, made Oct. 1, 1706, and proved Aug. 5, 1707, gave his estate, on the d. of his wid., to his two gd. sons, Stephen Martino (son of Stephen, dec.) and Vincent Fontaine, Jr. See *Clute's Annals of Staten Island*. It is to be regretted that the new and interesting work last cited contains so little relating to the original settlers upon that beautiful island; materials for their history are not entirely wanting. For some of these pioneers, see our Index under *Disosway*, *Journeay*, *See*, *Casier*, *L'sille*, *Cresson*, and *Boich* or *Buch*; also *Iakman*, *Markel*, and *Guion*. Many facts might also be gleaned respecting Jacques Haudoin, or Bodine; William Britton; Jean Crosseron, or Crocheron; his son-in-law, Jacques Poillon; Gerrit Crousen, or Cruser; Jacques La Reuiller, now Larzelere; Arend Prall; and Francois du Puis, or Depuy, the anc. of families still upon the Island.

the tools himself from defendant's house, and fined him 12 gl. and costs of suit.

Vexed at what he conceived to be a harsh judgment, Cresson, at the sitting of the court Dec. 1st, entered, and asked if he must satisfy the sentence given against him. He was answered "Yes." Now passion got the better of him, and he denounced the magistrates as "unjust judges," adding, with other abusive words, that "instead of judges they were devils!" On this the court ordered the constable to take Cresson into custody and convey him a prisoner to the High Sheriff at New York, to be duly proceeded against.

Cresson was soon released, but, now bent upon leaving the town, had his wife at Esopus apply for a building lot in that village, and this she asked for and obtained April 15th, 1671.

Marcus du Sauchoy brought a charge against John Archer, Dec. 1st, 1670, of some very bad usage, and cited Direk Everts to tell what he knew about it. The latter testified that, about four weeks before, Archer threw Du Sauchoy's furniture out of the house, but deponent knew not for what cause. The matter here rested for future action.

A case came up Dec. 14th which involved a principle of town law concerning the woodlands. Laurens Colevelt, married to a niece of Resolved Waldron, was neither a landowner nor resident, yet had been burning coals upon Waldron's lands on Van Keulen's Hook, to supply his forge. In so doing, by accident, as he said, he burnt some of Le Roy's palisades. The latter arrested his coals, when Colevelt called an extra court in order to recover them, pretending to nearly 400 gl. damages for the want of them. But the court (Delamater taking Waldron's place) held that no one, not an inhabitant or proprietor, had any right to cut wood within this jurisdiction, much less within the fencing. Colevelt was condemned to make good Le Roy's loss, and pay costs of court; being let off on these easy terms, and his coals released.

On Jan. 5th, 1671, the Town Court ordered a Pound built, at the common charge, to be seven rails high, and imposed for each hog impounded a fine of 1 gl. 10 st., and for every horned beast 3 gl., the damage, if any had been done by the creature, to be made good.

The subject of the town debts also came up as follows:

Exhibited by Resolved Waldron, as payable by the Lands of the Town:

To Mr. John Sharp	*f.*	93 : 9
" Abraham la Noy		68 : 4
" Daniel Tourneur		73 : 16
" Johannes Vermelje		24 : 0
" Resolved Waldron		41 : 4
" Joost van Oblinus		6 : 15
" Meyndert Maljaart*		3 : 0
" Pierre Cresson		2 : 10
" Glaude le Maistre		6 : 15
" David des Marest		2 : 0
" Jean le Roy		4 : 10
" Nicolls, for the Patent		137 : 0
" Paulus Richard, for the land at Spuyten Duyvel		300 : 0
" Johannes Verveelen		87 : 13

The last item involved a careful auditing of accounts for six years past, in which those of the town with Montagne as their

* MEYNARD JOURNEE, or, as now written, *Journeay*, is the person here intended. This metamorphose arose from the similar import of the Dutch word *maaljen*, and the French *journee*, as adopted by the Dutch. With these, the latter word, wrested from its usual meaning (a *day of battle*, or simply, *a battle*), had come to denote a *coat of mail*, which in Dutch was *maaljen*. The two terms being used synonymously by his Dutch neighbors, Journee was often called *Malyer*, as pronounced, but which Montagne wrote as in the text. The English records sometimes have it *Mallier Journee*—a tautological blunder. His given name, Meynard, became in Dutch *Meyndert*. Incidental notices of Journee, both before and after his emigration, will be found on other pages. On his arrival here he settled with Bogert in Brooklyn, where he united with the church Apl. 9, 1664, on certificate from Mannheim, and on June 2, ensuing, m. Elizabeth du Mont, a young lady b. at Middelburg. She was probably sr. to Margaret du Mont, w. of Pierre Noue, who, as we have seen, came out in the same vessel with Journee, and it is quite as apparent that Margaret was sr. to Wallerand du Mont, of Esopus. She who became Mrs. Journee was most likely the person that accompanied Noue and his wife in their voyage, and is called his "sister." Journee held honorable places in the town government at H., resigning that of magistrate when he removed to Staten Island toward the close of 1676; having sold his house and bouwery, Mar. 7, preceding, to Jan Nagel and Jan Delamater, for 2700 gl. His meadow on Sherman's Creek has till late years borne the name of *Meyndert's Fly*. On Mar. 26, 1677, he bought 80 acres of land on S. I., from Francis Charlier. Journee had lived there but a year, when he d. Jan. 30, 1678. Some months after his wid. m. "Boswell de Lisle, alias Francois;" the Court of Sessions held at Gravesend June 19, 1678, appointing Paulus Richard, with Obadiah Holmes, of S. I., as trustees for the chn., to "take care that the estate of said children be not embezzled." There were several drs., but the only son, apparently, was John Journeay, who m. in 1703 Elisabeth Deyo. But we have made no effort to trace his desc., who have become numerous, while some have been prominent on the island, to which, however, the name is by no means restricted.

collector, those of Verveelen as tapster—mainly his indebtedness to the excise, and his scores for liquors furnished the magistrates—as also the particular transactions between Montagne and Verveelen, were much mixed up. Curious as these details are, we must exclude them. The balances being struck, the town found Montagne its debtor for 208 gl., and itself indebted to Verveelen 87 gl. 13 st. Hereupon Montagne drew up the following, which Verveelen signed:

On this date, 13th Feb'y, I, Johannes Verveelen, acknowledge to have settled with Montagne for his accounts, and for the accounts of the Town, so that there is due me from the Town, by balance of accounts, seven and eighty guilders, thirteen stivers. Dated as above.

JOHANNES VERVEELEN.

To discharge these several debts an assessment was authorized to be made upon the lands and erven: on each erf, *f.* 10 : 18 : 12; and on each morgen, *f.* 2 : 16 : 14.

O cruel Cupid! ever seizing the favored opportunity to scatter his fatal darts where met the young and unwary to cheerily while the social hour, to crack walnuts and rustic jokes, or yet seeking a prouder conquest among those not strangers to his shafts; his triumphs the past winter are thus summed up:

PERSONS whose bans of matrimony are entered by consent of the Worshipful Mayor of this City, New York, and according to custom, published in the church.

Feb. 19th, 1671, *William Waldron*, born at Amsterdam, with *Engeltie Stoutenburgh*, of New York. Present, Resolved Waldron and Peter Stoutenburgh.

March 8th, *Martin Hardewyn* with *Madeleine du Sauchoy*, both living at Fordham. Present, the bride's mother Elizabeth Nachtegaal, and Jacques Cousseau; with a note from the bride's father, Marc du Sauchoy, that he beared consent to the same.

April 7th. *Jean le Roy*, living at New Haerlem, widower of Louise de Lancaster, with *Marie Taine*, widow of Philip Casier, living at New York.

April 29th. *Adolph Meyer*, young man, born at Ulsen, in Westphalia, with *Maria Verveelen*, born at Amsterdam.*

* MARIA MEYER, mother of a large and worthy progeny, identified as she was with Harlem from her early childhood for a period of eighty-five years, and, as daughter of the patentee, Johannes Verveelen, directly concerned in the principal distribution of the common land—she becomes a historic character. After a married life of forty years and thirty-seven of widowhood, and having survived all the Dongan patentees, except possibly Barent Waldron, death overtook her at the advanced age of 92 years, in

Johannes Pelszer sues Johannes Verveelen March 2d, 1671, for a claim of 24 gl., the balance of 90 gl. 12 st., his former indebtedness, of which Koopal (Archer) had paid him 66 gl. 12 st. He also complained that Verveelen had accused him of being "the cause that the defendant's house had come to be burnt." Verveelen answered that the plaintiff had said that he, defendant, kept two account-books. He maintained that his arrest was unlawful, since he was a resident, and plaintiff could have levied on his goods; he claimed 6 gl. for the ten days' arrest. The court having heard all they had to say, allowed Pelszer the 24 gl., and Verveelen to pay the costs. On the same date the old Indian interpreter, Claes Carstensen, a Norwegian, who had lived some thirty years in the country and several in this town, was granted a small house lot, to use during his lifetime, but without the right of succession. Carstensen had seen better days.

"WHEREAS the carriage road between this City and *New Haerlem* is impassable; and this Worshipful Court considering it necessary that a carriage road be maintained between this City and the above-named village: It is therefore ordered and directed by the W. Court that the magistrates of New Haerlem and the overseers of the highways beyond the *Fresh Water* shall lay out together the most suitable work, and that then, on the first day of the next coming mouth of May, the said road shall be made fit for use, by the inhabitants of the village of Haerlem, and the householders, both on this and the other side of the Fresh Water, each for his limits, and that on such penalty as shall be fixed by said magistrates and overseers."

The above order was passed by the Mayor's Court, April 18th, 1671, and Jan Jansen Langestraat, Dirck Siecken (*alias* Dey), and Jan Cornelisz de Ryck, were then appointed as overseers "on this and the other side of the Fresh Water."

Cornelis and Laurens Jansen, having for a year worked the farm bought in partnership of Mr. De Meyer, agreed to part. Laurens was about to lease the farm of Lubbert Gerritsen; the parties met for the purpose, Oct. 24th, 1670, and the contract was partly drawn, when they failed to agree. Cornelis having

1748. It afforded the author an agreeable surprise, while engaged some thirty years ago in the preparation of a work kindred to the present one, to discover that he was a descendant of this locally noted woman, and also of the redoubtable Spuyten Duyvel ferrymaster; and subsequently to find that a lineal chain, of nine intervening links, allied him to good old Hans Verveelen and Catrina Ollviers, of Cologne. See *Annals of Newtown*, pp. 277, 305, 317.

taken the De Meyer farm, Laurens on May 6th ensuing (1671) gave him a lease of his part for four years, to date from Sept. 25th, 1670, at the yearly rent of 400 gl. in grain. Their father, Jan Bastiaensc, and Bastiaen Elyessen, the father-in-law of Cornelis, were present and subscribed this agreement. Laurens went to Esopus and married, and is not found at Harlem for several years.

On May 18th, 1671, Jan Louwe van Schoonreweerd, of Bedford, L. I., later known as Jan Louwe Bogert, bargained with Jan La Montagne for his "piece of land named in the Dutch language Montagne's Punt, or by the Indians Rechcowanis," for the sum of 3000 gl. He reserved "the crop of grain, the hop plants, apple and pear trees, and twelve cherry trees." Full possession was to be given on receipt of the first payment, due May 1st, 1672. Some account will be given of the numerous and respectable family descendants of Bogert.

On Sept. 6th Meynard Journee sold to Dirck Storm his property at Bedford, Brooklyn, consisting of houses, land, meadow, etc., for 1400 gl. in wheat, peas, or rye, at the price of sewant. Jan Louwe van Schoonreweerd witnesses this deed.*

* DIRCK STORM, as already noticed, arrived here in 1662, with his w. Maria Pieters, and three young chn. He had in all, at least, sons Gregoris, Peter, and David, and dr. Maria, who m. Caspar Springsteen. In 1670 he succeeded Carel de Beauvois, dec., as secretary at Brooklyn; afterwards served some years as town clerk at Flatbush, was made Clerk of the Sessions for Orange co. in 1691, and held that office till 1703. In 1697 he and family were living at Philips Manor, Westchester co., where his desc. became numerous and noted. His son Gregoris Storm, m. at New Utrecht, Engeltie, dr. of Thomas Van Dyck, and had sons Derick, b. 1695; Thomas, b. 1697, etc. After Gregoris, or Goris, as commonly called, d., his wid. m. Jacques Tourneur, of H. Her son *Thomas Storm* becoming a widower, m. the dr. of Adolph Meyer, of H., and wid. of Johannes Sickels, 1st. Thomas remained on Philips Manor, holding a farm under Col. Frederick Philips, but he made three several purchases of land in Rombout Precinct, Dutchess co., on which he settled his sons Gerrit, Goris, Abraham, and John. His son Isaac took his place at Philips Manor. Other sons, Thomas, his eldest, and Jacob, were d. when he made his will June 28, 1763. It was proved Jan. 15, 1770. Abraham Storm m. Oct. 5, 1759, Catharine, dr. of Aaron Bussing, of H. An active whig in the Revolution, he was "made prisoner by the British troops," and his family saw him no more. On Mar. 22, 1784, his wid. released to Gerrit, Goris, and Isaac Storm the lands of said Abraham, in Rombout Precinct, and returning to H., obtained by deed of Aug. 18, 1784, from her fa.'s executor, John Sickels, the farm of 31 acres on Van Keulen's Hook, which she sold eleven years later to James Roosevelt. She d. Aug. 16, 1803, leaving no chn. The desc. of Dirck Storm take prominence for numbers and worth.

On the same day, said Jan Louwe and his wife Cornelia Everts, residing at Bedford, aforesaid, made their will at Harlem, as they expected to remove here. They "give to the poor of New Harlem the sum of ten guilders as a memorial." Speak of children, but name none. Make Johannes Pietersen Verbrugge and Teunis Gysberts Bogert executors. The witnesses are Cornelis Jansen and Johan Daniels, late under sheriff at New Castle, Delaware, under Beeckman, and who had before "held this position under Mr. Montagne." The testator signs *Jan Lu van Soodervoer.*

Mayor Delavall held his court at Harlem on Sept. 8th, 1671, at which were considered:

1. Complaint of *David Demarest* against John Archer, for mowing grass in his meadow at Spuyten Duyvel, being No. 1 on the Westchester side.

2. Complaint of *Martin Hardewyn*, of Fordham, against Archer, for breaking down his fences.

3. Complaint of *Marcus du Sauchoy*, of Fordham, against Archer, for throwing his furniture out of doors.

4. Complaint of *Johannes Verveelen* against Archer.

The first case was referred to the magistrates of Harlem and Fordham, the others to the arbitration of Daniel Tourneur and Jan La Montagne.

The "Inhabitants of the Town of Fordham" also preferred a charge against Archer, "that the defendant, several times, hath been the occasion of great troubles betwixt the inhabitants of the said Town, he taking upon himself to rule and govern over them by rigor and force; and do humbly desire relief and the protection of this Court."

"Upon the hearing of both parties, the court ordered the defendant John Archer to behave himself, for the future, civilly and quietly against the inhabitants of the said Town, as he will answer the contrary at his peril."

"AND *it is further ordered*, that all small differences, which for the future shall happen to fall out at Fordham aforesaid, shall be decided at Harlem by the magistrates of Fordham, with the assistance of two of the magistrates of Harlem aforesaid, except those of Fordham will be at the charge to satisfy the magistrates of Harlem for coming up to their Town of Fordham."

On Oct. 11th, 1671, John Archer executed at Harlem sundry new leases for farms at Fordham, viz.: to Hendrick Kiersen, Aert Pietersen Buys, and Cornelis Viervant; making the rent payable to Cornelis Steenwyck, of New York, to whom Archer, on Sept. 10th, 1669, had given a mortgage on his lands for 1100 gl. in wampum. Another mortgage to Steenwyck in 1676, for 2400 gl. sewant, ultimately gave him the full title and possession of the Manor of Fordham, which passed under his will and by certain deeds to the Dutch Church at New York.*

On Oct. 23d the voorleser's salary, 400 gl., became due, and to pay it a tax was authorized, "calculated $\frac{2}{3}$ on the Lands, and $\frac{1}{3}$ on the Erven; amounting for each morgen to *f.* 1 : 13 : 6, and for each erf, *f.* 6 : 7." But, notes Montagne in the margin, "It came to nothing." The reason is found in the strong aversion of the people to being *taxed* for religious purposes, especially the French and Walloons, who, cruelly tithed and amerced in their native lands to support the old church, had a mortal dread of this compulsory giving. Then, again, the present tax far exceeded any former call for this object. Montagne's allowance as voorleser was not over 150 gl. per annum, one third of which, derived from the Company, failed after the first year. But whatever he got from the people was by voluntary gift. Hence the present opposition to an assessment, and this proving effectual, led to a return to the former method of free-will offerings—a plan continued for several years, though, unfortunately, the earlier lists of contributors are missing.

* In getting possession, the church met with great opposition from the town of Westchester. This led in 1688 to a forcible entry by the officers and friends of the former. Elijah Barton, dwelling "near Harlem River, within the bounds of Westchester, at the house that formerly Aert Pietersen lived in," was with his father Roger Barton engaged "to keep possession for and in behalf of the town of Westchester," when on July 16, in the afternoon, "there came a great company of men with Nicholas Bayard of New York," demanding admittance. This being refused, Reyer Michiels and Teunis De Key, at Bayard's word, broke open the door, and the Bartons were ousted and roughly handled. With Bayard were also Nicholas Stuyvesant, Johannes Kip, Isaac van Vleeck, Michiel Bastiaens, his wife and sons Bastiaen and Reyer Michiels, Hendrick Kiersen, and Jacques Tourneur. Also "in the exployt" was Hannah (or Anna) Odell, wife of John Odell. Hendrick Vervelen and Jacob Valentine were there too. The Westchester authorities issued a warrant July 20, to "take the bodies of the said Reyer Michiels, with the said complycetors." But the church maintained its hold, and the lands were ultimately sold off in parcels between the years 1755 and 1760.

Two days later, a meeting was held at Cornelis Jansen's to adjust certain fines which had also caused no little excitement. It happened, July 7th preceding, that two of Jansen's horses were found upon the bouwland without a herder and driven to the pound, with one owned by "Mr. Aldrich," one of Waldron's, and one of Adolph Meyer's. The next day another of Waldron's horses and one of Meyer's, and the next day still, being Sunday, a pair of oxen of David Demarest's, one of Delavall's hogs, and two of Pieter Roelofsen's. Again on the 24th were put in pound three hogs belonging to Waldron and Nagel, besides a yoke of oxen owned by Jean le Roy, and found cropping the herbage "in the garden."

This enforcement of the law made some squirming, as the fines were put at 6 gl. for each horse, ox, etc., amounting in all to *f.* 74 : 6. But the matter was finally arranged, over sundry pots of Tapster Jansen's beer, for which his bill against the town was as follows;

CORNELIS JANSEN, *Credit.*

Drank at the settlement of the fines, the 25th Oct. 1671, at two bouts	*f.* 34 : 0
Also for Mr. Arent, engaged at writing, 3 vans beer*	1 : 18
Further, after the settlement was concluded, also drank 3 vans beer and 1 muts rum †	4 : 10
	f. 40 : 8

John Archer, to escape the interference of the Harlem magistrates, obtained from Gov. Lovelace, Nov. 13th, 1671, an ample patent for his domain, upon which "the new dorp or village is erected known by the name of Fordham." It was to enjoy "equal privileges and immunities with any town, enfranchised township, or manor within this government." Released from all dependence upon, or subjection to the rule, order, or di-

* ARENT EVERTSEN KETELTAS, here referred to, was, like his fa., "Mr. Evert Pietersen Keteltas," a voorleser and school-master. See Note on p. 107. In 1664 Arent is called *molenaar*, that is *miller*. He was here before Vander Vin was engaged as *voorleser*, maybe serving temporarily in that office. But he soon left, and on Oct. 6, 1670, Tourneur took his place as curator of Kier Wolters' estate. Arent's wife, Susannah de Boog, was sister to Mrs. Wilhelmus Beeckman. They were drs. of Hendrick de Boog, of Amsterdam, whose wife was a sr. of Mrs. Jonas Bronck. The *Keteltas* family desc. from Evert Pietersen Keteltas.

† A *vaan* was two quarts, and a *mutsje* one gill.

rection of any other riding, township, place, or jurisdiction; thereafter it was to "be ruled, ordered, and directed, in all matters as to government, by the Governor and his Council, and the General Court of Assizes only." It now took the style of the "Manor of Fordham." But not long after, "upon complaint of some disorders which were made at the town of Fordham, *in the Corporation of this City*, by reason they lie too far distant from any constable or overseers," his Honor the Mayor, on Feb. 13th, 1672, appointed Johannes Verveelen as constable and clerk, and Jan Pieters Buys and John Heddy as overseers of the said town, to serve during his mayoralty.

Valentine Claessen, founder of the Valentine family at Valentine's Hill, having sold his property in Harlem to Mr. Delavall, resolved upon a sea-voyage, and on Dec. 11th 1671, procured the governor's pass "to transport himself hence in the ketch Zebulon, whereof John Follett is commander, for the Isle of Providence, Curacao, and Jamaica, in the West Indies; and to return again as his occasions should present, etc." *

On Dec. 18th, certain Indians, some of them apparently the same that signed Montagne's deed for Rechawanes, convey to Daniel Tourneur, of New Harlem, all their lands "lying upon the Main, next to the land of John Archer, beginning at the Bay on the south side of Crab Island, and so running alongst the Creek parting the Main and Manhattan Island, to Broux-land, and thence extending east and west so far as the land of

* The VALENTINE FAMILY, of Westchester, from which most of this name in N. Y. City have sprung, has been quite misapprehended, as regards its common ancestor, who was not "Benjamin Valentine, a dragoon in the French military service, Canada," as per Bolton, ii. 544; but Valentine Claessen aforesaid, who as a soldier gained his laurels under Stuyvesant, not in Canada, but in an expedition to Esopus in 1660. His sons took and retained the patronymic *Valentine*. He was from Saxenlant, in Transylvania; m. in 1662 Marritie Jacobs, from Heest, and before settling in Westchester co., lived some years in H., where his *vrouw* found people from her native place, the Kortrights and Buys brothers. Valentine Claessen is named as late as 1688. His chn., Jacob, b. 1663, living 1690; Matthys, b. 1665; John, b. 1671; Mary, b. 1674, are all of which we find notice. Matthys, living 1710, probably d. before May 3, 1724, when a division of land was made by John and Matthias Valentine, of Lower Yonkers, his sons, if we are not much mistaken. John was b. in 1691. Matthias was b. in 1693—not '98, as his chn.'s ages show—and d. in 1781, being the "first proprietor of Valentine's Hill, Yonkers," as says Mr. Bolton; in whose work upon Westchester co., but more fully in the later *History of the Valentine Family*, may be found the several branches of the family tree, of which we have given the trunk.

the said John Archer." This was the same land as that granted Tourneur June 15th, 1668, but which the Indians afterward claimed, and therefore this purchase was authorized by the Governor, who added "a small tract behind it towards Broncks his river, the which doth properly belong to no person," and confirmed the whole to Tourneur, March 8th, 1672. Gov. Dongan, as we shall see, afterward retrenched this grant, otherwise disposing of that part since known as De Voe's Point.

On Dec. 29th, 1671, Daniel Tourneur, ruling magistrate, and his wife Jacqueline Parisis, both in health, made their will, and give 10 gl. each for the poor of New Harlem. The survivor to manage and use the estate till death or remarriage; then the children to share it equally. Witnesses, David Demarest and Glaude Delamater.

On Jan. 7th, 1672, Pieter van Oblinus, a boy of 9 or 10 years, driving through the village with his father's horse and sleigh, ran over David Demarest's child, Daniel, 5 or 6 years old, who was playing with other children, about the door of Cornelis Jansen's tavern. He died the next morning, and the magistrates then assembled to inquire into the circumstances. It was shown, by the statements of Cornelis Jansen, Arent Harmans Bussing, and Conrad Hendricks Boch, to have been accidental. Joost van Oblinus declared "that he did not know of the accident till informed of it by others, and that he was heartily sorry."

On Feb. 1st, David Demarest, ruling magistrate, and his wife Marie Sohier, in health, but "reflecting on the frailty of human life," made their will, giving, "each of them, 25 gl. to the poor of New Harlem, as a remembrance." The survivor to enjoy the estate until remarriage, and then "even though the laws of the land provide that the one child shall inherit more than the other," their will is that "all their lawful children, mutually begotten, shall inherit equal legatary portions." Witnesses, Daniel Tourneur and Glaude Delamater.

On Feb. 8th, the Town leased two parcels of meadow; the first not located being taken by Lubbert Gerritsen, Jan Nagel, and Johannes Vermelje for 6 years from May 1st, 1671, at 31 gl. a year. The other, "a piece of meadow at the North River" (called a little later Moertje Davids' Fly), was taken for the same term by David Demarest, at the yearly rent of 24 gl.

The same day, Jan La Montagne secured the signatures of the magistrates to the following deed for his Point, written in October preceding, but its execution for some cause delayed. It included also the meadows granted him some years before, in exchange for some others at Sherman's Creek. The effect of this deed was to release whatever claim the town might have acquired from Gov. Nicoll's Patent, and to place the property on a common footing with the other improved lands, so that from this date it became taxable for town charges, and at the same time invested with the right to a share of the common lands held by the freeholders in joint tenancy, whenever a division of said lands should be made. Hence the value of this deed to Montagne, and to Bogert, who was to succeed him in that estate.

We, Hon. Magistrates, with the vote and resolution of the Inhabitants of this Town, have granted forever and as hereditary, to Jan de La Montagne, a piece of land, with the meadows thereto annexed, named Montagne's Point, formerly possessed by his late father, lying within our Town's jurisdiction, bounded on the north side by a creek called Montagne's Kill; extending from the East River unto a little fresh water creek running between Montagne's Flat and aforesaid Point; on the south side bounded by a creek and a meadow and by hills, to the aforesaid little fresh water creek where the King's Majesty his highway goes over; with the Meadows lying in the Bend of Hellgate, which Montagne beforenamed has had in exchange for the Town Lot's meadows; with such rights and privileges as are granted us by patent and still remain to grant; provided he submit to such laws and servitudes as with us are common and may be imposed, without that we or our Inhabitants, now or in future days, shall have any claim thereupon, but as his other patrimonial property may enter upon and use or sell, as he may resolve and shall choose, saving the lord's right. For further security, and that our deed shall have greater force and legal authority, we the Magistrates and Constable the same subscribe, this 6th February, Anno 1672, in New Haerlem.

D. Tourneur.
Resolvert Waldron.
Johannes Vermelje.
David des Marest.
Pieter Roelofsen, *Constable.**

* The frequent use already made of this deed, has led us to give an amended translation of it from the original Dutch text of Montagne; and we also annex a *verbatim* copy of said original.

Wy, E. Magistraten, met toestemminge en goetvinden van de inwoonderen deser durpe, hebben vergunt, eeuwich en erffelyck, aen Jan de La Montagne, een stuck landt, met de valeyen daar aen, genaamt Montangis punt,

To all familiar with our modern Manhattan, with its fine avenues, its railways, and ample means of through transit, the following action of the Mayor's Court of February 13th, 1672, must at least prove amusing. It was in the Mayoralty of Mr. Delavall.

THE Court do empower Mr. Cornelis van Ruyven and Mr. Isaac Bedlo, aldermen, to cause the former orders for making *a good wagon path betwixt this city and the Town of Haerlem* to be put into strict execution.

The record proceeds to say that "it is still found unfinished," although recommended by the Governor, "at divers times," and enjoined by the Court upon the Overseers both of Harlem and the Suburbs. "For which reason many complaints have been lodged, yea, that people wishing lately to travel over that road on horseback have been in danger of losing their lives, by the negligent keeping of the said road." This had moved the Governor again not only to earnestly recommend, but to require its immediate completion, "forthwith, without any delay." The two aldermen commissioned to take charge of it were instructed, as often as they saw fit, to summon "the Overseers, as well of Haerlem as of the outside people dwelling hereabouts," to tell them "how very ill it has been taken that the previous orders regarding the aforesaid road have not been better observed," and "to devise means, not only to finish said road, but to keep it constantly in good repair."

eertyt door syn vader sl. geposseedeert, gelegen binnen onse onser durps jurisdictie, bepaalt aen de noort syde met een kil genaamt Monta— Kil, streckende van de oost revier tot aen een verse killeken streckende tussen Montangis Vlackte en voorm— punt. Aen de zuyt syde bepaalt met een kil en een valey en met bergen, tot aen de voorm— verse killeken daar syn Kon— Majis— syn hooge wech overgaat, met de valeyen gelegen in de boschs vant Hellegat die Montagne voorm— gereuylt heeft heest tegens durps lodts valeyen: met soodanige gerechticheeden en privilegen als ons by patent is vergunt, en noch staat te vergunnen, mits hem onderwerpende sodanige wetten en servituten als ons int gemeen is en sal opgeleyt worden, sonder dat wy ofte ons ingesetenen, nu oft ten eeuwigen dagen, daar iets op sullen te pretenderen hebben, maar gelyck syne andere patrimoniale goederen sal aenvaarden en gebruycken, of verkoopen, so als hy sal goetvinden en wille kueren, behoudens den heer zyn recht. Tot meerder verseeckeringe en op onser grontbrief meerder kracht en echt sal resorteren hebben, wy magistraten en konstapel de selve onderteeckent, Ay 8 Feb'y Anno 1672, in Nieu Haarlem.

D. TOURNEUR.
RESALVERT WALDRON.
JOHANNES VERMILJE.
DAVID DESMAREST.
PIETER ROELEFSEN, *Constapel.*

CHAPTER XVIII.

1672–1673.

THE DORP, OR VILLAGE; INCIDENTS AND INSIGHTS.

THE Town Court was busied April 23d, 1672, with an investigation sought by David Demarest as to an assault made upon him the day before by Glaude Delamater. The town's folk being at work, "making tight the fences of the Calf Pasture," Demarest fell into conversation with Ralph Doxey, Mr. Delavall's man; after which, going to Delamater, he charged him as the cause of Heer Delavall being at variance with the town; adding, that before he, Delamater, became intimate with him, Delavall let his cows go with the herdsman. Delamater retorted that "he lied like a buffoon and a bugger," and seizing Demarest by the coat kicked him. Instinctively the latter caught up a stone and threw it, hitting Delamater on the breast! Here further violence was stayed. As Demarest was a magistrate, the board had to refer the case to the Mayor's Court, and with that view took the evidence of Jean le Roy, Adolph Meyer, Gillis Boudewynsen, and Lubbert Gerritsen. Joost van Oblinus became bail for Demarest's appearance.

John de La Montagne's last official act as secretary was to record this affair of the Calf Pasture, and beneath the entry his successor, Vander Vin writes: "Here ends the register and protocol of the deceased J. de La Montagne, kept at the village of N. Haerlem." And years after, when growing infirmities foreshadowed his own departure, he added in a tremulous hand, "since the said Jan de La Montagne died in the year 1672." Stuyvesant, the old friend of his father and family, had but just preceded him to the grave. He made his will May 13th, 1672, of which we have only the date, but which must have given his consort the full control of the estate. Two years later the widow closed the sale of the farm to Bogert, by a warranty deed, dated March 30th, 1674, acknowledging the receipt of the 3000 gl., and conveying for herself and heirs; having power to do so, as is evident, either under the will or by the recognized rules of law, since she acted with the knowledge and official sanction of the public secretary, and one of the magistrates. Later still—that is, on Nov. 14th, 1679—she conveyed for 300 gl. to Mrs. Bogert, "authorized by her husband," to take the deed, the parcel called the Hop Garden at the rear of the farm, or "lying behind the land of John Louwe, over against the hill." Montagne left no other real estate here; that owned subsequently by his son Abraham Montagne (the only son that remained at Harlem), being derived through his mother, who bought a village residence, which fell to Abraham at her death in 1689. True the latter afterward indulged the idea that he was entitled to a share of the common land in virtue of his father's freehold, but the town held that such right had passed to Bogert.

The church at Harlem lost in Montagne a good and useful servant. It applied soon after for an elder to represent it in the Consistory at New York, under whose charge it had been up to this time. This was acceded to, and by an agreement made Wednesday, June 19th, 1672, the Harlem church were to nominate to the Consistory a double number of suitable persons as elders and deacons (the first institution of the former office here), out of which that body would choose one to serve with them. Then after each annual election made in this indirect mode—an exception to that usual in the Dutch churches—the pastor at New York was to preach at Harlem, and install the new officers. The deacon was to serve two years, so that there should always be two in office; but in regard to the eldership the usage of the church was not followed, as but one elder appears, for many years later. The communicants would still partake of the Lord's Supper at the Fort, and all seeking membership were to be received there as before. It was also agreed to pay "three hundred guilders to the preachers of New York," namely, Do. Drisius and his newly inducted colleague Do. Nieuwenhuysen, "for services at this village."

In this manner the church obtained its representative elder and deacon, the latter being Joost van Oblinus, with whom Daniel Tourneur, acting deacon, was to serve the first year. The elder's name is not given. For the installation services, "the preacher" received *f.* 24, and *f.* 6 were paid Teunis Cray for "fare," bringing and returning the domine, we presume. On July 26th Resolved Waldron paid over to Deacon Oblinus, as treasurer, the balance of *seewant* in the deacon's chest, *f.* 2 : 15. The new cash-book is thus prefaced: "Daniel Tourneur, Johannes Verveelen, and John de La Montagne, in their accounts, are remaining indebted to the deaconry, *f.* 21 : 19." So it seems that on revising Montagne's accounts, this sum expended in 1665 for the dinner to Stuyvesant, and charged to the deacon's fund, was disallowed. The collections from this time average about two florins, or eighty cents, per Sabbath, as shown by the record kept by Vander Vin, under whose lead, as voorleser, the Sunday services were continued with much regularity. Also, as appears, they religiously observed the *Voorbereyding*—that is, the *Preparation* for the Lord's Supper—on the Friday before its quarterly celebration, in March, June, etc.: as also *Kersdag*, or Christmas; Palm Sunday; *Paasche*, Passover or Easter; *Hemelvaarts-dag*, Ascension Day, and *Pinxter*, or Whitsuntide. *Allerheyligen*, or All Saints' Day, Nov. 1st, was excluded from the church days, but was often named as the date when a contract or term of service should begin or end.

With the farmers, *Allerheyligen* usually closed the grazing season. Then they began to prepare for winter. The cattle were taken from pasture, and the stock running in the commons hunted up and housed. The young swine often ran out all winter, but were liable to be missing when sought for. Indeed certain persons about Spuyten Duyvel did not scruple to embezzle them. It was an old trick with Tippett, who with others had been at it again the last winter. Arraigned and convicted at the Assizes, Oct. 3d, 1672, "Jan Hendricks, called Captain" (otherwise Bosch), for his "ingenuous confession," was excused; but fines and stripes were imposed on Thomas Hunt, Jr., and George Tippett, and fines only on John Heddy and William Smith.

An event which cast a gloom over the community at Harlem

was the death of Capt. Richard Morris and his wife, leaving a tender babe to the care and sympathy of strangers. Full of hope they came hither from Barbadoes, where they had been married (she as Sarah Pool) on Aug. 17th, 1669. Capt. Matthias Nicolls thus condoles with the brother, Col. Lewis Morris, of Barbadoes, in a letter written him from New York, Oct. 29th, 1672: "I cannot but reflect upon the transitory condition of poor mortals, when I frequently call to mind in how little time God hath been pleased to break a family, in taking away the heads thereof; first a virtuous young woman in the prime of life, and then a man full of strength and vigor, inured to hardships; while there is remaining only one poor blossom, of whom yet there may be great hope, with your kind friendship, for it is a lovely healthy child, and was well at Harlem, where it is at nurse, and I went to see it yesterday. I was also at the plantation on the other side," etc. The "poor blossom," an infant of a year old, afterward became the distinguished judge, Lewis Morris, proprietor of the manor of Morrisania, and ancestor of the Morris family.

An effort was now made to put a stop to the controversies "about some meadow in difference, beneath the Town of Fordham," being lots Nos. 1, 2, 3, 4, held by the people of Harlem. Though nothing appears to have come of it, the following order upon the subject is interesting:

WHEREAS the Meadow Ground or Valley by the Creek beneath the town of Fordham at Spuyten Duyvel is claimed by some of the inhabitants of New Harlem, but is at so great distance from them and lying unfenced, and so near the Town of Fordham that those of Harlem can receive little or no benefit thereby, as the inhabitants of Fordham cannot avoid being daily trespassers there, if the propriety there shall still continue to Harlem; To prevent all further cavils and contests upon that subject, as also for an encouragement to that new Plantation, as well as in compensation to those of Harlem for their interest which they shall quit at Spuyten Duyvel; I do hereby promise and engage that some convenient piece of meadow being found out at or near Bronx Land, in my disposal, I shall grant and confirm the same unto the persons concerned; provided the said grant do not greatly prejudice the rest of Bronx Land when it shall be settled; and I do refer this matter to Daniel Tourneur and David des Marest, with John Archer, to make inquiry hereunto, and make report thereof unto me with all convenient expedition. Given, etc., this 9th day of November, 1672.

FRANCIS LOVELACE.

A nomination for town officers having been made Nov. 2d, and the position of secretary, vacant since the death of Montagne, given to Vander Vin, he was confirmed Dec. 3d in that office for which he was peculiarly fitted, as a scholar and good penman. On Dec. 6th Pierre Cresson and Meyndert Journee were chosen fence-masters. Another quarrel between Daniel Tourneur and Resolved Waldron, now retiring magistrates, was brought to a friendly issue Dec. 12th. As in a similar rupture between them six years before, it ran so high that Tourneur struck Waldron. The latter made complaint to the Mayor's Court, on the day Vander Vin and the new magistrates were sworn in. The defendant being absent, the case was referred to the new board, with a request to use their best endeavors to reconcile the belligerents. In this they succeeded; the parties, binding themselves to drop all their differences of whatever kind as "from henceforth dead and of naught," agreed "to live hereafter in all charity, friendship, and peace," while the first one to raise a question should forfeit 50 gl. for the poor.

The 16th of the same December the deacons Tourneur and Oblinus, with consent of magistrates and community, let out at public auction "the loft over the church or school-house." Mrs. Maria Vermilye (Montagne's widow), as highest bidder, took it for a year at 20 gl., to be paid the deacons. On giving up the farm to Bogert, she removed to the village and soon bought a house and lot, undoubtedly that adjoining the river, and before owned by her brother, Johannes Vermilye.

The road to Harlem was at length finished or made useable; and a monthly mail between New York and Boston was officially announced, to set out for the first on Jan. 1st, 1673. Now the novelty of the mounted postman reining up at the tavern, with his dangling "portmantles," crammed with "letters and small portable goods," but tarrying only so long as necessary to deliver his mail and refresh himself and horse, added another to the sights and incidents which filled up the unwritten columns of village news.

Vander Vin being installed in his duties as secretary, Resolved Waldron on Jan. 16th, 1673, "with the advice of the constable and magistrates," delivered to him the valuable title papers of the town; and on March 6th he obtained from Sieur

Jacob Kip, brother-in-law of Montagne, the old protocol and other records kept by the latter. The papers handed over by Waldron were as follows:

No. 1. Patent of the town N. Haerlem, in the English.
" 2. Patent of the said town, in Dutch.
" 3. Two confirmations of the same, in English.
" 4. Patent in Dutch.
" 5. Ordinance of the Mayor's Court.
" 6. Extract from the Mayor's Court.
" 7. *Procuratie ad lites.*
" 8. Groundbrief of Spuyten Duyvel.

The mention of "patents in Dutch," in the above list, is likely to mislead. In questions affecting their landed rights and jurisdiction, the ordinance of 1658, under which Harlem was settled, is so often appealed to as to make it quite apparent that the inhabitants during the Dutch rule knew no other official grant or enactment upon which these rights and privileges were made to depend. The profound silence of the records as to any other general grant or patent to Harlem from Gov. Stuyvesant, and the omission to recite it, as was usual, in the English confirmatory patents, must be taken as proof that none was ever issued. And the references in the above list are plainly not to such, but only to the translations of the two English patents, into Dutch, which were made for the use of the inhabitants who did not read English. Thus a bill of Nicholas Bayard for services, in "the differences of the town with Fordham and Tourneur," contains a charge "for the translation of a groundbrief" (from Dutch into English, probably No. 8 in the foregoing list, being the Jansen and Aertsen Patent which Harlem now owned), and then comes the item, "For the translation of the town's patent, *f.* 20."

The new and old magistrates in joint meeting Jan. 16th, 1673, enacted:

It is, with the common consent, resolved and established, that from now forward the house lots (*erven*) which the several residents of this village possess, shall pay the charges, such as are already imposed, or may still be imposed, for the reduction of the debts and expenses of this town; unless some alteration therein shall happen, owing to the various hindrances to it that are liable to come; being owned as follows:

Resolved Waldron	2 erven.
Daniel Tourneur	2 "
Glaude le Maistre	2 "
Joost van Oblinus	6 "
Cornelis Jansen	2 "
Pierre Cresson	1 "
Lubbert Gerritsen	1 "
Adolph Meyer	1 "
Robert Hollis	1 "
Jean le Roy	1 "
Mr. Delavall	4 "
Johannes Vervelen	1 "
Meyndert Journee	1 "
David Demarest	1 "
Widow Montagne	1 "
Jan Nagel	½ "
Together	24½ erven.

This list is believed to embrace (see Map, page 292), the erven proper, marked *a* to *x* (*v* excepted); the small house lots granted Jean Demarest and Pelszer not appearing as yet among the erven.

By the death of Montagne the town accounts were left in some disorder. These needed careful revision, as there were various town debts which must be paid. It was concluded, in this connection, to write to Pieter Roelofsen, at Mespat Kills—and which was accordingly done—asking him to be present on the 20th, or, at farthest, the 21st instant, to give an account of his receipts and disbursements while serving here as constable. The business of Jan. 16th ended with making up the rate list for 300 gl. to be paid the ministers, as had been agreed upon. Meynard Journee being sick, Jan. 25th, made his will, naming his wife Elizabeth du Mont; alludes to "children." Appoints Sieur Demarest and Oblinus overseers of his estate.

After a second summons Pieter Roelofsen attended on Feb. 4th and gave a statement of his accounts while constable in 1671 and 1672, and by which it appeared that he had collected from sundry persons named the sum of 76 fl. 10 st. in wheat, sewant, and firewood, and paid the same to Mr. John Sharp toward the liquidation of his claim of 92 fl., the balance being more than cancelled by a load of wood, 20 fl. delivered to Sharp by Resolved Waldron.* The subject being resumed the following day, the 5th, it was resolved, with the advice of Mr. Delavall,

* JOHN SHARP was a "Public Notary," at New York; his appointment dating Dec. 1, 1665. This charge was probably for legal services.

to revise all the town accounts from the year 1664, and all creditors and debtors were notified to make up and hand in their statements on the 6th of March, to be examined by the old and present magistrates. The next day, at the request of the Voorleser (Vander Vin), the constable was directed to collect his salary as per the list of "free-will contributors."

Upon the investigation which took place, March 6th, it "was found that the accounts of J. de La Montagne and J. Verveelen upon their books concerning the town, were balanced on the 15th of February, 1671, and that there is due Verveelen from the town 87 gl. 10 st., and that Montagne is charged with 206 gl. for his particular, or as having been collector; so that the town have no further interest in their transactions but to let them rest, and from now forward to make up new accounts of the town's debts, and to find the means to discharge and pay the same." Then the debts follow:

Ao. 1673, the 6th March. List of the Creditors of the town of N. Haerlem, as a part were given in the 5th January, 1671, and now are found, to wit:

John Sharp according to account	*f.* 93 : 0
Abraham La Noy or Fredr. Gysbertsen	68 : 0
Daniel Tourneur	78 : 16
Johannes Vermelje	24 : 0
Resolved Waldron	41 : 4
Joost van Oblinus	6 : 15
Meyndert Journee	8 : 0
Peter Cresson	4 : 0
Cornelis Jansen	3 : 10
Glaude le Maistre	6 : 10
David des Marest	9 : 0
Jean le Roy	4 : 10
Capt. Nicolls for the patent	352 : 0
Johannes Verveelen	87 : 10
Paulus Richard for the land at Spuyten Duyvel	300 : 0
For two years' interest @ 6 pr. ct.	36 : 0
Metje Wessels	20 : 0
For the preacher when the confirming of elder and deacons happened	24 : 0
For fare to Theunis Crey	5 : 0
To victuals and drink	35 : 10
Total	1175 : 5
Also due Warner Wessels	8 : 6
and Cornelis Jansen	26 : 0

The above exhibits the original amounts in full, upon which partial payments had been made by some of the inhabitants who were to have credit for the same in the town rate now to be levied. Sharp's bill had been paid, as before seen, and a considerable sum on the patent.* Jaques Cresson, formerly constable, reported the receipt of 60 fl. 10 st. in wheat and sewant, from the following persons (upon the assessment ordered May 1st, 1676), and to have paid it on the patent, viz.:

Johannes Verveelen	*f.* 9 : 0
Joost van Oblinus	12 : 0
Jaques Cresson	7 : 15
Resolved Waldron	13 : 14
David Demarest	6 : 0
Peter Cresson	7 : 13
Jean le Roy	7 : 13
Isaac Vermeille	9 : 11

Ao. 1676, the 6th March; List of the Lands and Erven of the Town N. Haerlem, to contribute to and discharge the aforesaid debts, whereof ⅓ must come from the Erven, and ⅔ parts from the Lands; and amount for each erf to 16 gl. 6 st. and for each morgen of land to 3 gl. 14 st.

Thomas Delavall	4 erven; 48 morgen; 242 gl. 16 st. Nos. 3, 12, 19, 20, 21, 22 Jochem Pieters. Nos. 12, 13, 16, 22 Van Keulen's Hook.
Glaude le Maistre	2 erven; 15 morgen; 86 gl. 2 st. Nos. 14, 15 J. P. No. 21 V. K. H.
Cornelis Jansen	2 erven; 16 morgen; 92 gl. 4 st. Nos. 2, 18 J. P. Nos. 6, 15 V. K. H.
Jean le Roy	1 erf; 9 morgen; 49 gl. 12 st. No. 11 J. P. No. 1 V. K. H.
Daniel Tourneur	2 erven; 21 morgen; 110 gl. 6 st. Nos. 1, 17 J. P. Nos. 17, 18, 19 V. K. H.
Lubbert Gerritsen	1 erf; 12 morgen; 60 gl. 14 st. Nos. 4, 9 J. P.
Johannes Verveelen	2 erven; 15 morgen; 86 gl. 2 st. No. 10 J. P. Nos. 7, 8, 14, 19 V. K. H.
David des Marest	1 erf; 8 morgen; 45 gl. 18 st. No. 7 J. P. ½ of No. 5 V. K. H.

* Capt. NICOLLS transferred his bill for writing the patent to Reynier Willemsen, baker, to whom the town officers, Apl. 5, 1676, gave a Note in these terms:

"We Constable and Magistrates of the town of New Haerlem, acknowledge to be truly and honestly indebted, in name of the common inhabitants of this town, to and for the behoof of Reynier Willemsen, in the sum of 332 guilders, upon the Patent, on account of Capt. Matthias Nicolls, deducting what may be found to have been paid thereon: which aforesaid sum of 332 guilders we promise to pay in the first ensuing January, 1677, without default, under bond pursuant to the laws."

The amount yet due on the above Feb. 19, 1677, was 253 gl., on which sums were paid from time to time till 1683, when Constable Vermilye made the final payment of 15 gl.

Joost van Oblinus......3 erven; 12 morgen; 93 gl. 6 st.
No. 13 J. P. Nos. 10, 11 V. K. H.
Pierre Cresson.........1 erf; 9 morgen; 49 gl. 18 st.
No. 5 J. P. No. 20 V. K. H.
Resolved Waldron......2 erven; 15 morgen; 88 gl. 2 st.
No. 8 J. P. Nos. 2, 8, ½4, ½8 V. K. H.
Jan Nagel..............½ erf; 6 morgen; 30 gl. 7 st.
No. 16 J. P.
Isaac Vermeille.........1 morgen; 3 gl. 14 st.
½ of No. 5 V. K. H.
Meynard Journee.......1 erf; 9 morgen; 40 gl. 19 st.
No. 6 J. P. No. 14 V. K. H.
Jean La Montagne......18 morgen; 66 gl. 12 st.
The Point.*
Johannes Vermeilje......1 erf; 16 gl. 6 st.
Robert Hollis...........1 erf; 16 gl. 6 st.

Total.............. ..24½ erven; 216 morgen; 1198 gl. 11 st.

The following important document throws light upon the history of Montagne's Flat:

Upon this day, 8th March, 1673, appeared before me, Hendrick J. Vandervin, Secretary, admitted by the Hon. Mayor's Court at New York, residing at the village N. Haerlem; the undersigned inhabitants of N. Haerlem, as also owners and possessors of the land called *Montagne's Flat*, lying under this Town's jurisdiction; who together promised to inclose the aforesaid piece of land in a common fence, and to use, until the building, planting, or dwelling on, or as every of them shall think proper to do with his part; and if it happen that they in common or either separately should be troubled by any one, who would bring the ownership and possession in question, and would offer them jointly or either singly, any molestation concerning it, on account of the ownership of the aforesaid land; therefore the undersigned covenant, jointly or each separately, to defend them there-against, and to maintain one another in their rights (which they have in the same;) protesting against such as to all costs, damages, or losses which, by any interference, they jointly, or either in particular, may be put to. In witness of the sincerity of these above standing conditions, this has been written, and subscribed with our own hands. Thus done and passed at N. Haerlem, on the date as above.

David des Marest,
Glaude le Maistre,
Daniel Tourneur,
Cornelis Jansen,
Resolved Waldron,
This mark made
Lourens + Jansen,
by himself.
Jan Dyckman.

In presence of me

Hendr. J. Vandr. Vin, *Secretary.*

* Montagne was to deliver this property to Bogert free and unincumbered, hence this was properly charged to him.

Though not so much as hinted from what quarter trouble was apprehended, circumstances plainly point to the old Montagne patent or groundbrief. Montagne's Point, as we have seen, had just received a new owner, Jan Louwe Bogert. On Jan. 16th, 1673, the constable and magistrates, with a view of fixing a limit to Bogert's lands, held under the bill of sale from Montagne, had passed a resolution to estimate said lands at 18 morgen, which allowed 2 morgen for the Hop Garden. The deed, which only awaited the final payment, was soon to be given by Mrs. Montagne, and Bogert was already "in possession." It was, doubtless, in anticipation of some interference on the part of their new neighbor or the Montagnes, or both, which now led the owners to fence in the Flat, and to join in a covenant to protect themselves against any rival claimants.*

Indeed it appears that, in common with others who had built up claims upon the old defunct groundbriefs, some of the Montagne family indulged a hope of getting their groundbrief confirmed, with the view of claiming portions of the Flat. In this, as is apparent, neither of the sons of Dr. La Montagne took any part. The compromise with John La Montagne in 1661, which

* Op huyden 8 Marty 1673: Compareerde voor my Hendr. J: Vandr. Vin, Secreta: by de E. gr. achtbr. Mayor Court tot N: Yorcke geadmitteert; Ten Durpe N: Haerlem resideren: de ondergesn. ingesetenen van N: Haerlem, alsmede eygenaers enr. possesseuren van het lant genaemt *Montagnes Vlackte* gelegen onder desen durps jurisdictie, de welcke verclaerden gesamenlk. het voorsn. stuck lant, in gemeene heyningh te besluyten enr. te gebruycken, tot den bouw, planten, of wooning; of soo ider van haer voor syn gedeelt sal geraden duncken, enr. oft gebeurde, dat sy int gemeen of ider int bysonder, moghten werden getroubleert, door imant, die den eygendom enr. possessie wilde in twyffel trecken, met haerln. gesamenlk. of ider int bysonder, eenigh molest (dien aengaende), wilde doen, wegens den eygendom vant voorsn. lant; Soo verbinden sy ondergesn. gesamenlk., of ider int bysonder, haer daer tegen te beschermen ende malcanderen in haro gerechtigheyt (die sylidn. op het selve syn hebbende), te mainteneren: protesterende, tegens soodanige van alle costen, schaden enr. interessen, die haerln. gesamenlk. or ider int bysonder, door eenigh molest moghte werden aengedaen; Oirconde der waerheydt vant geene voorsn. staet, hebben dit doen schryven ende met eygen handen onderts: Aldus gedaen enr. gepasseert tot N: Haerlem, *dato ut supra.*

David des Marest,	Resolvert Waldron,
Glaude le Maistre,	dit merck by
Daniel Tourneur,	Lourens + Jansen,
Cornelies Yansen,	selffs gestelt.
	Jan Dyckman.

In kennisse van my
Hendr. J: Vandr. Vin, Secreta:

secured him the Point (for which the town gave him a deed in 1672), was to him and his children an estoppel to any further claim upon the Vredendal lands, and there is no intimation that he or they ever made any such claim. With his brother William the same was no doubt true, since his assent to the disposal of the Flat appears in that he not only drew and sold some of that land, but subsequently withheld his name from a petition to Gov. Fletcher for a confirmation of the old groundbrief. Without question the Flat came within the agreement of 1663, between Stuyvesant and Council and the inhabitants of Harlem, that the tithes, or tenths of the produce of their cultivated lands for the years 1666 to 1672, both inclusive, should be applied for the benefit of the original grantees who held the groundbriefs, their heirs or creditors. This agreement, by which the tenths were substituted for the 8 gl. per morgen, was alike binding on the government and the landholders, and was limited in its effects to the term of years named. If carried out in good faith, there must terminate the demands both of the said original grantees and their creditors. It seemed to favor the then owners, for the amount of tithes to be paid must depend upon what the land should be made to yield; but had the Dutch rule continued no doubt the government would have held these owners strictly to this condition, and the proceeds from Montagne's Flat would have been applied toward cancelling the debt due from Dr. Montagne to the West India Company. It might be argued that these payments being limited to seven years, had the Flat for that time been under tillage it would have taken a husbandry, then and there unknown, to have made the tenths pay Dr. Montagne's debt, which as early as 1662 amounted, by his own figuring, to 1130 gl., but by that of the public bookkeeper to not less than 1930 gl; and that the tithes being insufficient to satisfy this claim, the balance would still be against Montagne!

But the change of government, in 1664, was alike fatal to this provision for the payment of the tenths, and to the old groundbriefs on which it was predicated; the English, as we have seen, refusing to confirm the latter within the Harlem patent, and holding them to be null and void, while it also ignored the system of tithes which had worked badly for the country, and "did much hinder the populating of it." Montagne's Flat having lain as commons, unfenced and untilled, had indeed yielded nothing but pasturage, nothing for the payment of tithes. Therefore the owners (with whom must be named Capt. Delavall, who had a small lot there, of 4 morgen 320 rods, bought of Simon de Ruine), being released from their obligation to render the tithes, while the Montagne heirs were still liable to some demand from the government, which assumed to collect all other debts due the West India Company (even to small charges on their books for unpaid passage money), these heirs were easily led to look upon the agreement under which they had given up the Flat as thereby vitiated, and to fall back upon their old groundbrief as entitled to confirmation. Could they have succeeded it would have been a nice operation for them, as the lands had risen in value, and lots on the Flat now brought 44 guilders per morgen. But to the credit of the English rulers they did not attempt so unfair a proceeding as to enforce the claim against the Montagne heirs, while at the same time relieving the landholders of their obligation to pay the tithes. A majority, and no doubt all, of the eight proprietors of the Flat had documentary titles, five at least, as heretofore noticed, holding particular patents from government, and Demarest deriving through the Montagnes themselves. The aggregate of their lands, contained in nine lots, amounted to 54 morgen, as afterward rated and taxed; to which being added another lot which lay there vacated or untaxed till 1725, made 60 morgen, as reckoned, in the entire Flat. This came by a generous allowance to the morgen, the Flat being correctly estimated, in the Montagne groundbrief, at 100 morgen. Here was the real bone of contention. The Montagnes regarded as of right theirs the excess over the quantity the eight owners were entitled to. But the inhabitants took another view, and in which the government concurred, namely, that so much of the Flat as was undisposed of belonged to the common lands of the town, as granted and confirmed to them by Nicolls and Lovelace. The government adhering to the policy laid down by Stuyvesant regarding the old groundbriefs, saw no reason to make the Montagne groundbrief an exception. It respected the act of the Dutch government, which allowed the tenths to offset the Montagne debt, but also held the heirs to their act in the surrender of the Flat. Hence it could never be prevailed upon to confirm the old groundbrief.*

Pierre Cresson and Rachel Cloos his wife, "both being sound of body," made their joint will, March 15th, 1673; Cornelis Jansen and Jan Nagel witnesses. How sensible and wise thus, in health, to calmly weigh the fact of their mortality, and deliberately set their house in order! Leaving fifty guilders to "the church at New York," they say, "whereas their daughter Susannah has enjoyed as a marriage portion the value of two hundred guilders, so the testators will that at the decease of the longest liver each of their other children then living shall draw the like 200 guilders, and our youngest son Elie, if he is under the age of sixteen years, also a new suit of clothes becoming to his person, from head to foot."

Gabriel Carbosie, the miller, and his wife Bricta Wolferts, "both sound of body," also made their will, on April 18th ensuing, and which was witnessed by Jan Louwe van Schoonrewoerd and Cornelis Jansen. They gave six guilders "to the poor of the Lutheran congregation at New York." Each by former marriages had had children, but none had come from their own as yet.

On March 30th, "being Sunday and Paas," the quiet and good order of the village was broken by a most shameful affray, the more scandalous considering the standing of some of the parties. About four o'clock in the afternoon young Samuel Demarest falling in with Daniel Tourneur, Jr., began to tease him by asking why he had prated so much in Coenraet Ten Eyck's shop in New York, that Glaude Delamater's son should

* A PETITION was addressed to Gov. Fletcher in 1695, in the name of John Louwe Bogert, William Montagne, his sister Mrs. Jacob Kip, and nephew Johannes Van Inborgh, who claimed to be *seized*, and *by descent as well as mean assurance in the law*, owners of the patent granted by Gov. Kieft to Dr. Montagne; and prayed for a confirmation of said patent, as they were *now willing to divide the same*. But William Montagne, then of Ulster co., did not sign this petition; neither did Abraham Montagne, of Harlem (son of John), which is remarkable, considering the claim to the Montagne lands set up in our day, under a title purporting to be derived from him. The petition being referred to the Attorney General for his opinion received no further notice. A better knowledge of this old exploded claim than that afforded by the family traditions, might, in the case above alluded to, have saved a protracted and fruitless litigation.

fight (*plockhairen*) with him, and added that he, Tourneur, was a *blaffert*, a bully. Tourneur answered angrily, "Youngster, hold your mouth, or I'll give you some knocks." The other said he would not; on which Daniel made good his threat, with a blow or two. Now ran up Samuel's elder brother Jean, and then David, to take his part, and there was a free use of fists, stones, and sticks, which Mr. Gipsen (Gibbs), who saw the melee, tried in vain to stop, telling the Demarests, "Three against one is not fair." The fathers of the combatants now reached the scene of action, and with Tourneur came his prospective son-in-law, Dyckman, "with his drawn knife in his hand," and who clinched and got "the young David Demarest under," exclaiming, "This shall cost you your life!" At the same time Joris Jansen van Hoorn caught hold of Jean Demarest, and struck him several times in the face with his fist; while the elder Tourneur, who had turned upon the father, drew his knife and tried to stab him, but David, using only a stick, gave his assailant a stunning blow on the head, "so that he fell down." Gillis Boudewyns saw the whole affray from the beginning, and with Pierre Cresson testified to this stabbing; for by this time many of the villagers beside those named were drawn to the spot by the uproar, as Isaac Vermeille, Jean Delamater, Le Roy,* Vander Vin, and Nagel, with Pieter Claessen,

* SIMEON CORNIER had bought Le Roy's house and lands, Feb. 24, 1672, but it was not till May 2, 1674, that Le Roy, acknowledging payment, gave a deed and possession. Cornier and w. Nicole Petit (also called Petitmangin and Piemainte) joined the church at New Amsterdam, Oct. 2, 1662, having just arrived from Mannheim, *via* Holland, as has been noticed. Entering the military service, and promoted to a corporalcy, he was given his choice, at the English conquest, either to return to Europe with the Dutch forces or to remain here. As he chose the latter, the government remitted his passage money, which was yet unpaid. He went to Staten Island, and engaged in farming, his old calling in France. He received at H. the marks of respect due to his character and abilities. On the Dutch reoccupation in 1673, trouble being feared from the English, Cornier was fitly chosen as a corporal in the Night Watch, and two years later, during the Indian troubles, held the like command. He also served as deacon; but selling his lands, July 26, 1675, to Paul Richard, he removed to N. Y., a few months later. In 1686 he m., as a second w., Tryntie Walings van Winckel, wid. of Cornelis Jacobsen Stille, who had lived at H., anc. of the Somerindyke and Woertendyke families. See p. 151, and *N. Y. G. & B. Record*, 1876, p. 49. The day he bought it Richard sold Cornier's property to David Demarest, Jr. We know not when Cornier d., nor that he left chn., but take for his desc. *Capt.* Peter Corne, of N. Y., merchant, and commander of a privateer in the old French war, who still lived in the city during the Revolution. See *Dyckman* family.

Thomas Etherington, and Elias Bailey, who happened to be at the village. A stop was now put to the fight, but young Tourneur, still excited, said, "Wait, wait! this is not the last time." The elder Tourneur has the benefit of a doubt, as Jean Delamater, the innocent cause of the tumult, declared "that *he* had not seen that Daniel Tourneur stabbed David Demarest."

High Sheriff Allard Anthony, on being notified of this flagrant breach of the peace, held a court at Harlem, the next day, and took the testimony of several witnesses; but a hiatus in the minutes of the Mayor's Court probably deprives us of the sequel of this affair, in which, however, no lives were lost, and but slight personal injury sustained! Tourneur was about as usual, April 5th, when he leased to Jan Dircksen, or "Jan the Soldier," as before called, "a certain piece of woodland, lying at Monepas Kill," with meadow on "the kill of boor Aert and Jan de Pocp," for the term of three years, the lessee to build his own dwelling-house, and leave three morgen of land cleared and fenced; to all which Jan Dyckman and Ralph Doxey are witnesses.

Society was not very polished in those days, and was still wedded to the old ideas about personal prowess—pluck and muscle, never mind what called them forth, were things to boast of and applaud. The younger combatants might glory in this general knock-down, and little fear the opprobrium; but for the two elderly ones holding high positions, Demarest a magistrate, and Tourneur a deacon, sober retrospection no doubt brought shame and regret. But we must discriminate between Tourneur, rash, even dastardly, and Demarest, more temperate in his Picard impulses, and probably acting in self-defence only. The latter, a few weeks later (Aug. 23d) was re-elected to the magistracy; but then Tourneur, a man, mauger his faults, of generous instincts and of great energy, and to whose tact and abilities the town owed much of its success, had just closed an active life and been laid to rest. He is last noticed May 12th, when he subscribed as witness to an engagement of Thomas Selligh, late in his employ, to work a year for Wallerand du Mont, of Esopus. Tourneur's death made the first break in the company of Nicolls Patentees. It probably followed close upon Dyckman's espousal (June 15th) to his daughter Madeleine. We notice that Dyckman's old friend Arent Harmans Bussing, with whom he had left his native Bentheim, had just before married Susanna le Maistre, Glaude's daughter, both brides having been born at Flatbush, soon after their parents emigrated.*

This chapter of incidents may fitly close with a glance at the village of New Harlem as it was in the autumn of 1673.† How quaint an aspect has the Dutch settlement as e'en now its plain wooden tenements, embowered in foliage whose variegated hues already tell the declining year, rise modestly to view. Their humble eaves, keeping line with the street, lift themselves but one low story, yet the extraordinary slope of the thatched roof gives space to the loft above, so useful for many domestic purposes. Aside the house, quite too near for entire safety, stands the ample and well-stored "schuer" or barn, in its squatty eaves and lofty ridge the very counterpart of the dwelling, but by a noticeable contrast turning its gable with huge gaping doors to the highway. In the spaces between buildings and

* WALLERAND DU MONT (Dumont), whose desc. are still found in Ulster co., came to this country in 1657, from Coomen in Flanders; served as "cadet in the honorable Company of the Heer Director General," and m. at Esopus, Jan. 13, 1664, Margaret Hendricks, wid. of Jan Aertsen, who had been slain by the Indians. See *Van Patten*. Du Mont's sr. Margaret was w. of Pierre Noue, a Walloon, who emigrated with Demarest and company in 1663. See *Journee*. How will our revered friend and early pastor make Pierre the son of Elias Neau, the catechist, of N. Y., who was b. at Soubise in Saintonge, in 1662? *History of Elizabeth*, p. 267. Du Mont d. at Esopus, in 1713, having had sons, Wallerand, John Baptist, and Peter; and drs., Margaret, w. of William Loveridge, Jannetie, w. of Michael Van Vechten, and Francina, w. of Frederick Clute. Clute went to Schenectady. See *Pearson's Schenectady Settlers*. Peter Dumont, with his brethren Loveridge and Van Vechten, settled on the Raritan, N. J. Dumont and Van Vechten became justices of the peace. The latter was b. in 1664, being son of Derick Teunissen, who was b. in 1634, at Vechten, in the diocese of Utrecht, and when four years of age came with his fa. Teunis Dericksen, to Albany. William Loveridge was from the parish of Wool, in Dorsetshire, England, and d. at Perth Amboy, in 1703, leaving sons William, Wallerand, and John. He was br. to Samuel Loveridge, of N. Y., shipwright, who was b. in Albemarle co., Va., and m. at Esopus, in 1688, Hannah, dr. of George Meals. Their fa., William Loveridge, a hatter, came out to Connecticut as early as 1659, removed to Virginia, thence to Albany, and d. at Catskill, ab. 1683. He had drs., Temperance, who m. Capt. Isaac Melyn, of N. Y., and Sarah, who m. John Ward, of Ulster co. Hence the belief expressed in the *History of Elizabeth* that Samuel Loveridge was a son of Rev. William Leverich, though with seeming reason, is plainly not warranted.

† Consult the plan of the village at page 292.

homesteads flourish rows of choice imported fruit trees, apple, pear, peach, cherry, and quince, and the no less prized garden and ornamental shrubs, the Dutch currant, gooseberry, and evergreen box, dwarf and arborescent. Tidiness reigns, at least about the dwelling, and within reach of the busy housewife's mop and broom; but all betokens a plainness and frugality, in wide contrast with the elegance of modern living. The daily life of the villagers—but let us first note the occupants of the principal dwellings ere we cross the threshold, to explore the humble sphere of their domestic economy.

Here at the river end, where, about the tavern, smith-shop, church, and ferry, gather the stir and business activity of the village, is the comfortable home of the French refugee and newly-appointed *schepen*, David Demarest. His house and barn occupy a lot "abutting on three streets from which it is fenced," and extended "toward the strand, as far as he can," by virtue of a town grant of Jan. 5th, 1667. It contains a *double-erf*, or two *erven*, the upper, facing the Great Way, being that gotten from Montagne (and where *now* the oldest house and relic of the village stands), the other once Do. Zyperus'. This last looks out to the south upon the square or green about the landing place. Demarest's neighbor, over the cross-street, is Glaude Delamater, recent magistrate, testy but kind-hearted; his double-erf joining that of Cornelis Jansen, late constable, a young but rising man in the town, and at whose friendly inn—where swinging signboard and feeding-troughs mark it merely as the village hostel, but to Kortright, Bogert, and others, the veritable counterpart of Mynheer's inn at Schoonrewoerd—the passing traveller stops for refreshment, or the wiseacres of the *dorp* resort to swallow the latest bit of news or scandal in a bumper of Kortright's beer! Opposite the tavern, past the second cross-way, lives the Picard, good Pierre Cresson, from his occupation called by his Dutch neighbors, *de tuynier*, or *the gardener*, whose erf joins at its rear or north side to that of Daniel Tourneur, but just deceased, and westerly to that late of Hendrick Karstens, but now of the worthy Joost van Oblinus, *schepen*. Over the third cross-street are the two erven of Johan Verveelen, where his son-in-law Adolph Meyer now lives, and next him the "garden" and erf (strictly a double-erf), which had passed from Mr. Muyden to Jaques Cresson, and from him to Meynard Journee, present occupant, also called *Maaljer*, his surname *Belgicized*. Being sickly, Journee had just resigned his office of fence-master, which was given, Feb. 6th. to Laurens Jansen, the Low ancestor. Journee's grounds extend to those of Capt. Delavall, a small strip between them, "laid out for a street" (the fourth cross-way), having been added to Cresson's lot while his, by a grant of May 3d, 1667. In one of Delavall's houses, once the home of Simon the Walloon, had recently lived, till he removed to the city, Wouter Gerritsen, Delavall's principal farmer, and the old neighbor of Gillis Mandeville, in the Veluwe—the other of Delavall's houses had been occupied by Pieter Roelofsen, twice constable here. Beyond this point we soon reach the *Buyten Tuynen*, or Out-Gardens, the two farther ones soon to be the home of Arent Harmens Bussing, lately married and just appointed one of the schepens.

But from the quiet west end, retracing our steps, on the south side of the street, we come to the dwelling of the venerable Isaac Vermeille. Seated upon the end of lot 5, Van Keulen's Hook, "over against the garden of Jaques Cresson," as it was till of late; his erf, which extends back to a strip of flag marsh stretching across the lot, is well stocked with fruit trees, the pride of the Huguenot settlers, and in which culture they excelled. On either side of Vermeille lie vacant lots, but that on the west, No. 6, soon to be built upon and occupied by its owner, Laurens Jansen, aforesaid. Lot No. 4, on the east side of Vermeille, and which Adolph Meyer had gotten with his wife from her father, Verveelen, was at this end fit only for pasturage, being marshy, but a plot here was bought from Meyer Nov. 2d, 1673, by his friend Jan Dyckman, who for the many years before he moved to Spuyten Duyvel occupied a house built upon two of Tourneur's out-gardens, received by his wife Madeleine. Adjoining lot No. 4, and opposite to Oblinus, lives the most influential man in the town, Resolved Waldron, at present the *schout*, or sheriff, and next to him, easterly, his son-in-law Jan Nagel. Going still toward the river to the two small erven opposite Cornelis Jansen and Delamater (granted Jean Demarest and Johannes Pelszer, but seemingly never improved by them), on the corner of the Pelszer lot, where the road runs down by the green to the creek, stands or later stood the village smithy, where William Haldron, an Englishman, plied his hammer and bellows, waking the neighbors at early dawn with the music of his anvil, as did, within the same century, his successor in the smith-shop, Zacharias Sickels, whose descendants are yet among us.*

* ZACHARIAS SICKELS, the common anc. and fa. of Zacharias aforesaid, was from Vienna, in Austria. Finding his way to Holland, he went out to Curaçao, and served in the military rank of *adelborst* or cadet. When Stuyvesant returned from a visit to that Island in 1655, Sickels came with him, being soon after attached to the garrison at Fort Orange. In 1658 he was a tapster. He remained at Albany after the surrender in 1664, and worked as a carpenter, having m. Anna, dr. of Lambert van Valkenburgh, by whom he had sons, Robert, Lambert, Zacharias, and Thomas, and drs., Anna, Elizabeth, Maria, Margaret and Leah. Anna m. Abraham Isaacs, and Elizabeth m. William Peelen. In 1670 to '72, and 1681 to '83, Sickels was town herder, and had 18 gl. a head for the season. He next held the responsible place of *rattel watch*, so called from the *rattle*, used to give warning, in making his nightly rounds. He was also *town cryer*, to call the people together on needed occasions; and *porter*, or keeper of the city gates, to close and lock them at night, and to open them in the morning. His sons Robert and Lambert removing to N. Y., he, with his other sons, etc., followed them in 1693, his vacated office being given to his son-in-law Isaacs. In 1698 he was admitted a freeman of N. Y., and in 1703 was living in the East Ward. Robert, his son, m. 1686, Geertie, dr. of Abel Reddenhaus, and moved to Bergen co., N. J., where he d. in 1729; Lambert, b. 1666, m., 1690, Maria Janssen, from Albany, settled at Bedford, Brooklyn, and d. 1732; and Thomas, m., 1703, Jannetie, dr. of Jan Hendricks Brevoort, and remained in N. Y. All these left desc. See *Winfield's Land Titles*, the *Bergen Gen.*, and *N. Y. G. & B. Rec.*, 1876, 60.

Zacharias Sickels, blacksmith, and referred to in the text, was b. in 1670, at Albany, and after coming to H., m., Aug. 23, 1693, Mary, dr. of the aforesaid Brevoort. On Feb. 20, 1705, he bought of his fa.-in-law, who had then left H., the lands he still held there. See *Brevoort*. Of these, Sickels sold, Apl. 9, 1705, a meadow, once Pierre Cresson's, and lying at the head of Sherman's Creek, and northerly of the Kortright farm, to Jan Kiersen (with whose lands it was sold to James Carroll, in 1763), and on Jan. 23, 1706, he sold to Samson Benson, No. 1 New Lots, with "a garden" (originally two erven of Cresson and Tourneur), lying next west of the churchyard. He drew land in 1712, in 1st and 2d Divisions, having sold his 3d and 4th to Jan Kiersen, but obtaining in exchange Kiersen's lot in 1st Division. See *Appendix J.* For these drawn lands he received a patentee deed Dec. 24, 1712. Later, he sold his 1st Division to Joh. Meyer. He m., July 19, 1717, a second w., Wyntie Dyckman, wid. of Joh. Kortright. Being sick, he sold his property, Jan. 15, 1729, to his step-son, Nicholas Kortright. This consisted of lot No. 5, Jochem Pieters, a lot on Montagne's Flat, rated at 6 morgen or 12 acres (but in reality 20 acres), and No. 12, in 2d Division, 18 acres; in all, as rated, 43 acres. Zacharias Sickels d. Jan. 20, 1729, ae. 59 yrs. He had issue, *Johannes*, *Jacobus*, *Zacharias*, *Hendrick*, *Gerardus*, *William*, *Cornelius*, and *Robert*. Johannes, the eldest, was b. in 1694, m., May 2, 1718, Anneke, dr. of Adolph Meyer, and settled in Westchester co., on a farm of 100 acres, bought in 1720 and 1722. He d. in June, 1729; his wid. m. Thos. Storm. His chn., as far as known, were Zacharias, Johannes, and Maria, who m. Gerrit Storm, of Philipsburgh. Of these,

But for an inside view of the domestic life and home comforts of these villagers, let us visit the worthy and well-to-do Lubbert Gerritsen, late one of the magistrates, living near the west end. We enter. No carpet hides the well-scrubbed floor, and in vain we glance around the room for many articles which in our day imperious fashion, and even comfort, demand. The furniture goes but little beyond the practical and useful. A gilded mirror indeed adorns the whitewashed wall. The two beds have pillows and striped curtains. Two chests very convenient contain the clothing, one of the wife, the other of the daughter, fair Eva, who five years later married the Bussing ancestor. On one side is a small octagon table; and here a brass candlestick and a warming-pan. Upon hooks on the wall hang a musket and firelock. No stove is there; but in the ample fireplace the wood crackles and blazes cheerfully above the huge backlog and around the two iron dinner pots hung to the trammel by hooks and chain. On the table or shelves and in the pantry, we notice exactly 1 pewter bowl, 2 small pewter platters, 4 pewter trenchers, 6 pewter spoons, a pewter cup with a lid and another without, 2 white earthen jars, a copper cake pan, a small copper pot, a small brass kettle, 2 water pails, and 2 churns for butter-making. There is still place for 2 siths,* 2 sickles, and 2 augers.

We ascend to the "loft." Here are 4 milk pans, 2 iron hand-basins, 2 tubs, a lye-barrel, a cask filled with buckwheat, 2 ploughshares, a plough-chain and rope, a coulter, a yoke with

Zacharias became a merchant in N. Y., m. 1744 Catharine Heyer, and was the fa. of John Sickels, grocer, who had five chn., viz.: John, lawyer, Alletta, who m. John Tenbrook, Catharine, m. Com. Isaac Chauncey, Maria, m. James Heard, and Ann, who m. Nathaniel Griswold.

Johannes Sickels, b. 1720, son of Job. and Anneke, m. his cousin Margaret, dr. of Adolph Meyer, 2d, of H., where Sickels settled, inheriting in 1748, 84 acres from the Meyer estate. This embraced Nos. 2, 3, Jochem Pieters, No. 10, 2d Division, and No. 14, 4th Division. To this was attached the north garden (sold ten years later to John Livingston), derived originally by his gt-gd-fa. Verveelen from Jan Slot. See *App. F.* He d. in 1784, leaving one son, John S. Sickels, and a dr., Mary, w. of Samson Benson. John S. Sickels m. Sept. 29, 1763, Maria, dr. of Aaron Bussing, and d. June 4, 1804; his only ch surviving inf. being Mary, b. Apl. 9, 1764, who m. John Adriance, fa. of John S. and Isaac Adriance, Letitia, w. of Wm. B. Kenyon, and Margaret, w. of James Kenyon. Many write this name *Sickles*.

* See a description of the SITH and its use, under the year 1687.

a hook, 2 old sickles, an adze, and a sail mast, perhaps belonging to the "canoe at the strand."

Invited out to the barn: here is the garnered harvest, stores of rye, peas, and buckwheat in the sheaf, and 10 or 12 bundles of unswingled flax; also a fan, harrow, and 2 iron forks. On the premises, fat and sleek in their sheds and stalls, are the live-stock: 2 yoke of oxen, 2 cows, one black, the other red; 1 steer and 2 calves. Four young hogs are running upon Little Barent's Island. Other farming implements are at hand: 2 ox-yokes, 2 iron plough-rings, a wood-axe, 3 iron wedges, 2 hand-saws and a draw-saw, 2 iron-bound buckets, and an iron lamp. Ah! here stands the ox-cart, and here are 2 new cart-wheels. The plough is missing; left where Lubbert's last ploughing was done, out on one of the bouwlots, of which he has the Nos. 4 and 9 on Jochem Pieters, with salt meadow, and out-garden No. 11 beside. Busy bees still hum about, sucking sweets from the fall flowers, with which to store the seven hives in the garden, and hens as busily scratch and cluck about the barnyard. Not an item of Lubbert's effects has escaped our notice; all as enjoyed by him at the time of his decease soon after—affording us a reliable index to the average style of living observed here at that period.

And a grand political event had but just transpired in the highest degree pleasing to the Harlem community, because promising to its simple Belgian character and customs a happy perpetuity, while it restored, fresh and intact, the waning memories of dear Fatherland! This was the recapture of New York by the Dutch.

CHAPTER XIX.

1673–1674.

REOCCUPATION BY THE DUTCH.

"THIS day, 10th August, 1673, New Style, have the Holland and Zeeland fleets captured the Fort at N. York, in the name of their High Mightinesses the Lords States General of the United Netherlands and his Highness the Lord Prince of Orange; and the Fort is re-named *Willem Hendrick*, and the City obtained the name NEW ORANGE."

In these words did the secretary Vander Vin record in his protocol an event which, suddenly reducing the colony again to the obedience of Holland, at once startled and overjoyed the Dutch community at Harlem. The mother countries were at war, and this one of the fruits. They were therefore prepared for the following official letter:

To THE Inhabitants of the Town of *N: Haerlem.*

You will, by authority of the High Commanders and Council of War residing in the fort Willem Hendrick, appoint two persons from your village as deputies, and with the same send your constable's staff and town ensign, on the day after to-morrow, being Monday, in order then to talk with us; whereon depending, we remain, after greetings, your friends,

The SCHOUT, BURGOMASTERS and SCHEPENS
of the City of N. Orange.
By order of the same
N. BAYARD, *Secretary.*

N. Orange, 19th August,
1673, New Style.

To this the following reply was sent by the hands of the delegates:

To THE Noble, Honorable Lords, the Schout, Burgomasters and Schepens, at the City *of New Orange.*

WE, Inhabitants at the village N. Haerlem, pursuant to your Honors' writing of the 19th instant, by authority of the High Commanders and the Council of War, residing in fort Willem Hendrick, send by these the constable's staff (having no ensign), besides two deputies from us, to receive such orders as your Honors shall find to pertain to the welfare and benefit of this town; whereupon we shall rely, praying God to preserve your Honors in a prosperous, just, and enduring government; in the mean while remaining your Honors' dutiful, willing subjects, the Inhabitants of the town N. Haerlem, August 21st, 1673, New Style.

By order of the same,
H. J. Vander Vin, *Secretary.*

The delegates returned bearing the following letter:

To the Inhabitants of the town *New Haerlem.*

You are by these, by authority of the Noble Burgomasters and Schepens of this City of New Orange, ordered, for your town's folks and the dependant neighborhoud, on the morrow to assemble, and by a general vote to nominate eight from the same as magistrates (all such being also of the Reformed Christian Religion), out of which said nomination we then shall elect four as magistrates for your town; whereon we relying, remain your friends,

The Burgomasters and Schepens
of the City of New Orange, 22d August, 1673.
By order of the same,
N. Bayard, *Secretary.*

The town folks met pursuant to this order and nominated David des Marest, Joost van Oblinus, Lubbert Gerritsen, Cornelis Jansen, Resolved Waldron, Adolph Meyer, Arent Harmans (Bussing), and Jan Nagel, all good friends of fatherland, as magistrates, and Hendrick J. Vander Vin as secretary, from whom were appointed to the former office, Waldron, Des Marest, Oblinus, and Bussing, Waldron being named as schout; and as secretary, Vander Vin. These took an oath of fidelity "to their High Mightinesses the Lords States General of the United Netherlands and his Highness the Lord Prince of Orange."

By order of the Burgomasters and Schepens, the new board called the other inhabitants together on Aug. 25th, and administered to them the following oath of allegiance:

"We promise and swear, in presence of Almighty God, unto their High Mightinesses the Lords States General of the United Netherlands, and his Highness the Lord Prince of Orange, and their Governor already placed here, or hereafter to be appointed, to be beholden and faithful, and in all circumstances to behave us as trusty and obedient subjects are bound to do. *So truly help us, God Almighty.*"

The roll of names is as follows, being classified by Vander Vin, thus :

1st. Over 16 and under 60 years.

Lubbert Gerritsen,	
Cornelis Jansen,	
Meyndert Journee,	
Adolph Meyer,	
Simeon Courtier,	
Jan Laurens v : Schoonrewoert.	
Jean des Marest,	
Jan Dyckman,	
Daniel Tourneur,	
Jan Nagel,	
Samuel Pell,	*Englishmen.*
Robert Hollis,*	*Englishmen.*
John Smith,	*Englishmen.*
Jan le Maistre,	*Young Men (i.e. unmarried).*
David des Marest, Jr.,	*Young Men (i.e. unmarried).*
Samuel des Marest,	*Young Men (i.e. unmarried).*
Jaco el Roey,	*Young Men (i.e. unmarried).*
Evert Alrichs,	*Young Men (i.e. unmarried).*
Jochem Engelbert,	*Young Men (i.e. unmarried).*
Coenraet Hendricks,	*Young Men (i.e. unmarried).*
Cornelis Theunisz.	*Young Men (i.e. unmarried).*
Gabriel Carbosie, *Miller.*	

2d. Impotent, above 60 years.

Glaude le Maistre,
Pierre Cresson,
Jean le Roy,
Claes Carstensen,
Isaac Vermeille.

The Dutch rule was now re-established ; after two days came the Sabbath, when the people at worship expressed their gratitude in a practical way, by an extra large contribution of 4 florins ! To this, the next Sunday, Vander Vin added, as a special gift, a schopel of wheat, equal to 6 gl.

* Robert Hollis, says Gov. Nicolls, "came over with me into these parts, in his Majesty's service, a soldier under my command." He got a license Aug. 15, 1665, to m. wid. Mary Page. On July 18, 1667, he secured a patent for 26 acres of land in Brooklyn, having Jan Martyn on the north and Jan Damen on the south, "with his housing and accommodation thereupon," which he had bought early that year from Jean Mesurolle. He obtained, Jan. 4 ensuing, the sole right to tap strong drink in that town. In 1672 he bought an erf at H., where he was made a corporal in the Night Watch, Dec. 6, 1675, but must have left soon after, being last named at a settlement, Jan. 17, 1676, between the town and William Palmer, for whom Hollis had stood security.

The ready response to every demand of the new rulers also told the general satisfaction. Called upon to furnish "600 pieces of great palisades, 14 feet long, 1 foot thick and under," for the city defences, the inhabitants met Aug. 28th, and apportioned this heavy work *pro rata*, 10 posts to an erf, and 1½ to each morgen. An admirable spirit was also shown by the young men who owned no bouwland, four of whom—to wit, Coenraet Hendricks, Engelbert, Bussing, and Dyckman—volunteered 20 sticks each, and the loyal Jan Nagel and Jean Demarest each 25. Le Roy, Hollis, Pell, and Smith severally pledged 20 each, and Widow Montagne the same, to be cut by her hired man Evert Alrichs. Carbosie would spare time from the mill to furnish 16. The younger sons of Demarest, with his servant Jacob el Roey, offered together to cut 26, Jan le Maistre 12, and Oblinus' man, Cornelis Theunisz, 7. They agreed to draw all these to a suitable place at the strand.*

A new life and vigor seemed infused into the village; the overseers being especially occupied. Pursuant to orders from the Council of War, they had, on the 23d inst., visited the plantation of Capt. Richard Morris, and appointed Jean Demarest and Arent Harmans to take charge of it till further orders. The affairs of Capt. Delavall now demanded their care. His estates, which were scattered in different parts of the province, and valued by him at about £5000, had been attached by the Dutch commanders. A ketch building at Harlem, by Samuel Pell, ship carpenter, and of which Delavall was half owner, was to that extent included. John Smith, late in employ of Delavall, was instructed to take good care of his other property at Harlem till further notice.

Sundry claims against Delavall now came up; one by Pierre

* JOCHEM ENGELBERT VAN NAMEN, from Heusden, came out in the ship Hope, which sailed from Amsterdam, Apl. 8, 1662. He lived four and a half years with Burger Joris, and then entered the service of Verveelen, at H., Mar. 5, 1668, but complaining of ill-usage, was released by the Court, Sept. 10 ensuing. He bore a good name while with Burger, and seems to have sustained it afterward at Esopus, where he m., Nov. 3, 1676, Elizabeth, dr. of Evert Pels, by whom he had a family of chn., viz.: Dellantie, Evert, Engelbert, Johannes, Anna. Dellantie m. Barent Marteling. In 1702, Anna m. Isaac Marteling. See *Clute's Staten Island*.

EVERT ALRICHS, five years later, is found at Upland, on the Delaware, having m. Elizabeth, wid. of Hans Walter.

Cresson for what Delavall, in 1670, had agreed to pay to rebuild and keep up the fence between their gardens; another for repairs the last year at the mill on "the flume and door to the race," Carbosie still having charge. Meanwhile Smith, Delavall's man, intrusted with his cattle and goods, having suddenly absconded, the High Commanders on Sept. 9th directed Resolved Waldron to take the property in keeping, and which trust he accepted. This was officially made known to the people of Harlem on the 11th, and accompanied by directions that the ferry folks should set no strangers, "that is Christians, or negroes, or cattle," over the river, either at Harlem or Spuyten Duyvel, unless they could show a pass. These directions were afterward repeated.

On Sept. 25th the magistrates appointed Barent Waldron, the Court Messenger, who, on being sworn into office, was furnished with a commission, setting forth in general his duties, and warning all persons not to interfere with him in the proper discharge thereof. At the Court held next day, Carbosie, the miller, complained of Jan Louwe van Schoonrewoerd, for threatening to shoot his hogs, which had troubled him by running over the mill-dam. Louwe was told to repair his fences if he would not suffer from others' hogs or cattle, and Carbosie was ordered to make good his railing about the mill-dam, so that no cattle could run over.

The following day Joost van Oblinus made complaint that having sent Adrian Sammis, his wife's brother, living with him, to pasture the cattle "upon the point over against Simeon's land," he had been beaten off by Glaude le Maistre with a stick.* Le Maistre said that he chased the cattle from his own fence, and not from that of the point, and admitted to have struck Adrian, but not with a stick. Poor Adrian, who could not

* The POINT here referred to was undoubtedly that since known as *Bussings Point.* Simeon Cornier had agreed to buy lot No. 11, Jochem Pieters, but the reference is plainly not to him, nor to this land. We conclude it was the lot on Jochem Pieters, given up in 1661 by Simon (also called Simeon) de Ruine, and was No. 23 (afterward No. 22, one of Delavall's, whose title was just now uncertain), and that "Simeon's land," best known by its original owner's name, thus formed the north line of Jochem Pieters; and "over against" (that is, opposite to it, some space intervening) was said point early called *Glaudie's Point*, from Delamater, whose meadows lay there. Later, No. 22 formed the northernmost of the so-called "Six Lots," embraced in the large Myer tract.

speak for himself, being "deaf, dumb, and paralytic," had two good witnesses, Esther Tourneur and Cornelia Waldron. Esther being called in, said that Adrian coming along the fencing with the cattle, she saw that Glaude had beaten him with a stick. Cornelia testified the same, and that Glaude ran after them. The Court condemned Le Maistre "in an amend of 6 gl., to the behoof of the church here, with the costs hereby accruing." He was also directed to "draw in his fence by the point of his meadow forthwith, within the time of two months, without longer delay."

On the same date (Sept. 27th) the magistrates, with the advice of Cornelis Jansen and Jan Dyckman, passed the following curious regulation, respecting the lands in common fence:

"Is resolved and found good to establish that in the coming year, 1674, the tilled land on Jochem Pieters shall be exempt from any afterplanting of buckwheat, pumpkins, turnips, or any summer fruits, that the cattle of this village (after the crop is off the field) may pasture thereon; and the land Van Keulen's Hook shall in the same year, 1674, be sown and planted with summer fruits; and in the year 1675, on the contrary, Van Keulen's Hook from summer fruits shall remain unplanted and unsown, and Jochem Pieters again be sown as above; running so from year to year, alternately, the one to be sown by summer fruits and the other left unsown, for reasons as above."

The Dutch Commanders had now sailed for Holland leaving the administration of affairs in the hands of Gov. Anthony Colve, who on Oct. 1st issued the following:

PROVISIONAL INSTRUCTIONS to the Schout and Magistrates of the Town of *New Haerlem*.

1. The Schout and Magistrates each in their sphere shall have a care that the Reformed Christian Religion shall be maintained conformably to the Synod of Dordrecht held in the years 1618 and 1619, without suffering it, through any other persuasion thereto opposed, to be in any wise altered.

2. The Schout, so far as possible, shall be present and preside at all meetings. But when he acts for himself as a party, or respecting the right of his Lords Patroons, or in behalf of justice, on such an occasion, he shall stand up and vacate the bench, and at that time neither advise nor vote; but the oldest Schepen shall preside in his place.

3. All cases of government, of the security and peace of the inhabitants, also of justice betwixt man and man, shall be determined by the Magistrates of the aforesaid Town by definitive sentences to the amount of sixty

guilders in beavers, or less. But in all cases exceeding this sum, every one shall be free to appeal to the Hon. Governor General and Council here.

4. In case of diversity of voices, the minority must yield to the majority, yet permitting those of the contrary opinion to record and sign their protest; but in no wise to publish such outside the meeting, on pain of arbitrary correction.

5. Whenever in the Court any cases shall occur, in which any Magistrate shall be concerned as a party, in such case the Magistrate shall rise up and leave his seat, as before is directed in the case of the Schout.

6. All the inhabitants of the aforesaid Town shall be citable before the said Schout and Schepens, who shall hold their sessions and courts as often as the same shall be necessary.

7. All criminal offences may be referred to the Governor General and Council, saving that the Schout shall be obligated the criminal offenders to apprehend, to arrest and to detain, and as prisoners, under proper security, to deliver over to the High Magistracy, together with good and true information of the offences committed; at the expense of the offenders or the prosecutor.

8. Minor offences, such as quarrels, injuries, slanders, threats, fist blows, and such like, are left to the adjudication and decision of the Magistrates of each particular town.

9. The Schout and Schepens shall be authorized, for the peace and tranquillity of the inhabitants in their district, to make any orders for the regulating of highways, setting off lands and gardens, and whatever like things as relate to farm lands; also for the observance of the Sabbath, respecting the building of churches, of schools, and similar public works; also against fighting and striking and such like minor offences; provided the same do not conflict with, but are conformable unto the laws of our Fatherland and the statutes of this province; and to this end all orders of importance, before they are promulgated, shall be presented to the High Magistracy for their approval.

10. Said Schout and Schepens shall be held closely to observe and execute all the placards and ordinances which shall be enacted and published by the High Magistracy, and not to permit anything to be done contrary thereto; further to proceed against the transgressors according to the tenor of the same; and to execute promptly such orders as the Governor General from time to time shall send to them.

11. The Schout and Schepens shall also be bound to acknowledge their High Mightinesses the Lords States General of the United Netherlands, and his Serene Highness, the Lord Prince of Orange, as their Sovereign Rulers, and to maintain their high jurisdiction, right, and dominion in this land.

12. The choice of all minor officers and assistants to the said Schout and Schepens (alone excepting the Secretary's office) shall be made and confirmed by themselves.

13. The Schout shall personally, or by his substitutes, put in execution all the sentences of the Schepens, without releasing anybody, except with the advice of the Court; also take good care that the places under his control shall be purged from all rascality, gambling, baudy-houses, and such like immoralities.

14. The Schout shall enjoy the half of all civil fines accruing during his term of office, together with a third part of the allowance coming to

the respective towns from criminal cases; wherefore he shall receive no presents, directly or indirectly, forbidden by the laws.

15. At the time of election, the Schout and Schepens shall nominate a double number of the best qualified, honest, intelligent, and most wealthy inhabitants, and only those who are of the Reformed Christian Religion, or at least well disposed thereto, as Schepens, and to be presented to his Honor the Governor, from whom by him the election shall be made, with the continuation of some of the old, in case his Honor shall deem it necessary. Done at the fort Willem Hendrick the First of October Ao. 1673.

By order of the Honbl. Governor General
and Council of *New Netherland*,
N. BAYARD, *Secretary*.

On Wednesday, Oct. 4th, Gov. Colve visited Harlem and held a council there. Some of the people of Fordham presenting themselves complained "of the ill-government of their landlord John Archer," and asked the privilege of nominating their own magistrates. Archer being summoned, also appeared; and on hearing the complaint, he voluntarily yielded up the government there, retaining only the right to his houses and lands; whereupon the Court granted the people their request, and on the following day, pursuant to previous notice, all the inhabitants of that place appeared at Harlem, and took the oath of allegiance at the hand of Gov. Colve, and before the Heer Cornelis Steenwyck, Burgomaster Egidius Luyck, and Secretary Bayard; Resolved Waldron and David Demarest being also present. Within a few days Johannes Verveelen, Michiel Bastiaensen, and Valentine Claessen were elected magistrates at Fordham, the first being also made secretary.

The Harlem town court met Oct. 6th with reference to the affairs of Capt. Delavall, who had departed with Gov. Lovelace for England in the ship of the Dutch commander Benckes. A statement being drawn up, he was found indebted to the town as follows:

For his part of Preacher's salary, as per list of Jan. 16th preceding	*f.* 66 : 16
" his share of the general expenses of the town, as per list of Mar. 6th	242 : 10
" the 4 gardens sold him off the *Clover Pasture*	100 : 0
" wages for labor in making his fences	84 : 0
	493 : 12

The cutting and cartage of 140 palisades, for the city, was also to be added. His assets, in real estate, were found to be, "On Jochem Pieters in 9 lots, 54 morgen; on Keulen's Hook in 2 lots, 6 morgen; together 11 lots, 60 morgen. In the village two houses and erven. And meadows for hay in proportion."

The following petition, having reference to Delavall, was drawn up on the 10th of October:

To the Noble, Right Honorable Lord, the Governor of *New Netherland*.

Respectfully make known the Schout and Rulers of the Town New Haerlem, in the name and on behalf of their common Inhabitants, your Excellency's subjects, how that they the petitioners are entitled to a considerable sum of money from Capt. Thomas Delavall, on account of burdens and charges which by this town some years hither are borne upon the lands, houses, and house lots (*erven*), of the Inhabitants, being shown by the assessments and accounts thereof kept from time to time: and the aforesaid Thomas Delavall having possessed extraordinary parcels of land, as also houses and house lots, for his quota has done, contributed, or paid not one stiver to the discharging of the town's debts, to the great grievance of the community. 'Tis now such, that at this village lies a small strip of land, between the two common streets, reaching west to common land named the Clover Pasture, having appertained to the above-mentioned Delavall, who upon some of the same ground (*die op de gront deswijffe*), is now remaining indebted to this town one hundred guilders; So it is that they the petitioners, in quality as above, humbly request your Excellency to be pleased to grant and confer upon them, the petitioners, as property, in recompense for the said arrears, the said small strip of land, so that the inhabitants aforesaid may use it for a Calf Pasture (as the calves have little driving out), the which to nobody's prejudice in particular is tending, but which may serve for the common convenience and the inheritance (*oirbor*) of this town and its Inhabitants: hereupon awaiting your Excellency's favorable answer, remain meanwhile and at all times your Excellency's right willing servants, etc. N. Haerlem, 10th Octobr., Ao. 1673.

RESOLVERT WALDRON,
DAVID DES MAREST,
JOOST VAN OBLINUS,
ARENT HERMENSEN.

Answer. The Petitioners are allowed to use the small Clover Pasture requested, provisionally, till such time as order shall be taken about the affairs of Capt. Delavall. In the mean time the Petitioners to bring in their proper claim to the curators to be chosen thereto. Done in Fort Willem Hendrick, on the date 23d October, Ao. 1673.

By order of the Governor General of N. Netherland and the Hon. Council.

N. BAYARD, *Secretary*.

On the 1st of November Vander Vin's three years' service having ended, he was engaged for another year as clerk and voorleser, on the same conditions as of 23d October 1670, to wit: 400 guilders, dwelling house, and fuel. It was also stipulated that the people should keep the house and the garden fence in repair. The salary was to be paid half-yearly in grain at market value, and "according to *the old list of the free-will contributors,*" namely:

The Free-will Contributors to the Voorleser's office for this ensuing year:

Resolved Waldron		*f.* 30 : 0
Claude le Maistre		
Jean le Maistre		4 : 0
Joost van Oblinus		25 : 0
Daniel Tourneur		30 : 0
Adolph Meyer		30 : 0
David des Marest		15 : 0
Arent Hermans		8 : 0
Pierre Cresson		4 : 0
Lubbert Gerritsen		20 : 0
Cornelis Jansen		20 : 0
Jan Nagel		15 : 0
Jean le Roy		6 : 0
Jan Dyckman		8 : 0
Meynard Journee		16 : 0
The Widow of Jan La Montagne		
Jan Louwerens van Schoonrewoert		
Simeon Cornier		
Jean le Roy, rent of the Town's allotment		120 : 0
Rent of the meadows, beginning 1st May, 1671, of which are to pay each year:		
David des Marest	*f.* 24 : 0	
Jan Nagel	10 : 7	
Lubbert Gerritsen	10 : 7	
Johannes Vermelje	10 : 7	53 : 1

Claude le Maistre's annual contribution had been 25 guilders, but, for reasons which will hereafter appear, he declined to renew his subscription. The three others wanting the amount were new subscribers of the previous year. The items of rent for the town lands being added brought the figures up to 406 gl. 1 st.

Some of the neighboring English, exasperated at the recapture of the country by the Dutch, now began to make trouble; as will appear from the following minutes of proceedings at Harlem:

Ao. 1673, the 7th November, Tuesday.

Present, Schout, Magistrates and all the Inhabitants of this village collected.

Whereas by daily reports we are informed that some wicked and insolent persons, of the English nation, their riotings make about these countries, threatening to give one and another some molestation and trouble by robbing and burning; before which threats those of us who live outside will not prove secure. But as much that is feasible to be done rests upon our care, through heed and keeping watch upon such as may be disposed to do the same some hurt and damage, owing to their ability to escape away to a great distance; So it is that we, Schout, Magistrates, and the whole community, being assembled, have found good and deemed necessary to watch by turns during the nights; and that it may take place more orderly, we have thought it necessary to appoint a suitable person as Captain, to command as many as go on watch, to whom we promise obedience and submission in all that which he shall therein command, upon forfeiture of the fines also hereby ordered; and by a majority of votes is thereunto chosen and confirmed the person *Cornelis Jansen*, as Captain. And moreover the community are divided into four companies or corporalships, in order, by turns with their fellow soldiers, to keep the night watch, and to go the rounds as needful, and each his arms to keep ready, provided with powder and lead as required. Whoever neglects the watch without lawful reason, or those whose arms are not ready, wanting necessary powder and lead, or the command of the Captain, or his Corporal oppose, shall forfeit each time three guilders, for the use of the whole company. Thus done at N. Haerlem, the 7th November, 1673.

List of the Corporalships.

1. Jan Nagel, *Corporal*,
   Joost van Oblinus,
   Jan Helmont,
   Jean le Maistre,
   Jean le Roy,
   Robert Hollis.
2. Simeon Cornier, *Corporal*,
   Lubbert Gerritsen,
   Samuel Pell,
   Jacque el Roe,
   Barent Waldron,
   Samuel des Marest.
3. Jan Dyckman, *Corporal*,
   Arent Hermens,
   David des Marest, Jr.,
   Jan Tinker,
   Conradus Hendricksen,
   Cornelis Theunissen.
4. Adolph Meyer, *Corporal*,
   Laurens Matthysen,
   David des Marest,
   Daniel Tourneur,
   Jochem Engelbert,
   Meyndert Journee.

The gratitude of the Dutch inhabitants at the restoration of the country to Holland, now found expression throughout the colony in the observance, not of a day merely, but of a series of public thanksgivings. The following letter and proclamation from the new governor explains it:

Honest, Beloved, Faithful, the Schout and Magistrates of the village *Harlem*.

Honest, Beloved, Faithful,

These serve to accompany the inclosed proclamation of a general day of thanksgiving, fasting, and prayer, which you are required to publish at the usual time and place, and to take care that it be observed after the tenor thereof; let also the inclosed be seasonably sent on to the village of Fordham. Whereon relying, I remain, after greetings, your friend, A. COLVE.

Fort Willem Hendrick,
20th November, 1673.

*Proclamation.**

Honest, Beloved, Faithful,

Considering the manifold blessings and benefits wherewith the only good and merciful God has favored this province and its inhabitants, of which by no means the least is their fortunate restoration under their former lawful and natural rulers, and that which is above all to be prized, the continuance of the reformed worship, which also, like all other blessings and benefits to us, not only imposes a debt of gratitude, but also, in truth, humility and repentance for our manifold and weighty sins, so that the Almighty God may continue His blessings, and this land and people be freed from His righteous judgments and well-deserved punishment; Therefore it is that we have judged it highly necessary by these to ordain and proclaim a general day for thanks, fasting, and prayer, which everywhere within this province shall be observed every first Wednesday in each month, beginning on Wednesday, the 6th December next coming, and so following on each first Wednesday in the month. And that all may be the better practised and observed, so are by these interdicted and forbidden, on the aforesaid thank, fast, and prayer day, all labor, and play of tennis-court, ball-tossing, fishing, hunting, gaming, sailing, dice-playing, excessive drinking, and all tapping of liquors by innkeepers; the whole upon penalty of arbitrary correction. For the observance of the same, the Magistrates, Officers, and Justices of this province to whom these shall be sent, are required and charged strictly to provide that the transgressors be proceeded against as they should be; and to make known this our proclamation by timely publication where such is necessary. Herewith committing you to the protection of the Most High; Honest, Beloved, Faithful,

Your affectionate friend, A. COLVE.

Fort Willem Hendrick,
15th November, 1673.

* This interesting document is newly translated from the Dutch, the old translation printed in N. Y. Col. Doc. II., 655, being faulty.

In fitting mood was the community at Harlem to receive this message, for on that self-same day, Nov. 21st, one much esteemed in the town, Lubbert Gerritsen, late an overseer, departed this life.* The town was also full of the alarms which had dictated the institution of the night watch, and excited over the arrest at Spuyten Duyvel of one François Beado, aged about 27 years, a native of London, for being concerned, as was believed, in a conspiracy against the Dutch. From Verveelen's, where during his detention he had tried to induce one James Pinnot, of Fordham, "to assist him to kill the ferryman and other people, saying they were but Dutch," he was taken and lodged in the fort at New Orange. At his examination before the Governor and Council, Nov. 28th, Pinnot and George Tippett gave evidence against him. The following deposition was also taken:

"William Smith, aged about 46 years, inhabitant of Fordham, declareth upon oath that François Beado, now in prison, about six weeks ago came to the deponent at Fordham and inquired what neighbors he had; then saying further that he had a commission from the * * on this side, Canada, to burn, take, kill, and ruin all the Dutch; because he and his father and cousin had lost by them about 800 pounds, which he was resolved to get again; and when this deponent questioned his commission, the copy of which he did read to the deponent, he, the said Beado, replied that if he had no other, his sword and his half-pike (which he had in his hand) was his commission, the Dutch being his enemies—and the second day after

* Lubbert Gerritsen, having lived at Gravesend, L. I., till after his youngest ch. was b., appears at H. in 1661, when he bought the house and land of Matthys Boon, who then left the town. He was chosen *adelborst* in 1663, and held several town offices afterward, serving as overseer the year before he d. His property has been shown, as in his inventory taken Nov. 27, 1673. His chn., all b. in this country, and by his first w., Grietien Dircks, were Lysbeth, b. 1651, who m. Dirck Evertsen Fluyt and Joris Burger, both of N. Y.; Gerrit and Dirck, twins, b. 1653; Gerrit, b. 1655, and Eva, b. 1657, who m. Arent Harmans Bussing. Lubbert's second m. with the wid. Fermmetje Coenraets has been noticed. Their contracts, respectively providing for their former chn., are dated June 29, and their m. bans July 7, 1669. Lubbert chose as guardians of his chn.'s inheritance, Jan Gerritsen de Vries, from Workum, and Adrian Dircksen Coen, from Maasen, in Utrecht. Judging from their patronymics, these may have been, one his br., the other his first wife's br. Dirck and Gerrit Lubbertsen are not again named here; the last no doubt the "Gerrit Lubbertsen, from New York," who m. Allda Everts, at Albany, in 1684. *Pearson's Alb. Settlers.*

the said Beado came again to the deponent, and said he was beset by three rogues, but that he had two friends in the woods with whom he was resolved to meet them; inquiring further what woman Michiel Bastiaensen, his wife was, saying that he would burn Mr. Vervoelen's and the said Michiel's house, but he was afraid that the said woman would betray him, she having seen his half-pike; and desired further that this deponent would warn Mr. Gibbs, who quartered at Michiel's house, of his intention."

Beado also confessed "without torture," and being found guilty of disturbing and breaking the peace, was sentenced to be publicly bound to a stake and branded on the back with a red-hot iron, and then banished from the province, for a term of twenty-five years, which sentence was put in execution on Dec. 20th.

The intense excitement which these things created in the community at Harlem was heightened by the fears generally entertained that an attempt would be made by the English government to recover possession of the province. The following letter received from Gov. Colve has reference to this:

To the Schout, Magistrates, and Inhabitants of the Towns of *New Harlem* and *Fordham*.

Good Friends,

On last Tuesday week I had some conference in the town of Midwout with the Magistrates and chief officers of all the Dutch towns situated on Long Island, concerning the present condition of the country, and had wished indeed that time and the season of the year had permitted me to visit you the same as the rest; but time not allowing this, I have therefore deemed it necessary hereby to incite you to your duty, and with many of the other good inhabitants to fulfil your oath and honor, whereof I entertain not the least doubt, being herein partly assured by the Schouts of your respective towns. Therefore nothing remains but to recommend you to keep a wakeful eye on all designs which may be concocted against this province or yourselves in particular, and *always to be ready to transport your families and movables hither*, on certain information of the enemy's approach, or on special command from me; and that such may be executed in good order, Schout Resolved Waldron is hereby appointed chief officer of the militia of the towns of Haerlem and Fordham, with order to communicate these presents to the inhabitants of said towns, who, for the preservation of better order in each town, are hereby required to choose a Sergeant, and not to fail to give me information of all that occurs. Whereupon relying, I remain,

Your friend, A. COLVE.

Fort William Hendrick,
27th Xber, 1673.

This coupling of Harlem and the adjacent parts of Westchester in one jurisdiction, seen thus early to be expedient, was fully consummated just two centuries later, in 1873.

The panic at Harlem was almost as great as if the enemy were already at their doors. Influenced by rumors of their approach, many left for the city or other places, and the Sabbath congregations were reduced to a mere handful. The Secretary, Vander Vin, on Jan. 21st, 1674, makes this entry in the deacon's accounts: "Owing to the daily reports of the coming of the English, the inhabitants being fled with their families and movable goods, little was collected and found at the date of January 21st." But this excitement soon spent itself and subsided, things became more settled, the fast-days were regularly observed, and the Sunday services better sustained.

About this time complaint was made against Hendrick Kiersen and Reyer Michielsen, of Fordham, for shooting a hog belonging to Jean le Maistre. These two, according to their statement, came over to this Island, on Monday, Jan. 29th, to look for a hog which had strayed. In their hunt they shot a deer, and soon after that Kiersen, espying, as he thought, the missing hog, told Reyer to shoot it, which he did. As they could carry but one with them, they took the deer, and left the hog for another time. Reyer went for it two days after, when some one seeing it was curious enough to examine the head, and found upon the ear the mark of young Lodewyck Ackerman, from whom Le Maistre had gotten the hog. Reyer passed an examination before the magistrates at Harlem on Feb. 1st, and the case was referred to the Burgomasters—Cornelis Jansen, who was cousin to the accused, becoming his bail. The Burgomasters, Feb. 3d, sent the case back to the magistrates for further inquiry. This was made on the 5th, the testimony being sent to the Burgomasters, and from them to the Governor and Council, by whom the case was again referred back to the local court at Harlem, to be there decided, "unless they find it to be criminal." As a curiosity, we give the minute of the examination on Feb. 5th:

On 5th February, Monday.

Present, the Heeren, Resolved Waldron, Schout.
David des Marest, | Joost van Oblinus, | Arent Harmensen, } Magistrates.

Interrogatories to be put to Reyer Michielsen and Hendrick Kiersen, both living at Fordham, about the shooting of a hog, upon this Island, belonging to Jean le Maistre, &c.

QUESTION.	ANSWER.
1. *What is your name?*	1st. Reyer Michielsen. 2d. Hendrick Kiersen.
2. *Where were you born?*	1st. In the Prince's Land, about Schoonrewoert. 2d. At Giest, in the Land of Drent.
3. *How old are you?*	1st. About 20 years. 2d. About 23 years.
4. *Who has given you orders to shoot hogs upon this Island?*	1st. No one has given orders. 2d. Thought not that he was doing wrong to fetch his own hog.
5. *You knew well that you might hunt no hogs upon this Island without the knowledge of the magistrates of N. Harlem?*	1st. Well knew that such was the order under the English rule, but knew not that it continued under the Dutch. 2d. As above.
6. *Why do you shoot other people's hogs?*	1st. Knew not that it was another person's hog, but his brother-in-law, Hendrick Kiersen, said that it was his. 2d. Thought that it was his own hog.
7. *When you had shot the hog, did you not well know that it was not yours?*	1st. Knew well that it was not my hog, but my brother-in-law still knew not better than 'twas his own. 2d. Knew not better than 'twas his own hog.
8. *Why did you not take it away at the first?*	1st. Because that he, having shot a deer, thereupon for that time had enough to carry. 2d. That they had to carry a deer.
9. *Why did you skin the hog?*	1st. Because I saw that in the night it would freeze, and then the hair would not come off. 2d. Because that he thought it to be his, and therewith might do as he saw fit.
10. *Why did you carry it in sacks?*	1st. Because he thought that they could carry it better in sacks. 2d. Because it was to be better carried in sacks; but has not been near there.
11. *Why sought you to conceal it, when you perceived our folks?*	1st. Denied that; and said he had had no thought to hide the sacks.
12. *Why did you not fetch the hog the next day?*	1st. Because the kill was frozen, and the canoe could not get off. 2d. That he was busy with threshing, and also gave it no thought, as it was a lean hog.

The result was that proceedings were dropped, the evidence not clearly showing a criminal intent; but at the desire of the magistrates, the Governor and Council, on April 18th, issued a stringent order in regard to the offence of shooting hogs in the common woods of this Island, without consent of the Harlem or City authorities.

The attention of the government was also drawn to the matter of securing the horses of the late governor, Lovelace, and of Capt. Delavall and others, "now running in the woods upon Manhattan Island," and the magistrates of Harlem were notified to employ the whole community on the second day of the coming Whitsuntide, "to collect and drive into their village all the horses" belonging to the aforesaid persons, and other of the late English officials. This order was given by the Governor April 27th.

Little more of interest transpired in the "dorp" for some months succeeding, except a few transfers of property, from which may be had an idea of the value of Harlem lands at that period. On May 2d Jean le Roy executed a deed to Simeon Cornier for his farm, consisting of a house, barn, and erf, a lot on Jochem Pieters, and one on Van Keulen's Hook, with meadows; for which Cornier had a bill of sale, dated Feb. 24th, 1672, the price paid being 1400 gl. At a public sale, July 5th, of the estate of the late Lubbert Gerritsen, a lot of tillable land, No. 9, Jochem Pieters, with the crops thereon, and the meadows thereto belonging, and the erf with house and barn, were struck off to his stepson Conrad Hendricksen, for 875 fl. His lot No. 4, Jochem Pieters, with its meadows, and a garden (No. 11), for a building spot, "west of the village and north of the street," and "between Cornelis Jansen and Joost van Oblinus," was sold to David Demarest, Jr., for 925 fl.

But now came news of a peace in Europe, welcome enough in itself, but which cost the Dutch inhabitants a tearful regret when they learned that, by stipulation, the colony was to be again given up to the English. The news was officially communicated in a letter of July 3d, from Secretary Bayard, inclosing the Governor's proclamation of peace, dated June 30th, and postponing the fast-day for eight days, and changing it into a day of thanksgiving. It directed that on July 11th in the forenoon religious service should be held, and the proclamation of peace published.

Several months passed before an English government succeeded to the Dutch, and the interval was marked by a little shrewd preparation for it. This caused considerable litigation in the town court; several parties sued the Tourneurs, to recover for work done for Delavall, by direction of the elder Tourneur, while acting as his agent, and in connection with which suits the old story of Tourneur's having killed a man in France was again revived by the Disosways, and as the widow said, "to the great damage of herself and children." These demands for payment were generally sustained, though it appeared that the late Tourneur had declared to Martin Hardewyn, "I will no more pay the debts of Delavall, but I will give you an order upon him to pay you."

It is pleasing to note the regularity with which both civil and church affairs proceeded, amid all these disturbing causes. The new nomination for magistrates was made on Sept. 24th, and the choice and confirmation by the Burgomaster's court, Oct. 4th. Waldron was continued as schout, and Oblinus as schepen, the new schepens being Adolph Meyer and Jan Dyckman. On Oct. 29th, Do. Nieuwenhuysen came up and installed as new deacon Simeon Cornier, to serve with Joost van Oblinus, then holding the office. He was attended by the Heer van Cortlandt, one of the city elders, and the accounts of the church from July 26th, 1672, were taken up, audited, and pronounced correct.* During that period there had been collected on the Sabbath, fast-days, and Fridays, for preparation for the communion (as also on Christmas, when services were held and the largest collection realized), the sum of 184 florins, 0 stivers, and 8 pennings, from which 71 florins had been expended in alms, etc., leaving a balance of 113 fl. 0 st. 8 p.

* Olof Stevens van Cortlandt, the common anc. of the V. C. family in this country, was a wealthy brewer, occupying a residence in Stone street, adjoining his "malthouse;" and here he d. Apl. 4, 1684. His son Jacobus, a prominent merchant, bought of Jacques Tourneur, Sept. 28, 1705, about two acres of salt meadow on the Harlem side of the Spuyten Duyvel, which remaining in the family 168 years before it was sold, became very valuable. In a communication to Mr. Samuel E. Lyon, of New York, May 2, 1873, just previous to said sale, we had the pleasure of restoring the knowledge of the old title which had become lost to the owners.

in the deacon's chest. Thereupon Secretary Vander Vin closes the account with the following formal entry:

"On the date, 20th October, 1674, these accounts collected, and agreeing with the above donations, are found to be correct, with the assistance of the Heer Olof Stevens van Cortlandt, Elder of the Church of Jesus Christ in the city of New Orange, and the same are also closed."

Do. Nieuwenhuysen had already had a useful ministry; since he came, about twenty of the Harlem people had been received to church-membership, mostly young men and women. The last accessions were *Adolph Meyer*, *Cornelis Jansen*, *Conrad Hendricksen*, and *Jean le Maistre*, on March 1st preceding; and the next were received Dec. 10th following, namely, *Barent Waldron*, his sister *Ruth*, afterward *Mrs. Jean le Maistre*, and *Eva Lubberts*, afterward married to Arent Hermens Bussing.

Impatient to see the English rule re-established, a few restless spirits in Westchester, who had already given the Dutch much annoyance, now began to bluster about the country venting their spleen on the Hollanders, and vaunting their loyalty to the king. Of these was Thomas Hunt, Jr., who having at first refused to take the oath of allegiance, and been ordered to leave the province, was, at his father's request, allowed to remain on accepting the oath and giving security for its observance. On Monday, Nov. 5th, Hunt and five or six others came riding toward the village. Accosting Pierre Cresson, who was engaged fixing his fence, with a "How d'yo do," to which he replied, "So and so," they passed on, falling in with a flock of geese, which they began to chase, heeding not Pierre's remonstrance to "let the geese alone." At several houses in the village they stopped, demanding in an insolent manner feed for their horses and bread and beer for themselves. Mrs. Tourneur told them she had nothing to give, but said, "There is water; if you are thirsty, drink it." Her daughter, Madeleine (Mrs. Dyckman), pertly added, "If we had them we should not give them to you." Finding Jan Nagel at his house, they called out, "Here, give us oats for our horses; or else peas or wheat." Nagel, not the one to be intimidated, answered, "I have no oats; but peas and wheat are strange food for horses!" Said Hunt, "I must and will have some, nevertheless." Nagel repeated that he had none for him; whereupon Hunt asked "Does not Waldron live here?" Nagel signified that he did. "He does not," replied Hunt, "you know very well where he lives;" and so saying they rode on. Waldron was not at home, but his wife, Tanneke Nagel, like her namesake, showed a proper courage. "Give us oats for our horses," demanded Hunt; to which Mrs. Waldron replied, "I have none." "Then give us peas or wheat," said he. "There are none threshed, and I cannot get any," was the answer. With his usual oath, Hunt said, "I will have some, threshed or unthreshed;" then adding, "Or give us wine or rum; have you nothing for the king's soldiers?" "I know no king's soldiers," said the matron. "I am a soldier of the king, by the blood of God," said Hunt, striking his breast, "and I shall and will have it! Is not your husband the Constable?" he further demanded. "No," said the spirited Tanneke, "but my husband is the *Schout* of this town." Venting curses upon Waldron, Hunt turned and left with his companions.

Waldron entered a complaint to Gov. Colve, and by his order the magistrates on the 7th held a court of inquiry upon the matter. But Hunt just escaped merited punishment, owing to an important event which happened only three days after, and of which the careful Vander Vin makes the following minute:

"1674, the 10th November, New, or 31st October, Old Style, was the fort Willem Hendrick again to the English governor yielded up, and the governor, A. Colve, with his people, therefrom departed; the fort again named Fort James, and the city, New York."

CHAPTER XX.

1674–1677.

ENGLISH RULE RESTORED; REFUGEES; CAPTAIN CARTERET; INDIAN WAR; LAND GRANTS; SPUYTEN DUYVEL OCCUPIED.

SIR EDMUND ANDROS, the new governor referred to, was accompanied, besides his own retinue of officers and soldiers, by several families of French refugees who had fled to England from the Palatinate, lately invaded and laid waste by the ruthless armies of Louis XIV. under Marshal Turenne. Among these refugees were Nicholas de Vaux (whence our De Vouw, and De Voe), Isaac See, Isaac See, Junior, and Jean le Comte, all of whom were related. These, with Gerard Magister, evidently of the same band, came directly to Harlem; on account, as it would seem, of old Mannheim acquaintances, Demarest and others. Some brought their household goods, but as choicer treasures, the Holy Scriptures in French, the French Psalm Book, and the then highly prized *Book of Martyrs*. De Vaux, Le Comte, and their wives united with the church on the first opportunity, the 13th of December.

Andros restored the English form of government. The Mayor's Court again resumed its jurisdiction, and by its order the town, on Dec. 7th, nominated a double number of persons, from which to fill the places of constable and overseers. The next day the Court acted upon the nomination. Schout Waldron gave place to David des Marest as constable; Cornelis Jansen took his seat as an overseer, and with him the old schepens, Oblinus, Meyer, and Dyckman. They were not sworn in till Jan. 10th.

Several of the Dutch settlers about Spuyten Duyvel, probably distrusting the English and feeling unsafe, removed down into the village. Michiel Bastiaensen and his son-in-law, Hendrick

Kiersen, hired from the widow Tourneur and her son Daniel, Jan. 1st, 1675, their farm upon Jochem Pieters and Van Keulen's Hook, with house, barn, orchard, and meadows, stock and farming tools, for three years from May 1st ensuing. The Tourneurs apparently intended an early removal to their farm on Montagne's Flat, which was to be Daniel's inheritance. They were still annoyed by that injurious report, the more keenly felt, now the object of it lived only in their affections. But the widow, bent on putting a stop to it, had on Dec. 22d made complaint to the Mayor's Court, that Elizabeth Nightingale "had greatly defamed her husband deceased." Thereupon "the Court ordered that, it being formerly determined, the defendant shall either at Harlem or in this court make an acknowledgment and pay all costs." Lysbet had to comply, but preferred a journey to the city, to facing exultant adversaries whom she would meet at the town court. Her appearance, January 19th, the day the magistrates were sworn in, is thus noticed: "The Def^{t} brought into ye Court her suplicatory peticon, in wch was her acknowledgm^{t} for her wrong and injury to ye Plt^{s} husband; wch ye Court accepted off, conditionally she behaved her selfe well, and pay all costs." *

* MARC DU SAUCHOY, anc. of the *Disosway* family, has place in our introductory sketches of the French refugees, etc. As we follow these homeless refugees from exciting scenes in the Old World, when, no longer the suffering victims of despotism, we can only contemplate them amid peaceful walks and engaged in commonplace pursuits, we cannot but mark with interest the happy effects of the change in their ambitious and laborious efforts to provide a home and living for themselves and families—the admirable versatility, especially in the choice of new callings, with which they adapted themselves to circumstances every way extraordinary. Our Disosway, late wool-carder, on his first visit to this country found employment in clearing up some land at Flatbush for Cornelis van Ruyven. Well pleased with the island, and being present, June 17, 1655, when his countryman, Pierre Tetraçon, bought a farm at Mespat, Disosway went there on his return in 1657, and leasing Burger Joris' mill at Dutch Kills, the former wood-cutter now became a miller. This proving a failure, but by no fault of his, he gave it up for a plantation, and turned to farming in the town of Brooklyn, to which place he and wife, Apl. 10, 1661, transferred their church connection from New Amsterdam. Selling his farm a year later to Pierre Prae, from Dieppe, who had refuged at Leyden when Disosway was there, Marc appears at H., Jan. 3, 1664, as prosecutor of a claim against Glaude le Maistre for 95½ gl., and soon after removed here, and hired lands of Jean le Roy. How long was the lease, we know not, but it had expired Mar. 15, 1667, date of their settlement. Archer now induced him to take a farm in Fordham, where he continued to live a number of years.

The quarrel with the Tourneurs, grown bluer as many in feudal story, was shown in the mutual disposition to vex one another. The charge of

On Jan. 11th, 1675, the community renewed their engagement with Vander Vin, for two years' service as parish clerk and schoolmaster, running from Oct. 23d preceding. The terms were as before, to wit, 400 gl. per annum, with fuel, etc. The following persons promised, of their free-will, to give the sums set opposite to their names:

Resolved Waldron	*f.* 30
Joost van Oblinus	" 38
Cornelis Jansen	" 25
Jan Dyckman	" 10
Adolph Meyer	" 14
Jan Louwe van Schoonrewoert	" 30
Daniel Tourneur	" 30
Meynard Journee	" 16
Jan Nagel	" 18
Maria Montayne	" 10
Jean le Maistre	" 10
Arent Hermens	" 8
Conradus Hendricks	" 8
Lourens Jansen	" 8
Barent Waldron	" 6
Pierre Cresson	" 4
David des Marest, Jr.	" 4
Isaac Vermeille	" 8
Total	*f.* 272

homicide, reiterated so persistently, was met by recriminations even worse, till the local magistrates became weary of it. Wisely, the Mayor's Court cooled Dame Disosway's itching to push her adversary to the wall, by making good her charge; and but for the rejection of her offer to send to France for proof, we might know more of the affair in question. The settlement of some old accounts between the parties, Mar. 4, 1675, in presence of the magistrates, was another step toward a cessation of hostilities. Still Lysbet, but four days after, made another charge in the Mayor's Court against the widow T., but it was dismissed as "a vexatious suit," with costs to plaintiff; and no more is heard of this quarrel.

Disosway must have had means, to pay 80 gl. for "a book of martyrs and others," from the estate of Jean le Comte, as he did July 2, 1675. He bought lots Nos. 8, 9, on Hoorn's Hook, from Jan Delamater, Nov. 29, 1679, but presently sold them. On June 7, 1683, he and wife took letters from the Dutch to the French chh., newly formed under Rev. Pierre Daillé. He soon moved to Staten Island, where 225 acres of land near Daniel's Neck were laid out to him Apl. 5, 1684, and for which he got a patent July 16, 1685. In 1689 S. I. partook of the Leisler excitement. Disosway informed the government that many of his neighbors had left their houses and taken to the woods, "for fear of the Papists." He was still living, Oct. 1, 1706. His chn., as far as known, were Madeleine, b. 1657, who m. Marin Hardewyn (as the Dutch wrote it, but perhaps Ardenne); Marcus, b. 1659; Jeanne, b. 1662, m. Conrad Hendricks Boch, of H.; Jean, b. 1665; and Maria, b. 1669. Marcus joined the Dutch chh., N. Y., Nov. 30, 1676, but later took a letter to the French chh. Succeeding to his fa.'s lands, he petitioned

Glaude le Maistre and David des Marest, Sen., declined to subscribe; but the remaining deficiency was to be made up by rent from Jean le Roy for the use of the town lot, being 120 gl.

Few events worth naming marked the close of the winter. 1675. The town court was much occupied with petty cases. On Feb. 4th it was resolved to remind Jan Bos (Terbosch) to pay 25 gl. due "since the year 1667," for an erf charged to him (that bought of Robert le Maire), or to enforce payment in the Mayor's Court. On Feb. 6th, the Jansons, Cornelis and Lourens, completed a division of the lands bought of De Meyer:* Cornelis taking the farm (two lots) on Montagne's Flat, lots No. 18 Jochem Pieters and 15 Van Keulen's Hook, and the two Out-gardens; and Lourens, No. 2 Jochem Pieters and No. 6 Van Keulen's Hook, with the two erven, and also the orchard occupying two north gardens, later forming the John P. Waldron homestead. Lourens' part being of most value, as it included the buildings, he agrees to give his brother 600 gl. This property, as thus divided, composed the beginnings, respectively, of the Kortright and Low estates.

Among the newly-arrived French refugees before noticed was Jean le Comte, with his wife Mary Laurens and one child. For

Nov. 27, 1708, for two vacant tracts next to him, stating that he "hath been an inhabitant of Staten Island, and hath followed husbandry upwards of thirty years past, and hath nine children, four whereof are sons, brought up to husbandry along with him." This was no doubt granted, as by his will, made Dec. 23, 1713, and proved Jan. 27, 1714, he gives each ch. a farm, ranging from 88 to 95 acres. But three sons were then living, viz.: *Job*, who m. Sarah Deny; *Israel*, who m. Gertrude van Deventer; and *Gabriel*. His drs. were *Elizabeth*, w. of Peter Barberie; *Susannah*, w. of Daniel Hendricks; *Mary*, w. of Thomas Eyres; *Dinah*, w. of Hendrick Brees; and *Sarah*, unm. Part of the original Disosway farm, with the old stone house upon it, is still owned and occupied by some of the desc.

* NICHOLAS DE MEYER, originally from the city of Hamburgh, was one of the most enterprising and successful merchants of his day, often visiting Europe in the prosecution of his business. Few men enjoyed so much of the public confidence. He was several times an Alderman of N. Y., and once Mayor. He was chosen a member of Gov. Sloughter's Council, but when the Governor arrived, Mar. 19, 1691, Mr. De Meyer had just d. He left a fine estate, partly in Europe, as we conclude from his son William's will. He m. in 1655 Lydia, dr. of the *Fiskael*, Hendrick van Dyck, and in 1689 Sarah Kellenaer, wid. of Rev. John Weekstein, of Esopus. His chn. were, Johannes, b. 1656; Wilhelmus, b. 1657; Anna-Catrina, b. 1661; Deborah, b. 1664; Elizabeth, b. 1666; and Henricus, b. 1668. Johannes d. before 1689, without issue. (Johannes *De* Meyer, so called, of N. Y., who left a will dated Sept. 13, 1725, was a Meyer, not a *De* Meyer.) Anna-Catrina De Meyer m. 1680 Jan Willems Neering, from Bordeaux, and went

want of a dwelling, they were allowed by the constable, Demarest, to put their household effects in his barn. The father was now prostrated by a sickness which no efforts of the 'chirurgeons' employed could help, and he died May 24th. His personal estate, per inventory taken July 2d, amounted, less expenses, to 606 gl., of which the widow set apart 300 for her little son Moses, who afterward married Claude le Maistre's daughter and settled at Esopus, leaving descendants called De Graaf, which was the Dutch for Le Comte or Lecount.

There had recently arrived at Harlem "a person of quality," as he is styled, Captain James Carteret, descended remotely from the famous Lords de Carteret of the Cotentin in Normandy, and directly allied to the De Carterets, Lords of St. Ouen, in the island of Jersey, noticed in our opening chapter, and at which place various members of the family were now enjoying prominent civic positions.* The captain's father, Sir George De Carteret, Baronet, had been governor of that island as early as 1626, was knighted twenty years later, and now held a seat in the Honorable Privy Council of England, being also "Vice-chamberlain of His Majesty's household;" which eminence he had gained by marked devotion to Kings Charles I. and II. Capt. James Carteret, being the second son, was bred to the sea,

to New Castle, Del.; Deborah m. in 1684 Thomas Crundall, in 1691 Capt. Thomas Lyndon, and in 1697 William Anderson—all Englishmen; Elizabeth m. in 1667 Philip Schuyler, of N. Y., merchant, afterward of Kingston. Henricus De Meyer, of N. Y., merchant, m. 1689 Agnes, dr. of Jacob De Key. He bought his late fa.'s mansion near the Stadt Huys, July 20, 1691, but d. in 1692; in 1696 his wid. m. William Janeway, Esq. Henricus De Meyer left issue, *Lydia*, b. 1691, and *Henricus*, b. 1692. The latter d. in 1739, leaving a dr. Agnes, w. of Edward Nicoll, and of whom my friend Mr. Jos. O. Brown, is a desc. Wilhelmus De Meyer, called in the will of Nicholas the *eldest* son, m. 1678 Catharine Bayard, sr. of Col. Nich. Bayard. He settled in Kingston, Ulster Co., where he inherited property from his fa.; was made deacon in 1681, and elder in 1692. He was much in public life, became lieut.-colonel of militia, and d. in 1710, his w. surviving. His will, dated Jan. 10, 1705, proved Jan. 8, 1711, divides his property "as well in this province as in Europe," among his chn. therein named, being *Lydia*, b. 1681; *Nicholas*, b. 1683; *Anneke*, b. 1685; *Catrina*, b. 1689; and *Deborah*, b. 1693. Lydia m. Andries Douw. Nicholas De Meyer m. Elsie Schoonmaker, and d. on his farm, near Esopus Creek, in 1766, having sons, William, Jeremiah, and Benjamin, and a dr. Catharine, who m. Christopher Kiersted.

* AMICE DE CARTERET and Charles de Carteret, Esquires, were Jurats of the island; Mr. Nicholas de Carteret, Sergeant of Justice, in Greuville Parish; and Edward de Carteret, Knight (uncle of Capt. James), was first Gentleman Usher in Ordinary to the King, and Usher of the "Verge Noire Bailly;" as per an old legal parchment of July 29, 1678, in my possession.

took command of a merchantman in the India trade prior to the Restoration, and subsequently of a British man-of-war. He was captain-general of the forces which in 1666 attempted the recovery of St. Kitts from the French, and later had command of marines in the Duke of York's ship. In 1671, on being made a landgrave of Carolina, of which colony Sir George was part owner, he embarked directly for America to visit his new domains, but bearing also certain instructions and powers from the Lords Proprietors of New Jersey, advisory if not supervisory (as more than his own words plainly show), touching the affairs of that province, over which his younger kinsman, Gov. Philip Carteret, had for several years presided. On coming to New Jersey Capt. Carteret found the people full of complaints against their governor for alleged violations of their rights, and matters growing worse, soon led to an open revolt, and a pressing call upon the senior Carteret to interfere, which the latter felt himself justified in doing. For the details of this short but manly struggle of the people to rid themselves of a supercilious and incompetent ruler, with the sympathy and under the lead of the generous-hearted captain, reference may be had to the annals of that State.* Meanwhile our Carteret, in 1673, married Frances, daughter of Capt. Thomas Delavall; soon after which, submitting to a decision of the king and the Lords Proprietors in favor of Gov. Philip, and to the wishes of his father, he left New Jersey, and in July following, attended by his wife, sailed for Carolina. Unluckily the vessel was taken by the Dutch fleet on its way to the capture of New York, but the Carterets wishing to gain their destination, were set ashore in Virginia. Capt.

* CAPT. CARTERET, in a letter dated Elizabeth Town, in New Jersey, June 14, 1672, and addressed to Gov. Lovelace and Council, in reply to one of theirs, charges Capt. Philip Carteret with having "for several years past threatened and forbidden our people, upon pain of death, not to exercise themselves in military affairs or discipline," besides "other gross miscarriages;" by which he had "unjustly dissatisfied and impoverished the King's subjects in this Province." As to differences between himself and said Philip Carteret, he has no doubt "but they will in time be healed or cured by the Honorable Lords Proprietors, unto whom they are already presented and referred." But he deems "a true understanding," to still quote his words, "unnecessary to be declared to unconcerned persons, seeing that I am not under obligation to render the same to any but to his Majesty, and my superiors, the Lords Proprietors, *by whose orders and instructions I act.* I shall, in an orderly, meek, and peaceable way, endeavor to suppress such as do most falsely, without either show or color of truth, repute me a

Delavall meanwhile, his estates confiscated by the victorious enemy, had returned to England and engaged in merchandise in London. But on the eve of the new governor Andros' departure for New York, to reclaim it from the Dutch, Delavall procured the Duke of York's order for the restitution of all his estate in this colony, with the evident purpose of sending it by Andros. The order, however, was not placed on record here till January 23d, 1675, which was near the date of Carteret's reappearance, empowered to take charge of his father-in-law's property at Harlem; whence we infer that it was recorded and promulgated only when Carteret arrived from Carolina.

Taking part in the public affairs of the town, Capt. Carteret found himself courted for his abilities, and his influence with the ruling powers, Governor Andros being his kinsman. Consequently, when the inhabitants resolved to ask that governor to confirm their patent, Carteret was deputed with others as the bearer of their petition, which was couched in the following words, and for the governor's information was accompanied by "the Great Patent in English," and "the Confirmation in English," both being referred to in the petition.

To his Excellency the Governor General, at *New York*.

We the Constable, Overseers and common Inhabitants at the village of New Haerlem, declare to have constituted and empowered, as by these we do constitute and empower, the Hon. Capt. James Carteret, David des Marest, constable, Joost van Oblinus, overseer, and Resolved Waldron, for and in behalf of this town's jurisdiction and privileges, to request and obtain from his Excellency, the Governor of this province, the maintenance and confirmation of their Patent granted by the late Governor Richard Nicolls, dated the 11th October Ao. 1667, and confirmed by his Excellency, Governor Francis Lovelace, on the date 22d June Ao. 1670; promising for good, durable and of value, to hold and to

disturber of the country. These have very lately published me, by their writs, a rebel and mutineer, *who am proprietor of my father's interest in this Province*. And if God spare life, I will give his Royal Highness an account of them by the first occasion, and after, second it myself by a verbal declaration, how I am used in his territories, as also who they be that have appeared like enemies to king and country." This frank and spirited letter, which does the writer no discredit, may be found, with the one which called it forth, in vol. 4, *General Entries*, Secretary of State's Office, Albany. But advices from England put an end to Capt. Carteret's authority; the king, by letter dated Dec. 9, 1672, directing Capt. John Berry, Dep. Gov. of N. J., to enforce obedience to the laws and government established in that colony by authority of Lord Berkeley and Sir George Carteret.

ratify whatever by the aforesaid, our committee, in the premises, shall be done and executed concerning it, whether the case require greater or special burden, whereupon we shall fully rely and hold our peace; therefore humbly pray your Excellency to be pleased to maintain and protect our liberties and privileges, according to the aforesaid Patents, against every one who may design or think to trouble the same; Wherefor we shall remain your Excellency's good and obedient subjects, *etc.*, the Constable, Overseers and common Inhabitants at the village of N. Haerlem. Done N. Haerlem, 16th June, 1675.

By order of the same,

HENDR. J. VANDR. VIN, *Secretary.*

William Palmer, ship carpenter, was now engaged building a "ketch" at Harlem, and with his family occupied a house as tenant of Capt. Carteret. Etienne Rochelle,* employed by Carteret, went thither on Sunday, July 4th, to pick cherries. He was in one of the trees which stood beside Palmer's house, with Nicholas de Vaux, whom he had asked to assist him in picking, when Palmer came out and roughly bade them get down. Stephen refused, "saying that he had orders from his master to pick cherries." Then Palmer jerked Stephen by the foot, plied him with oyster-shells, and finally took a stick to him, when the latter was forced to leave the tree. Running to tell the constable, and then Waldron, neither of whom were found at home, he was overtaken by Palmer, who had followed him, crying "Papist, Papist!" and who first struck him with his stick, then seized him by the throat and tried to choke him; but Stephen breaking away fled into the house of Meynard Journee. Palmer then turned upon William Noird, Carteret's bookkeeper, who had come to Stephen's aid, and giving him a blow with his stick he also thought best to retreat. Palmer now spit out his spleen before the house of Journee, shaking

* GENEAU, or Gano. See Notes pp. 107, 120. He bought property in New Amsterdam, Apl. 29, 1662; again July 15, 1670, a house and lot in Broadway; and his wife *Lydia Metereu* another, on the Bever Graft, Apl. 22, 1672. In 1676, he was granted 80 acres of land on Staten Island, "near the commons." Geneau was a Huguenot. "Flight or the relinquishment of the Protestant religion was the only means of preserving his life. One of his neighbors had been martyred; he was determined on as the victim for the next day, information of which he received in the dead of the night. He therefore chartered a vessel, removed his family on board, and in the morning was out of sight of the harbor." From his son Francis, whom he brought with him, come all of the name, so far as known. The above extract is from Memoirs written by his desc. Rev. *John Gano*, chaplain in the Am. army in the Revolution, and afterward a pastor in N. Y., and who d. at Frankfort, Ky., in his 78th yr., Aug. 10, 1804.

his stick and uttering threats against the persons within, while Noird, finding Demarest the constable, got an order from him to restrain Palmer from picking the cherries, and delivered it to Palmer's wife. Many of the villagers, brought out of their houses by the uproar, as Cornelis Jansen, Jan Hendricks Kyckuyt (or Brevoort,) Jean le Maistre, Jan Nagel and his wife, and Mrs. Cornier, saw the affray, and the assaults made on Carteret's people. Palmer returning to his house and finding himself served with an injunction from the constable, boiled with rage, and going over to Noird's toward evening, found Daniel Tourneur there engaged in slaughtering a sheep, for which purpose Noird had sent for him. Palmer asked William by whose directions he had procured the constable's order forbidding him to pick cherries. "By my master's," said Noird, "and if I had no orders I should have done it, knowing well how to answer for it." On which Palmer retorted, "Had I been at home as well as my wife, I would have quickly paid you off, and made you find your legs, and possibly the constable the same, though it was Sunday; yes, even though your master had been present."

This breach of the peace was duly reported to the Governor, and an investigation ordered, which took place two days after, Noird taking a copy of the testimony; but we hear no more of it, for news of graver import now filled the minds of the community.

On that self-same Sunday, about three o'clock in the morning, Gov. Andros was aroused from his slumbers to hear the startling intelligence that the Indians had taken up arms at Narragansett, in New England, and murdered some of the settlers; at the head of this rising being the shrewd and powerful chief of the Wampanoags, from whom the bloody conflict which ensued took the name of "King Philip's War." The same evening the Governor sailed with a military force for Connecticut River, but soon returned on finding he was not needed there.

The possibility that the Indians in this province, from sympathy for their brethren at the east, might be induced either to join them or take up the hatchet against our own inhabitants here, led the Governor and Council to the precaution of inviting some of the chiefs to an interview to renew the bond of friendship; seeing no reason for breaking with these tribes "upon account of the war between our neighbors and their Indians." But it was enjoined upon the several towns to maintain a strict watch. And to allay or prevent excitement at Harlem, a message from the Mayor was published in the village, August 9th, charging all there at their peril not to beat the drum nor to hold any meetings, neither to ferry any stranger across the river, without the knowledge and sanction of the constable. This had reference to the practice long in vogue in the town before they had a bell, of beating the drum to call the people together, upon all occasions.*

Verveelen at Spuyten Duyvel was required to exercise all his vigilance. It happened that Jan Hendricksen, alias Kyckuyt, "inhabitant here," having been sent by the constable of Harlem to Fordham, with a warrant that came from New York, arrived at Verveelen's just after sunset. Presently there was a knock at the door, and a messenger from Fordham came in, who said, "Verveelen, I am sent to warn you to come to the watch." Verveelen replied that he could attend to no watch other than to pass people over the ferry, and that there was a person then in the house with a warrant, and who must be ferried over again. But as the other insisted, and argued the risk of refusing, "Let them call me before his Honor the Governor," said the resolute ferryman, "and I will answer them there." The messenger left, but at midnight there came three or four persons before the ferry-house making a great clamor, and trying to force the door, calling upon Verveelen to come to the watch. No heed being paid to them, they finally went away in a great rage. It was then suspected, as it afterward turned out, that no such order had been sent; and this *ruse* to decoy the ferryman from his post of duty while they executed some mischief which they were brewing, had succeeded but for Verveelen's firmness. At this

* The venerable BELL still in use at the Reformed church, 3d avenue and 121st street, is the first within the bounds of Harlem of which we have any knowledge. "It was cast in Holland expressly for this church. Among other metals, it contains twenty dollars' worth of gold and twenty dollars' worth of silver;" at least, so says a communication made by "Knickerbocker" to the *Harlem Traveler*, in January, 1863. The writer probably knew whereof he affirmed, but it would be gratifying could we trace this statement to its source. The bell, only relic of the old stone church erected in 1686, has the following inscription:

AMSTERDAM, ANNO 1734, ME FECIT.

time a most unfriendly feeling existed between Verveelen and Archer. The latter had cut the hay on Verveelen's meadows; the Mayor's Court, to which Verveelen complained Aug. 17th, appointed arbitrators, who decided "that the meadow in controversy belonged to the plaintiff." Nevertheless Archer carried off about four loads of hay, to recover which Verveelen petitioned the Governor and Court of Assize. And during the next winter, "about the month of January," Archer and his confederates went to Verveelen's, and "by force and arms" took out of his house "a quantity of wheat, and divers merchandises and household goods," to the value, as Verveelen alleged, of 980 gl., and to recover which he afterward sued Archer in the Mayor's Court. But we will not anticipate.

Mid-autumn, 1675, brought new alarms. In vain had the Governor a few weeks before issued a proclamation to assure the people of "the falsity of late reports of Indians' ill intents." King Philip's Indians were said to be advancing westward in order to destroy Hartford and other places this way as far as Greenwich. This done, what could stay their onward march to New York? The Governor, to prevent any co-operation on the part of our Indians, immediately directed that their canoes on the shores of the Sound should be laid up where they could not be used, and ordered the Wickquaskeeks at Ann's Hook, now Pelham Neck—then one of their summer haunts, and where to our day are many Indian graves—"to remove within a fortnight to their usual winter quarters within Hellgate upon this island."

This winter retreat was either the woodlands between Harlem Plains and Kingsbridge, at that date still claimed by these Indians as hunting-grounds, or Rechawanes and adjoining lands on the Bay of Hellgate, as the words "within Hellgate" would strictly mean, and which, by the immense shell-beds found there formerly, is proved to have been a favorite Indian resort. That this was the locality referred to, seems indeed to follow from the fact that the Indians, removing in obedience to the above order, attempted to pass up the Harlem River, but were stopped at the village by Constable Demarest. They said they were "going to Wickquaskeek," but could show no pass. Demarest thereupon detained them, and dispatched a letter to the Governor, to which came the following answer:

MR. CONSTABLE,

I have just now seen, by yours of this day sent express by Wm. Palmer, of your having stopt 10 or 12 Indian canoes, with women, children, corn and baggage, coming as they say from Westchester, and going to *Wickers-creek*, but not any Pass mentioned: So that you have done very well in stopping the said Indians and giving notice thereof. These are now to order all the said Indians to stay in your Town, and that you send some of the chiefest of them to me early to-morrow, and one of your Overseers for further orders; and that it may be better effected, you are to order them some convenient house or barn to be in, and draw up their canoes until the return of them you shall send: and that you *double your watch*.

Your Loving Friend,

E. ANDROS.

N. York, Octobr. the 21st, 1675.

A long and restless night, we dare say, was that to some timid souls, with these Indians, friendly but always distrusted, perhaps prowling about their streets and their very doors, despite the utmost vigilance of the watchmen; but the morning came without harm to any, and the unwelcome visitors soon departed.

All the settlements, indeed, were in a state of feverish anxiety, and taking measures for defence. The people of Fordham erected fortifications, and "Archer, proprietor of the Town," called upon all the neighbors round to come "into his town" and assist. But four families seated on the Yonker's Land near Spuyten Duyvel, including those of John Heddy, William Betts, and his son-in-law, George Tippett, "being removed from Mr. Archer his town above a mile, and being strong enough, or thought so, to resist this heathenish war, having a good and strong blockhouse," objected "to leave their houses and goods, to please the humors of the said Mr. Archer," and therefore at their request were excused by the Governor from going to Fordham.

On Oct. 16th Andros had ordered all the towns to keep "double and strict watches," and to the Harlem people on the 21st, as seen, had reiterated the caution, "Double your watch." This was complied with, so far as was practicable at that busy season, when much of the fall work was yet to be done, but with the setting in of winter the Night Watch was formally organized as follows; the Governor, at the town's charge, furnishing powder, "for the Indian war."

On the 6th December. Ao. 1675, Monday.

Present: Their Honors, Jan Dyckman, *Constable.*
Joost van Oblinus.
Resolved Waldron.
Meynard Journee.

The following are, according as they rank, appointed upon the *Night Watch*, organized by order of his Excellency the Governor-General, and divided into four *Corporalships*, each consisting of seven persons, to wit:

I.

1. Adolph Meyer, *Corporal.*
2. Meynard Journee.
3. David des Marest.
4. Daniel Tourneur.
5. Nicolaes de Vaux.
6. Isaac Kip.
7. Jan Hendricks Boch.

II.

1. Jan Nagel, *Corporal.*
2. Joost van Oblinus.
3. Jan Hendricks Kyckuyt.
4. Jan le Maistre.
5. Johannes Vermelje.
6. Jean le Roy.
7. Isaac le Maistre.

III.

1. Simeon Cornier, *Corporal.*
2. Cornelis Jansen.
3. Samuel des Marest.
4. Laurens Jansen.
5. William Palmer.
6. Jaco el Roe.*
7. Gerard Magister.

IV.

1. Robert Hollis, *Corporal.*
2. Resolved Waldron.
3. Arent Hermensen.
4. Coenrad Hendricks Boch.
5. David des Marest, Jun.
6. Cornelis Theunissen.
7. Isaac See, Jun.

1st. The whole or half corporalships, whose turn it is to watch, shall, in the evening, at the hour of eight, upon beat of the drum, be in full number at the watch-house, shall place their sentinels, and take the necessary rounds; and shall not retire before the beating of the morning *reveille;* upon a forfeiture, fixed or to be fixed, of 3 guilders.

2d. Whoever neglects the watch without a lawful cause, or making the same known to his corporal beforehand, shall each time forfeit 6 guilders.

3d. Each watchman coming to the watch shall be provided with suitable side and hand arms; also with sufficient powder and lead, upon forfeit of 6 guilders.

4th. The watch shall be kept quietly, without much calling or noise, upon penalty of 3 guilders.

* JACQUES LAROE was b. in 1657. From his name, and affiliation with the French refugees, we conclude he was himself French, though Vander Vin, usually careful, writes his surname, the first two or three times, *el Roey* or *el Roeyl*, and finally adopts the form of *el Roe.* As he must have had warrant for this, probably Jacques was of mixed blood, Spanish and Walloon. He is always called by Vander Vin, *Jaco*, a juvenile form of his name used by the Walloons. In 1677 Jacques joined the church in N. Y., but the next year accompanied the Demarests to Hackensack. Here he m. Wybrecht, dr. of Hendrick Teunisz Helling. She was five years younger than he, and bore him sons, *Peter, Hendrick, Samuel, Abraham, Johannes*, and as many drs. On the decline of the French Church of *Kinderkamack*, which he must have helped to form, he took a letter to the Dutch Church, Hackensack, Apl. 5, 1696. We think this family, under the name Laroe, has become widely extended, at least in the States of N. Y. and N. J.

The Indian excitement continued through the winter and spring, 1676. Suspicions were entertained that the Wickquaskeeks (or Wickers-creeks, as now commonly called) intended to join "the North Indians." But some eighteen of these, with their sachems and "Claes ye Indian," visited the Governor, Jan. 7th, bringing a present of venison and deer-skins, and renewed their pledge of friendship. The Governor assured them of his continued good-will and desire to protect them, but said that as they had now gone out of his reach he could not "mind them as before." Then, to quote the record of the interview, "the Governor in return would give them coates, but they desired drink, which is ordered for them."

Upon this hint the Indians asked leave to return to their old maize lands on Manhattan Island; whereupon the Governor and Council, on February 6th, passed the following:

"*Resolved*, That the Wickers-creek Indians, if they desire it, be admitted with their wives and children, to plant upon this Island, but nowhere else, if they remove; and that it be upon the north point of the Island near Spuyten Duyvel."

Still the settlers at Harlem were on the alert. On March 2d the Night Watch was reorganized, each corporal's squad being composed of five instead of six. The corporals were now: 1st, *Lourens Jansen*; 2d, *Arent Hermansen Bussing*; 3d, *Adolph Meyer*; and, 4th, *Jan Nagel*. For various reasons the following names disappear from the roll, to wit: Journee, Tourneur, Kip, Le Roy, Cornier, C. Jansen, Palmer, Hollis, and See; and the following new ones appear:

Barent Waldron,
Michiel Bastiaensen,
Reyer Michielsen,
Hendrick Kiersen,
Frederick de Vaux.

The last of these persons, born in the Walloon country, had lately left the Lower Palatinate, with many other French, on account of the troubles there; De Vaux coming *viâ* England to join his brother Nicholas in this country. He was now a widower, but a little later married a daughter of Daniel Tourneur deceased, from which union sprang the respectable De Voo family in the lower sections of Westchester County, first seated at

De Voe's Point, near which Frederick obtained by his wife a fine property.*

On April 8th the Council "ordered that all boats and vessels that pass through Hellgate do take a permit from the Custom House, by reason of the Indian troubles, which permit (unless for merchandise) to be given gratis and with all dispatch."

But now fear of the Indians gradually subsided; the Wickquaskeeks proving their friendship sincere, had their canoes restored to them. The close of the war at the eastward consequent upon the death of King Philip, who with many of his warriors was slain, Aug. 12th, in the great swamp fight near Mount Hope, was a principal means of allaying apprehension.

The ordinary domestic interests were not neglected amid all this public disquietude, and the extra drafts upon the time and energies of the inhabitants. Planting and harvesting allowed of no interruption. A common fence inclosed their cultivated lands on Jochem Pieters Flat and on Van Keulen's Hook, and no partition fences were yet set up; the lots being merely staked off that every one could know and make use of his own. Strict rules were required to maintain these common fences; so important since the entire planting of the community was at the mercy of any one member through whose neglect to keep up his part cattle might get in and destroy; and none so offending but had to meet the public frown, if not a lawsuit to recover losses. When new fence-masters were appointed April 24th, 1675—Cornelis Jansen and Conrad Hendricks, to succeed Arent Hermens and David Demarest, Jr.—it was resolved that each inhabitant

* Frederick de Vaux's passport, brought with him from Mannheim, is still preserved. We are indebted for a copy in German to one of his descendants, Col. Thomas F. De Voe, of New York. Here follows a translation.

"WE, DIRECTOR, SHERIFF, BURGOMASTER, and COUNCIL of the Electoral Paltz City MANNHEIM, hereby make known and publish, that the bearer of this, *Frederick de Vaux*, late a Burgher of this city, for his own business is intending to travel in Holland, and from thence further to England; in which behalf every one is requested to let the said *Frederick de Vaux* pass free, safe, and unmolested, at all places, and also to show him all good will and consideration; we engaging to do the same for every city, according to merit. In witness hereof, we have attached our usual Seal. Done at Mannheim, this 23d February, old style, Anno one thousand six hundred and seventy-five."

{ SEAL. }

should forthwith repair his part of the common fencing, and that by the spring of 1670 these fences should be generally renewed and made at least 5½ feet high, English measure; and any one failing it should be done by the town at his expense. Again, Nov. 22d, because of daily and manifold complaints of damage done by horses and cattle running upon the sowed lands, an ordinance was passed and posted up requiring the fences still unrepaired to be attended to within fourteen days punctually, under penalty of 25 guilders for every case of neglect; and also repeating the former order, that by the 1st of March ensuing all the common fences should be built anew, with posts and six rails, 5½ feet high English measure, upon the same penalty; and further, no one should let his calves or other beasts run within the sowed land *without a herder*, as any such being found trespassing upon another man's grain would subject its owner to a fine of 12 gl.

The yeomen were already much straitened in the breadth of their acres. In other words, the need of more arable land to meet the growing wants of the old residents and the newly-arrived families was becoming urgent. The town had reached a point in its history when the limited amount of improved land was mostly absorbed by the older and well-to-do settlers, who, aiming to enlarge rather than to reduce their area, held their lands at a high price. It was not easy to purchase any, except perchance an estate was to be closed up, or it happened that parties were leaving the town, as was the case this year with Journee and Le Roy, who removed to Staten Island: whither also went the Sees, father and son, unable to suit themselves with land here.*

With the immobility of Dutchmen, and moreover as a matter of policy, the present freeholders had been slow to move in a

* The See family, whose name in early records takes the several forms of *Cie, du Cie*, *Sieck*, *Zy*, and *Sie*, consisted, so far as appears, of the heads, Isaac See and w. Esther, their son Isaac, Jr., and dr. Maria, w. of Nicholas de Vaux. The w. of Isaac, Jr., was also named Maria. The Sees obtained two farms, 104 acres, on Karle's Neck, S. I., by patent of Sept. 29, 1677. But after living there some years, they removed to Philips Manor, Westchester Co., the fa. and son appearing as church-members at Sleepy Hollow, or Tarrytown, in 1697. Then the name was usually written *Sie*. Isaac and Maria had sons, *Peter*, b. in Europe; *Jacob*, b. 1675; *Simon*, b. 1679, etc. The family is still numbered among the most respectable residents there, and from its branches have come several well-known clergymen.

further division of the common lands, which might tend to lessen the value of the improved farms. Their aim was, if possible, to retain the control of these lands, and hence the anxiety to secure new confirmations of their patent from the successive governors. But the late petition to Andros for his confirmation, interfered with doubtless by the Indian troubles, had effected nothing; while, on the other hand, the governor was beset with applications for land upon Manhattan Island, and which he resolved to satisfy by dividing up various tracts of woodland among such applicants as were most worthy, and would undertake to clear and improve their grants. At this the Harlem freeholders took alarm, especially as they understood that these grants were to extend to the unappropriated lands within their own patent. No time was lost, therefore, in preparing a second memorial to Gov. Andros in these terms:

To his Excellency the Governor General at *New York*.

The Constable, Magistrates and Inhabitants of the Town of New Haerlem respectfully represent that your petitioners have understood and been informed by their Constable and Joost van Oblinus that your Excellency's purpose is to distribute the lands lying within their town's jurisdiction, for bouweries and plantations; wherefore they the petitioners and undersigned request that each may be allowed a part of the same to build upon and plant, etc. Remaining meanwhile your Excellency's most willing subjects. New Haerlem, Wednesday, 30th August, 1676.

Conradus Hendricks,	Gerard Magister,
Jan Hendricks,	David des Marest, Jun.,
Jan Nagel,	Jaco el Roe,
Arent Hermensen,	Samuel des Marest,
Jan le Maistre,	Adolph Meyer,
Cornelis Jansen,	Frederick de Vaux,
Laurens Jansen,	Isaac le Maistre,
Pierre Cresson,	Glaude le Maistre,
Nicholas de Vaux,	Abraham le Maistre,
Hendrick J. Vander Vin,	Barent Waldron,
David des Marest,	François Breteau.

Andros favored this application, but as none of the magistrates had signed it, he referred it to them to make out and present him a list of those to whom such grants might properly be made. This they prepared, omitting the petitioners Cresson, Vander Vin, David des Marest, Jun., El Roe, the Le Maistres, and Breteau; and designating instead Jan Dyckman, Resolved Waldron, Joost and Pieter van Oblinus, Jan Louwe Bogert, and

Jean Baignoux—but the last named, who was a tenant of Mr. Verveelen, was erased from the list, Andros making him a special grant upon Hoorn's Hook. The list was headed: "Persons for land in Harlem bounds, given in by ye Constable and overseers as fitt persons, ye 4th of 7^ber, 1676."*

Pending the new grants, the town employed Robert Ryder, government surveyor, to run out the lot lines on Van Keulen's Hook, in order to assign each owner his proper quantity or at least to equalize them, as these lots had never been accurately surveyed, and nearly all were known to much exceed the prescribed three morgen or six acres. The survey, finished before the close of 1676, put most of the owners who had inclosed and built upon the north ends of these lots to the necessity of shifting their fences.†

William Waldron, eldest son of Resolved, had learned the cooper's trade, and established himself in New York, where he married the daughter of the wealthy Stoutenburgh, city treasurer, and now enjoyed the position of inspector of pipe-staves. He and his partner Jan Pietersen, undertaking to cut timber for use in their business, in the common woods upon Hoorn's Hook, the town officers stopped them, upon the ground that they were non-residents. The coopers made their plaint to the Mayor's

* François Breteau, as he signs his name, was sometimes styled "Frenchman." Vander Vin wrote his name *Bertou*, showing how pronounced. If he, as we suspect, was the same with François *Beado*, mentioned on page 318, he was b. in London in 1646. About the date of this petition for land, Breteau was in the employ of Glaude de Maistre; but no land being granted him, he procured soon after 12 acres at Flushing. He petitioned, Sept. 28, 1680, for more land, giving as a reason that he had nine chn. to support. He was still living there, with his wife Mary, in 1698, having sons John and Francis. These two married and had families; John had sons, *John*, b. 1709, who removed to Vermont, and *Francis*, b. 1711, who settled at Hempstead, L. I., in which localities, respectively, their desc. are still found. See *N. Y. G. & B. Rec.*; and *Bartow Genealogy*, by Rev. Evelyn Bartow.

† The Out-Gardens, "lying at the west side of the village" (see pp. 246, 256, 292), were also "laid out by numbers," Feb. 5, 1677. On Jan. 5, 1667, record was made that Tourneur had gotten No. 1 from Claesten in exchange for No. 11, and 3 from Delamater for 19, and 4 from De Meyer for 10, "called Jan Cogu's garden." Later he got 5, 6, from Delavall, who let Verveelen have 7, 8. Lubbert Gerritsen exchanged No. 16 for 11; but Demarest buying 11, gave it back to the town, being allowed to "survey" 16 instead. The present owners were: *Daniel Tourneur*, Nos. 1 to 6; *Johannes Verveelen*, 7, 8; *Cornelis Jansen*, 9, 10; *The Dorp*, 11; *Joost van Oblinus*, 12, 13, 14; *Thomas Delavall*, 15; *David Demarest*, 16, 17, 18; *Glaude Delamater*, 19, 20.

Court, November 14th, against the "Constable of Harlem and several other Inhabitants, for discharging them from cutting of wood upon this Island, just against Hellgate, not being within fence." To the surprise of the defendants the case went against them; this decision being rendered:

IT is *Ordered*, That the said William Waldron and John Petersen may cut timber upon this Island, within one mile of any plantation fence; and the timber already cut they to carry away; and the town to pay the charges.

The approaching winter promised but little leisure. The inhabitants had been called upon to cut and draw to the water side 5000 stockades twelve feet long and four inches thick, to be used in making "a harbor before the City of New York." They met Oct. 3d, formed themselves into four corporalships, and apportioned the work; choosing as corporals Laurens Jansen, Arent Bussing, Adolph Meyer, and Jan Nagel. Another call was from Vander Vin, the clerk, whose house had become unfit to live in. At his request it was resolved at a meeting in October to remove him for the winter into the school-house (or church), after it should be repaired and adapted to the purposes of a dwelling by putting in a bedroom (*bedstede*), chimney, and mantel, and making the door and windows tight. It was further decided "to repair (*vermaeken*) the old house the following spring." In repairing the school-house, the elder Demarest was employed upon the work in "the loft," and also put a lock upon the door and glazed the windows, while Floris Gerritsen, mason, did the plastering. Gerard Magister at the same time made three new "sitting benches, in the church."

But David Demarest, Jr., offended, maybe, because he had been dropped from the list of those recommended to have land given them, declared to Daniel Tourneur that he would not contribute toward the repairs upon the town-house. Tourneur bade him consider that in such case he could have no privilege in the town. Demarest angrily replied, "What have you to say, since you have been magistrate a day or two? Hold your peace; I will not give to it; you do your best." The town court took the matter up Dec. 7th. Tourneur demanded that it should maintain its right and authority, in which view agreeing, it ordered the defendant to pay 12 gl. to the deacons and the court charges.

The elder Demarest and Glaude Delamater, giving reasons which will appear, had for some time ceased to contribute to Vander Vin's support, the first being two years in arrears and the latter three. The matter was referred to the Mayor's Court, which on Nov. 7th, passed an order that "the Clerk of the Parish be continued in his place, and have his pay what is behind, and for the future as formerly."

The two refractory persons paying no heed to this order, were now waited upon, Dec. 19th, by the constable, Resolved Waldron, and Adolph Meyer, magistrate, to demand from them the payment of their dues. Demarest refused, but added, "*If the Heer Governor* order that I pay it, I shall do it." Said Delamater, "If you will have it, you must fetch it out of my house, for I will not give it." Again after ten days the same persons, taking another magistrate (Tourneür) with them, repeated the demand. Demarest, still stout in his refusal, answered, "I will not pay before the Court of Sessions decide that I must." Delamater's answer now was, "I must first see the town accounts for six years; would you otherwise have it, you must take it out of my house." On Feb. 5th the same officers, with another magistrate, Jan Louwe Bogert, went to Demarest's house, but he was not at home. They then called upon Delamater, but with no success. "I shall not pay," said Glaude, at this third interview; "you must take it out of my house, and then I will appeal to the High Council."

The baffled officers hesitated to distrain upon their goods for the debt; but after another month's delay again applied for power to do so to the Mayor's Court, which on March 6th, 1677, issued the following ample order:

FROM the City of *New York* to the Town of *Harlem*.

THE Court order, *that* Hendrick Jansen Vander Vin, the Clerk of the said Town, be continued in his place according to former order, and have his pay, what is behind and for the future as formerly by the Inhabitants; and if they or any of them refuse to pay what is due from them for the time past, and for the time to come, then the Constable is hereby ordered to levy the same by distress and sale of the goods, for satisfaction of what is or shall hereafter become due to the said Clerk.

On April 3d citations were issued to Demarest and Delamater to appear before the town court on the 5th instant. Glaude appeared. The constable as plaintiff, demanded that the order of

March 6th should be enforced. The defendant stated that they of the French congregation, in the time of Gov. Francis Lovelace, having received a preacher, the aforesaid governor had said that "the French of the Town of New Harlem should be free as to contributing to the Dutch voorleser."* He demanded that this might be deemed sufficient, and that the court should carry out the order they had from the Mayor's Court so as they were advised to. But the court would not allow this plea, and directed execution for the amount of the debt and costs. Forthwith the magistrates (except Arent Hermensen, Delamater's son-in-law) proceeded in a body to the defendant's house to levy upon his goods. Finding nothing suitable at hand, the constable told him that on Wednesday evening (April 11th) he would take one of his cows out of his stable and sell her at public vendue, to satisfy the debt. Delamater replied scornfully, "You may as well take her now; why have you to wait so long?"

* Rev. PIERRE DAILLÉ is said to have been the first "pastor" of the French Church in New York. But according to the reference in the text, a "preacher" had preceded him by ten years or more, whose name, however, is unknown to us. The statement is of interest as showing that the refugees at N. Y. and H. joined to introduce and sustain the French service as early as 1674. A better organization followed on the arrival of Mr. Daillé, of whom Do. Selyns, in a letter of Oct. 21, 1683, thus speaks: "Do. Peter Daillé, late professor at Saumur, has become my co-laborer, and conducts the French worship. He is full of fire, godliness, and learning. Banished on account of his religion, he maintains the cause of Jesus Christ with untiring zeal." With others of his family, Mr. Daillé first took refuge in Holland; but must have been some months in this colony at the date of Selyns' letter, as he organized a church at New Paltz, Jan. 22, 1683. (*Du Bois Reunion*, p. 8; and compare *Doc. Hist. of N. Y.*, iii. 472, 1167.) The date of the organization at N. Y. may be nearly indicated by letters taken from the Dutch chh. in order to unite with the French, the earliest of these noticed being those of our Marc Disosway and wife, which are dated June 7, 1683. Mr. Daillé extended his labors to neighboring French communities, and probably aided in organizing the church of Kinkachemeck, near Hackensack, of which the Demarests were chief promoters. He evidently revived that upon Staten Island, where the church established as early as 1664, by Demarest and others, had declined, till there was "neither church nor minister," as the French residents told the Labadist travellers in 1679. The Revocation of the Edict of Nantes added to his flock many French families, who came by way of London, South Carolina, and St. Kitts. Though disapproving Leisler's course, Mr. Daillé's sympathies were so stirred at his impending fate, that he circulated for signatures, at Harlem and elsewhere, a petition for his pardon, but for this humane act was called to account by the General Assembly. Rev. Pierre Peiret, before a minister in France, but expelled for the cause of religion, arriving, with other refugees, at New York from London, Nov. 19, 1687, soon after formed a second church, and

On April 11th the court ordered another citation to be served on Demarest, who had not appeared, and meanwhile to delay the execution against Delamater. Demarest, in no very amiable mood, appeared before the court on the 14th. The constable inquired why he had neglected to obey the order of the Mayor's Court after being so many times notified. Demarest said that he was not cited to answer before the Mayor's Court, and that the Heer Governor had told him that he was not bound to pay. He said further, that the Mayor's Court was wrongly informed of the case; adding that the constable, Jan Louwe, and Daniel Tourneur were parties in this prosecution, and the secretary the instigator. Yet as he intends to remove out of this town, he will pay or cause it to be paid, but not if he should not leave. "You people," said he, meaning all the magistrates, "are my enemies, and seek but to drive me into costs." The court seem to have let this ebullition of feeling pass unnoticed. The contest was ended as to Demarest, who having promised, kept his word. Delamater, however, held out, and the magistrates hesitating to use extreme measures, the case thus rested for several years.

became its pastor. He was deemed very learned. In 1692 the two French churches united, agreeing to give an equal support to both pastors; Mr. Peiret to perform service in the city, and Mr. Daillé in the country, as he had loved to do. The latter, in 1696, accepted a call to Boston, returning the next year to marry a second wife, and occasionally thereafter coming to N. Y., as in 1703, when he sold a house and lot in Broadway, and again three years before his death, which was probably his last visit to his old flock. This devoted minister, long remembered by the Harlem French for his eloquence and excellence, closed his earthly labors May 21, 1715, in his 67th year. Mr. Peiret continued to serve the church in N. Y. with general approbation, to the time of his death, Sept. 1, 1704, having attained his 60th year. He was buried the next day "in the common cemetery of this city." The consistory and people agreed to pay his widow an extra year's salary. He was succeeded by Rev. James Laborie, late Indian missionary at Oxford, Mass. For some years the church had worshipped in a plain structure near the Fort; that is, on the south side of Marketfield Street, also called Petticoat Lane, which had become in a sense the French quarter. Only the year before Mr. Peiret's death they bought a lot in Pine Street, and were engaged in building the unique stone church which stood till 1834, and witnessed the labors of Peiret's successors down to the late Dr. Verren. Trinity Churchyard contains Mr. Pieret's tombstone, with an inscription in both Latin and French, the first, as follows, copied some years ago with difficulty, it being almost illegible.

Hic jacet Reverd. Dom. Petrus Peiretus, V. D. Mr. qui ex Gallia religionis causa expulsus, verbum Dei in hujus civitatis Ecclesia Gallicana per annis 17 cum generali approbatione prædicavit quique. Cum vitam prædicationibus suis conformem duxerit usque, ad 60um ætatis suæ annum tandem in manus Domini spiritum humiliter deposuit 1 mens. Sept. Ann. Dom. 1704.

Demarest was now engrossed with a scheme of some magnitude—the purchase from the Indians of a large tract of land on the Hackensack River, with the "declared purpose of making a settlement of 30 or 40 families, to be transported from Europe." He and his son David contracted with Paulus Richard, of New York, merchant, apparently on the same date, March 12th, 1677, to sell him their property in Harlem, but only the deed from David, Jun., has been found, given April 12th, pursuant to the articles of sale previously executed. On June 8th ensuing, Demarest effected his Indian purchase of 2000 acres, to which he prepared to remove with his entire family, including Jacque el Roe, on the 1st of May, 1678, until which date the two Davids had reserved the use of their respective dwellings, the father then occupying his "new house." *

* RICHARD had an old claim of 1600 gl. against Demarest, sen., and the late Tourneur. How it originated we know not, unless from what follows. Demarest having bought Montagne's farm, failed to meet the second payment (but had paid Jacob Vis, on Montagne's order, 180 gl. sewant); when Montagne sued him, Oct. 6, 1666, and citing the articles of sale, demanded back the farm. Demarest said his default was caused by Allard Anthony having stopped the payment—that yesterday, Daniel Tourneur, acting for said Anthony's brother-in-law, had arrested 300 gl. for claims against Montagne. The court ordered the land to be given up, but on an appeal to the Mayor's Court, Oct. 9, it reversed the decision, holding "that the sale of the land in question shall stand fast." But Demarest must pay his second instalment (less the 180 gl.) within fourteen days. The amount due could hardly have exceeded 600 gl., but Richard (we only presume that this was the occasion) advanced Demarest and Tourneur together 1600, and the town officers became their surety. This appears from the following letter (suggesting that Tourneur's loan was for the town's use), indorsed by Richard, "Obligation to pay from Daniel Tourneur and David Demarest."

Ao. 167$\frac{3}{4}$ the 23d Feb., N. Harlem.

Honored friend Cellile Richard :

Whereas we have duly received yours of the 19th, so these serve for answer: As your husband has agreed, with Daniel Tourneur and David Demarest, that he will wait yet one year, by their paying interest upon the sixteen hundred guilders, so it is that we by these accept it, and shall take measures the next year for the payment, as this year we have some other burdens. Farewell.

D. Tourneur.
David des Marest.
Pieter Roelefsen, *Constable*,
Resolvert Waldron.

This was cancelled, Mar. 12, 1677, upon the elder Demarest selling out to Richard, and the letter returned, with the following on the back:

"Acknowledged paid, etc., being from date for standing obligation. Done, New York, the 12th March, 167$\frac{6}{7}$. Paulus Richard."

The 19th of February, this year, was given to making provision for the town debts and the discharge of other public business. Quoting from the record :

At a meeting held Monday, 19th February, 1676–7. *Present:* Their Honors, Resolved Waldron, constable; Jan Louwe van Schoonrewoerdt, Adolph Meyer, Arent Hermens, Daniel Tourneur; with the advice of Joost van Oblinus, old magistrate, and Jan Dyckman, late constable.

It is resolved and found good to reckon up the debts, for which the town is now in arrears, and must pay; and to make an assessment upon the lands and house-lots (*erven*) lying within this town, to discharge the said debts; and there is found to be due to—

Reynier Willems, balance	*f.*253: 0
Paulus Richard, balance	21:15
Jan Louwe	5: 0
Joost van Oblinus	26: 0
Hendr. J. Vandr. Vin	31: 0
Glaude le Maistre, 2 schepels wheat	12: 0
Resolved Waldron, ½ vat of beer	15: 0
Jan Dyckman, board money to Surveyor	8: 0
Frederick Gysberts	57:10
Nicolaes Bayard	24: 0
For extraordinary expenses	46:15
Total	*f.*500: 0

An assessment made on the lands and house-lots, to pay and discharge the foregoing 500 guilders; whereof one third was put upon the house-lots and two thirds on the lands, and upon each house-lot comes 8 guilders and on each morgen 2 guilders, to wit :

Richard took this property, obviously, in payment of this claim; or at least the claim was part of the consideration paid by Richard for said property. He got his deed from David, jun., Apl. 12, 1677, and the same day reconveyed what it covered (house and lot, barn, lot 11 Jochem Pieters, lot 1 Van Keulen's Hook, and meadows) to Joost van Oblinus, for 2400 gl. in sewant. He disposed of the property late of David, sen., in the course of the year, as follows: On July 1, the 2 houses and lots, barn, and 7 Jochem Pieters, to Oblinus, for 4000 gl., in grain; on Aug. 1, No. 4 Jochem Pieters to Adolph Meyer, for 845 gl., in grain, and 3 Out-gardens, Nos. 16, 17, 18, to Arent Harmans, for 700 gl.; on Nov. 17, the half of No. 5, V. K. Hook, to Laurens Jansen, for 400 gl., and lot No. 4 Montagne's Flat (since in the Nutter farm) to Cornelis Jansen, for 400 gl. All these to pay in grain or tobacco. Two north gardens, described in the senior Demarest's patent, 1671, as "betwixt Glaude le Maitre and the Poor's Garden," meaning the Church Farm, were added to the latter. On Nov. 27, 1691, Paul Richard gives a receipt, having "settled in full with Joost Obline's wife, for two farms (*twee bowery*) lying in the town of New Harlem." Richard (see p. 53) was twice alderman. He m., 1664, wid. Celitie Vanderwal, from Christianstadt. A dr., Hester (Mrs. Le Fort), was mysteriously murdered Oct. 19, 1699. Their son Stephen, b. 1670, had 10 chn., one being Paul Richard, mayor of N. Y. from 1735 to 1739.

Glaude le Maistre*	2	erven.	15	morgen.	*f*. 46
Laurens Jansen	2	"	9	"	34
Cornelis Jansen			9	"	18
" " on the Flat			2	"	4
David des Marest, Jr.	1	"	9	"	26
Daniel Tourneur	1½	"	18	"	48
Jan Dyckman	½	"			4
Conrad Hendricks	1	"	6	"	20
Johannes Verveelen	2	"	9	"	34
Adolph Meyer	1	"	6	"	20
David des Marest	1	"	14	"	36
Joost van Oblinus	3	"	12	"	48
Nicholas de Vaux	1	"	9	"	26
Resolved Waldron	2	"	15	"	46
Jan Nagel	½	"	12	"	28
Johannes Vermelje			1	"	2
Jan le Maistre	1	"	3	"	14
Jan Louwe			16	"	32
Isaac Kip	1	"			8
Arent Hermens	½	"			4
Pieter Cresson	¼	"			2
					f. 500

The foregoing sums must be paid, at furthest, by the last of March next ensuing, punctually, without any delay, or exception, in good merchantable grain, upon penalty, etc.

Most of the inhabitants were present at this meeting of Feb. 19th, 1677. Some action was expected "in regard to the shifting of the fences on Van Keulen's Hook," but nothing was resolved upon. Weightier matters claimed attention. No little concern was felt at the silence of Gov. Andros in regard to his promise to distribute more land among them, and at reports of the large grants he was intending to make in their immediate vicinity and even within their limits. It was therefore resolved to send another committee to his Excellency, requesting him to grant the lands lying within their jurisdiction only to the actual residents, according to their petition of August 30th preceding, "and further to be maintained in the rights of their patent."

Capt. James Carteret was named first on this committee. Apparently he had just returned from a voyage to England. He had taken from Vander Vin, April 5th, 1676, a statement of Capt. Delavall's indebtedness to the town, being 243 gl. 16 st.

* "N.B. Glaude le Maistre has not more than 9 morgen of land, so that in the foregoing is put by mistake 6 morgen too much." Note in the original.

Between the dates of May 9th and Dec. 5th ensuing, no mention of him here has been found, and he now held deeds of lease and release, dated London, Aug. 7th and 8th, 1676, from his father-in-law, for the mill property, the Moesman farm, and Little Barent's Island; in which instruments Delavall is described as "late of New York in America, and now of London, merchant," and Carteret also as "of London." Delavall had been prompted to this gift, as he says, "in consideration of the natural love and affection which the said Thomas Delavall beareth to the said James Carteret and Frances his wife, the daughter of the said Thomas Delavall, and for divers other good causes." With his usual caution, Delavall signed the lease only, reserving his signature to the deed till he should return himself to America. Perhaps Delavall was afraid the captain's creditors might get it. A little episode may suffice here.

On his first coming to Harlem, about the 1st of April, 1675, "having occasion for a horse to employ," Carteret sent his man Willer to borrow one of William Sturt. But it happened that the horse took sick and died "within three or four days after his return." Sturt declared that the animal "was overridden and much misused," and when more than a year had passed sued the captain for damages. But Willer having left, the captain was placed at a disadvantage in the matter of witnesses when the trial came on, Dec. 5th, 1676. "Daniel Tourneur, sworn, saith that he saw the horse in question at Harlem, and that the man told him that the horse failed him at Freshwater, and that he was forced *to lead him* forewards and backwards between York and Harlem." Sturt demanded £12 for the horse and £5 "for the want of said horse and expences in his sickness." The jury and court found for the plaintiff. But Carteret objected to the price put upon the steed; and this point was referred to arbitrators, who reduced the valuation to £8; whereupon the court, March 20th, 1677, "order a horse of that value to be delivered before next court day, or judgment to be entered against Carteret to that amount and costs of suit." Carteret was delinquent, and on April 3d execution issued; but the next year came round and it was not yet satisfied, when Sturt, getting the court to reaffirm its former judgment, left soon after to become town clerk at Pemaquid. But to return.

Besides Carteret, the committee to wait upon the governor consisted of Adolph Meyer and Daniel Tourneur from the magistracy, and Jan Dyckman and Laurens Jansen from the community. The committee reported on Feb. 24th that at their interview with Andros he said he had understood from David Demarest that the people of New Harlem had not needed nor desired any land. But that now he would send the surveyor, within eight days or thereabouts, and "they of New Harlem might themselves lay out the land as was convenient, because he had no knowledge of this place."

It is hard to say what designs Andros may have had regarding the Harlem lands, or whether he ever seriously intended to override the Harlem patent. There is some reason to believe that he did. But if so, he came to think better of it; and while he did not formally confirm their patent, he recognized it by allowing the Harlem people to dispose of their common lands in their own way. Nothing could have suited them better, and the concession was important as tending to settle their rights. They had to congratulate themselves on their own vigilance and efforts, and especially to thank Capt. Carteret, whose name with six others was now added to those who were to draw land.

Ryder finally came, and spent fourteen days in making the surveys. He had been occupied during the intervening time in laying out several farms along the East River, in a range extending from Kip's Bay to Hoorn's Hook; forming, within the recollection of many, the charming rural seats of Winthrop, Hoffman, Buchanan, Pearsall, the Beekmans, Jones, Riker and Lawrence, the Delafields and Schermerhorn. Beginning at Kip's Bay, the grants were 30 acres to Gabriel Carbosie, 60 to David du Four and son, 60 to Rev. Jacobus Fabricius, 30 to Cornelis Matthysen, 60 to John Bassett, 38½ to George Elphinstone, 32½ to Jacob Young, and 30 to Jean Baignoux. The last three fell partly within the Harlem patent.* That to Elphinstone, which lapped upon the southern end of this patent (at 74th Street, including within its limits the Saw Kill); and that next, granted to Young and "bounded to the north-east by the

* See Notes on these Titles from Carbosie to Bassett, in the *N. Y. Corp. Manual* for 1869, pp. 881–887; also *Abstracts of Farm Titles*, by H. Croswell Tuttle.

commons or a certain run of water"—were surveyed on April 25th. Beignoux's farm was run out adjoining to Young, on July 20th. The grants were "to be confirmed by patent when begun to be improved." The first patent was issued to Young, May 1st, 1677, the other two not till Sept. 29th following, and they were subject severally to a quit-rent or annual render to the government of "half a bushel of good winter wheat." In the interim, 30 acres on the North River side, upon the hills next below Moertje Davids' Fly, and running into "the Commons of Harlem," were granted and set off July 9th to Hendrick Bosch, a sword-cutler, and originally from Leyden. Elphinstone had erected a leather mill and other buildings upon his tract, with the assistance of a copartner, Abraham Shotwell, late of New Jersey, to whom (probably in view of what followed) the patent was made out. On Oct. 30th Elphinstone sold all his interest in the farm, houses, and mill to Shotwell, who in payment gave his obligation, in the form of a mortgage, for £52:10s.*

With genuine sagacity, the people of Harlem resolved to secure the two extremities of their patent from further encroachment. Under their direction Ryder first laid out five lots at Spuyten Duyvel, upon the old Matthys Jansen patent—"beginning by Johannes Verveelen," who as ferryman occupied the upper end of that patent; and ranging down the Harlem River to "the hills and the meadows," or the northern line of the Jansen and Aertsen patent, which touched the river at what is now 211th Street. These lots were "given out by lot." We annex the numbers, owners, and acres of those—

At Spuyten Duyvel.

No. 1.	Johannes Vermelje	18 acres.
" 2.	Jan Nagel	14 "
" 3.	Conrad Hendricks Boch	14 "
" 4.	Jan Dyckman	14 "
" 5.	" "	14 "

The unappropriated meadows behind these lots on the Spuyten Duyvel Creek (with the exception hereafter noticed) were given to Dyckman and Nagel, who at once purchased Vermilye and Boch's lots.

Upon Hoorn's Hook ten lots were laid off, these running

* For more relating to this and the adjacent farms, see App. H.

in from the East River north-west, and ranging from Jean Baignoux's line upward to the bend since called Gracie's Point; the last lot in the range containing 12 acres, but all the others 8 acres each. These were allotted as follows:

Upon Hoorn's Hook.

No. 1. Adolph Meyer,
" 2. Laurens Jansen,
" 3. Johannes Verveelen,
" 4. Jan le Maistre,
" 5. Maria Vermelje,
" 6. Jan Louw v. Schoonrewoert,
" 7. Daniel Tourneur,
" 8. Barent Waldron,
" 9. Jan Hendricks Boch,
" 10. Pieter van Oblinus.*

Another ten lots, each eight acres, were laid off upon Jochem Pieters' Flat, in continuation of "the old lots." Running east and west, they began "at the land of Capt. Carteret," ranging northward to what has since been called Bussing's, but then Glondio's Point, so named from Le Maistre, who owned meadow there. These, often distinguished as the "New Lots," were drawn by the following persons:

On Jochem Pieters' Flat.

No. 1. Jan Hendricks Brevoort,
" 2. Glaude le Maistre,
" 3. Frederick de Vaux,
" 4. Resolved Waldron,
" 5. Arent Hermens,
" 6. Cornelis Jansen,
" 7. Gerard Magister,
" 8. Joost van Oblinus,
" 9. Capt. James Carteret,
" 10. Pieter Jansen Bogert.

We observe in these allotments a preconcerted design to occupy what remained of the three old groundbriefs given to Matthys Jansen, Claessen, and Kuyter: a shrewd stroke of policy, truly, but which we are not to interpret into a distrust of the equity of their claim to those lands, of which they had been legally put in possession by the deliberate action of the constituted authorities.

* For the after history of these lots, which were mainly included in the *Waldron farm*, see App. H.

Ryder dates his certificates of the above surveys on August 6th. They were recorded August 17th. While here surveying, he boarded with Resolved Waldron, the town paying for it, and also for six gallons of rum drank during the progress of the work. The surveyor's bill, including the survey of Van Keulen's Hook, amounted to 429 gl.

A parcel of meadow land lying on the Spuyten Duyvel, to the westward of the first lot there granted, had been the object of some contention, but was finally disposed of, by a vote of the magistrates, August 10th, as follows:

"*Whereas* a dispute has arisen among the inhabitants of this town respecting a certain parcel of meadow lying on the Spuyten Duyvel, which each of them claims to have, and the said meadow is too small to be divided amongst them all; and because some have no meadow annexed to their land, to wit, *Arent Hermens, Johannes Vermelje,* and *Gerard Magister,* We the Court, pursuant to the order of his Honor the Governor-General given to the Land Surveyor, also give directions to said Surveyor to measure out and give the said meadow to the aforesaid persons."

It was then further resolved, that "a piece of meadow lying at the north point of this Island, and Moertje Davids' Vly, shall remain to the town's lot."

More wrath seems to have been stirred up at this action of the magistrates in giving away the meadows, than at the larger grants made by Andros impinging on their patent, though this caused, from first to last, a deal of excitement. Adolph Meyer, now a magistrate, but opposed to the grant, had the temerity to take an active part with the dissatisfied people in getting up a remonstrance. Andros took this as a grave offence, and issued his warrant, Aug. 14th, for Meyer's arrest, charging him with having "occasioned disturbance by siding with the commonalty and petitioning in a factious manner." He was admitted to bail, on condition of appearing before the Governor and Council when required, to answer what should be alleged against him, "and in the mean time to be of the good behavior." At the next election his townsmen renominated Meyer for magistrate, and he was even confirmed in the office. But when brought to the notice of the Mayor, Van Cortlandt, he removed Meyer,

Nov. 3d, because he was "under recognizance for his good behavior;" and ordered a new nomination, which resulted in putting Laurens Jansen in the vacancy.

Scarcely was the survey at Spuyten Duyvel made, when Dyckman and Nagel bought out Vermelje and Boch, and thereby became the owners of the whole five lots, containing 74 acres of upland, with the meadows granted them as before stated, being about 8 acres; the beginning of the fine estates subsequently held there by the Nagel and Dyckman families. With no intention of yet quitting their old homes in the village, they agreed with Michiel Bastiaensen and his son-in-law, Kiersen, to take these lands upon lease for a term of twelve years. We have thought the contract, here translated from the Dutch, worthy to be preserved, as it relates to the first successful effort to make improvements in that section of Manhattan Island, on which as yet there was not another white man's hearthstone north of Harlem village.

On this date, 26th October, Ao. 1677, appeared before me, Hendrick J. Vander Vin, by the Honorable Mayor's Court admitted Secretary, residing at the Town of New Haerlem, and the after-named witnesses; the honest *Jan Nagel* and *Jan Dyckman*, on the one side, and *Michiel Bastiaensen* with *Hendrick Kiersen*, on the other; the which agree to contract with the others and are agreed in the following manner. Jan Nagel and Jan Dyckman have conjointly leased, and by these do lease to the before-named Michiel Bastiaensen and Hendrick Kiersen in company, certain the lessors' lands, contained in five lots, marked No. 1, 2, 3, 4, 5, with the meadows thereto belonging, all lying upon this Island Manhatans, at Spuyten Duyvel, and under this town's jurisdiction, as appears by the surveys thereof existing, the which the lessees take and accept on lease upon condition as follows, to wit: The lessees shall occupy and use the aforesaid lands and meadows for the time of twelve consecutive years, to count from now on, expiring in the year 1689 after the crops and fruits are off the land, and the lease of the houses shall end at May in the year 1690; in particular, the lessees shall possess and use the aforesaid lands and meadows the first seven years free, by paying as an acknowledgment, each one hen, every year; the three following years shall the lessees pay each a hundred and fifty guilders per year: the last two years to pay each two hundred guilders in the year; the lessees shall have authority to build and erect houses, barns or stables, after their own satisfaction and contentment, for their accommodation; on condition that the same, at the end of the lease, with the fences which then shall be upon the lands and meadows, be delivered over all in good repair; the lessors promise to furnish the lessees—in order upon the aforesaid lands, wherever the lessees decide, to place an orchard—with fifty fruit trees, both apple and pear, and all the trees which they the lessees shall come to set out and raise shall at the end of the lease.

except the fifty trees aforesaid, be divided half and half; the lessees holding their option as to their circumstances, to be permitted to remove or give up this present lease at their pleasure, with the same to the lessors, upon mentioning it one year before; the lessors promise the lessees freedom in the real possession of the aforesaid lands and dependencies, without any charges standing thereon, reserving the lord his right; all the before-written conditions, the appearers declare to be their contract and accord, promising the same on both sides to conform to and fulfil, each in his regard, without craft or cunning, under obligation as according to laws. Thus done and passed at New Haerlem in presence of Joost van Oblinus and Conradus Hendricx, as witnesses hereto requested and solicited, who beside the appearers and me secretary, have undersigned these, on the date as above.

Witness,
J. VAN OBLINUS,
CONRADUS HENDRICKS.

JAN NAGEL.
JAN DYCKMAN.
This mark * of
MICHIEL BASTIAENSEN
by himself made.
HENDRICK KIERS.

With my knowledge,
HENDR. J. VANDR. VIN, *Secretary.*

Subsequently Dyckman and Nagel became the joint owners of the adjacent tract, known as the Jansen and Aertsen Patent, but in our day as the *Dyckman Homestead;* as also of that part of the Papparinamin Patent which had been occupied by Verveelen.*

* The *Papparinamin*, or *Matthys Jansen Patent*, in the view of the Harlem people, was in the same category with that of Jansen and Aertsen, and other of Kieft's grants which had lapsed for want of the required improvement; and hence they claimed it under their general patent as part of their common land, notwithstanding Gov. Nicolls' confirmation to Matthys Jansen's heirs. Verveelen, on or after removing to Spuyten Duyvel, had inclosed some sixteen acres off the north end of the patent; and the grants of 1677 engrossing the remainder, the Jansen heirs had nothing left them.

These held to their claim, however, and many years later, when Verveelen had vacated, made an attempt to recover. On Aug. 2, 1700, John Matthyssen, eldest son of Matthys Jansen, late of Ulster County, deceased, in behalf of himself and others, the co-heirs of the said Jansen (see Index, *Van Keuren*), petitioned the General Assembly for relief, representing "that by reason of the uncertainty of some bounds in said patent contained, he was wholly dispossessed of his father's inheritance, and therefore humbly prayed that the bounds of the said land might be settled, and the said patent confirmed unto the co-heirs of the said Matthys Janson." Leave being granted, a bill for that object was introduced the next day, passed on the 8th, and sent to Gov. Bellomont for his signature.

After reciting the original grant by Kieft to Matthys Jansen, Aug. 18, 1646, of "one hundred acres," at Papparinamin on Manhattan Island, its confirmation by Nicolls, May 23, 1667, and the petition of Jan Matthyssen, this bill provided "that the limits and bounds of the said Patent be, and are hereby forever declared to be, at a place called Papparinamin, which said Papparinamin is upon the island of New York, joining to the river

The ensuing winter found nearly all of the inhabitants busily employed in the woodlands cutting 5000 palisades "for the use of the city," pursuant to an order from the Governor, of Nov. 27th, 1677. They were to be "under 4 inches thick and 12 to 13 feet long, to be delivered at the water side in a convenient place to be taken away." The inhabitants on Nov. 29th were divided into four corporalships, "as was done formerly;" the corporals being Laurens Jansen, Arent Bussing, Adolph Meyer, and Jan Dyckman. The labor was probably turned to advantage in the clearing of some of the newly-drawn lands. All those who had shared in the late land drafts took part in this work, save Constable Nagel, Johannes Verveelen, ferryman, and Capt. Carteret; Maria Vermilye represented by her husband, Isaac Kip. In addition were enrolled David Demarest, David Demarest, Jr., Michiel Bastiaensen, Reyer Michielsen, Pierre Cresson, Abraham Delamater, Jan Kiersen, Hendrick Kiersen, Nicholas de Vaux, François Breteau, Jan Jansen (F. Bogert's man), and Jan Petit (Baignoux) "and his mate."

upon which the bridge called King's Bridge is built, according as the Indian name Papparinamin did anciently signify." It also declared "that all and singular the estate, right, title, and interest contained in the said patents shall be, and hereby are, confirmed and ratified unto the said John Matthyssen and other of the said co-heirs of the said Matthys Jansen, his and their heirs and assigns in equal proportions and divisions, any law, usage, or custom to the contrary hereof in anyways notwithstanding."

But the governor withheld his signature, and the bill failed to become a law. Matthyssen petitioned the Assembly again, Oct. 26; it "was read, and referred for further consideration," but not again taken up. The Harlem folks had meanwhile, by their deputy, Peter van Oblienis, taken counsel and put in their plea before the governor, and doubtless with effect. His Excellency informed the Assembly, Nov. 2, that he had declined to meddle with certain bills presented for his approval, because as matters of property they should be referred to the Courts of Judicature, soon to be established. But no further proceedings in the case have been found. The Dyckmans soon took possession under their grant of 1701 from the town, of which we shall hereafter speak.

There was really no injustice done the Jansen heirs, for the land had lain neglected and unclaimed by them, now more than thirty years since the confirmation by Nicolls. This groundbrief stood in no wise different from others which had been declared void, except said confirmation, which was probably an oversight. As it had never been sold, there was no such reason for compensation as there was in the case of the Jansen and Aertsen patent; and to have admitted its validity at that late day would have been a bad precedent, and one which the holders of other vacant groundbriefs would have been only too ready to take advantage of.

The parcel which Verveelen had had the use of passed from Jacob Dyckman to his son Jacob, and formed part of the 30 acres sold Feb. 11, 1773, to Caleb Hyatt.

CHAPTER XXI.

1677–1682.

THE FRENCH LEAVING; NEW TOWN-HOUSE; LAND QUESTIONS; LABADISTS; CAPT. CARTERET; SALE OF MOERTJE DAVIDS FLY.

A SUIT of Nicholas de Vaux *versus* Pierre Cresson, for some time pending in the local court, was decided November 15th, 1677. Defendant having sold plaintiff his house and lands, October 27th, 1676, the bill of sale was cancelled on April 23d ensuing, when De Vaux gave Cresson a parcel of fence rails, and was promised in return the use of enough land to sow a schepel of flaxseed, Cresson to receive of the flax every fourth sheaf. Jean Baptiste de Poictier, *Sieur* Dubuisson, was present and heard the bargain. But before De Vaux was ready to put in his seed Jan Hendricks Brevoort leased and planted Cresson's land on Jochem Pieters, leaving to De Vaux only a small corner, where it was sandy and unfit for his purpose. De Vaux then demanded of Cresson the use of his lot on Van Keulen's Hook; but the latter objecting, De Vaux on September 6th appealed to the magistrates. On a hearing it was agreed to "hold the case in advice till the coming of Jean Baptiste Bison." On the date first named it again came up, when Cresson presented Dubuisson's written declaration. The Court now decided that Cresson "restore to the plaintiff the 250 rails which he has wrongfully taken from him; and as the plaintiff has failed to perform his part of the contract, that he be condemned in the costs hereby incurred." De Vaux removed soon after to New Jersey, and with his wife Marie Sec joined the church at Bergen, April 5th, 1679. His descendants, under the name of

De Vouw, or De Voe, were long to be found at Hackensack and Tarrytown.*

The French refugees were gradually leaving, drawn principally to Bergen County, N. J., Staten Island, and up the Hudson, where they found other French families, and land more abundant, and to be had at a trifling cost. Gerard Magister was of the number that left. He had lately drawn one of the New Lots, and at the same time, by deed of August 9th, 1677, bought from Joost van Oblinus, for 400 gl. in grain, the erf, house, and barn lately owned by and yet in the occupancy of David Demarest, Jr. On Dec. 26th ensuing he and wife Madeleine l'Admiral made a joint will before the secretary, magistrate Tourneur, and Frederick de Vaux, after the form usual with the French refugees. All this looked to a fixed residence; but within two years Magister left the town. He sold his lot No. 7, Mar. 22d, 1679, to Jan Delamater, but no sale of his dwelling-house is to be found.|

* NICHOLAS DE VAUX had a dr. Esther, b. at H., who in 1698, m. Ulderick Brower, of Hackensack, whither De Vaux had removed, and where, in 1706, he m. a second w., Margaret Jans, wid. of Jacques Button. He d. prior to 1717, when his wid. m. Hendrick Cammega, whose first wife was Anna M. Verveelen. De Vaux had other drs., Susanna, b. 1680, who m. Thomas Brickers and Jacobus Van Gelder; Mary, who m. Jacob Buys, of Bergen; and Rachel, who m. Abraham Martelingh; also, by his second w. another dr. Esther, b. 1711, his first, so named, Mrs. Brower, having just d. His son, Abraham de Vaux, or *de Vouw*, joined the Hackensack ch. in 1694, but removed to Tarrytown, to which place his mo.'s kinsfolk, the See family, had gone, and where he and w. Mary appear as chhm. I believe he had sons Nicholas and Johannes. He served as deacon in 1709, and as elder in 1724; offices afterwards held by said Johannes de Vouw.

| JEAN LE ROY had owned this domicil as early as 1670, and apparently it was the north garden No. 2, next Tourneur; on which account I suppose Le Roy was led to get it. This garden was in Simon De Ruine's allotment, bought in 1666, by Capt. Delavall; and when Le Roy sold Delavall his lands bought of Presto, he probably took this garden in part payment, and built on it. Le Roy sold out entire in 1674. The owners after him were Cornier, Richard, Demarest, Jr., Richard again, and Oblinus. The latter agreed to sell Magister the house, barn and houselot, for 400 gl., to run on interest, if he could not meet the payment. The rate lists indicate that Oblinus took it back. His sons John and Hendrick evidently held this garden No. 2, then an erf, in 1706 and 1708, and John alone in 1712, though Marcus Tiebaut at this date had some interest in it, and was in possession in 1713. I think he had bargained for it, but d. before the sale was closed; and that then, 1714, his step-son, John Lewis bought it. This is probably its history, but, resting in part on other proof than deeds of transfer, it cannot be given with absolute assurance. See note on *John Lewis* for more about this lot, which later formed a part of the William Brady plot.

Again came up the matter of the town finances, and prominently that of the voorleser's salary. The record of Feb. 7th, 1678, runs: "Is proposed and resolved that the accounts of this Town, as well the debts as credits, revised on the date of 19th February, 1677, shall with the first opportunity be taken up and disposed of; and the Secretary is authorized henceforth to keep a separate register thereof." From the register so begun and yet preserved have been culled many interesting items relating to the settlers.

On the same date we also read:

Is further resolved and concluded that the magistrates shall go about among the common inhabitants and see how much each is willing to contribute yearly to the maintenance and salary of the Voorleser, beginning the 23d October of the previous year, 1677, and following. The Voorleser must have yearly for salary, according to the agreement entered into the 23d October, 1670, the sum of 400 guilders; the magistrates remain held to furnish the money.

List of the Free-will Contributions for the support and salary of the Voorleser of this Town, etc., and the following are to contribute yearly:

Jan Nagel	*f.* 18
Daniel Tourneur	" 15
Joost van Oblinus	" 40
Jan Dyckman	" 12
Laurens Jansen	" 10
Resolvert Waldron	" 30
Conradus Hendricks	" 10
Jan Hendricks	" 6
Maria Vermelje	" 8
Johannes Vermelje	" 10
Glaude le Maistre	" 12
Michiel Bastiaensen	" 6
Hendrick Kiers	" 6
Arent Hermens	" 8
Jan Hendricks van Brevoort	" 10
Jan le Maistre	" 6
Adolph Meyer	" 14
Cornelis Jansen	" 12
Gerard Magister	" 6
Jan Louw	" 20
Jan le Maistre } Arent Hermens } rent of the land	" 63
Jan Nagel, rent of the meadow	" 18
	f. 342

Upon the 4th April, "The Constable was authorized and empowered to collect and receive the debts which to this town must be paid, according to the assessment of the 19th February, 1677, *as* from Jan Louwe, David des Marest, Glaude le Maistre, and others."

Demarest settled up in full with the town on April 26th, his son David had done so on the 23d. and soon after this the whole family, with Jacques Laroe, removed to their new home on the Herring River, now the Hackensack. All the adults, being eight persons, united "by certificates" (in part from the French church), with the church at Bergen, on October 7th succeeding.*

* DEMAREST'S "two miles square" purchase from *Mendawasy* and other Tappan chiefs was commonly called "The French Patent." From what is now New Bridge, on the Hackensack, two miles above Hackensack village, it reached up the river to a little beyond Old Bridge; and from the river eastward to the "North River Mountains," or present line of the Northern Railroad. On the part lying above the Old Bridge, upon the bank of the Hackensack, in a charming situation, Demarest built his dwelling and a grist mill, with a dam across the stream. He called his home *Esia*, perhaps from the old family seat in Picardy, Oise Mont, or Oise, which the Latin authors called *Œsia* or *Æsia*. Afterwards buying lands on the west side of the river, he put up there a saw mill, and also a more capacious grist mill. This last was called the *Great Mill*, and its older neighbor opposite, the *Little Mill*. Demarest's plan of forming a French colony on his tract, failed; though he drew to him several families, as those of Daniel du Voor, Jean Durie, Jacques Laroe and Nicholas de Vaux, and they together organized what was called "The French Church of Kinkachemeck," and built a house of worship on Demarest's land, near his dwelling, upon a knoll just below the Old Bridge, where still remains "The French Burying Ground." In midsummer, 1693, David Demarest, the patriarch, d., and his remains, with those of his wife, who d. first, no doubt rest in the old burial ground aforesaid. His last will, made Aug. 26, 1689, gave his estate equally to his three sons. David junior had meanwhile d., and his wid. m. John Durie. On Aug. 13, 1693, some days after the d. of David the elder, a division was made, in presence of Rev. Pierre Peiret, by John and Samuel Demarest, and by John Durie for the chn. of David junior; the homestead and Little Mill falling to John, the lands and mills west of the river to Samuel, and heirs of David. After losing its chief patron, the French church declined; Rev. Pierre Daillé, Peiret's colleague who usually preached here, removing to Boston, his visits ceased, and the Demarests and others took letters to the Dutch church at Hackensack. Demarest's cherished creations, the church, the mills, have alike disappeared; only a few piles, the remains of the mill-dam, show their heads at very low water.

John Demarest was b. 1645, on the Island of Walcheren, Zeeland; m. 1668, Jacomina, dr. of Simon De Ruine, again in 1692, Marritie Van Winckel, wid. of Peter Slot, and in 1702, Magdalena Laurens, wid. of Jean Tullier. In 1689, he was of the committee of safety which commissioned Gov. Leisler. He d. in 1719, having parcelled his lands among his chn. These were, (w. or hus. given in parentheses,) *David*, b. 1669, (Antie, dr. of Jan Slot); *John*, 1671, (Deborah ———); *Maria*, 1673, (Jacobus Slot); *Sarah*, 1675, (Abraham Canon); *Rachel*, 1678, (Thomas Hyatt); *Jacomina*, 1680, (John Stewart, from Sterling, Scotland); *Leah*, 1682, (Abraham Brower); *Magdalena*, 1684, (James Christie, from Iverden); *Peter*, 1688, (Maria Meet

Again on the 8th of May resolutions were passed as follows:

WHEREAS it is found that the Voorleser, from the contributions, for this current year since the 23d October past, with the rent of the town's lot and meadow reckoned in, will not draw for his salary more than 342 guilders, instead of 400 which he must have yearly; the said Voorleser has, to the constable and magistrates assented, that (because of other burdens) he shall have for this current year till 23d October first coming, no more than the said 342 guilders; and the constable and magistrates shall then make a new and reliable assessment for the full sum of 400 guilders yearly as salary, according to the first accord of 23d October, 1670. The whole aforewritten provision is by the Voorleser agreed to, declaring therewith to be content.

Is also taken into consideration about the rebuilding of the town's house for the Voorleser; it is found good to take the same in hand by the first opportunity, as the most necessary work to be done by the inhabitants, and they having leisure to properly hew and make ready the timber for the same; thereupon called in Gerard Magister, wheelwright, to contract with him for the carpenter work, according to a plan to him submitted. Demands 200 guilders; whereupon it was not ordered, but the magistrates said that they would think upon it and inform him when they should be able to have him do it; thereupon separated.

Circumstances led to a change of plan. Mrs. Montagne had ended her widowhood, but within a short three years had lost her second husband, Mr. Isaac Kip; the magistrates being called upon July 25th, 1678, to inventory the household goods "which the deceased in his lifetime had brought to the widow." The plan to build a new house, the timber for which was already

and Maria Button). David Demarest was b. 1652, at Mannheim, and m. 1675, Rachel, dr. of Pierre Cresson. He d. ab. 1691. His wid. m. John Durie, and in 1702, Roelof Vanderlinde. Demarest's chn. were *David*, b. 1676, (Sarah, dr. of Rev. Guilliaem Bertholf); *Peter*, 1677, not again named; *Susanna*, 1679, (Peter Westervelt); *Rachel*, 1680, (Andries van Norden); *Jacobus*, 1681, (Leah, dr. of Peter De Groot, and Grietie, dr. of Cosyn Herring); *Samuel*, (Sitske, dr. of Siba Banta); *Mary*, (Wiert Banta); *Daniel*, (Rebecca, dr. of Peter De Groot); *Benjamin*, (Elizabeth, dr. of Peter De Groot); *Jacomina*, (Andries van Buskirk); *Leah*, (Rynier van Houten); *Lydia*, (Stephen Terhune).

Samuel Demarest was b. 1656, at Mannheim, and m. ab. 1678, Maria, dr. of Simon De Ruine, who survived him. He d. in 1728. His sons who reached manhood, were *David*, b. 1681, (Mattie Debaun); *Samuel*, (Annetie van Hoorn); *Peter*, (Margaret Herring); *Simon*, b. 1699, (Vrouwtie Herring); and his drs. were *Magdalena*, b. 1680, (Cornelius Banta); *Jacomina*, (Samuel Helling and Cornelius van Hoorn); *Judith*, (Christian Debaun and Peter Durie); *Sarah*, (John Westervelt); *Rachel*, (Jacobus Peek); *Susanna*, b. 1703, (Benjamin van Buskirk). To most of these Samuel assigned portions of his lands before his d.

We cannot extend these interesting details, so far, we believe, entirely reliable; but invite some one to fill out the genealogical lines, which, in 1820, were said to embrace seven thousand names!

contracted for with Daniel Tourneur, was suddenly arrested, and the widow turned her contract over to the town. Thereupon the following resolution was passed September 7th:

> The Constable and Magistrates, with the advice of the whole Community, have found good and resolved to rebuild and renew the town's house for the Voorleser; and Daniel Tourneur has agreed to cut the timber needed therefor, as he was held to do for Maria Vermelje, for 130 guilders (on condition it shall cancel her whole debt in the town's account); to wit: 3 beams twenty feet long, broad in proportion; 18 posts ten feet long, 4 sills twenty-two and twenty feet long, 2 rafters, 2 girders, 1 other spar, all twenty-two feet; also split shingles for the roof; all finished to deliver at the stump, and they of the community shall ride out the said timber, as it is ready, and bring it to the work, etc.*

Leaving Tourneur to perform his toilsome work of hewing, and good Vander Vin to make the best of his straitened circumstances—for owing Gerrit van Tright, of New York, merchant, "64 gl. 13 st. in beaver, 100 gl. 17 st. in sewant, and 2 pieces of eight in silver," he was obliged, July 27th of this year, to mortgage his house and lot on the Beaver Graft, whence he derived a part of his support,—other matters now claim a notice.

Changing the lines on Van Keulen's Hook was a fruitful cause of misunderstanding between adjoining owners during this and the preceding year. Hendrick Kierson's lease of the Tourneur lots had not yet expired. Pierre Cresson, who joined Tourneur on the west, summoned Kierson to court, June 7th,

* Isaac Kip was of a worthy and well known family, for an account of which see *Holgate's Am. Gen.*, and the *N. Y., G. & B. Rec.*, for 1877.

Mr. Kip was b. at Amsterdam in 1627. He was much respected at H., and was nominated for magistrate Oct. 27, 1675. He had no chn. by Maria Vermilye; but his first w. Catalina, dr. of Hendrick Jansen, bare him Hendrick (see p. 163), Tryntie, Abraham, Isaac, Jacobus, Johannes. Tryntie m. Philip de Forest. Jacobus was the gt. gt. gd. fa. of Rev. Francis M. Kip, and Rev. Wm. I. Kip, D.D. Johannes, bapt. Jan. 20, 1660, is the subject of a letter in my possession, written in Dutch, on a sheet four by six inches, and which reads thus:

Mrs. Mary Kip. After salutation; These friends come to counsel with you as to the best and most proper way to manage it with Johannesie Kip, the youngest child of your husband, my brother deceased. 'Tis such I should also have come, but have just now in daily employ four strange masons, and cannot leave them. Therefore request that you with the friends will please consider all that is needful to do for the welfare of the child, and further provide that which is necessary. What you and the friends do, shall be acceptable to me. Hoping that both sides may agree in all friendship, for the best; whereof not doubting, commend you to God's protection, and remain,

1678, the 26 July
Kipsberry.

Your affectionate
Jacob Kip.

1677, demanding that he should give up the strip of his land on which he had sowed. Kiersen said he had only used the land he had hired of Tourneur.

"The Honorable Court having maturely considered the case in question, and finding it to be a mistake general among the users and owners of these lots, consent and order that, as it is now sowed, it shall remain as it is till the crop is off the land; and that then each one shall plough and sow his land according to the last survey made and staked off by the sworn surveyor."

Again, Glaude le Maistre claimed and put under arrest the grain which had been sowed by Joost van Oblinus on a strip of land that fell within Le Maistre's line. On a complaint by Oblinus July 12th, 1677, the town court, a little mystified in this instance, directed "the plaintiff to cut and carry in his grain, but that he shall take account how much has stood upon the strip of land in question, and keep the same separate till further order." *

Again, on September 5th, 1678, Cornelis Jansen complained of Jan le Maistre, "concerning a strip of bouwland upon Van Keulen's Hook;" that he "had not fixed his land properly according to promise." Defendant said that he had regulated the land as it should be, and that the plaintiff might have ploughed it; proves that he had proposed and plaintiff had refused an arbitration as to the fitness. After hearing parties the Court went out and viewed the situation, "in order afterwards to judge as they should;" and then the parties came to an agreement—Jansen to have his strip of land, etc., and the costs to be borne half and half. Then the Court passed the following general order:

"Is moreover resolved and established that from now forward, to prevent further questions concerning the fences upon Van Keulen's Hook because of the changing of some strips, those intending to reset their new fence in stead of old, remain bound to remove the old from the new, and to set it properly; according to which each one must conform himself."

* COIN was then so rare an article in the colony, that Vander Vin makes a note to this case as follows: "The Plaintiff paid for the extraordinary session a double gold ducat, 9 guilders Holland; in sewant 36 guilders." So it then took four guilders in sewant, to make one in coin.

The year 1678 at the dorp wore away with no other noticeable incident except the usual choice of town officers, and the visit from Do. Nieuwenhuysen to install an elder and deacon. On the latter occasion, Glaude le Maistre, at the expense of the town, furnished "a half-vat of good beer" for the entertainment of the domine and the congregation, and Waldron, Dyckman, Bussing, and Oblinus advanced the domine each 3 guilders (in all 12) for his services, while Jan Nagel provided the wagon to bring and return his reverence; the visit costing the town in all 41 guilders.

An episode of the current year was a marriage in high life at New York, that of Thomas Codrington, merchant, to Margaret, daughter of the then mayor, Capt. Delavall. Having resumed active business on his return from England, the Captain was now in the height of his prosperity, and enabled to do handsomely by his daughter, upon whom Oct. 9th, in view of her nuptials soon "to be solemnized," he settled the sum of £500. Twenty years later, Capt. Codrington, meanwhile risen to wealth and official distinction, became a freeholder of Harlem, by the purchase of the Daignoux farm; the good services which he rendered the town in its public affairs only ending with his death in 1710.

It speaks well for the prevailing security at this period, that but seldom an act of robbery comes to notice. A flagrant case which occurred in the spring of 1679 made the greater excitement at Harlem as one of the thefts was committed at "the house of Daniel Tourneur's sister," the wife of Frederick De Voe. The thief was one Williams, who having stolen a horse at Stamford had also robbed several persons in Fordham. Being arrested, and, by an order from the Governor of March 3d, "delivered pinioned into the hands of the constable of Harlem," Waldron conducted him to New York for trial. He was convicted on May 8th, of horse stealing, upon several affidavits taken at Stamford.

This year another French refugee left the town with his family. This was Pierre Cresson. After selling out his farm May 23d, 1677, to Jan Hendricks van Brevoort, who had had it a year under lease, he built upon and occupied his outside garden No. 14. This he now sold, March 5th, 1679, to Jan Nagel, who owned No. 13, for 100 guilders in goods or grain, a pair of oxen, one cow, and a half-firkin of soap! Cresson removed to Staten Island, having already secured a lot of land at or near Long Neck, on the north-west side of the island, for laying out which an order had issued from the Secretary's office, May 14th, 1678. A small stream, on which lay his meadow at Sherman's Creek, was long called after him "Pieter Tuynier's Run."

This year gave rise to a protracted law-suit between Daniel Tourneur and Cornelis and Laurens Jansen, as plaintiffs, and Col. Lewis Morris, defendant, concerning certain meadows on Stony Island, which the plaintiffs claimed to have owned "upwards of sixteen years." This carried their title back to Stuyvesant's grants, in 1663, to Tourneur, Cogu, and De Meyer. Morris claiming the meadows as within his purchase, had sent his men in haying time to mow and gather the grass. The others complaining of this trespass, obtained from the Council the following mandate in their favor:

"Ordered that the Petitioners do continue in quiet possession of the said meadows at Stone Island, according to their grants. And if Col. Morris have any claim or pretence thereto, the same is to be heard and determined at the next General Court of Assizes."

Thus the matter rested till the next annual return of the haying season.

The signal event of the year was the visit of the two Labadist travellers, Sluyter and Dankers, from Wieword in Friesland. Their journal affords us this interesting description of their visit.

Under date of October 6th, 1679, they say: "We left the village called the Bouwery, lying on the right hand, and went through the woods to *New Harlem*, a tolerable village situated on the south side of the Island, directly opposite the place where the north-east creek and the East River come together." Their object was "to explore the Island of Manhatton," which in their view ran east and west, but in this respect we correct their account in italics. "This island is about seven hours' distance in length, but is not a full hour broad. The sides are indented with bays, coves, and creeks. It is almost entirely taken up;

that is, the land is held by private owners, but not half of it is cultivated. Much of it is good woodland. The *south* end on which the city lies is entirely cleared for more than an hour's distance, though that is the poorest ground; the best being on the east or north side. There are many brooks of fresh water running through it, wholesome, and fit for man and beast to drink, as well as agreeable to behold; affording cool and pleasant resting-places, but especially suitable for the construction of mills, for while there is no overflow of water, yet it can be shut off and so used."

With eyes accustomed only to monotonous plains and pastures, they viewed with delight the variety of landscape. Mount Morris and the heights lying westward of the flats they describe as "two ridges of very high rocks, with a considerable space between them, displaying themselves very majestically, and inviting all men to acknowledge in them the majesty, grandeur, power, and glory of their Creator, who has impressed such marks upon them." The last reference is probably to the outcropping of the gray stone along the entire face of the west heights. "Between them runs the road to *Spyt den duyvel.**

* HARLEM LANE. See Note p. 282. The road from *Harlem village* to Spuyten Duyvel had been laid out recently by order of the Mayor's Court of Nov. 7, 1676, and pursuant to which the inhabitants on Dec. 7, met and "resolved to make the road between this village and Spuyten Duyvel; to begin on Saturday the 9th of this month." Harlem Lane was probably regulated about the same time. Its first house was put up by the Tourneurs as early as 1679, and stood "about where 7th avenue intersects 115th street." Says one looking back over half a century, "I remember the depression where the partly filled up cellar was, and the two large old ox-heart cherry trees that stood probably in front of the house." The only ancient dwelling left on Harlem Lane is the old Van Bramer house, on the east side of the Lane midway between 117th and 118th streets, its gable end to the road, and fronting to the south. It was built not long before the Revolution, probably by Hendrick van Bramer, who lived there in 1774. Fifteen years ago we noted: The front and the west end were laid up of hammered red or free stone. Query, why were not all sides of stone? The oldest portion measured 18 by 31 feet; for the frame addition of 15 feet 6 inches on the east end was modern. Its exterior was tasty. The eaves were low, the roof had a moderate pitch; while the short beveled chimney tops, and the quaint dormer windows, with flat roofs sloping downward toward the front, had a decidedly antique air. The weather-beaten clapboards, (on the rear and on the gable above the eaves the same,) were very thick, rabbeted deep, finished with a half-inch bead, and put on with large *wrought* nails. The window sills, etc., were of blackwalnut, the sash stiles very heavy and the glass all 7 by 9. The two front doors were in halves after the old fashion, and hung on strap hinges. The ceilings low, not plastered, showed the bare heavy oak timbers, planed and beaded; and the

THE VAN BRAMER HOUSE.

The one to the *west* is most conspicuous; the *east* ridge is covered with earth on its *west* side, but it can be seen from the water or from the mainland beyond to the *east*. The soil between these ridges is very good, though a little hilly and stony, and would be very suitable in my opinion for planting vineyards, in consequence of its being shut off on both sides from the winds which would injure them."

With Gerrit van Duyn of Long Island, who had volunteered to show them the way, they reached Harlem. "As our guide Gerrit had some business here and found many acquaintances, we remained over night at the house of one Geresolveert (meaning Resolved Waldron), constable of the place, who had formerly lived in Brazil, and whose heart was still full of it. This house was constantly filled with people, all the time drinking; for the most part that detestable rum. He had also the best cider we have tasted.

"Among the crowd we found a person of quality, an Englishman named Captain Carteret, whose father is in great favor with the king, and he himself had assisted in several exploits in the king's service. This son is a very profligate person. He married a merchant's daughter here, and has so lived with his wife that her father has been compelled to take her home again. He runs about among the farmers and stays where he can find most to drink, and sleeps in barns on the straw. If he conducted himself properly, he could be not only governor here, but hold higher positions, for he has studied the moralities, and seems to have been of a good understanding; but that is all now drowned. His father, who will not acknowledge him as his son, as before, allows him yearly as much only as is necessary for him to live.

"Saturday, 7th.—This morning about half-past six we set out from the village, in order to go to the end of the Island; but before we left we did not omit supplying ourselves with peaches which grew in an orchard along the road. The whole ground

stair to the loft was a *perpendicular ladder!* Some claim it to be the very house that De Forest and Montagne built on this Flat in 1637, which had *two doors* and was 18 *feet wide*. But that was 42 feet long, and measured by Dutch feet. Plainly no such antiquity can be assigned it, as the deed for the land given by Arent and Louteus Kortright to Benjamin Benson, Feb. 9, 1755, mentions no tenement.

was covered with them and with apples, lying upon the new grain with which the orchard was planted. The peaches were the most delicious we had eaten." Proceeding up the Island, they add :

"We crossed over the *Spyt den duyvel* in a canoe and paid 9 stivers fare for us three, which was very dear. We followed the opposite side of the land and came to the house of one *Valentyn*"—this was the ancestor of the Valentines of Westchester. He was not at home, but his Dutch *vrouw*, who was from Beest. in Gelderland, glad to see Hollanders, entertained them at breakfast; after which they came down on that side to Col. Morris's, meeting his nephew Walter Webley, ready to cross the river. "He carried us over with him and refused to take any pay for our passage, offering us at the same time some of his rum, a liquor which is everywhere. We were now again at *New Harlem*, and dined with *Geresolveert*, at whose house we slept the night before, and who made us welcome. It was now two o'clock; and leaving there we crossed over the Island, which takes about three quarters of an hour to do, and came to the North River, which we followed a little within the woods, to *Sappokanikke*." A few days after at Staten Island they fell in with Pierre Cresson.* Had the elder Tourneur been living,

* PIERRE CRESSON, or Moy Pier Cresson (*me* Piet Cresson,) as he always wrote his name, is the subject of interesting notice in the journal of these Labadists. Under date of Oct. 13, 1679, they say, "We pursued our journey this morning from plantation to plantation, the same as yesterday, until we came to that of *Pierre le Gardinier*, who had been a gardener of the Prince of Orange, and had known him well. He had a large family of children and grand children. He was about seventy years of age, and was still as fresh and active as a young person. He was so glad to see strangers who conversed with him in the French language about the good, that he leaped for joy. After we had breakfasted here they told us that we had another large creek to pass called the Fresh Kill, and there we could perhaps be set across the Kill van Kol to the point of Mill Creek, where we might wait for a boat to convey us to the Manhattans. The road was long and difficult, and we asked for a guide, but he had no one, in consequence of several of his children being sick. At last he determined to go himself, and accordingly carried us in his canoe over to the point of Mill Creek in New Jersey." Here they "thanked and parted with Pierre le Gardinier." Pierre and his son Joshua, had each obtained a grant of 83 acres on the west side of the Island, which were surveyed for them Dec. 24, 1680, and patents issued Dec. 30. This is the latest notice found of Pierre. His chn., so far as appears, were Susannah, Jaques, Christina, Rachel, Joshua and Elias. Susannah, b. at Ryswyk, m. 1658, at N. Amsterdam, Nicholas Delaplaine. Her fa. gave her a m. portion of 200 gl. Christina, b. at Sluis, m. Jean Letelier and Jacob Gerritse Haas. Rachel, b. at Delft, m. David

this visit of the Labadists must have restored faded reminiscences of the father of the sect, Labadie, when by his eloquence he so moved the hearts of the people of Amiens. If others had personal knowledge of those scenes, as Demarest, Disosway, Cresson, they had removed, and the interest which the travellers awakened at Harlem was probably confined to the objects of their visit, their character and movements. Professing the doctrines of the Dutch Church, but warmly advocating a higher religious life, they appear to have won the respect of all till they began to make proselytes to their peculiar social ideas, which nearly resembled those of the Shaking Quakers. But they gained over to their views members of several respectable families, as those of Beekman, Bayard, Cresson, and Montanye, some of whom were persuaded to join the community established by Sluyter at Bohemia Manor, in Maryland.

The travellers, staying a night with Waldron and dining with him the next day, should have made no mistakes in speaking of him. Yet we suspect they have. Waldron's history is sufficiently known to make it improbable that he had ever visited Brazil. But the voorleser, Vander Vin, whom they must have seen and conversed with, had spent some of his earlier years in that country, when clerk of the High Court of Justice at Maurits-stadt, during the presidency of the Heer Johan van Rassvelt. He kept the minutes of this court. Here he had met with Hon. Matthys Beck and his uncle Jacob Alrichs—both afterward *vice-directors*, the one at Curaçao and the other on the

Demarest, Jr., Jean Durie, and Roelof Vanderlinde. Joshua Cresson, b. 1659, and Elias, b. 1662, both lived upon S. I., the latter, we presume, succeeding to his fa's. farm. He was high sheriff of Richmond co., under Leisler. One Joshua Cresson lived at North Branch, N. J., in 1720.

Jaques Cresson, of good repute and much respected at H. where he owned property and held office, m. 1663, Marie Renard, of whom we have given some account. They had issue *Jaques*, b. 1665, *Maria*, 1670, *Susannah*, 1671, *Solomon*, 1674, *Abraham*, and *Isaac*, 1676, *Sarah*, 1678, *Anna*, 1679, *Rachel*, 1682. Jaques' injury, Jan. 31, 1677, and sad d., Aug. 1, 1684, we leave unrecorded. His wid., with her son Jaques or Jacobus, sold their house in Stone street Sept. 9, 1685, and taking a church letter Nov. 25, she sailed, with her family, for the Island of Curaçao. Later they returned, and Mrs C. reunited with the church at N. Y., May 28, 1701, but it is evident they soon left again for Philadelphia. Solomon Cresson served as constable there in 1705, and others of the family are found in that vicinity. Their desc. include the late eminent philanthropist Elliot Cresson, and the present Dr. Charles M. Cresson. The name of late years has worked up the valley of the Susquehanna into N. Y. State.

Delaware—who were then among the Heere Electors of Schepens at Maurits-stadt. Vander Vin might well retain vivid impressions of his experiences in Brazil at a very exciting period in the history of the Dutch occupation there, to which we have before alluded, and have been "still full of it," as the travellers say of Waldron. Mistakes easily find place in the hastily-written notes of tourists, and the journal of these travellers forms no exception.

"Great injustice has been done to the memory of Capt. James Carteret," says the historian of Elizabeth; and a truer remark was never uttered. We do not believe all the hard things said of him by the Labadist travellers, for we recall the oft-told story of his illegitimacy, now at length admitted to be a fiction. In quest of information wherewith to embellish the narrative of their tour, and strongly inclined to the hypercritical, the tourists were likely to swallow any bit of scandal which their fellow Dutchmen at Harlem were ready to deal out to them against the English in general, and Delavall's family and kin in particular; one-sided stories, which the brevity of their stay gave no opportunity to correct. Into these old prejudices none probably entered more heartily than Waldron, who, albeit he was of English extraction, evidently cherished no affection for the land of his ancestors.*

Carteret, it is true, had been unsuccessful in business ventures, incurring debts which, maugre his willingness and promises, he found it hard to pay; but it is difficult to believe him so utterly the vagrant he is represented, being still a landholder at Harlem. That Mrs. Carteret, having young children, should prefer a comfortable city home under her father's roof, was not so strange for one to whom the society at Harlem was uncongenial, or could offer little that was attractive. And so

* The Labadist views were embraced by Nicasius de La Montagne, Jaques Cresson, Petrus Bayard, William Beekman and his aunt, Susanna wid. of Arent Keteltas, named p. 309. Cresson could hardly have joined the community, as he d. but a year after Peter Sluyter's second arrival at N. Y. July 27, 1683, on his way to Maryland. Beekman and Montagne were but young men. Bayard left his w. Blandina Kierstede in N. Y., but returned and d. here in 1699. His son Samuel, b. 1675, m. Susanna Bouchelle, Sluyter's step dr., and in 1698, Sluyter conveyed him part of the manor. Sluyter had m. Anna Margareta Coude, then the wid. Bouchelle. She d. in 1721, he in 1722, and the community dissolved. See *Jour. of Dankers and Sluyter*, and *N. Y. G. & B. Rec.* 1878, 188.

there was room for dislike or prejudice to put the worst construction upon it. But why argue about that which could have been scarcely more than a matter of temporary convenience, as Mrs. Carteret, while her father was still living, accompanied her husband to Europe, to look after his landed interests there; probably making their principal home in the Island of Jersey, where their only daughter was married in 1690, and so respectfully noticed as "daughter of the Honorable James De Carteret." Certainly Capt. Carteret was treated with much consideration at Harlem, where on Oct. 20th, 1677, he received a nomination for magistrate. If he was a hard drinker, he lived in a day and community when indulgence was the rule. He was well read in the Scriptures: and also reverenced them, if his apt quotations in his letter referred to be taken as evidence. That his heart had a tender side, let an incident show. It was in the winter of 1676; Jean le Roy became embarrassed, and unable to pay his last year's rent for the town lot. When told to the generous Captain, he headed a subscription for his relief with 10 gl.; more than was given by all the rest besides.

The last mention of Capt. Carteret at Harlem is under date of Nov. 21st, 1679, when he sold his land on Montagne's Flat to Glaude Delamater, "for 200 guilders and a wether." Certain provisions in the will of his father, Sir George Carteret, whose death occurred Jan. 14th ensuing, made it necessary for him to return promptly to England and Jersey; and he appears no more in this country. He still held the farm and mill property with Little Barents Island, the title to all which descended to his daughter, Mrs. Pipon, of Jersey.

On the 6th of November, 1679, died at the house of Johannes Vermelje, the worthy old Norwegian settler, Claes Carstensen,*

* Claes Carstensen being from Sant, in Norway, was called "the Norman." He was here prior to the Indian war of 1643, had learned the Indian language, and figures as public interpreter, at the forming of treaties &c. In 1646 he m. Helena Hendricks, served in 1653 as corporal in the burgher corps at New Amsterdam, and was admitted to the small burgher right in 1657. After the English came in power, he removed to Harlem, and on March 2, 1671, was granted a small house lot for the term of his life. On his decease, and at the request of Resolved Waldron, elder and constable, the deacons Arent Hermens and Jan Nagel took an inventory of his effects, found in his house and at Vermilye's where he died; these being sold Nov. 10, 1679, at public vendue for 268 gl., 16 st. "for the benefit of the deaconry here."

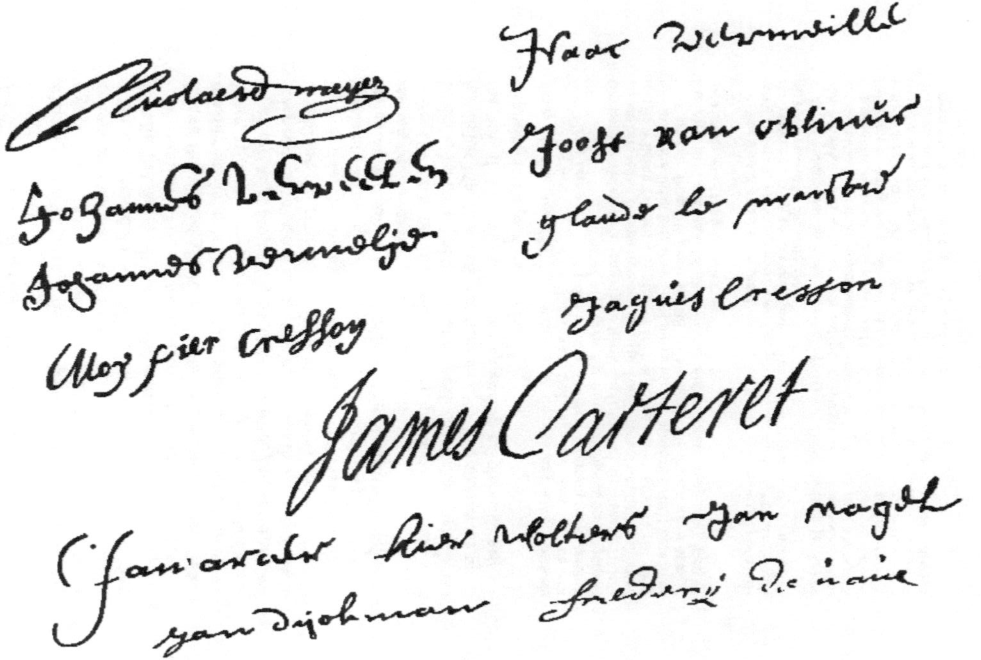

Nicolaes Meyer

Johannes Verveelen

Johannes Vermelje

Mos Pier Cresson

Isaac Vermeille

Joost van Oblinus

Claude le Maistre

Jaques Cresson

James Carteret

Jan Arcer   Kier Wolters   Jan Nagel

Jan Dyckman   Frederick De Vaux

whose age was 72 years. He had been for some time in needy circumstances and was aided by the deacons, having been a church-member for many years.

On the same date Abraham Shotwell sold the Sawkill farm to John Robinson, of New York, merchant.

A question of some local interest had arisen between Jan Louwe Bogert and Joost van Oblinus, touching a piece of salt meadow at Hoorn's Hook, which Oblinus (in behalf of his son Peter, still a minor) claimed as belonging to the lot laid out to Peter on Aug. 6th, 1677, by Robert Ryder, the surveyor, and described as "a parcel of land being the tenth lot in the row, in breadth on the river side twelve rods, bounded south-west by the land of Jan Hendricks, stretches north-west into the common woods one hundred and sixty rods, and north-east by the river, including all points and morasses therein comprehended, containing twelve acres."

On the 12th of November Louwe procured a citation for Oblinus, requiring him to answer next court day "why he has forbidden him to set off his meadows." The case came up on the 4th of December, Oblinus appearing as plaintiff, and the following is the minute:

JOOST VAN OBLINUS, *Plff.*, vs. JAN LOUWE. } WHEREAS a dispute has arisen between Joost van Oblinus and Jan Louwe van Schoonrewoert over a certain small meadow lying in the Bay of Hellgate, which each of the parties claims as belonging to him; after several debates and rebuts on either side, it was decided by the Honorable Court (the said small meadow being the most southerly in the range under against the steep hill next the little kil) that Jan Louwe for his meadows shall have those that stretch from his great kil till to the little kil *from anckers house*;* the rest to Joost van Oblinus. And ordered that each shall bear his own costs attaching to this case."

* The Dutch word used (*anckers*) may be either the possessive or plural form. Here it probably means *ancker*, perhaps the *anchorage* house; though the reference is by no means clear. For those whom it may interest, we give the record in the original.

Alsoo questie was geresen tusschen Joost van Oblinnis ende Jan Louwe van Schoonrewoert over seecker valeytge, gelegen in de boght vant Helle-gat die elck van parthyen sustineerde hem toe te behooren, naer v'scheyden debatten en rebatten ten weder syde, is by den E gerechte verstaen dat het geseyde valeytge synde het suydelyckste in die rygh onder tegen de steyle bergh naest het killetge, dat Jan Louwe voor syn valeyen sal hebben die haer strecken van syn groote kil tot aen het killetge van anckers huys, de rest aen Joost van Oblinnis. En° ordonneren dat ider syn eygen costen over dese saecke gevallen, sal dragen.

The line of partition here indicated was apparently the same as that afterward fixed and described in the deeds for the adjacent upland, given by the town, March 2d, 1701, to Jan Louwe Bogert and Jan Delamater, the latter then owning the Hoorn's Hook or Waldron farm, which included the Oblinus lot. By the above decision Oblinus plainly took a small share of the meadows claimed by Bogert under the town's grant to his predecessor Montagne.

Bogert's shrewdness in protecting his own interests more than once exposed him to the charge of being disobliging, if not churlish. Some time before—in 1675—he had forbidden David du Four and others from passing over his land, as they had been wont to do, to shorten their travel from Hoorn's Hook to the mill, the village, and church. It happened that Du Four and wife, in passing this way on Sunday, April 18th, in the said year, noticed a cow, one of two which Bogert had taken of Hans Jacobs Harding, "to winter, and to feed and water with his own cattle," lying out in the road alone, while Bogert's cattle were grazing in the meadows. Harding's cow died, as he charged, from neglect; and the honest Swiss finding such fruits of a friendship with Bogert running back to their emigration in the same ship, brought his suit, Du Four being a witness for him.* Hence Du Four and others, going that road again August 5th, were forbidden and threatened by Bogert, who called them "rebels and highwaymen." David complained

* Hans Jacobs Harding was a weaver, and then lived at Stuyvesant's Bowery, where he had bought a small place, Feb. 12, 1669, from Jan. Pietersen Slot. He was a native of Bern, and m. here July 29, 1668, Geertie, dr. of Lambert Moll, of Bushwick. She was b. 1648. Her older sister Marritie, also b. here, m. in 1646, *Gerrit Hendrickse Blauvelt*, from Deventer, who d. in N. Y. a. 1684, his sons Hendrick, Huybert, Johannes, Abraham and Isaac, who all had families, removing to Tappan or Orangetown, Rockland co., and whence sprang the numerous Blauvelts. Harding d. in 1685. The next year his wid. m. Thys Franse Oudewater, of Tappan, whither she and her chn. went to live. This name took the form of Outwater, and probably Atwater. Thys had a br. Thomas, of N. Y.; they were both b. at Albany, and were sons of Frans Jacobson, who lived at Fort Orange as early as 1657. Dr. Thomas Outwater, of Rockland, of Revolutionary merit, was a desc.

The Harding chn. were Tryntie, b. 1670, Frena, 1672, Conrad, 1673, Lambert, 1676, Reyer, 1678, Johannes, 1679, Jacob, 1681, Lambert, 1683, Emeline, 1685. The last m. Johannes Verveelen. All the sons m., except perhaps Lambert, and the Hardings in time spread through the counties of Rockland, Orange and Ulster, some being sturdy patriots in the Revolution.

Sept. 2d, but the Court so far sustained Bogert as to decide "that there is no common way over defendant's land." At another time, William Waldron, of New York, cooper, accused Bogert of having for spite unfastened and taken to his house a cutting bench, two of which Waldron had been using, and left nailed to stumps in the woods on Bogert's point. But Bogert denied doing it, and after a long debate, pro and con, they were reconciled. It was the tradition—so said a descendant of Jan Louwe, the late excellent James Bogert, Jun.—that Louwe's credit with the Indians for veracity led them to call him in their language Schoonreweerd, or *True Lips!* But as this term is Dutch and not Indian, alas for the tradition.*

The winter of 1679–80 was barren of noteworthy incidents, unless it were a bear hunt which took place on the farm of Mr. John Robinson, at the Saw Kill; for bears, wolves, and other noxious animals still infested the woods on Manhattan Island, and were so troublesome, especially the latter, even years after, that official encouragement was given to destroy them.† In the bear hunt here noticed "very good diversion and sport" was afforded those who took part in it, one of whom was the Rev. Charles Wolley, chaplain of the garrison at New York. Bruin was chased and treed in Robinson's orchard; "and," says the chaplain, giving an account of it in his Journal, "when he got to his resting-place perched upon a high branch; we dispatched a youth after him with a club to an opposite bough, who knocking his paws, he comes grumbling down with a thump upon the ground; and so we after him again." The sequel is not told;

* SCHOONDERWOERD, as more correctly written, was obviously so called from the Dutch SCHOONDER, signifying *fairer*, *finer*, &c. and WOERD, another term for *polder*, a tract of low land recovered from the overflow of the sea or surrounding rivers by dykes and drainage; this term (*woerd*) applying as well to islands that had undergone the same reclaiming process. Very many such places throughout Holland bear names, of which this term forms the ending; variously written *waard*, *waert*, *woerd*, *woert*, etc. Schoonderwoerd was simply the *Fairer polder*. We suspect the "tradition" aforesaid came from mistaking this term *woerd* for the more familiar *woord*, so taking Schoonderwoerd to mean *fairer word*; and fancy supplying the rest.

† The modern annotator of Woolley's Journal, aware of the prevalence of "bears" about Wall street, may be pardoned for locating Robinson's farm, the scene of this bear hunt, near that section of the city; *Journal*, Note 33. He only failed to *bear* in mind, that the old species, more cautious, and less disposed to *risks*, seldom ventured so far down.

we know the youth was *dispatched*, but whether the bear was, is more than doubtful, since Mr. Wolley says they had neither gun nor weapon, except "a good cudgel;" whence also it may be inferred that the hunt was not prearranged, but incidental to one of those not agreeable surprises, which till years later often awaited the astonished farmer, on visiting his barnyard upon a winter's morning.

We naturally connect Mr. Wolley's visit to Robinson's farm with the sale which Robinson made, Jan. 1st, 1680, of the half of said farm, with the leather mill, etc., to John Lewin, Esq., and Mr. Robert Wolley, of London, merchants, the latter probably a brother of the chaplain; which purchase was effected through the immediate agency of William Pinhorne, who had returned from England in 1678, in the same vessel with Chaplain Wolley, directly after a business interview with Lewin and Wolley in London, at which the chaplain was present. Lewin soon visited his purchase, as he arrived in New York on October 16th ensuing, commissioned by the Duke of York to inquire into and report upon the administration of Gov. Andros.

Jan Nagel, Jan Dyckman, Arent Hermens Bussing, Adolph Meyer, and Jan Delamater were busy hewing timber to fill a contract made Jan. 2d, 1680, with Nicholas de Meyer as agent for Hendrick Cuyler, of Albany, for whom they were to furnish timber for a house, including "beams, posts, rafters, plates, sleepers, door-posts, and casings, according to the plan thereof," to be delivered in the ensuing May, part at the water side, and part in New York, at the Burgher's Path; and for which they were to receive "the sum of 1300 guilders with a half-ancker of rum, to wit: one third in silver money or sewant, one third in good winter wheat, and one third in goods at such price as he (De Meyer) sells the same at his store for current sewant." *

* HENDRICK CUYLER, tailor, was b. in 1637. His br., Reynier, button maker, resided at Amsterdam. Hendrick m. at New Amsterdam Anna, dr. of Jan Schepmoes, and about 1664 went to Albany, where he acquired property. He eventually returned to N. Y., and with his w. united with the chh. by letter Nov. 29, 1688. He d. soon after, in 1690. His drs. Maria, Sarah, Rachel, and Eva, m. respectively John Cruger, Peter van Brugh, Myndert Schuyler, and Rev. Petrus van Driessen. His son Johannes Cuyler, b. 1661, was mayor of Albany in 1725–6. He m. Elsie, dr. of Major Dirk Ten Broeck. From him and his brs., Henry m. to Maria Jacobs, and Abraham, whose w. was Catrina, dr. of Hon. Jan Jansen Bleecker, come the respectable family of Cuyler, allied from an early day to many others noted in the annals of New York.

The timber for the town house had been ready for some time. As early as December 20th preceding, a vote was taken to give out the contract for building it, but it had been delayed in order that debts due the town might first be collected in. On May 6th, 1680, action was taken regarding the house for the clerk; a visitation of the outside lands was authorized with a view to assessing those in fence; several small pieces of land were sold or granted; and a resolution was passed to sell Moertje Davids' Fly. But to particularize:

Constable Johannes Vermelje and Daniel Tourneur were appointed and empowered to employ a carpenter to build the house, "for the least cost to the town." It was to be made 22 feet long and 20 feet broad, and all complete with chimney, mantlepiece, doors and windows. Adolph Pietersen De Groot, carpenter at New York, took the job at 250 guilders.* The inhabitants agreed to work at the building a certain number of days gratis.

The visit to the outside lands under the town's jurisdiction was to ascertain the quantity inclosed within fence, with a view to making an assessment for town expenses. It was intrusted to the constable, with Arent Harmens and Joost van Oblinus, and who reported as follows:

Hendrick Bosch, at Moertje Davids Fly, 1 erf, 1 morgen.
John Robinson, at the Saw-kill, 1 erf.
Jacob Young, 1 erf, 3 morgen.
Jean Balgeoux, on Hoorn's Hook, 1 erf, 1 morgen.
Jean Belin and } on ditto, 1 erf, 1 morgen.
Etienne Bullon, }
Jan Dircksen, on ditto, 1 erf, 1 morgen.
Michiel Bastiaensen and } (No quantity
Hendrick Kiersen, at Spuyten Duyvel. } reported.)

* Gerard Magister, and his w. Madeleine l'Admiral, had now left the town, possibly to join Demarest's colony. But inquiry, even an appeal made and repeated in the columns of that valuable medium, the N. Y. G. and B. Record, fails to recall this worthy Huguenot pair from their subsequent obscurity. A bill for carpenter work, written by Magister's own hand, reads as follows:

Memoire de l'ouvrage que ici fait pour le communaute de Harlem.
le 14 *fevriere* 1677, *fait une bariere* .... 10 *franc*
fait une riviere à Peter le mort .... 10 *franc*
le 17 *decembre* 1677, *reclose une table et fait* 2 *banc pour le maitre d'ecole* .... 4 *franc*
le 16 *fevriere* 1678 *fait* 2 *banc* .... 8 *franc*

la somme est .... 32 *franc*
fait par moi
Gerard Magister.

Cornelis Jansen purchased of the town a small piece of land lying next to his land upon Montagne's Flat next the run (*de fonteyn*), paying therefor to this town at once 25 guilders." Johannes Vermelje "was granted and allowed the place before his house extending into the street, from the corner post of Jan Dyckman, on a line straight to the corner of Laurens Jansen's house, as broad as his erf and land may stretch, for him to set off and use." Laurens Jansen was in like manner allowed to take in the street so far as his land stretched, and Arent Hermens was permitted to set off for his use a place 33 feet in the street "along his two gardens;" for which he was charged 12 gl.

It was resolved to sell *Moertje Davids Fly* at public vendue, on Monday, the 10th instant. Whoever wanted it was invited to come, hear the conditions, and benefit himself. The constable was authorized to extend the notice, and the secretary to post a handbill. On May 10th, 1680, toward evening, the time appointed, the constable and magistrates being present, the terms of sale were made known as follows:

CONDITIONS AND TERMS on which the constable and magistrates have a mind to sell to the highest bidder a certain meadow lying in this town's jurisdiction, at the North River, named *Moertje Davids Vaily*.

1st. Whoever remains purchaser shall be held to pay in the following February, 1681, punctually, with good winter wheat, without any default.

2d. The costs attending this sale, as silver money and other expense of writing, shall be borne and paid by the buyer.

Vander Vin started the sale with a bid of 50 gl. from Resolved Waldron, between whom and Hendrick Bosch was the principal contest. Finally, Barent Waldron gave the sixteenth bid, advancing 50 gl. and calling out *mine*, as was then the custom, when it was struck off to him at 205 gl.

Meanwhile Daniel Tourneur and the Jansens commenced a prosecution against Col. Lewis Morris for the trespass upon their meadows at Stony Island the previous year. This case assumed a graver importance, as upon its legal decision seemed to hang other landed rights which the inhabitants had upon that side of Harlem River.

On June 5th a formal declaration was entered in the Mayor's Court, or Court of Record, at New York, as follows:

DANIEL TOURNEUR, CORNELIUS JANSEN and his brother LAWRENCE JANSEN, *Plaintiffs*, against LEWIS MORRIS, SEN., *Defendant*.

The Plaintiffs declare against the Defendant in an action of Trespass upon the Case, for that he the Defendant sometime in or about the month of July or August, in the year of our Lord one thousand six hundred and seventy-nine, contrary to law and against the public peace, did enter into and upon Plaintiff's meadow upon Stone Island, over against New Harlem, and then and there by force and arms did with scythes mow and cut down the grass which was growing upon the said meadow, and with force and arms carried the hay away, whereby the Plaintiffs were much damnified for want of hay for their own cattle in the winter season, which is to the damage of the Plaintiffs, Forty Pounds. And thereupon the Plaintiffs bring their Suit and crave Judgment, with costs of Court, *et dam. aul guoque.*

To which Col. Morris entered this counter plea:

CITY OF NEW YORK, Ss. And the said Col. Lewis Morris comes and defends the wrong and injury to him done, etc., and saith that the said Daniel Tourneur, Cornelius Jansen, and Lawrence Jansen their action against him ought not to have, for that he knoweth not of any such place as Stone Island over against New Harlem, as in the Declaration is set forth, or that any Trespass is by him committed. But if by it shall be meant a certain Island called Stone Island adjoining to his Plantation and belonging to him, and that thereon the pretended Trespass should be committed, he the said Col. Lewis Morris doth plead in bar to the said action, that the said Island is not within the Jurisdiction of this Court, and therefore not triable in this Court. And therefore prays Judgment, that the Plaintiffs may be nonsuited and pay costs, etc.

Having thus joined issue, the case came to trial as follows:

City of New York. The COURT OF RECORD of the City aforesaid, holden at the *City Hall* within the said City, the 6th day of July, 1680. Before Francis Rombouts, *Mayor;* William Beeckman, Johannes Van Brugge, Peter Jacobs, Gulian Verplanck, Samuel Wilson, *Aldermen*.

Daniel Tourneur *et alii*,
against
Col. Lewis Morris,
} about a Trespass upon a marsh.

Mr. William Pinhorne,	Mr. Jacob Leisler,	
Mr. Paul Richard,	Mr. James Matthews,	
Mr. William Cox,	Mr. Baltus Bayard,	
Mr. Thomas Codrington,	Mr. Norton Claypole,	*Jurors.*
Mr. John Lawrence, Jun.	Mr. Albert Bush,	
Mr. John Robinson,	Mr. Philip Smith,	

The Deposition of *John Delamater* saith, that as he was going to the Mill-dam, he saw three canoes laden with hay, and he asked the negroes where they had the hay so soon; they answered they had it at Stony Island.

The Deposition of *John Dyckman:* Being at the meadow where the hay was cut which is now in question; seeing negroes cut grass there, asked the negroes who set them to cut the hay; they told him that their master Col. Morris set them to do it. This deponent said that he could find it in his heart to take away the hay which was made. The negroes answered, he should not This deponent asked why he should not carry it away. The negroes answered, for because they were stronger than he.

Mr. *Nicholas Demeyer* sworn, saith that Col. Morris did confess that he did send his negroes to cut the grass off the land in question, and said he would send them to cut it again this year.

Verdict. The Jury find for the Plaintiffs; fifty shillings damage, and costs of court.

The Court agree with the verdict, for all charges whatsoever.

Morris had relied with too great confidence upon the inability of the other side to prove that *he* cut and took away the hay, or ordered it done. He insisted "that they prove their damage how much it is," and declared the Jury was "not lawfully impanelled," that "the Smith"—alluding to Bush—was "no juryman." *

Morris paid no heed to the decision, but soon made good his threat by again mowing the meadows. Of this Tourneur and the Jansens complained July 20th, and the next day the Mayor issued his warrant to the constable of Harlem to "give warning unto the said Col. Lewis Morris, his agents, workmen, and servants, that they presume not to mow, cut, or carry away, any

* HENDRICK BOSCH, anc. of the *Bush* family, was a native of Leyden, his fa. bearing the same name, Hendrick. The son m. Anna Maria Rembach, from which union was Albert Bush, named in the text, b. at Leyden in 1645. Losing his w., Hendrick m. Maria, dr. of Gerrit Eshuysen, with whom, his said son Albert, and an infant of two yrs., (which last d. early), he embarked for America, Dec. 23, 1660—a wrong year being given in *N. Y. Col. Mss.*, vol. XIV. He established himself as a sword cutler in N. Y., where he had other chn., viz.: Dorothy, b. 1661, who m. Isaac Caspars Halenbeck, of Albany; two Gerrits, b. 1663, and 1665, both d. early; and Hillegond, b. 1666, who m. Lodewyck Ackerman. By a third w., Egbertie Dircks, wid. of Hage Bruynsen, of H., he had also Cornelia, b. 1672, who m. Peter Gerard Cavalier; Hendrick, b. 1674, Samuel, 1677, and Joshua, 1678. His farm near Moertje Davids Fly, referred to elsewhere in the text, was sold before his death to Thomas Tourneur. Being of a "great age," he made his will Apl. 23, 1701, when all his chn. were living, save those above excepted, and said son Albert. He cut off from sharing his estate, his two eldest drs., for "stubborn and disobedient carriage towards me these many years," &c. All the sons had families. Albert learned his fa.'s trade, m. 1668, Elsie, dr. of Jurian Blanck, and had chn., *Jurian*, b. 1669, *AnnaMaria*, b. 1672, *Justus*, b. 1674, *Albertus-Conradus*, b. 1681, and *Casparus*, b. 1683. The dr. m. Edward Marshall, tailor. On May 24, 1721, Albert's wid. and chn., except Jurian, petition the Assembly; wish to sell his house and lot. The registers of the Collegiate Chh., N. Y., give the desc. of Albert and others. Joshua Bush settled on Staten Island, his posterity being still there; Justus Bush removed to Rye: others of the family went to Hackensack. Marshall, b. in Barbadoes, d. June 1, 1704, æ. 37 yrs.

the grass or hay from off the said marsh or meadow late in controversy as aforesaid, as they and every of them will answer the contrary at their perils," etc.

Nor did this notice move Morris, who still denied the jurisdiction of the Mayor's Court. Whereupon the plaintiffs appealed to Gov. Andros. In this appeal they say:

"That your petitioners about seventeen years past did buy and was possest of our several lands lying at Harlem, to which belongeth a certain marsh or meadow ground called by the name of Stony Island; for which land and meadow ground your petitioners hath and can produce patents signed in Governor Stuyvesant's time and afterward renewed by Governor Nicolls, yet notwithstanding and although it is our just right, Col. Morris the last year did send his servants and workmen to cut the grass off our said meadow and carried the same away before we had knowledge of it; and the 6th day of July last past we had a trial in the Mayor's Court, where we obtained a judgment against him, with damage and costs of court; yet notwithstanding the same, he hath sent his servants and workmen to mow the said meadow and make it into hay, and saith he will carry it away, although he hath been forewarned to the contrary. Whereupon the Mayor hath directed a warrant to the Constable of Harlem to forewarn them from such unjust, illegal actings, and to forbear; yet would he take no notice thereof, and did say that he wondered that the Mayor was so bold as to issue forth his warrant there. Which, if we are deprived of this our just right, we shall be destitute of food for our cattle in the winter time, and must be constrained to turn our stocks out into the woods, where we shall be in danger of being damnified by several inconveniences that attends the same; it being the chiefest of our pasture-ground." They pray for his Excellency's consideration, etc.

On the above being submitted to Col. Morris, he indorsed upon it the following answer:

"I have seen the contents of this petition, and in answer say, that what hay hath been cut and carried away has been from and off my own land, which I am ready to make appear and justify in the Court at Jamaica, (in which precincts, as I am informed, the land lies), and to make good my title, or pay the condemnation for the trespass thereon committed, according to the verdict of the jury. New York, the 28th July, 1680.

"LEWIS MORRIS."

To Morris's proposal to change the *venue* to Jamaica, exception could hardly be taken, that town being the seat of justice for the North Riding, in which Westchester was included. But a year now slipped by, when Tourneur again essaying to mow his meadows was forcibly ejected by Morris, who seized his hay. And thus the matter rested for another two years.

Things went on as usual in the village. On September 1st, 1680, there was a full turnout of the inhabitants to repair the king's highway. Barent Waldron was missing, and thus liable to a fine of 6 gl., which was to be put upon every delinquent. The four magistrates conferring together, repaired in the evening to the house of Constable Johannes Vermelje, and in the name of the community requested him to collect the fine from Waldron. Vermelje, who was a brother-in-law to Waldron, refused, said he was not bound to, that they were fools to ask it, and moreover that they had no right to command him; that being constable it was his prerogative to command in this town, and not the magistrates', who could not hold a court without him. On September 4th, the court having met, Vermelje, whose dignity had been touched because the magistrates had presumed to act in his absence, took them to task for it. In vain they explained that they had held no court, but only a conference; Vermelje protested that his authority as constable should be maintained or he would appeal to the High Court. The magistrates also insisted that their authority should be respected; and so the affair ended.

The work upon the town house drew largely on the time of some of the inhabitants, especially Daniel Tourneur and Jan Delamater; and these, with Jan Hendricks Brevoort, Arent Hermens, Jan Nagel, Adolph Meyer, Jan Dyckman, and Laurens Jansen, all took part in riding the shingles and clapboards. It took 400 clapboards and 1800 shingles to inclose the house. Four hundred and thirty feet of sawed planks were obtained from Gabriel Legget, of Westchester, "wood-sawyer," for flooring the loft; and Henricus de Forest, of New York, did the glazing of the windows. The inhabitants had credit in their accounts for whatever articles they furnished, or extra time they spent; the allowance for a day's labor being 5 gl., or two dollars.

The building of a bridge across the Spuyten Duyvel had been under consideration for a year; on January 7th, 1680, the Council had taken order to have the passage viewed for that purpose. It caused Verveelen some uneasiness, as his lease would run out on November 1st, 1680. The time had even expired when he succeeded on December 30th in getting from Gov. Andros an extension of his ferry privileges for seven years longer.

The *Sieur* Dubuisson visited the village March 28th, 1681, to give testimony in a case pending before the court. Marked respect seems to have been shown this Huguenot stranger, regarding whom we know so little.* On April 8th Paulus Richard, as administrator of the estate of Meynard Journee, late of Staten Island, deceased, confirmed to Jan Nagel and Jan Delamater the sale made them by Journee before he left Harlem. A painful incident of the summer was the drowning of five persons, in Hellgate, caused by the upsetting of a canoe. It happened at night, August 23d. Thomas Palmer, tanner and currier, and Matthew Smith, in his employ, set out to row to Flushing, having in company Anna Marlett and Ann Coffin, of Staten Island, with Mary Marshall and one other person. Getting into the

* JEAN BAPTISTE DE POICTIERS, Sieur *Dubuisson*, of whom just enough is recorded to whet our curiosity, was evidently a person of character, and of standing and influence among the refugees. His interest in their affairs, and the friendly offices performed for them, which incidentally appear, present him in an amiable light. He remained a number of years in or about New York, being first noticed at Harlem in 1676 and last in 1681. If we are not mistaken, it was he who at a time of popular excitement and fear of a French invasion from Canada, was the subject of the following order:

"Whereas we are informed that one *Dubison* is intending to transport himself and family to Canada, being suspected to have kept a secret correspondence with the French there, and it being judged dangerous to suffer such a person to live at Saratoga, or any place in this county, at this juncture of time, where he may have conveniency to keep such a correspondence. You are therefore hereby required, in his Majesty's name, to bring the said Dubison and family forthwith here, in order that they may be secured from any such dangerous designs; in doing whereof this shall be your sufficient warrant. Given, etc., in Albany, the 14th of June, 1689.

To Anthony Van Skaick, Constable of the Halfmoon."

As Dubuisson is found at Kingston, Nov. 12, 1693, standing as godfather for two chn. of Pierre Mouras, who had renounced Romanism, we presume nothing was found against him. One Sieur Dubuisson was sent from Quebec in 1711 to take command at Detroit.

Pot, and being "by the eddy tide overset," all but Smith were drowned. Mr. John de Forest, of New York, "Chirurgeon," bought, November 30th, from Jan Delamater his lot No. 4 on Hoorn's Hook, containing eight acres, for the sum of 130 gl. or $52! At the choice of new town officers this year was afforded a striking instance of the precaution taken by the appointing power to prevent favoritism on the part of the ruling magistrates in procuring the choice of successors. In presenting a nomination to the Mayor and Aldermen, if any of the candidates were nearly related to each other or to either of the retiring magistrates, the fact was to be expressly stated. Jan Nagel and Johannes Vermelje, two of the nominees returned Dec. 10th and acted upon the next day, were brothers-in-law, and also sons-in-law of Resolved Waldron, retiring magistrate. Hence Vermelje only was accepted. Cornelis and Laurens Jansen, being also candidates, Cornelis only was chosen, and his brother thrown out. Similar cases might be cited.

The town house had been finished, and must be paid for. To provide for this and certain other claims against the town, a meeting was held Feb. 14th, 1662. On a careful audit of the accounts, the public debts were found to amount to 1190 fl.,* and the sums due the town from sundry persons to 406 fl. 12 st. To meet the deficiency of 783 fl. 8 st. a tax of 600 fl. upon the lands and *erven* was voted.

The following is the assessment list, with a *description of the property* annexed; the whole showing the exact state of the occupied lands as they stood at this date, and the changes which had taken place since the last list. According to what had become the established practice and so continued, two thirds of the gross tax was assessed upon the lands, and one third upon the erven. Now each erf was taxed 7 guilders, and each morgen 2 guilders 14 stivers. Hitherto only the lands of Jochem Pieters Flat and Van Keulen's Hook, with Bogert's Point, had been subject to tax. But to make up for Delavall's 54 morgen, here for some reason omitted, an equal quantity (short half a morgen) was taxed upon the outside lands, that is to say, Montagne's Flat, the New Lots, Hoorn's Hook, Spuyten Duyvel, etc.

* Costs incurred in making the Town's House, and some old balances, of debts, etc., which must be paid from the present assessment, to wit:

It will be observed that the New Lots, so far as taxed, are reckoned at two morgen each, or half their actual contents; and the other outside lots, so far as included, at one morgen per lot, excepting those at Spuyten Duyvel. For the first time also the outside erven are included, swelling the list to 37 whole and 2 half erven, without the two erven of Delavall or Carteret. The lands in the list in brackets are either not assessed or only in part as indicated. Dr. De Forest's lot on Hoorn's Hook is not in the list. Delavall's 54 morgen embraced Nos. 15 to 22 of Jochem Pieters, and Nos. 21, 22 on Van Keulen's Hook.

To *Daniel Tourneur*, 13 days' work, @ 5 gl. per day	*f.*	65 : 0 : 0
Riding 1650 shingles, @ 5 gl. per 150		55 : 0 : 0
Also for shingles and clapboards		16 : 5 : 0
2½ lbs. nails, @ 30 st		3 : 15 : 0
Paid Kleyn Jan for fixing the town's drum		9 : 0 : 0
1 gallon of rum to the carpenter		6 : 0 : 0
A cord to the drum		3 : 0 : 0
To *Jan le Maistre*, 6 days' work, @ 5 gl		30 : 0 : 0
3 lbs. nails, @ 30 st		4 : 10 : 0
Riding shingles and clapboards, etc		16 : 5 : 0
Taking a warrant to Spuyten Duyvel		4 : 0 : 0
To *Adolph Pieters* for building the town's house		250 : 0 : 0
To *Resolved Waldron*, 10 schepels wheat delivered		60 : 0 : 0
48 lbs. nails, @ 30 st		72 : 0 : 0
Also 10 lath nails		5 : 0 : 0
A cord to the town's drum		6 : 0 : 0
Old payment (see page 396)		3 : 0 : 0
Paid to the carpenter		120 : 0 : 0
Board for the carpenter		40 : 0 : 0
Barent Waldron, taking a warrant to Spuyten Duyvel		4 : 0 : 0
To *Joost van Oblinus*, 1 lb. nails delivered		1 : 10 : 0
Paid the carpenter		30 : 0 : 0
Old payment (see page 396)		3 : 0 : 0
To *Jan Nagel*, 3 lb. nails, @ 30 st., delivered		4 : 10 : 0
Riding shingles and clapboards, etc		20 : 5 : 0
Taking a warrant to Spuyten Duyvel		4 : 0 : 0
To *Adolph Meyer*, 2 schepels wheat delivered		12 : 0 : 0
Riding shingles and clapboards, etc		16 : 5 : 0
Taking a warrant to Spuyten Duyvel		4 : 0 : 0
To *Jan Dyckman*, 1 schepel wheat delivered		6 : 0 : 0
Riding shingles and clapboards, etc		16 : 5 : 0
Old payment (see page 396)		3 : 0 : 0
To *Arent Hermans*, 1 schepel wheat delivered		6 : 0 : 0
Riding shingles and clapboards, etc		16 : 5 : 0
Old payment (see page 396)		3 : 0 : 0
To *Lawrens Jansen*, riding shingles, clapboards, etc		20 : 5 : 0
To *Jan Hendricx Kyckuyt*, riding shingles, clapboards, etc		26 : 5 : 0
To *Johannes Vermelje*, beer, wine, and rum, etc		33 : 0 : 0
To *Isaac le Maistre*, taking a warrant to Spuyten Duyvel		4 : 0 : 0
To *Glaude le Maistre*, ¼ vat beer, old account (see page 396)		15 : 0 : 0
To *Reynier Willems*, the baker, balance		15 : 0 : 0
To *Nicholas Bayard*, for services, old account		24 : 0 : 0
To *Hend. J. Vander Vin*, writing-book, paper, and ink		12 : 0 : 0
To *De Forest* and *Leggett*, glass and planks to the town's house		110 : 0 : 0
	f.	1190 : 0 : 0

OWNERS. Feb. 14th, 1682.	ERVEN.	MORGEN.	TAX.	DESCRIPTION OF PROPERTY BY NUMBERS, ETC.
Joost van Oblinus.....	4	28½	ƒ104 : 10	J. P. Nos. 7, 11, 13; V. K. H. 1, 10, 11, ½ 16. [N. L. 8; H. H. 6, 10.]
Resolved Waldron.....	3	24	81 : 2	J. P. No. 12; V. K. H. Nos. 2, 3, ½ 4, ½ 9; N. L. Nos. 3, 4, 9, 10.
Jan Nagel............	2½	18	66 : 8	J. P. Nos. 6, 8, 9; ½ erf on Out Gardens Nos. 13, 14.
Daniel Tourneur........	2	18	62 : 0	J. P. No. 1; V. K. H. Nos. 17 double lot, 18, 19.
Jan Hendricx Kyckuyt[1]	3	10½	42 : 8	J. P. No. 5; V. K. H. ½ 16, 20. [N. L. No. 1.]
Laurens Jansen[2]......	3	11	50 : 14	J. P. No. 2; V. K. H. ½ 5, 6.
Arent Hermens[3].......	1	1½	10 : 18	V. K. H. ½ of No. 13. [N. L. No 5.]
Glaude le Maistre......	3	14	51 : 16	J. P. No. 14; V. K. H. No. 12; M. F. 3 lots 12 *morgen*; N. L. No. 2.
Adolph Meyer.........	3	12	46 : 8	J. P. Nos. 4, 10. [H. H. No. 7.]
Cornelis Jansen[4].......	1	12½	40 : 12	J. P. No. 3; V. K. H. ½ 14, 15; N. L. No. 6. [M. F. 18 *morgen*.]
Joannes Verveelen.....	1½	9	34 : 16	V. K. H. Nos. 7, 8, ½ 9, ½ 13. [H. H. No. 3.]
Joannes Vermelje.....	1	1	8 : 14	V. K. H. upper ½ of No. 5.
Jan le Maistre.........	1	1½	10 : 18	V. K. H. ½ of No. 14. [N. L. No. 7.]
Maria Vermelje........	1	0	7 : 0	[Hoorn's Hook No. 5.]
Jan Louwe Bogert....	1	16	30 : 4	"On the Point."
Wid. Daniel Tourneur	1	5	20 : 10	M. Flat, 3 lots 18 *morgen*; H. H. Nos. 1, 2.
Michiel Bastiaensen[5]...	1	4	17 : 16	At Spuyten Duyvel. [Dyckman and Nagel had 74 acres there.]
Hendrick Kiers........	1	4	17 : 16	
John Robinson........	1	0	7 : 0	At Saw-Kill. [Had 38½ acres, with Lewin, &c.]
Hendrick Bosch.......	1	1	9 : 14	At Moertje David's Fly. [Had 30 acres.]
Jacob Young..........	1	2	12 : 8	Below Hoorn's Hook. [Had 33½ acres.]
Jean Petit[6]............	1	1	9 : 14	On Hoorn's Hook. [Had 30 acres.]
Dirck vander Clyff....	1	1	9 : 14	Hoorn's Hook No. 8.
Jan Dircksen..........	1	1	9 : 14	Hoorn's Hook No. 9.
Jan Gerritsen de Vries[7]	1	0	7 : 0	
Jan Dyckman.........	0	2	5 : 8	V. K. H. ½ 4, with house-lot on the end called 8 *morgen*.

[1] Brevoort. [2] Low. [3] Bussing. [4] Kortright. [5] Kortright. [6] Balgooux. [7] Dolsen.

CHAPTER XXII.

1682—1685.

INCIDENTS; DEATH OF DELAVALL, ARCHER, DELAMATER, AND VANDER VIN; TOURNEUR vs. MORRIS; DONGAN'S ASSEMBLY; TOWN COURT REMODELLED; HALF-WAY HOUSE; GLOUDIE'S POINT OCCUPIED, ETC.

FAR up the winding Neckar which joins the Rhine at Mannheim, in a fruitful part of Germany, was the little town of Lauffen, where Gabriel Carbosie was born. Finding his way to Holland, and thence to this country while under the Dutch, Carbosie, used to a rich soil, tried divers places, at both farming and milling, and by the way had served on the "rattle watch" at New Amsterdam in 1658; but yet this "very clever fellow" had accumulated little. Again at Harlem, after years on the Delaware, to which he had gone when his Lutheran domine, Fabricius, was called thither, he was now too old to do much. Asking the use only for his lifetime of "a small piece of land in the bend of the Hellegat," whereon to set a small house, and by it make a garden, from which, with fishing, to support himself and his Brieta; Constable Oblinus assembled the whole community March 14th, 1682, and, the matter having already been talked over one with another, his request was granted. But it must be to no one's prejudice, and Carbosie was not to keep over three or four swine, lest they should damage "the meadows there lying, belonging to Jan Louwe." But were Carbosie to die, his widow, should she *marry again*, must give up the land, unless the grant were renewed; a wise provision (yet to Brieta perhaps too palpable a joke), since Carbosie was her third husband, and with another chance she might extend her tenure indefinitely. All which was as hard to foresee as what might be her next fancy; for herself, a Swedish woman from Gottenburgh, she had already taken to her heart a Dane, Frieslander, and German.*

While Carbosie was miller for Delavall, his swine running over the milldam had, as we have seen, caused Bogert not a little annoyance. Whether he was now the more troubled at the liberties just granted Carbosie, or at being himself fined 20 gl., "for the loss of four days' work upon the Town House," we know not; only some things had crossed him. On May 4th, when called to pay the late assessment and other arrears which, aside from the fine aforesaid, relieved him of 52 fl. 10 st., in *silver*, and 10 st., in *sewant*, Bogert tarried in the court-room, a full bench being present, and demanded that he might have the same justice as was done to other inhabitants. When asked wherein justice had not been done him, he answered, that in various ways he had been treated with injustice; and then losing his usual control, he outright charged their honors with being unrighteous rulers, and "vomiting forth the same in great rage and railing," left the room.

Recovering from their astonishment, the magistrates resolved to cite Bogert to appear on the next court day and answer for his abusive language. They also ordered the debts still standing out to be collected, if necessary, by execution. Bogert failing to appear July 6th, another citation was sent him. But ere the time arrived he came before the board, which met August 3d at his request; and expressing hearty sorrow for what he had said, alleged it had resulted from passion, and promised, if forgiven that time, never to repeat it. Thereupon the following

* CARBOSIE's first w. was *Teuntie Straetsman*, whom he m. at New Amsterdam in 1657. Her history has a touch of romance. She had lived in the Dutch colony at Fort Margariete, in Brazil, and had already had three husbands, viz.: Jan Meyer, George Haff and Tileman Jacobs Vander Myen. By the first she had a dr. Margaret Meyer, (w. of Hendrick Wiltsee, common anc. of our *Wiltsee* family.—See *Annals of Newtown*;) by the second hus., "in his lifetime, field-trumpetter in Brasil," she had a son Laurens Haff, (who was b. in Brasil, lived at Flushing, L. I., m. in 1676, Kniertie, dr. of Peter Mool, and originated the respectable N. Y. family of *Haff*;) by the third, a dr. Annetie Tilemans, (who m. Dirck Hattem, of Gowanus, and Hendrick Van Pelt, of New Utrecht,—See *Bergen Gen.*, 2d edit., p. 232;) and by Carbosie, a son David, b. 1659. Teuntie, whose posterity thus remains among us, d. at Gowanus, Oct. 10, 1662, and a dozen years later, one of her former husbands in Brasil, Vander Myen, thought to be d. when she m. Carbosie, arrived safe and sound in N. Y., found his dr. Annetie, m. in 1678, the wid. of Jan Thomasz Van Dyck, of New Utrecht, and lived there for some years after.

action was taken : "The magistrates of this Court having heard the petition, do excuse the petitioner his fault this time ; nevertheless that this Court may maintain and defend its rights and authority, and that such conduct may not happen in future from him or any one else, they condemn him in a fine of 25 gl. to this town." The fine was paid to the constable, and so the affair ended.

Next day, August 4th, the Court held its regular monthly session. A summons had been issued to Glaude le Maistre, pursuant to a motion of the constable, Oblinus, passed at the July term, to the effect that the old verdict of July 12th, 1677, against Le Maistre, be confirmed, and the debt, 85 gl., collected by execution. Le Maistre not appearing, the Court proceeded in a body to his house, but found him as unwilling as ever to admit the claim, he telling them, among other things, that he had "nothing to do with the town or town books." On this they proceeded to attach and seize three pieces of new linen, which they measured in the presence of witnesses, and found to contain 56 ells. Notice was then given by the constable, and also posted up in writing, that on Thursday, the 16th instant, Delamater's linen, unless redeemed, would be publicly sold. But the very next day (Aug. 5th, 1682), John and Isaac Delamater, in behalf of their father, came and recovered the linen, giving security for the debt and costs, 93 gl. 10 st. So this vexatious matter, many years pending, was finally arranged ; the brothers duly met their obligation, and Glaude having died, his account with the town was closed by John Delamater paying a small balance "for his mother," Oct. 3d, 1685.

Petty troubles with the English residents on or near Hoorn's Hook also drew upon the time of the magistrates. John Smith, "miller at the mill of Mr. Pinhorne," on the Saw-kill, having taken "French leave," his creditor, John London, seized a horse, which he understood belonged to the runaway. But Robert Barlowe brought Ralph Ross and William Engel, persons in his employ, to prove that he was the owner, whereupon Barlowe obtained his steed, and London pocketed the costs, for which Jacob Young became his bail. This suit was decided July 6th, 1682.

Young himself now had an issue with some of the town's folks. Daniel Tourneur and Johannes Verveelen, owning lots on Hoorn's Hook, accused him of taking their fence-posts. Cited to appear and answer on Aug. 4th, he gave no heed, nor to a second citation, but finally came, Dec. 7th, in no amiable mood. He denied the charge, declared that he bought the posts and would prove it; further saying that "the whole town was against him, and that Jan Dyckman (one of the magistrates) had threatened to burn his house." The Court directed defendant to bring evidence regarding the posts on the next court day, and also "to prove his scandalous words," on pain of correction. The *finale* is not given, but within a year Young left the town and went to other parts, having sold his farm, Sept. 27th, 1683, to William Holmes, of Turtle Bay; the sale, including "buildings, barns and outhouses," with 8 cows, 1 heifer, 2 calves, 4 ewes, 1 ram, and 4 stocks of bees, all for £50.

The ministerial labors of Domines Drisius and Nieuwenhuysen had been productive of much good among the Harlem people, as results prove. The pastoral visits, oftener devolving upon Nieuwenhuysen, but infrequent, and, aside from weddings and burials, almost restricted to the annual induction of new church officers, became for this reason signal events among the villagers, and occasions for much sociality. But death had recently taken away these two beloved pastors, to the great grief of the people. In sympathy to the bereaved Annetie Maurits Sluyswachter, whose good man, Nieuwenhuysen, had gone to rest Feb. 17th, 1681, Jan Nagel, "on account of the town," took her "two schepels of wheat," and Resolved Waldron also "two schepels, and a bottle of rum."

The loss to the church was in a measure repaired by the arrival from Holland, during the summer of 1682, of Do. Henry Selyns, who had now returned as pastor at New York, but was also to follow up the custom of preaching at Harlem at least once a year, for the purpose of confirming the elder and deacons; the flock here, except when called to the city on sacramental seasons, to continue its usual Sabbath exercises by the voorleser, as before. The first installation of an elder and deacon the next fall, chosen in the way then observed, was a time of unusual interest. A few still remained here to welcome Selyns, of his former members at the Bowery—Joost van Oblinus and Glaude le Maistre, with their wives, and the two worthy widows, Jacqueline Tourneur and Maria Kip. And there was Verveelen, the genial old deacon, who, to greet his good domine, must surely for this once have left his ferry at Pappirinemin, with its weighty responsibilities, in charge of his son Daniel, now living with him. But while to not a few others Selyns' features were familiar, though eighteen years had passed, to Abram de La Montanie, who could only know him by hearsay, was reserved the gratification of taking the hand which had been laid on his infant head, at his baptism, just before the domine left for Holland. It must have been a pleasant reunion, evoking gratitude to God; while, with the flow of good feeling, freely flowed Johan Vermeljo's "good bier," a half vat nearly being consumed before it broke up. Arent Hermens Bussing was the newly installed deacon; the elder's name is not mentioned.

Captain Thomas Delavall died in the summer of 1682, in New York City, over which, during three respective terms, he had presided as mayor. The event necessarily caused a sensation at Harlem, owing to his long and peculiar relations to the town, both as a proprietor and a patentee. Being sick and weak, John Tuder, attorney, was called in, June 9th, and drew up his will, which he signed with tremulous hand; the next day adding a codicil disposing of some property not before specified. His death directly ensuing, his will was proved July 11th.

He bequeathed to his son-in-law William Darvall, Esq., "all his lands lying and being in the bounds of Harlem," as also "Great Barnes Island, lying near Harlem," and his mill at Esopus, besides all the debts due him, contracted since the year 1664; the said Darvall out of the same to pay such money as was due from the testator to Mr. Samuel Swynock, of London, merchant. To his son John Delavall, whom he made his sole executor, he gave all his houses and lands at the Esopus (the mill excepted), and his share of "the Yonker's Mill, lying in Hudson's River," with such debts as were due him, the testator, and were contracted *before* the year 1664; and charging upon him the payment of certain legacies and charities. To his son-in-law Thomas Codrington, he gave all his land and houses at Gravesend, on Long Island; and to his (testator's) grandchild, Frances Darvall, his piece of ground "lying beyond the Smith's Fly, in New York, called by the name of the Cherry

Garden." This grandchild, then but a year old, afterward married Richard Willett, whose name will occur again. Capt. Delavall omits any reference to the Moseman farm, the Mill and Little Barent's Island, already conveyed to his daughter Frances and to her husband Capt. James Carteret, whom he does not name, and who at this date were no doubt in Europe.

We may simply add here, that subsequently, to wit, on Nov. 24th, 1684, William Darvall conveyed his lands in Harlem, with Great Barent's Island, to Samuel Swynock, aforesaid, of London, and Jacob Milborne, of New York (formerly Captain Delavall's book-keeper), as trustee for said Swynock; and that the latter buying Swynock out, Aug. 9th, 1687, afterward sold the island to Thomas Parcell, as will be further noticed. Abraham Gouverneur marrying Milborne's widow (who was a daughter of the noted Capt. Jacob Leisler), eventually came in possession of one third of Capt. Delavall's lands in Harlem—the other two thirds, with Little Barent's Island, going to the Pipons, as heirs of Captain Carteret. But not till sixty-five years after the death of Capt. Delavall were these respective claims fully adjusted, and the estate—much enhanced meanwhile by drafts from the common lands—finally closed by the sale of the property. This interesting title is especially treated of in the Appendix, under the head of *The Delavall Lands*.*

Jacqueline Parisis, widow of Daniel Tourneur, being "sick and weak of body, and lying in bed," made her will Aug. 31st, 1682, to which were witnesses Resolved Waldron and Joost van Oblinus. The property, comprising "lands, houses, house

* JACQUES COUSSEAU, another old merchant of N. Y., and a Huguenot exile, (see pp. 53, 111,) associated with H. in its infancy, survived Capt. Delavall but a short time, after being present as a witness to his will. He himself d. intestate. His account and letter books running from 1653 to 1677, and described in his inventory taken Dec. 7, 1682, evidence a long and active business career, chiefly at La Rochelle and New York. He was latterly a shipping merchant: in business affairs "esteemed a person of credit and honesty, and in no manner suspected of fraudulent dealings." In 1665 he visited Hamburgh, and again went to Holland in 1668. He had served as schepen at New Amsterdam, and was one of the commissioners who arranged the capitulation in 1664. His connection with H. had previously ceased, on the sale of his lands to Tourneur. A warm friendship had long subsisted between Mr. Cousseau and Simon Fell and his w., be a Huguenot from Dieppe, (probably anc. of Judge John Fell, of N. J.,) and, in 1680, Cousseau m. Fell's wid., Anna Vincent. Her br. John Vincent was Mr. Cousseau's administrator. Martha Cousseau, his dr., as would appear, m. Daniel Poireau, of N. Y.

lots, cattle, ready money, credits," was to be shared equally by her children, Daniel, Madeleine, Esther, Jaco and Thomas, except as follows: "Whereas, Jan Dyckman, married to Madeleine, has a lot of land on Montagne's Flat, and an erf and garden here in the village, already in possession;" her son Daniel shall have the lot of land on Hoorn's Hook, which he has procured in his own name, with a lot on Montagne's Flat, and also the carpenter's tools. Jaco and Thomas are each to have "a weaver's loom and its fixtures." Daniel and Jaco are to engage to give her youngest son, Thomas, a good trade, whichever he is best suited for, either wheelwright or weaver, which they themselves understand. Her two daughters to divide her clothing. But Mrs. Tourneur survived this illness eighteen years. Not "sackcloth and mourning" came to her house, but a happier event, the marriage, the ensuing winter, of her eldest son, Daniel, to an English maiden, "Ann Wodhull, of Seattalcot, spinster." By what unbidden chance or love's deep art was brought about this alliance with a distant Long Island family, we are not told. The Governor's license was obtained Feb. 5th, 1683, and the nuptials were probably celebrated at Setauket, in the hospitable home of the Woodhulls. The next summer the son Jacques married into the Dutch family of Kortright, and went to live on the farm on Montagne's Flat, on the expiration of the lease to Thomas Holland, who had taken it Oct. 30th, 1679, for four years, "with the house and *hoyberg*h," engaging, the first year, to clear and fence three morgen of land; the lessor (Daniel Tourneur) and lessee to use the barn in common, and together to dig a well.

By a later will, and a contract between the children, both dated Sept. 7th, 1690, the Tourneur lands were divided somewhat differently. Daniel took the land and buildings on Montagne's Flat, then occupied by his brother Jacques, giving him his own included three lots together (in which the late Wood farm was embraced), with the meadow on the adjoining creek; Jacques and Thomas took "the buildings and house lots and orchard, and the five lots lying at this village, to wit: a lot behind the aforesaid orchard (being No. 1 Jochem Pieters) and four lots of land lying on Van Keulen's Hook; with *the meadows to the same belonging, at Stony Point*, and at Spuyten Duyvel, in the

Round Meadow." The children of Madeleine Dyckman, deceased, were to have the inheritance from their grandfather and grandmother, namely, a lot on Montagne's Flat and two Outgardens at the village; and Esther was to retain the land on which she then lived (in Westchester), with the meadow on that side of the river at Spuyten Duyvel. Jacques and Thomas were to pay their sister Esther 400 gl., and the children of their sister Madeleine 1000 gl.; all the lands were to pass into full possession in May, 1691, and the children were to pay their mother for her support, each the sum of 40 gl. yearly. Daniel's death, which happened only a few days after, made no change in this arrangement of the lands; for the further history of which and of the partition between Jacques and Thomas, see Appendix E, F, G.

Jan Hendricks van Brevoort leased the town lot (church farm) and meadows, Jan. 12th, 1683, for the term of ten years, at 85 gl. per year. According to custom, it was set up at public auction, and struck off to Brevoort as highest bidder. On March 15th, Resolved Waldron, Johannes Vermelje, Jan Nagel, and Joost van Oblinus, curators and guardians of the estate of Thomas Hedding, deceased, advertised for creditors to present their claims within six weeks.* After further notice, his stock, etc., was sold at auction May 12th and June 2d, 1683, bringing 608 gl. Buyers, Johannes Vermelje, Jan Dyckman, William Bickley, Barent Waldron, Reyer Michielsen, Lourens Jansen, and Jan Gerrits de Vries. Three cows, with each a calf, brought respectively, 132, 145, 150 gl.

Jean Baignoux sold his farm on Hoorn's Hook, May 15th, to Isaac Deschamps, a French refugee, and well-to-do merchant at New York. On June 8th ensuing, Deschamps got a lien on Jacob Young's farm adjoining, to secure the payment of £20; but three months later, Young sold to Holmes, as before stated.

* THOMAS HEDDING, who leased a farm in the town, had lately died. He made his will June 2, 1682, when "sick in body and lying in bed." He was then the "widower of Maria Huyberts," and devised what he had to his chn. equally, after gifts to Catherine, the ch. of his dr. Sarah, and to his youngest dr. Maria. Sarah was then the wife of John Watson. Lawrence Hedding, his only son known to us, and who was b. in Amsterdam, in 1665, became a "mariner" or sea-captain, and m. in 1698, Johanna, dr. of Laurens Colevelt. The next year he took a dismission from the H. chh. to that of N. Y. He was naturalized in 1702.

The Saw-kill farm was now held jointly by Robinson and Pinhorne (the last as agent for Lewin and Wolley), but Robinson, within a short time, to wit, on Feb. 12th, 1684, disposed of his half to William Cox, a prominent New York merchant, largely engaged in the West India and foreign trade. Deschamps eventually sold the Baignoux farm to John Spragge, Esq., of New York. The lands about this lower section of the town, already acquiring value, were thus passing from the hands of the sturdy yeomen who first settled and improved them, in part to become, under the touch of wealth and refinement, the charming rural seats of affluent tradesmen and shipping merchants, noted mariners and others. Later occupants of the Saw-kill farm were Capt. Samuel Bradley and his son-in-law, the famous Capt. William Kidd, whose wife was the former Mrs. Cox.*

Col. Thomas Dongan arrived at New York, August 25th, 1683, with a commission as governor. He was instructed to convene a General Assembly, to frame new laws for the province, and in Council, Sept. 15th, ordered a writ sent to the Sheriff, "to summon the freeholders of the City of New York, the Boweries or Farms, and Harlem, to choose four Representatives." Due respect must have been paid to this notice, though the records are silent in regard to the effect upon the Harlem people, or their action thereon. Exciting less enthusiasm here than it produced among the English population, we presume none of the delegates were from Harlem. On Sept. 24th, John Delamater's two horses were "pressed" for some urgent public service, and he accompanied them and was paid for it, but we are left to surmise the object.

* JEAN BAIGNOUX bore a good character, but is little known. It was he, we presume, who, as Jan Binjou, joined the chh. Apl. 12, 1665, at the same time with Abraham du Toict. Binjou, (*Beenyou*) approaches his name in sound. Montagne writes it *Benu*; the English scribes usually *Benew*. The cultured Vander Vin using a latin prefix, (see note p. 120.) writes it *Abigeau*, i.e. *from* Baignoux, the latter a Burgundian town, whence Jean probably came. Twice he calls him "Jean Abignou, alias Jan Petit." The French called him Jean Petit, the Dutch *Kleyn Jan*, both meaning *Little John*. Kleyn Jan was paid at 11. 9 fl. for "putting the drum in order." I suspect he had been one of Gov. Nicolls' soldiers. He had license Dec. 6, 1670, to m. Elizabeth, dr. of Ralph Hall, but his w. in and after 1673, was Anna Hoede. In 1680, he m. Jenne Stevens. Later, if we mistake not, sailing a coasting vessel, he met with disaster. Abm. Gouverneur writing from Boston, Oct. 12, 1692, relates "the sad mischance of Little John and his son," who, bound thence for N. Y., "were cast away on Nantucket Shoals, and both drowned."

Indeed, a home matter of great interest to the freeholders had for some months occupied the public mind. This was another suit brought by Tourneur and the Jansens against Col. Morris, for the recovery of the meadows at Stony Island. On May 31st, 1683, at the instance of the plaintiffs, Justice Willett, of the Court of Sessions for the North Riding, issued a summons for Col. Morris; an entry and record of the case being also made as follows, by John West, the clerk:

Jamaica Sessions Ss: Col. Lewis Morris was summoned to answer Daniel Tourneur, Cornelis Jansen and Lawrence Jansen, of a Plea, for that he the said Col. Lewis Morris them, the said Daniel Tourneur, Cornelis Jansen and Lawrence Jansen, out of a certain parcel of Meadow Ground at Stone Island, being *four lots*, hath ejected, and from them unjustly and unlawfully dues detain, etc. And thereupon the said Daniel, Cornelis and Lawrence say that for divers years last past, they, the said Daniel, Cornelis and Lawrence, have been quietly, peaceably, and lawfully seized of the before-mentioned four lots of Meadow Ground, and to their own proper use and behoof have held, occupied, and enjoyed the same; but the said Col. Lewis Morris the right, title, and interest of the said Daniel, Cornelis and Lawrence not at all regarding, into the said four lots of Meadow Ground hath entered, and therefrom the said Daniel, Cornelis and Lawrence hath ejected, and by force unlawfully and injuriously the same doth withhold and detain, by which they say they are damnified the sum of Sixty Pounds; Whereupon they bring this their suit, praying Judgment against the said Col. Lewis Morris, for the said four lots of Meadow Ground, with their Damage and Costs, etc.

The summons was in these terms:

Jamaica Sessions; To Col. Lewis Morris.

You are in his Majesty's name required to be and personally to appear at the next Court of Sessions to be holden at Jamaica for the North Riding of Yorkshire on Long Island, on Wednesday, the 13th day of June next ensuing, then and there to answer Daniel Tourneur, Cornelis Jansen and Lawrence Jansen, for that you them, the said Daniel Tourneur, Cornelis Jansen and Lawrence Jansen, out of a certain parcel of Meadow Ground at Stone Island, being four lots, have ejected, and unjustly and unlawfully from them do detain and withhold, to their damage Sixty Pounds; and thereof you are not to fail at your peril. Dated the 31st day of May, 1683. Thomas Willett.

This summons was served on Morris, June 2d, and at the time appointed the case came to trial. Plaintiffs produced the Harlem patent, and the special patents to Tourneur and De Meyer, in support of their claim. Witnesses were heard. Adolph Meyer testified that he had been at Harlem twenty-two years, and never heard that any others laid claim to the meadows in question at Stony Point; further that the two brothers, Jansens, mowed the hay before Gov. Colve's time, at Stony Point and Stony Island, and that the island belonged to Daniel Tourneur fifteen or sixteen years ago. Defendant endeavored to show that the island so called was not such till "David Demarest made the Ditch between Stony Neck and the Main, in the time of the Dutch, he being then overseer of the Plantation." Hence he held that it was part of his land. The case being submitted, the jury returned a verdict for the plaintiffs; but Morris's attorney put in a plea for an arrest of judgment, which being allowed by the court, the verdict was quashed, and the plaintiffs were ordered to pay the costs.

Thus the case stood till after the arrival of Col. Dongan, when, single-handed, Tourneur determined to renew the contest. On Sept. 25th, he petitioned and obtained an order of the Governor and Council, allowing him to carry his suit to the Court of Assize. Thereupon the following summons was issued:

By the Governor.

You are, in his Royal Highness' name, required to be, and personally to appear at the next General Court of Assizes, to be holden at the City of New York, beginning the first Wednesday in October next ensuing, by nine of the clock in the forenoon of the same day; Then and there to answer Daniel Tourneur in an Action of Trespass on the Case, for ejecting the said Daniel Tourneur out of a certain lot of Meadow Ground lying on Stone Island, in the Precincts of Harlem, and therefore you are not to fail under the Penalty of One Hundred Pounds. Given under my hand at Fort James, the 25th day of September, 1683.

THO. DONGAN.

To Col. LEWIS MORRIS.

Tourneur's statement, duly entered, was as follows:

Declaration *ad Ami*, Daniel Tourneur *vs.* Col. Lewis Morris.

Province of New York: To the Honorable Court of Assizes, etc. Col. Lewis Morris was summoned to this Court to answer Daniel Tourneur, of the Town of Harlem, in plea of *Trespass on the Case*, for that he the said Lewis the said Daniel out of a lot of meadow ground lying on Stony Island, in the precincts of Harlem, within the jurisdiction of this Court, did eject, expel, and from his quiet possession thereof did remove: And whereupon the said Daniel sayeth, that in the month of June, in the year of our Lord 1681, he the said Daniel stood quietly and lawfully possessed of a certain lot of meadow, marked Number 3, lying on Stony Island, on the east part of the said Island, containing by estimation about four acres; And being so quietly and peaceably possessed, he the said Lewis Morris, upon the 2d day of July, in the year of our Lord

1681, with force and arms, upon the said lot of meadow ground did enter, and him the said Daniel from his quiet and peaceable possession thereof did eject, expel, and remove, and the hay which he the said Daniel had mowed with force did take and carry away, and him the said Daniel from his quiet possession thereof doth keep, contrary to the peace of our Sovereign Lord the King, etc., and to the damage of the said Daniel Forty Pounds; which causes the said Daniel to bring this his suit, craving Judgment of this Honorable Court, that he may be repossessed of the said meadow, and such damage and cost may be awarded him as your Honors in your grave Judgment shall think meet. And the Plaintiff will ever pray, etc.

Morris's answer, prepared with care, was in these terms:

Ad Ami, Aº. 1683.

Daniel Tourneur, *Plt.*
Col. Lewis Morris, *Deft.* } *In Trespass and Ejectment.*

Declaration. The Plt. declares in Trespass and Ejectment, that the Deft., the 2d July, 1681, with force and arms, etc., did eject him out of a lot of meadow ground lying on Stony Island, on the east part of the said Island, in the precincts of Harlem, containing by estimation about four acres, and the hay which he had there mowed did take and carry away, to his damage £40.

Plea. Deft. pleads not guilty, etc., and puts himself on the country, etc. Claims the meadow in question belongs to the Deft. He derives his Title as followeth, *viz.*:

Oct. 20th, 1644, a patent was granted by the Dutch Governor Wm. Kieft unto Arent van Curler, who married the widow of Jonas Bronck, for a certain tract or parcel of land formerly in the tenure or occupation of the said Jonas Bronck, and by the English called Bronck's Land, lying and being on the main to the east and over against Harlem town, having a certain small creek or kill which runs between the south-west part of it and little Barnes Island, near Hellgate, and so goes into the East River, and a greater creek or river which divides it from Manhatans Island; containing about 500 acres or 250 morgen of land, and including all the fresh meadow thereunto annexed or adjoining.

July 10th, 1651, the said Arent van Curler conveyed the said land unto Jacob Jans Stoll.

Dec. 19th, 1662, Mattheus de Vos, as attorney of Geertruyt Andries, the widow of the said Jacob Jans Stoll, conveyed the said land unto Geertrica Hendricks, formerly the widow of Andries Hoppen. Upon the same day the said Geertrica Hendricks, with the approbation and consent of Dirck Gerrits van Tright, then her husband, conveyed the same land to Harman Smeeman.

Oct. 22d, 1664, Harman Smeeman sold and conveyed the same land, for a valuable consideration, to Samuel Edsall.

1668, Col. Nicolls, by patent, makes recital of all the former conveyances and ratified and confirmed to the said Samuel Edsall, his heirs and assignes forever, all the aforesaid land and premises, with its appurtenances, and all meadow ground, marshes, etc., to the same belonging or in any wise appertaining.

June 4th, 1668, The said Samuel Edsall and Jannetien his wife, by deed indented, for the consideration of £140, sold and conveyed the same to the Deft. with all the meadows and marshes thereto belonging; and had actual possession thereof.

1673. The Deft. remained in possession until Anno 1673, when the Dutch taking the place, his negroes were seized, and his family forced to leave the land, in which time the Plt. cut a ditch in his meadow to make that an Island which was not so before.

1674. By the Articles of Peace, and surrender of the place, the Deft. was again possessed of the land and premises, and so remains.

March 25th, 1676; The before-mentioned land, meadows and premises, with an addition of a larger quantity of land, was by patent from Sir Edmund Andros confirmed to the Deft. who is in possession thereof, and therefore says that the meadow in question is part of the land and meadow mentioned and contained in all the former grants and conveyances; and that he ought to hold and enjoy the same, for that his title as aforesaid is far preferable and more ancient than the Plaintiff's pretences, which are but of late, and on uncertain grounds.*

Upon the trial, which came on at the time appointed, and at which Gov. Dongan presided, Engeltie Burger, widow of Burger Joris, Thomas Hunt, Sen., Thomas Hunt, Jun., Walter Webley, John Archer, Mr. Osborne, and Thomas Wandell gave the following testimony in behalf of the defendant; that for the plaintiff has been substantially anticipated:

Burger sayeth that Bronck mowed the meadow on the Neck about 40 years ago, three times; and made a bridge, and put their cattle there.

Hunt, Senr. had knowledge of the land in Gov. Kieft's time, and saw fences of Bronck's land standing on the east side of the creek; and a bridge went over it, and the land was generally called by the name of Bronck's land, and that Stone Island is a new name.

* The HOPPER FAMILY, of this country and of good Holland antecedents, are desc. of *Andries Hopper*, who with his w. Geertie Hendricks emigrated hither in 1652. He was enrolled in 1653 in the burgher corps at New Amsterdam, and granted the small burgher right in 1657, when he owned considerable property in the city; but this honor he survived little more than a year. Having agreed with Jacob Stol for the purchase of Bronck's land, and made a payment on it, he and Stol both d. before the deed passed. The two widows concluded the transfer. In view of her m. with Van Tright, which took place in May, 1660, Mrs. Hopper secured to each of her four chn. the sum of 200 gl. These were Catharine, b. 1652, who m. Frederick Thomasz, of N. Y.; William, b. 1654, m. Minne, dr. of Jurck Paulus; Henry, b. 1656, m. Maria, dr. of John Van Blarkum; and Matthew-Adolphus, b. 1658, who m. Anna, dr. of Jurck Paulus. Part of this family settled at Bloomingdale, part in Bergen Co.; and from the former came Yellis Hopper, of Hoorn's Hook, gd-fa. of Mrs. Wm. H. Colwell, of H. And the author, making his home in Jersey City while passing his work through the press, has prepared this brief note under the mayoralty of an estimable desc. of Andries Hopper, the old New Amsterdam burgher; we refer, as is obvious, to the Hon. Henry J. Hopper.

Hunt, Junr., that when Col. Morris' brother came, a report was that he had got the land as far as Bronck's river; and meeting with Daniel Tourneur, father to the plaintiff, he told him thereof; and in discourse the said Tourneur showed him the bounds of Bronck's land, and that the land in controversy was contained therein; that till the time of the Dutch governor Colve, the same was a firm, entire neck, and horses and carts could go over, when a ditch was made; and that he never knew it to be called Stone Island, and that the defendant's land comes to the East River only in that place.

Webley understanding that some Harlem men had been on the land to mow the meadow, he forewarns them; they went away. Next year the place being taken by the Dutch, Tourneur hired one to make a ditch round the meadow, etc. In discourse after, with Tourneur, in presence of Capt. Nicolls and Capt. Knapton, the draft being shown, they agreed; and the defendant thereon procured a patent for it.

Archer sayeth that long time since, the town pretending want of meadow, obtained liberty of Stuyvesant to mow, until the owners appeared to forewarn them, and when Col. Nicolls came, they underhand got a patent of him, and had none before, but hired land of the Indians.*

Osborne sayeth he was overseer on Col. Morris's land; the plaintiffs by Capt. Morris's leave mowed there at halves, and afterwards were by him discharged, and that the meadow was then fast and firm, without any ditch.

Wandell, the same.

The following is a copy of the decision:

At a *General Court of Assizes* held in *New York*, beginning the 3d and ending the 6th day of October, 1683.

Daniel Tourneur, *Pltf.*
Col. Lewis Morris, *Deft.*

Upon an Action brought into this Court by the Plaintiff against the Deft. for being ejected, expelled, and from his quiet possession removed out of his lot of land lying on a certain piece of ground called Stony Island, which the Deft. alleged to be within his purchase as belonging to the land bought by his brother, of Samuel Edsall, on his behalf: the Case having been fully heard and debated, and witnesses on both parts produced, the Jury brought in their Verdict in writing: *We find for the Plaintiff, with Costs of Suit*; and the Court gave their Judgment accordingly. The Defendant petitioning the Court for a review of his case, and desiring that the Jury may be of the neighborhood, it was *Ordered*, that Col. Lewis Morris have a review or a hearing at the next General Court of Assizes, and that there be a Jury appointed, the one half whereof is to be of this City of New York, and the other half from Long Island, to view the said Land, and to have the patent of Arent van Curler along with them.

By order of the Governor and Court of Assizes,

J. Spragge, Secretary.

* Archer's unfriendly thrust at the Harlem people regarding their patent, and to be readily accounted for, cannot impair his direct statement, that they had no patent prior to that of Gov. Nicolls. Thus the position taken on page 319, that Harlem had no general patent under the Dutch, is sustained.

Again this matter hung in suspense. By having it submitted to a jury "of the neighborhood," the defendant hoped to gain a verdict in his favor, but to this the Court would not consent. As it stood, the prospects were not very flattering for a reversal of the decision given and sustained in three several courts.*

Other matters were pending of great import, touching the public interests. The General Assembly met on Oct. 17th, and the next day that august body, the Town Court, also sat as usual for the discharge of business. "To prevent as much as possible all accidents by fire, which may God avert"—so reads the minutes of the latter body—an ordinance of Sept. 6th, 1677, was re-enacted, to wit: "That every one shall bring his compost heap and refuse straw within his inclosure, and not throw them into the street." A disastrous fire the next spring showed that human foresight could not always prevent such calamities. On the day the General Assembly performed its crowning act, the town magistrates and clerk were busy with Robert Hudson, of Westchester, concluding a settlement respecting a horse which Hudson had attached in the hands of Jan Dyckman a full year before. Hudson sold the horse to Resolved Waldron, paying the costs of keeping and clerk fees, which amounted to "£1 : 11 : 0, or 62 guilders."

The General Assembly, in session within the walls of Fort James, were framing a *Charter of Liberties* for the province, which being adopted on the 30th of October, 1683, was published on the 31st, with great acclamation. It provided for similar assemblies, to meet as often as every three years; admitted

* As a *precedent* for modern courts we copy "A Bill of Court Charges at the Assizes 1683; Daniel Tourneur, *Plt.*, Col. Lewis Morris, *Deft.*

	£	s	d
The special warrant of summons	£0	12	0
The entry for trial		5	0
Filing the Declaration		2	6
Copy		3	4
Filing the Answer		2	6
Copy		3	4
The High Sheriff's fees		12	0
The Cryer and Marshall		3	8
Seven witnesses sworn in Court		14	0
To the Cryer for swearing them		4	8
The Charges to the Publick	1	0	0
The Judgment of Court		10	0
The Copy		2	6
	£4	15	6

the people, with some limitations, to a voice in legislation, by their representatives; declared entire freedom of conscience and religion to all professing faith in God by Jesus Christ; and forbade any tax, assessment, or impost being laid upon any of His Majesty's subjects, or their estates, "but by the act and consent of the Governor, Council, and Representatives of the People, in General Assembly."

By another act, the province was divided into shires and counties, in place of the ridings; the city and county of New York to embrace, beside Manhattan Island, also Manning's, or Blackwell's Island, and the two Barne Islands.

Another act reorganized or erected Courts of Justice: the Town Court, the County Court, or Court of Sessions, a General Court of Oyer and Terminer, and a Court of Chancery. The town court was to be composed of three "Commissioners," chosen by the freeholders, and to be called the "Commissioners' Court;" having power to hear and determine small causes to the value of forty shillings. This law, passed on the 1st of November, was of special advantage to Harlem, as against the assumptions of the city government.

The city authorities were aiming to secure enlarged prerogatives, and were now in conference with the Governor upon this subject; but passing over details which have no place here, it is sufficient to say that a check was put upon their aspirations. To the first proposition submitted by the Mayor and Aldermen, Nov. 9th, viz., "That all the Inhabitants on the Island Manhattans are under the government of the City of New York," the Council took exception. They regard it but "reasonable that the Town of Harlem shall have liberty to determine all matters that come before them under forty shillings at their own Town Court." Whereupon the Mayor and Aldermen hastened to explain thus: "The *Town of Harlem* is a village within and belonging to this City and Corporation, and for the more easy administration and dispatch of Justice, officers have been annually appointed by the Mayor and Aldermen, to hold Courts and determine matters not exceeding 40s., both at *Harlem* and the *Bowery*, and shall do the like for the future."

The *Out Ward*, one of the six wards into which the city, pursuant to a resolution of the Mayor and Aldermen, of Dec.

8th, was now divided, embraced "the town of Harlem, with all the Farms, Plantations, and Settlements on this Island Manhattans, from the north side of the Fresh Water." It was to be subdivided into the *Bowery* and *Harlem Divisions.* The separating line between these two divisions, as by a resolve of Dec. 10th, was to "continue as formerly at the Sawmill Creek," and each division was to have its local court; the people to nominate a double number of persons fit to be commissioners, and the Mayor and Aldermen to make the appointments.

Harlem, upon being notified, made its nomination; and on Dec. 18th "*John Dyckman*, *John Nagel*, and *Arent Harmans* were appointed Commissioners for the Harlem Division, in the Out Ward," and took the oath of office. *Resolved Waldron* was named Assessor, and *Daniel Tourneur* Constable and Collector. *William Cox*, chosen Alderman for the said ward, soon secured a freehold here, as part owner of the Saw-kill farm, a fact already noticed. The militia was organized the next year, when the inhabitants of the Out Ward capable of bearing arms were formed into a company, under Capt. *Nicholas William Stuyvesant*, with *Daniel Tourneur* as lieutenant, and *Adriaen Cornelise van Schaack* as ensign.

Nothing much happened till the meeting of the new court. Resolved Waldron and Johannes Vermilye, the guardians of Cornelia Viervant, offered at auction, Jan. 16th, 1684, a horse left by her late father, but did not succeed in selling it, only 37 gl. being bid. It was afterward bought for 120 gl. by Jan Postmael (the Post ancestor), who at the same time, March 3d, hired 3 cows left by Viervant, for six years, for half the increase.*

*Cornelis Arents Viervant was a native of Leamont, in the Land of Vianen, Utrecht. He m. at Kingston in 1668, Jeanne le Sueur, sr. of François, the [illegible] anc., and d. at Fordham, in 1675, leaving an only ch. Cornelia, [illegible] m. William Innis, of Kingston, a son, we suspect, of Rev. Alexander Innis, chaplain at N. Y., in 1686. William Innis had chn. Alexander, b. 1694, Cornelius, 1696, etc. Desc. are yet found.

Jan Jansen Postmael, whose chn. shortened the name to *Post*, came from Harlingen, in Friesland, and lived some years in N. Y., where he seems to have gotten his surname, from being employed as mail-carrier: a family legend gives it this origin, but names no place. He m. Jeanne, dr. of François le Sueur aforesaid, and leased Laurens Jansen's farm at H., Apl. 23, 1679, but the lease was cancelled July 3, under a new agreement. Removing about 1684 to Kingston, there he d. a few years later. His chn. were Jan, b. 1680, Abraham, 1682, Anna Catrina, 1684, Elsie, 1686, Anthony,

On Feb. 8th the Constable and Commissioners, Dyckman as *President*, held their first court. The old officers were also present. It was resolved to take up and examine the town accounts, both debits and credits, and to transfer them to a new book, "as the old book C is written full." *Adolph Meyer* and *Resolved Waldron* were chosen inspectors of chimneys and fire-wardens; and *Barent Waldron* and *Isaac Delamater*, surveyors of the common fences. These fences were ordered to be repaired and made of four split rails; good and suitable. Barent Waldron, on his request, was voted a deed for Moertje Davids Meadow, which he had purchased four years previous. The deed was duly passed by the Commissioners, April 8th, 1684.

On Feb. 21st, Jan Dyckman and Arent Harmans Bussing, "deacons of the Christian congregation of New Harlem," were called to visit the aged Gabriel Carbosie, whom finding in bed sick at the house of Jan Louwe Bogert, they first "instructed as far as practicable, with words of comfort." To an inquiry as to the disposal of his effects, "in case God should with this sickness take him out of this world"—for his wife Brieta had gone before him—he answered "that he should leave his goods to those who had been kind to him;" evidently the Bogerts. Soon after, he passed away, and on March 3d the deacons made a record of what was said at this interview, for the benefit of those interested.

Near this time also, "John Archer, Lord Proprietor of the Manor of Fordham," met with a "sudden and unexpected death." His son, John Archer, Jun., by this event "become a poor orphan, void and destitute of all support," as he himself alleged, applied to the Council, on March 1st, to appoint administrator's upon his father's estate. A similar application

1688. His wid. m. Thomas Innis. Anna C. Post m. Jan Pearson. Jan Post, for so he was called, was b. at H., and married at Kingston, 1702, Cornelia, dr. of Martin Isselsteyn; he has desc. in Ulster co. Abraham returned to H., and in 1701, then calling himself Postmael, became farmer for Capt. Jacob De Key. In 1709, as witness in a suit to which De Key was a party, he is called Post. He was no doubt anc. to the Post family given in *Bolton's Westchester*, ii, 537. He had, however, a son Hendrick Post, who m. 1737, Rebecca, dr. of Jan Nagel, of Kingsbridge, and d. before 1756, his chn. being John, Abraham, Hendrick, Elizabeth, and Lena. One of his drs. m. Henry Tison, who with John and Hendrick Post, came into possession of the Nagel lands at Kingsbridge, on the d. of their uncle William Nagel, in 1508.

was made by Cornelis Steenwyck, to whom Archer was indebted £993 : 16, secured by mortgage on the manor; and appraisers were appointed, one of whom was Daniel Tournour.

On March 11th, in the evening, the village was alarmed by the cry of fire. It proved to be Jan Nagel's barn; which was not only burnt to the ground, but with it 12 head of cattle, including 7 milch cows. It was found to have been set on fire by his own negro, who then ran away, and was discovered next morning "hanging to a tree at the Little Hill by the common." A letter was sent to the Mayor and Court asking what they should do with the body; to which, on the 14th, came an answer to hang it on a gibbet, in any place they thought proper. But the magistrates and community, fearing the effect of such a spectacle upon "their children, who are in the habit of going daily to the fields and woods, and who might be terrified thereby," cut the body down, and burnt it to ashes. No pen has revealed the incentive to actions so desperate, on the part of the poor bondman, by which we may judge of this particular case. But the chains of slavery were sufficiently galling even then and there; and the wonder is that the free spirit of the native African, chafing under an involuntary servitude, did not oftener avenge itself. Another case occurred, within a year, on Col. Morris's plantation. His slave Cuffy, being guilty of arson, was hung and buried, but afterward disinterred and placed in gibbets.

The first direct step toward the renewal or confirmation of the town patent by Governor Dongan was taken at a Council held on March 31st, of this year, by the passage of an order "that the Inhabitants of Harlem bring in their Patents and Indian Deeds on Thursday." As for Indian Deeds, the town of Harlem had none; but this was the form in which the order went forth to the several towns. The "patents" were delivered to the Council, April 10th, by Mr. Jacobus Van Cortlandt, who, in behalf of the inhabitants, proceeded "to treat about Quit Rent;" to secure which was the object had in view by the government in calling for the old patents. A year or more later this negotiation ripened into a formal demand upon the freeholders "to make up the quit rent for the Heer Governor."

An event locally interesting was Cornelis Jansen's removal to his land on Montagne's Flat, since known as the Nutter Farm. On April 30th, 1684, he engaged Adrianus Westerhout to build him a house there, 22 by 36 feet, to be ready in six weeks, or at farthest by the 20th of June; for which he agreed to pay "800 guilders in fat cattle, wheat and rye;" the cattle to be delivered on All Saints' Day, and the grain the next January. Here Jansen established the famous tavern and stopping-place, "commonly called the Half-Way House," and which continued to be kept after his death in 1689, by his widow. It stood on the west side of Harlem Lane, at the foot of the hill about 109th Street. A little above this site, Valentine Nutter, on getting possession of the Kortright farm after the Revolution, built a new residence, which remained till swept away by the opening of 6th Avenue, on which it stood, its north corner touching 110th Street.

Mowing-time was again at hand, and Daniel Tourneur petitioned the Council, July 9th, that whereas the review of the case between him and Col. Morris could not take place before the Court of Assize, since that court had been "wholly taken away, and other courts constituted," he might be secured in his possession by a "writ of *habere facias possessionem.*" But Col. Morris, being present as a member of the Council, "desired a writ of error, which was granted." The old Cromwellian officer, though his fighting principles had yielded to the pacific tenets of the Quaker, had thus far proved himself so good a tactician as to maintain his ground against every attempt to dislodge him. But emboldened by success, he now determined, if possible, to force the case to an issue before the Court of Oyer and Terminer in his own county, where he might have the advantage of his opponent; and thereupon petitioned as follows:

To the Hon. Col. Thomas Dongan, Lieutenant and Governor-General, etc. etc.

The Petition of Lewis Morris, the elder, commonly called Colonel Lewis Morris, *Sheweth:* That at a General Court of Assizes held in New York, beginning the 3d and ending the 6th day of October, 1683, an Action was commenced against your Petitioner by Daniel Tourneur for being ejected, expelled, and from his quiet possession removed out of his lot of land lying on a certain piece of ground called Stony Island; where on trial the Jury found for the Plaintiff with costs of suit, and the Court gave Judgment accordingly; whereupon your Petitioner, according to the usual custom and practice of that Court, petitioned for a Review of his Case, and that the Jury might be of the neighborhood, to view the land in controversy; which was ordered accordingly to be done at the next General Court of Assizes, since which said General Court of Assizes is made void and null, and Court of Oyer and Terminer appointed in each County, for the trial of causes of this nature. Your Petitioner not being willing that the difference between him and the said Tourneur should be longer delayed, but that some speedy issue may be put to the same, humbly prays your Honor that the said Daniel Tourneur may be ordered to commence his action at the next Court of Oyer and Terminer to be holden in the County where the land in controversy lyeth, that the same may be reviewed and reheard, and a Jury of the neighborhood, who shall view the said land, to pass thereupon, etc. And your Petitioner shall pray, etc. LEWIS MORRIS.

In acting upon this petition, Morris's plan was again amended as to having "a jury of the neighborhood;" but care was taken to secure a fair and impartial hearing. The record reads:

At a Council held at Fort James, the 13th September, 1684; *Present*, The Governor, etc.

This Petition being read, the two Judges, Capt. Matthias Nicolls and Capt. John Palmer, were consulted, who gave their advice, and it was ordered by the Governor and Council that a Special Commission be given to the Judges, and to Mr. Cortlandt, Mr. Pell, Jacques Cortilleu, Justices; and a particular writ be sent to the Sheriff of New York, and another to the Sheriff of Queens County, one to return twelve men and the other twelve more, for a Jury in the Action between Col. Lewis Morris and Daniel Tourneur, the Cause to be tried at New York, to begin on the 6th of October next ensuing; the Jury is to view the land, and the trial is not to continue above six days; and it is farther ordered that Col. Lewis Morris is to be at the charges of the Review.

Twenty-two days only were to intervene before the meeting of this Court, and as the Council did not revoke the order, no doubt it met accordingly, though its minutes, we regret to say, have not been found. But from several considerations, we infer that it changed nothing. The New York Court of Record of July 6th, 1680, had found for the plaintiffs, so had the Jamaica Sessions of June 13th, 1683, and then the Court of Assize of Oct. 3d ensuing. This last allowed a rehearing, because that was "the usual custom and practice of that Court." But no change in the status had occurred to warrant any reverse of judgment. It was a simple question of fact. These courts had assumed that when Stuyvesant granted these meadows, he acted from the knowledge that no one else had a prior title. After the last hearing, to wit, on November 24th,

1684, Col. Morris paid to Secretary Spragge the amount of the bill given on page 434, as we find by an indorsement thereon. And the Tourneurs appear to have remained in possession. See page 420. As a piece of early litigation, this case is interesting; but it assumes real importance as evidence of the high respect with which the early English courts regarded Stuyvesant's official acts, touching landed interests. His grants were not to be lightly set aside. And if this view obtained at a date the most favorable for knowing the real merits of such cases, how wise the reticence of modern courts to meddle with questions of title reaching back into times so remote!

Tourneur, now Lieutenant of the Out Ward Militia, under the Governor's commission of the 10th of September, was succeeded as constable of the Harlem Division by Adolph Meyer, who was appointed Oct. 13th, and took the oath of office the 18th of November.

Vander Vin, the venerable secretary and voorleser, who had served the town so long and faithfully, and exhibited much wisdom and ability in the discharge of his duties, now entered into rest, having reached his seventieth year. As he lives in the work of his pen, Vander Vin shows his culture, and incidentally his knowledge of Latin and Spanish. He was remarkable for his accuracy, very methodical and precise in small as well as greater matters. Clerk of the Court, both drafter and registrar of deeds, wills and contracts, accountant for the town and church, all these added to his specific duties as voorleser and schoolmaster, it is amusing to find minuted in his clear, neat hand, "Set hen to brood, 15th July, 1675." He left no family, and his wife had died within a few years; therefore, on Jan. 28th, 1685, the Mayor's Court passed an order, "That Daniel Tourneur and Cornelis Jansen do appraise the estate of *Hendrick Jansen Vander Vin*, deceased; and that the same be disposed of by Resolved Waldron and Johannes Vermeljo, to satisfy his funeral charges and debts; and to make report thereof to this Court."

On the same date Joost Oblinus, Johannes Vermeljo, and Jan Delamater were "appointed and sworn Commissioners for Harlem, for the year ensuing;" and Jan Tibout, by birth a Fleming, and late schoolmaster at Flatbush, was made Clerk for the same term. Tibout had entered upon his duties Jan. 20th, at a salary of 300 gl.; he and his family to occupy "the town's house."*

Barent Waldron, soon to marry, prepared to occupy his land, being two of the New Lots purchased by him Nov. 21st, 1677, the one No. 9, from Capt. James Carteret, "for 277 lbs. of beef," and the other, No. 10, from Pieter Jansen Bogert, "for

* JAN TIBOUT was b. at Bruges (see p. 76), and after emigrating lived for a short time at Fort Casimer, on the Delaware, where he was in 1656, and whence coming, he and his w., Sarah vander Vlucht, joined the chh. at New Amsterdam in January, 1660. There and at Flatbush (save while at Bergen, where he was court messenger in 1662, and took the oath of allegiance to the English, Nov. 20, 1665), he spent most of the ensuing years till he came to H. He was voorleser here from 1685 till 1690, when for a year Guiliaem Bertholf took his place, but resuming his office in 1691, he served yet six years, and probably till Adrian Vermeule was employed in 1699. Thence, and at least till 1709, he held the same office at Bushwick. He m., in 1687, the wid. of Glaude Delamater, and on her *erf* right drew Lot 13 on Jochem Pieters Hills, which was sold to Jan Dyckman. Of his dozen chn. we give only such as appear to have reached maturity (with the reservation hereafter made as to the first), viz., Marcus, Theunis, Johannes, Andries, Jacomina, who m. Reyer Michielsen, and Jannetie, who m. Hendrick van Oblinus. Andries Tibout m. Maria De Grawe, settled at Hackensack; had chn., Johannes, Peter, Andries, Jacobus, Jacomina, and Annetie. He d. in 1704, and his wid. m. Albert Terhune. Johannes Tibout, son of Jan, was a turner; m. Teuntie van Rommen; was a zealous Leislerian soldier, 1689; made a freeman at N. Y., 1699, then alderman, and d. chless. June 29, 1729, leaving his property after his wife's d. to his brs. and srs. Theunis Tibout, b. in N. Y., 1663, m., 1690, Mary, dr. of Hendrick Vandewater, was a carpenter; made freeman at N. Y., 1698; proposed, 1712, to erect a horsemill in the city, "never before seen in these parts;" had eight chn., and d. July 27, 1754, æ. 90 yrs. His will was dated Nov. 8, 1753. His dr., *Sarah*, b. 1692, m. Jan Ewouts; he also had sons, whence the Tiebouts of New York, viz., *Hendrick*, b. 1694, m. 1720, Elizabeth Burger; *Johannes*, b. 1696, m. 1719, Maria van Deventer; *Theunis*, b. 1705, m. 1729, Margaret D[illegible], and *Albertus*, b. 1708, who m. 1728, Cornelia Bogert, and was a captain in the old French war. Johannes, a blockmaker, living in N. Y. Jan. 2, 1763, when with his sr., Sarah, he sold some property of his late fa., d. Sept. 12, 1773.

Marcus Tiebaut, as he wrote his name, was b. at Ghent, Flanders, and was probably a son of the voorleser; for though nowhere so called, he was also a Fleming; lived at H. before, as well as after, his marriage, and acted as town clerk after Vermeule, as would appear from records of 1710, written by him. Marcus m. May 29, 1699, Aefie, wid. of Jonas Lewis, and dr. of Cornelis Jansen, and in 1713 was "in possession" of a house and lot on the north side of the Church Lane, next but one west of the *kerk erf*, which no doubt came from John van Oblinus, and went to John Lewis, from whom it passed, in 1749, to Dr. Josiah Paterson. Marcus bought from Caspar Mabie, Mar. 26, 1700, a dwelling, with its lot, which had formed Nos. 5, 6, of Daniel Tourneur's out-gardens. Here Marcus lived after John Lewis m. in 1713, but dying in 1714, without chn., so far as appears, his wid. sold it the next year to John van Oblinus, the trusty friend of Marcus, and also his kinsman, if we are right as to the latter's parentage.

one heifer of three years old." Waldron now bargained with the magistrates for a house lot "on the north side of Pieter Jansen"—that is, lying at the west end of his lot No. 10, where it joined the highway, and for which he was to pay the town after two years, namely in January 1687, "30 gl. in cash, and a gallon of rum." Soon after this the magistrates concluded to sell the "piece of land called *Cloudie's Point*, with a *house lot* lying between the swamp and the King's Way, next to the house lot of Barent Waldron." It was put up at auction March 15th. Johannes Vermelje offered 1200 gl., but Resolved Waldron, wanting it for his son Barent, bid 1500 gl., and took it. Security was given for the payment, which was to be made in two equal instalments, in one and two years. Fifteen years after—that is, on March 7th, 1700—Barent got a deed from the town for this property, which he occupied till 1740, being that since known as the *Bussing Point Farm.*

While the process had thus begun, by which the new lands were to be brought under the plough, or otherwise utilized, sundry large tracts beyond and adjoining the patent lines, or too near to be matter of unconcern to the Harlem people, were being eagerly sought for and taken up. On the North River side, settlement pushing out from the city, beyond Sapokanikan, or Greenwich, to the region already called *Bloemendael;* here Theunis Idens van Huyse, apparently by buying up the title to several lesser grants, had come to own an immense tract, 460 acres, by actual survey, which extended from the present 89th Street to 107th Street. From the Hudson it ran within direct and parallel lines into the woods, nearly 220 rods, touching at its easterly corner the Harlem patent line. Here Theunis, after toiling hard "to make tillable land out of the rough woods," built his dwelling and barns, and set out an orchard, for a lifelong home.

The high lands, stretching north from Van Huyse's line to Hendrick Bosch's farm at Moertje Davids Fly (and which, being sold a few years later to Jacob De Key, became, after his time, the seats of the De Peysters and others, and on portions of which stand the Asylum for the Insane, and the Leake and Watts Orphan House), were yet in native woods; as was also the case with the greater stretch of heights and hollows which reached northerly from Harlem Plains to Sherman's Creek; but here the plough was soon to begin its work, in an Indian field, near the present Fort Washington, called the Great Maize Land.* Col. Morris's trusty friend, William Bickley, had made an application, July 9th, 1684, for a parcel of vacant land on the east side of the Harlem River, which, in the survey, made by Philip Wells, Aug. 10th, 1685, is described as:

A certain neck of land—lying upon the main, and joining upon Harlem River; beginning at a certain spring or run of water to the south of Crab Island, which is the south-west corner of the land of John Archer, and runs into the woods by his line east, by a range of marked trees, forty chains, to a marked tree by a small run of water which is the west bounds of the land of Daniel Tourneur, and so by the run to a creek,† and so round by the creek to Harlem River, and then by the Harlem River to the said small spring or run of water to the south of Crab Island; the whole bounded north by the land of John Archer, east by a run of water, the west bounds of Daniel Tourneur, south by a creek, and west by Harlem River: containing in all one hundred and eighty-four acres and a half.

After an opportunity had been given for presenting objections, a patent issued to Bickley May 13th, 1686. Bickley sold this tract June 25th, 1694, to Tourneur's son-in-law, Frederick De Vaux, whose descendants long owned it, and whence it was called De Voe's Point. *Highbridgeville* is on this tract.

* The *Mayor, Aldermen, and Commonalty*, of the city of New York, convey, July 31st, 1701, to *Jacob De Key*, of the said city, bolter, for £237, "all that certain tract or parcel of land situate, lying, and being on the Island Manhattans, within the Out Ward of the city of New York, lying on the north side of the land of Teunis Ides, and beginneth at a certain old black oak tree marked with three notches, which stands in the south-east corner of the fence of Teunis Ides, and ranges along the fence of the said Teunis Ides north-west sixty chains to Hudson's River, and from thence along the said river north-east and by north (nearly) seventy chains, and from thence south-east and by east till it cuts the line of Harlem, ten chains, and from thence it runs directly south along the line of Harlem Commons eighty-eight chains to the place where it first began; containing in all *two hundred thirty-five acres, three roods, and eighteen perches, or thereabouts*, all English measure; being bounded on the east by the Commons of Harlem, southerly by the land of Teunis Ides, and on the north-west side or thereabouts by Hudson's River, and upon the corner northerly by land of Thomas Turneur; together with all and singular the pastures," etc.—*Grants, City Comptroller's Office*, vol. 2: 28.

† The *Mannepies*, or Cromwell's Creek, before named (see pp. 280, 310). *Crab Island*, to which other references will be found, lay "in Harlem River, at or near the outlet of a small stream, near the old boundary line between Morrisania and the Manor of Fordham, which point is just below the Aqueduct or High Bridge." Communicated, as the result of his inquiries, by Hon. *Lewis G. Morris*, and which is corroborated by the documents here quoted.

CHAPTER XXIII.

1685—1687.

WOLVES; DELAVALL ESTATE; TENURES; TENTHS CANCELLED; NEW STONE CHURCH; GREAT MAIZE LAND; DONGAN'S PATENT; QUIT RENT; CORPORATION RIGHTS; INDIAN CLAIM; COMMON LANDS; FRENCH GUNS; DUTCH MANNERS AND CUSTOMS.

AS the neighboring woodlands were gradually taken up, and here and there the ancient forest, subdued by the axe and burnings, gave place to new fallows and corn-fields, it greatly disturbed the noxious animals still infesting this section of the island, and which, driven from their old haunts and feeding places, were led to prowl about the open fields in search of food or prey, and even to intrude within the paling of the barn-yards. The wolves were especially annoying, and very destructive to the young cattle and stock running at large in the woods. The following order of the governor, authorizing a general foray upon these dangerous animals, to take place on the 6th of August, shows how serious was the evil, and no doubt afforded a day of rare and exciting sport for the young hunters of the town:

> Upon the many complaints of the great mischief done by Wolves on the Island of Manhatans, and at the request and desire of several of the inhabitants of the said Island that they may have liberty and license to hunt and destroy the same: These may certify that liberty and license is hereby granted to any of the inhabitants of the said Island to hunt and destroy the said Wolves on Thursday next after the date hereof. Given under my hand at Fort James, this 1st day of August, 1685.
>
> THO. DONGAN.
>
> Passed the office, J. SPRAGGE, Secretary.

There was a piece of woodland, about twelve acres, for which a bargain had been pending between the town and the late Capt. Delavall, the latter wanting it in exchange for two village lots. This bargain was now completed by John Delavall. On September 2d, 1685, he and the town officers passed deeds in which they "acknowledge to have agreed upon an exchange of two house lots (*erven*), lying north of Johannes Verveelen,* and south of the highway, that belonged to Capt. Delavall, which said house lots he, John Delavall, releases and delivers over to the aforesaid Constable and Magistrates, for the behoof of the said Town, for a parcel of woodland lying behind the lots of the said John Delavall, on Jochem Pieters, being the piece of woodland the before-named Capt. Delavall applied for." This woodland, in a release of the "Three Lots," by Abraham Gouverneur to Johannes Meyer, dated May 2d, 1725, is referred to as "lands in possession of the heirs of James Carteret, deceased;" and by a subsequent division it came to be included, part with the Three Lots, and part with the Six Lots. Upon the lower end (defined by a double elbow in the old Harlem and Kingsbridge road, at 127th Street), the 7th Avenue and 128th Street cross each other, and upon the upper end, the 8th Avenue and 131st Street.

John Delavall, as heir at law, had succeeded to the remainder of all and singular the rights and prerogatives at Harlem which had pertained to his late father in his twofold capacity of freeholder and town patentee. As his sole executor he took the custody of all the lands and *erven* given by his father to his sons-in-law Carteret and Darvall. This last became necessary for the due discharge of his trusts as executor, the respective interests requiring adjustment, while the devise to Darvall was subject to the payment of certain debts due by the testator, in the settlement of which it was requisite for the executor to become a party. It does not appear that the disposition of his lands made by Capt. Delavall was ever called in question, and as for the undivided common lands, there is no intimation that John Delavall, or his widow, ever pretended to any interest in these, after the 14th of January, 1687, when he gave Swynock and Milborne a full and absolute release of the lands conveyed to them conditionally by himself and Darvall, on the 24th of November, 1684. Although such claim must have been excluded under the rule which obtained in making the divisions,

* VERVEELEN's lots on Van Keulen's Hook are here referred to. The *house-lots* were afterward included in the John P. Waldron farm.

namely, that the common lands belonged only to those who held the *erf* and *morgen rights.**

The kind of tenure under which the freeholders held their lands was justly regarded as of vital importance, and invites a notice. The grants made by government, both the Dutch and English, and whether to individuals or communities, were always conditional, imposing a counter obligation upon the grantee or grantees, to recognize the superior right of the lord or sovereign, and his claim upon their obedience and service. Some visible token of this was required annually, and whether the trivial gift of a pepper-corn or fat capon, or a render of greater intrinsic value, it was none the less an act of homage, an acknowledgment of fealty on the part of the subject toward the superior. A remnant of feudal polity, it had this important advantage that the superior

* JOHN DELAVALL, quite young when his fa. first came to this country in 1664, probably remained in England, and arrived here with the family a few years later. He was brought up to a mercantile life in the city of N. Y., where he united with the Dutch church Aug. 29, 1678. On Oct. 14 ensuing, he sailed in the ship Blossom, upon a visit to England. Returning to his business here, his fa., on Nov. 24, 1680, in consideration of "natural affection and love," conveyed him a house and lot in Brewers or Stone street. After the d. of his fa. two years later, the care of a large and somewhat involved estate did not hinder him from engaging in public duties. On Sept. 10, 1684, he was commissioned captain of militia; but this honor he was soon constrained to renounce. It was consequent upon that radical change in his religious views which made him a non-combatant, a Quaker, and which is alluded to as follows, in a notice of the excellent woman who became his w.: "Being earnestly solicited in marriage by John Delavall, who, though a worthy man, was not at that time of the same religious communion, she, by her prudent conduct and pious resolution to maintain the principles she professed, without deviating therefrom in a matter of such importance, did not agree thereto until he, after some time, embraced the truth in sincerity of heart, and bore his cross like an humble follower of Christ. He received a gift in the ministry, and continued faithful therein to his death." She was wont to say of him that "he never used to her an expression of anger, or the product of a disturbed mind." This lady, to whom he was m. May 31, 1686, was Hannah, dr. of Thomas Lloyd, of N. Y., afterward governor of Pennsylvania. She was b. in Wales in 1666, and was therefore some years his junior. Mr. Delavall subsequently removed to Philadelphia, where he continued his business, associated with Mr. John White, his late partner in N. Y. Here he d. on Aug. 10, 1693. "Faithful and zealous for the truth, a man of a tender, broken spirit," wrote one of Mr. Delavall who had known him personally, "he finished his testimony with a heart full of love to God and his people."

None of his chn. reached maturity. Eight years after his d. his wid. m. Richard Hill, for some years Mayor of Phila., and who survived her. She entered into rest Feb. 25, 1727. See *Memorials*, etc., *of the People called Quakers*; Phila., 1824. Also *The Friend*, Phila., vol. 27, p. 216. For the history of the property at H. subsequent to the d. of John Delavall, see *The Delavall Lands*, App. I.

was no longer some imperious lord or suzerain, but a sovereign amenable to a constitution, and a government limited by laws framed with regard to the rights of the subject. So little of feudal law remained under the Dutch, as to impose few if any hard conditions upon the colonists, or to render the tenure of land in any degree precarious. With the English, feudal law survived till the Restoration. But in the 12th year of Charles II., which was prior to the capture of New Netherland, the tenure by military service was abolished, and all sorts of tenures held of the king or others, with some unimportant exceptions, were converted into tenures by *free and common socage*, a species of tenure of great antiquity, and which, as then also modified, was neither military nor burdensome, but whose requirements were moderate, well defined, and fixed. It was the specific nature of the service, duty, or render, which made this species of tenure such a safeguard against the wanton exactions of the feudal lords, and had given it an incalculable value with the English. When the service under this tenure was commuted to an annual payment in money or the produce of the land, such render was called *Quit Rent*.

The *Tithes* (or tenth part of the crop), which by arrangement between the freeholders of Harlem and Gov. Stuyvesant, the government was to receive annually, in and *after* the year 1666, were never exacted by the English rulers, and no specific charge of quit rent was made in Gov. Nicolls' patents to said free-holders. Nor were they called upon to pay such rent till the time of Gov. Dongan. But now, in order to enhance the revenues of his master, the Duke of York, and by his direct instructions, Dongan set about introducing a system of quit rents throughout the province, and making it retrospective in its operation. The negotiations had with him by the Harlem people on this subject resulted in a compounding for all back rents, for the full years expired since the English took possession of the country, beginning with 1665, at the nominal charge per year of *one bushel of wheat!* Having an obvious reference to the old claim for tenths above referred to, it at once took the place of and cancelled every such claim, while it acquitted the inhabitants of all liability touching the same.

At a meeting of constable and magistrates, Dec. 3d, 1685,

"for making up the quit rent for the Heer Governor," the lands were assessed at the rate of 8 stivers per morgen, and the house lots, 1 guilder 17½ stivers each. Within a few days "this quit rent was paid to Mr. Cox, according to the order of the governor," and consisted of eighteen bushels of grain, which Adolph Meyer delivered, we presume at the mill on the Sawkill. This payment was in full up to (but not including) the year 1683, when Dongan became governor.

The tax list, which here follows, embraces only the *erven* actually built upon, and also excludes the *half erven.* As to the outside lands, Montagne's Flat is taken at the full number of morgen, less one vacant lot; the New Lots, at three morgen per lot, as far as assessed, those omitted being apparently such as were unimproved. At Spuyten Duyvel the rate is partial, as will be seen, and on Hoorn's Hook, only Peter van Oblinus is assessed, his eighteen morgen being reckoned at half.

As exhibiting the state of the occupied lands, just prior to the granting of the Dongan patent, this list has special interest. Its value, with that of those previously given, may not indeed be at once apparent to the reader. Had the author's work been only for the present, and his object simply to gratify the popular taste for something novel and entertaining, he should hardly have burdened his pages with these tables, much less have imposed upon himself the task of preparing them. But he has done both, and with the deliberate conviction that the exact information which these tables embody will prove them to be one of the most valuable features of this work. Time will not render them obsolete, so long at least as any question remains to be raised which will involve the landed rights of the Dongan patentees (and of those deriving under them); inasmuch as the estate of each patentee respectively, as exhibited in these tables, determined his share and interest in the yet undivided common lands. Taken in connection with lists of these lands given in the Appendix, they present a full and consecutive statement in regard to the original and early ownership, situation, quantity, etc., of the Harlem lands, such as in all probability can be shown of no other territory of equal extent, and undergoing like subdivision. Will some one, keeping to the record, do as much for the lower section of Manhattan Island?

Owners, December 3, 1663.	*Erven.*	*Morgen.*	*Tax.*	*Description of Property.*
Joost van Oblinus	1	30	*f.* 13:17½	J. P., Nos. 7, 11, 13; V. K. H., Nos. 10, 11, 13, 16.
Resolved Waldron	1	24	11: 9½	V. K. H., Nos. 2, 3, ½4, ½9; N. L., Nos. 3, 4, 5, 9, 10.
Barent Waldron	1	9	5: 9½	Gloudie's Point.
Jan Nagel	2	20	14: 8	J. P., Nos. 6, 8, 9; S. D., 8 *morgen.*
Daniel Tourneur	1	6	4: 8½	Montagne's Flat, 6 *morgen.*
Wid. Daniel Tourneur	3	30	15:15	J. P., No. 1; V. K. H., Nos. 17 double, 18, 19; M. F., 13 *m.*
Jan Kyckuyt,[1]	1	13	6:13½	J. P., No. 5; V. K. H., No. 20; N. L., No. 1.
Laurens Jansen,[2]	1	11	6: 8½	J. P., No. 2; V. K. H., ½ of 5, 6.
Arent Harmans,[3]	1	6	4: 5½	J. P., No. 12.
Wid. Glaude Delamater	3	13	9:15	V. K. H., No. 12; M. Flat, 12 *morgen* (3 lots).
Adolph Meyer	1	15	7:17½	J. P., Nos. 4, 10; V. K. H., No. 14.
Cornelis Jansen,[4]	1	30	13:17½	J. P., No. 3; V. K. H., No. 15; M. F., 18 m.; N. L., No. 6.
Johannes Verveelen	0	7½	3: 0	V. K. H., Nos. 7, 8, ½9.
Johannes Vermelje	1	1	2: 8½	V. K. H., ½ of No. 5.
Jan Delamater	1	3	3: 1½	V. K. H., No. 1.
Maria Vermelje,[5]	1	0	1:17½	*Erf*, since known as the Judah Plot.
Jan Louwe,[6]	1	16	8: 5½	Bogert's Point.
Jan Dyckman	2	14	9: 7	V. K. H., ½ of 4, or 2 m.; M. F., 6 m.; S. D., 6 m.
Pieter van Oblinus	1	9	5: 9½	Hoorn's Hook.
William Haldron	1	0	1:17½	
John Delavall	3	66	30: 3	J. P., Nos. 14 to 23 @ 6½ *morgen*; V. K. H., 21, 22.
William Cox	1	0	1:17½	Hoorn's Hook.
William Holmes	1	0	1:17½	Hoorn's Hook.
Isaac Deschamps	1	0	1:17½	Hoorn's Hook.

[1] Brevoort. [2] Low. [3] Bussing. [4] Kortright. [5] Widow Kip. [6] Bogert.

At the meeting, Dec. 3d, each householder was ordered to make a ladder to his chimney, within a month, or to be fined 6 gl., and Jan Nagel was mulct 25 gl. for putting his compost heap on the public street, contrary to the town regulation. In that era of straw roofs and wooden tenements special precaution against fire was necessary; and several fires had actually happened in the village, causing great alarm and heavy losses.

This, no doubt, was one of the reasons which led to the gradual abandonment of the small village plots, and removal to their outside lands, for which we now observe a growing inclination. Especially after the grants of 1677, the old rule against building out of the village, the necessity for which had ceased, fell into disuse, as it was found to seriously hinder the growth of the town, which could best be promoted by the occupation and improvement of the new lands as farms and homesteads. So the privilege to build was granted whenever applied for, usually by selling the party an *erf* convenient to his land; the dwellings so erected on these farms being generally substantial stone houses, of which a very few are still standing. By a careful computation made at a meeting of the old and new magistrates, Jan. 20, 1686, for laying a "repartitie," or assessment, to pay the parish clerk's salary due this date, "so are found 25 *erven* (house lots), and 393 *morgen* of land; each house lot must pay 4 gl., and each morgen of land 10½ st., for making up 300 gl." * This rate was levied, and

* This enumeration is valuable as embracing all the lands then taken up, excepting the small parts of the three farms below Hoorn's Hook which lay within the patent line. The list of *erven* is obviously the same as that of Dec. 3, 1685; the last three, on the said farms, being omitted. The list of *morgen* is made up as follows:

Jochem Pieters Flat, 13 lots @ 6 *morgen* each...	78 m.
Do. Delavall, 9 lots @ 6⅔ *m*....	60 "
Van Keulen's Hook, 22 lots @ 3 *m*..................	66 "
Do. for Tourneur's No. 17, add.	3 "
Montagne's Flat, 7 lots @ 6 *m*., 3 @ 4 *m*.........	54 "
Hoorn's Hook, 9 lots @ 4 *m*., 1 @ 6 *m*...........	42 "
Bogert's Point..	16 "
New Lots, 9 lots @ 4 *m*., 1 @ 6 *m*..................	42 "
Gloudie's Point, now rated at....................	12 "
Spuyten Duyvel, Dyckman and Nagel.*..........	20 "
	393 "

* D. and N. owned 74 acres at S. D. How they came to be rated at 20 *morgen*, is shown in App. J.

received in grain. Also this year, as in the last, the inhabitants contributed toward Domine Selyns' salary.

The care taken to keep up the common fences inclosing the farming lands appears in another order, needed to stay the damage being caused by swine.

THERE was good cause found by the Constable and the old and new Magistrates for an order in regard to the running of the hogs; So it was *Resolved*, to keep tight the fencing of JOCHEM PIETERS up *to the land of Cupt. Delavall*, and *from the village to art it off till into the river*; and to keep tight the fencing of VAN KEULEN'S HOOK *from the village off till into the creek of the mill*. And all shall be held within one year from the ensuing May, being the year 1687, to make the whole fencing around tight and sufficient. And if any hogs still be found out of the limits of the fencing, the owners shall be compelled to keep up their hogs—and shall continue till the year 1687. By order of the Constable and Magistrates, this 4th Feb., 168¾.

Measures were now taken to build a new church. The old church was no longer adapted to the needs and improved tastes of the community, though still answering the purposes of a school-house. An invitation given them in 1680, to aid in the erection of a new church in the city, a work not yet begun, had perhaps suggested the present movement; and, not unlikely, it was part of a new agreement already made with Do. Selyns, by which he was to administer the Lord's Supper at Harlem twice a year, in the spring and fall, during the intervals between its occurrence in New York. It was to be observed on a *week day*, and this arrangement had gone into effect on Wednesday, April 22d, 1685, when the first celebration of the Supper here, as a stated observance, took place. An extra large collection was taken by the deacons, Adolph Meyer and Jan Dyckman, amounting to 14 florins 9 stivers. On the next occasion, and for some years, while this arrangement lasted, the Supper was observed on Thursday, and the preparation for it the day before. From this time also obtained the practice of receiving new members here.

The church was to be built of stone, and upon a new site; an arrangement being made with Laurens Jansen and the Delamater family, who gave up their two north *erven* for this purpose, and which also afforded ample ground for a new churchyard or cemetery. The community pledged themselves liberally, and assumed the labor of preparing and bringing the stone, lime, timber, shingles, lath, etc., all which was to apply on their subscriptions.* Tobias Stoutenburgh and Hyman Koninck, masons, the first brother-in-law to William Waldron, were employed, and by the 29th of March the foundation was begun; Resolved Waldron, with due ceremony, placing the first stone, and Johannes Vermelje the second. The following day the contract was made for the carpenter work with William Hellaker of New York, half-brother of Tounis Ides, a good mechanic, and honest, though "a little rough." Here is the agreement:

SPECIFICATION of the *Church at Harlem:* The size of the church, across it either way, is 36 Dutch feet; upon which William Hellaker undertakes to construct the roof, with an arch therein, and a small steeple upon it, and to cover all properly with shingles, and to make a scuttle thereto; upon condition that the people of the town shall be obligated to deliver the timber at the building place. For which the Constable and Magistrates promise to pay the aforesaid William Hellaker, the sum of Seven Hundred and Fifty Guilders, in Wheat, to be paid in the month of January following this year, 1686, the wheat to be delivered at the current price. Thus arranged and agreed to in the presence of the after-named witnesses, and which, with our usual hand, is subscribed. Done at New Haerlem, this 30th of March, 1686.

Witnesses.	
JOHANNES VERMELJE,	WILLEM HELLAKER,
RESALVERT WALDRON,	JAN DE LAMETER, *Constable,*
	DANIEL TOURNEUR,
	JAN NAGEL.

Before me,
JAN TIBOUT, *Clerk.*

* *Subscription for building the Church,* 1686.

Daniel Tourneur	*f.* 100
Jan Dyckman	" 100
Isaac Delamater	" 30
Cornelis Jansen Kortright	" 100
Jan Louwe Bogert	" 100
Jan Hendricks van Brevoort	" 100
Jan Delamater	" 75
Barent Waldron	" 50
Laurens Jansen	" 70
Jacques Tourneur	" 25
Adolph Meyer	" 60
Jan Nagel	" 100
Joost van Oblinus	" 100
Arent Harmans Bussing	" 75
Resolved Waldron	" 100
Abram Delamontanie	" 25
Thomas Tourneur	" 25
Pieter van Oblienis	" 50
Johannes Vermelje	" 50
	f. 1365

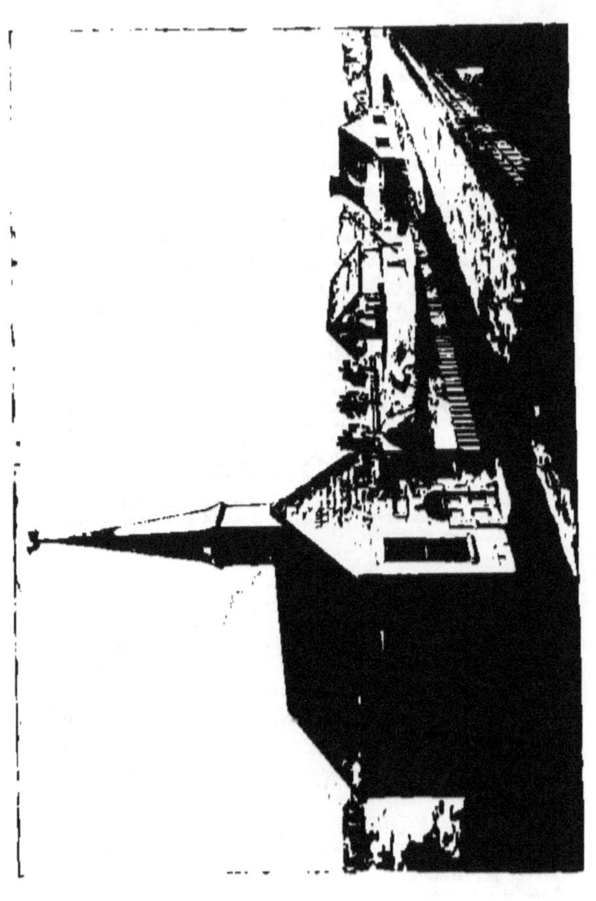

The walls, laid in good mortar, were soon up; the "bent timber" for the arch being placed in position, was well secured with clamps, the rafters were set, and the roof shingled. William Haldron, the village smith, kept his forge and anvil busy on the iron work, of which he furnished 139 pounds, at 1 gl. 10 st. a pound. And then came a proud moment for the villagers; it was when the gilded "haen," or weather-cock, with the cap on which it perched, was raised to its lofty position on the tip of the steeple." *

On Thursday, April 15th, the people had gathered around the Lord's table, for the last time in that humble but hallowed sanctuary where, through their early struggles, they had sought and found inward strength and comfort. The collection was large and significant, being 24 florins. The work upon its successor was pushed forward so rapidly, that on Thursday, September 30th, Domine Selyns preached the first sermon in the new church, and administered the Lord's Supper. A liberal collection, 22 florins, was taken up. This item is also recorded, "1686, Septemb. 30th, to bread and wine, 12 florins 10 stivers." Before the people separated they took the opportunity to nominate new town officers; those appointed being sworn in, at New York, on the 2d of November. They were Jan Hendricks van Brevoort, constable, and Jan Dyckman, Lawrence Jansen, and Isaac Delamater, magistrates. On November 4th the constable and magistrates resolved that the churchyard (*kerckhof*) should be inclosed with clapboards, within the ensuing two months.

The secretary, Tibout, on December 13th, made up the accounts for the building of the church, and a glance at which will show their way of doing things. Jan Hendricks van Brevoort offsets his pledge of 100 florins, by the following work done, materials furnished, etc.

13*th December*, JAN HENDRICKS VAN BREVOORT, *Credit.*

For stone broken and drawn to the church	*f.*	30 : 0
" timber cut and drawn to the church	"	14 : 15
" 300 shingles, delivered at the church, 7 gls. the hundred	"	21 : 0
" making lath	"	6 : 5
" 10 ton lime, 1 gl. 10 st. per ton	"	15 : 0
" payment of masons, carpenters, and laborer	"	17 : 18

* JAN DELAMATER has credit Jan. 14th, 1687, "Aen een ketel tot de haen van de toorn *f.* 9." *Schult Boeck* (or Ledger), page 74.

Essentially the same are the credits to Daniel Tourneur, Jan Dyckman, Isaac Delamater, Cornelis Jansen, Jan Delamater, Barent Waldron, Laurens Jansen, Adolph Meyer, Jan Nagel, Joost van Oblinus, Arent Harmans Bussing, and Resolved Waldron, most of whom exceeded the amount of their pledges. Others did less as they were able.* On the same date Barent Waldron, in presence of the court and community, accounted for the moneys he had disbursed for nails, stone, and other things, and which amounted to 576 florins. Resolved Waldron was given credit for 12 florins, and Jan Delamater, Adolph Meyer, and Laurens Jansen, each 6 florins, all "earned at the bent timber."

Mr. John Delavall being in arrears, Tibout and Dyckman were sent to "the Manhattans," to see him about it. His indebtedness, as made out Dec. 13th, was, "for stone, timber, lime, and *morgen money*, 236 florins; for 2 years' salary of voorleser, 95 florins; for quit rent, 32 florins." Having embraced Quaker principles, Delavall had scruples as to paying toward the church or voorleser, and had rather submit to a distraint upon his goods. So the town by its constable Brevoort levied on 61 schepels of wheat belonging to him, in the hands of Laurens Jansen, Adolph Meyer, Jan Delamater, and said Brevoort, then the lessees of Delavall's lands.

The voluntary subscription being insufficient, a tax was laid of 2 gl. on the morgen, and afterward, on Feb. 24th, 1687, an additional tax of 8 st. per morgen. A special contribution was made up for glazing the windows. The people brought in their wheat to the town house, depositing it in the loft; others delivered it to the mechanics, or at the sawmill, in payment for

* ARENT HARMANS has credit in the church accounts:

"Jan. 15, 1686-7, For riding stone to the city of New York, *f.* 1 : 0
" " 2 schepels wheat.................... 12 : 0."

It would have been extraordinary, a departure from the universal practice in Fatherland, had the builders omitted to place over the portal of the church the usual inscription, giving the date of its erection, with perhaps a scripture text in Dutch. Over the entrance to the church in the fort they had often read: "Ao. Do. MDCXLII. W. Kieft, Dr. Gr. Heeft de Gemeenten dese Temple doen Bouwen." It could hardly have failed to be imitated, and this, we think, explains the credit to Arent Bussing; one florin for taking the stone to New York, to be cut, and twelve florins, paid for it.

boards and plank, receiving credit therefor in their accounts.* Jan Delamater paid to the laborer (*opperman*) a remnant of wheat left in his hands, after the last payment of the town's quit rent, three schepels, amounting to 18 guilders. Constable Brevoort afterward paid him 2 schepels, or 12 guilders, and the balance of his wages, 35 guilders, on February 24th, 1687. To Jerome van Bommel, of New York, "smith," was paid 126 florins. At this date the new patent had also to be paid for, and the mechanics gave time on their bills. The 14th of March, 1688, the sum of 528 florins yet due the masons (their contract was 600 florins) was paid to Stoutenburgh, by Barent Waldron. William Hellaker had received "for the building of the church," from Jan Dyckman 45 florins 12 stivers, from Constable Brevoort 153 florins, from Jan Louwe Bogert 125 florins, and from Adolph Meyer, Constable, 275 florins. At a final reckoning with him March 14th, 1689, there was found due him a balance of 163 florins 13 stivers, which included 12 florins 5 stivers, for extras, over and above his contract; and on April 16th, Barent Waldron was authorized to pay this balance from funds in his hands. Besides the work done by the people themselves, and the materials they furnished, the church cost them over 2600 guilders. It was spacious and substantial, but obviously of the plainest finish, according thus with the simple tastes and strictly utilitarian ideas of the builders, of which the following item from the deacon's book for 1687, is quite suggestive: "July 21, gave to the Smith for making of a bolt, also a latch, for the church, 8 guilders." During the first year of

* 168⅞ the 25th February; List of those who have paid to Adolph Meyer, Constable, for the *Glass* at the Church:

Adolph Meyer	*f.* 14	Jan Louwe Bogert	*f.* 9
Arent Harmans	" 14	Daniel Tourneur	" 9
Jan Dyckman	" 9	Pieter van Oblinus	" 9
Jacqueline Tourneur	" 9	Jan Nagel	" 9
Joost van Oblinus	" 9	Jan H. Brevoort	" 9
Cornelis Jansen	" 9	Maria Vermelje	" 9
Laurens Jansen	" 9	Resolved Waldron	" 9
Jan Delamater	" 9	Barent Waldron	" 9
Isaac Delamater	" 9	Samuel Waldron	" 9
Johannes Vermelje	" 9	Johannes Waldron	" 9
Jacques Tourneur	" 9		

its occupancy, the collections amounted to 171 guilders 4 stivers, averaging 3 guilders 5 stivers per Sabbath.*

* THE REFORMED CHURCH.—It was three fourths of a century after the new chh. was built before the congregation secured a pastor to live among them. The ministry of Do. Selyns seems to have gone smoothly till the breaking out of the Leisler troubles, in 1689. The Dutch at H., and with them Tibout the voorleser, generally approved Leisler's course. Selyns took the opposite ground, and this caused an alienation. It went so far that after the celebration of the Lord's Supper, Oct. 9, 1690, the arrangement with Selyns was broken off, and this ordinance suspended here for a series of years. Tibout had closed his services on preparation day, Apl. 23, 1690. Selyns, in writing to the Classis of Amsterdam, says Harlem had fallen off, "under the idea they can live without ministers or sacraments." The chh. had been much afflicted in the loss of several of its old members, Cornelis Jansen, Jan Nagel, and Mrs. Maria Kip, formerly Montanye, all in 1689, and Resolved Waldron and Daniel Tourneur in 1690. Repairs were needed on the chh. and chh. yard, and on Sept. 13, 1690, Joost van Oblinus and Adolph Meyer were chosen chh. masters to superintend this work. The Sunday services were kept up, however, without interruption: for the first year under the lead of Guillaem Bertholf, who came here from New Jersey as voorleser, and began serving Apl. 24, 1690. He also acted as town clerk at Harlem, but performed his last service here as voorleser, Sept. 13, 1691: Tibout resuming his old place the next Sabbath. See note, page 77. Tibout continued to serve the H. chh. six, if not eight years, when he entered on a term of service at Bushwick. The breach with Selyns had meanwhile been healed; indeed, his labors here had never been wholly suspended. A young man, named Adrian Vermeule, from Vlissengen, in Zeeland, bringing a chh. letter addressed to "Henry Selyns, Minister of Harlem and York, in America," was now engaged to fill Tibout's place as voorleser, etc., and entered upon his duties Nov. 4, 1699. Judging from his penmanship, he was a scholar; the town immediately built "a new house, as a dwelling for the voorleser, and as a school and town house," beside repairing the chh.; and that the latter might be taken out of the control of popular meetings, and placed directly under the chh. officers, a deed was secured Nov. 2, 1699, from "all the residents or proprietors of the town," conveying "the church" to the consistory; but those who helped build the chh. to retain their seats. We have not seen this deed, but only the record by the clerk of its having been given. Whether it included, in express terms, the *kerk lot* or "church farm," and the *kerk erf*, we do not know; but nevertheless these had always been held as appurtenances of the chh., for whose use and benefit they were originally set apart (the church farm being expressly recognized in records as early as 1665, as also at various subsequent dates, as "the church lot"), so that not merely by an implied right, or with the tacit consent of the town, but under the original allotment, always held to give a title, the consistory continued to possess the church farm, even down to our own time.

Adrian Vermeule having served here with acceptance for eight years, "was requested to be the voorleser at Bergen;" and in a meeting of the consistory at N. Y., Jan. 1, 1708, the elder Peter van Oblienus, and deacons Samuel Waldron and Samson Benson, being present, it was agreed to dismiss him with a recommendation. He closed his term on Feb. 1, ensuing. While here he m. Dinah, dau. of William Hellaker. He m. again at Bergen, Christina Fredericks, gd. dr. of Andries Hopper, and here he d. in 1735. The chh. left without a voorleser, Col. Morris, of Morrisania, "endeavored to persuade the Dutch in his neighborhood (that is, the H. people) into a good opinion of the Church of England," and induced Rev. Henricus Heys, of Esopus, to come and preach at H., as a missionary of

Coeval with the church enterprise, was another looking to the opening of a new section of the township to the plough and husbandman, and to the ultimate increase of the town revenues. Midway of the long range of heights stretching from Moertje Davids Fly to Sherman's Creek, and not far below Fort Washington, was an Indian clearing known as the Great Maize Land. This was now leased to Capt. Jan Gerritsen van Dalsen and his son-in-law, Jan Kiersen, upon the following curious terms :

On this date, We the Constable and Magistrates hereby acknowledge to have consented and agreed in manner hereafter written. Jan Gerritse van Dalsen and Jan Kiersen own and declare to have received from the aforesaid Constable and Magistrates, a piece of land named *The Great Maize Land*, belonging under the jurisdiction of New Haerlem ;

that chh., with a view to accepting Episcopal ordination. The attempt seemed to promise success, and Mr. Beys labored here in the years 1711 and 1712, having the support of Col. Morris, Capt. Congreve, and some other English residents, but the Venerable Society in England gave him but little encouragement, and he was obliged to give it up. For the next half century the history of the chh. is scanty. It was still ministered to by the pastor at N. Y., now the Rev. Gualterus Du Bois, called in 1699, as colleague with Do. Selyns, who d. July 19, 1701 In a few years they secured another voorleser, Johannes Martinus van Harlingen, a young man from Amsterdam. He m. here, Sept. 17, 1722, Mary, youngest dr. of Arent Bussing. The next year, June 19, he was naturalized by act of assembly. He afterward, by the d. of his nephew, Jan de Cerfl, Lord of Old Hyerland, fell heir in fee tail to that lordship. In 1741 he removed to New Brunswick, N. J., where he was an elder in 1765. He was the fa. of five sons, of whom the eldest was the Rev. Johannes M. van Harlingen, of Neshanic and Sourland. The question between the *conferentie* and the *cœtus* (or the adherents of the Classis of Amsterdam, and those who favored an American classis) now greatly disturbed the H. chh. The chh. was mainly of the latter, but the domines now acting, Ritzema and De Ronde, were strongly in favor of the old *régime*. These took it very hard in 1755 because the H. folks subscribed toward founding an American college, proposed by Do. Frelinghuysen. But in 1765 the chh. called Rev. Martinus Schoonmaker, of the cœtus, who divided his services with Gravesend, but took up his residence at H., where he bought, Aug. 10, 1768, a farm of 28 acres, just north of the village, afterward owned by Lawrence, and later by Wagstaff. Being an ardent Whig, he spent the period of the Revolution within the American lines, as did many of his flock. He returned at the peace, but left in 1785. The chh. edifice having been ruined during the war, another was begun in 1788, and in 1791 the Rev. John F. Jackson was called as pastor. His ministry continued till 1805. His successors have been : Jeremiah Romeyn, 1806 to 1813 ; Cornelius C. Vermeule, D.D. (a desc. of the former voorleser), 1816 to 1836 ; Richard L. Schoonmaker, 1838 to 1847 ; Jeremiah S. Lord, D.D., 1848 to 1869 ; G. Henry Mandeville, D.D., the present pastor, settled 1869. For details of these several pastorates, we refer to "Golden Memories," treasured by the excellent pastor in his valuable discourse of April 20, 1873. Until the organization of the St. Mary Episcopal Church, at Manhattanville, in 1823, the Reformed Church was the only one of any denomination within the entire limits of H.

which aforesaid piece of land the before written Jan Gerritse van Dalsen and Jan Kiersen shall use, build and live upon, for the time of twelve successive years, to commence in the month of August of this year, 1686, and ending in the month of August, after the harvest is off; and the hirers shall be permitted the last year to sow two schepels of buckwheat and to plant a piece of maize (corn); also the lessees, for the first seven years, shall occupy it free, only each giving to the lessors a *fat capon* yearly, as an acknowledgment, and shall be obligated for the last five years to pay each year two hundred guilders in good wheat, rye, peas, or barley, at the market price; from each parcel the just fourth part to be given to God the Lord. The lessees shall be allowed to make an orchard, and at the end of their years, shall have the right of taking up half of the same, from the large fruit trees or the nursery; and the lessees shall be required to clear fourteen morgen of land in the first years, which will be two morgen yearly, and if the lessees shall have need of more land, the lessors shall be required to assign more land to the lessees, at the most convenient time; also is leased with the land a piece of meadow lying at the farthest point at the North River. So also the lessees are required to deliver up the buildings in good condition at the end of the years, as also to deliver the fencing of the land tight and sufficient. To the extent of fourteen morgen, the lessees shall be obligated to bear the ordinary town charges, but no extraordinary. The lessees shall be allowed to continue living on the aforesaid land till May of the last year, being the year 1699. The lessees shall have the liberty of removing, upon condition that they signify one year before, their intention to give up the lease. All thus performed and agreed to, and with our usual hand undersigned. Done at New Haerlem this 30th of March, 1686. [*Signed* by Jan Delamater, as Constable, Daniel Tourneur, Jan Nagel, Jan Kiersen, and Jan Gerritsen van Dalsen, in the presence of Jan Tibout, *Clerk.*]

Some progress had been made in clearing and cultivating the Hoorn's Hook lands, since known as the *Waldron Farm*. On Jan. 8th, 1687, Peter van Oblienis leased his erf and four lots here (Nos. 6, 8, 9, 10), to David Devoor, junior, for six years, to commence with the ensuing May.* He was to have it rent free

* DAVID DU FOUR, senior, thus wrote his surname, but it soon exchanged F. for V., then took the form of Devoor. Some now write De Voe, which confounds it with the name of another and distinct family, herein noticed, descended from the brs. Nich. and Fred. de Vaux, or De Voe. Early at H., as an original proprietor, the elder David left again on selling his allotment to Jacob Elderts, who directly resold it, June 1, 1662, to Jean le Roy. In 1668, Du Four passing in a canoe up the East River, and with him his ch. Anthony; when, between Turtle Bay and Blackwell's Island, John Copstaff, a drunken soldier, in another boat, let off a gun which wounded little Anthony; this was on Aug. 18, and he d. Aug. 31. Copstaff was convicted of manslaughter. Du Four being very ill, he and w. Jannetie made a will Sept. 14, 1671, naming the places whence they came in Hainault, probably for the reason that the survivor is to enjoy all the property both here and "in their fatherland." But David recovered and lived long. In 1677, Gov. Andros granted, for him and his son John, 60 acres of land "on the Coale Kill," Turtle Bay, and here David spent the rest of his life. His will was

for the first year, for the second, pay 100 gl., and for the remaining time, 150 gl. yearly; "in good wheat, rye, barley, peas and buckwheat." Devoor engaged "to pay toward the salary

proved May 1, 1699. It names his chn John, David, Peter, and Glaude; Peter not named again, and Glaude not after 1687.

John Devoor, b. during his fa.'s sojourn at Sedan, m., in 1676, a Leyden girl, Jannetie, dr. of Jan. Willems van Isselsteyn, otherwise called Jan of Leyden. He bought a farm at Bloomingdale, where he d., leaving a wid., Mary. She was dr. of Capt. Peter van Woglum, of Albany. The twelve chn. of John, senior, were all by his first w. and all living July 24, 1717, when, being sick, he made his will; it was proved Apl. 13, 1724, after his youngest ch. became of age. These chn., who shared equally in his estate, were: *Maria*, b. 1677, who m. Gerrit Roelofs Vander Werken, of Half Moon, near Albany; *John*, b. 1680; *Margaret*, b. 1681, m. Teunis Pier; *David*, b. 1683; *Peter*, b. 1686; *Rachel*, b. 1687; *Adriana*, b. 1688, m. Conrad Vanderbeek and Jacob Montanye; *Jannetie*, b. 1690, m. Andrew Bisset; *Elizabeth*, b. 1693; *Teunis*, b. 1696, m. Georgie Barheyt and Sarah van Oblinus; *William*, b. 1698, and *Abraham*, b. 1701. John, eldest son, m., in 1706, Catharine, dr. of Roelof Gerrits Vander Werken, of Half Moon, to which place he removed, and on Apl. 1, 1724, sold his interest in his fa.'s farm to his brs. David and William. He d. in 1746, and his desc. are called *De Voe*. See *Pearson's Albany Settlers*. David, last named, lived for a time at H., where he m., in 1726, Anna, dr. of Thomas Wakefield, and wid. of Jacob van Bremen, anc. of the Van Bramers, late of Harlem Lane. Devoor and w. owned a place on the upper side of the Church Lane, which they sold in 1745 to Capt. Daniel McGown. It was the old Hanel garden, bought by Van Bremen in 1715, from Abraham Meyer.

David Devoor was b. in 1659, and m., 1689, Elisabeth Jansen, from the Delaware. When his Hoorn's Hook lease expired in 1693, he returned to the homestead at Turtle Bay, of which he became the owner. He had five chn., viz.: *Margaret*, b. 1690; *David*, 1693; *Jannetie*, 1695; *John*, 1697, and *Elizabeth*, 1700. David, the eldest son, who succeeded to the Turtle Bay farm, m., 1715, Jannetie, dr. of Abram Delamontanie, of H., by whom he had issue David; Elisabeth, m., 1741, John Burger; and Jane, m., 1749, Nicholas Burger. David, last named, b. 1717, m., 1740, Mary van Vleckeren. On May 2, 1760, his fa. conveyed him 12½ acres off the north side of his farm; but the former, then living retired in the East Ward, d. November 12, ensuing, leaving the remainder to David, jointly with his two srs., whose interests he acquired. He added to it 10½ acres next south of him, by purchase in 1769. All this, at his d. in 1780, fell to his dr. Ann, who m., successively, Abraham Brevoort and Gen. Jacob Odell. See *N. Y. B. & G. Rec.* IX., 48.

John Devoor, b. 1697, and son of David 2d m., 1722, Aefie (Eve), dr. of Bastiaen Michiels Kortright, and had three chn., to wit: Jelante, b. 1723, m. Abm. Ackerman; John, b. 1728, and Aefie, b. 1730, who m. *John Courtright*, of Sherman's Creek, gd. son of Bastiaen aforesaid. In 1731, Devoor bought the Saw-kill farm (See App. H.), of which at his d., in 1780, he left 14 acres on the upper side to his son John, and the remainder, 24½ acres, to his dr. Aefie Courtright. Jelante received a house and lot in town. John Devoor, Jr., b. Oct. 1, 1728, bought and occupied 4 acres of the Young farm, adjoining the 14 afterward received from his fa., which 18 acres subsequently formed the southerly part of the Dr. Baker farm, now vested in the trustees of the Trinity Church School. Devoor m., May 19, 1752, Beltille, dr. of Hendrick Bogert, by whom he had a son John, b. 1757, and other chn. His property here passed into other hands under mortgages, one for the 4 acres dated Feb. 16, 1774, and another for the 14 acres, dated Mar. 17, 1783.

of the Voorleser," and to allow Oblienis liberty to build a house and live there, but not to the limiting of Devoor "in syn wey ofte int bos;" *in his pasture or in the woodland.*

The neighboring Baignoux farm had already passed, by a transfer of Oct. 12th, 1686, from Isaac Deschamps, also known by the name of Saviat Broussard, to John Spragge, Esq., one of Dongan's councilors.

Great Barent's Island was now to become productive under the well-directed toil of a new proprietor and experienced farmer, Thomas Parcell, late of Newtown. He contracted with Jacob Milborne, Feb. 17th, 1687, for the purchase of the Island for £600; Milborne being empowered to sell it by Samuel Swynock. Having paid his three instalments, Parcell, on June 23d, 1690, obtained a full deed from Milborne, to whom, in the interim, Swynock had conveyed the Island, Aug. 9th, 1687.

Meanwhile a matter of common interest and of great importance to the freeholders, the renewal or confirmation of the town patent, had been pressed upon them by the governor, who in behalf of his sovereign, now King James II., was aiming at a large increase of the revenue in the form of quit rent, and also to fix the amount, and the time and mode of payment, by the general issue of new patents. Cogent reasons were brought to bear upon the people. James, Duke of York, had ascended the throne, Feb. 6th, 1685; but as king it was by no means certain that he would be bound by his acts as duke; and hence the wisdom of taking out new letters patent directly under the crown, by the hand of its accredited agent. Indeed, assuming the old town patents to be invalid unless confirmed, Dongan avowed his intention to appropriate, as belonging to the king, and at his disposal, all such tracts of common land as could be found within the several townships, and not yet purchased of the Indians. So the inhabitants "were willing rather to submit to a greater quit rent, than to have that unpurchased land disposed of to others than themselves."

While the Harlem people were thus given to expect great trouble and loss, should they neglect to secure the confirmation of their patented rights, the utmost benefit was, apparently, to accrue from such a confirmation, and especially in view of a certain clause contained in the charter just granted by Gov. Dongan, to the City of New York (being dated April 27th, 1686), and which clause read as follows :

> AND I do by these presents give and grant unto the said *Mayor, Aldermen*, and *Commonalty* of the said *City of New York*, all the waste vacant unpatented and unappropriated lands lying and being within the said City of New York and on Manhattans Island aforesaid, extending and reaching to the low-water mark in, by, and through all parts of the said City of New York and Manhattans Island aforesaid, together with all rivers, rivulets, coves, creeks, ponds, waters, and watercourses, in the said City and Island, or either of them, *not heretofore given or granted by any of the former Governors*, etc.

As rights and privileges within the township of Harlem very akin to some of these, and in some respects more ample, had heretofore been granted the inhabitants by the patent of Gov. Nicolls, its confirmation was now deemed imperative to preserve and insure these valuable franchises to them, their heirs, or successors. A pledge to bear *equally* the expense of the new patent had been circulated in the town, and signed by the whole community. This was entered on the records at the meeting held Nov. 4th, 1666, when the resolution passed to fence the churchyard.

To digress a little : At this time action was also taken for protecting the common woodlands. "Whereas, great damage has happened therein by the destruction of the timber," so the order read, "every one is hereby forbidden to cut any wood within the limits of the Town more than he wants for his own use, under the penalty of £5, being 200 guilders."

But the court on this occasion found itself "weakened by animosities." The old board had been invited to sit with the new ; but one from each, namely, Cornelis Jansen and his brother Laurens, were absent, the latter having just left on a visit to his kinsfolk, the Roosas, at Esopus, where he and his cousin Reyer Michielsen had been only the year before.* Two of the

* The ROOSA family, since so multiplied in Ulster and adjacent counties, and known also as *Rosa* and *Rose*, came from Herwynen, Gelderland ; sailing from Holland for this country, in the ship Bonte-koe, Apl. 15, 1660. There were Albert Heymans Roosa, his w. Weilke de Jonge, and eight chn. between the ages of 2 and 17 yrs. Directly on arrival Roosa went to Esopus (no doubt at the instance of Roelof Swartwout, a fellow-passenger returning to that place); where he and his w. united with the church, of which, two years later, he became an elder. Gov. Stuyvesant giving a name to Wiltwyck, May 16, 1661, appointed Roosa one of its first schepens. Here he took up land, for which he got a patent Aug. 19, 1664. He was a man

other members had a quarrel, one of the old and one of the new board, Jan Nagel and Jan Dyckman, before such good friends—all because a *goose* of Nagel's, getting into Dyckman's grain, had been bitten by his dog. To settle this weighty matter Joost van Oblinus and Adolph Meyer were, "for this time," called to the bench.

On further deliberation upon the subject of their patent, another paper, designed to amend the former action, was drawn up and signed by the inhabitants, as follows, and the value of which consisted in this, that it pledged them to a *pro rata* distribution of the lands held in common, and which plan was adhered to in all the general allotments subsequently made. Those with the signs made their marks.

The underwritten Persons subscribe to pay *according to their estate*, and are *to draw in proportion to their estates*, of the common woods:

Resolvert Waldron,	Pieter van Oblienis,
Joost Van Oblinus,	Johannes Vermelje,
Daniel Tourneur,	Jan Delamater,
Jan Hendricks van Brevoort, 8,	Arent Harmans,
Laurens Jansen, +	Abram de Lamontanie,
Isaac Delamater,	Jan Louwe Bogert,
Jan Nagel,	Jacqueline Tourneur,
Cornelis Jansen,	Jacques Tourneur, 8 T,
Jan Dyckman,	Hester Delamater, H,
Barent Waldron,	Adolph Meyer, AD.

New Haerlem, 8th January, 1681.

Jan Tibout, *Clerk.*

Meanwhile the new patent was drawn up. The names of those who had subscribed the paper of January 8th were entered as patentees, only that Jacqueline Tourneur stood also for her son Jacques, and Peter Parmentier took the place of Jan Louwe Bogert. Then four others were added, namely, John Delavall, in the stead of his father, the councilor Spragge, Johannes Verveelen, and William Haldron, the smith, all freeholders. Being submitted to the attorney-general, James Graham, who found "nothing contained therein prejudicial to His Majesty's

of firm will and great energy, being also "wonderful strong and quick." Roosa d. Feb. 27, 1679, leaving a good estate to his chn., who were: Heyman, b 1643, Arien, b. 1645, and Jan, b. 1651—by all whom the name was perpetuated—and drs. like, Mary, Neeltie, and Jannetie. The last was m. to Matthys Ten Eyck, of N. Y., like to Roelof Kierstead, Neeltie to Henry Pawling, and Mary to Laurens Jansen, of H.

interest," the patent was approved in council March 7th, and signed by the governor.* It read as follows :

Thomas Dongan, Captain-General, Governor-in-Chief, and Vice-Admiral in and over the Province of New York, and its dependencies thereon in America, under His Majesty James the Second, by the Grace of God, of England, Scotland, France, and Ireland, King, Defender of the Faith, &c., To all to whom these Presents shall come, sendeth *Greeting* :—WHEREAS RICHARD NICOLLS, Esq., formerly Governor of this Province, hath by his certain writing or Patent, bearing date the Eleventh day of October, *Anno Dom.* One Thousand Six Hundred Sixty Seven, DID GIVE, ratify, confirm, and grant unto THOMAS DELAVALL, Esq., JOHN VERVEELEN, DANIEL TOURNEUR, JOOST OBLINUS, and RESOLVED WALDRON, as Patentees, for and on the behalf of themselves and their Associates, the freeholders and inhabitants of New Harlem, their heirs, successors, and assigns, ALL THAT TRACT, together with the several parcels of land, which they then had, or after should be purchased, or procured, for and on the behalf of the said Town, within the bounds and limits hereafter set forth and expressed, *viz.* That is to say, from the west side of the fence of the said Town, a line being run due west four hundred English poles, without variation of the compass, and at the end thereof another line being drawn across the Island north and south with the variation, that is to say, north from the end of a certain piece of meadow ground, commonly called the Round Meadow, near or adjoining unto Hudson's or the North River, and south to the place where formerly stood the Saw Mills, over against Verkens or Hog Island in the Sound or East River, shall be the western bounds of their lands, and all the lands lying and being within the said line so drawn north and south as aforesaid, eastward to the end of the Town and Harlem River, or any part of the said River on which this Island doth abut, and likewise on the North and East Rivers, within the limits aforementioned described, doth and shall belong to the said Town ; As ALSO *four lots of meadow ground* upon the Main, marked with Number 1, 2, 3, 4, lying over against the Spring, where a passage hath been used to ford over from this Island to the Main, and from thence hither, WITH *a small Island commonly called Stony Island*, lying to the east of the Town and Harlem River, going through Bronck's Kill, by the little and great Barn's Islands, upon which there are ALSO *four other lots of meadow*

* JOHN SPRAGGE, being a member of the Governor's Council, and owning the Haignoux farm, managed to get his name into the Patent. He was present in Council when the Patent was passed upon, Mar. 7, 1687, but directly after sailed with dispatches for England, and appears not to have returned to this country. On Dec. 6, 7, 1690, he conveyed his farm aforesaid to Dr. Daniel Cox, of London, who on Apl. 28, 1692, empowered his agent Jeremiah Bass, Esq., of New Jersey, to sell it. No common land was ever laid out within the Harlem Patent, in virtue of this freehold. The next two farms south of Spragge's, also partly within the patent line, fared no better ; except that William Holmes drew a five-morgen lot in 1691. He owned the centre farm and had paid a small sum on the Patent. But in the subsequent divisions these three farms had no share ; the rule obtaining that those only who had helped bear the expense of the general Patent, were named therein, and held morgen and erf rights under it (the three farms holding under special patents), were entitled to draw of the common land.

ground, marked with Number 1, 2, 3, 4 ; TOGETHER WITH *all the mills*, creeks, quarries, woods, meadows, pastures, marshes, waters, lakes, fishing, hawking, hunting and fowling, and all other profits, commodities, emoluments and hereditaments to the said land and premises, within the bounds and limits set forth, belonging, or in any wise appertaining. AND ALSO *freedom of commonage* for range and feed of cattle and horses, further west into the woods upon this Island, as well without as within their bounds and limits set forth and expressed : TO HAVE AND TO HOLD all and singular the said lands, island, commonage, hereditaments and premises, with their and every of their appurtenances, and of every part and parcel thereof, unto the said Patentees and their Associates, their heirs, successors, and assigns, to the proper use and behoof of the said Patentees and their Associates, their heirs, successors, and assigns forever. AND WHEREAS Richard Nicolls, Esq., did likewise ratify, confirm, and grant unto the said Patentees and their Associates, their heirs, successors, and assigns, *All the rights and privileges belonging to a Town within this government*, *With this proviso*, or exception, that in all matters of debt or trespass of or above the value of Five Pounds, they shall have relation unto and dependence upon the Courts of this City, as the other Towns have upon the several Courts of Session to which they do belong ; AND that the place of their present habitation shall continue and retain the name of New Harlem, by which name and style it shall be distinguished and known in all bargains and sales, deeds, writings, and records ; AND *that no person whatsoever* should be suffered or permitted *to erect* any manner of *house* or *building* upon this said Island, *within two miles of the limits* and bounds aforementioned, *without the consent* and approbation of the major part of the inhabitants of the said Town ; AND WHEREAS *the said Town lies very commodious for a Ferry*, to and from the Main, which may redound to the particular benefit of the inhabitants, as well as to a general good, the freeholders and inhabitants of the said town should, in consideration of the benefits and privileges therein granted, as also for what advantage they might receive thereby, be enjoined and obliged, at their own proper costs and charge, to build or provide one or more boats fit for the transportation of men, horses, or cattle, for which was to be a certain allowance given by each particular person, as should be then ordered and adjudged fit and reasonable : THEY, the said Patentees and their Associates, their heirs, successors, and assigns, *Rendering and paying* such duties and acknowledgments as then were or after should be established by the laws of this government, under the obedience of His Royal Highness, his heirs and successors, as in and by the said Patent, remaining upon record in the Secretary's Office, reference being thereunto had, doth fully and at large appear. AND WHEREAS, the present inhabitants and freeholders of the Town of New Harlem aforesaid have made their application unto me for a more full and ample confirmation of their premises to them, their heirs, successors, and assigns forever, in their quiet and peaceable possession : NOW KNOW YE, that by virtue of the commission and authority to me derived, and power in me residing, in consideration of the premises, and of the Quit Rent hereinafter reserved, I HAVE GIVEN, *granted, ratified, and confirmed*, and by these presents do give, grant, ratify, and confirm unto JOHN DELAVALL, RESOLVED WALDRON, JOOST VAN OBLINUS, DANIEL TOURNEUR, ADOLPH MEYER, JOHN SPRAGGE, JAN HENDRICKS BREVOORT, JAN DELAMATER, ISAAC DELAMATER, BA-

RENT WALDRON, JOHANNES VERMELJE, LAWRENCE JANSEN, PETER VAN OBLINUS, JAN DYCKMAN, JAN NAGEL, ARENT HARMANSE, CORNELIS JANSEN, JACQUELINE TOURNEUR, HESTER DELAMATER, JOHANNES VERVEELEN, WILLIAM HALDRON, ABRAHAM MONTANIE, PETER PARMENTIER,* as Patentees, for and on the behalf of themselves the present freeholders and inhabitants of the said Town of New Harlem, their heirs, successors, and assigns, *All and singular* the before recited tract, parcel and parcels of land and meadow, butted and bounded as in the said Patent is mentioned and expressed, together with all and singular the messuages, tenements, houses, buildings, barns, stables, orchards, gardens, pastures, mills, mill-dams, runs, streams, ponds, woods, underwoods, trees, timber, fencing, fishing, hawking, hunting, and fowling, liberties, privileges, hereditaments, and improvements whatsoever to the said tract of land and premises belonging, or in any wise appertaining, or accepted, reputed, taken, or known, or used, occupied, and enjoyed, as part, parcel, or member thereof, with their and every of their appurtenances; *Always provided*, that nothing contained therein shall be construed to prejudice the right of the City of New York, or any other particular right; and saving to the said City of New York, and their successors forever, and also saving to every particular person, his heirs and assigns, that have any right, interest or estate within the limits of the said Town of New Harlem, as well as without the limits of the said Town of Harlem, full power, liberty and privilege to build, cultivate and improve all such tracts and parcels of land as the said City of New York now have, or hereafter shall have, within or without and adjacent to the limits of the Town of Harlem aforesaid: *And also the commonage*, of the Town of Harlem aforesaid, is to be confirmed within the limits aforesaid, and the right of commonage to extend no further, any grant or thing contained herein to the contrary in any wise notwithstanding: TO HAVE AND TO HOLD the said several tracts and parcels of land and premises, with their and every of their appurtenances, unto them the said John Delavall, Resolved Waldron, Joost van Oblinus, Daniel Tourneur, Adolph Meyer, John Spragge, Jan Hendricks Brevoort, Jan Delamater, Isaac Delamater, Barent Waldron, Johannes Vermelje, Lawrence Jansen, Jan Dyckman, Jan Nagel, Arent Harmanse, Cornelis Jansen, Peter van Oblinus, Jacqueline Tourneur, Hester Delamater, Johannes Verveelen, William Haldron, Abraham Montanie, Peter Parmentier, as Patentees for and on the behalf of themselves, their heirs, successors, and assigns, to the sole and only proper use, benefit, and behoof of the said Patentees, their heirs, successors, and assigns forever: TO BE HOLDEN of His Most Sacred Majesty, his heirs and successors, *in free and common soccage*, according to the tenure of East Greenwich, in the County of Kent, in His Majesty's Kingdom of England; YIELDING, *rendering and paying* therefor, yearly and every year forever, on or before the Five and Twentieth day of March, in lieu of all services and demands whatsoever, as a *Quit Rent*, to His Most Sacred Majesty aforesaid, his heirs

* These names are strangely distorted in the Patent, as "Recorded for the Inhabitants of Harlem," in Liber 6, page 192, of Patents, in the Secretary of States Office, Albany; showing gross carelessness somewhere, either on the part of the recording clerk, the draftsman, or the person who made out the list. They are here corrected from indisputable data; and the entire document is also relieved from the crudities of the old spelling, which serve no purpose but to mar the text.

and successors, or to such officer or officers as shall be appointed to receive the same, *Sixteen bushels of good winter merchantable Wheat*, at the City of New York. IN TESTIMONY whereof I have caused these presents to be entered upon record in the Secretary's Office, and the Seal of the Province to be hereunto affixed, this Seventh day of March, 1686, and in the Third year of His Majesty's reign.*

THO. DONGAN.

It now remained to discharge the arrears of quit rent, and pay for the patent. To this, for the time being, some of the payments on the church had to give way, as before stated. On March 20th Jan Louwe Bogert brought in his wheat to the constable, as did others on the same date, and on April 5th nearly all the rest. It was deposited in the loft of the town house, over 130 schepels, preparatory to being taken to New York. Constable Brevoort carted from the loft, April 29th, four bushels of wheat as the balance due for quit rent, under the commutation, to wit, for the years 1683 to 1686, inclusive.‖ On June 3d William Holmes paid 11 florins on the patent, though not named as a patentee, for which he was allowed to

* The *Manor of East Greenwich* was an ancient Crown domain, which had been given successively to several monastic institutions, but was finally recovered from one of these, in exchange for other lands, by Henry VIII. in the 23d year of his reign. On the sale of the Crown Lands, under Cromwell, this Manor was reserved for the use of the State, and at the Restoration fell again to the Crown, in which it continued till the accession of James II. to the throne in 1685, when it was bestowed on his queen as part of her jointure. It was apparently in compliment to the queen that it was now taken and cited as a pattern tenure, enjoying all the advantages of the *free and common socage*, briefly explained on a former page. The term *socage* as here used is derived by Blackstone from the Saxon *soc*, a *privilege*, and hence here denoting a privileged tenure, but others very plausibly refer it to *soca*, a *plough*. (See *Blackstone*; the chapters on *English Tenures*.) The date of the above Patent is given in Old Style, by which the year began March 25. According to our present reckoning it should be 1687.

‖ The *Quit Rent* charged by the Dongan Patent continued to be assessed upon the freeholders, and paid to the Receiver-General, down to the opening of the Revolution, from which time no further payments were made for a term of forty years. The State Legislature had passed a law in 1786, providing for the commutation and collection of all quit rents due on the numerous land patents granted by the English colonial governors; but nothing was done in relation to the Harlem Patent till 1815. In this year it was advertised, with many others, to be sold for the arrearages; but the claim was then cancelled by the Comptroller of the City of New York, Thomas R. Mercein, who on Nov. 1, 1815, paid to the State Treasurer, in three per cent stock, the sum of $547.50, in full satisfaction of all the quit rents which had accrued upon the Harlem Patent since Mar. 25, 1774, and also in commutation of all the prospective rents. This exaction of the quit rent premises the validity of the early colonial patents; but this point is clearly admitted by the constitution of this State, which annuls all colonial grants and charters made subsequent to Oct. 14, 1775, but affects none given prior to that date.

draw of the common land in the first general allotment, in 1691. On Oct. 18th Johannes Vervelen made the last payment, 9 florins, 12 stivers in money, by the hand of his daughter, Mrs. Meyer. The whole cost of the patent was something over 800 guilders.

The Dongan patent was professedly designed for quieting the freeholders and inhabitants in their ancient rights and privileges. Save that it annuls the restriction upon the erection of buildings, and cuts off the outside commonage (a most unwarrantable measure), it simply confirms what Nicolls' patent had granted. The several persons holding under Andros' grants to Elphinstone and others, and not named in the patent, were held to be thereby excluded from its provisions, and from any share with the other patentees in the common lands. The limits of the patent, recited somewhat awkwardly, but never meant to be indefinite or uncertain, plainly included so much of Manhattan Island as lay to the east and north of the given line, and bordering upon the "Harlem River, or any part of the said River on which this Island doth abut, and likewise on the North and East Rivers." It expressly comprehended "all the soils, creeks, quarries, woods, meadows, pastures, marshes, waters, lakes, and all other profits, commodities, emoluments, and hereditaments to the said lands and premises, within the bounds and limits set forth, belonging, or in any wise appertaining."

If these premises be admitted, and if the vacant lands, etc., granted by Dongan's charter to the Corporation of New York, were, as that charter says, only those "not heretofore given or granted by any of the former Governors," we may fairly question whether Dongan did not violate the ancient rights of the Harlem people, not only as to their commonage, but in giving the Corporation the control of the water-line along the exterior shore of the Harlem patent. But while greater wrongs must inevitably follow any impairing of this now venerable and generally conceded prerogative, how can the claim hold that it extends alike to the *interior* vacant lands, creeks or marshes, the title to which we submit is rightfully vested in the heirs or assigns of the Dongan patentees?*

* This view is taken in an Opinion, given by the late Hon. Murray Hoffman, March 13, 1873, respecting a piece of land owned by Mr. Voorhis;

At the date of Dongan's patent all was woodland and commons north of Moertje Davids' Fly (Manhattanville), that is, from what were called Jochem Pieters Hills, all the way to Spuyten Duyvel; the claims of Dyckman and Nagel and the salt meadows owned by individuals excepted. To this section of the island the Indians still laid a claim, but which they surrendered to the town, in lieu of "sundries delivered to the natives" by Col. Stephen van Cortlandt, in behalf of the inhabitants, Feb. 28th, 1688, and a balance which was not made up till March 1st, 1715, when a tax was raised by the freeholders for that purpose.

Beside the above, the yet unappropriated woodlands embraced a few inconsiderable parcels here and there on the Flats, a larger piece between Hoorn's Hook and the Bogert (since Benson or McGown) farm, and the tract lying between the village and Montagne's Flat, hitherto kept for pasturage, containing some 250 acres. It was bounded east by Kingsbridge road, west by the creek, and stretched from where 111th Street and 5th Avenue now intersect (and where said creek was then crossed by the road from Harlem to New York), northward to 131st Street and 8th Avenue. The allotments and sales made under the Dongan patent, in and between the years 1691 and 1712, disposed of most of this tract and nearly all the other common land within the patent lines, though several small pieces were not sold till 1753. The exact plan and history of these several allotments, hitherto unknown to modern conveyancers, and which

situated on Harlem Creek, between 2d and 3d avenues, and extending from 105th street toward 109th. It lay in a cove of the creek and was part of the 12 acres (two of the Van Keulen Hook lots) owned at an early day by Capt. Thomas Delavall, and sold to Benjamin Benson by Simon Johnson, 1747. We quote one or two paragraphs from the Opinion.

"We can here draw a natural and, we think, legal distinction between the River proper and a creek of it. The former is defined by the general course (*filum*) of the body of the stream, and such course is from point to point where there is an indentation into the land, properly a cove. The latter is that indentation. And we could very consistently hold that the land under water within the cove, between high and low water mark passed, but not outside of it. This view would be tenable even if that was an indentation from Harlem River; *a fortiori* when from Harlem Creek. But the creek itself, we contend, passed; and the case is then much stronger."

Again, alluding to the language of the Harlem Patent, quoted in the text, granting all the *soils*, *creeks*, etc., Judge Hoffman very pertinently remarks, "It would be difficult to get together terms which would more fully embrace anything of land, of water, and of any combination of the two."

will be found in Appendix J, not only supply a vast deal of curious information upon a new subject, but, as we conceive, have an intrinsic and permanent value, in connection with the subsequent titles, on which they throw much light.*

There were now remaining here but few witnesses to those trials in Fatherland which had so largely contributed to people the town. Of the French refugees, filling heretofore so considerable a space in its history, nearly all were either dead or had gone with their families to other parts. Spirited and litigious as were these refugees, wearying the courts with their petty disputes, the recital of which may seem beneath the dignity of history; they did but betray in all this the underlying national trait, extreme jealousy of their rights, the legitimate fruit of former and sharper conflicts. For them, in the fullest sense, "self-preservation was the first law of nature." But we may not forget their many good qualities, nor their valuable agency in building up the town, in which quickness of perception, promptitude and efficiency, whether in official or business relations, and greater skill in various industries, supplied elements in which the Dutch were not their equal. A principal cause of the removal of so many of these families was the better facility for obtaining land in the places to which they went; but the fact is also obvious that they could not well fraternize with the Dutch, for while the latter were generally prosperous, the French were commonly "poor, and therefore forced to be penurious." Strongly attached, moreover, to their own frugal mode of living, their language and church service, intuitively they sought out the place and society where these advantages could be best secured and enjoyed. A few of the wealthier families remained here, as the Tourneurs, Montanyes, Delamaters, and De Voes, held either by property ties, or intermarriage with the Hollanders, to whom by degrees they became assimilated.

The court proceedings are curious and quite enjoyable, as exhibiting the prevailing causes of dispute between neighbors, the

* The 250 acres included the late Myer homestead, in the angle formed by the forking of the road from Kingsbridge, together with the Isaac Day plot 1½ acres, the William Molenaor 17 acres, the Lawrence or Wagstaff 38 acres, the Samson A. Benson or Race Course farm, Mount Morris Park, Elizabeth Benson 25 acres, and Samson Benson 45 acre tract. See notices of *Myer* and *Benson* families, and *App. J., 1st Division.*

usual grounds of legal action, and the court customs and jurisprudence of the times. Not less valuable are the court records as an index of the public morals. Cases of trespass, slander, and breach of the peace were indeed too common, but flagrant crime was almost unknown. Not a single manslaughter, or action for divorce, or bastardy, or a clear case of petty larceny, is reported for the entire half-century under review. The case of arson by a slave, as before noticed, and the beating to death of a negro child in June of this year (1667), are not to be cited as against the general devotion to law and order, which indeed was shown in both these cases by a prompt report to the mayor, and in the last case, an inquest; though no particulars are given, not even the name of the party implicated. The doings at town meetings also prove beyond question the capacity of this early community for self-government, and for handling the perplexing questions which came up from time to time. No superior ability is shown in the advanced periods of the town's history.

Did not the scope of this volume limit it to the "origin and early annals" of the town, it would be easy to find in the varied exigencies of succeeding times much food for sober thought. The Leislerian troubles; how deeply they affected some Harlem families! The arbitrary suspension of the local court for eight long years after the colonial government was settled in 1691; what embarrassment it caused, till it was finally restored after long soliciting the General Assembly! Unswerving friends of the Dutch Church, with what alarm they beheld the efforts of Col. Morris and others to introduce the English service, through the ministrations of Rev. Henricus Boys! And then grave questions and difficulties attended the distributions of the common lands. Coercive measures taken by the King's Receiver-General, in 1713, to levy quit rents not justly chargeable, subjected six of the principal inhabitants to legal prosecution in the Court of Chancery. Other questions which arose respecting their lands could only be settled by a reference to the Supreme Court. And the Pipon-Gouverneur imbroglio, and questions growing out of it, kept the whole town disquieted till finally ended in 1747. Then came the sad discords and division in the Church between the *Cœtus* and the *Conferentie*. A desultory warfare with the Corporation of New York, concerning the

"Commons," began with the century and ended only the year before the Revolution.* And a volume of itself might be written upon those seven years of unprecedented trial, under the galling domination of British and Hessian soldiery, before the distressed inhabitants could realize the blessings of independence. Aside from these and a few similar passages, their history as a community is meagre during the colonial period proper. The recovery from the ruin of the war, and the successive steps by which a sparsely settled rural district was transmuted into the teeming city, with its wonderful concomitants of churches, schools, railways, parks, boulevards, etc.—which latter change may be dated from the sale of the Commons in 1825, and the first disposal of some of the farming lands as city lots—forms a history of much and varied interest, but still within the knowledge of the living, and easily traced as compared with that of the obscure initial period to which this volume is chiefly devoted.

Not to enlarge, therefore, upon these more modern times (though some of the matters touched upon and others pertaining to those periods will claim attention either in the succeeding chapter on the patentees, or in the notes or appendix), the social condition, at and after the period under review, presents some interesting features yet to be noticed.

The inhabitants, in their ways and mode of living, preserved all the characteristics of Fatherland. Wedded to their plain and primitive habits, the portrait of our early Dutch yeomanry, as others have drawn it, is here true to the life, with but slight retouching.

The village seats or scattered farm-houses: let us enter one, bidden welcome by mine host, smoking his evening pipe, in his wonted seat on the porch. An air of hospitality has the premises, even to the old well, with watering-trough beside it, which, placed conveniently *before* the house, with mossy bucket hung from the primitive well-pole, invites the gentle kine to

* The history of this tract is particularly set forth in the *Deduction of the Title to Harlem Commons*, forming pages 117 to 175 of a volume prepared by the late Isaac Adriance, and entitled "Conveyances on record in the Register's Office by Dudley Selden, from the 1st January, 1825, to the 1st January, 1838. Printed by Alexander S. Gould, 144 Nassau Street, N. Y., 1838." It contains Maps of the Commons, as divided into city lots.

come freely to water, or the wayfarer to stop and slake his thirst. These houses have begun to be constructed with greater regard to permanence, and even to style, being solidly built of stone, and of more ample dimensions than formerly, though only of one full story. The low ceilings, still void of lath and plaster, expose the heavy oak beams as roughly hewn, or, if taste has dictated, planed and beaded. Similar taste sometimes demands wainscoting, either plain or in panels, around the rooms and hall, and up the broad stairway, with its oaken balustrade, leading to sleeping-chambers in the loft. Outer doors, swung upon heavy strap hinges, are invariably divided in halves horizontally, the upper one usually open by day in the warm season, for the admission of air and light. Above it perhaps is a sash, with three or four small panes of thick green glass, blown with a curious knob or swell in the centre. The panes in the windows measure not over seven by nine inches, and are sometimes set in leaden cross-bars, being protected by strong, close shutters, instead of the less secure modern blinds. The fireplace, with usually no jambs (but having supports built into the wall), gives ample room for all *around* the fire. Thus suspended, as it were, overhead, the chimney mouth opens wide and flaring to catch the fugitive sparks and smoke, and forms a convenient place in which, at the proper season, to hang up hams, sausage, and beef to cure. If the fireplace is built with jambs, these are often faced with glazed earthern tiles, imported from Holland, on which are pictured Bible stories and other scenes. These amuse and instruct the juvenile part of the family, who make it a favorite pastime to study out the curious designs. The last of these ornamental fireplaces now recollected was in the Peter Benson stone house, which stood in 109th Street, between 2d and 3d Avenues, and was demolished in 1865.

Plain and substantial were their dwellings, and in perfect accord with the manners and tastes of the occupants, which were simple, unaffected, and economical. Slow and deliberate in what they did, it was made up by patience and application. And no people could have been more independent of the outside world. The farmer burnt his own lime, tanned his own leather, often made all the boots and shoes worn by himself and family, and did much of his own carpenter and wheelwright work.

Their help in the heavy farm work was mainly African slaves, who, at this time, numbered as one to four whites.

Primitive were their methods of farming; it was not the era of iron ploughs, horse-rakes, and reapers. The scythe was used in mowing grass. The cradle was then unknown, and instead of which all grain was cut with sickle, or with the *sith* and *hook*. The sith had a blade similar to that of the scythe, but only half as long, to which was attached a snath of about the same length, having at the other end a loop like that of a shovel-handle. The hook was made of a slender wooden stock, three feet long, from the end of which ran out at a right angle a small iron prong about eight inches long. When used the hook was held in the left hand near the middle, where, to prevent its turning, was a socket for the thumb to rest in, the prong being turned from the person. The hook, pressed against the standing grain, served to hold it in place, while it was cut by a swing of the sith, which was held in the other hand. The cut grain was thus left leaning against that still uncut, till the reaper, or his attendant following after him, gathered and bound it into sheaves. Nothing was deemed more important than to cut and lay in a good supply of salt hay, which was then thought indispensable for the healthy subsistence of cattle through the winter. It was for this reason that a piece of salt meadow was regarded as a necessary appendage to every farm, and was not less valuable in the view of the early settlers than so much upland.

The children were brought up to those habits of industry which the parents themselves found so profitable. The sons were invariably given a useful trade, and the daughters well taught in all household duties. While the men were engaged in the out-door work of the farm, the women, in short gown and slippers, the common indoor dress, were as busy at their special avocations. The spinning-wheel was brought out and set in motion as soon as wool and flax could be prepared in the fall, and so each family made its own "homespun," as it was termed, both white and colored, to supply its members with clothing; while she was considered but a poor candidate for matrimony who could not show her stores of domestic linens, and other products of her maiden industry. The dames, so saving were they of their time, usually took their spinning-wheels, on going to spend a social afternoon with a neighbor. Nor were the females unwilling to help in the field during the busy season of harvest or corn-gathering. Side by side with their fathers, brothers, and husbands, they vied with them in raking hay or carrying sheaves; and their presence gave a charm to the merry time of *husking*.

Broom and scrubbing-brush, with a periodical *white*washing, frequently tinted *yellow* or *green*, kept their apartments cleanly and neat. The carpet, when first introduced called in derision a *dirt-cover*, was in those days unknown here. The bare floors, as scrupulously clean as the bare table on which they ate their meals, were regularly scrubbed, then sprinkled with the fine beach sand which was brought to the city by the boat-load, and peddled in carts through the streets and roads of the island. On cleaning-day it was spread moistened in little heaps over the floor, the family being taught to tread carefully between them. To disturb these would sadly mar the economy of the good housewife, and maybe provoke some good honest scolding in Dutch! The next day the sand, now dry, was swept in waves, or other figures, by drawing the broom lightly over it. It was in truth but a sample of the general tidiness which ruled the premises.

Living so largely within themselves, they knew little of the dangers and diseases incident to luxury and indolence. Their clothing, bedding, etc., all of their own homespun, most that their table required the farm supplied, to which a mess of clams or fish often gave variety; but no dish, with the Dutch farmer, could compete with his *speck en koole*, pork and cabbage.

Their pride was of a kind that was no bar to pleasure, if their only coach *was* a common wagon, or perchance an ox-cart! Home-made linsey-woolsey gave content equally with the finest imported fabrics, and, says a contemporary, "though their low-roofed houses may seem to shut their doors against pride and luxury, yet how do they stand wide open to let charity in and out, either to assist each other or relieve a stranger." Another bears this testimony: "They are sociable to a degree, their tables being as free to their neighbors as to themselves." And hospitality could not do too much for the guest if welcome; the acme only reached if he tarried for the night, when, soon after sunset, he was snugly ensconced in the best bed, made of softest down, and between homespun linen sheets, from which, if cold, the chill was taken by the indispensable warming-pan! At the same time the idea of warming the church was yet unfledged, nor was this provided for till early in the present century, when a stove was introduced. Before this, each church-going matron took to comfort her her little *foot-stove* and her Dutch Bible with silver clasps! Intermarriages among the resident families was the rule, and he was thought a bold swain truly who ventured beyond the pale of the community to woo a mate. And with the unaffected welcome, a keen-eyed scrutiny also awaited the blushing bride, on her first arrival from the charming vales of Bloomingdale, the hills of Westchester, or rural home at Bergen, Hackensack, or Esopus. When friends gathered socially, or happened to meet, as at the village tavern, conversation running in mellifluous Dutch, turned, as usual with farmers, upon their crops, or on horses or cattle, or modes of farming, unless some special topic intruded. With the good *Juffrouws*, church matters and the domines last visit were always in order. Not many survived who could speak from personal recollection of the Fatherlands; yet we cannot misjudge of the themes on which a few gray heads could still dilate, with all the effect of eye-witnesses or actual participants. Good Joost van Oblinus—the thrilling incidents of the French invasion of Flanders, his escape with parents to Holland, sojourn at Mannheim, second flight before French invaders, and final adieu to the dear shores of Europe. Mrs. Tourneur, in tender childhood a victim of that cruel war, and driven with others of her family from her native Hesdin, probably on its capture by Louis XIII., in 1639; hers was a tale of trials, of which we have but the veriest outline. And Mrs. Delamater, the daughter of a refugee, depicting her young life at Canterbury, and the humble abode where she was born and reared, whence also, on the quiet Sabbath, she was wont to accompany her parents to the grand old cathedral, and down by a flight of stone steps into the solemn crypt or vault, where the French and Walloons used to meet for divine service, a privilege long before granted them by good Queen Bess. And Frederick De Vaux, or De Voo, who lived to a patriarchal age, and probably was the last survivor of the refugees experimentally familiar with persecution and hair-breadth escapes in fleeing his native land; facts still among the lingering traditions of his family.* Now Bogert and the Jansens grow mellow over the good old times at Schoonrewoert; or the other trio, Meyer, Dyckman, and Bussing, draw parallels between the soils or productions of Harlem and their native Bentheim, so famed; or again the well-companioned Waldron and Verveelen live amid former scenes in busy old Amsterdam—the shop-keeper's son, perchance, garrulous over shrewd bargains in trade, and the "book-printer" of the *Teerketels-steeg*, once more among his type and forms, and, as of old, throwing off from his new press, which his townsman Blaeu, the map-printer, and former assistant to Tycho Brahé, had brought to such perfection, fresh sheets of learned folios, full fifty impressions per hour! But should conversation chance to turn upon some controverted question, either of politics or theology, and the latent fire once

* FREDERICK DE VAUX, the anc. of the *De Voe* family, has already had a partial notice. Born on Walloon soil, as records inform us, tradition has handed down some touching particulars of the flight, the pursuit of bloody persecutors, and the escape into Holland. How long Frederick de Vaux sojourned at Mannheim is unknown, but long enough to obtain citizenship. He emigrated in 1675, bringing a passport from the authorities of that place, a copy of which is given on a former page. He was then a widower, but in 1677 he m. Esther, dr. of Daniel Tourneur. To the lands in Westchester, since the Cromwell farm, gotten with his w., he added, as we have seen, the Bickley tract, or De Voe's Point. He also provided his sons, Daniel and Abel, with large farms at Fordham and New Rochelle. Living in his later years among his several chn., he d. in New Rochelle, in 1743, at the venerable age of ab. 90 yrs., and was buried on the farm of his son Abel. His chn. were Frederick, Daniel, Joseph, Abel; Rachel, who m. Johannes Dyckman; Esther, m. Levi Vincent; Susannah, m. Andrew Nodine; Mary, m. Evert Brown and Joshua Bishop; Leah, m. Nathaniel Bailey; Dinah, m. Louis Guion and Tobias Concklin; Judith, m. Johannes Barhite, and Abigail, who d. unm. Daniel De Voe settled in Fordham, and Abel in New Rochelle, upon the farms conveyed to them by their fa. before his d. Joseph removed to the city of N. Y., where he d. in 1764, leaving a family. Frederick, the eldest son, succeeded to the paternal estate at De Voe's Point, under a deed of June 13, 1731, and where he d. in 1753. He m. twice, and had chn. *Frederick* (3d of the name), *Daniel*, *David*, *John*, *Thomas*, *Abraham*, *Abigail*, *Hester*, *Sarah*, *Mary*, and *Leah*. This old and respectable family is now widespread and numerous. The brs. Isaac, Thomas Farrington, James, Moses (of Fordham), John Appleby (dec.), George W., and Frederick W. De Voe, are sons of the late John De Voe, of N. Y., who d. Aug. 29, 1853, æ. 68 yrs., having attained the same age as his fa., John De Voe, of Yonkers, or Philips Manor, who d. Sept. 24, 1824, being the son of Frederick De Voe, 3d, aforesaid. To the estimable Col. Thomas F. De Voe, of N. Y., we are indebted for many of these particulars.

kindle, the dispute was sure to run high; for only then their tobacco-pipes lost the power to soothe—that solace alike of their working and their leisure hours, and by no means confined to the males; but yet the good domine set the example!

Large productive farms, and a convenient market for all they had to sell, led to certain wealth, and no thriftier farmers were to be found anywhere. They were proud too—of their broad acres, fine stock, lands well tilled and barns well filled! But not the alluring example ever before their eyes could win them to the display and ceremony of city life; though the latter, simplicity itself as compared with the demands of modern fashion, sets in stronger contrast the style of living, so unpretentious yet rational, which obtained in even the wealthier families, as the Waldrons, Meyers, Bensons, and Bussings. English modes and manners could make but slow advance among a people so tenacious of the Holland tongue, who for half a century later kept their records in Dutch, and their accounts in *guilders* and *stivers*.*

This picture of the former times, so rudely drawn and void of limner's art, is yet worthy of thoughtful study. As every age has had its virtues as well as its vices, things which men admire and emulate, so the initial days of our colonial history teem with instructive lessons in all that pertains to manly aims and right living, the study of which is calculated to make one wiser and better. If the present effort to restore a knowledge of the Harlem founders shall subserve so useful a purpose, and the sequel to their history, as now to be given in that of the patentees and their families, shall in any degree contribute to the same result, we may count our labor not wholly lost.

* In 1658 the valuation of Real Estate in the several Wards of the City of New York was as follows.

Out Ward, Harlem Division	£1,723
do. Bowery Division	4,140
North Ward	7,625
West Ward	9,600
East Ward	9,648
Dock Ward	16,241
South Ward	29,254

CHAPTER XXIV.

NOTICES OF THE PATENTEES AND THEIR HEIRS OR SUCCESSORS.

BENSON.

WITH those whose recollections of Harlem run back a generation or more, to the time when it yet retained all the charms of a quiet rural suburb—ere "trade's unfeeling train usurped the land and dispossessed the swain"—the name of this locality finds almost a synonym in that of Benson; so largely identified was this respectable family with the history and landed interests of the town. Standing first in alphabetical order, we cheerfully accord it the precedence, which it may properly claim among these genealogical notes.*

Capt. JOHANNES BENSON, the first of the family to locate here, is not named in Dongan's patent, as he was not then a resident, nor till some ten years after; but, purchasing the Bogert farm, he thereby acquired the rights of a patentee, before the final division of the common lands, in which he shared; and his desc. continued, as we shall see, among the largest proprietors at Harlem till it ceased to be an agricultural community. His fa., Dirck Bensingh, as commonly called, was not a Hollander, but a Swede, according to the tradition in the family, as old Lawrence Benson used to say; and this is borne out by the original form of the name. Perhaps, to be more exact, Dirck was a Dane. We have traced him from Groningen to Amsterdam, and thither, with his w. Catalina Berck, to New Amster-

* These sketches do not claim to be complete genealogies, but are designed to preserve, in the case of each family, enough of its history to interest its living members, and to enable many of them to identify their connection with the parent stock; while others, wishing to perfect their line of descent, will here find a valuable beginning for such a work. As serving to elucidate the land titles, by showing the transmission of real property in the several families—and this, by including all the patentees, necessarily embracing all the lands within the township or patent lines—these sketches have a special importance. The result of many years' search among authentic records, they are believed to be substantially correct and reliable, whether as genealogies or otherwise; any venerable hearsay or family traditions, so called, to the contrary notwithstanding.

By observing that the grandchildren of the ancestor (or patentee) are named in *italics*, the first three generations may be more readily distinguished and the relationships traced. For a key to the abbreviations used see table at the end of the General Contents.

dam. See page 103. Here he bought a house and lot near the fort, Aug. 23, 1649, and the next year another on Broadway. On June 29, 1654, at his desire, the Director and Council allowed him "to leave this place to promote his own affairs." Going to Fort Orange, he built upon a lot which had been granted him Oct. 25, 1653, and proved himself an industrious and worthy citizen. He worked as a carpenter on the new church built in 1656; in 1658 he loaned the deacons 100 gl. He d. Feb. 12, 1659. Three years later Dirck's wid. m. Harman Tomasz. Hun.

Dirck Benson's chn. were Dirck, b. 1650; Samson, b. 1652; Johannes, b. 1655; Catrina, b. 1657, who m. Doctor Reynier Schaets and Jonathan Bradhurst; and Maria, b. 1659, who m. Volckert van Hoesen. The three sons of Benson grew up in Albany much respected, and all became chh. mem. Samson set up a pottery, and was known as the "pottebacker." Dirck became a skipper on the Hudson, sailing the sloop *Eendraght* between Albany and New York. Johannes was probably an innkeeper, for in 1689, when apprehensions existed of a French and Indian invasion from Canada, a committee of safety, of which *Lieut.* Joh. Benson was a member, directed "that the people of Patcook do make their retreat to Johannes Bensing's upon occasion." Raised to a captaincy soon after, he performed useful service during those fearful times. The midnight massacre at Schenectady, Feb. 8, 1690, in which their br.-in-law, Doctor Schaets, then a justice of the peace at that place, was slain, together with one of his sons, and the continuance of French and Indian hostilities, quite unsettled the Bensons and their families (for the three brs. were now m.), and they finally transferred their residence to N. Y., Dirck in 1693, and Samson and Johannes in 1696, when the public alarm became so great as to cause many such removals.

Dirck and Samson remained in the city, while Johannes came to H., and bought a place in the village from Peter van Oblienis.* It consisted of the two *erven* lying easterly of the

* The BENSONS, *of New York City*, became numerous; we subjoin a brief notice of them, as of interest to their desc., and to save the mistaking of persons of similar Christian name, so often recurring in both branches of the family, a plan we have also pursued in regard to some other names, for a like reason.

DERICK BENSON, b. 1650, m. Thysie Claes, dr. of Claes Jansen Slavast, of Albany, by whom were all his chn., and secondly, Jannetie, dr. of Barent Pietersen Coeymans, of Albany, who survived him. Derick became wealthy; owning, among other property, 1000 acres of land on the Raritan, which he sold, in 1697, to his fa.-in-law, Coeymans, and on which his son, Andries Coeymans, afterward settled. In 1701, Benson leased the ferry between N. Y. and Brooklyn, for seven yrs. at £130 a yr., but lost money at it. For additional items respecting Derick Benson, see the *Bergen Gene-*

third cross street, which Peter's fa. had gotten from Lubbert Gerritsen, as heretofore noticed, and which he formally conveyed to Peter Dec. 28, 1699, after the latter had sold it to Benson. It formed a part of the late Dunning plot of 4 acres. Benson was still here Nov. 16, 1700, when he acted as an arbiter in settling the Tourneur estate, and on Dec. 13 ensuing he voted for building a new bridge "at the stone bridge," which crossed the Mill Creek at 111th Street. But in the mean time his br.-in-law Van Hoesen, also quitting Albany, had settled as a farmer and innkeeper at the Indian *Sappokaniken*, just without the city on the North River side; otherwise called by the Dutch *New Nordwyck*, and also from Gerrit Bas, a proprietor there, *Bassen Bouwery*, a contraction of "Bas syn bouwery." It has since been known as Greenwich Village. At this place lived the Mandevilles, the Van Schaicks, etc., and here Jacob

alogy. He d. June 26, 1717, having had chn., Catalina, b. 1683, m. John F. Vandermeulen and John Kelly; Eve, b. 1686, d. young; Rachel, b. 1689, m. Hans Bergen; Eve, b. 1693, m. 1717, Anthony Duane, fa. (but by a second w.) of Hon. James Duane; Derick, b. 1696, d. Aug. 30, 1734; and Thysie, b. 1699, who m. James Henderson, of N. Y., merchant. As Derick, last named, left no desc., his uncle Samson becomes the head of all the later N. Y. Bensons, not of the H. branch.

SAMSON BENSON, the potter, b. in 1652, m. first, Tryntie van Deusen (sr. to the w. of Job), by whom were all his chn. but one; and secondly, Grietie, dr. of Abm. Kermer, and wid. of Capt. Jacob van Tilburg; Benson being her third hus., and surviving her. We have not located Benson's pottery, but he owned a house and lot in Smith street (now William, below Maiden Lane), bought of Dr. Lucas van Tienhoven, and which his executors sold to his son Harman, Feb. 4, 1732. He d. June 2, 1730, having had 13 chn., viz: Catalina, b. 1675, d. 1706, having m. 1697, Stoffel, also called Theophilus, Pelts; Derick, b. 1677; Teuwes, or Matthew, b. 1679; Harman, b. 1681; Samson, b. 1684; Robert, b. 1686; William, b. 1687; Elizabeth, b. 1689, m. Egbert van Borsum; Johannes, b. 1692; Helena, b. 1694; Maria, b. 1696, who, with Wm., Joh. and Helena, d. early; Hendricus, b. 1698, and Catalina, b. 1707 (after the elder ch. so called was d.), and who was unm. in 1726.

Derick Benson, b. 1677, also a potter, lived in Crown street (now Liberty), and d. in 1725. By his w., Elizabeth Radcliff, who survived him, he had *Samson*, b. 1712 (who m. Catharine Peck, and had Derick, b. 1741; Johannes, 1744, etc.; perhaps went to Albany); *Catharine*, b. 1714, who m. Capt. Abraham Eight, of N. Y. (fa. of the excellent Abm. Eights, Esq., of Albany, dec., fa. of the late Dr. Jona. Eights: See *Pearson's First Settlers*); *Rachel*, b. 1716, who m. Frederick Fine, of N. Y.; *Johannes*, b. 1718; *Derick*, b. 1721; *Matthew*, b. 1723; and *Elizabeth*, b. 1725. On Apl. 9, 1754, the wid., Elizabeth, and her two drs., Catharine (with her hus., Capt. Eight) and Rachel, the last being also a wid., sold the residence in Crown street to Rem Rapelje, bolter, for £300.

Matthew Benson, mason, b. 1679, d. 1721. He m., 1706, Catrina, dr. of Jonathan Provoost, and their chn., that reached maturity, were *Samson*, b. 1713; *Catharine*, b. 1716, and *Catalina*, b. 1719. His will, made May 9, 1721, was proved Dec. 9, 1755, on the oath of Henry Riker, one of the witnesses. On Apl. 30, 1753, the wid., with Catharine and Catalina, the sur-

Cornelissen Stille (see *Woertendyk* and *Somerindyk*) had an improved farm of 100 acres which Joh. Benson bought Dec. 6, 1699, for 2000 gl. Hither Benson soon removed, having agreed, Nov. 12, 1701, to sell his house and lot at H. (for which he had obtained a deed Mar. 15 preceding), to his eldest son Samson, now m. to a dr. of Adolph Meyer. With it Samson bought "a negro, with a plough, and iron-work for a wagon, as also 37 schepels of seed rye and wheat," all for £130, which he had till May 1705 to pay for, and then to receive his deed.

After several years at the Bassen Bouwery, Capt. Benson bought the farm of Jan Louwe Bogert, Sept. 21, 1706, and the next spring returned to H., to spend the rest of his days. In the divisions of 1712 he drew his proportion of land, for which see App. J. He added otherwise to his acres, which numbered 182 in 1715. Capt. Benson d. this year; his wid., Elizabeth

viving children—the last unm., and Catharine, then the w. of Thomas Moore, weaver—sold property of Matthew Benson, to Charles Johnson, schoolmaster. But it would appear that Samson m., 1735, Jannetie Arment, and had issue, Matthew, 1741, Jonathan, 1744, Lucas, 1746, Cornelius, 1748.

Harman Benson, carpenter, b. 1681, m., 1702, Aeltie, dr. of Victor Bicker, and surviving her six years, d. Oct. 7, 1743. Their chn. were *Catharine*, b. 1703, who m. John Leake; *Claesie*, also called Cloe, b. 1705, m. David Scott, and *Mr.* John van Aernhem; *Samson*, b. 1707; *Catalina*, b. 1711, m. John Walker; *Victor*, b. 1714; *Annetie*, b. 1716, m. John Man; and *Harmanus*, b. 1719, who m., 1742, Judith Castang.

Samson Benson, cooper, b. 1684, m., 1710, Maria, dr. of Abraham Boker, and d. Nov 29, 1732. His chn., except three that d. early, were *Abraham*, b. 1712, living 1763, m. Anna Tilly, 1739, and had a family; *Samson*, b. 1714, was a mariner, m. Elizabeth Williams, 1737, had a Samson, 1739, etc., his wid. appointed administratrix June 1, 1743; *Catharine*, b. 1715, m. James Taylor; and *John*, b. 1725, who d. before 1763, leaving his property, by will dated July 2, 1754, to his br. Abm. and sr. Catharine.

Henricus Benson, potter, b. 1698, m., 1722, Catharine, dr. of Gerrit van Laer. He d. Oct. 27, 1742. Three chn. named *Gerrit*, d. in inf., beside which he had *Tryntie*, b. 1722; *Henricus*, 1726; *Samson*, 1729, and *Dirick*, 1737. On Dec. 29, 1737, Henricus sold a house and lot in Smith street, deeded him Feb. 24, 1727, by his fa.; we trace his chn. no further.

Robert Benson, b. 1686, m., 1708, Cornelia, dr. of Johannes Roos, but d. in 1715; and the next year his wid. m. Anthony Rutgers. Benson had chn., Elizabeth, b. 1708, who m. Harmanus Rutgers, 1729; *Tryntie*, b. 1710, d. y.; *Tryntie*, b. 1712, m. Col. Martinus Hoffman, 1733; and *Robert*, b. 1715, d. 1762, who was a brewer, m., 1738, Catharine, dr. of Egbert van Borsum, became wealthy, and served in the Common Council from 1740 to 1754. He was fa. of Robert Benson, b. Oct. 30, 1739, d. Feb. 25, 1823, asst. alderman 1766–68, aid de camp to Gov. George Clinton, in the Revolution, clerk of the State Senate, and later, clerk of the N. Y. Com. Council; also of Capt. Henry Benson, b. Nov. 17, 1741, d. unm. Aug., 1823; and of the late Judge Egbert Benson, b. June 21, 1746, d. unm. Aug., 24, 1833. Robert, last named, was the fa. of Hon. Egbert Benson, of N. Y., and later of New Utrecht, and his sr. Maria, who m. Judge Leffert Lefferts, and was the mo. of Mrs. J. Carson Brevoort.

van Benson, surviving till 1740. She was the dr. of Teunis (Matthew) van Deusen, of Albany, where she was m. in 1676. Their chn. were Samson; Helena, who m. Lawrence Kortright; Derick; Catalina, m. Jacob Sammon; Rachel, m. Joh. Couwenhoven, of Bergen Co., N. J.; Matthew; Catharine, who m. Abm. Delamater; Marritie, m. Ryck Lydecker, of Bergen Co., and Johannes.

Johannes Benson Jr., or, as he wrote his name, *Janni*, was b. 1701, and m. in 1724 Elizabeth, dr. of Gerrit Lydecker, of Bergen Co. The same year, June 26, he bought from his br. Samson, lot 12, in 1st Division, which their fa. had drawn. On Feb. 10th ensuing he also bought from Samson two other parcels of land, in 1st and 2d Divisions, as hereafter further designated, which gave him in all 60 acres. He and his wife conveyed these lands to Peter Bussing, Mar. 14, 1733. That same spring they removed to Bergen Co., and on June 3 joined the church at Hackensack, by certificate from H. They had issue *Elizabeth*, b. 1725; *Gerrit*, b. 1727; *Johannes*, b. 1732; *Catrina*, b. 1734; *Matthew*, b. 1736.

Matthew Benson, son of Capt. Joh., was by trade a cooper; he m. in 1716 Elizabeth, dr. of Arent Bussing, and in 1727 Hannah, dr. of John Edsall, and wid. of Gerrit DeGroot. In 1716 he bought 30 acres of land at H., from his br.-in-law, Lawrence Kortright; sold it in 1719 to John Delamater; in 1724 bought 60 acres from his br. Samson, being lots 2 and 18 in 2d Div. These he sold in 1730 to Nicholas Kortright, and went to Bergen Co., he and his wife uniting with the church at Hackensack, May 29, 1731, by certificate from H. Matthew was afterward a "vintner" in N. Y., owning a house and lot in Dey Street, and where he d., leaving sons *Gerrit*, *Benjamin*, and *Samuel*, and dr. *Charity*, who m. William Sloe 1755; all living till 1758, when Gerrit d. unm., æ. 30 yrs. Samuel, of N. Y., house-carpenter, m. Ann Steel 1759. Benjamin, b. 1732, succeeded to the property in Dey Street, which he still owned in 1773, when he resided on a farm at Haverstraw.

Derick Benson, son of Capt. Joh., m. 1707, Jannetie Vandewater, and in 1711 Catalina, dr. of Abm. Bokee. In 1715 he owned 57 acres of land, which included the old Resolved Waldron farm on Van Keulen's Hook, bought 1714 from John van Horn, and since known as the Bogert or Morris Randell farm. He got an increase of 40 acres at the settlement of his fa.'s estate, in 1721; by releasing to Samson the parts of the lots in 1st, 2d, and 4th Divisions drawn with him in 1712 (see App. J.), and taking No. 4, 2nd Div., No. 4, 3d Div., No. 6, 3d Div., and No. 2, 4th Div. Of these he sold in 1724 the first and last to Joh. Meyer, and 3½ acres of No. 6 to John Lewis. The last named passed in 1726 to the Kortrights, later to Peter Waldron, and from him, May 5, 1768, to John Bogert, Jr. In 1731 Derick bought Nos. 19, 20, Van Keulen's Hook, from Grietie Kortright. Thus his estate stood till his death in 1751. Derick was several times constable of the H. division of the Out Ward, and was named as collector, in Montgomery's Charter, 1731. His chn. were *Elizabeth*, *Tanneke*, *Helena*, *Catalina*, *Maria*, and *John*; of whom Elizabeth m. Abm. Lydecker, Helena m. Peter Bants, and Catalina m. Dr. Josiah Paterson.* Said *John Benson* m. 1747 Marritie Lydecker, of Hackensack, and came to own his fa.'s lands at H. He sold the farm aforesaid, Mar. 12, 1766, to John Bogert, Jr., and, I believe, removed to Bergen Co.

Samson Benson, eldest son of Capt. Joh., was b. in 1678, at Albany; and with Maria Meyer, whom he m. in July, 1699, and a negro servant, he began life in his own house at H. village, purchased from his fa. On Jan. 23, 1706, he bought from Zach. Siekels part of the Brevoort property, being No. 1 of the New Lots, and two *erven* on the east side of his own, and adjoining the cross street on which were the chh. and chh. yard. On making a larger purchase he sold Lot 1 to his br. Derick, from whom it passed in 1712 to Joh. Meyer. In 1711 Samson bought the property of Daniel Tourneur, Jr., dec., embracing the farm on Montanye's Flat, and lot No. 2 in the Division of 1691, the first of which he sold soon after to Metje Cornelis (reserving the *morgen rights*), and in 1715 he sold lot No. 2 to Adolph Meyer. For his own drafts in 1712 see App. J. On Mar. 28, 1721, by buying out the wid. and co-heirs, Samson became owner of the paternal farm at the Point, and the lots drawn by his fa. in the Four Divisions; his br. Derick, by an arrangement already noticed, taking other of his father's lands. On May 4, 1721, he exchanged land with Barent Waldron for lot No. 6, 1st Div., lying between his farm and the highway, and by a decision of the Supreme Court, of Nov.

* JOSIAH PATERSON, of N. Y., "surgeon," bought the property of John Lewis, at H., in 1748. Beside the house and lot named in note on page 442, it embraced two others in the village, with eleven acres of woodland in 2d, 3d and 4th Divisions. Dr. Paterson was probably the son of John Paterson, of N. Y., "surgeon," who bought land at the Fly, Mar. 25, 1719. Josiah owned property in Queen street and in Crown street. His wid., etc., sold the latter to Gualterus Du Bois, in 1767. He also owned "part of Leonard Lewis's right" in the Great Patent in Ulster co. He disposed of his property at H. after holding it ten years. Dr. Paterson was admitted a freeman in N. Y. in 1750, and there he d. Oct. 23, 1766, leaving by his w., said Catalina Benson, chn. John, Richard, Josiah, Abraham, Elizabeth, Ann, and Mary. John became a merchant in Dutchess co., and, I believe, m. Catharine, dr. of Robert Livingston, proprietor of the Manor of Livingston, and was a Justice of the Peace, at the Manor, in the time of the Revolution. Col. Peter R. Livingston, who owned the Judah place, (see note p. 191,) was a br. of Mrs. John Paterson. See *Doc. Hist. N. Y.*, 8vo, IV., 448.

29, 1723, was quieted in his title to his drafted lands. See account of *Abm. Delamontanie.* Lot No. 6 lay mostly within the 64 acres (erroneously called 80) which Benjamin Benson conveyed to his br. Adolph in 1743, and which descended to Adolph's son, Lawrence Benson. For notice of Samson's grant of the Mill Camp, and the erection of a mill, etc., see App. F. This mill stood on the south side of the creek, and had two run of stones, only some eighteen inches in diameter. While building it, in 1740, Samson Benson died. His chn. were *Johannes; Adolph; Benjamin; Elizabeth*, who m. Joh. Waldron, Jr., and John Romer; *Mary*, m. Samson Pelts, of N. Y.; *Catharine* m. Captains Luke Shourd and Daniel McGown; *Helena*, m. Peter Bussing, of Fordham; *Anne*, m. John Odell, of Fordham, and *Catalina*, who m. Jacob Dyckman, Jr. of Kingsbridge.* The homestead and other lands of Samson Benson were sold by deeds of Sept. 23, 1740, and Jan. 28, 1743, to his son Benjamin, who the next day, after the last deed was given, conveyed the 64 (called 80) acres of the homestead before noticed (its western part), to his br. Adolph, with lot No. 18, 4th Division (the latter reconveyed to Benj.): Johannes at the same time getting the 5 a. 3 q. 2 r. lot, being No. 18, 3d Division. Benjamin took the mill and his fa.'s rights in the Mill Camp, obtaining a full title for the latter from the town in 1753. With additions, it became that since known as the Peter Benson farm. The old mill south of the creek being burned during the Revolution, while the British had possession and the Bensons were in exile, Benjamin built a new mill on this farm, on the north bank of the creek, which remain-

* Luke Siogrts, also called Shourd, was a "mariner," as were others of his race, at a later day. The name is evidently derived from the Swedish Christian name *Shute*. The anc., Sioert Olfertsen, emigrated from Heerenveen, a large village 18 miles s. e. of Leeuwarden, and for its beauty called the Friesland Hague. He sailed from Amsterdam Sept. 27, 1663, in the ship Statyn and with him his w. Ilie Roolofs, their ch. Olfert, and servant, Foppe Johannes. In the same vessel came Minne Johannes, also from Friesland, whose desc. in Rockland co. have borne the name of Minne or Manny. Sioert was a mason, and hence usually called *Sioert de metselaer*. He and w. joined the chh. in N. Y. Aug. 24, 1671, at the first communion under Do. Nieuwenhuysen. He was asst. ald in 1658 and 1689. He m. secondly, in 1697, Heyltie Pieters, wid. of Cornelis Clopper, and again in 1701, Janneke Snediker. He d. in 1702, leaving all his property to his son Olfert. His dr. Maria, b. 1664, m. Joh. Clopper. Olfert Sioerts, as called, b. at Heerenveen, in 1661, took his fa's trade, a bricklayer, but abandoned it for the sea. He m. in 1682, Margaret, dr. of Cornelis Clopper, and in 1703, Hillegond, dr. of Skipper Lucas Andriessen. Capt. Sioerts died in N. Y. in 1710. His chn. that reached maturity were *Mary*, b. 1686, *Heyltie*, 1688, *Sioert*, 1691, *Aeltie*, 1695, *Johannes*, 1701, *Luke*, 1704, and *Cornelius*, 1707. *Heyltie* m. Joh. Roosevelt, and has many desc. Luke m. Catharine Benson Jan. 6, 1728, but within five yrs. left her a wid. Some of this family removed to Rockland co. long prior to the Revolution.

ed till the construction of the Harlem Canal, when it was taken down. See App. F.

Johannes Benson, son of Samson, was b. in 1700, and was the third of the name in the order of descent; but being a year older than his uncle Joanni, was designated as "de oudste," *the eldest*. He m. Sept. 17, 1722, Tanneke, dr. of Samuel Waldron, and the next year, pursuant to a town custom, was made constable. In 1727 he bought Theunis Delamontanie's place in the village, being three acres, the upper half of No. 4, Van Keulen's Hook, near to which Benson lived; adding, in 1742, the adjoining Peto lot, one acre. See App. F. In 1733 he bought 31 acres from Nich. Kortright, 6 of which were off the north side of lot No. 17, 3d Division, and 25 acres lay on the west side of the Harlem and Kingsbridge Road, and included the *Ronde Gebergte*, or Mount Morris (see p. 136), being lot No. 5, 1st Division; both lots having descended to Kortright from his gd.-mo., Metje Cornelis, for whom they were originally laid out. The last, as enlarged by a strip of land taken off the highway in 1744 (when the latter was narrowed to a width of three rods) and sold to Joh. Benson by the town, May 11, 1747, for £10, came to form part of a title, hitherto but imperfectly understood. Joh. Benson was serving as deacon at H. Aug. 30, 1753, but was probably dead Nov. 27, 1756, when his lands in 3d Div. were in possession of and sold by his br. Adolph. On Feb. 21, 1773, his wid. Tanneke made her will, which was proved May 25, 1778, in Dutchess Co., whither she had gone with her nephews, the Waldrons of Hoorn's Hook, and other kinsfolk, at the opening of the Revolution. Joh. Benson's 4 acres on Van Keulen's Hook were bought by his br. Benjamin (in possession in 1766), and his other lands by his br. Adolph.

Adolph Benson, son of Sampson, and b. 1703, was made constable in 1732, soon after his m. with Eve, dr. of Lawrence Kortright. He bought his first land in 1737, from his br.-in-law John Delamater, being 30 acres to the south of lot No. 1 (of 1691), said tract having been purchased from the town in 1712 by Benson's fa.-in-law, Kortright, who sold it in 1715 to Matthew Benson, and he in 1719 to said Delamater. It was the nucleus of the large farm of 90 acres, lying central of Harlem plains, and known in our day as the Samson A. Benson or Race Course Tract; its title indisputable, but its origin hitherto an enigma to the professional conveyancer. The farm contained two other parcels. One of these embraced the land lying between the 30 acres aforesaid and the old Kingsbridge Road, (contents not given), for which Adolph agreed with the town, in 1747, for £30; this sale being confirmed May 30, 1753, by an award of arbitrators, touching the disposal of this and other parcels of the common land, pursuant to which the price, with six years' interest, was paid, and the title secured. The other was the adjoining 25-acre tract of his br. Johannes (No. 5, 1st Div.), as enlarged on the north-east and east by the strip from off the road, purchased by Johannes from the town as aforesaid; of which lot Adolph also became the owner.

Adolph also acquired the 6 acres of lot 17, 3d Div., which his br. Joh. bought of Nich. Kortright, and lot 18, 3d Div., 5 a. 3 q. 2 r., originally of his gd-fa. Capt. Joh. Benson, both which, making 11 a. 3 q. 2 r., he sold on Nov. 27, 1756, to Jacob Rapelje. This formed part of the late Dyckman Fort George tract. Adolph Benson m. in 1768 a second w., Martha Van Dyck. He d. in his 99th yr., Apl. 30, 1802, in his old homestead, which stood till 1854 on the line of 122d Street, one hundred feet or more east of 7th Avenue, and on his first purchase.

Adolph Benson had two sons, Samson and Lawrence. The latter m. in 1765 his cousin Mary, dr. of Benj. Benson, with whom he obtained the 4-acre plot on Van Keulen's Hook, late of his uncle Johannes, and the house, still standing, venerable and sole relic of *old* Harlem village, and now occupied by Mr. Cowperthwait. His fa. conveyed to him, March 10, 1781, the so-called 80-acre tract set off to him from the Point farm, by deed of Jan. 29, 1743. As Adolph, in 1746, had become the owner of the 10 acres as estimated, west of the highway (lot 23 of 1691), originally granted to Abraham Delamontanie, possibly this tract also passed to Lawrence under that deed, and with which it may have grown to 80 acres. Lawrence also bought, April 26, 1785, from the heirs of John Bogert, the 42 acres, since known as the Lawrence Benson Homestead (see App. E.), on which he thereafter lived till his d. in 1822. His chn. were Adolph, who d. unm.; Benjamin L.; and Susannah L., who m. Rev. Philip Milledoler, D.D. Benj. L. Benson, who died in 1852, was fa. of the present Benjamin L. and Lawrence A. Benson; the latter, empowered by the Court of Common Pleas, May 19, 1875, having taken the name of George Gardener Grennell.

Samson Benson, also called Samuel, eldest son of Adolph, succeeded to his fa.'s lands under his will, dated Aug. 2, 1793. He m. in 1769 Rebecca, dr. of John Dykman. In 1776 Capt. Benson, with his Harlem company, rendered important service in standing guard and carrying out the orders of the Convention while it met at H., and till forced to retire before the enemy. His fa. and br. Lawrence remained at H. Samson d. on the Race Course farm at an extreme age, Nov. 22, 1823. Under his will, made Apl. 28, 1823, the said farm passed to a gd-son, Samson Adolphus Benson, while to his other heirs he gave that other tract of 45 a. 3 q. 22 r., which Samson bought, May 6, 1787, from the estate of Aaron Bussing, and further described in App. J., in notice of 1st Division. Mount Morris Park, 20$\frac{44}{100}$ acres, was taken from the Race Course farm, by the city, Sept. 4, 1839. Capt. Benson's chn. were John; Susan S., who d. unm. 1825; Eve, who m. Benj. Vredenburgh, and Jane, who m. Aaron Bussing. John Benson m. Apl. 27, 1820, Maria B., dr. of Dr. Milledoler, and was named as an executor by his gd-fa. Adolph. He d. shortly before his fa., leaving but one ch., said Samson Adolphus Benson, b. 1821, who m. in 1848 Miss Louisa Aman, of Fishkill, where Mr. B. d., Aug. 6, 1851, having two chn., viz., Maria-Louisa and Edward A. Benson.

Benjamin Benson, youngest son of Samson who d. in 1740, has been mentioned as next owner of the homestead or Point farm, and mill, and as having purchased the Mill Camp and adjacent lots, together forming the large Benson farm north of the Creek. In 1748 he received 35 acres (with 2 *erven*, we believe those originally Slot's) from the estate of his gd-fa. Meyer. See App. F. For another purchase see App. G. On May 1, 1770, he gave his son, Samson, a deed for 20 acres, off the south side of the homestead, bounded by the river, the land of William Waldron, and the commons, but twenty years later, viz., on May 2, 1791, conveyed him the entire farm; having on Apl. 2 preceding given his other son, Peter, a deed for the farm north of the Mill Creek, including the mill-pond and stream, and the mill which Benj. had recently built. He now bought the homestead farm of John Bogert, Jr., dec., by deed of May 9, 10, 1791, and removed thither, but d. the following year. Mainly by his instrumentality in securing funds was the new church erected at H., in 1788. By his w. Susannah, dr. of Peter Bussing, who survived him, he had said sons Samson and Peter, and drs., Mary, who m. Lawrence Benson; Rebecca, m. 1765 Matthias Vredenburgh (whose son Benj. m. Eve Benson); Susannah, who m. Benj. Lightbourn (their dr. Maria m. Edward Elting, of N. Y.); and Elizabeth, who d. unm. 1795.

Peter Benson m. Hannah, dr. of John Horn, of the Bloomingdale Road, and who, after his d. in 1802, m. Rev. John F. Jackson, then pastor of the church at H.* Peter left two chn.,

* Rev. John Frelinghuysen Jackson was a son of the Rev. William Jackson, whose fa., Patrick Jackson, was a son of William Jackson, from Edinburgh, Scotland, a zealous Presbyterian, who came out to East Jersey, in 1683, with George Scot, Laird of Pitlochie, and settled in N. Y., where he m. 1694, Anna, dr. of Dr. Hartman Wessels. Rev. John F. Jackson and the widow Benson were m. Feb. 2, 1804. He built and occupied till his d., which occurred March 26, 1836, in his 68th year, the stately frame house on 124th street, between 2d and 3d avenues, now the residence of his son Dr. William H. Jackson.

viz., Benjamin P., and Wilhelmina, who m. Dr. Peter Van Arsdale, of N. Y., whom she still survives. Benj. P. Benson, m. Apl. 7, 1821, Mary-Ann, dr. of Jonathan Ferris, of Peekskill. The distinguished artist, Eugene Benson, now of Rome, Italy, is his son.

Samson Benson, "Jr.," oldest son of Benj. and Susannah, was b. Sept. 13, 1736, and m. in 1764 Mary, dr. of John Sickels. He succeeded to the ancestral farm, as before stated, on which he lived till his d., Jan. 31, 1821. From a weakness of the eyes he was familiarly called "Crying Sam." His wid. d. æ. 90 years, Nov. 14, 1835, when the farm fell to their dr., Mrs. Margaret McGown, the only ch. then living. Samson had but two chn. who survived inf., viz., said Margaret, who was b. Mar. 10, 1766, d. May 25, 1851, and m. Nov. 21, 1784, Andrew McGown, son of Capt. Daniel McGown, already named in this article; and Benjamin, b. June 21, 1770, d. April 15, 1815, who m. Eliza, dr. of Xavier Gautro, but left no issue. Said *Capt.* McGown, a shipmaster of N. Y., m. Mrs. Sheard in 1740, after her widowhood of ten years. He owned a residence in the village, on the north side of the Church Lane, and adjoining westerly on Petrus Waldron, which had once belonged to Do. Zyperus. See note p. 461. It was a one-morgen lot, like others in this range, but having been divided and each part built upon, was called two lots. McGown sold the whole, June 1, 1758, to John Livingston, and it has since made a part of the Brady plot. See note p. 191.* Capt. McGown was lost at sea some years before the Revolution, and his wid. soon after bought from Jacob Dyckman, Jr., a few acres on the hill back of the old Benson farm, at what became known as McGown's Pass, where she and her son Andrew kept a public house (in part the identical building in Central Park since known as Stetson's Hotel), her house being a favorite resort, before and during the war, of gentlemen coming from the city with their hounds to indulge in the sport of fox-hunting. Mr. Andrew McGown, who d. Oct. 16, 1820, æ. 78 years, was the fa. of the late Major Andrew McGown, b. 1786, d. Mar. 2, 1870, and of Ald. Samson B. McGown, b. 1797, who still occupies the ancestral seat of the Bensons. A few years since he removed the venerable stone farm-house, erected by his gt-gd-fa., Benj. Ben-

* John Livingston, b. 1714, d. 1788, and whose country seat was at H. from 1758 to 1780, was an eminent merchant of N. Y., the uncle of Col. Peter R. Livingston, named in note on p. 485, and son of Philip Livingston, second proprietor of the Livingston Manor. John Livingston was an asst. ald. from 1750 to 1755. He took a principal part in the proceedings for settling the division line of the N. Y. and Harlem Commons, in the years 1772 to 1775. His w. was Catharine De Peyster. See *Holgate's Am. Gen.*

son, on the south shore of the Mill Pond, and built upon its site his present residence, 106th Street, south side, between 3d and 4th Avenues.

BOGERT.

JAN LOUWE BOGERT, otherwise, from the place of his nativity, called Jan Louwe from *Schoonderwoerd*, claims a place among the patentees, for reasons given in the annexed note.* Many references to him will be found in the preceding pages. Having spent nine years at Bedford, Long Island, he came to H., in 1672, as proprietor of the Montanye farm, the history of which, up to its purchase by Bogert, has also been given. He was chosen a magistrate in 1675, was re-elected in 1676, and on Nov. 30th of this year, with his wife, Cornelia Everts, was received at N. Y. as a mem. of the H. chh. In 1677 Bogert drew lot No. 6, on Hoorn's Hook, but sold it Dec. 9, 1679, to Joost van Oblinus. He drew, in 1691, lot No. 25, adjoining his farm on the south side; and which in the deed from the town, Mar. 21, 1701, is thus described:

"There is set off for Jan Louwe Bogert, for the *right* of sixteen *morgen* of land and an *erf right*; a piece of land lying in the bend of Hellgate, beginning from the southwest corner of the Hop Garden, by a birch tree, till to a white oak tree which stands by a small swamp (*crempelbosje*,) marked I L B and I D L, thence towards the River, past a rock marked I L B and I D L, and so on to the beach, till to the end of a meadow, north of a rocky hill; as it is at present fenced in." The initials (I for J), are those of Jan Louwe Bogert and Jan De Lamater.

Bogert having spent 35 years at H., sold his farm to Capt. Joh. Benson, Sept. 21, 1706, for £650, and the next spring removed to N. Y.; with his w. uniting with the chh. there by certificate from H., on May 27, 1707. His chn. were Peter,

* PETER PARMENTIER was one of the Mannheim refugees who came out in company with Jan Louwe Bogert, in 1663, as heretofore noticed. He and his w., Antoinette Terrin, bringing letters from Mannheim, were received to the Brooklyn chh., Sept. 23, of that year. Parmentier and Bogert lived neighbors at Bedford for some years, and the former was one of four named as trustees for the inhabitants at large, to whom the Indians, in 1670, sold lands in that vicinity. Parmentier became the owner of a farm and grist mill in Bushwick, where in 1675, one other excepted, he paid the largest tax on land and stock. Selling his farm to his only son Michiel, he kept the mill and eight morgen of land, but these he also conveyed to Michiel some time after, and probably when he sold, (May 31, 1684,) certain lots in Brooklyn to Jacques Lasillere. He soon came to H., and assuredly took Bogert's place in Dongan's patent; for which there seems no accounting, except on the ground of a contract to buy Bogert's farm, whose mill-

Gysbert, Nicholas, Johannes, Elizabeth, m. Harman Knickerbacker, of Dutchess Co.; Catharine, m. Elbert Harmense, of N. Y.; Margaret, m. Peter J. Haring, of Tappan; Cornelis, m. Wouter Quackenbos, of Albany; and Jenneke, who m. George Holmes. Johannes, b. 1670, m. Claesie, dr. of H. C. van Schaick, but d. in 1711, without ch.; his wid. m. Joh. De Graaf.

Gybaert Bogert, b. 1663, at Bedford, m. Annetie, dr. of Laurens Jansen, of H., and near the time that his parents left the town, removed to Tappan, or Orangetown, where he bought land from Hendrick Lamberts, Oct. 6, 1707, served the same month as a grand juror, and was living in 1729 on his farm on the Sparkill. He had chn., *John*, b. 1705; *Mary*, 1707; *Lawrence*, 1710; *Cornelius*, 1715; *Nicholas*, 1718.

Peter Bogert was b. in 1656, in Leerdum, Holland; we presume the county, as it included Schoonrewoerd. He is also called in Harlem records, *Peter Jan Louwe*. He m. 1686 Feytie, dr. of Matthys Vlierboom, of Albany. Peter Bogert served as a soldier under Leisler, in holding the fort at N. Y., in 1689 and '90, and in 1717 was paid for arms given up in 1691 to the government. His chn. were *Cornelia*, b. 1687, m. Gysbert Crom; *Maria*, b. 1689, m. Daniel Gautier; *Elizabeth*, b. 1694; *Catalina*, b. 1697; *Johannes*, b. 1700; *Matthew*, b. 1702; *Peter*, b. 1705; *Willemtie*, b. 1708. Matthew and Willemtie were bapt. at Hackensack.

Nicholas Bogert, b. 1668, at Bedford, m. 1695 Bellitie, dr. of Hendrick C. van Schaick, aforesaid, and in 1703 Margaret, dr. of John Conselyea and wid. of Joh. van Tilburg. He lived in N. Y., was a "baker and bolter," and d. Jun. 5. 1727, leaving issue, *John*, b. 1697; *Cornelius*, b. 1700; *Hendrick*, b. 1705; *Cornelia*, b. 1710, m. Albertus Tiebout; *Margaret*, b. 1713, m. Joh. Quackenbush; *Elizabeth*, b. 1714, m. Elbert Haring; *Annetie*, b. 1718 and *Petrus*, b. 1720. Five other

ing facilities probably attracted him. Nevertheless no sale took place; Bogert kept the farm, and Parmentier is not again named among the freeholders. He d. at Kingston, Ulster co., in 1701, evidently in reduced circumstances, as the church officers attended to his burial and the wants of his widow.

Michiel Parmentier sold his mill property in Bushwick, Jan. 26, 1696, (owned soon after by John Mesurolle, Jr., and Charles Fountain,) and on May 6, 1699, bought from Sanders and Harmanse, land at "Wareskeech," in Dutchess county, to which he removed. He was living there in 1714, at the age of 60. He m. Neeltie, dr. of John Damen, of Brooklyn, by whom he had issue, *Peter*, b. 1680, m. Sarah Van Kleek, 1702, and Helena Vanden Bogert, 1714; *John*, b. 1682; *Antoinette*, b. 1684, m. Barent Van Kleek; *Michael*, b. 1687, m. Maria Tissoort, 1717; *Neeltie*, b. 1690, m. Myndert Bogert; *Damen*, b. 1694; *Elizabeth*, b. 1699, and *Johanna*, b. 1702. *Damen* and younger members of the family were still occupying the paternal lands in "Poughkeepsie Precinct," in 1770, under the name *Palmatier*.

chn. d. young. *Hendrick Bogert* was a baker, m. 1724 Cornelia, dr. of Gerrit DeGraw, by whom he had chn. viz., Bellitie, b. 1725, who m. John Devoor; Gerrit, b. 1729; Henricus, b. 1735, and Cornelius, b. 1738. *Cornelius Bogert*, b. 1700, m. 1720 Cornelia, dr. of Cornelius Verduyn, lived in N. Y., was a baker, accumulated a good property, and d. Apl. 19, 1793, æ. 93 yrs. His chn. were Cornelius, b. 1721, d. young; Cornelius, b. 1725; Nicholas, b. 1727; Sarah, b. 1728; Rachel, b. 1731; Henry, b. 1732; Nicholas, b. 1734. The last two, known as Henry C. and Nicholas C. Bogert, were eminent merchants in N. Y.; the latter fa. of Cornelius N. Bogert, and Rev. David S. Bogert. For interesting details of this branch, see *Thompson's Long Island*, and *Stevens' Chamber of Commerce.*

John Bogert, b. 1697, eldest son of Nicholas, son of Jan Louwe Bogert, was by trade a mason, m. Mar. 10, 1716, Hannah, b. 1695, dr. of Jan Peeck, by his w. Elizabeth, dr. of Dr. Gysbert and Rachel (Montanye) van Imbroch. He and his brs. Cornelius and Hendrick owned land at Fishkill; they sold three fourths of it to Jacob Haff, Dec. 17, 1736, for £2,000. John d. in N. Y., in 1775, having had chn. John, b. 1718; Isabella, b. 1719, m. Francis Wessels; Elizabeth, b. 1720, m. John Leary; Margaret, b. 1722, m. Jacobus van Antwerp; Nicholas, b. 1725; Anna, b. 1728, m. Jacobus Roosevelt; Rachel, b. 1731; and Jacobus, b. 1734. Of these, Nicholas, b. in N. Y., Apl. 2, 1725, d. in Beekman, Dutchess Co., N. Y., Jan. 28, 1814. He m., Apl. 27, 1747, Maria Quick, and Feb. 2, 1762, Alida, dr. of Rev. Johannes Ritzema; having by the two wives twenty-one chn., one of whom was the late Cornelius, of N. Y., lawyer, b. Aug. 14, 1775, and fa. of Horatio G. Bogert. See other details in *N. Y. Gen. & Biog. Rec.*, 1878, 191.

John Bogert, Junior, b. 1718, m. March 16, 1737, Abigail, dr. of Jacobus Quick. A distinguished and prosperous N. Y. merchant, he served as an alderman from 1756 to 1766, and during the same period was a deacon and elder for several terms. On Mar. 12, 1766, he bought John Benson's farm at H., lying on Van Keulen's Hook, adjoining Harlem River, and thither he removed, devoting his remaining years to husbandry. He afterward bought the property known as the Lawrence Benson Homestead. In 1776, when the Revolution opened, the Provincial Convention, on leaving N. Y., met for a month in the church at Harlem, and Mr. Bogert being a good Whig, the records were kept at his house, which stood on the same site as the present Morris Randell house, at the foot of 125th Street, Harlem River. John Bogert, Jr., d. in 1782, having only the year previous m. a second w., Elizabeth, dr. of Philip Daly and wid. of Abm. Brasher. His chn. were, Jacobus, John J.,

Nicholas, Cornelius J., Peter, Henry, Anna, m. 1758 Peter Byvanck, and Mary, who m. 1760 Capt. Willett Taylor. Of these, Henry, a lieut. in Col. Lamb's artillery, d. during the Revolution. Peter was the fa. of Cornelius, James, and Henry K. Bogert, and their sisters. Cornelius J., lawyer (see *Thompson's L. I.*, 2 : 127), was fa. to the late John G. Bogert, Russian Consul at N. Y. (fa. of Dr. Cornelius R. Bogert, Mrs. Gerardus Clark, and Mrs. Henry Kneeland), and of his sister Abigail, who m. Robert I. Thurston. Jacobus Bogert, b. 1738, son of John Bogert, Jr., m. 1756 Elizabeth Peacock, of a French Huguenot family. He d. in 1811, having had two sons, viz., John and James, Jr., as also six drs. Said James Bogert, Jr., b. in 1767, was m. thrice; in 1795 to Miss Elizabeth Benezet,* who was the mo. of all his chn. Mr. Bogert eventually came to H., and after two or three years' residence bought (by two purchases in 1811 and 1812) the farm on Van Keulen's Hook before owned by his gd-fa., John Bogert, Jr. In 1816 he joined the Reformed Dutch ch. at H., to whose interests his hands and purse were devoted. After living here some years, his house being burned, he sold his farm, in 1825, to Morris Randell. Highly respected during a useful life protracted to his 91st yr., Mr. Bogert d. in N. Y., Mar. 31, 1858. He had four sons and four drs.; two sons and a dr. surviving him : the latter, an estimable lady, now deceased, was the wife of Dr. Edward L. Beadle, of Poughkeepsie, but formerly of N. Y., to whom I am indebted for some of these details.

BREVOORT.

JOHN HENDRICKS BREVOORT, of humble origin, but attaining to wealth and honorable station, presents one of many instances among our early colonists of similar rewards meted out to honesty and industry. When Harlem village was first settled, Brevoort was a boy of fourteen years, and living at Bushwick, with Hendrick Jansen van Brevoort, his father, we assume, who had leased a farm from Reyer Moll, owned later by Jean Mesurolle, and from an eminence called the *Kyckuyt*, or Lookout, known as the Kyckuyt Farm. Hence its occupant, living there from 1650 to 1665, came to be distinguished as *Hendrick Jansen Kyckuyt*. Though Brevoort in *Guelderland* has hitherto had

* This lady was of the Benezet family of Philadelphia, whose anc., Jean Benezet, d. at Abbeville, France, Aug. 13, 1710. A ms. account of the family, yet preserved, opens with this entry made by Jean Benezet.

"Le 16ee Aoust, 1682, Je mesiers marie avec Marie Madelaine Testart, fille de M. Pierre Testart et de defunte Rachel Cromellin, de la ville de St. Quentin, en Vermandois." See also *Bartow Genealogy*, p. 53.

the credit of giving name to our Brevoort family, the ancestor really came from "Brevoort in the diocese of Utrecht." It was a hamlet to the north-west of Amersfoort, and but little over a mile from its walls, and here Hendrick Jansen was born —in 1630, taking his own statement as to his age, made at various times. Before leaving the Kycknyt farm he got land at Dutch Kills, in Newtown, "which was laid out for him by Jacques Cortelyou, the surveyor, by order of Gov. Stuyvesant." This became his home, and was confirmed to him by Gov. Lovelace, May 20, 1672, the main tract lying between lands then of *Jan Hendricks* and *Frans Hendricks*.

About this time John Hendricks Brevoort, or Jan Hendricks Kycknyt, as he was then called, removed to N. Y., where his wife's parents were living, for he was now *m.* Hendrick Jansen Kyckuyt followed him, and bought property in the city Feb. 24, 1680, having, in or after 1675, sold his farm in Newtown to one Laurens Cornelisz, who soon conveyed it to a neighboring owner, Joris Stevens van Alst, whose dr. was w. of Hendricks' son, Frans Hendricks.* Hendrick's dr. Marritie had m. in 1673 Hendrick Bastiaens, of N. Y., br. to Annetie Bastiaens, Jan Hendricks' wife. Metje Bastiaens, wife of Cornelis Jansen, of H., being a sr. of Annetie, this may account for Jan Hendricks' going to Harlem, as he soon did. The three Bastiaenses

* Doubts have arisen as to the relationship between Hendrick Jansen and Jan Hendricks Brevoort, because of a too close approximation in their ages (only fourteen years intervening, as shown by their own statements), and an apparent difference of birthplace; for Hendrick and his chn. Frans and Marritie were born at Brevoort, while Jan Hendricks' marriage registration names him as "from Amersfoort." As against the last discrepancy, we should say it would be quite as natural for Jan, in stating where he came from, to name a well-known city, near which he was born, as the obscure village (Brevoort) in its suburbs; and we judge this the explanation, for while in the one instance only is Jan called "van Amersfoort," he is many times called "van Brevoort." The difficulty arising from his being so nearly of an age with Hendrick is relieved by the record of many similar and well-attested cases. We premise, for reasons deemed sufficient, that neither Hendrick nor Jan had fallen into an error regarding his age, however common this is, as we know, especially with the uneducated. But it may be urged further in favor of the blood paternity in Hendrick, that the almost imperative custom of that day would require the eldest son of *Hendrick Jansen* to be called *Jan Hendricksen*; while the birthplace of the father and younger children being the same (indicating a fixed residence), we should look for his to correspond therewith. But if (as has been suggested, by way of solving this problem) our Jan were only an *adopted* son of Hendrick, we should not expect to find, as we do in his case, the three requirements—birthplace, name, and priority as eldest son—to be all exactly met.

These difficulties obviated, all doubt as to the paternity of Jan Hendricks Brevoort, must be dispelled by the direct testimony of the Newtown court records of [illegible], where on two separate occasions Hendrick and Jan are named as *father* and *son*.

were chn. of Bastiaen Elyessen (as he wrote his name), from Werckhoven, a wheelwright, and who by several purchases, the last in 1684, became the owner of 40 acres of land west of the Bowery Road (4th Avenue), extending from 10th Street northward, and forming subsequently the lower half of the well-known Brevoort estate.

John Hendricks Kyckuyt, living in N. Y., in 1673, on its recapture by the Dutch, was among the patriotic carmen who volunteered to work gratuitously on the defenses one day in a week. The city being restored to the English, he was sworn anew as a carman, Nov. 13, 1674. He removed to H. the next year. On Mar. 13, 1676, he took Pierre Cresson's farming lot on Jochem Pieters, No. 5, on a four years' lease; but bought Cresson out Mar. 23, 1677, house and house lot, said lot on Jochem Pieters, and No. 20 Van Keulen's Hook, with meadows at Sherman's Creek. He drew the same year, No. 1 of the New Lots. He now began to use the surname Brevoort, and is sometimes called by the clerk, "Jan Hendricks van Brevoort, *alias* Kyckuyt." Natural abilities making up in a good degree his lack of education, Brevoort arose to be an overseer of the town in 1678, and was reappointed the next year. He bore an active part in the building of the new church in 1686. In 1691 Brevoort drew lot No. 6, on Jochem Pieters Hills, 14 morgen, to which, on May 27, 1698, he added No. 7, being 10 morgen; by purchase from Jacques Tourneur. He was living on this property Feb. 21, 1701, when he sold it to Johannes Myer. The same year, Nov. 15, he bought the farm of his fa.-in-law, Bastiaen Elyessen, before noticed, and to which he removed; he and w. Anna selling their remaining lands and interests at H. to their son-in-law, Zacharias Sickels, Feb. 20, 1705. Brevoort's acres were subsequently doubled by the purchase of another tract of 45 acres which lay adjoining, and ran up to 18th Street.

Mr. Brevoort was elected assistant alderman of the Out Ward in 1702, and filled the same office from 1707 to 1713. He d. in 1714, leaving four chn. viz., Hendrick, b. 1670; Marritie, b. 1673, m. Zacharias Sickels; Elias, b. 1676; and Jannetie, b. 1679, w. of Thomas Sickels, br. of Zacharias. To these the fa. gave an equal share of his farm. It was appraised at £400, and offered for sale, but having no purchaser, was bought (we believe the entire tract) by Hendrick Brevoort, from whom it passed to his heirs. Elias Brevoort followed his trade as a carpenter, in the city of which he was admitted a freeman in 1698. He m. in 1701 Margaret, dr. of John Sammons, by whom he had eight chn., the last two being sons, viz., *John*, b. 1715, and *Elias*, b. 1718. He acted as an executor of his fa.'s estate, with his br. Hendrick, whom he survived. *John Brevoort*, b. Sept.

14, 1715, was a goldsmith in N. Y., and m. July 30, 1739, Louisa-Abigail, dr. of Rev. Joshua Kockerthal. His only ch. that survived inf., Charlotte, b. May 22, 1740, m. Hon. Whitehead Hicks, Mayor of N. Y. from 1766 to 1773. See *Thompson's Long Island*, 2 : 510.

Hendrick Brevoort, after that excellent Dutch usage which gave each son a trade, was bred a weaver, but followed farming. He m. in 1699 Maria, dr. of Johanes Couwenhoven, dec., "late Secretary between Harlem and Bowery;" and in 1705, Jacomina, dr. of Abm. Bokee. Hendrick d. in 1718, leaving chn., viz., by his first w.: *John*, b. 1700; and by his second, *Abraham*, b. 1707; *Hendrick*, b. 1711; *Elias*, b. 1715; and *Jacob*, b. 1717. His wid. m., in 1721, Jacob Harsen, the Harsen anc. Of the sons, *John* m. Oct. 8, 1726, Anna, dr. of Eide van Huyse, of Bloomingdale; had by her a dr., Mary. His w. d. May 20, 1730. By a second w. he had Henry, b. Feb. 12, 1735, d. Oct. 2, 1782, fa. by Maria Anthony, of Abraham, b. June 24, 1763, d. Nov. 12, 1794, fa. by Ann Devoor (see p. 461), of Henry, b. Feb. 16, 1791, d. Apl. 4, 1874, fa. by Jane Stewart, of Mary S., Ann and Jane, m. respectively to Stevenson Towle, John H. Riker, and Ulysses D. Eddy, Esqrs.

Hendrick Brevoort, b. 1711, m. Sept. 20, 1739, Catharine, dr. of Abraham Delamater, and had eight chn., to wit, Henry, Abraham, Elias, John, Isaac, Anna, Catharine, and Jemima. Henry, the first of these, b. Oct. 29, 1747, m. May 25, 1779, Sarah, dr. of Capt. Wm. Whetten, and d. Aug. 21, 1841, being fa. of Henry, b. Sept. 25, 1782, fa. of Mr. J. Carson Brevoort. For other details of this respectable family see the *Todd Genealogy*, and the *N. Y. G. & B. Record*, for 1870.

BUSSING.

Arent Harmans Bussing, one of the most worthy of the H. settlers, appears in the earlier records only as Arent Hermens (Harmens or Harmans, for he thus varied the spelling), and is so called in the Dongan patent; but he finally dropped the patronymic, and took his proper surname. To the former frequent mention of him little need now be added. By his m. in 1673 with Susannah Delamater he obtained two of the west gardens, Nos. 19, 20, on which he built a house and barn, and lived the rest of his life; being the place afterward of his gt.-gd-dr., Mrs. Catharine Storm. When about to m. again, Bussing bound himself, Mar. 8, 1678, to pay his two chn. by said w. Susannah, when they should be of lawful age, the sum of 900 gl., being the portion gotten with their mo.; and he then to own the said two gardens, valued at 400 gl. He had recently added to these the three Demarest gardens on the east side, but those were sold by his heirs, at a later period, to Petrus Waldron. He drew No. 5 of the New Lots, but sold it to Barent Waldron. Serving often in the magistracy, and bearing office in the chh., Arent Bussing was not inattentive to his worldly estate, which he enhanced with a lot on Van Keulen's Hook and three lots lying together on Jochem Pieters Flat, the latter the same tract sold by John Adriance to Charles Henry Hall, June 27, 1825. He drew lot 8 in the Division of 1691, being 12½ morgen, to which 4 acres were added in 1720, making it 28 acres, as sold by the Bussing heirs to John Myer, Nov. 6, 1790. For his lands drawn in 1712, see App. J. At his d. in 1718 he owned 127 acres, then valued, as per sale to his son Peter, at £511.

Arent Bussing had by his first w. three chn., viz., Peter, b. 1674; Harman, b. 1675; Harman 2d, b. 1677. Only some strong incentive could have led him to ignore custom and call his first born Peter instead of Harman. By his second w., Eva Lubberts, he had Dirck, b. 1679, d. early; Margaret, b. 1681, who m. Lawrence Kortright; Susannah b. 1684, in 1718 was yet unm.; Engeltie, b. 1686, m. Abraham Myer; Elizabeth, b. 1692, m. Matthew Benson; Geesie, b. 1694, m. Teunis Delamontagne; John, b. ab. 1697, and Mary, b. ab. 1700, who m. Joh. M. Van Harlingen, clerk at H. See note p. 458.

John Bussing, who m. Sept. 2, 1723, Metje, dr. of Joh. Kortright, was a weaver, and perhaps left the town; certainly did not hold any real estate here. His dr. *Eva* m. Oct. 30, 1756, Alexander Forbes, shopkeeper, afterward of the Out Ward, farmer, to whom administration on the estate of wid. Metje Bussing was granted Jan. 27, 1774.

Harman Bussing, b. 1677, became a carman in N. Y., m. Jan. 27, 1707, Sarah, dr. of Isaac Selover, and had the following chn.: *Susannah*, b. 1708, m. Joh. Montanye; *Isaac*, b. 1710; *Anna*, b. 1712; *Eve*, b. 1715; *Arent*, b. 1718; *Jacobus*, b. 1721; *Abraham*, b. 1724. Isaac, also a carman, m. 1738 Elizabeth Tilly, lived in Lombard Street, now Trinity Pl., was dec. in 1765, and had chn., the eldest being Timothy, of Albany. Arent, carpenter, m. 1749 Sarah Roome, and had issue William, Harman, Peter, Sarah, Mary, and Anna.

Peter Bussing, b. 1674, m. June 7, 1700, Rebecca, dr. of Capt. Joh. Vermilye, and went to Westchester Co., but on the d. of his fa. he returned to H., buying out the interests of the other heirs in the paternal lands, Dec. 30, 1718, for (less his own share) the sum of £454 : 4 : 6. He also purchased, Mar. 14, 1733, from Joanni Benson, the 60 acres bought by the latter from his br. Samson, and which included No. 12, 1st Div., and 6 acres in No. 8, 2d Div.; besides Nos. 1 and 2, 1st Div., being the tract north of the road and the Benson or Mill farm (and opposite the old Bussing house), containing 41 a. 1 q. 23 r., which the executors of his son Aaron sold to Samson Benson, May 6, 1787. In 1726 Peter Bussing had gotten all Jacques Tourneur's lands, viz., his lots drawn in the 4 Divisions, and those on Van Keulen's Hook which adjoined southerly to the said Bussing house lot (when the road between them was closed up), and westerly to the Mill farm aforesaid, and, with said house lot, since composing the Catharine Storm farm. Peter's fa. had purchased from Samuel Waldron, Jan. 3, 1711, the two north gardens next to the Church Farm, previously owned by his fa.-in-law Glaude Delamater, from whose surviving chn. and heirs Peter Bussing obtained a quit-claim deed June 1, 1726. This plot being built upon was held by his desc. till sold by John S. Adriance to Christopher Heiser, June 7, 1820. In 1733 Bussing sold Nos. 11, 12, 13, 1st Div., and his 6 acres in No. 8, 2d Div., to Adolph Myer, whence they descended to Wm. Molenaor. Peter Bussing d. in 1737, leaving his house and lands in H. to his son Aaron, and to his sons Peter and Abraham each a farm at Fordham. His chn. in all were *Aaron*, b. Dec. 27, 1703; *John*, b. Jan. 20, 1705; *Peter*, b. Jan. 1, 1707; *Arltie*, b. Jan. 20, 1710, m. Jacob Myer; *Abraham*, b. May 31, 1714; and *Susannah*, b. May 19, 1716, who m. Benjamin Benson. *Peter Bussing*, last named, m. Helena, dr. of Samson Benson, was an elder at Fordham, and left his lands to his dr. Mary Bussing and his son Peter. The last d. in 1790, leaving sons Peter and John Bussing and several drs.; of these, Margaret was w. of Isaac Valentine, and Mary w. of Walter Briggs.

John Bussing, b. Jan. 20, 1705, m. June 15, 1725, Mary, dr. of Evert Bruyn, of Westchester Co. On Aug. 26, 1729, he contracted to complete the chh. at Fordham for £4. He d. before his fa., leaving sons Evert, Peter, and John, of whom Evert was living in Westchester in 1757. Peter last named, who, I believe, m. a dr. of Abraham Myer, bought of Abraham Myer, Jr., Apl. 16, 1753, the two southerly lots (called 40 acres), of the old Tourneur farm on Harlem Lane, to which about a year later he added the upper lot by purchase from the widow Grietie Kortright. The three lots taking in the land outside the patent line in the rear, up to the hills, made about 74 acres, of which, in 1784, after the d. of their fa., the three sons of Peter, namely, Adolph, Abraham, and John Bussing, conveyed that part of the upper lot which lay west of Harlem Lane, and containing 14 acres, to the brs. Henry and Abraham Van Bramer. The remainder of the farm was equally divided by the three Bussing brs. by deeds of Apl. 7, 1787. See App. G. These occupied their respective portions, and here Adolph closed his life, on Feb. 3, 1820, and John on May 1, 1830. The latter, though m. twice, left no issue. Adolph Bussing, by his w. Anna, left an only ch., Susannah, w. of Obadiah Sands, and mo. of John B. Sands. Abraham Bussing m. Nov. 3, 1782, Elizabeth Brett, and secondly Sarah Brown. He sold his farm west of Harlem Lane (since of David Wood) to John N. Grenzebach, Jan. 17, 1794, and removed to Bedford, Westchester Co. Abraham had four chn., to wit, John, Peter, Anna, who m. George Warner, and Susan, who m. Benj. Banks and was mo. of Wm. W. and Alvah C. Banks. Peter Bussing (Rev.), left issue Wm. J. Bussing, Julia A., w. of Horatio W. Thompson, and Elizabeth, w. of George Peck.

Aaron Bussing m. Oct. 21, 1730, Maria, dr. of Johannes Myer, the next year was named as constable in the Montgomery Charter, and succeeded upon the d. of his fa. to all his lands at H., rated at 201 acres, and which he held nearly intact till his d. He parted with the Tourneur lots, No. 14, 2d Div., and No. 2, 3d Div. He d. in 1784, æ. 81 yrs., having had issue Catharine, b. Aug. 31, 1731, m. Abraham Storm; Rebecca, b. Jan. 8, 1734, m. John Waldron; Abraham, b. Dec. 31, 1736; Maria, b. Nov. 20, 1738, d. Sept. 17, 1744; Maria, b. Jan. 8, 1745, m. John S. Sickels; and Aaron, b. Mar. 18, 1747, who d. July 6, 1750. Pursuant to the will of Aaron Bussing, made May 1, 1782, and proved May 27, 1784, his lands were sold by his executors to various parties, the homestead being purchased by his dr., Mrs. Storm. His son, Abraham, m. Dec. 27, 1764, Margaret, dr. of Aaron Myer, and d. (we believe just before his fa.) leaving a son, Aaron, and a dr., Susannah, who m. successively John Myer and Peter Montfort. By devise of his gd-fa. Myer, Aaron became joint owner, with his sr. Susannah, of the old Barent Waldron or Bussing Point farm; and afterward its sole owner, by purchase from the other heirs, Mar. 18, 1794. (See note on this title, under *Myer*.) He m. Jane, dr. of Samson Benson, and d. May 22, 1835, æ. ab. 70 yrs. His property passed to his chn., who were John, Samuel, Abraham-Barker, Margaret, who m. Peter Myer, and Rebecca D., who m. the present Hon. Nathaniel Jarvis, formerly Alderman, County Clerk, etc.

DELAMATER.

Glaude le Maistre, as his autograph is, anc. of the entire Delamater family in this country, having d. before the date of the Dongan patent, his wid. Hester, and sons Jan and Isaac, took his place among the patentees. An exile from his home at Richebourg, in Artois, it was while living in the *Loyerdwars-*

straet, at Amsterdam, in 1652, that Glaude m. Hester Du Bois, who was his second w., and, as we have seen, also of a French refugee family. Glaude spent some of his first years in America at Flatbush, working as a carpenter, and there four of his six chn. were b. With Meyndert Coerten, Walraven Luten, Pierre Billiou and others (Mrs. Billiou, a Du Bois, was probably related to Mrs. Delamater*), he applied, Aug. 22, 1661, for land on Staten Island; but only Billiou and Luten settled there, while he and Coerten soon came to H., where Delamater served four terms as a magistrate, between 1666 and 1673. He bought two allotments of land, from Daniel Tourneur, for which he took out a patent June 25, 1668. In 1675 he was chosen a deacon, but his sympathies were with the French church and service, whence arose the controversy with the town regarding the parish clerk's salary, which so disturbed his latter years. If impetuous, Glaude was not incapable of generous acts when approached kindly; and his obstinacy in maintaining what he conceived to be his rights can hardly be deemed a defect in his character. He d. in or ab. 1683, his yrs. having exceeded threescore and ten. His chn. were Jan, Abraham, Isaac, and Jacobus, Susannah, b. at Flatbush, who m. Arent Harmans Bussing, and Hester, b. at Harlem, who m. Moses Le Count, of Kingston, N. Y. See p. 360. On Nov. 6, 1687, Glaude's wid. m. Jan Tibout, the parish clerk. In view of this event, she and Tibout had entered into an agreement, Sept. 23, preceding, with her sons Jan and Isaac, and son-in-law Bussing (who together took the real estate, having power to do so from the absent heirs, Abraham and Jacobus Delamater, and Moses Le Count), by which she was to "have the free use of the house and *erf* at the strand," while she lived, and Jan and Isaac were to pay her twenty-seven schepels of wheat yearly. "Should any land be drawn during Hester du Bois's lifetime, it shall belong to them both, to wit, Jan Tibout and Hester Du Bois."

Abraham Delamater, b. at Flatbush, in 1656, removed in his early manhood, with his br. Jacobus, to Kingston, Ulster Co.

* PIERRE BILLIOU was a Walloon from near Lille, and m. at Leyden, Apl. 20, 1649, Françoise du Bois, a sister of Louis du Bois, later of Esopus; both, we think, of the Canterbury family of which was Mrs. Delamater, this kinship, probably, the cause of three of the Delamater chn. going to Esopus. Billiou had two drs. b. at Leyden. He embarked at Amsterdam, May 9, 1661 (see note p. 203), accompanied by his w. and 4 chn., aged 9, 7, 6 and 2½ yrs. They had an Isaac baptized four days after landing at New Amsterdam. Isaac was living in 1707. A son Peter, b. here in 1663, m. Maria Bresse in 1701. Pierre Billiou was schout of Staten Island during the Dutch reoccupation. He and "his two sons" received a grant of three farms, 270 acres, on the south side of that island, next to Jacques Guion, laid out to them Oct. 18, 1675. He also acquired land at Piscataqua, N. J. Billiou has desc., but now much scattered.

He there m., in 1682, Celeste, dr. of Cornelius Vernoy. He m. a second w., Elsie, dr. of Jurian Tappen and wid. of Hillebrant Lochier. A magistrate and elder at Kingston, and prominent in public affairs, he closed a useful life Nov. 20, 1734. His chn. were *Cornelius*, b. 1683, who m. Margaret van Steenburgh; *Susannah*, b. 1685; *Adriana*, b. 1694, m. Aldert Kiersted; *Johannes*, b. 1697, m. Christina Wynkoop; *David*, b. 1701, m. Laurentia Tenbrook; *Jacobus*, b. 1705, m. Catrina Schoonmaker; and *Abraham*, b. 1707, who m. Rachel, dr. of Abm. Low. Said *Abraham Delamater* d. July 13, 1776, having had nine chn.; his son Johannes, b. Apl. 30, 1747, d. July 18, 1811. From *Cornelius*, b. 1683, was desc. (through Cornelius, Benjamin, and Jacob), his gt-gt-gd-son, the late distinguished Dr. John Delamater, of Cleveland, O.

Jacobus Delamater, Glaude's youngest son, was b. at H., and m. at Kingston, in 1688, Gertrude, b. 1666, dr. of Martin Cornelisz. Ysselsteyn, of Claverack. He was a trustee of Kingston, and a firm supporter of the chh. there for some years, till he settled in Marbletown upon land (296 acres), bought in 1715, and where he d. in 1741, leaving this property to his sons Isaac and Martin, and a farm at Claverack to his eldest son Glaude. The chn. of Jacobus were *Glaude*, b. 1692, d. at C. ab. 1770, having had by his w. Christina, sons Jeremiah, Jacobus, John, and Derick, and drs. Gertrude, m. John M. Van Valkenburgh, Catalina, Christina, m. John Van Deusen, and Rachel, m. John Leggett, Jr.; *Isaac*, b. 1694, known as Capt. Delamater, who m. his cousin, Rebecca Delamater, removed from Marbletown to Amenia, Dutchess Co., served in the French war, was a justice of the peace, and d. 1775; *Martha*, b. 1696; *Jacobus*, b. 1699; *Martin*, b. 1701, who m. Elizabeth Nottingham, and was succeeded in his large property in Marbletown, in 1768, by his son Jacobus; *Ruth*, b. 1703, m. John Leg; *Hester*, b. 1706; *Cornelius*, b. 1708, m. Catalina Osterhout; *Jannetie*, b. 1711, m. Joris Middagh, and *Susannah*, b. 1713, who m. Thomas Nottingham. The *N. E. Hist. & Gen. Register*, for 1860, gives a Delamater Genealogy, which abounds in errors, but may afford some aid in extending the foregoing branches of the family.

Jan Delamater, of H., eldest son of Glaude, was b. in 1653, at Flatbush, m. in 1678 Ruth, dr. of Resolved Waldron, and was, as we have seen, a worthy and useful resident. He operated considerably in lands. On Mar. 7, 1676, he and Jan Nagel bought Journee's property. Dividing it July 14, 1677, Delamater took the house and lot and No. 14 Van Keulen's Hook. He soon sold the latter, but afterward acquired Nos. 10, 11, in the same tract, and No. 7 of the New Lots. He also succeeded to an *erf* and 9 *morgen* of the paternal lands; this giving him the lower half of the farm on Montanyo's Flat, lot

No. 12 Van Keulen's Hook, and the 2 north gardens next the chh.-lot. He now sold No. 7 New Lots to Samuel Waldron, Apl. 21, 1688, leased his 3 lots on V. K. H. to Joost van Oblinus, and on the same date conveyed the Journee *erf* to Peter van Oblinus, who sold it to Jacques Tourneur, Aug. 7, 1691. In May, 1690, Delamater bartered his V. K. H. lots for others on Hoorn's Hook, to which he removed. See App. H. On Oct. 25, 1702, being "sick in bed," he made his will, giving his w. a life use of his estate. The will was proved Sept. 9, 1703, only a few days before the wid. m. Henry Bogert, of Marbletown, to which place she removed with some of her chn. The Hoorn's Hook farm and other lands of Jan Delamater were sold, in 1710, to Samuel Waldron. His chn. who survived inf. were *Susannah*, b. 1682, who m. Albert Low, of H., and went to Somerset Co., N. J.; *Cornelia*, b. 1685, who m. her step-br. Cornelius Bogert; *Abraham* b. 1689, m. Jan. 19, 1711, his step-sr., Sarah Bogert, and settled at North Branch; *Tanneke*, b. 1692, m. her step-br., Martin Bogert, who had previously lived at H.; *Hester*, b. 1694, who m. John Lewis; and *Catharine*, b. 1697, who, I believe, m. Wm. Van Gaasbeek, of Kingston.

Isaac Delamater, of H., third son of Glaude, was b. 1658, at Flatbush, and m. ab. 1681 Cornelia Everts (van Ness?), of Albany, a sr. of Rebecca Everts, w. of Jerome Barheyt, of that place. Both Isaac and w. united with the chh. at N. Y., Dec. 3d, 1681, though living at H., where he was afterward a deacon. Later, he served the town as a commissioner, also as constable. Isaac obtained the upper half of his fa.'s farm on Montanye's Flat, called 6 *morgen* or 12 acres. He leased it, with house, garden, orchard, and half the meadow, to Jan Tibout, Feb. 13, 1688, for 12 yrs. Isaac drew lot No. 11, Jochem Pieters Hills, which he sold to Jan Dyckman. He resumed his farm, and occupied it as late as Dec. 9, 1720, on which date he conveyed all his lands to his son John. He or his son Isaac bought No. 6 New Lots from Nich. Kortright, in 1729, and sold it in 1731 to Johannes Waldron. His chn. were *Hester*, b. 1683, at Albany, who m. Simon van Ness, from that place, but in 1716 a farmer at Newark, N. J.; *Evertie*, b. 1685, m. 1713 Bernardus Verveelen, of Rockland Co., N. Y.; *John*, b. 1687, of whom hereafter; *Abraham* and *Isaac*, twins, b. 1693; *Rebecca*, b. 1696, who m. Capt. Isaac Delamater, of Marbletown and Amenia; *Jacob*, b. 1699, not further noticed; *Susannah*, who m. Johannes B. Waldron, and *Cornelia*, who m. Cornelius Quackenbos, of H. *Abraham* m. Feb. 21, 1718, Catharine, dr. of Capt. Joh. Benson, and was owner from 1727 to 1742 of the Louvre, or Jones' Woods Farm. He lived for some yrs. at Tappan, on the Hudson, but returned to N. Y., where he d. Dec. 8, 1771. His chn. so far as known, were 1. Catharine, who m. Henry Brevoort; 2. Isaac, who m. Nov. 26, 1744, Maria Richardson, and had issue Catharine, b. Dec. 24, 1745, William, b. Jan. 19, 1747, Abraham, b. Sept. 7, 1749, John, b. Apl. 22, 1752; 3. John, m. Phebe Maby, and had Abraham, b. Jan. 20, 1751, Catalina, b. Feb. 19, 1753, etc.; and 4. Elizabeth, who m., 1750, Cornelius Vanderhoof. *Isaac* m. Aug. 9, 1717, Helitie, dr. of Barent Waldron. They had, 1. Barent, b. at H., 1720, m. 1745 Rachel Jewel, bought a farm in Mount Pleasant, Westchester Co., was a deacon, 1773, of Tarrytown chh., had a son Isaac, and drs. m. to Knapp, Devoe, Shule, and Lanigan, and d. 1812, leaving his farm to Isaac; 2. Isaac, m. Jannetie Flierboom, and was fa. of Isaac, b. at Tappan, Sept. 1, 1751, who m. Jannetie Myer, and was fa. of Jacobus Flierboom Delamater, b. Jan. 27, 1782, and John Delamater, b. July 4, 1787; 3. John, of N. Y., carpenter, m. Jannetie Pon. 1755, and had Isaac, b. 1757, John, 1762, d. y., Evert, 1770, and John, 1773; and 4. Abraham, b. in 1732, m. Maria, dr. of Harmanus Vandewater, of Bloomingdale, and had 8 chn., one of whom, Isaac, was the fa. of Mrs. Jacob Weeks, and another, Catharine, m. John Wilson, of N. Y., fa. of James B. Wilson, Esq., formerly president of the Bank of the Commonwealth.

John Delamater, b. 1687, m. in 1714 Anneke, dr. of Joh. Waldron, and in 1718 was elected constable. In 1715 he bought the property of his aunt, Aeltie Vermilye, who removed to Westchester. This consisted of lot No. 5, of 1691, and her drafts in the four divisions, 31 acres in all, with a village seat. In 1719 he added 30 acres from Matthew Benson (since in the Samson A. Benson farm), and next, in 1726, his fa.'s lands, giving him a total of 99 acres. In 1729 he sold 4 acres (the Vermilye 1st Div.) to Joh. Waldron, and in 1737 the 30 acres aforesaid, to Adolph Benson. The rest of his lands, 65 acres, in which was included the farm on Montanye's Flat, and said lot No. 5, he sold, Mar. 15, 1742, to Arent Kortright, who afterward m. his dr. John Delamater d. soon after, and on Mar. 24, 1744, his will was admitted to probate, and his son-in-law Myer allowed to administer. His drs. were Anneke, who m. Samuel Waldron, of Newtown; Cornelia, who m. John Myer, Jr.; Susannah, who m. Isaac Day, blacksmith, of Hackensack, later of H., and who kept the noted Day Tavern; Margaret, who m. Aaron Kortright; Rebecca, who m. Lewis Williams, and Hester. His sons were 1. John, the eldest, of N. Y., carpenter, who m. Elizabeth Post, and had issue John, b. 1754, Rebecca, b. 1757, Isaac, b. 1759, Elizabeth, b. 1762, Isaac, b. 1764, Abraham, b. 1765; 2. Isaac, who m. Anna Pearse, and had John, b. 1750, Anna, b. 1755, Joseph, b. 1761 (sold their house in Frankfort Street, Mar. 17, 1775); 3. Samuel, "of the Out Ward, cordwainer," Oct. 3, 1756, when he m. Catalina, dr. of Benjamin

Waldron, of Harlem. He had sons John S., and Samuel, and dr. Ann, who m. John Vandenburgh. John S., b. 1757, served in the artillery in the Revolution. He m. Margaret Cronk, and was for many years health officer in N. Y.

Samuel Delamater, b. March 28, 1759, became a tanner and currier in N. Y., m. 1779 Hannah Vandenburgh, and d. at his residence, 20 North Moore Street, June 8, 1843. His chn. were Hannah, b. 1780, who m. Peter Stryker (their dr. Hannah was mo. of Hon. Schuyler Colfax); Catalina b. 1782, m. Gysbert B. Vroom, of N. J., nephew of Gov. Peter D. Vroom; Samuel, b. 1784; Garret, b. 1787, d. 1797; Maria, b. 1790, m. Rev. Johnson, and Abel Hine; John, b. 1792; Benj. Waldron, b. 1795; and James-Horn, b. 1799. Of these, Samuel, b. July 23, 1784, was a "shipmaster;" d. unm. He made his will Nov. 25, 1818, "expecting to sail to-morrow for Matanzas." It was proved Oct. 23, 1819. James H. Delamater, b. Oct. 11, 1799, removed to Ohio. John Delamater, b. July 1, 1792, for many years a builder, and formerly alderman, and much esteemed, d. Dec. 21, 1877. He m. Sophia J. Ostrander, and has living, sons Benjamin, etc. His br. Benjamin W. Delamater, b. Mar. 28, 1795, formerly grocer, is now pres. of the *L. I. Ins. Co.*

DYCKMAN.

JAN DYCKMAN—*Deckman*, as then pronounced—the anc. of the Dyckmans of Kingsbridge and vicinity, and ultimately one of the wealthiest of the patentees, came, as already stated, from Bentheim in Westphalia,* probably in company with his early and life-long friends, Adolph Meyer and Arent Bussing, jointly

* JOANNES DYCKMAN, fa. of Cornelis, anc. of the Bloomingdale family, was the son of Joris Dyckman and Aeltie Roos, of Amsterdam, and not related, so far as appears, to Jan Dyckman, of Kingsbridge. He had been "first clerk" to the W. I. Comp., came out in 1651, and served as clerk and commissary at Fort Orange or Albany, but in 1655 was laid aside by insanity. He d. in 1672, leaving by his w., Maria Bosyns, who survived him, two sons, said Cornelis, b. 1647, and Johannes, b. 1662. The last m. Jannetie, dr. of Cornelis Viele, of Schenectady, and by her received land at the All Plaats, on which they had lived but two years, when the French and Indian massacre of 1690 happened. Dyckman and family made their escape to Albany, and went to Dutchess Co., but in 1715 removed to the Manor of Livingston, where he enjoyed some prominence and left posterity. He had a son, Johannes, b. 1690, and one dr.

Cornelis Dyckman, some of whose desc. write the name *Dikeman*, m. Jannetie, dr. of Dirck Claessen, potter (see p. 261), and settled in Albany Co., at Canastigione (Niskayuna), buying lands, which he occupied five years or more, but abandoned in 1690, on the French and Indian invasion; finding a temporary home in Bergen Co., N. J., but removing thence to H., where he lived in 1694, and was made constable in 1698. He was yet here Sept. 5, 1701, when he and w. sold 80 a. of their Niskayuna lands to Evert

with whom he first became a landholder, Mar. 13, 1666, by the purchase of Simon De Ruine's farm. But with little means of their own, the borrowed purchase money, 2000 gl., was appar-

van Ness. Cornelis finally buying a farm at Bloomingdale, there d., leaving chn., *Johannes*, *Derick*, *George*, *Cornelius*, *Nicholas*, *Wyntie*, m. Johannes Kortright, *Cornelia*, m. Jacob Harsen, *Geertie*, m. Derick Vander Haan, and *Elizabeth*, m. John Sprong. By his will, made Nov. 1, 1711, when he was "sick and weak," Cornelis left his farm to his sons George and Cornelius, who were to remunerate the other chn. But "the executors not sworn, and no administration granted," we infer that Derick and Nicholas bought it, as they owned parts of this farm, subsequently, of about equal size and extending together from 70th to 78th Streets, on North River, and from 68th to 77th, on 7th Ave. *Johannes*, the eldest son, b. in Albany, leased a farm at Bloomingdale Dec. 29, 1701, for six yrs., from Jurien Rynchout, and the next yr. m. Rachel, dr. of Frederick De Voe, by whom he had Elizabeth, b. 1703, Janneke, 1705, Cornelius, 1707, Hester, 1709, Frederick, 1711; the last two bapt. at Hackensack, whither Johannes seems to have gone when his lease expired. *Derick* learned the art of weaving from Hendrick Brevoort. He m., 1711, Wilhelmina Bass, from Newtown. His will, dated Feb. 16, 1730, was proved October 12, 1762. He left his farm at B. to his wid. and chn. The latter were, Cornelius, b. 1713, Anna, 1716, Cornelia, 1718, Johannes, 1720, Derick, 1723, Aaron, 1726, and George, 1729. His dr. Anna m. Jacobus Myer, and dr. Cornelia m., 1745, Teunis Somerindyke. *Nicholas*, b. in Bergen, 1692, m., 1716, Anneke, dr. of John Sevenhoven, who by her fa.'s will received half of the Fabricius farm on the East River side, and which she and Nicholas sold in 1751. Dyckman's homestead, at Bloomingdale, embraced 94 a., which ran up to 73d Street at 7th Ave., and a little higher on the river. Pursuant to his will, dated May 29, 1752, it was sold, Mar. 1, 1763, by his executors, John Harsen and Garret Cosine, to Jacob Harsen, who two days later reconveyed the northern half to said John Harsen (nephew of Dyckman, and also m. to his dr. Rachel), and the southern half to said Cozine, whose w. was Jannetie Dyckman. The southern half, with east portion of the northern, formed the well-known Harsen Estate.

George Dyckman m., May 17, 1712, Catalina, dr. of Teunis Idens van Huyse, of Bloomingdale, and went to Bergen Co., but returned to occupy 115 a. conveyed to him, June 23, 1720, by his fa.-in-law, from off his farm. See *Van Huyse*, p. 522. In 1729 he bought an adjoining section of the farm from his br.-in-law, Abm. Montanye, with 20 a. in the rear, lying within the Harlem line; also Montanye's *erf*, at H. In 1748 he sold the *erf* and 20 a. to Adolph Benson and Jacob Dyckman, Jr. Jacob sold his 10 a. to Mrs. Daniel McGown, being the place on which she lived at McGown's Pass. See p. 470. George Dyckman owned a part of the old Tourneur Meadows on the little Mill Creek, "two acres more or less," gotten, we presume, with Montanye's land, and bought by Montanye when the adjacent Tourneur farm, to which it had belonged, was sold to the Kortrights. Dyckman sold these meadows, Oct. 19, 1734, to Nicholas Kortright, m. to his niece, whence they passed to Abraham Myer, June 12, 1740, and from Myer to Peter Bussing, April 16, 1753. Dyckman d. Jan. 16, 1753. He had issue, Jannetie, b. 1714, Teuntie, 1716, Cornelius, 1718, Maria, 1720, Teunis-Eidesse, 1722, George, 1725, and John, 1728. John *Dikeman* last named, first a baker in N. Y., with w. Rebecca (who was a dr. of John Buys), sold their city property in 1759 and returned to Bloomingdale. He was ald. of the Out Ward, 1769 to 1773, and d. some yrs. after the Revolution, leaving chn., Teunis-Eidesse, Matthew, John, Catharine and Rebecca. Catharine m., in 1780, Peter Grim, Jr. These divided the paternal lands in 1793. Of this family and branch, we believe, was Judge John Dikeman, of Brooklyn,

ently too heavy a burden to carry, for the associates, on Apl. 7, ensuing, turned over their bargain to Capt. Delavall. Dyckman united with the chh. at N. Y., on Feb. 26, 1673, together with Busing and others, his young acquaintances, of both sexes, to one of whom, Madelaine, dr. of Daniel Tourneur, Dyckman was m. during the next summer. Obtaining by her a farming lot upon Montanye's Flat, and two of the out-gardens on which to build and begin domestic life, Dyckman bought of Meyer, Nov. 2, following, "a certain *hook* of marsh land," on the north end of lot 4, Van Keulen's Hook. We have taken notice, p. 380, of his grant and purchase at Spuyten Duyvel in 1677, in connection with Jan Nagel. The latter d. in 1680, and the next year Dyckman, then living at Spuyten Duyvel, m. his wid., Rebecca, who was a dr. of Resolved Waldron. By this means the union of the Dyckman and Nagel estates was maintained. They drew jointly of the common land in 1691, but in 1712, the Nagel heirs being of age, the drafts were made in separate lots, in the names of Jan Dyckman and Jan Nagel respectively.

The land drawn in 1691 lay in two places; one parcel, No. 14, of 20 morgen, being on Jochem Pieters Hills (see App. J), and the other, No. 24, drawn mainly on their joint rights at Spuyten Duyvel, embracing *all the common land north of Sherman's Creek*, as shown by the annexed extract from the deed (*groundbrief*), having the written consent of the freeholders, and signed by the town officers, Mar. 21, 1701.

No. 24.

THERE is set off for JAN DYCKMAN and JAN NAGEL, on account of 26 *morgen* and 2 *erven*,* a piece of land upon the end of York Island, north of the Round Meadow and the Half Creek, commonly called Pieter Tuynier's Fall, till to the little Sand Bay lying at the North River; ALL the common land north of this abovewritten boundary; ALSO a suitable King's Way shall remain over the said land.

The quantity of land strictly due upon the given *erf* and *morgen* rights was 40 a., but the grant was estimated at 140. The additional 100 a., with 16 more on Jochem Pieters Hills (known as Lot 17, Last Division), all woodland, were gotten by agreement between Dyckman and the town, in exchange for cleared land on Jochem Pieters Flat (20 a.), which had belonged to Nagel, but was now wanted in order to make up the quantity claimed by the heirs of Capt. Delavall, in that tract. In this exchange Dyckman got four acres of woodland for one of tillable land, being the relative value of the two at that date. See this matter further explained in App. E.

* These *erf* and *morgen* rights had been adjusted as early as 1686. See Note, p. 454. How they were made up is shown in a Note in App. J.

The deed of necessity included the lands covered by the old Jansen and Aertsen patent, and known latterly as the *Dyckman Homestead.* Dyckman and the Nagels also bought in company three lots, Nos. 11, 12, 13, adjoining their lot 14, on Jochem Pieters Hills. Thus in 1715, when Dyckman d., his estate and Nagel's together were rated at 300 a.; which was exclusive of the said lots 11 to 14, being 90 a., then held in his own name by Dyckman's son Gerrit, and also of the three Nagel lots on Jochem Pieters Flat, except 11 a., also of the Dyckman lot on Montanye's Flat, which had passed to Zacharias Sickels, and the Nagel drafts in the four divisions which had been disposed of to Abm. Myer and Joh. Waldron.

Jan Dyckman's d. was followed, after four yrs., by that of his wid. His chn. by his first w. were Daniel, b. 1673, who d. y.; Maria, b. 1676, who m., in 1695, Capt. James Hewett, and in 1713, Peter Ubregt, from whom Tubby Hook took its name; Gerrit, b. 1678; Magdalena, b. 1680, who m. John Nagel, 2d; John, b. 1682, who d. y.; and Grietie, b. 1685, still in 1719 a *spinster*, i.e. unm. His son Jacob, b. 1692, was by his last w., as was also his dr. Rebecca, b. 1695, who m. Joseph Hadley, of Philipsburgh, or Philips Manor.

The Dyckman and Nagel chn., under the marriage articles between Dyckman and Mrs. Nagel, dated May 12, 1690, and their joint will of Nov. 2, 1702, were to share equally of the patrimonial estates. Before Dyckman d. his eldest son Gerrit, as already seen, had come to possess the 90 a., or lots 11 to 14, on Jochem Pieters Hills; and other of the separated parcels had been disposed of. But the ample domain above Sherman's Creek and Dyckman's drafts in the four divisions remained intact and undivided till Nov. 10, 1719, when the heirs of both names made a settlement. Gerrit Dyckman took 30 a. more of his father's estate, embracing his lots in 1st and 4th Divisions, and half of No. 17 Last Division, being 8 a. near Kiersen. Jacob Dyckman and John Nagel, Jr., on the date aforesaid, bought the interests of their co-heirs respectively, in the remaining lands, which gave Dyckman 120 a. and Nagel 151 a.; the latter taking the Dyckman lots in 2d and 3d Divisions. Each had an equal quantity above Sherman's Creek, to wit 112 a., and these lands, excepting the homesteads, were held in joint tenancy for another ten years. Their possessions were made up thus:

NAGEL:	Half the 5 lots of 1677	38 a.	0 q.	0 r.
	" No. 24 of 1691	24 "	2 "	0 "
	" 100 acres	50 "	0 "	0 "
	2d Div., No. 17	19 "	0 "	30 "
	3d " " 10	8 "	3 "	11 "
	On Jochem Pieters Flat	11 "	0 "	0 "
		151 a.	2 q.	10 r.

DYCKMAN: Half the 5 lots of 1677	38 a.	0 q.	0 r.
" No. 24 of 1691	24 "	2 "	0 "
" 100 acres	50 "	0 "	0 "
" No. 17 Last Division	8 "	0 "	0 "
	120 a.	2 q.	0 r.

Gerrit Dyckman was constable in 1710-11. He d. in 1729, his property being held by his wid. till 1748, when her son *Jan Dykman*, who dropped the *c* from his name, came in possession. Twenty years previous he had m. a dr. of Abraham Myer, 1st. He was constable in 1734-5, was chosen, May 10, 1744, with Jacob Myer and Benj. Benson, to sell certain remnants of common land, and in 1753 was acting as an elder. Dykman sold lots Nos. 20, 21, 1st Div., to Lawrence Low, and bought instead No. 19, 1st Div., from the heirs of Joh. Waldron. But on Nov. 13, 1767, he sold to John Watkins his farm, with its several appendages, including, on the north side, lot No. 15, 22 a., the Lawrence Low homestead, which he had lately purchased of John Low. John Dykman d. five yrs. before the Revolution, and on Oct. 8, 1770, his sons-in-law Benson and Myer were appointed his administrators. His residence, a substantial stone house, built by him or his fa., is yet standing on Kingsbridge road, west side, corner of 152d Street. Of his drs., Rebecca m. Samson, or Samuel Benson, and Eve m. John Myer, fa. of Jacob, and gd-fa. of the late Peter Myer, etc. Jacob Dykman, younger br. of John, was constable of H. in 1739-40, and 1741-2. He m. Rebecca, dr. of Isaac Vermilye, of Yonkers, and, I believe, lived in that vicinity.

Jacob Dyckman, b. 1692, and from whom the late Isaac of Kingsbridge was desc., m., in 1716, Jannetie, b. 1693, dr. of Jan and Gerritie Kiersen. He and Nagel, joint owners of all the lands from Sherman's Creek to Kingsbridge, passed deeds May 15, 1729, for their homesteads, then computed at 38 a. each; parted by the creek at 211th Street (where on either side near Harlem River stood their respective dwellings), and a line running westerly, in the direction of said street, to 12th Avenue. The Dyckman tract so conveyed was limited south by the Kingsbridge Road, which then deviated from its present course at 204th (say Inwood) Street, and ran nearly straight to the foot of 208th Street, at Harlem River; then for some distance northward followed the shore. On June 9, 1744, Dyckman and Nagel completed the division of their lands, passing deeds. Dyckman took the 16 a. at the extreme end of the island; Nagel the next 38 a. which came down to his homestead farm, also estimated at 38 a., and which Nagel now transferred to Dyckman, though he or his sons subsequently bought it back. The highlands next the Hudson, from Tubby Hook upward, which had been set off by a line run from the little Sand Bay, north 59 degrees east, to the Spuyten Duyvel Creek, and surveyed into six lots singularly corresponding in contents to the parcels before disposed of on Jochem Pieters' and Montanye's Flats, were also divided on the above date.

Jacob Dyckman took part with others, in 1758, in building a free bridge over Harlem River. By a letter from him to Sir William Johnson, the Indian Agent on the Mohawk, dated Mar. 22, 1765 (see *Doc. Hist. N. Y.*, ii. 810), it appears he gave attention to raising choice fruit trees, and farm stock "of the right old England breed." He lived to a good age, his will being dated Aug. 10, 1767, and admitted to probate June 16, 1774. His sons were, *John*, who d. y.; *Jacob* and *William*; and drs. *Magdalena*, m. Evert Bruyn; *Gerritie*, called Charity, m. John Vermilye; *Rebecca*, m. Abraham Odell, and *Margaret*, who m. Jonathan Odell; the husbs. all residents of Westchester Co.

Jacob Dyckman, Jr., a person of some prominence in the town, m. ab. 1742, Catalina, dr. of Samson Benson, and at first lived near his fa., at Spuyten Duyvel. In 1748 he and his br.-in-law Adolph Benson bought from George Dyckman 20 a. of land adjoining the highway, in the rear of the Benson Point farm, which they divided; and here Dyckman kept a public-house for about ten yrs., till he sold his place to Mrs. McGown (see p. 490, and note, p. 506), and returned to Spuyten Duyvel. It was here that the Colonial Assembly met in 1752, from Oct. 24 to Nov. 11; the Governor and Council while in attendance staying at the neighboring house of Benj. Benson, which stood where is now the residence of S. Benson McGown, Esq. Jacob Dyckman obtained from his fa. the 16 a. lying next to Kingsbridge, and from Nagel 14 acres adjoining, giving him 30 a.; whereon he built the tavern since kept up, which, on account of the free bridge, became popular, but not a financial success for Dyckman, who becoming insolvent made an assignment. His farm, then occupied by his son Samson, was advertised and sold at the Merchants' Coffee House, Sept. 30, 1772 (deed given Feb. 11, 1773), the purchaser being a N. Y. innkeeper, Caleb Hyatt, whose son Jacob Hyatt owned it after him. See note, p. 388.

Jacob Dyckman's chn. were, 1. Jacob, the fa. of Jacob and John; 2. Samson, m., 1770, Rebecca, dr. of Isaac Odell, was in public service in the Revolution, and had drs. Hannah and Catharine, the last m. to Mathias Valentine; 3. Benjamin, post-rider, m. Martha, dr. of Jacob Lent, and had William, John, Samson, and Jane; 4. Jacobus, m. Margaret, dr. of Martin Post, and had Martin, Samson, Benjamin, Staats-Morris, Catharine, m. Pell C. Vought, Martha-Maria, m. Isaac Mandeville, and Elmira, who m. Louis Levines; 5. John, m. Aletta Goetchius, and had Samson and Rachel-Goetchins; 6. Garret, m. Joanna, dr. of Jonathan Odell, and d. May 7, 1816, æ. 60 yrs., being fa. of William N., lawyer, and Jacob G. Dyckman; 7. William-Nagle, m. Rebecca, dr. of Jonathan Odell, and was fa. of Samson, Jonathan, William, Catalina, Maria, and Rebecca; 8. Maria, who m., 1771, John Clark; 9. Jane, who m., 1777, John Vredenburgh; and 10. Catalina, who m. Daniel Hale. Staats Morris Dyckman, esteemed for his benevolence and cultivated manners, m. Eliza Corne, a gd.-dr. of Capt. Peter Corne. He d. Aug. 14, 1806, æ. 51 yrs., leaving a son, Peter C. Dyckman (fa. of Mrs. Col. John P. Cruger), and a dr., Susan Matilda, the late Mrs. Wheaton.

William Dyckman, son of Jacob, and gd.-son of Jan Dyckman, was b. Aug. 23, 1725, and m. Mary, dr. of Michael Tourneur. She was b. Feb. 4, 1728. William succeeded to the homestead at Sherman's Creek, occupying the old residence which stood on 210th Street, near Harlem River. In the times which tried men's souls, the patriotic Dyckman and his family warmly espoused the cause of their country, and upon the invasion by the British army left their home for a seven years' exile. The sons, very active during the war in aiding the American operations, immortalized themselves as the "Westchester Guides." The survivors returned at the peace, and their dwelling having been burnt by the enemy, built another on a new site, where it yet remains on Kingsbridge Road, west side, between 208th and 209th streets, or more properly a little north of Hawthorne Street. Here William Dyckman closed his life Aug. 10, 1787, and his wid. Feb. 14, 1802. Their chn. were, Jacobus, b. Sept. 18, 1749; Mary, b. June 2, 1752, m. Jacob Vermilye; Abraham, b. Aug. 25, 1754; Michael, b. Aug. 9, 1756; Jane, b. June 26, 1759, who d. March 24, 1772; William, b. Dec. 9, 1762; John, b. July 28, 1764, who d. April 15, 1774; Jemima, b. Feb. 25, 1765, who m. Evert Brown; and Charity, b. May 18, 1770, who m. Benjamin Lent. Of these, Abraham, unm., was one of the *Guides*, and was killed in that service, March 4, 1782. Michael, similarly distinguished, m. Sarah Oakley, and d. in Jan., 1808, having had drs. Sarah and Maria. William, after the war, m. Mary, dr. of Martin Post, before named, eminent as a *Guide*, in which service William, though but a youth, had done himself credit. He removed to Western N. Y., where he d. some years ago. He had sons William, now d., and Evert, residing in Michigan.

Jacobus Dyckman, eldest br., m., 1773, Hannah Brown, and became chief owner of the Kingsbridge estate, to which he added the Courtright farm (see note, p. 297), and several lots in 3d Div. He was a memb. of the Constitutional Convention in 1821, and alderman in 1822. He d. in his 84th yr., Aug. 20,

1832, having had nine chn. that reached maturity, viz., William, Frederick, Abraham, Jacob, James, Isaac, Michael, Maria, and Hannah, who m. Caleb Smith. Of these Jacob, a physician, at one time health-commissioner of N. Y., d. Dec. 8, 1822, æ. 34 yrs. Abraham m. Margaret, dr. of Isaac Vermilye, and d. Apl. 20, 1815, æ. 33 yrs., leaving issue Jane-Odell, John Honeywell, and Isaac Vermilye Dyckman. Isaac and Michael, then the only surviving sons, took all the real estate under their father's will, and of which, on the d. of Michael in 1854, Isaac became sole owner. The latter dying unm., Jan. 6, 1868, his nephew, James F. D. Smith, was made his principal heir, and took the name of Isaac Michael Dyckman, but is since dec.

KIERSEN.

JAN KIERSEN claims a notice among the patentees as the direct successor of William Haldron. He chose to write his name *Cierssen*, a departure neither warranted by the derivative word nor followed by Kiersen's chn., for which reasons we adopt the usual spelling of the records. He was the son of Kier Wolters (see note, p. 294), and was b. at Arnhout, in Drenthe. In 1685, at about 30 yrs. of age, he m. Gerritie, dr. of Capt. Jan van Dalsen. She was b. in New England. The next year Kiersen and his fa.-in-law obtained from the town a lease of part of the Great Maize Land, on Jochem Pieters Hills (Harlem Heights, below Fort Washington), for a term of 12 years. See p. 459. But the lands there being laid out and allotted to the inhabitants in 1691, Kiersen, on July 2, 1694, bought "for 1000 gl. in money," the lots, Nos. 16 and 18, from Thomas Tourneur, as purchased by him from Holmes and Waldron, the original drawers. In March, 1696, Kiersen obtained the signatures of "every inhabitant of the town" to a paper granting him "a *half morgen* of land from the common woods, lying at the south-east *hook* of the land that Samuel Waldron has drawn out of the common woods, which half morgen of land he may build upon, thereon setting a house, barn and garden, for which he promises to let lie a *morgen* of land upon the north-east *hook* of the aforesaid lot; leaving a suitable road or King's way betwixt his house and the lot of Samuel Waldron." Kiersen built his house, etc., and on March 7, 1700, the town officers gave him a deed. This was the first settlement on the well-known Jumel homestead, and we believe the first spot permanently occupied on these heights. Kiersen, by purchasing the lands and patentee rights of William Haldron, deceased, came to own the lot lying between his two, west of the road, and which lot (No. 17) Henry Haldron, eldest son of William, released to Kiersen Nov. 7, 1701.* A resurvey of that tract in 1712 united those three in one lot as No. 18, and it was subsequently called 40 a. Kiersen sold Haldron's smithshop lot to Samuel Waldron, as it joined southerly on Waldron's meadows, but reserved the *erf*, on which he drew land in 1712. When those drafts were made, Kiersen enlarged his half morgen or house lot east of the road to 8 a., but from whom he got it is not a matter of positive record. To this, in 1720, he added an adjoining 4 a., being a remnant left after the 1st Div. was laid out. He afterward got the Vermilye lot, No. 6, 2d Div., which joined his homestead on the north, and which gave him 20 a. east of the road. For his drafts in 1712, etc., see note, p. 333, and App. J.

Kiersen joined the chh. in 1682, and later served as deacon. He was also town collector and constable, and was a party, in 1738, to the Mill Camp grant. When he d. does not appear. His 90 a. (upland) stand in the tax lists in the name of "Jan Kiersen," down to 1753, but we might conclude that John senior was not living at so late a date, and that his son John, b. 1690, had succeeded him. Yet, if we mistake not, we find the

* WILLIAM HALDRON, referred to p. 333, etc., first comes to notice in 1685, as the owner of a house and lot (*erf*), by virtue of which he was numbered with the patentees. By a clerical error, as we must regard it, his name is entered in the official record of the Dongan Patent as *W*aldron; but fortunately contemporary records remove all doubt of Haldron's identity as the patentee. Being a blacksmith, he made most of the iron-work for the chh. built in 1686, but the next year he was unfortunately drowned in the river, on or about Dec. 7, 1637, date of the coroner's inquest. His wid. survived him but a short time, for in April, 1690, the town court ordered "that the property found in the house where William Haldron's widow died, according to the inventory; and also the smithshop, shall be given over to the deaconry of New Harlem, and to Johannes Vermilye." On June 1, 1693, Zacharias Sickels, a smith from Albany, was put in possession as tenant of the "house, with smithshop and garden" (smith tools included), by the deacons, who on Apl. 18, 1694, gave him a formal lease for 3 yrs. from the date of occupancy. We find the following, written in English, signed and dated Apl. 17, 1696: "I, Henry Haldron, son of William Haldron, deceased, do hereby acquit and discharge the Overseers and Poormasters of Harlem, and by these presents do give them full power to sell and dispose of all the goods and movables that did belong to my father, William Haldron, deceased." It was soon after this that Jan Kiersen bought the Haldron property, in which was included lot No. 17, on Jochem Pieters Hills, set off to Haldron's *erf* right in 1691.

Haldron's chn., so far as known, were Henry, John, and Anna, who m., 1705, John Allen, of Milford, and, in 1720, Thomas Cox, of Boston. Of Henry we have no further account than is here given. John Haldron, b. at H., m., May 18, 1707, Cornelia, dr. of Dr. Lucas van Tienhoven, and wid. of Andries Holst. She was b. in 1678. About 1712 they removed to Tappan, on the Hudson, where their desc. became quite numerous. Their chn. were *William*, b. 1708, *Elizabeth*, 1709, *Lucas*, 1711, *Elsie*, 1713, *Sarah*, 1716, *John*, 1719, *Cornelius*, 1721. William m. and had 9 chn., whose births are recorded. John and Cornelius also had families.

peculiar signature of John senior to a town document of Mar. 28, 1749. If his, he lived to a great age. His chn. were John, Abraham, and Jannetie, who m. Jacob Dyckman, of Kingsbridge. John and Abraham, on Apl. 23, 1756, join in selling part of their salt meadow, at Kingsbridge, which the elder John bought of Joh. Waldron, Jan. 16, 1703.

The names of the two sons appear upon the roll of Capt. Stuyvesant's company in 1738; but devoted to husbandry, their quiet, unobtrusive lives seldom bring them into notice. John, especially, is rarely named otherwise than herein stated, nor is there any intimation that he left desc. His br. Abraham, b. 1695, was constable in 1728, and probably had no family. He acts alone with the freeholders in signing deeds, etc., in 1747 and 1753, neither his fa. nor br. being named. It would seem that his sr., with her hus. and chn., had either purchased, or been empowered to sell (perhaps by the will of John senior), the Kiersen property in H., because these join in a deed, Jan. 29, 1763, conveying said lands to James Carroll, of N. Y., for £1000. Abraham Kiersen is named therein as a grantor, but does not subscribe. A clause in Jacob Dyckman's will of Aug. 10, 1767, devising a share of his property to John and Abraham Kere, and directing that they "be supported as I have done," shows a state of dependency in their old age, whatever else it may imply. With their dec., the name disappears here, though probably perpetuated in the Westchester branch. From Carroll the Kiersen property passed to Col. Roger Morris, whose stately mansion, better known as the Jumel house, still remains, being owned and occupied by Mr. Nelson Chase.

KORTRIGHT.

Cornelis Jansen, with whom the preceding pages have made us acquainted, will be further named only as introductory to a notice of his desc., who composed the principal part of the late Kortright family of H. Born in 1645, at Beest, in Gelderland, he came out with his fa., Jan Bastiaensen, in 1663 (see pp. 74, 106, 227, and note, p. 288), and in 1665 m. Metje, dr. of Bastiaen Elyessen, and wid. of Claes Teunisz van Appeldorn; a lady who, after Jansen's early d. in 1689, proved her ability both to manage his business and enhance his estate, the use of which, under his will dated Feb. 25, of said year (but not proved till Mar. 18, 1706), she was to enjoy till her d. or re-m. Having been a trooper, he gave his eldest son Johannes "the best horse, and the best saddle, and the best boots, and the best pistols, and holsters, and carbine and cutlass." He also left him, over and above his share of the estate, "the lot of land at Jochem Pieters, to wit, the lot by the great gate." This was No. 3 of the old lots (afterward Sickels'), and the gate must have stood at the upper corner of the Church Farm, where the road going north to Myer's narrowed from 4½ to 3 rods, as finally fixed by vote of the town in 1744. Cornelis Jansen left four chn., at first called *Cornelissen*, viz., Johannes, Laurens, Aefie, who m., in 1688, Jonas Lewis, an Englishman, and, in 1698, Marcus Tiebaut, and Annetie, who m. Adrian Quackenbos.*

The wid., from her hus., is usually called Metje Cornelis, once Metje Jansen, and sometimes, from her fa., Metje Bastiaens. As the lists show, she drew largely of the common lands in the several divisions; but survived those of 1712 only a short time. Under that of 1691 she obtained an annex to the farm on Montanye's Flat; in the deed dated Mar. 21. 1701, "bounded by a line leading from the southwest corner of the kitchen as the fence runs, to a small brook, and along the brook till it meets with the patent line of Harlem, thence along said line northerly till it meets with the old lots of Cornelis Kortright, deceased." In 1715 her family held 246 a., of which Laurens Cornelissen held exclusively 77; and he and the other heirs jointly 169, which, from 1715 to 1726, stood in the name of "Metje Cornelis' heirs." Laurens' 77 a. included 30 a. sold by him the same year, and since in the Race Course Farm (see p. 467), with No. 1, 2d Div., and half of No. 17, 3d Div., both which finally passed to the Nutters. In the 169 a. was the farm on Montanye's Flat (since Nutter's), rated as 36 a., the adjoining Tourneur farm (later of Peter Bussing), 36 a., No. 10, Jochem Pieters Flat, No. 16, Van Keulen's Hook, No. 6 New Lots, No. 10 of 1691, No. 5, 1st Div., and ½ of No. 17, 3d Div. Widow Tiebaut and her son John Lewis, in 1715, held each 13½ a. in the 4 Divs.; the widow's lots reverting the same year to John van Oblienis, in whose name they had been drawn.

Johannes Corn. Kortright was b. in 1673, and m. in 1701, Wyntie, dr. of Cornelis Dyckman. The next year he was made constable. He d. in 1711, and in 1717 his wid. became the second w. of Zacharias Sickels. Johannes left chn., *Metje*, m. John Bussing; *Nicholas*, and *Jannetie*, who m. Johannes Van Wyck. *Nicholas*, who was constable of the town in 1729, and afterward collector, m., in 1731, Elizabeth, dr. of Eide van Huyse,

* ADRIAN QUACKENBOS, or Quackenbush, was b. at Albany, and probably the br. of Wouter (m. Cornelia, dr. of Jan Louwe Bogert), a son of Pieter Quackenbos, brickmaker, from Oestgeest, in Holland, the common anc. See *Pearson*. Adrian m. Annetie Kortright, Aug. 22, 1701, and for some yrs. occupied the Kortright lot, No. 10, on Jochem Pieters Hills, being part of the Dr. Samuel Bradhurst tract. He had a son, Cornelius, who m. Cornelia Delamater, and Metje, who m. Resolved Waldron, afterward of Haverstraw. Cornelius had a son Adrian, b. 1725.

of Bloomingdale, and in 1739, wid. Elizabeth Peltrong. On the d. of his uncle Laurens in 1720, the Kortright lands were divided, and Nicholas took as his portion 101 a., viz., 10 a. from the south lot of the Tourneur farm, No. 10, of 1691, 40 a., No. 10, Jochem Pieters Flat, 12 a., No. 5, 1st Div., and ½ of No. 17, 3d Div. The middle lot of the Tourneur farm (on which were the buildings), and 2 a. of the south lot, making 14 a., were set off for the use of his mother, Wyntie Sickels. In 1729 he bought his step-fa., Sickels' lands, No. 5, Jochem Pieters Flat, 2 q. 23 r. of 16, 1st Div., No. 12, 2d Div. and a lot on Montanye's Flat, in all 42 a. 3 q. 19 r. This gave him 144 a. In 1730 he bought Nos. 2 and 18, 2d Div., from M. Benson, and in 1739 succeeded to the Tourneur middle plot, 14 a. In 1729 he sold No. 6, New Lots, to Isaac Delamater; in 1731, Nos. 5, 10, Jochem Pieters Flat, and No. 12, 2d Div., to Abraham Myer; in 1733, No. 5, 1st Div., and upper 6 a. of 17, 3d Div. to Joh. Benson; in 1737, No. 10 of 1691, to Lawrence Low; in 1740, the Sickels lot on Montanye's Flat to wid. Grietie Kortright, and the remnant of his lands, being the 2 southerly Tourneur lots, and Nos. 2, 8, 2d Div., to Abm. Myer. Kortright again, in 1742, bought 21 a. of land in H., which at his d. passed to John Van Zandt. He d. Nov. 19, 1751. He had sons John, b. 1732, and Nicholas, b. 1743. His dr. Frances, b. 1741, m. John Norris, peruke-maker. Nicholas, a sail-maker, owned property in N. Y., where he lived, was a vestryman of Trinity Church, 1787 to 1792. His w. Elizabeth d. in 1789, æ. 46 yrs., and he in 1820. He had chn., Nicholas, James, etc.

Laurens Corn. Kortright, from whom sprang the main branch of the family at H., was b. here in 1681. On Dec. 9, 1704, his mo. leased him for 4 yrs. the farm "lying on the flats about New Harlem," and also "the lot on the Maize Land," or Jochem Pieters Hills. He m., in 1703, Helena, dr. of Capt. Joh. Benson, and in or ab. 1708, Margaret, dr. of Arent Bussing. Laurens served as constable in 1708–9. He succeeded to the homestead on Harlem Lane (since Nutter's), which at his d. in 1720 fell in the division to his wid. Grietie, together with the upper Tourneur lot, and Nos. 19, 20 (the last got in 1720), on Van Keulen's Hook, No. 1, 2d Div., ½ of 17, 3d Div., and 3½ a. of No. 6, 3d Div. bought 1726 from John Lewis. In 1740 she bought from Nich. Kortright the Sickels lot on Montanye's Flat, and in 1747, from Simon Johnson, the parcels below Montanye's Flat, and being part of No. 8, 1st Div., and mostly within the late Valentine Nutter Farm. These lands (except Nos. 19, 20, V. K. Hook, sold, 1730, to Derick Benson) descended to her surviving sons Aaron and Lawrence Kortright. Lawrence took the homestead and No. 1, 2d Div.; the upper Tourneur lot was sold to Peter Bussing, and the adjoining Sickels lot, Feb. 9, 1755, to Benj. Benson, the deed also covering the next lot, which Benson had inherited from his fa., bounded by Vandewater's gore in the rear. Laurens Kortright's chn. by his first w. were *Cornelius* and *Elizabeth*, the last of whom m., 1753, Gilbert Garrison, of N. Y.; and by the second w., *Aaron*, *Lawrence*, *Eve*, who m. Adolph Benson, *Mattie*, who m. Abraham Myer, and *Susannah*, who m. Aaron Myer.*

Lawrence Kortright, last of the name to hold the homestead, d. in 1761, unm. He had devised all his estate to one Sarah Gilmore, wife of William Nutter, and afterward, on Apl. 5, 1760, gave her a deed for the farm (which is described, from the old groundbriefs, as in four contiguous parcels) and two woodland lots. But by another will, of Nov. 8 ensuing, he revokes, to quote his words, "a pretended last will and testament said to have been made by me in favor of Sarah Nutter, which last will and testament (if any such there be), and also certain deeds of lease and release for my real estate (if any such there be), pretended to have been made and executed by me to her, I do hereby, on the faith of a christian, declare to have been obtained from me by fraud and circumvention, and without any valuable consideration received by me for the same." By this second will he divides his property among his kindred. The Kortright heirs refusing to give up the premises, Valentine Nutter, only ch. and heir of Sarah, brought an ejectment suit in 1771; but after "divers differences, controversies, and disputes about the said lands," a compromise was made, *Aaron Kortright* and his co-heirs, for a consideration, releasing their claims, by deeds dated Sept. 12, 1789, and Feb. 28, 1799. Upon getting possession, Mr. Nutter erected a new dwelling-house and outbuildings (see p. 439); living here till 90 yrs. of age (1831), when he went to pass his remaining days with his gd-son, Gouverneur M. Wilkins, Esq., at Westchester, where he d. in 1836, æ. 95 yrs.

Aaron Kortright m. Margaret, dr. of John Delamater. He had purchased, Mar. 15, 1742, the Delamater farm on Montanye's Flat, and accompanying lands. The latter embraced all Isaac Delamater's draft lots of 1712, and Aeltie Vermilye's, of

* JOHN LEWIS was b. at H., m., May 22, 1713, Hester, dr. of Jan Delamater, and the next fall was chosen constable. He succeeded to the allotment drawn in 1712 by Marcus Tiebaut, his step-father, from the common lands; but not to the half-erf and three morgen on which it was drawn. His house lot was on the north side of the Church Lane, and has since formed the easterly lot of the Brady plot. See Notes, pp. 390, 418. In 1740 Lewis sold his lot in 1st Division to Adolph Myer, and in 1748 the rest of his property in Harlem to Dr. Josiah Paterson. It included two house lots (*erven*) besides that he occupied, one of which he bought of Simon Johnson, in 1747, out of Pipon's estate. One of Lewis's drs., Tanneke, m. Abraham Montanye, and another, Ruth, m. John Ewouts.

1691 and 1712, except No. 20, 1st Div. (see App. J.) We believe 2 a. of No. 5, V. K. Hook, were also included. Of these Aaron sold No. 10, 1st Div., to Adolph Myer in 1751; part of the large Molenaor tract. He sold No. 5, of 1691, to Jonathan Odell, May 11, 1753, since of Jacob Schieffelin; and No. 6, 2d Div., to John Kiersen. He recovered, by purchase from Peter Waldron, the lower half of the Delamater farm, which together now embraced 12 a. east of the Lane, on which were the buildings, and west of the Lane, 40 a. on the Flat, and 19½ a. (in it part of No. 8, 1st Div.) on the heights. In 1762 and 1765 Aaron gave liens on some of the lands bought of Delamater to his nephew Lawrence Kortright, of N. Y., merchant, and finally the two made an exchange, Apl. 28, 1772, Lawrence taking the farm and some woodlands, and giving Aaron and his w. a deed for 241 a. of the Wawayanda patent, in Orange Co.—to go after their d. to their sons Lawrence, John, and Aaron Kortright—whither they removed, and where their desc. are still found.

Cornelius Kortright, eldest son of Laurens Cornelissen, was b. in 1704, m. Hester, dr. of John Cannon, of N. Y., and owned property in Queen (now Pearl) Street, where he carried on the baking business. He was assist. ald. of Montgomery Ward, 1738–40. His two slaves, implicated in the Negro Plot in 1741, were transported to San Domingo. After his d., which happened Apl. 15, 1745, his business was continued by his wid. and son Cornelius. He had six chn., viz.: Lawrence, b. 1728; John, b. 1731; Cornelius, b. 1732; Maria, b. 1736, m. John Wilkinson Hanson, merchant; Helena, b. 1739, m. Abraham Brasher, merchant; and Elizabeth, b. 1742, who m. Wm. Ricketts Van Cortlandt, merchant. Lawrence, the eldest son, also a merchant, became wealthy and prominent. In the old French war he was part owner of several privateers fitted out at N. Y. against the enemy. He was one of the founders of the Chamber of Commerce in 1768. He had a large interest in Tryon Co. lands, and on his purchase the township of Kortright was settled. He had identified himself with the Episcopal Chh., and during the Revolution remained quiet at his residence, 192 Queen Street; but his sympathies were with his country. In 1778, partly on his surety, Judge Fell, then a prisoner in the Provost, obtained his release. Before his death he conveyed his farm at H., with some woodland, to his only son, John. Mr. Kortright d. in 1794. By his w. Hannah Aspinwall, whom he m. May 6, 1755, beside said son Capt. John Kortright, he had four drs., viz.: Sarah, m., in 1775, Col. John Heyliger, of Santa Cruz; Hester, m., 1790, Nicholas Gouverneur, Esq.; Elizabeth, m., 1786, Hon. James Monroe, afterward President of the U. S.; and Mary, who m., 1793, Thomas Knox, Esq. Capt. Kortright m., May 2, 1793, Catharine, dr. of Edmund Seaman, who, after his d. in 1810, m. Henry B. Livingston, Esq. His farm on Harlem Lane, with the new mansion built west of the Lane, descended to his chn., who were John L., Edmund, Robert, and Nicholas G. Kortright; Eliza, m. Nicholas Cruger, and Hester-Mary, who m. Billop B. Seaman.

LOW.

LAURENS JANSEN, b. in Holland in 1651, and anc. of the Low family of H., was the youngest son of Jan Bastiaensen, whose two elder sons bore the name of Kortright. For notices of their emigration see pp. 74, 106, 227, 288; other references to Laurens after he established himself at H. may be found in subsequent pages. His share of the De Meyer lands, bought jointly with his br. Cornelis, laid the foundation for the ample estate he acquired here; but which, with his gd-sons, passed out of the name. His election as an overseer, in 1677, and repeatedly afterward, and the other responsible duties intrusted to him, evince the respect in which he was held. In the division of the De Meyer lands, Laurens took lot No. 2 on Jochem Pieters Flat, No. 6 on Van Keulen's Hook, the two north gardens, or orchard, and the two *erven*, on one of which the new chh. was built in 1686. To said Lot 6, on which he afterward built, he added the lower half of No. 5 (rated at 2 *morgen*), by purchase from Paulus Richard, Nov. 17, 1677. See note, p. 379. He drew 61 a. in the several divisions, for which see App. J. Prior to 1715 he sold No. 4, 2d Div., to Joh. Benson, and conveyed the orchard to Peter van Oblienis, tho last the plot which passed to Peter Waldron, and since owned by James Chesterman, who built thereon the Chesterman house still standing. Laurens m., in 1672, Mary, dr. of Albert Heymans Roosa, of Esopus. See p. 436. On Apl. 13, 1706, she and Laurens joined in the sale of her father's estate to her br. Arien Roosa. Laurens Jansen d. in 1727. His chn. were Annetie, b. 1674, who m. Gysbert Bogert; Albert, b. 1676; Wyntie, b. 1679; Neeltie, b. 1682, who m. Conrad Lamberts; John, b. 1685; Gysbert, b. 1687; Belitie, b. 1693, and Lawrence, b. 1698. Of Gysbert we know nothing further. The other sons took the name of *Low*. Albert m., in 1702, Susannah, dr. of John Delamater, and with his br. John removed to Somerset Co., N. J. Having served as a deacon at Raritan, Albert d. in 1739, leaving his farm to his sons *Abraham* and *Cornelius*. His dr. *Mary* m. Pettinger. John Low m. in 1707, Jannetie Corsson, and in 1721 was a deacon at North Branch.

Lawrence Low, m., on June 12, 1725, Jannetie, dr. of Marinus Roelofs van Vleckeren (whence Fluckra and Flack), of Bloomingdale. He succeeded to his *fa.*'s lands at H., as we have described them, and which his br. Albert, as heir-at-law, released to him Dec. 8, 1731. On May 22, 1732, he sold to wid. Maria Myer his lot and a half (now called 9 a.), on Van Keulen's Hook, and built upon his Lot 15 of 1691, on the Heights, where he was living May 9, 1738, when he and his w. conveyed Lot No. 2, Jochem Pieters Flat, to Isaac Myer. Low also made several considerable purchases; in 1737 he bought Lot No. 10 of the division of 1691, to which in 1747 he added the upper half of the adjoining Lot 9, laid out to Delavall, and called "the 33 *morgen* lot" (this half, with No. 10, forming the tract since of Samuel Bradhurst); and also half of Delavall's No. 9, 4th Div. Low made his will Nov. 25, 1754, which was proved Nov. 4, 1755, and by which his wid. was to enjoy his estate during her life. But ten years before her d., which happened in 1772, in her 70th yr., her two sons made a formal division of the property, and sold some of it, whence it would appear that they had acquired the interests of their mo. and sr. The chn. of Lawrence Low were *Dinah*, *Marinus*, and *John*. The first, b. 1730, m. Jacobus Tourneur, of Haverstraw.

On the division of the lands by Marinus and John, Feb. 2, 1762, embracing, as at their fa.'s d., 149 a., Marinus took the 73 a. in Lots 9 and 10 of 1691, with No. 16, 1st Div., and No. 5, 3d Div. He conveyed to John No. 15 of 1691, being the homestead, Nos. 20 and 21, 1st Div., and No. 11 and ½ of 9, 4th Div. Marinus Low, b. 1734, m., in 1754, Deborah, dr. of John Oblinus. Having given sundry mortgages on his lands, he sold out, in 1766, to John Maunsell, Esq., afterward Lieut.-General in the British army. His br., John Low, m., in 1765, Bridget, dr. of Adolph Myer. He added considerably to his lands; including No. 4, 2d Div., 17 a., originally of his gd-fa. Low, and which had passed from the Bensons to Joh. Myer. He also bought No. 1, 2d Div., 41 a., and No. 16, Last Div., 51 a. But he, too, sold out, in and between the yrs. 1762 and 1767; his No. 11, 4th Div., to Jacob Dyckman, Lot 15 of 1691 to John Dykman, No. 1, 2d Div., to Benj. Waldron, Sen., and Nos. 20, 21, 1st Div., No. 4, 2d Div., ½ of 9, 4th Div., and No. 16, Last Div., to John Watkins. Thus within a few yrs. after getting possession, the brs. Low had disposed of all their lands here. In 1770 they kept a public-house at Freshwater, in the suburbs of the city. This family must be distinguished from another of the same name, to which it bore no relationship, that of Ulster Co., named p. 203; members of which also lived in N. Y. and N. J. It is indeed difficult to separate the two after the one left Harlem, and in regard to the latter family we should welcome further information.

MONTANYE.

ABRAM DE LA MONTANIE, — he so wrote his name, — claims a separate notice here as one of the patentees; though representing only a lesser branch of this numerous family, of which more extended notes will be found in Appendix B. The prefix *De La*, adopted by all the sons of Dr. Johannes La Montagne, was more generally retained, perhaps, by his desc. of this branch, than of any other, but still was so far common to all of the name, and yet so generally treated as of doubtful utility, — to be used or omitted at pleasure, — that it becomes a very unreliable means of identity. See note, p. 120.

Abram Delamontanie, b. in 1664, and but eight yrs. of age when his fa. John, d., was the only son that remained at H. He was bred a weaver, and afterward gave instruction in that handicraft to other young men of the town. He m. in 1689, Rebecca, eldest dr. of Theunis Idens van Huyse, of Bloomingdale, and by the d. of his mo. soon after, near the close of that yr., succeeded to her house and lot in the village. His rights as a patentee were by virtue of this freehold; and upon this he drew, in 1691, lot No. 23, five *morgen*, which in the deed given by the town Mar. 21, 1701, is described as follows:

> There is set off to Abraham de La Montanie, (for the right of one *erf*,) a piece of land lying west of the King's way, bounded against the Harlem limits to a steep rock standing in the run, upon it four rods northerly a small maple tree of Metje Cornelis; and southerly on along the King's way to a run where the King's way passes over.

This piece of land, now within Central Park, lay opposite to and below the old McGown place, stretching along the west side of the road from 99th to 104th Street, or thereabouts, and upon its southern end afterward stood the *Black Horse Tavern*, of Revolutionary notoriety. The west side of this grant lay in proximity to the lands of his fa.-in-law, Theunis Idens. Samuel Waldron, in 1712, had drawn No. 7 in 1st Div., which was in two parts, one of nearly 10 a., being identical with the McGown place aforesaid; the other, some 2½ a., lying opposite, west of the road, between Delamontanie's grant above described, and a lot laid out to the Delavall heirs, and later included in the Nutter farm. Delamontanie, by an exchange, added Waldron's lot to his own, giving Waldron his drafts in 2d, 3d, and 4th Div. His lot in 1st Div., No. 17, containing 3 a. 1 q. 24 r., lay on the hill about 145th Street, on the east side of Kingsbridge Road. He sold this to Barent Waldron, from whom it passed with his farm, in 1740, to John B. Myer, and from him to Abm. Myer; being the piece improperly described as in "first *fourth* division," and which experts even have been puzzled to locate. Delamontanie's lands in H. continued to be rated at 20 a. On June 22, 1720, his fa.-in-law conveyed to him and his w. an eighth part of his farm, said part being 57½ a., running in a strip from near Delamontanie's land north-westerly to Hudson River.*

There is not a circumstance to show that Abraham Delamontanie ever set up any claim to the lands sold and conveyed by his parents to Bogert: but he early conceived the idea, drawn apparently from some clause in his fa.'s will, as well as the tenor of the deed to Bogert, that said deed merely conveyed the Point and meadows attached, but did not carry the *morgen right*, or a share in the undivided common lands. This gave rise to the following letter:

N. Haarlem, 5 Decemb. 1700.

To the Overseers of *N. Haarlem.*

Honorable Sirs,

Abram de Lamontanie, inhabitant of this town, inquires of your Honors, whether you or your predecessors have laid out any ground or land for the deed of John de La Montanie, deceased, which deed is remaining on the records of this town, and dated 8 February 1671.

ABRAM DE LA MONTANIE.

To this, two days after, the following reply was given:

N. Haarlem, 7 Decem. 1700.

WE, Laurens Jansen, Jacques Tourneur and Peter Van Oblienis, Overseers of N. Haarlem, having read the writing of the 5 Decemb., 1700, sent to us by Abram de La Montanie, think proper to answer that the

* THEUNIS IDENS, as his autograph is, but also called Theunis Eldese van Huyse, has been noticed as the owner of a large farm between 89th and 107th Sts., on the North River side. He was b. in 1639, probably in Holland, being son of Iden van Huyse, by his w. Tryntie Jacobs, afterward m. to Jacob Helliker (or Hellaker), alias Swart, who has desc. of both names. Theunis spent his early life on Long Island. A curious account of him there and after he came to N. Y. is given by Dankers and Sluyter—of his reckless youth and his reformation. He became a chh. mem. June 17, 1680. When and from whom he purchased at Bloomingdale is not ascertained; the line between his land and Harlem patent was run in 1690, the town paying 24 gl. toward the survey. In his old age Theunis had his farm laid off by Peter Berrien into lots of 57½ acres each, being in breadth 42 rods, or thereabouts, at the river and rear, and numbered 1 to 8, from south to north. On June 22 and 23, 1720, he and w. Jannetie (dr. of Thys van Pelt), conveyed these several parcels to their chn., as follows (giving possession, after the ancient usage, "by turf and twig"): No. 8 to their son-in-law, Abraham Delamontanie, and his w. aforesaid; Nos. 6, 7, to their son-in-law, George Dyckman, m. to their youngest dr., Catalina; Nos. 4, 5, to their son, Eide van Huyse; No 3, and ½ of 2, to their son-in-law, Myndert Burger van Evera, m. to their dr. Sarah; and No. 1 and ½ of No. 2, to their son-in-law, Marinus Roelofse van Vleckeren, m. to their dr. Dinah. Of these lots, Nos. 1 to 5 were owned subsequently by Charles Ward Apthorpe, and Nos. 6 to 8 were held many years by the Dikemans, desc. of Joris Dyckman. To his dr. Maria, m. to Jurien Rynchout, Theunis gave the farm noticed p. 506.

before named La Montanie may examine whether he can obtain any advantage from the deed which John Louwe Bogert shall get from our hands. Also, he can then take a copy thereof. . Witness

ABR: VERMEULE, *Secretary.*

It was a disturbing question to Bogert, who had drawn lot No. 25. adjoining his farm, and which now seemed to be menaced. Not to rely wholly on the deed given him Mar. 21, 1701, he took occasion to fortify himself by another from Joost van Oblinus, the surviving Nicolls patentee, dated Feb. 14, 1702, and still another from the town trustees, Sept. 14, 1706, soon after which he sold out to Benson. The question was not put to issue during the lifetime of the latter, but enough of uncertainty hung over it to make Benson unwilling to pay quit rent on that part of his farm. After Samson Benson came in possession, Delamontanie entered an action of ejectment in the Supreme Court of the Province, Oct. 5, 1723, which came to trial at New York, Nov. 29, following, in the name of *John Simson*, "on the demise of Montanye," *against Samson Benson.* Lewis Morris, Chief Justice, and Robert Walters, Second Justice, presided. The best counsel were employed on both sides. Defendant confessed lease, entry, and ouster.* Delamontanie had clothed himself with due power in the premises, by deeds obtained from his elder br. John, and several other of the co-heirs. These and various public records and writings were read, including the proceedings of the freeholders, the agreements subscribed to, and rules adopted, for the division of the common lands. A number of witnesses were also sworn. Mr. Abraham Gouverneur acted as interpreter, *ex parte*, for the prosecution. Mr. Edward Blagge, Zacharias Sickels, and Johannes Waldron were called to testify for plaintiff, and Peter van Oblienis, Samuel Waldron, and Barent Waldron, for defendant. But Delamontanie failed to make out a title, and the jury found for the defendant. This was final, and we hear no more of the matter.

In 1729 Abraham sold out to his br.-in-law, George Dyckman, who owned an adjoining part of the Van Huyse farm. See note on Bloomingdale *Dyckmans*, p. 505. Abraham was

* This presupposes that Montanye had forcibly entered, or by a legal fiction was held to have so entered upon the land; that he had given Simson a *lease* and *entry* of the premises; and that Simson had thereupon been *ousted* by Benson. All this taking place, entitled Simson, as Delamontanie's tenant, to his action of ejectment. To avoid being non-suited, Benson must have applied to be made a defendant, which could only be allowed upon condition that he comply with a rule of court to confess at the trial of the cause, the *lease*, *entry*, and *ouster*, as aforesaid, these making three of the four requisites for the maintenance of the plaintiff's action, and which being done the trial stood solely upon the merits of the *title*. (*Blackstone.*)

living Jan. 16, 1734, having a second w. named p. 593. His grave, as believed, was in the old cemetery, beneath a rude stone inscribed A. L. M., Feb. 12, 173½. His chn. were John, Teunis, Isaac, Jacob, Ide, Jannetie, who m. 1715, David Devoor, Maria, m. 1714, John Buss, and Hannah, m. 1727, John Buys, and 1732, Andries Albody, *alias* Anderson, she having by Buys, chn. Matthew, called *Boice*, and Rebecca, w. of John Dikeman, and by Anderson, sons Abraham, Elias, and John. A marked taste for the sea and relative pursuits is noticed among the desc. of Abm. Delamontanie. His son Jacob was a blockmaker in N. Y., some of his kinsmen, the Pells, being shipbuilders at the Smith's Fly.* Isaac, then (1738) lived near his brs.-in-law, Devoor and Albody, at Turtle Bay, noted for its shipyards, in which he was probably employed.

Teunis Delamontagnie, b. 1695, bought a place in H. village, in 1719, having m. the yr. previous; see pp. 487, 498. He and Ide were living in Somerset co. in 1731; the latter had sons Abraham and Ede, or Edward, who bore arms in the Revolution. In 1735, Teunis owned 100 a. in Franklin township, and had a second w., Rebecca. He seems to have returned to N. Y., where in 1751, his dr. Bregie m. Peter Zenger, son of the famous printer. There are reasons for believing that the fa. of Teunis, Robert, Joseph, and William Delamontagnie, all, except Robert, mem. of the N. Y. Marine Soc., and shipmasters in the Bermuda and W. I. trade, was an older son of Teunis. But unfortunately neither his worthy desc., living in N. Y., nor the parish registers of Bermuda, where he resided when his chn. were born, are able to tell us any more about the fa. of these brave "toilers on the sea." William was b. June 27, 1750, and joined the Marine Soc. in 1774. His drs. Mrs. Woodward and Mrs. Asson, of Phila., still survive. Teunis, b. Jan. 17, 1744, m. 1771, Sarah, dr. of Edward Nicoll, named p. 600, and the next year was admitted to the Marine Soc., but d. prior to 1783. Capt. Joseph Delamontagnie, b. in Bermuda, Nov. 10, 1747, d. in N. Y., Apl. 16, 1820. His w. was Elizabeth, dr. of Teunis Tiebout; his chn., Sarah, b. Oct. 7, 1785, who m. Rev. Wm. Gray; Anna, b. Mar. 24, 1787, m. Wm. J. Crolius: William, b. Nov. 11, 1788, the veteran boatbuilder, of Water Street, d. June 15, 1877, sons William, John, Joseph E. and Albert; Edward, b. May 5, 1792, boatbuilder, d. Mar. 19, 1872, sons Robert and Alexander; Elizabeth, b. Dec. 27, 1794, d. in inf.; and Joseph, b. Jan. 6, 1797, d. Sept. 23, 1820, leaving no issue.

* JOHN PELL and his brs. William, Thomas, and Samuel, of N. Y., were sons of Samuel, of Harlem, ship-carpenter, named p. 338, etc., who was from London. Thomas was fa.-in-law of said Jacob Delamontagnie.

Jacob Delamontagnie, blockmaker, m. in 1729, Maria Pell. He was one of the city firemen, appointed in 1738, all "strong, able, discreet, honest, and sober men." He had sons Abraham, b. 1734, and Thomas, 1736. The last d. Dec. 18, 1791.

Abraham Delamontagnie, as he called himself, took the trade of his fa. Jacob, a blockmaker. He was admitted to freemanship in 1769, and also to honorary membership in the Marine Soc. He m. in 1755, Mary, dr. of Jacob Remson, of Brooklyn, and ultimately became a "vintner," or innkeeper, in which he was engaged in 1769, his house being near the Commons, and then and thereafter a famous resort for the "Liberty Boys." It was probably the same place, "opposite the Green, near the Bridewell," or, to exactly locate it, at the corner of Broadway and Murray Street, where he leased, Mar. 25, 1773, five lots of ground from Trinity Church, for 99 yrs. Abraham did a good thing for his heirs, but he himself d. the very next yr., aged only 40, and on Oct. 17, 1774, letters of administration were taken out by his wid. She continued the house, 253 Broadway, m. in 1777, John Amory, whipmaker, and d. in 1797, in her 66th yr.

Jacob Delamontagnie, b. Sept. 15, 1765, is understood to have been the only son of Abraham and Mary, and is remembered as one of the best of men. He studied law, opening an office at 9 Beekman St., but removed before his mo. d. to 253 Broadway. He had m. Mary Elizabeth, dr. of Capt. John Armour, shipmaster. In 1792 he was lieut. and adjt. of the 1st N. Y. Regt., was ald. much of the time from 1796 to 1806, and in 1798 mem. of assembly. The 99 yr. lease being sold in 1812, Jacob was one of three purchasers, but sold out, 1817, to Benj. Ferris and Amos Butler. He d. at his residence in Beaver Street, Apl. 9, 1823, without chn., and leaving large legacies to mem. of the Armour and Moore families, beside providing amply for his w., Mary E. Delamontagnie. She survived him twenty-five yrs., and d. at Belleville, N. J. For a portrait of Mr. Delamontagnie, see *Doc. Hist. N. Y.*, iv., 1024.

MYER.

Adolph Meyer, the anc. of the Myer family of H. (whose name, at first pronounced *Mayer*, has changed its sound as well as form), emigrated, as before noticed, from Ulsen, a parish of Bentheim, in the German province of Westphalia. He arrived at H. in 1661, where he gained a good standing; and in 1671 m. Maria, dr. of Johannes Verveelen. Three yrs. later he united with the chh., his w. having done the same some months before. At their m., Verveelen gave them the two out-gardens,

Nos. 7, 8, with most of the land in the Hanel patent, the rest being promised, and the patent eventually transferred to Meyer, Oct. 13, 1683. Meyer sold the lot on Montanye's Flat, Jan. 28, 1673. Adrianus Jansen van Westerhout built him a house 25 by 18 feet, with a leanto; the contract dated Aug. 18, 1675. It cost 300 gl., as appeared at their settlement Jan. 6, 1676. Meyer bought the Demarest lot, No. 5, on Jochem Pieters, Aug. 1, 1677. On Sept. 4, 1679, he and John Delamater leased for 10 yrs. the Slot lands on Van Keulen's Hook, with house lots, garden and meadows; but just before the lease expired Meyer, whose house and barn had been burnt, stating to his fa.-in-law that he wished to build a new barn, but was afraid of another accident, as he and Joost van Oblinus were living so near; Verveelen sold him the Slot patent, June 3, 1689, for 300 gl., "silver money or in wheat as silver," Meyer engaging, should Verveelen die before receiving the money, to pay Daniel Verveelen and his sr. Anna their respective shares of 1000 gl. each. Meyer no doubt met his engagements, as he continued in possession, and later, Daniel released to his sr., Mrs. Meyer, all his interests at H., by deeds of June 12, 1710, and June 30, 1712; in the latter expressly including all "the right and property of Johannes Verveelen deceased, by reason of his being patentee of said town and patent." The Hanel and Slot patents laid the foundation of the large Myer estates.*

* The HANEL patent is unrecorded, and I am but too well convinced that the original (in fragments when I saw it) has perished. Luckily a copy was taken which saves to us the text of this ancient Dutch grant:

WY PETRUS STUYVESANT, Directeur-Generael ende RAEDEN, wegens de Ho: Mo: Heere Staten Generael der vereenighde Nederlanden, syn Hoogheyt van Oranjie, ende Edele Heere Bewinthebberen der geoctroyeerde West Indien Compagnie, in Nieuw Nederlant residerende, oirkonde en verclaren mits deesen, dat wy, op hurden dato ondergeschreeven, hebben toegestaen en vergunt aen JURIAEN HANEL, resident van het eylant van Manhatans, en in de dorp *Nieuw Haerlem*, een parceel lant gelegen op Van Keulen's Hook, geteykent No. 4, suylen wederzyde zuyden, breet twaelf roeden, groot drie morgen; alzo een stuck op Jochem Pietersen's Lant, tusschen Hendrick Carsense en Jan Le Roy, suylen wederzyden west wel so noordelyk, breet sestien roeden, groot ses morgen vier hondert roeden: alzo een stuck lant op Montagne's Lant, geteykent No. 7, breet seven en twintigh roeden, vier en een half voeten, suylen van de kil tot het gebergte west, groot vyf morgen en vier hondert roeden: een erf bezuyden Montagne, langh seven roeden negen voeten, breet seven roeden ses en een half voeten; item een thuyn bewesten Jan Pietersen, beoosten Nicolaes de Meyer, breet vyf roeden, langh twintigh roeden; item een stuck valey geteykent No. 5, gemeen met Lubbert Gerritsen, synde het noordelyk streek tot eylant by 't Springh, als mede het noordelyk streek in de Groot Valey. Met expressererde conditie ende voorwaarde dat hy Juriaen Hanel, of die uyt krachte deses syn actie macht genomen, de Ed: Heeren Bewinthebberen voornaemde voor syn heeren en patroonen sal erkennen, onder de souvereigniteyt van hare Hooge Moogende

Mr. Meyer often held office in the town, was asst. ald. of the Out Ward, 1693–95; also served as an elder. Between 1691 and 1701, chosen with others for that purpose, he had much to do with the first allotment of the common land under the Dongan patent, and signed the deeds. The first four lots in that allotment embraced that part of Harlem Flats which lay north of the Samson A. Benson line, and extended up between the two roads to the point or forks at 131st Street. See list of these lots in App. J. Myer drew lot No. 4, at the forks, in conjunction with his son Johannes, who owned a 7½ *morgen right* upon the lots on Van Keulen's Hook, which came from his gd.-fa. Verveelen. Here, at the fork of the roads, Adolph or Johannes built a substantial stone house, as early as 1706. Mr. Meyer d. in February, 1711. By will made the 13th of that month, he left the use of his property to his wid. To his gd.-sons named for him he gave each a pair of gold buttons, and to his gd.-drs. named for his wife, each a gold ring. His chn. were Johannes, Hendrick, Anna-Catrina, Maria, Abraham, Isaac, Jacob, Adolph, and Anneke. Of these Anneke, b. 1698, m. Johannes Sickels and Thomas Storms; Maria, b. 1679, m. Samson Benson; and Anna-Catrina, b. in 1677, m. Abraham Lent. See *Annals of Newtown*, p. 317. Anna-Catrina's name, derived from the Verveelens, is yet worthily borne by desc. of her gd.-dr. Anna-Catrina Riker; an example of the almost religious adherence, in our Dutch families, to the ancestral christian names.

The Myer estate was much increased, both by purchase and by the drafts from the common lands, before Mrs. Meyer d., which was not till 1748. We except the Delavall lands, the bulk of which

de Heeren Staaten Generael, en hier haren Directeur ende Raeden en alles gehoorzamen als goede ingezetenen schuldig syn te doen, mits hem wyders onderwerpende al sulcke lasten ende gerechticheden, als by de Ed: Heeren reets is beraemt ofte noch te bemeemen; Constitueerende oversulcx den voornoemden Juriaen Hanel in onze staet reele en actueele possessie vant voornoemde parceel lants, hem gevende mits desen volkomen macht, authoriteyt, ende speciael bevel, omme t voorschreeven lant te moogen aenvaerden, bebouwen, bewoonen ende gebruycken, gelyck hy met andere syne patrimoniale landen ende effecten doen soude moogen, sonder dat wy cedenten inde qualite als vooren, daer aen eenige part actie oft gerech int minste meer syn hebben te reserveren oft behouden, maer ten behoeve als vooren, van alles te desisteren, van nu en voor eeuwigh, beloovende voorts dit transpoort vast, bondich, onverbreckelyk ende irrevocabel te behouden, naer te komen ende te volbrengen, alles onder t verbont naer rechten daer toestaende. 'tOirkonde is desen by ons geteeckent en met segel bevestight; actum int Fort Amsterdam in Nieuw Nederlant, 16 May, 1664.

P. STUYVESANT.

Ter Ordonnantie van den E: Hr: Dr Generael
ende Hooge Raeden van Nieuw Nederlant, etc.

CORNELIS VAN RUYVEN, *Secretaris.*

were bought by the Myers, but held separate from the common inheritance. Adolph Meyer's will was proved Sept. 2, 1748, after the d. of the wid., but when his chn. were all yet living, and by whom a final division of the property was made Nov. 15, 1748, and deeds passed. How the lands were parcelled out will be shown as we speak of the sons respectively; here we need only mention that Benj. Benson, gd-son of Adolph Meyer, succeeding to his mo.'s share, took 35 a., which included Lots 7, 8, 9, Van Keulen's Hook; and another gd-son, Johannes Sickels, intended by his uncle Myer as his sole heir, received said uncle's portion, to wit: No. 3, Jochem Pieters, No. 40, 2d Div., and No. 14, 4th Div., as also the remaining north garden, which Sickels sold July 1, 1758, to John Livingston. No. 2, Jochem Pieters, and No. 6, ½ of 5, Van Keulen's Hook, he took under Isaac's will. Isaac Myer, b. 1684, purchased from Gideon and Bernardus Verveelen in 1710, jointly with his br. Jacob, a tract of land in Bergen Co., N. J., Jacob selling him his share in 1743. By his will, dated Sept. 12, 1743, he gave "all his lands in the provinces of N. Y. and N. J." to his nephew Johannes Sickels. He could have left no chn.; maybe he was called "widower Myer." It would appear that he lived with Sickels, on the lower street, I think on the old Laurens Jansen place, at the north end of No. 6, V. K. H., the lots attached to which, ½ 5, 6, his mo. bought of Lawrence Low in 1732, and conveyed to Isaac in 1735. Low sold him No. 2, J. P., in 1738. But it is singular that Isaac's name never occurs in the tax lists.

Hendrick Myer, b. 1673, removed to N. Y., m. Wyntie, dr. of John Ray, and had by her ten chn., half or more of which d. in inf. or childhood. His eldest son *Adolph*, b. 1701, d. unm. Oct. 7, 1732. *Henricus*, b. 1713, m. Maria, dr. of Abraham Gouverneur; they parted; he, discarded by Mr. Gouverneur, d. Dec. 15, 1740, without surviving issue; his wid., who was a gd-dr. of Capt. Jacob Leisler, m., in 1742, Capt. Jasper Farmer. *John Ray Myer*, the youngest ch. of Hendrick, and b. 1710, m., in 1747, Anna, dr. of Charles Crommelin, of N. Y., where Myer became a wealthy merchant, and having outlived his second w. (Helena Rutgers, wid. of Hon. John Morin Scott), and attained to near 90 yrs., as one who knew him informed us, d. Aug. 31, 1807. He had a son, Henry R. Myer, of N. Y., merchant, 1774, and two drs., Ann, who m., 1760, Thomas Sowers, of N. Y., "Capt. of Engineers in His Majesty's service," who d. 1774, and Mary, who m., 1772, Henry Bowers, Jr., of Swansea, Mass. Mrs. Bowers inherited her fa's estate under his will. Hendrick Myer, the elder, bought the farm of Barent Waldron, Gloudie's Point; but the deed, dated Aug. 6, 1740, was made in the name of his son John (or properly John R.) aforesaid. He sold it July 21, 1743, to his uncle Abraham, who bought it for his son Arent Myer, and to whom Abraham gave a deed March 21, 1747.* Hendrick Myer d. in N. Y., Oct. 31, 1753, æ. 80 yrs.

Jacob Myer, b. 1686, m. Anna, dr. of his cousin Hendrick Cammega, and settled at Closter, Bergen Co., N. J., where, losing his w., he m. secondly, in 1725, Rachel Baton. Jacob was a purchaser of some of the Delavall lands in 1747. His sons were *Adolph*, b. Mar. 20, 1720; *Jacob*, b. ——, 1726; and John, b. Dec. 21, 1728. Adolph m. at Closter, and had a family, but John romoved to Fishkill.

Adolph Myer, b. 1692, m., 1716, Margaret, dr. of Joh. Waldron, and, secondly, in 1723, Catharine, dr. of Peter Haring. He had four sons and five drs., viz.: *Adolph*, *John*, *Isaac*, *Peter*, *Ann*, who m. William Waldron, *Margaret*, who m. John Sickels, *Mary*, who m. Benjamin Vandowater, *Bregie*, who m. John Low, and *Sarah*, who m. Elias Degrush, Jr., rope-maker. Of these, Peter, b. 1729, m. Mary Bunn in 1762, and had issue, Adolph, b. 1763, etc. Adolph, senior, made his first purchase of land in 1715, when he bought from Samson Benson Lot No. 2 of 1691, his fa., as we have seen, having drawn No. 4 of the same tract. Adolph eventually acquired Nos. 1, 3; as also the several parcels beyond the highway to the westward, originally Nos. 8 to 14, 1st Div., laid out to Capt. Delavall's heirs and others, and forming the 84 a. tract, afterward sold, with Lot 3, etc., by his son Adolph, to Charles Duryee, and purchased soon after by William Molenaor. To specify: Adolph bought several lots in the 84 a. tract in 1733 (see p. 499), and in 1740, No. 14, from John Lewis. He had already built on his No. 2 of 1601, and in 1717 bought No. 3 from Aaron Bussing. In 1748 he got from his mo.'s estate No. 16, 3d Div., and by prearrangement with Abraham, No. 1 of 1601, which gave him Nos.

* The *Glaudie Point Title* has its beginnings set forth on pp. 442, 443. Barent Waldron drew, in 1691, a piece of land between his Point and lot No. 10, which in his deed of Mar. 21, 1701, is thus described: "There is set off to Barent Waldron, for 4 morgen, more or less, a piece of land north of his house lot (*erf*), east of the King's Way; saving that a suitable road remain along the swamp (*creupelbosch*), to the meadow of Isaac Delamater, as the fence at present stands."*

The Bussing Point farm was therefore made up of five parcels, viz.: the Point, and adjoining tract above described, with lots 10, 9, and ½ of 8 of the New Lots. See account of *Johannes Waldron*. This is exclusive of Barent Waldron's drafts in the Four Divisions and the lot 17, 1st Div., lying on the hill, "four acres more or less," which he got of Abm. Delamontanie. Barent owned No. 3, 1691 (late Molenaor 17 a. tract), bought of his br. Samuel prior to 1715, and not sold with the farm, 1740, but apparently to Aaron Bussing, 1746, who sold, 1747, to Adolph Myer.

* In making the four divisions in 1712, all the lots embraced in this farm enjoyed the *morgen right*, and drew of the common land, except this single piece, which, as drafted land, bore no such right; a curious distinction.

1, 2, 3 in that tract. These lands, excepting the "homestead," or Lots 1, 2, of 1691, fell to *Adolph* 3d under his fa's will, dated May 10, 1760, and proved May 5, 1762. To these he added Nos. 9, 10, 1st Div., and some other parcels. His br. *John* succeeded to the homestead, 28 a., and m. in 1761, Antie Waldron, but d. in 1767, leaving his wid. with chn. Adolph, Catharine, and Mary. On Aug. 10, 1768, his br. Adolph, as executor, sold the homestead (the rights of dower having been released) to Rev. Martinus Schoonmaker, then pastor at H. *Adolph Myer* was an elder at H., and signed the articles of union in 1772 which healed the divisions in the Dutch chh. He occupied his lands, aforesaid, till the Revolution, when, being a Whig, he retired to Dutchess Co., and, at the close of the war, concluding to remain there, traded farms, May 1, 1784, with Charles Duryee, of N. Y., merchant; as shown by the deed from Duryee to Myer, for his lands in Rombout Precinct, given, as it states, "by virtue of a mutual exchange of farms;" the fact of said exchange being also corroborated by the late Simeon De Witt.*

Abraham Myer, b. 1682, m. Engeltie, dr. of Arent Harmans Bussing. On Aug. 12, 1713, he bought from John van Oblienis Lot No. 1 Jochem Pieters, with the one morgen houselot attached, both owned originally by Daniel Tourneur. This be-

* William Molenaor, in some records called *Miller*, this being the English of his name, was a desc. of Joost Adriaens Molenaer, who was b. at Pynacker, a village three miles east of Delft, and came to this country in the ship Faith, which sailed from Amsterdam, Dec. 23 1660. At Esopus, where he went to live, he m., May 20., 1663, Femmetie Hendricks, from Meppel. On June 7, ensuing, the Indians rose against the white settlers and killed and wounded many, carrying others into captivity, among whom was Molenaer's w. She was soon ransomed, and a yr. later their first ch., Marritie, was b. Joost m. a second w., Lysbeth, dr. of Willem Krom, Oct. 28, 1668, having first, on Sept. 2, made his will. By this w. he had issue, Jane, b. 1672, who m. Jellis de la Grange, of Albany, Adrian, b. 1675, William, 1678, and Henry, 1681. He served as deacon, and from 1672 to 1678 as schepen. On July 9, 1681, he m. his third w., Maria, dr. of Jacob Hayes, and wid. of Philip Leeuw, or Lyon. By this w. he had a dr. Sarah, b. 1682. Removing to a farm in Bushwick, of 50 a., he and his w. joined the chh. at N. Y., May 30, 1683, but he d. that same yr. (his will being admitted to probate at Kingston, Oct. 17, 1683), and the next yr. his wid. m. Capt. Peter Praa. See *Annals of Newtown*, p. 382, and *Stiles' Brooklyn*, II., 321, etc. Adrian Molenaer m. at Kingston, in 1700, Anna de la Grange. Did he not settle on the Raritan? William Molenaer m., 1704, Gertrude, dr. of Caspar and Maria Springsteen, and d. in Newtown, "an aged man," May 11, 1753. His son David, who m. Catherine Meserole, was the fa. of William Molenaor, b. 1754, the first of the name at H. The latter, then living in Bushwick, bought the Adolph Myer farm, Apl. 1, 1790. He d. in 1812, leaving by his w., Mercy, issue, David, William, DeWitt C., and Catharine, w. of Charles W. Gordon. Dr. William Molenaor, long a practitioner at H., m. but left no chn.; his brs. have desc. We remember the old Molenaor house, while yet standing, but in ruins. It stood in a hollow, on the north side of 124th Street, 200 feet west of 8th Ave.

came Abraham's home. In 1715 he had acquired 85 a., which included No. 1 of 1691, late Thomas Tourneur's, with Jan Nagel's 1st Div., and half of his drafts in 2d, 3d, and 4th Div. In 1722 he bought from Nagel 11 a. on Jochem Pieters, and from Zach. Sickels, No. 4, 1st Div. In 1731 he bought Nos. 5, 10, Jochem Pieters, and No. 12, 2d Div., from Nich. Kortright; and probably at this date exchanged with his mo. No. 1, 1691, for No. 4, Jochem Pieters. Before 1748 he had evidently anticipated by possession what land was due him from his mo. Subsequently buying another lot on Jochem Pieters, he held, under Nos. 5, 7, 10, lying together, and then called 40 a. (see App. E.) the tract later known as "the homestead farm of Lawrence Benson," containing 42 a., 2 q., 10 r., the title to which, after six years' litigation, was settled by the Supreme Court of the United States, Jan. 19, 1863. Mr. Myer was appointed clerk of the town, May 11, 1747. He made his will Apl. 3, 1754, which was proved Feb. 18, 1756. He had five chn., viz.: *Abraham, Arent, Susannah, Maria*, and *Eve*. Of the drs. I believe Maria was m. to John Dykman, and Susannah to Peter Bussing. Mr. Myer had also purchased from Nich. Kortright, June 11, 12, 1740, for his eldest son Abraham, 40 acres of the old Tourneur farm, on Montanye's Flat, with some meadow east of the creek, and Lot 18, 2d Div. He had also provided for his younger son Arent, as we have seen, by the purchase, in 1743, of the Gloudie Point farm, of which Arent took immediate possession. The latter m. Susannah, dr. of Lawrence Kortright, and had two drs., Engeltie, who m. Peter Waldron, and Margaret, who m. Abraham Bussing. The last were m. by license, and Bussing's bondsman was no less a person than George Clinton, afterward Governor. By Arent Myer's will, made Nov. 23, 1773, and proved Sept. 21, 1784, he left half his estate to his gd-chn., Arent and Susannah Bussing, and half to his gd-dr. Susannah Waldron.

Abraham Myer, br. of Arent, was b. in 1716, and m. Mattie Kortright, sr. of Arent's w. He succeeded to his fa.'s lands, having sold his farm on Montanye's Flat. See p. 499. Abraham served as deacon. He d. in 1772, his w. Mattie surviving, and also five chn., viz.: Abraham, Lawrence, Margaret, Engeltie, and Bregie. The first three, with the wid. and executor Adolph Myer, conveyed the 42-acre tract, Apl. 20, 1773, to John Bogert, Jr., whose heirs sold it to Lawrence Benson. Abraham's son, Abraham, a weaver, m. Agnietie Boome, in 1771, and Lawrence m. in 1765, Engeltie, dr. of Samuel Waldron. The latter, a blacksmith, was fa. to Samuel Myer, carpenter, who m. Mary, dr. of Capt. John Waldron, and ultimately removed to Claverack, being fa. to the late Abraham Myer. These were the last of the family to occupy the ancient stone house, removed by Judge Ingraham when 125th Street was opened, the well remaining on the south side of the street, and in use till within a few yrs. This house stood on the Tourneur home-lot, bought by Abm. Myer in 1713, and which Samuel sold to Alexander Phœnix, Mar. 27, 1806, with the old church lot joining it on the easterly side; his fa. Lawrence holding that the fee of the last named lot (whereon the first chh. had stood) was in *his* fa. Abraham Myer, and passed by devise to his chn. These two lots have since formed the Eliphalet Williams plot. There was a house of later construction on the adjoining farm lot, probably built by Johannes De Witt before the Revolution, which was burnt in 1811, and on whose site Nathaniel G. Ingraham erected the present Judge Ingraham house.

Johannes Myer, b. 1671, m. Tryntie, dr. of Capt. Jan van Dalsen,* and became a large landholder; his first acquisition being a share of Lot No. 4, in the Div. of 1691, drawn in

* Capt. JAN GERRITSEN VAN DALSEN, elsewhere called *de Vries* (see pp. 103, 263), was a ship carpenter, and m., 1660, at New Amsterdam, Grietie, dr. of Teunis Cray. After the Dutch lost N. Y. he lived somewhere in New England; there his dr., Mrs. Kiersen, was b. But coming, 1667, to H.—for the inducement, possibly, see p. 348—he put up a house, and built one or more vessels here. In 1670 he sold his place to Resolved Waldron, but subsequently owned another, and appears among the erf-holders, 1681–83, having his home here, and sailing an "open boat" out of N. Y. While thus engaged he is noticed as follows in the Council minutes, Jan. 28, 1684: "John de Vries desired that he might have some land at Harlem. They of Harlem said he formerly had land and sold it; he said he bought it; they said it was given to him, and he was obliged to sell it (if he parted with it) to no stranger. He, not being able to produce any witness or writing of said purchase, it was agreed by those of Harlem to give him a piece of ground, for him and his children; provided that he should not sell it, but for want of heirs it should relapse to the township." After this he and Kiersen got a lease of the Great Maize Land. See p. 450. Capt. Van Dalsen subscribes to Do. Selyns' salary in 1685 and '6, and was living in 1697. His chn. (omitting the first two, who d. y.) were, Teunis, b. 1664; Gerritie 1667, m. Jan Kiersen; Annetie, 1669, m. Joh. Waldron; Peter, 1671; Tryntie, 1674, m. Joh. Meyer; Jacob, 1679; Lysbet, 1682; Jannetie, 1685.

Teunis van Dalsen, in an obituary published at the time of his death, is stated to have been "the first male person born in this city (N. Y.) after it was ceded to the English by the Dutch;" and with this the family tradition accords. He lived at H. when he m. Sarah, dr. of Capt. Joh. Vermilye, in the fall of 1696, having, on May 21, preceding, bought No. 8 of the New lots from Joost Van Oblinus. This he sold, Jan. 1, 1701, to Barent and Joh. Waldron, for 1070 gl.; in 1721 was a farmer at Mamaroneck, in Westchester, but removed to Goshen, Orange Co., where he d., Aug. 30, 1766, æ. 102 yrs. The Dolsens of that county are his descendants. They were great Whigs in the Revolution, and from them *Dolsentown* takes its name. See *Eager's Orange Co.*, p. 412. We are not to confound with these the numerous Dolsens of Rockland and other counties, desc. of Jan van Dalsen, from Haarlem, Holland, who, bringing certificates from that place, with w., Anna van Raasvelt, joined the chh. in N. Y., Feb. 27, 1702. He d. ten or fifteen yrs. later at Tappan, where he had served as *voorleser*.

partnership with his fa., the whole of which he ultimately owned. On Feb. 21, 1701, the Brevoort farm, on Jochem Pieters Hills, being Lots 6, 7, of 1691, was purchased in his name, and on March 11, 1712, he bought of Derick Benson, No. 1, New Lots, also once Brevoort's. See p. 485. Joh. Myer drew jointly with his mo. of the common lands in 1712, on his 7½ *morgen right*, which entitled him to just 17 a. 1 q. 22½ r. They agreed that he should hold No. 15, 1st Div. (all but 10 a. at the lower end), with No. 6, 1691, and that she should hold in her name the lots No. 1 and 7, aforesaid; however, on Nov. 10, 1713, she conveyed the 10 acres to Johannes, and in 1715 gave him possession of the No. 1, New Lots. Among Myer's purchases was Sickels' lot, No. 16, 1st Div., on Mar. 9, 1722. See also p. 484. He bought 114 a. of the Delavall lands from Abm. Gouverneur, Mar. 25, 1720, but Philip Pipon reclaimed this land, on his arrival the next year. After Pipon and Gouverneur had had their claims settled by a legal decision, the latter sold Myer, on May 1, 2, 1725, the three most southerly of the "Nine Lots," on Jochem Pieters Flat, with a third of the Delavall drafts from the common lands. Joh. ultimately got a full half of the Delavall drafted lands; for more of which see App. I. Simon Johnson, assignee of Elias Pipon, also sold him that part of "that piece of land formerly belonging to the heirs of James Carteret," which lay at the west end of the "Three Lots," but separated by the road, and which Myer sold to John Sickels, Apl. 4, 1751, called 5 a. more or less; Sickels the next yr. buying the Three Lots, when the road was altered and carried around this piece. See p. 445.

Johannes Myer living to take part in the settlement of his fa.'s estate in 1748, came in legal possession of the homestead (No. 4 of 1691), and No. 7 of the same allotment. He then gave his sons *Jacob* and *John* his ⅓ of No. 9, 1691, and of No. 15, 3d Div., both Delavall land. In 1750, he further conveyed to Jacob No. 6, 1691, and No. 15, 1st Div. On May 5, 1753, he conveyed to Jacob No. 6, 1691, and to his other son John, No. 7, adjoining; the latter sold his lot to Jacob, Mar. 21, 1758. Johannes Myer d. 1755 in his 84th yr. His will, dated Feb. 7, 1729, was admitted to probate Apl. 5, 1756. He devised all his lands, after the d. or re-m. of his wid., equally to his two sons, but required them to satisfy their srs., by paying each £100, so that all should have an equal share of his estate. The drs. were *Jannetie*, b. ab. 1705, m. Resolved Waldron; *Maria*, b. 1711, m. Aaron Bussing, and *Elizabeth*, b. 1714, who m. Petrus Waldron.

John Myer, m., by license of July 20, 1738, Cornelia, dr. of John Delamater. He was constable in 1740–1. In the division of their inheritance, between him and his br. Jacob,

John obtained the "Three Lots," which he and wife sold, Oct. 1755, to John Sickels, and which subsequently formed the well-known Richard Harrison and Gabriel Furman tracts. John Myer's home was afterward on west side of Kingsbridge Road, near Breakneck Hill (on Lot 16, 1st Div., reaching from 140th to 145th Streets, and part of Lot 9 of 1691, in the rear, in all about 20 a. which had fallen to his share), and here he kept a public-house till his d. in 1773, at ab. the age of 57 yrs. A second w. Amy survived him. He had chn. John, Adolph, Catharine, etc. Catharine m., in 1770, Jonathan Randell, anc. of the worthy H. family of that name.*

Jacob Myer, eldest son of Joh. and Tryntie, was b. Mar. 26, 1709, and m. Aeltie, dr. of Peter Bussing. By lease and release from Simon Johnson and others, trustees of Elias Pipon, dated Feb. 11, 12, 1741, Jacob Myer came to own that part of the Delavall estate called the Six Lots, with two thirds of the adjacent Carteret Lot. This purchase, with the adjoining Lot No. 1, New Lots, which Jacob received from his fa., gave him that large square tract since known as the Myer farm, bounding upon the Harlem River, its lower angle on 128th Street just west of 7th Avenue; its upper angle on 139th Street, a little east of 6th Avenue. The fine large tract on the heights which Joh. Myer had gotten from Brevoort came, as we have seen, to be vested in Jacob, and reached (where intersected by the Bloomingdale branch of the Kingsbridge Road) from just below 138th Street to 139th Street. His son John added the Bussing lot, next north, 28 a., by deeds dated 1790 and 1791. Jacob Myer at forty yrs. of age was a prominent man in the town, and at a later period its treasurer. He d. Nov. 25, 1758, leaving all his property to his wid., who survived till 1765, when his son John, b. 1731, came in possession, either under his mo.'s will, or as heir-at-law. John, provided in his will for an unm. sr. Rebecca, who lived with him.

John Myer was many years town clerk, we believe the last holding that office here. He m. Eve, dr. of John Dykman, who d. in her 78th yr., Nov. 1, 1809. He d. æ. 86 yrs., Feb. 23, 1817. From Johannes, if not from Adolph the anc. down, this branch of the family all occupied the old stone house which stood, till of late, at the northern angle of Lot 4, of 1691, at the junction of the two roads; or to otherwise locate it, about

* JONATHAN RANDELL came from Greenwich, Conn., being by trade a carpenter. After his m. he lived for some time upon Harlem Heights, but on Nov. 29, 1784, purchased Randell's Island for £2,400, and by his energy and industry as a farmer paid for it in ten yrs. Here he resided, greatly respected, till his d., at the age of 88 yrs., Jan. 27., 1830. Leaving this fine property to his heirs, these sold it, five yrs. later, to the Corporation of N. Y., for $50,000.

an hundred and fifty feet west of 8th Avenue, on the lower side of 131st Street. John Myer's chn. were, 1. Jacob, b. Apl. 23, 1757, d. Oct. 29, 1813, m. twice, and was *fa.* of the late Peter Myer, John Myer, Phebe, Mercy, who m. Smith Valentine, and Eve, who m. Frederick Dyckman and Edward Riker; 2. Peter, b. Aug. 9, 1761, d. Mar. 4, 1834, m. Mrs. Sarah Westervelt, his chn. being Eva-Maria, who m. Capt. Joseph P. Dean, Cornelia-Frances, who m. John J. Deitz, and Abraham Dyckman Myer, fa. of Mary-Matilda, now w. of Dr. Wm. T. Lusk, and Anna-Maria, w. of Orlando Lines; 3. John-Dyckman, b. Dec. 25, 1759, d. May 15, 1802, and fa. of John, b. Sept. 9, 1783, m. and lived at Hackensack (*fa.* of John Myer, of Boonton, N. J.), Gilbert, b. Sept. 14, 1785, Hannah, b. June 25, 1794, m. David D. Myer, of Fishkill, and Peter, b. Nov. 15, 1800; 4. Abraham, b. Jan. 20, 1767, d. unm. Apl. 2, 1819; and 5. Garret, b. Mar. 20, 1775, m. Jane Bogert, Dec. 18, 1799, d. Jan. 6, 1860, resided at Hackensack; issue, John G., b. Aug. 30, 1800, d. Mar. 15, 1834, m. Ellen Kip, no heirs; Harriet, b. June 7, 1803, d. Oct. 23, 1873, m. John C. Z. Anderson, and Robert C. A. Ward; and Eve, b. June 11, 1807, d. April 17, 1859, m. Adolf W. Campbell.

NAGEL.

JOHN NAGEL has no desc. of the name at H., though yet to be found in Rockland Co. and other localities.* The name is now oftener written *Nagle*, or *Naugle*, the last expressing its original sound. Jan Nagel, having been "a soldier in the service of the

* JAN GERRITSEN HAGEL—Hagel is often written for Nagel in our early records, a mistake easily made—was a passenger by the ship Faith, which left Amsterdam Dec. 23, 1660, bringing also the Molenaer and Bush anc. Prior to this date our Nagel is not named, while another Jan Nagel of that period, whom we shall presently notice, had just died, and therefore was not the passenger referred to. Was this passenger our Nagel? As against it, apparently, Nagel calls neither of his sons Gerrit, but his eldest, Barent, which would indicate that his own patronymic was *Barentsen*, judging from common usage. In such case, and considering his relations to the Waldrons, he might be taken for a br. of Tanneke Barents Nagel. But, on the other hand, those relations may have been alone due to his marriage with Rebecca Waldron, and the child's name, Barent, have come from her br. Barent. Further, we notice that Nagel, though a chh.-mem., is not enrolled on the very full register extant, either as Hagel, Nagel, or Barentsen, while the name *Jan Gerritsen* occurs twice, at the same date with those of persons uniting, from Harlem, in 1670 and 1673. The presumption is that one of these was Nagel, and renders probable his identity with the emigrant of 1660. But with the uncertainty as to our Nagel's patronymic, whether Gerritsen or Barentsen—or again, since he called his second son John, whether he may not have been a son of Sergt. Jan Nagel, hereafter mentioned—we will not assume to decide the question.

honorable West India Company," up to the surrender to the English, in 1664, then quit the service and retired in disgust to H., with avowed intention to leave the country. He saw fit to remain, but was slow in becoming reconciled to the English rule. His first essay as a freeholder and m. with Rebecca Waldron (see p. 296) require no further notice. On the division, in 1677, of the lands bought jointly with John Delamater (see pp. 303, 503), Nagel took lot No. 6, Jochem Pieters Flat, with out-garden No. 13, and half the meadows. In 1679 he bought the adjoining garden, No. 14, with the dwelling-house on it (see p. 306), which he may have occupied thereafter. On Aug. 16, 1678, he bought a third lot on Jochem Pieters. See App. E. His acquisitions at Spuyten Duyvel have been noticed, pp. 383, 386. In 1675 Nagel was chosen deacon, and he seems to have been a man of sterling principles. Owing probably to his known dislike of the English government, his nomination for office was several times rejected by the Mayor's Court, but at length he was confirmed as constable in 1677, and later served twice as commissioner. He died in 1689. The next year his wid. became the w. of John Dyckman, then of Spuyten Duyvel, and there they were m. Their marriage contract, made at *Harlem*, May 12, 1690, says: "As it is found by the testament of Jan Nagel that his surviving children should receive the exact half of his estate, part of which is lying here at this *dorp*, and the other part at Spuyten Duyvel, but, as is thought, the part of the aforesaid estate lying at the dorp is the greater part; yet Rebecca Waldron assigns to her children by Jan Nagel deceased, all that is situated and lying here at this dorp." These lands, for a time, stood in the name of her son Barent. Four of Nagel's chn. d. y., viz., Barent, b. 1671; Jannetie, b. 1672; Jacobus, b. 1683, and William, b. 1689. His other chn. were John, b. 1673; Anna-Catrina, b. 1676, m. Johannes Berck, of Albany; Barent, b. 1678; Johanna, b. 1680, m. William Waldron; Deborah, b. 1684, m. Robert Westgate; and Resolved, b. 1687.*

* JAN NAGEL—not ours, for he, as well as Dyckman, had a contemporary of like name—was also a soldier; but nothing is found to prove a relationship between the two Nagels, or any intercourse between the families. *Sergt.* Nagel was from Limburg, and is called an *Oosterling*. After five years or more of military service at New Amsterdam, he m. Grietie Dircks, in 1652. It may be that he had had a former w. in Europe, as in his marriage record the customary mention whether he was a young man or widower is omitted. It was usual for persons coming out as soldiers to leave their family at home. His present w. was a dr. of Dirck Volkertsen, Norman, of Bushwick, and her uncle, John Vinge, was the first male person born in the State of N. Y.* Grietie was the young wid. of Nagel's fellow-

* Is there not room to distrust the accuracy of the Labadist travellers as to John Vinge's age? (*Dankers and Sluyter's Jour.*, p. 114) inasmuch as he—and an older sister, Rachel, b. in *Europe*, and afterward w. of Cornelis van T[illegible]—were

Barent Nagel was constable at H. in 1700. He and Resolved went to Rockland Co., where, in 1710, they had purchased 1000 a. of land from Lancaster Sims. Resolved joined the chh. at Hackensack, on certificate from Harlem, in 1713, and that yr. m. Clara, dr. of Gerrit Lydecker (son of Ryck Leydecker, of Bushwick), by whom he had issue, *Rebecca*, who m. Teunis van Houton; *Elizabeth*, m. Stephanus Stevenson; *Marritie*, m. Petrus van Houten; *Catrina*, m. Roelof van Houten; *Janneke*, and *Cornelia*, who m. Arie Arieanse. Resolved, in 1729, was elder and trustee at Orangetown. Barent Nagel, br. of Resolved, was a justice of the peace in 1731. His w. was Sarah Kiersen, by whom he had *John*, *William*, *Hendrick* and *Jacob*, besides drs. *Rebecca*, who m. Gerrit Bruyn, *Sarah*, m. Peter Oblinus, and *Johanna*. Of the sons. *Jacob*, b. 1720, m. Margaret Lozier. *Hendrick*, b. 1716, m. Catharine Blauvelt and Mary De Clerk, and by the first had, besides drs., sons John, b. 1751, who m. Elizabeth Riker; Isaac, b. 1753, who m. Maria Arianse, and Barent, also b. 1753, who m. Maria Benson, and was deacon at Tappan in

soldier, *Sergt.* Jan Hermans Schut, m. but three yrs. before, and lately murdered by the Indians, leaving her with a ch., Phebe, b. 1651, afterward w. of the *Conselyea* anc. (See p. 227.) By Nagel she had two chn., viz., Juriaen, b. 1653, and Christina, b. 1655. Nagel was enrolled as a burgher, Apl. 13, 1657, but d. soon after, and in 1658 his wid. m. Barent Gerritsen. Christina m. Wm. Aertsen, of N. Y. Juriaen Nagel, b. in N. Y., but living at Bushwick, m. 1679 Jannetie, dr. of Philip Langelaan. That yr. Mrs. Nagel joined the chh. at N. Y., as did Juriaen in 1683, when they went to live there, but subsequently returned, and, in 1695, transferred their connection to the Bushwick chh. Nagel, in 1689 and '90, served 22 months as a soldier under Leisler. How his independence revolted at the official exactions of his time appears from an incident in *Stiles' Brooklyn*, 2:352, where he is called *Hagell*. He served as deacon at Bushwick, and took part in building the new chh. there in 1706; then owning a farm of 95 a. He died in 1732. His chn. were *John*, b. 1679, d. y.; *Philippus*, b. 1682; *Margaret*, b. 1684, who m. Conselyea and Covert; *Jacobus*, b. 1687; *Benjamin*, b. 1690; *John*, b. 1693; and *Cornelia*, b. 1697, who m. Andries Stockholm. In *First*. Philippus Nagel, the military taste still showed itself. He settled in Flatbush, and was supervisor in 1719, constable 1731, etc. By his w. Anna, whom he m. in 1703, he had sons Jurian, Cornelius, and Philip, beside drs. Philip was long a judge of Kings Co., and county treasurer. He d. May 11, 1797, aged 84 yrs. See *Strong's Flatbush*. Some of this family early migrated to Bucks Co., Pa., and have desc. in and about Philadelphia.

minors, and yet to be educated and put to trades, on the date of Apl. 30, 1632, when their mo., Adriana Cuvilly, contracted a second m. with Jan Jansen Damen. *N. Y. Col. MSS.*, I. 6. On the assumption that John's birth was as early as 1614, *eleven years* must have transpired (a remarkable interval if there were families here thus early) *before a girl was born*, that girl being Sarah Rapelye. Our opinion is that Gulian Vinge came over with the first Walloon colonists in 1623, and that his son John was b. in that or the ensuing year. It might otherwise have been rather stale news which was sent to Holland, Sept. 23, 1626, that "the women also have borne some children here." *Col. Hist. N. Y.*, I. 37. What has been said on p. 130 must be our apology for alluding to this matter. Vinge was an anc. of Gulian C. Verplanck.

1783. *William*, b. 1716, m. Lena Alger; issue, Rebecca, b. 1755, Barent, b. 1762. *John Nagel*, b. ab. 1709, m. Elizabeth Blauvelt and Magdalena Nagel. By the first he had issue, Sarah, b. Jan. 18, 1731; John, b. July 11, 1733; Barent, b. Nov. 2, 1734; Catharine, b. Aug. 16, 1736; Maria, b. Mar. 2, 1738; Elizabeth, b. Oct. 11, 1739; Hendrick, b. Aug. 14, 1741, and David, b. Sept. 4, 1750. David m. Dirkie Haring, and Barent m. Jannetie Westervelt; John m. 1756 Elizabeth Lydecker—issue, Magdalena, b. Dec. 19, 1760; Maria, b. Oct. 18, 1762; Catharine, b. Sept. 9, 1764; John, b. Oct. 6, 1766; Gerrit, b. Oct. 26, 1768, and Elizabeth, b. Jan. 11, 1771. But we leave to others to complete these Rockland branches.

John Nagel, second, of II., was taught to weave by Abm. Delamontanie. He m. Jan. 2, 1708, Magdalena Dyckman, and on Nov. 10, 1719, became sole owner of the paternal lands, by deed from his brs. and srs.; Jacob Dyckman and his sr., Mrs. Hadley, also joining in the conveyance. On May 15, 1729, and June 9, 1744, Nagel and Dyckman passed partition deeds. See *Dyckman* family. In 1736 Nagel built him a stone dwelling, which continued to be the residence of the family, and is that yet standing on the bank of Harlem River at 213th Street, and known as the "Century House." Nagel was constable in 1712, signed the Mill Camp grant in 1739, and deeds given for common lands, sold in 1747. His will, made when "far advanced in years," Dec. 14, 1754, was proved Oct. 11, 1763. He had three sons, *John*, *Jacob*, and *William*, all of whom d. bachelors; John, at the age of 70 yrs., in 1780, Jacob in 1806, and William in 1808. He also had four drs., viz., Rebecca, m. 1737 Hendrick Post; Magdalena, m. in 1754 her cousin John Nagel, of Tappan; Deborah, m. Benjamin Waldron, and Catharine, unm.

The Nagel estate descended by devise from the other brs. to William, the youngest, who in his will, dated Aug. 31, 1806, left all his property to his four nephews, Hendrick, Dennis and Abraham Post, and Henry Tison, and to his niece Lena Post, living with him. Making ample provision, in money, for Abm. and Lena Post, he distributed the real estate as follows: To *Hendrick Post*, "the upper lot of land of my farming, running from the Post Road to Harlem River; likewise the opposite lot of land running from the Post Road westerly to Spuyten Duyvel Creek, with the salt meadow joining to the said lot on Spuyten Duyvel Creek; likewise that lot of land adjoining said lot, bounded north to land of Caleb Hyatt, near Kingsbridge; also two lots of woodland, the one adjoining the Fishing Rock, at the North River, the other the last lot of woodland adjoining Spuyten Duyvel Creek." To *Dennis Post*, "all the lands belonging to the Homestead whereon I live, except about ten rods square of the burying ground, with free access from the road to the same for interments; also the Clove lot of woodland; also that lot of land known by the name of the Barrick, with the three Huckleberry Islands, and the salt meadow called Minderache Fly." To *Henry Tison*, "the house and lot of land whereon John Oblenis now lives, and a woodlot lying between the lots belonging to Jacobus Dyckman, joining the North River; also a lot of salt meadow lying near the Round Meadow Creek, three acres, more or less." He empowered his executors to sell his meadow, lying on the other side of Harlem River, opposite his house.

OBLENIS.

JOOST OBLINUS, or, as his autograph is, *Van Oblinus*, being the person named in the patents of Nicolls and Dongan, was the son of Joost, who bought out the heirs of Philip Casier, Nov. 8, 1663 (see pp. 220, 227), and who with his wife Martina and a younger son soon after disappear from our records. Probably they returned to Europe, where some of the chn. seem to have remained; as in a letter written by the younger Joost, after the English took N. Y., to his "virtuous, well-beloved brother and sisters"—the first of whom he calls Jan van Oblinus—he says: "Know, my beloved brother, that we are here in a land before this called New Netherland and now New England, by the English mastered, being to the injury of our Dutch nation," etc. Joost, second, succeeded to his fa.'s property aforesaid, and made large additions thereto; see pp. 300, 373, 379, 384, 390, and the App. It was a deserved tribute to his worth when in 1666 he was made a magistrate, and soon after one of the five patentees. To the former office he was often chosen, besides serving as deacon and elder, and it was his peculiar fortune to be the last survivor of the Nicolls patentees. Mr. Van Oblinus d. in 1706. He had, by his wife Maria Sammis, sons Peter, John, and Hendrick, and drs. Maria, w. of Thomas Tourneur, and Josyntie, who m. Teunis Corssen in 1702, and Isaac Vermilye in 1707.

Peter van Oblienis, as he wrote his surname, was b. at Mannheim in 1662, the yr. before his parents emigrated. He was bred a weaver. At nineteen yrs. of age he became a chh.-mem., afterward serving many times as deacon and elder, and for most of his life, protracted to over 80 yrs., took the lead in all the affairs both of the chh. and town. On June 8, 1685, he was joined in m. by Do. Selyns, to Cornelia, dr. of Resolved Waldron. Three yrs. later, namely, on Apl. 21, 1688, he bargained with Jan Delamater for the house and lot in the village, originally Jaques Cresson's, for 400 gl., and on the same date his fa.

leased Delamater's lots on Van Keulen's Hook, Nos. 10 to 12, next his own. This resulted, May 10, 1690, in an exchange of property, Delamater giving Peter Oblinus 1100 gl. and deeds for these three lots and the Cresson place, and taking a deed for the farm on Hoorn's Hook. Oblienis sold the house and lot to Jacques Tourneur, Aug. 7, 1691; his fa. turning over to him three *erven*, two originally bought from the estates of Casier and Karstens, and one (joining the Karstens lot), gotten by Joost from Lubbert Gerritsen, in exchange for another bought of the Casiers. Peter sold the Karstens and Gerritsen lots to Capt. Joh. Benson. See p. 482. In the division of 1691 Peter van Oblienis drew Lot No. 20, being 10 morgen, "by the Round Meadow;" and the town gave him a deed for it March 21, 1701. On Sept. 19 ensuing he conveyed it to Bastiaen Kortright, in whose family it remained till after the Revolution. It formed a part of the late Dyckman "Fort George Tract." See p. 297. On Aug. 24, 1705, Joost van Oblinus, being near his last days, conveyed to Peter, for £425:

ALL his certain dwelling house, barn and orchard, in the Town of Harlem aforesaid, being formerly called four lots, and containing between two and three acres of ground, lying between the lot of Arent Harmense and the Town lot; *Also* three lots of land in said Town lying together, having the lot of said Peter van Oblienis joining to the eastward, and the lot of Metje Cornelisse adjoining to the westward; *Also* another lot of land on the north side of Harlem aforesaid, lying between two lots belonging to Barent Nagel; *Also* a piece of meadow joining to the meadow which did formerly belong to Thomas Delavall; *Also* another piece of meadow at Spuyten Duyvel, joining meadow of Johannes Waldron; *As also* all his right in the undivided lands under the Patents of Nicolls and Dongan.

The homestead named in this deed, and where Peter afterward lived, comprised four of the *buyten tuynen*, or out-gardens, being Nos. 12 to 15; the three lots of land were Nos. 13 to 15 of Van Keulen's Hook, and the lot described as between two of Barent Nagel, was No. 7 Jochem Pieters. The next day Peter conveyed to his br. Hendrick the meadow at Spuyten Duyvel, and half the right in the undivided common lands named in said deed from his fa. But after the d. of Joost, the brs. and srs. of Peter gave him, Sept. 6, 1706, a quitclaim of all the property covered by the deed from his fa., which restored the whole to Peter again, and hence he is credited in the quit-rent list of May 24, 1708, with his fa.'s full rights; saving one *erf* right then held by John and Hendrick, but in 1712 by John alone.

As oldest son and heir of the last survivor of the Nicolls patentees, Peter van Oblienis held a commanding position, when the great division of the common lands was made in 1712, all the deeds for which had to have his approval and signature. Those allotments lay in four general divisions, and in each of the four every freeholder drew a lot, which were scattered from 94th Street to Sherman's Creek. Oblienis alone enjoyed the privilege of drawing his four shares in one parcel, and this he located at an intermediate point near Fort Washington, adjoining the farm of his br. Hendrick, to whom he sold it. Before this date, as we conclude, Peter had secured for his own special use and behoof the 100 acres lying at Manhattanville (since of Lorillard and others), of which he was certainly the recognized owner in 1712. See App. J. The adjoining meadow, called Moertje Davids Fly, Oblienis must have gotten from his brs.-in-law, Samuel and Johannes Waldron, to whom it had been sold Jan. 15, 1702, by their br. Barent. On Oct. 18, 1715, Abm. Gouverneur conveyed him a piece of the adjoining Delavall woodland, being a part of No. 8, 1st Div. In 1718 Oblienis transferred all his lands in H. to Samuel Waldron, reserving only 10 a., not till then named in the tax lists, and not located with entire certainty, but we believe forming the island adjoining to Gloudie's Point and Oblienis' meadows. This also he passed to Waldron two yrs. after; but in 1728 Oblienis regained possession of his lands, said 10 a. only excepted. Certain suits brought against him, at this period, may explain these transfers.

Peter van Oblienis, who d. in 1743, left no chn., though twice m., his last w. being Agnietie, wid. of William Brett, whom he survived, and of whose six chn. by Brett he made kind remembrance in his will, dated Sept. 20, 1742, when he was in health. He further left his niece, Tanneke Benson, £50, to his "well-beloved brother Hendrick, one British shilling," and his whole estate otherwise to his nephew, Peter Waldron; to whom, on the same date, in consideration of good causes and £700, he gave a deed for the real estate, all therein described. *Deeds*, Sec. of State's Off., *Lib.* 26 : 219. This deed did not cover the two home-lots (4 a.), on the north side of the Church Lane, bought by Oblienis from Laurens Jansen, and since Chesterman's, nor the lot on Jochem Pieters Flat; but all these, if not already sold to Waldron, he must have taken under the will, which was proved Jan. 17, 1744.

John Oblienis, br. of Peter, was made poundmaster in 1699, but took no prominence in town affairs. He made weavers' reeds, and was apparently well to do, owning a house and lot in Smith (now Cedar) Street, which he bought Mar. 27, 1707, and an *erf* at H. village, on which he and Marcus Tiebout drew land together, in 1712. Marcus' step-son, John Lewis, became the owner in 1714. See notes, pp. 390, 442, 517, and App. J. That Oblienis purposely had nothing to do with making the 4 Divisions, in which his br. Peter bore so important a part, would appear from his not signing the preliminary agreements, nor any of the patentee deeds. He subscribed to articles of May 2, 1713, by which the freeholders bound themselves to pay their proportions of quit-rent, and to defend their titles. He d. at H., in 1717, without issue. We judge favorably of his character and tastes from the items in his inventory: "The Book of Martyrs in Dutch; a Dutch Psalm Book, with silver clasps; one book of poetry, one book of history called *Euphems*, one book of Common Prayer." In his will, dated May 11, and proved Aug. 10, of that yr., he made various bequests of £25, gave others gold rings, to br. Peter a shilling, to br. Hendrick his clothing and sleigh, and the rest of his estate equally to "brother Hendrick Oblienis, Mary Alderick, and Josantia Vermillia." The last was his sr., but if Mary Alderick was, she must have m. again after the d. of her hus., Tourneur, and we notice that Laurens Jansen's w. was commonly called *Mary Aldricks*.

John Oblienis' lands stood in his name, intact, for thirty years, his br. Hendrick and br.-in-law Vermilye, named as his executors, in the mean time paying Mary Alderick "her proportion." On Nov. 17, 1747, John Romer bought lot No. 11, 2d Div., being 6 a. 9 r., from Isaac Vermilye and Johannes Oblenis, the last acting instead of his fa. Hendrick, then dec. His lot 9, 1st Div., was sold to Adolph Myer, but those in 3d and 4th Div., held in common with John Lewis, who sold his shares to Dr. Paterson, we have not traced later than 1753.

Hendrick Oblienis, b. 1672, m. in 1692 Jannetie, dr. of John Tibout, and was the only son of Joost who left desc. He bore his part in town affairs, being constable in 1705, etc. His fa. gave him his allotment of 1691, being No. 19, containing 22½ morgen, "upon the south end of the Long Hill," or just below Fort Washington. Here he had built and was living when his fa. d. In 1712 he added the larger tract adjoining, as before stated (see App. J.), and which increased his farm to 130 a., salt meadows excluded. In 1709 he was a petitioner, with others, for 1500 a. of land in the Highlands. At his d. in 1745, his fine property in H. passed to his son *Johannes*. He had also a son *Peter*; and drs., of whom *Mary* m., in 1717, Michael Tourneur, and *Jacomina*, in 1720, Jacobus Tourneur, brs., with whom they went to Haverstraw; *Josyntie* m. in 1726 Benj. De Voe, of Westchester, and *Sarah*, who m. Teunis Devoor, in 1731. *Peter Oblenis* also went to Rockland Co., and settled upon a part of the Kakiat patent, at New Hempstead, now Ramapo. By Sarah, dr. of Barent Nagel, he had issue, Hendrick, b. 1731; Sarah, b. Dec. 4, 1733, who m. James Tourneur; Jannetie, b. July 26, 1735; Barent, b. May 8, 1737; Maria, b. Oct. 5, 1739, who m. Johannes Blauvelt, and John, b. June 26, 1743; all, except Barent, living at the time of

Peter's d. in 1764. Hendrick m. in 1757 Antie Lydecker, of Schraalenburgh, was alive during the Revolution, when he had a son wounded in the service of his country. Of this branch, we believe, was Barent or Bernard Oblenis, of N. Y., 1796, who m. Gertrude Sanders, and was clerk of police from 1805 to 1819. He had sons Henry, John, and Peter.

Johannes Oblenis, son of Hendrick 1st, was constable in 1736. Coming into possession of the paternal farm at Fort Washington, which he occupied many years, he sold 100 a. of it, May 23, 1769, to Blazius Moore, of N. Y., tobacconist; and conveying the remainder—the lower part—to his son Hendrick, he removed to the Manor of Cortlandt, where he d. in 1775, leaving him surviving his w. Mary, sons Hendrick, Dennis, and John, and dr. Deborah, w. of Marinus Low, of N. Y. He gave his lands there to Dennis and John. Hendrick Oblenis, son of Johannes, m. Maria Devoe, Nov. 12, 1753, and still held his farm on the Heights at the opening of the Revolution; but it subsequently passed to Jacob Arden. Hendrick was fa. of John Oblenis, who m. Elizabeth Ostrom, Sept. 1, 1783, and of Helen, who m., Feb. 5, 1782, John Ostrom, of H. The Oblenis name, now quite extinct on Manhattan Island, is yet found in other sections of our State, taking in some cases, by an odd fancy, an Irish form, *O'Blenis!*

TOURNEUR.

DANIEL TOURNEUR being deceased at the date of the Dongan patent, his wid., Jacqueline, represented his rights among the patentees; while her son Daniel was named in virtue of an *erf*, and six *morgen* lot, which he owned on Montanye's Flat. The peculiar circumstances under which the elder Tourneur left his native Picardy and retired to Leyden, with his m. in that city, and departure for this country a few months after the baptism, July 30, 1651, of his son Daniel at the Walloon church, are already familiar to us. On coming here he first lived at Flatbush, where a dr. Maria was b., who d. in inf., and where Tourneur, with some military prestige, as would seem, was made corporal of a company formed April 7, 1654, for protection against marauders. Soon after this he was granted a corner lot in New Amsterdam, with a view to put up a house, but a year or more passing before the timber was ready, he renewed his request, Apl. 11, 1657, for leave to build, but, we suspect, without success. He afterward built a house on the Prince's Graft, where he had bought a lot, May 31, 1660, and on Aug. 16 of the same year was appointed a magistrate for H.; but probably yet continued in business at New Amsterdam, as, on Oct. 15 ensuing, he was made one of the "sworn butchers." The next winter he put up a barn on his village plot at H., where he had already built a house, and whither he soon removed, serving in the magistracy at various periods, and for several years as deputy sheriff. He was repeatedly chosen deacon, besides which he was a delegate to the General Assembly of 1664, and also one of the Nicolls patentees. He d. in 1673, leaving a goodly estate, as heretofore particularized, and five chn., who all m. and left desc., viz., Daniel, Jacques, Thomas, Madeleine, who m. John Dyckman (whence the elder, or Gerrit Dyckman, branch of that family), and Esther, w. of Frederick de Vaux, anc. of the De Voe family of Westchester, etc. See pp. 425–427. The wid. Tourneur survived her hus. 27 yrs., and d. in 1700, and her personals, as per inventory taken Aug. 22, that year, were divided Nov. 16 ensuing, each ch. (Daniel's heirs in his stead) getting in cash 167 gl., with a fifth part of the goods.

Daniel Tourneur, the eldest son, was made "a free denizen of this place and province," by special letters, dated Jan. 13, 1672, he having been born in Holland, with which England was now at enmity. He served as magistrate, and was lieutenant of militia, still holding the latter office under Leisler, whose cause he actively supported, and by whom he was sent to Hartford, in March, 1690, to arrest Robert Livingston. But his d. the ensuing fall spared him the pain of witnessing the tragic fate of his chief captain, perhaps of sharing it. His inventory, taken Oct. 13, begins with "The bouwery lying upon *Montanie's Vlackte*, consisting of three lots of land, house and barn, orchard, and a piece of meadow lying on the kill of the *Vlacte*. Also another three lots of land lying upon *Hoorn's Hook*." See p. 398. By his w., Ann Woodhull (see p. 426), he had issue *Dorothea*, *Woodhull*, and *Daniel*. The last owned land in Westchester, which he sold in 1727. Woodhull, by trade a weaver, is named in 1706 and 1708 as holding his late fa.'s farm on Montanye's Flat, but in 1711 he sold it to Samson Benson and went to Newtown, L. I., where he is found the next yr., and on Jan. 27, 1713, bought the farm since of Cornelius Purdy. Here he m., May 13, 1715, his cousin Hannah Lawrence, but sold his farm Apl. 8, 1714, and removed to Rockland Co., whither most of the Tourneurs, on leaving H., seemed to gravitate. He was living in 1728. He had issue Anna, Daniel, James, and perhaps other chn. James Tourneur m. 1752 Sarah Oblenis; issue, Sarah, b. Jan. 13, 1753, Woodhull, b. Oct. 23, 1754, etc.

Thomas Tourneur, youngest son of Daniel 1st, was b. at H., and m. Apl. 5, 1692, Maria, dr. of Joost van Oblinus. He had just come in possession of his share of the paternal lands, embracing lots No. 19 Van Keulen's Hook and No. 1 Jochem Pieters, with the adjoining "orchard," or one morgen lot, reaching from the latter down to the Church Lane, and on which stood the house and barn. The out-gardens, Nos. 1 to 4, also fell to his share; and prior to 1701 he became the owner of the Bosch or Bush farm, on the North River side. Thomas seems to have inherited largely the tastes and spirit of his fa. Besides filling lesser town offices, he was the ald. of the Out Ward in 1696–7. Being appointed surveyor of highways in 1707, he sided with the H. people who felt aggrieved because required by the mayor and aldermen to join in working the newly surveyed roads outside of their limits; and Tourneur refusing, was fined 6 shillings by Constable Sickles, who levied on his goods. Tourneur thereupon procured a writ of the Supreme Court, and had the constable arrested for trespass. The mayor and ald. resolved to defend the constable. It caused much excitement, but pleased the inhabitants, and the next year Tourneur was made constable. But the city council, on the plea of his "having served in the office of alderman," declared him exempt, and ordered a new election! On Sept. 29, 1709, he was chosen town collector. Tourneur probably d. in 1710, as his son Jacobus is charged for back quit-rent in his stead, and that year all his lands were sold. His farm last named was bought by Capt. Jacob De Key, his Van Keulen Hook lot by John Dyckman, his out-gardens by Maria Meyer, and his lot No. 1, etc., by Capt. Charles Congreve. The latter sold in 1713 to John van Oblienis, and he directly to Abm. Myer. Thomas Tourneur had issue, *Jacobus*, b. 1693, *Magdalena*, b. 1695, *Martina*, b. 1698, *Thomas*, b. 1702. We know not of any others, nor whither these went. The chn. and their mo. are remembered in John Oblienis' will in 1717. Jacobus, familiarly called *Cobus*, to whom his uncle John Oblienis left a legacy of £25, was probably the "chirurgeon," Jacob Tourneur, who practiced in the families of Frederick De Voe, Louis Guion, and other French residents of Westchester, and d. Mar. 9, 1719, at the house of Frederick Bolt, at New Rochelle.

Jacques Tourneur, son of Daniel 1st, and b. in H., m. June 17, 1683, Aefie, dr. of Michael Kortright, and May 29, 1714, Engeltie Thomas, wid. of Gregoris Storm, of Philips Manor. He served as a deacon, and also as constable and overseer of the town; succeeding, in 1691, to that part of his fa.'s lands on Van Keulen's Hook, known as Lots 17, 18, but in quantity three lots, and since the Bussing or Storm farm. On Aug. 7, 1691, he bought from Peter van Oblienis, for 600 gl., the old Jaques Cresson residence, which became his home. On May 27, 1698, he sold his lot No. 7, of the draft of 1691, to Joh. Myer. See also p. 353. His d. is not noticed, but his farm, and lots in the several divisions, in all 60 a., were sold to Peter Bussing in 1726. Jacques Tourneur had three drs., viz., *Anna*, b. 1686, *Adriana*,

b. 1689, who m. Jacob Gerritsen, of Flatbush, and *Maria*, b. 1691; as also sons *Michael*, b. 1693, *Jacobus*, b. 1695, *Abraham*, b. 1698, and *Isaac*, b. 1701, the last living at Fordham in 1733.* The two elder sons m. srs., the drs. of Hendrick Oblenis, and settled in Haverstraw, where the family became quite numerous.

Jacobus Tourneur, son of Jacques, and born in 1695, m., May 26, 1720, Jacomina Oblenis, of H., and died at Haverstraw, leaving sons Jacobus, Hendrick, John, and drs. Aefie, who m. Johannes van Dalsen, and Jannetie, who m. Teunis Blauvelt. Of these three brs., John m. his cousin Jannetie Tourneur (issue, Jacobus, b. Nov. 17, 1756, Daniel, b. May 30, 1763, etc.); Hendrick m. 1753 Mary Kuyper, issue unknown, and Jacobus, who d. on his farm in Haverstraw, in 1773, left by his first w., Grietie Kuyper, chn. Jacobus (b. Feb. 28, 1747) and Margaret, and by his second w., Grietie Blauvelt, m. in 1763, and who survived him, issue, Rachel, Jacomina, and David. The Turnures of Rockland were good Whigs in 1776, as the lists of associators witness. The name took that and other forms.

Michael Tourneur, aforesaid, m. Maria Oblenis, Feb. 1, 1717. In 1743 he bought the old residence of his fa. and 12 a. of his land, being lot No. 2, 3d Div. and 9 a. of No. 14, 2d Div. He got from Bussing, in 1750, the remaining 6 acres of the last named lot. See p. 500. But selling out within ten yrs., he removed, and d. at Haverstraw in 1775, æ. about 82 yrs., leaving chn. Jacobus, Hendrick, Jannetie, w. of John Tourneur; Aefie, w. of Derick De Clerck; Sarah, w. of Edward Salyer; Mary, w. of William Dyckman, and Jemima, w. of William Chappell, of N. Y. Of these, Hendrick succeeded to the homestead part of the paternal farm, and m. 1758 Margaret Blauvelt; issue, if any, not ascertained. Jacobus m. Dinah, dr. of Lawrence Low, of H.; issue, Michael, Lawrence, Jacobus, John, Hendrick, Jane, Mary, Maria, and Sarah. Undoubtedly Lawrence aforesaid, who resided at H. was the gd. fa. of the brs. Lawrence and David M. Turnure, of N. Y. City.

VERMILYE.

JOHANNES VERMILYE, the patentee, was common anc. of all who in this country bear the name of Vermilye or Vermilyea.

* The TURNER family, of Westchester Co., are not to be mistaken for the Tourneurs. The former were desc. of Lawrence Turner, who as early as 1646 had dealings with English residents at Manhattan. He removed from Newport to Greenwich, and thence into "the borough and town of Westchester," where he d. in 1668, leaving a wid., Martha. His dr. Mary m. John Ferguson, Jr., and his son Daniel Turner, of Westchester, yeoman, d. May 24, 1705, leaving his wid. Margaret, a son *Daniel*, and drs. *Martha*, *Mary*, and *Rebecca*, the last of whom m. Eleazar Gedney, of Mamaroneck.

His fa., Isaac Vermeille, has been already the subject of notice, before as well as after he emigrated with his family, in 1662. Welcomed to H. by some of his former acquaintances, Vermeille's worth was recognized by an appointment to command a military company in 1663. Later he served two terms as magistrate. Buying the northern end (a morgen) of lot No. 5, Van Keulen's Hook, probably from Montagne, his son-in-law, he built a house, planted fruit-trees, and here made his home. His house occupied a spot nearly central of the block between 1st and 2d Aves. and 122d and 123d Sts. Vermeille held no other farming land, no doubt having some other calling suited to his now advanced yrs., perhaps with his son in the brewery. He was living Aug. 29, 1676, when he witnessed the will of Aert Pietersen Buys and w. Jenneke Cornelis, of Fordham, and on Sept. 4 ensuing, Vermilye, either fa. or son, is called "clerk." Observing that on the d. of Jean le Comte, in 1675, there was paid "To Isaac Vermeille, for the burial, *f.* 12;" we think he performed the office of "clerk" for the French residents at H. He probably d. in 1676, and is not among the proprietors Feb. 19, 1677, when his house and lot stand in the name of Johannes.* Isaac's chn. were Johannes aforesaid, Abraham, who had no issue, Maria, b. 1629, who m. John La Montagne and Isaac Kip, and Rachel, b. 1637, who m. John Terbosch and Derick Wessels.

Johannes Vermelje, as he wrote his name, was b. in 1632 at Leyden.† Coming here in ripe manhood, and uniting in his character the sterling traits of the French and Dutch, he was made court messenger in 1665, and constable in 1667, being for this year also farmer of the excise; previous to which he had set up a brewery. In 1670, then holding the position of magistrate, he m. Aeltie, dr. of Resolved Waldron; when he probably built upon an *erf*, procured some yrs. before, but which is first taxed in 1671. It lay in the Judah plot. See pp. 263, 264, 318. Mr. Vermilye took a leading part both in civil and church affairs. In the political crisis of 1689 he was chosen one of the Committee of Safety, which, on June 8 of that yr., appointed Capt. Jacob Leisler to be "captain of the fort," and on Aug. 16 signed his commission as "commander in chief" of the province. Taking a seat in Leisler's council, Dec. 11 en-

* Bolton, Hist. Westchester Co., II., 327, under date of 1694, copies the name of Capt. Isaac *Van Vleck*, as *Vermilyea!* Such carelessness is reprehensible.

† The letter *j* (with Hollanders) having the sound of our English *y* when the latter begins a word or syllable; Johannes only conformed to the Dutch mode of writing his name, without changing its terminal pronunciation, which is well preserved in the modern spelling Vermilye, but better (since *e* in Dutch, as in French, takes the sound of *a*), by Vermilyea.

ening, he was sent soon after upon an embassy to New Haven. He continued a member of the council till a sudden end was put to Leisler's rule by the coming of Col. Sloughter, Mar. 20, 1691, by whose orders Leisler and his council (Vermilye included) were "committed to the guards," on a charge of high treason. The execution of Leisler and Milborne, but two months later, seemed to Vermilye and his fellow-prisoners to forebode a similar fate. But after a painful suspense of over seventeen months they were liberated by Gov. Fletcher, on his arrival, and were pardoned by the king Feb. 20, 1693. Vermilye survived this trying ordeal but a short period, as he was dec. in March, 1696. His wid. sold out her lands at H. in 1715, to her nephew John Delamater (see p. 504), and d. at Yonkers in 1734. Their chn. were Rebecca, b. 1671, who m. Peter Bussing; Sarah, b. 1673, who m. Tennis Dolsen; Rachel, b. 1675, who m. Charles Vincent; Abraham, b. 1679; Isaac, b. 1682; Maria, b. 1684, m. Peter Kierse; Jacob, b. 1686, d. y.; John, b. 1688, and Hannah, b. 1690, who m. John Odell. The three sons became farmers in Yonkers. Abraham, named after that uncle supposed to have been killed in the Esopus war, was living, in 1730, but, it is said, left no issue.

John Vermilye, b. 1688, became rich in landed property, by buying up farms in Yonkers, about Kingsbridge, from William and Benj. Betts, Anthony Barley, etc. He lived till "far advanced in years," as he says in his will, dated June 3, 1776, and proved Nov. 2, 1786. He m. Sarah Odell, Oct. 29, 1713, but before his d. contracted a second m. He distributed his lands among his sons. These were *John*, *Abraham*, *David*, *Gerardus*, *Frederick*, *Joshua*, and *Benjamin*. His drs. were Aeltie, Antie, Mary, Sarah, and Rebecca; Aeltie m. John Kortright, of H. Of the sons, *Abraham* d. in Yonkers in 1784; issue, John, William, Abraham, Edward, and Sarah, w. of Solomon Hustis. *Frederick* m. 1763 Catharine Noulue, d. 1814, and was fa. of John and Frederick. *Joshua* d. in Westchester Co. in 1782; issue, Thomas, Isaac, Anna, and Mary. Some of these removed to N. Y. as early as 1792. *John*, *Gerardus*, and *David*, before the Revolution, removed from Yonkers to Lagrange, Dutchess Co. They, in common with their kindred, had now yielded their French characteristics, at least as to their speech, for it is known that John, called Hannes (Johannes), was wont to ask blessings in Dutch. *David* was fa. of Isaac Dyckman Vermilyea, who had Sarah, Jane, Jerome, and Gideon; the last had John and Maria. *Gerardus* m. in 1762 Jane Valentine. He contributed toward building the Ref. Dutch chh. at Hopewell. He was the fa. of Isaac G. Vermilyea, fa. of John Kip Vermilyea, Esq., of Cold Spring. We would willingly extend these branches, had we the materials.

Isaac Vermilyea, b. 1682, m. Jan. 16, 1707, Josyntie, dr. of Joost van Oblinus, and wid. of Teunis Corssen, who left her with a ch., Teunis, living in 1748. Isaac was an executor of his br.-in-law, John van Oblinus, and well sustained the good reputation so generally characteristic of the family. His will, made Mar. 1, 1748, was proved Mar. 5, 1767. He had chn. *John*, of Kingsbridge; *Isaac* and *Petrus*, of Croton Valley; Aeltie, who m. John Teller; Marritie, who m. Jacobus Teller; Sarah, who m. Valentine; Rebecca, who m. Jacob Dyckman, and Hannah, who m. Odell. *Petrus* had issue, Isaac, Peter, John, Philip, William, Cynthia (Josyntie), and Mary. Philip, b. 1760, d. 1790; issue, Nathaniel, of N. Y., chairmaker, who d. Feb. 2, 1826, æ. 33 yrs., having had Nathaniel-Drake, b. 1807, Philip, and Frances, who m. Shapter. *Isaac* had John, Isaac, Joseph, Rebecca, Cynthia, Hannah, Nancy, and Hester; of whom John was fa. of John, fa. of Isaac, who d. in N. Y. 1875, being fa. of ex-treas. Isaac Vermilye.

John Vermilye, of Kingsbridge (Yonkers), eldest son of Isaac and Josyntie, succeeded to the land his fa. bought of Anthony Basley. He m. Charity, dr. of Jacob Dyckman, and had issue Isaac, Jacob, William, Jane, who m. 1767 Edward Prior, of N. Y.; Rebecca, who m. 1765, Wm. Maharry, of N. Y.; Cynthia, and Aletta. Of these, Isaac, of Yonkers, eldest son of John and Charity, m. 1756 Susannah, dr. of Jacob Myer, and had sons, John, who m. Ellie Clark; Jacob-Myer, who m. Phebe Vail, and Isaac, who m. Jane Odell. Jacob, son of John and Charity, was b. 1740, and d. Jan. 31, 1814. He m. 1766 Susannah Dyckman, and in 1773 Mary Dyckman; his sons were, 1. John, m. Rebecca Fowler, and d. Oct. 15, 1823, æ. 55 yrs. 0 m. 3 d., being fa. of Jacob, Benjamin, Dorothea, Gerardus (fa. of Mary and John), Susan, Maria, Amelia, Abraham, and Isaac—Abraham being fa. of George, Frank, Oakley, Irving, and William; 2. Gerardus, d. Aug. 3, 1823, æ. 52 yrs. 2 m.; 3. William, d. unm. Mar. 8, 1822, æ. 46 yrs.; 4. Isaac; 5. James, m. Mary Greenway; issue, Susan, Michael, Julia, Jane, Euretta, and Charity, of whom Jane m. Wm. D. Smith; and 6. Michael, who m. his cousin Susan Vermilye; issue, Abraham and Isaac. The drs. of Jacob (son of John and Charity) were Jane, Susan, and Rebecca; Susan m. Jacob Cregier. William Vermilye, b. 1748, son of John and Charity, went to N. Y. as early as 1792, was a builder, and from 1812 till his d. surveyor for the Eagle Ins. Co. He d. Mar. 8, 1822, æ. 73 yrs. 11 m. Maria, dr. by his 1st w., Miss Brower, m. Wm. Chardavoyne; issue, Rebecca, m. Matthew McIlwaine, M.D. (fa. of Rev. Joseph McIlwaine, of Essex, N. J.); Eliza, who m. John H. Buckle; Jane-Magdalene, m. Thos. E. Vermilye, and Wm. Chardavoyne. By his 2d w., Mary Taylor, W. Vermilye had William W., Thomas B., Robert, (of Ohio), and Joanna, who m. *George B. Smith*; having issue Mary-Vermilye, Edwin, Sarah, m. Chas. G. Rockwood, Emily, m. Wm. H. Sage, George-William, Joanna, m. Gardner Sage, Charlotte, m. Wm. H. Sage, Clara-Green, m. George S. Conover, and Charles Green Smith. Thomas B. Vermilye m. Mary Hoagland; issue, Robertanna, d. y., Thomas-Edward, William-Henry, John-Robert, d. y., Isaac-Dyckman, John-Hoagland, and Theodore-Chardavoyne. Of these, William H. was fa. of Daniel Babbit Vermilye; Isaac D. was fa. of Thomas-Edward, William-Henry, Isaac-Ward, Henry-Fisher, Joseph-Fenelon, Charles-A.-Townsend, Lewis-Chauncey, Annie-Ward, Robert-C.-Halsey, Marion-Hoagland, Hobart-Potter, and Mary-Josephine; John H. was fa. of Thomas-Brower, Mary-Caroline, John-Dewint, and William-Gray; Theodore C. was fa. of Theodore-Chardavoyne, Mary-Hoagland, Cornelia-Tompkins, Hannah-Tompkins, Isaac Dyckman, and Sarah-Hatch Vermilye.

William W. Vermilye, b. Dec. 24, 1780, began business in N. Y. as a printer with Langdon & Son. He m. Mary Montgomery, Jan. 11, 1800, whom he survived two yrs., and d. Nov. 14, 1819, at the residence of his son, Rev. R. G. Vermilye, Clinton, N. Y. His chn. were William-Montgomery, b. Sept. 30, 1801; Thomas-Edward (Rev.), b. Feb. 27, 1803; Joanna-Maria, b. July 20, 1804, d. Jan. 4, 1877, m. Benj. R. Ruton; Margaret-Louisa, b. July 23, 1806, d. Aug. 31, 1874; Robert-George, b. June 24, 1808, d. Jan. 20, 1810; Washington-Romeyn, b. Sept. 29, 1810; Robert-George (Rev.), b. Mar. 3, 1812, d. July 5, 1875; Mary-Ann, b. Apl. 19, 1814, is dec.; Jacob-Dyckman, b. July 15, 1817; Rebecca, b. Nov. 15, 1818, m. to Fergus A. Hathorn; Erskine-Rockwood, b. Dec. 20, 1821, now dec.; and Ebenezer, b. Jan. 20, 1823, d. same date; of whom, *William M.*, banker, who d. on June 18, 1878, m. Hester Ann De Reimer, having issue William-Edward, Robert-Montgomery, and Charles-Augustus-Morford, with others; Rev. *Thomas E.*, the venerable senior pastor of the Col. Ref., Chh., N. Y., whose w. Eliza B. was dr. of Ebenezer Hazard, former postmaster of the U. S., is fa. of Rev. Ashbel G. Vermilye, and of Thomas E. Vermilye, banker; *Washington R.*, banker, who d. Dec. 23, 1876, m. Elizabeth Dwight Lathrop, having with other chn. Washington-Romeyn, and Emily-Augusta, who m. Elbert A. Brinkerhoff; and *Jacob D. Vermilye*, now pres. of the Merchants' Bank, who m. Mary Cornelia Lathrop, and is fa. of Mr. William G. Vermilye, treas. of Union India Rubber Co.*

* To the gentleman last mentioned, whose tastes and foresight led him years ago to investigate his family history, are we indebted for most of the later details here presented.

VERVEELEN.

JOHANNES VERVEELEN held a prominent place in the history of the town, and as one of the five original patentees. As before stated, his anc. were German, and citizens of Cologne, at the terminus of the highlands of the Rhine; whence his gd.-fa., Hans Verveelen, with his family, removed, about 1610, to Amsterdam, obviously to escape the oppressive policy dealt out to those of the reformed faith at Cologne—a fact in the family history to be cherished by the present numerous desc. of Hans and Catrina Verveelen. To our account of Johannes, his b. and m. at Amsterdam, emigration, and subsequent career at H., a few particulars may be added. A first step after his arrival, with his w. Anna Jaarsvelt, at New Amsterdam, was to enroll his name, Apl. 24, 1657, among the burghers, and to unite with the chh. here, where Verveelen, whose social habits, if we rightly apprehend him, won him friends and popularity, soon found himself at home and engaged in the brewing business in partnership with Isaac de Forest. He also bought a house and lot in the Marckvelt-steeg, from John La Montagne, Jr., June 27, 1659. Nominated for schepen, first in 1660, then in 1661, but not a successful candidate, he removed to H., in which place from the first he had taken an interest, and where he was made a magistrate in 1663, a delegate to the General Assembly of 1664, and, as intimated, a patentee in 1667. By the purchase of the groundbriefs of Jan Pieterson Slot and Jurian Hanel, one dated Jan. 4, the other May 16, 1664, Verveelen had become a large proprietor. For the subsequent history of these patents, see *Myer* family. The public duties intrusted to Verveelen, and his long retention as ferrymaster, evidence the favor in which he was held. When his second lease of the ferry expired, his son Daniel, in his behalf, petitioned Gov. Dongan, April 2, 1688, for its renewal. He was told to "hold the premises until farther order to the contrary." Four years later Frederick Philips brought a suit in the Supreme Court to eject Verveelen from the island Papparinamin, which Philips claimed under a title derived from Vander Donck. Verveelen complaining, the council, Feb. 25, 1692, resolved to defend their tenant and his Majesty's title. But the same year the governor proposed that the city build a bridge across the Spuyten Duyvel; the mayor and aldermen were quite willing to oust Verveelen, and hereupon Philips, on his petition, readily procured an order, Jan. 19, 1693, for converting his lands in Westchester County, with the neck or island, Papparinamin, into the Manor of Philipsburgh, and empowering him to build a drawbridge, across the Spuyten Duyvel, to be called *King's*

Bridge, and to collect certain tolls from passengers. This was amply assured by the charter of June 12, ensuing, erecting the said manor; and the bridge was built forthwith. See *Bolton's Westchester.**

Verveelen, now grown to be an old man, is known to have been living Mar. 13, 1693, when, styling himself "of the county of Westchester, *yeoman*," he sold a house and lot in N. Y. On Jan. 10, 1699, Johannes Verveelen brought a suit in the Mayor's Court, against one Huling, a citizen, to recover pay for 8 bls. of beer. If this was our Johannes (and not his gd.-son), he was 89 yrs. of age. Witnesses were cited, Nov. 24. 1701, to prove the deed last named, whence we conclude he was then dec., as he certainly was Feb. 14, 1702, having outlived all but one of the Nicolls patentees. He made a will, in which he gave his lands at H. to his dr. Maria. Of Mr. Verveelen's chn. (see p. 105). Anna was b. in 1636, joined the chh. at New Amsterdam in 1662, and two yrs. later m. Derick Looten, commissary, with whom, as before noticed, she returned to Holland. Maria, b. in 1656, m. in 1671 Adolph Meyer; see pp. 304, 525.

Daniel Verveelen, who was nearly of an age with his sr. Anna, preceded his parents to this country, coming, as is believed, in 1652, with Rev. Gideon Schaets, whose dr. he afterward m. At Albany (then Beverwyck), Daniel, a mere youth, engaged in trade, as early as 1655, but several years later joined his fa. at New Amsterdam, uniting with the chh. there Jan. 2, 1661. It was probably during the next summer (when he visited Albany, and on Aug. 25 sold an interest in a house and lot there), that he m. Aletta Schaets, who as his w. joined the chh. at New Amsterdam, Oct. 2 ensuing. The next month (Nov. 7) Daniel and his fa. secured a lot adjoining to one owned by the latter, on the Prince's, now Beaver Street, and on Feb. 14 following, they also bought out Isaac de Forest's interest in the brewery in Prince's Street, of which for some yrs. Johannes had been part owner. At the surrender Daniel was opposed to resisting the English, and took the oath of allegiance. The next year he had

* An application by Jasper Nessepott to the common council, Jan. 16, 1700, for leave to build a grist-mill at Kingsbridge, was submitted to a committee, which reported in favor, "on condition that he take out of the way the stones and rocks on the other side thereof, that the same may not hinder the passage of boats and canoes, and when any is to pass, at their reasonable request, he is to shut his sluices; and on the other side of the bridge erect a post in the water, and have a rope ready to assist them in passing." John Marsh, millwright, "being projector and contriver of the mill," Nessepot bought him out, when the mayor and aldermen formally granted Nessepot said "mill or mills, under one roof," and "the ground whereon the said mill or mills doth stand," with toll for grinding, and other mill privileges; by deed of Jan. 29, 1700, or 1701, N. S. *Grants, City Comptroller's Office*, vol. 2 : 388.

a narrow escape from some riotous soldiers, one of whom cut him with his sword. Several years later he left the city, and went to New Utrecht, with his w. taking letters to the chh. there, of which Verveelen, in 1678, was chosen an elder. He next went to Spuyten Duyvel, whether "to live at Fordham," as Archer had expected, does not appear. Subsequently he and his family settled in the neighborhood of Hackensack, where Daniel was living in 1712. His dr. Anna-Maria, b. 1666, m. Hendrick Jansz Cammega, and Johanna m. Johannes Schuerman and Nicholas Petersen. Daniel's sons were *Hendrick*, *Bernardus*, *Reynier*, *Gideon*, and *Johannes*. Of these, Hendrick, b. 1668, is last named in 1688; and we have failed to find evidence that Reynier had a family. He was named for his uncle, Dr. Reynier Schaets, slain at the burning of Schenectady.* Johannes, b. in New Utrecht, m. in 1703, at Hackensack, Emeline, dr. of Hans Jacobs Harding, named p. 407. He had Alida, b. 1704, and Francina, b. 1706, but dying, his widow m. 1710 Wouter Willemsen. I believe Alida m. Rev. Fredericus Muzelius.

Bernardus Verveelen joined the chh. at Hackensack in 1704, at the same time with his br. Reynier. In 1708 he obtained a patent for a large tract of land in Rockland Co., described as between the Hudson and Overpeck Kill, part of which he sold his br. Gideon; the two conveying 1000 a. to Lancaster Sims, in 1709. Bernardus m. Evertie, or Titie Delamater (see p. 503), and had issue, Alida, b. Jan. 14, 1714, who m. Hubartus Blauvelt; Isaac, b. Apl. 12, 1715, m. Tryntie van Scheyven; Cornelia, b. Dec. 23, 1716, m. Peter van Scheyven; Daniel, b. ———, 1719, m. Jannetie van Scheyven; Johannes, b. June 13, 1723, m. Sarah Westervelt; Hester, b. Oct. 9, 1725, m. Jacob Cool; Fredericus, b. Nov. 13, 1728; Abraham, b. Apl. 26, 1731, who m. Elizabeth Allen. By a second w., Jannetie Vanderbeeck, Bernardus had further issue, Jacobus, b. Aug. 28, 1734, m. Sarah Nagel; Elizabeth, b. Feb. 8, 1736; Bernardus, b. Oct. 30, 1737, who m. Mary Blauvelt; Gideon, b. Aug. 1,

* Rev. GIDEON SCHAETS, the worthy minister of Albany, and of whose blood are all the Verveelens, is too well known through the works of O'Callaghan, Brodhead, and Pearson to require further notice here. But, strangely enough, all the printed accounts ignore his dr. Alida, who m. Verveelen. Another mistake occurs in regard to his son Bartholomew, who is confounded with a later person of that name. The first, said to have gone to Holland in 1670, d. prior to 1680, when his wid., Willemtie, dr. of Hugh Barents de Kleyn (see p. 107), m. again. Bartholomew, who came from Albany to the city of N. Y. in 1706, and whose posterity are noticed upon its records down to the Revolution, was probably the son of Gideon, son of Dr. Reynier Schaets, as the name Reynier ran in the N. Y. family. Do. Schaets' first w. was Agnietie Mortaens. He m. his second in 1683, survived her five yrs, and d. Feb. 27, 1694, in his 87th yr.

1739, m. Maria Banta; John, b. July 18, 1741, and Cornelius, b. Aug. 24, 1745. Of these, Isaac and Jacobus removed to the City of N. Y. years before the Revolution. Jacobus was a grocer, and d. at 22 Walker Street, Feb. 8, 1816. We presume Henry and James, then of 20 Walker Street, were his sons.

Gideon Vervelen, b. 1680, at New Utrecht, m. in 1712 Marritie Kock, and in 1714 Susannah, dr. of Moses and Hester De Graaf. He removed from Rockland to Dutchess Co., and, on May 20, 1740, bought 3115 a. of land in Rombout Precinct, from which he sold off twelve parcels, but kept enough to give his four chn. each 252 a. These, named in his will, dated Jan. 25, 1755, and proved June 26, 1762, were Marritie, b. Apl. 12, 1715, who m. William Rogers; Hester, b. Dec. 20, 1716, m. Johannes Roeger; Alida, b. Oct. 15, 1718, m. Isaac Cole, and Moses, b. 1723. Gideon had five younger chn., not named in his will, to wit: Daniel, b. Sept. 12, 1722; Johanna, b. Aug. 19, 1725; Gloudie, b. Nov. 12, 1727; John, b. June 6, 1731, and Johannes, b. Oct. 18, 1733. If all these were dec. without issue, at the date of his will, it appears remarkable; if living, they must have been otherwise provided for. Moses, to whom was devised the homestead, but who d. before his fa., had by w. Hester, issue, Gideon, Moses, John, Daniel, Jeremiah, Elizabeth, and Hannah, of whom Gideon succeeded to the homestead farm, and was an active patriot during the Revolution. This name has assumed various forms, as *Vervalin*, *Vanvalin*, *Vanvaler*, etc.

WALDRON.

RESOLVED WALDRON, the most noted, as he was one of the most intelligent, of the Harlem settlers, needed not the titular dignity of baron, which some of poetic humor claim for him; yet might he have well graced the title. As we have seen, he had been in the printing business at Amsterdam, and emigrated with his family to New Netherland, late in 1654. Received with his br. Joseph, and their w., to the fellowship of the chh. at New Amsterdam, the first care was to secure a home, and on Apl. 3 ensuing the brs. bought a house and lot on Broadway, near Wall Street. Both entered the public service, Resolved being made "overseer of the workmen."* On Apl. 17, 1657,

* JOSEPH WALDRON, "living near the *beeck* of Passenger Street" in Amsterdam, and on the eve of his second marriage, appeared before the orphan masters, May 12, 1649, according to custom, and gave bonds for the maintenance of his two chn. by his late w. Aeltie Hendricks; as "the children by the former marriage had no property." One of these perhaps was left at Amsterdam with its gd.-mo., Maria Govetts, since it is not named in our records here, and Waldron was wont to order part of his sal-

he applied for the burgher right, and under May 3 occurs this entry: "Resolved Waldron being admitted a burgher, hath on this date taken the oath of fidelity." His salary was increased soon after. Found to be efficient, the Director and Council, on May 25, 1658, appointed him deputy to the *schout-fiscael*, or attorney-general, de Sille; the Burgomasters being ordered, Oct. 28, to recognize him as deputy sheriff. Very exact in carrying out his orders and in enforcing the laws, he was charged by the Quakers, some of whom he arrested, with being "hard-hearted." He visited, upon public errands, every part of the province, and even the neighboring colonies; and in 1659 was sent with Augustine Heermans to Maryland, to vindicate the Dutch title

ary to be paid his said mo.; the last time noticed was on Aug. 30, 1661, being two months' wages, 48 florins. He was butler to the garrison, and had charge of the magazine of the company. Waldron d. in 1663. Just before his end, sending for a notary to draw up his will, he said "there would be nothing left—but if anything should remain, it should not be touched, but go to pay the passage of his widow, who intended to leave for Fatherland." Upon these representations, and it appearing that there were "six minor children, two of whom are by a former marriage," the orphan's court of New Amsterdam, Dec. 10, 1663, at the desire of the wid. Annetie Daniels, appointed Resolved Waldron, "her husband's brother," and Hendrick Jansen vander Vin, "who is her oldest and most intimate friend," as guardians of her surviving chn. It is uncertain whether she visited Holland, as she was m. here, in 1668, to Harman Smeeman, and again, in 1682, to Coenraet Ten Eyck. Joseph Waldron's chn. known to us were Sarah, Daniel, Mary, Anna, Deborah, and John. Deborah d. in inf., and John, when not quite 8 yrs. old, was accidentally killed in his step-fa.'s mill, Jan. 23, 1669. Sarah, b. ab. 1646, at Amsterdam, m. in 1662 Jan Gerritsen van Voorst, and in 1666 Laurens Jansen Colevelt, by whom she had chn. whose desc. are yet found. Mary, b. 1652, m. Hendrick Gerritsen Blauvelt (see p. 407); and Anna, b. 1657, m. John Delamontagne. To her son Daniel and son-in-law Delamontagne, Annetie Daniels, then for the third time a wid., conveyed some city property May 10, 1688. She was afterward allowed pay by government "for tending sick soldiers." Daniel Waldron, b. 1650 at Amsterdam, m. in 1673 Sarah Rutgers, dr. of Rutger Willemsen. He was a gun-stock maker, but while serving in the city guards against Leisler, lost an eye and was otherwise badly hurt by the premature discharge of "a great gone," Mar. 19, 1691, and which killed several persons, including Jacob De Key, the De Key anc., and Major Patrick MacGregory, from whom are desc., I believe, the *Gregory* family of Orange Co., of which was the late Dr. H. H. Gregory, of H. Daniel Waldron and his son Joseph were admitted freemen Aug. 30, 1698. He had chn., *Joseph*, b. 1674; *Judith*, b. 1675, m. Mr. Isaac Selover; *Rutger*, b. 1677; *Annetie*, b. 1681, m. Francis Huys and Isaac van Duersen; *Sarah*, b. 1683, m. Carsten Burger; *John*, b. 1685; *Maria*, b. 1686, m. Frederick Williams; *Cornelia*, b. 1688, m. Gerrit de Forest; and *Catharine*, b. 1689, m. Isaac Boelen. The last d. in her 83d yr., in 1772, her srs. Sarah and Cornelia surviving her; and of the others, Judith lived to be 85, Annetie 84, and Mary 86. Their mo. d. Jan. 7, 1735, having reached her 93th year. Truly a long-lived race!

Joseph Waldron, a "cordwainer," m. in 1696 Anna Woodward; his will, dated N. Y., May 5, 1715, was proved Oct. 10, 1722. His chn. that survived inf. were Jannetie, b. 1698, who m. Henricus Boelen; Sarah, b.

on the Delaware. The next year the directors in Holland would have made Waldron sheriff of the Dutch towns on Long Island, but Stuyvesant wrote them, June 25, 1660: "Respecting the person, Resolved Waldron, we may be permitted to remark, that when appointed as a deputy to the *fiscael*, and as *schout-by-nacht* in this city, he conducted himself with so much fidelity and vigilance that he gave to us and the magistrates great satisfaction, so that his services, both as respects the Company and the *fiscael*, can hardly be dispensed with, besides that he would not be so well fitted for the shrievalty of the said villages, as he cannot well wield his pen; wherefore, till your further orders on this point, we shall ask his continuance in that office." Stuyvesant was allowed to retain his favorite officer while his own rule lasted.

On the accession of the English, Waldron took the oath of allegiance (Oct., 1664), but retired to private life at H. with the disappointments of one whose interests, as well as sympathies, all lay with the former government. It was still a pleasure to correspond with kindred in Holland. Mortien Govert, of Am-

1701; Catharine, b. 1703, m. 1726 Hendrick van Winckel, of Bergen, N. J.; Joseph, b. 1708, cordwainer, m. 1731 Elsie Hellaker, both living, 1758, at Pembelpogh, on Bergen Neck (parents of Jacobus, of Staten Island, blacksmith, who m. 1762 Elizabeth Holland, wid., and had issue Joseph, 1765, etc.); Benjamin, b. 1711, hatter, m. Maria Debevoise (by whom a dr. Maria, who m. Isaac Meet), and was living in 1758 with his second w. Bridget Haviland, at Newtown, L. I.; Daniel, b. 1713, a cordwainer, admitted freeman, N. Y., 1737, where he d. ab. 1756, having m. three w., viz., Maria Pell, 1735; Maria Gautier, 1743; and Teuntie Bogert, 1746, and leaving two sons, Daniel, house-carpenter (m. 1759 Catharine Turner), and Joseph, b. 1740, feltmaker (m. 1761 Mary Foshay); and Jacobus, b. 1717, who d. July 22, 1730.

Rutger Waldron, a turner, made freeman Feb. 3, 1699, m. 1700 Deborah Pell, and 1714 Cornelia Morse. He d. 1720, leaving Daniel, b. 1703 (fa. of William, of N. Y., baker, who m. 1752 Hillegond Mintborne, and d. 1762, leaving chn. Jane, John, Daniel, and Richard); Samuel, b. 1705, of N. Y., blockmaker, m. 1746 Mary Kip, and d. Apl. 2, 1772, leaving son Richard; Richard, b. 1707, made freeman 1732, m. 1734 Anna de Graaf, wid. of John Langedyke, made property as a baker and shopkeeper, and d. Jan. 4, 1775, without surviving chn.; Johannes, b. 1713, m. 1741 Margaret Van Noss, was living 1774, with chn. Christopher, b. 1743, Deborah, b. 1745, and Rachel, b. 1746; Sarah, b. 1716, living unm. 1774; and Cornelia, b. 1718, who m. Jurlaen Blaau, issue William, Cornelia, Sarah, and Henry Blaau, or Blaw.

John Waldron was a turner, and m. Rachel Lefferts, dr. of Leffert Pietersen van Haughwout, of Flatbush, to which place Waldron removed, and was there living in 1755, a farmer. He had issue Daniel, Leffert, Benjamin, etc., of whom Leffert, who d. 1748, was fa. of Johannes, of Middlebush, N. J.: see *Leffert Genealogy*, pp. 28, 29, from which we differ somewhat. Daniel and his w. Hepzibah, also went to N. J., had Johannes, b. 1737, etc., and one of their younger sons, Leffert, b. 1754, d. Aug. 20, 1847, was the fa., by his w. Sarah Colthar, of the present respected Cornelius L. Waldron, of Martinville, N. J., fa.-in-law of Charles H. Horton, M.D.

sterdam, writing to Resolved, Apl. 12, 1660, says, "Brother: Tall Anna has gone over with the supercargo who lived in Nicholas Carman's house." Waldron had secured some property at H. (see pp. 280, 294, 297), and was soon called to public office, from which he seldom had a respite for the rest of his life. He was one of the five patentees named in Nicolls' patent, and also served in the eldership. He d. in 1690; his inventory taken that year, May 17, embracing lands, slaves, farm-stock, etc. The following items stand first: "Three lots of land lying upon Van Keulen's Hook, with one lot of land lying upon Jochem Pieters, and a house with its lot (*erf*), comprising buildings and plantation, as it is situate and lying at this village; as also a piece of meadow lying in the Round Meadow."*

But Waldron owed so much that the heirs agreed to let his son Samuel take all the property, real and personal, on condition that he assume the debts and the support of the widow. This was subscribed to May 10, 1690, and pursuant to which, on the 17th, the town clerk, Bertholf, took a list of the lands and effects, in presence of the constable, etc., and on June 5 the magistrates appointed Adolph Meyer and Daniel Tourneur to appraise the same. But on the 14th the heirs executed a paper assigning "two thirds of the estate of our deceased father, aforesaid, to his creditors, for the payment of his debts, and the widow agreeably to law shall retain one third." On July 16 ensuing, the wid., for 1200 gl., conveyed to Arent Harmons, "a lot of land on Jochem Pieters, being No. 12, on the survey." On the 25th ensuing, a public sale of part of the farm-stock, etc., took place; and the next day the wid. sold to John Hendricks van Brevoort, for 600 gl., "a half lot lying upon Van Keulen's Hook, being No. 9, the other half belonging to Adolph Meyer." On Nov. 25, 1690, the wid. and heirs sold to Samuel Waldron, for 3800 gl., "the farm of his deceased father, Resolved Waldron, consisting of two lots and a half of land, lying upon Van Keulen's Hook, with the meadows, buildings, and planting;" on the same date released to John Dyckman, for 400 gl., "a certain piece of meadow lying in the Round Meadow, at Spuyten Duyvel, next to the meadow of Coenraet and Meyndert;" and also ratified the sale of Nos. 3 and 4, New Lots, which Resolved Waldron had deeded to Samuel, Feb. 20, 1686, and he to his br. Johannes, May 21, 1689.

Resolved Waldron's chn. by his first w., Rebecca Hendricks, all b. at Amsterdam, were William, b. 1647; Rebecca, b. 1649,

* The statement in the *Annals of Newtown*, p. 381, that Resolved Waldron "acquired a large property at Hoorn's Hook, within the limits of Harlem, on which he located," was made on the authority of Mr. Isaac Adriance, seldom inaccurate in such matters; but was found, on fuller investigation, to apply to Samuel, son of Resolved Waldron.

who m. John Nagel and John Dyckman; and Aeltie, b. 1651, who m. Capt. Johannes Vermilye. By his second w., Tanneke Nagel, he had Barent, b. 1655; Ruth, b. 1657, who m. John Delamater and Hendrick Bogert; Cornelia, b. 1659, who m. Peter van Oblienis; Johannes, b. 1665, and Samuel, b. 1670: three b. in New Amsterdam, the others at H.*

William Waldron, of N. Y., cooper (see p. 373), was made viewer of pipestaves, June 7, 1676. On Dec. 17, 1679, he and the other coopers, in all twenty-two, formed a combination to maintain their prices upon casks and barrels, and prevent underselling. For this they were proceeded against before the governor and council, and fined each fifty shillings, for "the church or pious uses." The cullers of pipestaves were dismissed, and Waldron and his partner, Petersen, were sworn as cullers, Feb. 16, 1680. Waldron was appointed one of the public measurers Dec. 1, 1702. He was still living in 1710. By Engeltie, dr. of Peter Stoutenburgh, m. in 1671 (see p. 304), he had issue, *Rebecca*, b. 1672, *Peter*, b. 1675, *Hendrick*, b. 1677, *William*, b. 1680, *Aefie*, b. 1682, *Annetie*, b. 1692, *Wyntie*, b. 1694. Of Hendrick, Aefie, and Wyntie, no more is found. Rebecca m. John Davenport and David Kent, and Jannetie m. Thomas Powell and William Adams; Powell being a young man from St. Christopher. *William Waldron* m. Johanna, dr. of John Nagel, of H., and had issue Resolved, b. 1706, Rebecca, 1709, William, 1713, Johanna, 1715, and Deborah, 1717: but two yrs. later we lose track of William and his family, who seem to have left the city. On his petition an act was passed in 1717 to exempt his sloop, the *Mary and Hannah*, from paying tonnage. His br. *Peter* went to Albany, m. in 1698 Tryntie, dr. of Cornelis Vandenbergh, and d. at that place, in 1725, leaving issue, William, b. 1700; Cornelia, b. 1702, m. to Derick Bratt, Jr.; Cornelius, b. 1705; Engeltie, b. 1708, d. single; Catharine, b. 1711, m. Hendrick van Wie; Eva, b. 1711, m. John Witbeck; Peter, b. 1717, d. 1728; Rebecca, b. 1710, m. John G. Yates; and Gerrit, b. 1723. Of these, Cornelius m. in 1732 Jannetie van Ness, and d. in 1756; he has desc. about Half Moon, Bethlehem, and Waterford. The brs. William and Gerrit, both masons, removed to the city of N. Y., but William eventu-

* Capt. JOHN WALDRON, who commanded his Majesty's ship Greyhound, was probably not from either of our Waldron families. He m. at N. Y., by license of Oct. 27, 1704, Cornelia Hardenberg. About 1721 he gave up his command, and became a merchant; was vestryman of Trinity Ch., 1725 to 1732, and captain of the Blue Artillery co., and as such had charge of the military stores for some 20 yrs. He d. ab. 1762. His dr. Mary m. Daniel Stiles. His son John, b. 1709, m. 1732 Elizabeth Bresteede, and Gerardus, b. 1713, m. 1736 Elizabeth Rose, but both d. soon after their m., (Gerardus in 1737, at Hurley, Ulster Co.), leaving no issue. The wid. of John, Jr., m. 1737 Johannes Remsen.

ally returned to Albany, where he left a family, by his w. Elizabeth Beekman. His will, made 1768, was proved 1774. See *Pearson*, and *Todd Gen.* Gerrit m. 1744 Maria de Forest, and in 1765 became a freeman. He was fa. of Catharine, b. 1748, who m. Alexander Exceen; Peter, b. 1751, Cornelius, b. 1753, and John, b. 1758; said Peter known as Peter G. Waldron.

Barent Waldron, whose possession of Glondie's Point gave him a place among the patentees, m. Sept. 25, 1687, Jannetie, dr. of John Meyndertsz. See p. 236. Having much of his fa.'s aptness for public business, he served the town in various trusts, especially in that of collector. His name as assessor stands in Montgomery's charter, 1731, and he signs the Mill Camp grant in 1738. At this date Jochem and Jacob Gardenier appear to occupy his farm. Being aged, he sold his farm, Aug. 6, 1740, to John R. Myer, of N. Y. See pp. 500, 528. Barent had chn., *Tanneke*, b. 1688, who m. John Adriaens, of Hackensack; *Belitie*, b. 1690, m. Isaac Delamater, Jr.; *Johannes*, b. 1692; *Resolved*, b. 1695, not further noticed; *Catharine*, b. 1698, m. John Foshay; and *Margaret*, b. 1700, who m. Cornelius Lydecker, of Hackensack. *Johannes Waldron* m. June 5, 1719, Susannah, dr. of Isaac Delamater, and some yrs. later removed to Philipsburgh, Westchester Co., both living to an advanced age, and having sons and drs. Of the former, we believe, were Barent and Isaac; and of the latter, Cornelia, who m. Jacob Gardenier, Catharine, who m. Reynier Quackenbush, and Rebecca, who m. 1759 Jacob Flierboom, of Tappan. Isaac Waldron m. Francina Flierboom, his only son known to us being John, b. Dec. 13, 1760. Barent Waldron was b. at Harlem, and m. at Philipsburgh, June 9, 1744, Lena Gardenier; issue, Johannes, b. July 25, 1752; Barent, b. Nov. 20, 1754; Jacobus, b. Feb. 24, 1757; Isaac, b. June 7, 1759; Jannetie, b. May 22, 1761; Rebecca, b. Dec. 18, 1763. There was also *Johannes Waldron*, who lived at Philipsburgh, probably related to, but not easily identified with, our Waldrons, if, as his marriage record says, he was b. "at Utrecht, in Holland." He m. in 1720 Janneke Bogert, of Tappan, probably a dr. (not named p. 492) of Peter and Feytie, and, if we mistake not, was fa. of Peter Waldron, b. in Fordham, who, while living at Philipsburgh, m. Oct. 10, 1747, Marritie Ackerman.* He became a freeman of N. Y. in 1752, and

* DAVID ACKERMAN, whose desc. are very numerous, was from Berlikum, in Brabant. His departure from Amsterdam for this country, in 1662, is mentioned p. 106, but considering the silence of our records regarding him it may be doubted whether he survived the voyage. He had six chn., who came over, viz., Lysbeth, b. 1642, Annetken, b. 1644, David, b. 1646, Lourens, b. 1650, Lodewyck, b. 1654, and Abraham, b. 1656. Lysbeth being the eldest, upon her seems to have devolved the care of the younger chn. She and her st. joined the chh. at New Amsterdam Jan. 6, 1663, being the

had sons David, b. 1754, and Isaac, 1756; the first, by trade a gunsmith, and a much respected citizen, m. 1773 Elizabeth Tremper, and d. Nov. 9, 1811, at 418 Broadway.

Johannes Waldron, son of Resolved, m. in 1690 Anna, dr. of Capt. Jan van Dalsen; and living close under Jochem Pieters Hills (133d Street, between 8th and 9th Aves.), he was usually called *of the Hill*, to distinguish him from his namesake of Hoorn's Hook. His house-lot, which lay at the end of the New Lots, but west of the highway, was bought from the town, May 10, 1688, for 12 gl., by his br. Samuel, who, after building on it, sold it to Johannes, May 21, 1689, together with the New Lots, Nos. 3, 4, 5, 7, which had come to Samuel from his fa. and others. On Apl. 3, 1690, the town sold Joh. an addition to his house-lot, making it 17 rods on the road, and to extend back to the foot of the hill. Joh. and Barent together bought No. 8 of the New Lots, Jan. 1, 1701, from Johannes' br.-in-law, Teunis van Dalsen, who had obtained it, May 1, 1696, from Joost van Oblinus. This lot they divided, Joh. taking the

first communion season after their arrival. They lived in the *Marckvelt Steeg*. In 1664 Anneke m. Nathaniel Pietersen Hennion, from Leyden; and in 1668 Lysbeth became the w. of Kier Wolters, of H., whence for several yrs. some of the family are found here and at Fordham, where Lourens rented a farm; see pp. 278, 350. In 1679 Lourens m. Geertie Egberts. David, living in N. Y., m. in 1680 Hillegond, dr. of Abram Isaacs Verplanck. Lodewyck m. at Kingston, in 1681, Janneke, b. in New England, dr. of Jacob Blaeck, of N. Y., (see p. 228) and Abraham, living at Bergen, m. in 1683 Aeltie, dr. of Adrian van Laer. All the family ultimately went to Hackensack; David, Lourens, and Lodewyck, with their w., helping to organize the chh. there in 1686, the nearest chh. previously being the newly formed French society at *Kinkachemeck*, or Kinderkameck. Abraham also joined in 1696. Lodewyck losing his w., m. in 1699 Hillegond, dr. of Hendrick Bosch, and removed to Philipsburgh, Westchester co. We give a list of chn., but incomplete. David had issue, *David*, b. 1681, m. Gerbrecht Romeyn; *Johannes*, b. 1684, m. Jannetie Losier; *Marritie*, b. 1690, m. Swain Ogden, of Newark. Lourens had *Lysbeth*, b. 1680, m. Cornelius Vanderhoof, from Albany; *Jannetie*, b. 1682, m. Jacobus van Voorhees; *Egbert*, b. 1685, m. Elizabeth Bryant; *Catharine*, b. 1687, m. John Verwey; *David*, b. 1689, m. Sarah Culver; and *Johannes*, who m. Jacomina Demarest. Abraham had *David*, b. 1684, m. Margaret Jurcks; *Gerrit*, b. 1685 m. Jannetie van Voorhees; *Abigail*, b. 1687, m. Andries Hopper and Derick Brinkerhoff. *Lysbeth*, b. 1689, m. Johannes Doremus; *Annetken*, b. 1691, m. Thomas Doremus; *Adrian*, b. 1695, m. Mary van Blarcom; *Johannes*, b. 1696, m. 1721 Maria Wakefield, and 1728 Elizabeth Stagg; *Gulian*, b. 1697, m. Rachel van Voorhees; *Anna-Maria*, b. 1701, m. Albert Terhune; *Abraham*, b. 1702, m. Hendrica Hopper, and *Sarah*, b. 1703, m. Cornelius Boers. Lodewyck, of Philipsburgh, had a dr. *Lysbeth*, b. 1684, m. Arent Pootman (Putman), of Schenectady, but who moved to the "Maquaas country;" and dr. *Francina*, b. 1696, m. Samuel Williams, of Albany. His son *David*, b. 1694, m. 1719, Mary See, was a deacon in the Philipsburgh chh., and fa. of Mary, who m. Peter Waldron, as in the text. We have not space for fuller details, but hope this brief sketch may aid some desc., with a becoming pride in his ancestry, to fill out the family tree.

western half. He had already secured No. 2, originally Claude Delamater's, from his son-in-law, Arent Bussing, and in 1731 bought No. 6, from Isaac Delamater, who had gotten it in 1729 from Nich. Kortright, gd.-son of Cornelis Jansen, the first owner. Thus Johannes came to hold Nos. 2 to 7 and half of 8, being 6½ lots. His large acquisitions from the drafted lands are shown in App. J. He d. in 1753, having survived his w. and all his chn. except his son Resolved. He had *Ann*, b. 1692, who m. John Delamater; *Margaret*, b. 1693, who m. Adolph Myer; *Cornelia*, b. 1696, who m. Ryck Lent; *Johannes*, b. 1698; *Resolved*, b. ab. 1702, and *Samuel*, b. ab. 1705. The last bought his fa.'s farm and stock, Nov. 17, 1748, but d. in 1752, his wid., Engeltie, occupying the farm till the Revolution. His heirs sold it to John Delancey, July 10, 1776, the principal heir being his dr. Engel, who m. 1765 Lawrence Myer, fa. of Samuel Myer.

Resolved Waldron, son of Johannes "of the Hill," m. 1729 Mattie, dr. of Adrian and Anna Quackenbush (see p. 515), and removed to Hackensack, joining the chh. there in 1731. On Apl. 10, 1751, he bought a farm of 135 a., on Floris' Fall, at Haverstraw, to which, after his dec., his sons John and Jacob succeeded, purchasing from the co-heirs, June 17, 1769, and making a division Oct. 23, 1600. Resolved being weak, made his will, Dec. 22, 1756; it was proved June 1, 1761. His chn. were John, Adrian (also called Edward), Jacob, Anna, who m. Johannes Springsteen,* Elizabeth, m. Patrick Hine, Mary, m. Abraham Lent, and Catharine, who m. Alexander Bulen.

Johannes Waldron, the son of Johannes of the Hill, m. in 1719 Elizabeth, dr. of Samson Benson, but died in 1724, leaving two sons, Johannes, b. 1721, and Samuel, b. 1723. His wid. m. John Romer, and went to live in Bergen Co., N. J., but returned to H., where Romer purchased, in 1744, and held till the Revolution or later, the square plot in the village, south of the Church Lane, which John P. Waldron devised, in 1806, to his dr. Cornelia, who m. S. D. Ingraham. Johannes Waldron, b. 1721, built a house on the Commons, at 90th Street, at the junction of Kingsbridge Road with the *Bloomingdale*

* The SPRINGSTEENS have a good claim, in the matter of ancestry, to the traditional "three brothers;" for to Joost and Johannes Springsteen, named in the *Annals of Newtown*, p. 130, as coming from Groningen in 1652, must be added Melle, or Melchert, at Bushwick, 1663, who m. Gertrude Bartelsen, became a freeman of N. Y., Jan. 23, 1676, but ultimately removed to Rockland co. He had sons Casparus, Jurian and Isaac; the first the miller who went to Schenectady. See Pearson's *Albany Settlers*. Caspar, of Haverstraw, 1702, son of Johannes aforesaid, also left a family, whence, probably, Johannes named in the text. We have gathered other items respecting the Springsteens, which would aid in making up a genealogy. The first were Swedes. The Delaware branch shortened the name to Spring.

New Cross Road, also called Apthorpe's or Jauncey's Lane. Though originally we believe without a written title to the land he had inclosed, he continued in possession till his d. in 1813, at the age of 91 yrs. His old house, which stood in Central Park, was afterward burned. He was twice m., first in 1745, to Wyntie Terhune, of Hackensack, and secondly in 1781, to Maria Vermilye, of Yonkers; by the first having a large family, his son Samuel B., b. 1755, succeeding to his "possession." His eldest son John, b. 1746, is still remembered; another son, Albert, was b. 1749; another son, Peter, m. Hannah van Blarcom, in 1774, but d. in N. Y. in 1780, without issue; another son, Benjamin, d. at his residence near St. Mark's Church, ab. 1823; another son, Oliver, of N. Y., freeman, 1770, was fa. of Mrs. Eliza Byrne, wid. of Edward Byrne. Of Johannes Waldron's drs., Elizabeth, b. 1747, m. William Sandallan, Mary m. William Shaw, and Anna m. Jones.

Samuel Waldron, youngest son of Resolved 1st, purchased the paternal farm upon Van Keulen's Hook, Nov. 25, 1690, as before mentioned. He m. Neeltie, dr. of Francis Bloodgood, of Flushing.* Waldron was among the first to discard the common fences. On Oct. 26, 1704, he gave notice that he should do so, and, within a year and six weeks, fence in his lands on Van Keulen's Hook. The same notice was given by Arent Bussing; and also by Johannes Waldron, Joost and Peter van Oblienis, and Barent Nagel, owning lots on Jochem Pieters. Waldron had a share in the Hoorn Frigate, a somewhat noted vessel, which, being sent out by Gov. Sloughter on the public service, was captured by the enemy. In 1710 he bought the John Delamater lands, including the Hoorn's Hook farm, two north gardens (see p. 499), a lot on Montanye's Flat, and No. 1,

* Captain FRANS JANSEN BLOODGOOD, or *Bloetgoet*, as then written, was from Amsterdam, and one of the early colonists to New Amstel, whither he was accompanied by his w. Lysbeth Jans, a native of Gouda, and an infant, Geertie. In 1659 he came to New Amsterdam, but settled in Flushing, owning, when he died, land, cattle, and sheep. On May 24, 1674, he was commissioned chief officer of the Dutch militia of Flushing, Hempstead, Jamaica, and Newtown. Two yrs. after, "being sorely wounded and very weak," he gave directions as to his property, and d. Dec. 29, 1676. His wid. three yrs. later, m. Wouter Gysberts, from Hilversum. His chn. were Geertie, b. 1658 at Amsterdam, m. John Marston; Adriana, b. 1660, m. Hendrick Hegeman; Isabella, b. 1662, m. Ide van Schaick; Judith, b. 1665, m. Johannes Wynkoop; William, b. 1667; Neeltie, b. 1670, m. Samuel Waldron; John, b. 1672, and Lysbeth, b. 1675, and unm. in 1698. At this date John, and his w. Mary, were living at Flushing. William belonged to Lt. Schuyler's troop in 1687, was elected one of the first vestrymen for Jamaica parish in 1703, and in 1714 was justice of the peace. Desc. of Frans Bloodgood went to Albany in the next century (*Pearson*); and the N. Y. Directory witnesses to their increase in this city, some of them distinguished for their wealth.

Van Keulen's Hook, the last joining his farm there, which embraced lots 2, 3, and half of 4. This farm he sold, Mar. 23, 1711, to Capt. Charles Congreve and John James, reserving the *morgen rights*, but allowing the puchasers "all those undivided sixteen acres of land in the commons of Harlem, of the first and second draft belonging to the said Samuel Waldron." On selling this farm to John van Horn, Mar. 27, 1711, Congreve substituted for this 16 a. his lot No. 7, 2d Div., retaining his lot in 1st Div., which he sold, Dec. 26, 1713, to Johannes Waldron. Removing to Hoorn's Hook, Samuel Waldron secured a patentee deed for his new farm, of 115 a., Dec. 20, 1712. For his draft lots, see p. 521, also App. J. He sold, prior to 1715, his lot in 1st Div. to Abram Delamontanie, his 2d Div. to Samson Benson, and 3d Div. to Johannes Benson. He got an additional 10 a. from Peter van Oblienis in 1720. Its situation is not clearly shown; but what is said p. 541 may be compared with the further reference to it here. Waldron d. in 1737, his lands, now rated 150 a., passing to his son Johannes, and from him in 1741 to his br. William, who the yr. following conveyed part of the farm (17 a., say the Hopper place), to his br. Benjamin, and the lot on Montanye's Flat, with lot No. 12, 4th Div. and 4 a. of the 10 a. lot aforesaid, to his br. Peter. William kept 3 a. of the last lot, and the remaining 3 a. were bought by Hendrick Myer, apparently because adjacent to the Gloudie Point Farm, which Myer had recently purchased; see p. 528. If not here, we know not where to locate this 10 a. lot. From William and Benj. the title to the farm is readily traced. See App. H. Samuel had the following chn., namely, *Johannes*, b. 1693; *Francis*, b. 1695, d. y.; *Francis*, b. 1697, *Resolved*, b. 1699, *Elizabeth*, b. 1700, *Tanneke*, b. 1703, *William*, b. 1705, *Peter*, b. 1708, *Samuel*, b. 1710, and *Benjamin*, b. 1713. Elizabeth m. Martin Beekman, and Tanneke m., Johannes Benson.* *Johannes*

* MARTIN BEEKMAN is named by two respectable authorities (*Our Home*, p. 402. *Bergen Genealogy*, p. 348), as a desc. of Wilhelmus Beeckman, noticed on p. 179. This is a mistake. Martin was the son of Hendrick and gd.-son of Marten Hendricksen, of Fort Orange, or Albany, apparently the person so-called, from Hamelwaard, in the duchy of Bremen, who came out in 1638, in the service of the Patroon Van Rensselaer. Marten Hendricksen Beeckman was a sturdy blacksmith, such a character, we may judge, as gives dignity to labor, for during a residence of some years he maintained a good credit with the deacons, who loaned him considerable sums, in 1652 and later. By his w. Susannah Jans, he had, as identified, five chn., viz., Hendrick, Johannes, Marten, Meije, who m. Cornelis Vanderhoof, of Albany, and Jan Bebout, of Brooklyn, and Neeltie, who m. Jacob Bennett, of Brooklyn. Johannes Martensen Beekman, who m. Machtelt, dr. of Jacob Schermerhorn, and Eva, dr. of John Vinhaegen, is noticed in the works of *Holgate* and *Pearson*. His br. Marten m. Neeltie, dr. of Teunis and Engeltie Slingerlant, of Albany, removed in 1692 to N. Y., and had, so far as known, seven drs. but no sons.

probably d. in 1741, and if he m.. evidently left no issue. He was assist. ald. of the Out Ward from 1731 to 1737, excepting one yr. A stone, rudely inscribed IW+D+23+AO+1693+ and rescued by Mr. Rufus Prime from the venerable Waldron house (88th Street, north side, a little east of Avenue A), when its walls were demolished in 1870, takes us back to the boyhood of Johannes Waldron; his own record, no doubt, of his initials and birthday, "Johannes Waldron, Dec. 23, Anno 1693."

Samuel Waldron, b. Feb. 13, 1710, was a blacksmith, m. Apl. 25, 1735, Anna Delamater (b. July 15, 1715), and removed to Newtown, L. I., where he bought a small farm Feb. 6, 1736. His chn. were Anne, b. Jan. 29, 1736, m. Richard Repelye; Samuel, b. Mar. 13, 1738; John S., b. June 18, 1741, d. unm., Feb. 18, 1795; Elizabeth, b. Jan. 29, 1744, m. Samuel Beck-

Hendrick Martensen Beekman, of Scotia, near Schenectady, m. Annetie, dr. of Peter Quackenbos, and had issue *Martin*, b. 1685, *Susanna*, b. 1688, *Lydia*, b. 1689, *Hendrick*, b. 1692, *Mary*, b. 1695, *Peter*, b. 1697, and *Magdalena*, b. 1701. He removed to Somerset co., N. J., where he was living on Nov. 13, 1710, when he bought from Octavio Conraets, of N. Y., a large tract of land on the Raritan river, about three miles above Somerville, part of which is now occupied by the wid. of Ex.-Sheriff Van Dorn Vredenburgh. Wilhelmus Beeckman's sons also owned various tracts on the Raritan, some of which Dr. Gerardus Beekman conveyed and devised to his son Hendrick, a merchant in N.Y.; and the two Hendricks being taken as one person has led to the error pointed out at the beginning of this note. Hendrick M. Beekman d. prior to Sept. 20, 1735, as we find by an agreement of that date between his sons Martin and Peter, and which states that they, with their br. Hendrick, had "hitherto jointly enjoyed" his lands. *Peter Beekman*, who d. in 1773, left a w. Grietie, and drs. Leentie, m. Fernandus Gulick, Annetie, m. Peter Peterson, and Neeltie, m. Bernardus van Zandt. *Hendrick*, br. of Peter, d. a bachelor, in his 77th yr., March 19, 1769, and by will gave his property to the five chn. of his br. Martin, dec., said Martin having d. Oct. 27, 1757, æ. 72 yrs. These chn. (all by his w. Elizabeth Waldron, of Hoorn's Hook, whom he m. June 21, 1724, and who d. Nov. 27, 1760, æ. 60 yrs.), were Elizabeth, b. Aug. 30, 1725, m. Francis Brasier, and d. Nov. 9, 1810; Hendrick, b. Mar. 24, 1727, m. Phebe Bloomfield, and d. Jan. 26, 1796; Samuel, b. Nov. 26, 1729, m. Elizabeth Waldron, of Newtown, L. I., and d. Oct. 19, 1808; Anna, b. June 28, 1734, m. Johannes Waldron, Nov. 12, 1766, and d. Sept. 5, 1795 (he d. Sept. 10, 1795), and John b. Nov. 5, 1741. Of these Hendrick and Phebe had eight chn., of whom Benjamin (b. Oct. 26, 1766, m. Cornelia Beekman, and d. Mar. 21, 1838), was fa. of Bloomfield Beekman, and of Elisabeth, now the respected wid. of Van Dorn Vredenburgh, Esq., dec. Samuel and Elizabeth had five chn., of whom were two sons, viz., Samuel and Martin, the last (b. May 14, 1773, m. Matilda Brokaw and Mary Powelson, and d. Aug. 26, 1844, in Somerset Co.) having fourteen chn., of whom Joseph B. was fa. of Revs. John S. and Abraham J. Beekman. Martin's br. Samuel (b. Sept. 21, 1766, m. Helena Ten Broeck, and d. Mar. 4, 1850, at Harlingen), was fa. of Rev. Jacob Ten Broeck Beekman, (b. Apl. 10, 1801, m. Ann Crawford, and d. Apl. 23, 1875), being the fa. of Hon. George C. Beekman, of Freehold, N. J., without whose friendly co-operation we may have been less successful in correcting the current mistakes regarding the early history of this important branch of the Beekman family.

man; Margaret, b. July 13, 1746, m. Jacobus Waldron; Cornelia, b. Sept. 11, 1749, d. unm., Apl. 5, 1760; William, b. Oct. 22, 1752, d. Apl. 8, 1824; and Benjamin, b. Feb. 25, 1757. See *Annals of Newtown*, p. 381.

Francis Waldron settled near North Branch, N. J., where he and w., Catalina van Nest, were chh. mem. in 1725, and he afterward a deacon. He d. in 1764 or 1765, leaving sons Samuel, Jerome, and Johannes, who shared his farm; and William, who received £100. He had also drs. Neeltie and Agnietie.

Resolved Waldron m. 1722 Jannetie, dr. of Joh. Myer, settled near Harlingen, N. J., where he was a deacon and elder; returned eventually and lived at Eastchester, then became a baker in N. Y., and later a farmer in Brooklyn. He d. there Oct. 21, 1772, and was buried in N. Y., administration on his estate being granted on Oct. 23 to his youngest son Adolph, also of Kings Co., yeoman. Resolved had three sons, to wit, Samuel, John, and Adolph; of whom the first m. 1749 Mary Bassett, was a farmer at the ferry in Brooklyn, and d. the year before his fa., having had issue, Catharine, b. 1750, Maria, 1753, Margaret, 1755, Samuel, 1757, Elsie, 1759, John, 1761, Jane, 1763, and Eve, 1765. His dr. Catharine m. Capt. Nich. P. Bogert, and Mary m. Elias Nexsen, of N. Y., merchant. John Waldron, b. 1726, son of Resolved, and "of N. Y., mariner," m. 1759 Rebecca Bussing, by whom he had Mary, b. 1762, and John, b. 1771; the first m. Samuel Myer. Adolph Waldron, of N. Y., baker and shopkeeper, m. Mar. 15, 1758, Catharine, dr. of Capt. Alexander Phœnix, removed to Eastchester, returned to N. Y., sold out here after the d. of his br,. Samuel, and became a farmer and innkeeper at Brooklyn ferry. In 1775 he was made capt. of the troop of light-horse and soon called into active service to guard the coast. During the war he lived at Preakness, N. J. In 1795 he sold his Brooklyn property, and d. in 1802. Issue, Elizabeth, b. Apl. 13, 1761, d. y.; Resolve, b. Aug. 13, 1763; Alex.-Phœnix, b. Sept. 13, 1765; Catharine, b. Dec. 12, 1768; Elizabeth, b. Sept. 3, 1777, d. unm. June 9, 1802. Alex. P. Waldron, of Hackensack, a most excellent man, m. a dr. of Rev. Hermanus Meier. His br., Capt. Resolve Waldron, of N.Y., a shipmaster, m. 1782 Elisabeth Godwin; issue, Adolph, b. Oct. 22, 1783; Abraham-Godwin, b. Aug. 12, 1786; Elizabeth, b. Sept. 10, 1789, and perhaps others.

Peter Waldron, also called Petrus, was named for his uncle Peter van Oblienis, to whose lands he afterward succeeded. He m. Elizabeth, dr. of Joh. Myer, and was made constable in 1735. In 1738 he occupied the plot before of Peter van Oblienis, and since of James Chesterman; see pp. 191, 541. Coming into possession of the Oblienis farm on Van Keulen's Hook, Peter Waldron made additions to that part of it which joined on the

Church Lane. One piece, known as "the *hoeck*," corner or end, "of the *Klaaver wey*," or Clover Pasture (see pp. 343, 344), and described as "lying in the village of Harlem, aforesaid, bounded west against the land now in the possession of Peter Waldron, north by the highway, east by the street or lane, south by the old lots of Van Keulen's Flats," was sold him by the town, May 11, 1747, for £16 : 10, "upon condition that Maria Meyer may have a convenient way to her land." A question between him and Benj. Benson, who owned lots 7 to 9, Van Keulen's Hook, was settled by the award of May 30, 1750, which decided "that Peter Waldron hath a just right to, and that he be at liberty to take in and enclose to his own use and possession, a small slip of land which lies within the fence of th said Benjamin Benson, behind the *Cloverwey*, so as the same is now staked out to him for that purpose." Waldron d. July 12, 1772, being fa. of 1. Cornelia, b. Dec. 19, 1733, who m. her cousin, David Waldron; 2. Peter, b. Dec. 15, 1736 (m. Engeltie Myer, Jan. 29, 1765, and was fa. of Susannah, b. Jan. 20, 1766, who m. Peter Myer); 3. John, b. June 30, 1741, d. æ. 5 months; and 4. John P. Waldron, b. Apl. 1, 1748, who m. Elizabeth Bend, a niece of Grove Bend, Esq., and was fa. of Peter, Grove-Bend, John P., Jr., and Cornelia, who m. Samuel Dana Ingraham. At a meeting of the H. freeholders, held at Marriner's Inn, Dec. 19, 1801, John P. Waldron and five others were chosen commissioners to carry into effect a plan for dividing up the Harlem Commons among the freeholders, and laying an annual ground-rent which should be applied to the support of an academy in said town. Register's Off., *Deeds*, 73 : 420. Mr. Waldron d. in 1806.

Benjamin Waldron m. in 1736 Elizabeth, dr. of Jacob Sammon. Obtaining the two lower lots of the Hoorn's Hook farm, known as Nos. 3, 4, of the grants of 1677, he exchanged with John Brown, owning the Codrington farm, giving the easterly half of these for the westerly half of his lots Nos. 1, 2, by which both tracts were made nearer square. Waldron built on his part, and for many yrs. carried on a tannery and shoe factory. He d. in 1782, and the property passing to Yellis Hopper, was thence known as the Hopper place, the quaint old stone house standing till late on 2d Ave., west side, between 83d and 84th Sts. Benjamin's chn. were John, Jacobus, Benjamin, Catalina, who m. Samuel Delamater; Elizabeth, m. Yellis Hopper, aforesaid; Cornelia, m. Ide Hennion, and Eve, who m. Robert Boyle. Benjamin m. Hannah van Sise; their dr. Gertrude, b. Jan. 5, 1784, m. her cousin, Samuel Waldron. Jacobus m. his cousin, Margaret Waldron, of Newtown, where he settled.

William Waldron, b. Feb. 10, 1705, m. in 1729 Aagie, dr. of Jacob Sammon; in 1734, Catharine, dr. of David Mandeville, and as his third w., Antie, dr. of Adolph Myer, who survived him. He was made constable in 1734, and soon after sergeant in the company of Capt. Stuyvesant. Enjoying the confidence of his townsmen, by whom on various occasions he was intrusted with the public interests, Mr. Waldron fairly represented the stability and respectability so largely characteristic of the family. He d. Dec. 5, 1769, and was buried with his fathers in the old graveyard at H. His sons were David, Samuel, Adolph, John, Peter, Benjamin, and William; and drs. Tanneke, eldest ch., b. 1730, who m. Matthew Mandeville, Mary, who m. John Vredenburgh, and Margaret, who m. Abraham Lent. Of the sons, William d. without issue, making his br. Adolph his heir at law; Benjamin and Peter removed to Fishkill. John, tailor, m. Elizabeth Oaks and Aletta Bicker, and had with other chn. issue, by the first, William J., b. 1774, grocer, assist. ald., 1811, and by the second, John-Vredenburgh, b. 1788, metal-fan-sash maker, and Victor-Bicker, b. 1798, merchant-tailor. Adolph, house-carpenter, m. Christina Zabriskie, and was fa. of Benjamin A., coachmaker, and Tunis A., tailor, the last fa. of Adolphus, of Newark. Samuel, blacksmith, who held part of the old farm, and d. 1798, left by his w. Aefie, sons Samuel and David; the last d. unm. in 1814. Samuel, the elder br., b. 1780, m. his cousin, Gertrude Waldron, and d. Dec. 31, 1824, being fa. of Col. Samuel Waldron, of H. David Waldron, b. 1737, eldest son of William, m. Cornelia Waldron, Dec. 1, 1763, and d. Oct. 10, 1813; issue, William, of Yorkville; Peter, of Oyster Bay; Catharine, who m. Jonathan Randell, Jr., and Eliza, who m. John Dawson.

Cheerfully the author puts the final period to these family sketches, with the untold labor they have involved; yet not without regret, as in parting with old friends, does he take leave of the familiar names and scenes to which it has been his grateful office to introduce the reader. Well has one expressed it in the couplet:

> "These to the feeling heart are hallowed haunts,
> Though but in ruins seen and faintly traced."

But the condensed form which it was found necessary to give to these details has at once precluded sentiment and restricted the author to naked fact; a method, however, deemed most in keeping with the object before referred to and steadily pursued, namely, to make these sketches the medium of useful information respecting the lands and titles, and which, it is believed, must give them a permanent interest and value with intelligent property-holders throughout this section of the city. Under the precise descriptions given—when not by metes and bounds, by the ancient lot numbers—the transmission from party to party of every original parcel of land has been so clearly indicated as to point with certainty to the origin and history of nearly every title; while also giving the most positive contradiction to the foul slander, uttered with a "zeal without knowledge," that the old settlers here were nothing but "squatters."

But if the practical information here embodied (we refer to the volume at large) shall commend our work, as we believe it must, to the notice of such as seek information of this kind; not for these alone will it possess an interest so long as the love of kin and ancestry shall remain a virtue innate within the human breast. What a nursery was Harlem of sterling old Holland and Huguenot names, which, with the lapse of generations, have migrated beyond the banks of the Hudson and the confines of neighboring States, to nearly every part of the Union. To all claiming this descent, and who would add to their reminiscences of a worthy ancestry all that is now recoverable from the crumbling records of their times, this volume is respectfully commended.

APPENDIX.

CONTENTS OF THE APPENDIX.

APPENDIX.

A. Page 167.

THE DE FOREST FAMILY.

THE history of the De Forest ancestors, as the pioneer settlers at Harlem, early engaged the author's attention, since it promised him the leading historic thread for the yet unwoven fabric of his story. Extending his inquiry to the Fatherlands, the result is already known to the reader. Driven by persecution from the French Netherlands, the De Forests became identified in Holland with the beginnings of our colonial emigration—some of its phases, developed in their unpretentious yet eventful career, in a manner equally novel and touching—till it culminated in the first settlement upon the then wild and solitary "Flats of Manhattan." Hence the pre-eminence here given them: a deserved tribute to their trials in their own and other lands, and to their well-conceived enterprises, of no less local significance because thwarted or marred by disasters beyond human control. As supplementary to these interesting details, we here add some further notes upon the family in this country, premising that this name, which under the Dutch took the form *De Forest*, is quite distinct from those of *De la Forest*, and *Van Forest*, the last an old titled family of Holland.

ISAAC DE FOREST, younger of the two brs. who emigrated in 1636, was the common anc. Born at Leyden in 1616, as elsewhere stated, he m. at New Amsterdam, in 1641, Sarah, dr. of Philippe du Trieux (Truax), and Susannah de Chiney, Walloons of the early migration, Sarah being b. here in the semi-fabulous days of Peter Minuit. The same yr. De Forest built at H. a dwelling and tobacco-house on his plantation, subsequently the site of Harlem village. In 1643 he leased it to John Denton, for raising tobacco on shares, and opened a tobacco wareroom on the Strand, now Pearl Street, in what had been the first church. Coming to own that property, he built there a fine house, "an ornament to the city." In 1650 he sold his bouwery at H. to Wm. Beeckman. Later he became a brewer; his malt-house and residence was in Stone Street, north side, near Whitehall. He also had "a hop-garden and orchard at Norman's Bight." He was among the affluent citizens who loaned 100 gl. each for repairing the city defences in 1653. On Apl. 6, 1657, "Isaac de Forest requests by petition the privileges of the Great Burgher right, as he has been in this country *over twenty years*, has built considerably in this city, and performed many services." The burgomasters deferred his request, but on Jan. 28, 1658, as one of six "suitable persons" recommended by Stuyvesant and council, De Forest was made a Great Burgher. The same yr. he was elected *schepen*, having served sundry times in the board of selectmen. In 1664, when the English fleet, which took N. Y., entered the harbor, among some persons seized was De Forest;

released Aug. 31, he afterward swore allegiance. His will is dated June 4, 1672. He d. in 1674, but his wid. not till Nov. 9, 1692. She sold the property "called the Old Kerck," June 30, 1682; that in Stone Street was sold by the chn. May 2, 1693, to Harman Rutgers, brewer, from Albany. Isaac de Forest's chn. were Jesse, b. 1642, Susannah, 1645, Gerrit, 1647, Michael, 1649, John, 1650, Philip, 1652, Isaac, 1655, Hendrick, 1657, Maria, 1666, and David, 1669; of whom, the three elder sons d. early. Susannah m. 1665 Peter De Riemer, and Maria m. 1687 Bernard Darby, from London, mariner, and 1706 Ald. Isaac De Riemer, son of Peter.

John De Forest was educated a "chirurgeon," or physician; his brs. were given trades—Philip a cooper, Isaac a baker, Hendrick and David, glaziers. Dr. De Forest m. June 8, 1673, Susannah, dr. of Nich. Verlet; bought a house and lot in Beaver Street, Feb. 20, 1682; on Oct. 4, 1687, sold for £6:5, lot No. 4, Hoorn's Hook, to Wm. Presker. See p. 417. Of several chn., but one survived ch.-hood., viz., Susannah, b. 1676, m. Robert Hickman, 1703. Philip De Forest m. Jan. 5, 1676, Tryntie, dr. of Hend. Kip, and removed to Albany, served as high-sheriff, etc., and d. 1727, having had sons Isaac, Jesse, Johannes, David, Abraham; David being anc. of Col. Jacob J. De Forest, of Duanesburgh. See *Pearson's Albany Settlers.*

Isaac De Forest, b. 1655, only son of Isaac that remained in N. Y., m. Sept. 4, 1681, Elizabeth, dr. of Lawrence Vanderspiegel, was serving the Dutch chh. as deacon, 1690 and 1696, and 1699 was appointed an overseer of public works. He d. within a yr. or two, his wid., it seems, continuing his business; she furnished provisions for the expedition to Canada in 1711. In 1741, in her 80th yr., she changed her chh. relation to Hackensack, the home of her dr. Elisabeth, w. of Rev. Antonius Curtenius. Isaac De Forest left nine chn., of whom reached maturity: *Johannes*, b. 1684; *Sarah*, 1686, m. John Myer; *Margaret*, 1689, m. Harman Rutgers; *Maria*, 1694, and *Elisabeth*, 1697, who, 1732, m. as aforesaid. *Johannes De Forest* was a baker, m. June 23, 1705, Catharine, dr. of Gerrit van Ravenstein, and buying property Mar. 22, 1715, in Marketfield St., resided in N. Y. till his d., July 30, 1757. His chn. named in his will, Dec. 25, 1746, were Isaac, b. 1705; Nicholas, 1710; Johannes, 1711; Maria, 1718, who m. Gerrit Waldron; Lawrence, 1720; Gerrit, 1723, Elizabeth, 1725. Of these, Lawrence m. 1744 Sarah, dr. of Mansfield Tucker; issue Mansfield, b. 1746, perhaps others. Isaac became a freeman, in N. Y., 1734, his br. Nicholas 1735, and Johannes 1748; the last probably fa. of Theodorus, grocer at Fly Market, who m. 1778 Mary Doughty; issue John, b. Aug. 11, 1780; Mary, Dec. 22, 1782; Theodorus, May 11, 1786, etc. Nicholas m. Maria Parker, Oct. 17, 1736, and had a son John, b. 1739, probably the sailmaker, freeman 1765, who m. 1768 Jane Albouy; in 1780 a wid., when she m. George Scott, mariner. Bernard De Forest, shopkeeper, freeman 1768, apparently br. of the sailmaker, m. 1767 Martha Albouy, in 1773 a wid., and m. Nathaniel Harriott, mariner. Isaac, b. 1705, removed to Adamsville, Somerset Co., N. J., d. ab. 1800; issue by w. Maria Brokaw, Maria, b. 1740, John, 1743, Catharine, 1745, Abraham, 1749. His son John, b. July 28, 1743, d. in N. Y. May 16, 1825, leaving five chn. by his w. Maria Van Nest, viz., Isaac, b. Mar. 3, 1764; Catharine, Jan. 17, 1766; Abraham, Apl. 2, 1774; Lawrence-Vandeveer, May 11, 1782, and John, May 8, 1784; of whom Catharine d. Nov. 19, 1846. John d. in his 81st yr., Nov. 16, 1864, having m. Surviah Whitehead; his only ch. being Mr. Isaac De Foreest, Sen., of No. 2 Old Slip. Abraham aforesaid m. Catharine Fulkerson, and d. in his 57th yr., Aug. 30, 1830, was fa. of Richard and Maria; his br. Isaac, who m. Kneertie Wortman, and d. Mar. 13, 1808, was fa. of the late Peter and John I. De Foreest, of N. Y., grocers, and their srs. Maria, Sarah, Catharine, and Margaret; and Lawrence V., of N. Y., merchant, who m. Jane, dr. of Peter Davis, of Somerville, N. J., and d. May 7, 1858, æ. nearly 76 yrs., was fa. of the late Ald. Theodore Romaine De

Forest, M.D., John Abeel De Forest, and Jane Lawrence De Forest, the accomplished and lamented Mrs. Dr. Hull of N. Y., murdered in her bed, June 11, 1879, by the burglar Cox. Gerrit De Forest, b. 1723, called Gerardus, m. 1744 Sarah Hardenbrook, and had issue John, b. 1745, Andrew, 1751, Gerardus, 1753, Theodorus, 1756, etc., of whom Theodorus m. 1779 Susannah Leggett. Gerardus was a shipwright, m. Rachel Kingsland, and d. Apl. 19, 1802, in Harrison Street, leaving his wid., who survived many yrs., and sons John, Gerardus, and David, besides seven drs., of whom Sarah, the eldest, m. Hugh Fairley.

Hendrick De Forest, b. 1657, m. June 5, 1682, Phebe, dr. of Barent van Flaesbeek, and settled at Bushwick, L. I., was commissioned justice of the peace 1698, in 1705 bought land at and removed to Madnan's Neck, and d. in 1715, having issue *Barent*, b. 1684; *Sarah*, 1686, *Gerrit*, 1689, *Henricus*, 1691, *Susannah*, 1693, *Phebe*, 1695, *Maria*, 1696, and *Jesse*, 1698; of whom Susannah m. Abraham Koning, and Phebe m. Henry Cole. Several of the sons returned to N. Y. *Henricus* was probably the sea-captain, of 1747. *Barent* m. 1708 Catalina, dr. of Anthony Sailey, and 1723 Elisabeth, dr. of Cornelius Verdoyn. He was teacher of the Dutch chh. school, serving as late as 1726, in which yr. he probably d. His wid. d. Mar. 1, 1736. His chn., save some who d. in inf., were, so far as known, Henricus, b. 1712; Phebe, 1714, m. Benj. Stout; Sarah, 1717; Catalina, 1720, m. Hendrick van Beuren; Cornelius, 1725. Cornelius m. Antie Van Winkle. *Gerrit* m. 1716 Cornelia Waldron; he d. Oct. 14, 1744, she May 9, 1772; issue Sarah, b. 1719, m. Hendrick Vandewater; Henry, 1722; Phebe, ab. 1725, m. Andrew Gewara; and Gerrit, 1731. Henry last named was perhaps the blockmaker, made freeman 1770, and Gerrit, the storekeeper at Fly Market, 1776. Henricus, b. 1712, freeman 1734, m. that yr. Susannah, dr. of Benj. Bill, and wid. of Wm. Golding, and was a printer in King (now Pine) Street, in 1753. His wid. sold part of the property Aug. 2, 1766. His chn. known but in part; his dr. Susannah m. 1754 Samuel Brown, stationer, and dr. Caroline, m. 1759 Richard King, mariner. *Jesse* m., June 14, 1719, Teuntie Titsoort. He d. Apl. 12, 1755, she Sept. 3, 1761. Their chn. who reached maturity were Abraham, b. 1722, Henricus, 1724, and Margaret, 1732, who m. Capt. Wm. Long. Of these, Henricus, blacksmith, m. Elizabeth Young, and d. prior to Aug. 21, 1772, when adm. on his estate was granted his wid. Abraham, hatter, m. in 1744 Elizabeth Myer; in 1758 went out as master-at-arms in the privateer Peggy; in 1760, '1 and '2, commanded companies from N. Y. against the French, on the frontiers. His w. d. Apl. 6, 1761. Capt. De Forest removed to Dutchess Co., and was living in 1774. His chn. were Jesse, b. 1745, Elizabeth, 1746, Peter, 1748, Anna, 1752, Abraham, 1754, Henry, 1756, Cornelia, 1758, Deborah, 1759.

David De Forest, b. 1669, removed to Stratford, Ct., subsequent to 1693, where he m. in 1696. His w. was Martha, her maiden name Blagge, as says tradition, with probable truth. Evidently she was related to Edward, Samuel, and Benjamin Blagge, of N. Y., but not a sr., as we conclude from the will of their fa., Capt. Benj. Blagge, dated June 6, 1695, and other records. David d. in Apl. 1721, his wid. (after a second m.) in 1740, æ. 63 yrs. For a list of his male desc., who have mostly lived in Connecticut, see *Bronson's Hist. of Waterbury*. His chn. were Mary, Sarah, Martha, David, Samuel, Isaac, Edward, Henry, Elizabeth, and Benjamin.

The last, b. 1716, m. Esther Beardslee, and was fa. of Benjamin, b. 1749 (who m. Mehitable Curtis), fa. of Benjamin, b. 1780 (m. Alma Southmayd), fa. of John de Forest, M.D., of Watertown, Ct., whose w. was Lucy S. Lyman. His only ch. is Mr. Erastus L. De Forest. Said Benjamin, b. 1749, was fa. of David C., b. 1774, founder of the "De Forest Fund," of Yale College, and whose son, Carlos M. De Forest, b. 1813, removed to Troy, Penn., where his chn. now reside. Hezekiah, b. 1745, a son of Benjamin,

b. 1716, was fa. of Samuel A., of Stratford, b. 1784, d. 1852, who settled in Danby, Tioga Co., N. Y., and was the fa. of Mr. Charles De Forest, of Waverly. Samuel De Forest, b. 1704, son of David and Martha, was fa. of Joseph, b. 1731, whose son Gideon removed to Edmeston, Otsego Co., N. Y., d. in 1840, and had sons Abel B., Lee, Cyrus H. (of Buffalo), Charles A. and Tracy R. De Forest. Nehemiah, b. 1743, a br. of Joseph, was fa. of Lockwood, b., Mar. 5, 1775, who m. Mehitable Wheeler, and began business as a merchant, in Greenwich Street, N. Y., in 1816, but three yrs. later, with his son William, founded the well-known mercantile house of De Forest & Son at 82 South Street. Mr. Lockwood De Forest d. Nov. 28, 1848. His sons, like himself nearly all merchants and enterprising business men, were William W., George B., Alfred, Frederick L., James G., Henry G. (lawyer), and Frederick L. 2d. His drs. were Mary L., who m. Roger Sherman Skinner, of New Haven; Susan, who m. Daniel Lord; Eliza, who m. Samuel Downer; Jane, who m. Burr Wakeman; Ann, who m. Simeon Baldwin; Sarah, who m. Walter Edwards, and Louisa, the w. successively of Samuel Woodruff and Thomas F. Cock, M.D.

B. Page 300.

THE MONTANYE FAMILY.*

Dr. JOHANNES LA MONTAGNE, prominent in the affairs of New Netherland, has a relatively important place in Harlem history, as is set forth in the preceding pages. We give briefly the sequel of his life; then notice his desc. Derick Corssen Stam, supercargo in the vessel which brought the De Forests over, had a br. Arent, whose wid. Agnes, a dr. of Gillis Ten Waert, was wooed by the Doctor, after the d. of his w., Rachel de Forest. As Arent had been lost at sea (see p. 166), it proved an obstacle to their union, but this was overcome, as is shown by the following proceeding of July 18, 1647: "Mr. Johannes La Montagne appeared before the council, and requested leave to marry Angenietie Gillis Ten Waert, widow of Arent Corssen. Being fully persuaded that he perished, as the Lords Directors have written, that they had left nothing untried to learn about him, but were entirely ignorant of his fate; therefore if Mr. La Montagne, and she Angenietie, have no scruples regarding it, they are at liberty to marry." Two months later they were m.

Montanye was commended for his discreet rule as vice-director at Fort Orange, which lasted till 1664; much of his official correspondence with Stuyvesant is preserved. He prudently swore allegiance to the new government, but from this date is lost sight of, and probably accompanied his old friend Stuyvesant on his errand to Holland in 1665, to defend his course in surrendering the country to the English. There is reason to conclude that Dr. Montanye d. abroad in 1670. He had eight chn., viz., Jolant, b. 1627, Jesse, 1629, John, 1632, Rachel, 1634, Maria, 1637, William, 1641, Gillis, 1650, and Jesse, 1653. The last two d. y., as had Jolant. The first Jesse was

* We cannot follow here the various spellings of this name which occur, but observe the form *Montanye*, as most accordant with modern usage, and with its original, the Latin *Mons*, in French *Montagne*, Mountain; see p. 53. The change of the *a*, in some branches, to *u* and *i*, seems unfortunate. After he came to this country, Dr. Montanye, previously signing his name "Mounnier de La Montagne," invariably wrote it "La Montagne," omitting his family name *Mounier* or *Monier*, which however was sometimes used by all his sons, and even grandsons, before it was finally dropped. See pp. 67, 521.

commissary of stores, 1647, but d. soon after. Rachel m. Dr. Gysbert van Imbroch, and Maria m. Jacob Kip, whose desc. have been locally prominent.*

William Montanye (he styled himself *de La Montagne*) joined the chh. at New Amsterdam Oct. 2, 1661, when he came to H. Called to be *voorleser* at Esopus, he held that office till 1678; from 1668 adding the duties of secretary. He m., May 19, 1673, Elenora, dr. of Anthony De Hooges, and that yr. drew 300 gl. from the Orphan Chamber, at Leyden (whence derived is left to conjecture); to obtain which he chose as guardians his cousins Panhuysen and Du Toict, the sons-in-law of Gerard de Forest.† Leisler made him high-sheriff of Ulster Co., Dec. 24, 1689. He had removed to Mombackus, town of Rochester, and was living 1695. His chn. were Rachel, b. 1674, who m. Harman Decker; Johanna, 1676, living 1699; William, 1678; Maria, 1680, m. Nicholas Westfall; Johannes, 1682; Jesse, 1684; Eve, 1686, m. Derick Krom; and Catharine, 1688, who m. John Bevier. Ulster Co. records are strangely silent as to William's sons.

John Montanye was b. at Leyden, and first appears as Jean Monier de La Montagne, Jr., later as Jan La Montagne, Jr. He early joined the chh. at New Amsterdam, where, in 1652, he taught school a few months, under an appointment from the directors in Holland; then was made commissary of accounts. Entering into trade with Vincent Pikes, in 1654, Montanye, about midsummer of that yr., sailed for Holland, and while there (as noticed p. 105) m. Peternella Pikes, two yrs. his junior. Returning alone to this country, he bought a residence on *Marckvelt steeg*, from his uncle De Forest, Sept. 26, 1655, preparatory to the coming of his w., who soon arrived, with her infant, John, b. at Amsterdam, and there baptized, at the Walloon chh.,

* Dr. GYSBERT GYSBERTS VAN IMBROCH, desc. of whom in N. Y. and N. J. write their name *Van Emburgh* and *Van Amburgh*, was a physician; had a sr. Barbara, the first w. of Thomas Verdon; see p. 182. In 1655 Van Imbroch, then for two yrs. a shopkeeper at New Amsterdam, was permitted "to make a lottery of a certain number of bibles, testaments and other books." His m. probably took place at Fort Orange, whither he went to live, Rachel being his second w. They removed to Wiltwyck or Kingston, joining the chh. by letter, Dec. 16, 1662 (see pp. 222, 225), and here Van Imbroch practiced medicine, being one of the *schepens* from 1663 till his d. Aug. 29, 1665, his w. having d. Oct. 4, 1664. Their chn. were Elizabeth, b. 1659, Johannes, 1661, and Gysbert, 1664; all of whom removed to N. Y. Elizabeth, m. John Peeck. Gysbert, shoemaker, came to N. Y. in 1686, m. 1688, Jannetie, dr. of Peter Mesier, and acquired property; see *Deeds* N. Y., 26, 327, and Albany, 14, 11. He had nine chn., some d. in inf. See *N. Y. Corp. Manual* for 1863, p. 805, and 1864, p. 820. Johannes van Imbroch was "doctor of physic;" m. in 1687 Margaret, dr. of Arie van Schaick, and later Catharine, dr. of Capt. Wm. Sandford, of Bergen Co., N. J., where Dr. van Imbroch then lived, and where he made his will, June 6, 1739, proved Sept. 11, 1742. He had sons and drs., the former, Gysbert, William, and John. His dr. Mary m. John Sandford, Catherine m. Richard Gibbs, of New Brunswick, and Elizabeth m. Jacobus Bertholf, 1739.

† We, Commissaries of the Court at Kingston, do certify that before us has appeared William Monier de La Montagne, son of the elder deceased Johannes Monier de La Montagne, begotten by Rachel de Forest; that said William Monier de La Montagne has given to Mr. Gabriel Monvielle, merchant at New York, a bill of exchange for three hundred guilders Holland money, reckoned at twenty stivers per guilder: And that Mr. Monvielle or his order may receive the same, therefore the above named William Monier de La Montagne by these constitutes and makes, even as he is himself authorized and fully empowered to do, his guardians or friends, Sieur Johannes Panhuysen and Mr. David du Toict, living in the city of Leyden, on his behalf and in the constituant's name, to take up from his money due from the Orphan Chamber of the said city, the beforenamed three hundred guilders, and to deliver the same according to the bill of exchange, to Mr. Gabriel Monvielle or to his order, promising to hold good that which they shall do in the premises. In witness whereof, we with our own hand, as also the Hon. Commissaries, Cornelius Wynkoop and Joost Adriaens, have subscribed this on the date, 27th March 1673, at Kingston, in the Esopus.—*Esopus Records.*

Oct. 21, 1655. On the institution of the *burgher right*, Montanye's name was the first enrolled on the list of Great Burghers, Apl. 10, 1657. That yr. he was Farmer of the Retail Excise, and was made a Fire-warden, Dec. 23, 1658.

One of the first, if not the first, to take up land at the proposed New Haerlem, in which enterprise he felt a special interest, owing to the proximity of his fa.'s lands, Vredendal; he sold his house on the Marckvelt-steeg to Joh. Verveelen, June 27, 1659, and removed hither, being chosen deacon in 1660. He was living here the next winter, when he bought "a horse, with a saddle and bridle," for 300 gl., "in good strung current wampum." His next appointment was that of schepen of the new village, where all his interests centred, after the sale, Feb. 14, 1662, of another house and lot, adjoining one owned by his fa. in Beaver Street. His service as schout, secretary, and voorleser has been duly noticed. Having lost his w., he m., June 10, 1663, Maria, dr. of Isaac Vermilye, Domine Selyns officiating; the bride's sr. Rachel being also m. to John Terbosch. How Montanye acquired the property known as the Point, before patented to his fa., as also its history till sold to Bogert, has been stated in the general history of the town, to which it properly belongs. As Montanye left the village within two yrs. after getting permission to build on his Point (see p. 363), but remained "in the jurisdiction of New Haerlem," it may be inferred that he put up buildings there, yet neither the bill of sale nor deed to Bogert mention any. They may have been destroyed. He or Bogert built the stone house whose ruins have disappeared within the last fifty years: it stood nearer the Mill Pond, and westerly a little from the late farm-house, torn down by S. B. McGown, Esq., when about to erect his present dwelling. It antedated the late house, itself considerably over 100 yrs. old, and built in the early childhood of Samson Benson, b. 1736.

In May, 1670, Montanye dropped the *Jr.* from his name, indicating his father's dec. He himself d. in 1672. His wid. surviving another hus. (see p. 393), was buried Nov. 23, 1689. Montanye had chn. *John*, b. 1655; *Vincent*, 1657; *Nicasius*, 1659; *Abraham*, 1664; *Jelante*, 1667; *Isaac*, 1669; *Peternella*, 1671, and *Johanna*, 1673. Jelante m. Bastiaen Kortright; Peternella m. Peter See, and Johanna, posthumous, m. Johannes Vredenburgh.* For Abraham and desc., see p. 521. Nicasius, named for his god-fa., Hon. Nicasius de Sille, joined the Labadists at Bohemia Manor (see p. 403), and was of those who shared the lands in 1698. He then returned to N. Y. and bought a lot on Broadway, June 10, 1702. His only chn., Samuel, b. June 2, 1698, and Jesse, b. Nov. 21, 1699, were baptized June 26, 1703, near which date Nicasius d. His wid. Christina, a dr. of Nich. Martensen Roosevelt, m. John Hammell; they sold said lot Feb. 20, 1704, and are traced no further.

Isaac Montanye, usually called Isaac Monier de La Montagne, on Apl. 26, 1679, when 10 yrs. old, was bound by his mo. for 3 yrs. to John Dyckman, who was to clothe him and send him "to the day or evening school." When grown up he served as a soldier in His Majesty's fort at New York,

* PETER SEE was son of Isaac and Maria, named p. 371, and fa. of Isaac See, b. 1703, who m. Eve Forbay, Oct. 5, 1734. Their son Peter, b. Mar. 20, 1737, m. June 20, 1765, Sophia De Revere, and d. Oct. 18, 1800; issue Isaac, b. July 12, 1766; John, Apl. 18, 1768; Abraham, Apl. 16, 1770; Jacobus, Jan. 1, 1772; Catrina, Nov. 21, 1774; Maria, June 22, 1780; and Leah, Oct. 13, 1784. John last named m. Maria Seaman, Dec. 2, 1797, and removed to N. Y. Their chn. were John D., b. Sept. 20, 1799; Isaac, July 14, 1801; Clara, Aug. 2, 1803; Eliza-Ann, Jan. 13, 1806; Mahala, June 7, 1809; Harvey, Jan. 27, 1812; David, Nov. 16, 1813; George-Comb, Aug. 24, 1818; Catharine, Oct. 7, 1820; and Maria, Aug. 4, 1822. Isaac last named m. Grace Sands Hudson, July 19, 1821, and d. Dec. 25, 1829; being fa. of Rev. John L. See, D.D., Rev. Wm. G. E. See, and Rev. Isaac M. See.

under Capt. Leisler. In 1696 he m. Hester van Voorst, from Albany, and d. in 1703; the next yr. his wid. m. Alex. Phœnix. Isaac left issue Sarah, b. 1696, Johannes, 1698, Jacobus, 1700, and Isaac, 1702. Sarah m. 1717 James Mackintosh, and 1730 Samuel van Naamen. Jacobus was in N. Y. 1738; Isaac, not named, appears to have gone to N. J.; neither traced further. Johannes, b. 1698, remained in N. Y., m., Feb. 7, 1726, Susannah, dr. of Harman Bussing. She d. Apl. 27, 1736; he on Sept. 26, 1762. Their chn. were Sarah, b. 1726, m. Daniel Brand; Isaac, 1729; John, 1730; Hester, 1733, m. Capt. Lazarus Peperall; and Harman, 1736, the last a mason, and living 1763. His br. John, painter and glazier, m. 1760 Catharine White, and d. in 1772, his wid. in 1814, æ. 87 yrs. John left issue Susannah, b. 1763, m. Wm. Gibson; John, 1766, not in his mo.'s will, 1811, perhaps he who d. Apl. 1, 1802; and Catharine, 1768, who m. Wm. Gamble. Isaac, b. 1729, d. Apl. 26, 1814, in Cedar St., had by w. Anna Speer, sons Isaac, b. 1763, John, 1765, and Harmanus, 1769, besides drs. Harmanus was a house-carpenter, m., Nov. 1, 1794, Anna Tabele, and lived in 1798 at 46 Cortlandt St. Isaac and John, like their fa., were masons: the first m., Sept. 18, 1785, Sarah Sitcher, had known issue John, b. 1786, and Ann, 1788, and lived in 1798 at 34 Lumber St. John, b. Feb. 1765, m. Mary Weldon, May 3, 1788, and d. Dec. 13, 1820; issue that reached maturity, Catharine, b. Dec. 18, 1790, m. J. Wyckliffe Donnington, printer; Isaac, Aug. 8, 1793; William, Nov. 14, 1796; Abraham, Mar. 8, 1799; and Ann Maria, Nov. 2, 1803, who survives. William, lapidary, who m. Elizabeth Marshall, and d. Feb. 3, 1842, æ. 45 yrs., was fa. of Wm. H. Montanye, coffee and spice dealer, 62 Barclay St.

John Montanye, often called Delamontagne, was b. 1655 in Amsterdam, became a "master cooper" in N. Y., m., Sept. 4, 1678, Annetie, dr. of Jos. Waldron. He m. secondly, Sept. 8, 1701, a wid., Elizabeth, dr. of Fred. A. Bloom; see p. 143. Mr. Montanye lived on Broadway, where he had bought, May 10, 1688, as on p. 555. From his 22d yr. a chh. mem. he was long the sexton, both in the fort and in Garden St.; and as an elder, was named in the charter granted the Coll. Dutch Chh., May 11, 1696.* He d. July 12, 1730, in his 75th yr. His chn. sold his residence May 31, 1748. These were Annetie, b. 1679, m. Frederick Bloom and John Peterse; Johannes, 1681; Peternella, 1683, m. Jacob Brower; Joseph, 1684; Jesse, 1687; Abraham, 1688; Rachel, 1691, m. Patrick Smith; Jacobus, 1693, and Maritie, 1695, who m. Adrian Bogert. Smith, an innkeeper, d. Dec. 6, 1755; his wid., who survived but two yrs., having no ch., gave her property to her M. kindred. Of John Montanye's sons, Abraham removed to Foster's Meadow, L. I., early as 1715; subscribed that yr. for building a Dutch chh. at Jamaica. His son John, b. 1723, farmer, received as chh. mem. at Success, in 1766, d. without issue during the Revolution; his wid. Mercy in 1784. Jesse Montanye, b. 1688, m. Charity Yates, May 29, 1714, and d. in N. Y. Apl. 25, 1745; the city granted his wid., Feb. 12, 1751, the water lot No. 4, in Montgomery Ward. She d. Mar. 28, 1762; issue John, b. 1715; Ann, 1716; Joseph, 1718; Charity, 1720, d. Apl. 18, 1751; Jesse, 1722; Mary, 1725, m. Wm. van Sise; and Sarah, 1727, who m. Robert Finley. Jesse d. Jan. 6, 1756; Ann, named in Rachel Smith's will of Sept. 17, 1757, d. May 4, 1758; of the others, nothing certain known; Joseph, freeman 1740, probably m. Maria Bragaw, of Newtown, and went to N. J. Joseph, b. 1684, m. Margaret Roll, Mar. 2, 1728; his son Joseph, b. 1732, lived at Stroudsburgh, Pa., and m. Mary Brodhead. Their son Abraham, b. 1772, d. 1825,

* BOLTON, *Hist. Westchester*, ii. 332, wresting this charter to his purpose, makes *John Montagne* minister at Fordham, and Henry Selyns an elder; whereas Selyns was minister at N. Y., and Montanye an elder! This error is copied in *Corwin's Manual*, last edit.

m. Elizabeth Buffum, and was fa. of the estimable Joseph D. L. Montanye, of Towanda, Pa., b. Nov. 12, 1802, d. May 18, 1880.

Johannes Montanye, b. 1681, m. Sarah Parcell, Jan. 27, 1706, was admitted a freeman 1716, succeeded his fa. as sexton, and d. very aged. His will, made in health Dec. 12, 1770, was proved Oct. 17, 1774. Judge Benson, "in his earliest youth," saw and conversed with Montanye, when, "approaching to four-score," he went his round to collect the domine's salary. See *Benson's Memoir*. His chn., all living 1770, were Sarah, b. 1708; John, 1710; Ann, 1716, m. Capt. John Tomkins; Joseph, 1719; and Abraham, 1722. The sons, all made freemen 1743, became tradesmen. Abraham, b. Aug. 25, 1722, carpenter by trade, m. 1749 Tanneke Lewis; she and inf. John d. next yr. He then m. Sarah Christeen, of English Neighborhood, N. J., where he took up his residence on a farm, and served as an elder. His fa. left him his own dwelling in N. Y., and on Mar. 26, 1775, he and his brs. bought a house in Cortlandt St., formerly of their aunt Rachel Smith. He d. Feb. 7, 1801, and was buried on his farm, now in possession of Mr. Samuel Edsall. Under his will, dated Oct. 30, 1789, his ex. sold his property corner of Cedar and Lumber Sts., May 14, 1801. Joseph, in 1770, occupied a house in Cortlandt St., given him by his fa. He m. Phebe Barnes; issue Sarah, b. 1756, Rachel, 1757, John, 1759, Phebe, 1762, Anna, 1765, Joseph, 1770. On June 2, 1796, John J. Montanye, blacksmith, and w. Martha, and Simon Kiersted, blockmaker, and w. Sarah (Montanye), sell to John Moore, mason, their *two thirds* interest, in said house, "formerly the property of Joseph Montanye, dec." John J. removed the same yr. to Haverstraw. By his w. Martha Strachan, he had Phebe, b. 1785, Sarah-Christeen, 1787, Nancy, 1790, Joseph, 1791, John 1792.

John Montanye, b. 1710, was a carpenter; perhaps constable of Dock Ward, 1734. He m., Mar. 14, 1741, Mary, dr. of Philip Daly, and later set up a bakery. He in turn became sexton, serving "till the dispersion of the congregation, on the invasion of the city in 1776." Returning, he d. at 24 Pine St. in 1796, having had issue Sarah, b. 1743, who m. John Harry; John, 1744; Philip, 1746; Cornelia, 1751, m. Demarest; Catharine, 1753, m. Philip Minthorn; Mary, 1755, m. Wm. Ash; and Abraham, 1759. Of these, John, then a baker, m. 1767 Abigail Wilsey, and perhaps was the builder, living in Brooklyn, 1796–1812. Abraham was a brass-founder, named 1786 to 1796, d. at 38 Cedar St., near Nassau, where his wid. Ruth Decker lived in 1798; issue John, b. Mar. 13, 1794.

Jacobus Montanye, b. 1693, m., July 6, 1717, Adriana, dr. of John Devoor, and wid. of Conrad Vanderbeck. She d. Jan. 5, 1758; he on Dec. 5, 1761. Their chn. were John, b. 1718; Ann, 1722, m. Benj. Paine; William, 1725, d. 1737; Maria, 1728, m. John Tomkins, and Adriana and Elizabeth, twins, 1730, who m., the first, 1750, to Stephen Callow, the last 1751, to George Giffing. Callow, upholsterer, left sons in the city, and was gd.-fa. of Mrs. Wm. Stackhouse, of Columbus, O. Giffing d. 1771; was fa. of the Giffings, formerly of 40 Chapel St., now College Place. Rachel Smith's will names Jacobus' four drs.; omits his son John. Perhaps he was the felt-maker, or hatter, long at 187 Broadway. The hatter probably m. twice. He lost a ch. Aug. 17, 1770; on Apl. 30, 1773, bought his place in Broadway, then known as Pell's Ropewalk, and sold the rear part May 3 ensuing, naming no w. His dr. Mary, by his w. Mary Lowry, was b. Mar. 29, 1774. He d. June 21, 1798. On May 10, 1800, Mary and Elizabeth Montanye, spinsters, Jas. Anderson, gunsmith, and Ann his w., sold *three fourths* of the lot on Broadway, and on Aug. 19, 1801, John Montanye, bookbinder, "one of the heirs" of John, hatter, conveyed his *one fourth* of said lot. He lived at 20 Christie St. in 1822.

Vincent Montanye, b. 1657, m. Mar. 5, 1684, Adriana, dr. of Jan Thomasz Aken (see p. 186); first lived in New St., being chh. mem.; afterward "at

Sclavonia. In Bowery Division of Out Ward;" Vincent, then a brickmaker, constable there in 1695. Here, fourteen yrs. later, his domestic peace was interrupted by the wiles of one Cordus, a neighbor brickmaker, who, found guilty, was fined by the Court of Sessions. Vincent left the city, perhaps temporarily; was living 1713. His chn., save two which d. y., were John, b. 1689, Thomas, 1691, Apollonia, 1694, Jesse, 1696, Petrus, 1698, Peternella, 1701, who m. Godfricus Bennoe; Annetie, 1703, who m. Henry Dyer; Vincent, 1705, and Rachel, 1707. John, we suspect, was he who d. in Great Britain, leaving a son Henry, for whom Geo. Harrison, of N. Y., was allowed to administer, Oct. 24, 1743. Vincent, b. 1705, m. 1737 Elizabeth Murray; issue Vincent, b. 1738. Petrus m. Jannetie Dyer, Apl. 17, 1723, was constable of Montgomery Ward in 1734, and d. June 1, 1751; issue Maria, b. 1724, Adriana, 1728, Vincent, 1731, Rebecca, 1732, Thomas, 1735; of whom Rebecca m. Capt. Richard Martin and Capt. Richard Richards. Was this the Thomas, cabinet-maker, who d. in the Island of Grenada, adm. on his estate being granted Philip Pelton, at N. Y., Dec. 9, 1774?

Thomas Montanye, b. 1691, m. Nov. 25, 1718, Rebecca Bruyn, was ultimately a shopkeeper, but d. Oct. 12, 1761, his wid. not till Sept. 15, 1775. His dwelling-house in Prince St., sold by his son Peter, as ex., May 15, 1784. Of 15 chn. there reached maturity, Vincent, b. 1721, Peter, 1723, Adriana, 1724, m. Abm. Lefoy; Martha, 1726, m. Abm. Allener; Thomas, 1731, d. unm. June 19, 1758; Rebecca, 1735, Hannah, 1737, m. Morris Earl; Jane, 1739, m. John Wright; Apollonia (called Prudence), 1741, m. Elbert Amerman; John, 1743, Benjamin, 1745, and Peternella (called Nelly), 1747, who m. Isaac Vredenburgh. Of these, John T., as called, m. Mary Blain, lived in N. Y. when the Revolution opened, and the brs. Peter, Isaac, and Jacob Montanye, who early removed to Central N. Y., are believed to have been his sons; a conclusion arrived at after careful inquiry: still an intelligent desc. says they were sons of *Jesse*, and from Morris Co., N. J. Isaac, who d. 1825, æ. 45 yrs., was fa. of Joseph B. Mintonye, now of Conquest, and of the late John, of Lysander; Peter, b. 1775, d. 1850, at Sempronius, was fa. of John, late of Westfield, Pa., Elijah, who removed to Ohio, and William, fa. of Wm. J. Mantanye, lawyer, Marathon, N. Y. Vincent, shop-keeper, m. May 8, 1743, Catharine Harte, who d. Aug. 29, 1760; m. Apl. 12, 1761, Gertrude Vonck, who d. Sept. 15, 1766; m. July 6, 1767, Mary Brundige, who survived him. He d. May 26, 1773, æ. 52 yrs. Dr. O'Callaghan (*Hist. N. N.*), misled by those who confounded the two Vincents, makes the latter 116 yrs. old! the "connecting link between Stuyvesant and Washington." We regret to spoil this pretty fiction, which we see is copied in our *N. Y. B. & G. Rec.* vii. 119. Vincent had chn. (with 4 that d. y.) Thomas, b. 1745, John, 1747, Isaac, 1751, Rebecca, 1752, Peter, 1757, and Mary, 1768, who d. unm. Aug. 14, 1814. Rebecca m. Peter Truman, gd.-fa. of the late James A. Cosse, known for his persistent but ineffectual efforts to recover the Montanye lands at H. Thomas last named m. May 4, 1766, Catharine Smith, who d. Sept. 20, 1770, and by whom he had two sons, viz., Vincent, b. 1767, who, with the fa., was dec. in 1789; and Henry, b. 1769, who removed to Tappan, and m. in 1803 Rebecca Nagel; issue John, b. Apl. 1, 1805; David, Dec. 12, 1808, etc.* Peter, b. 1757, son of Vincent, was a tailor, removed to Orange Co., and had sons George, Isaac, and Abraham; Isaac, b. 1783, d. 1840, being fa. of the late John, fa. of Wm.

* This Thomas, b. 1745, is named in his fa.'s will, Feb. 3, 1773, but not in the list of citizens, May 9, 1774: *N. Y. Corp. Man.*, 1850, 427. Moreover, his gd-mo. Rebecca, in her will of Oct. 25, 1774, gives a tenth of her estate to her son Vincent's "five children;" whence it would follow (as the others were living) that Thomas was dec. Most likely he was the cabinet-maker before noticed, who had lately d. in the West Indies.

D. L. Montanye, M.D., of Rondout. Isaac, b. 1751, grocer in N. Y., 1786-98, m. 1780 Geesie Banta. John, b. 1747, tailor, m. Mary Briggs, and lived at Tappan before and during the Revolution; then returning to N. Y., lived from 1810 in Elm St., where he owned property, and d. Sept. 24, 1820. His w. d. Mar. 29, 1825, æ. 70 yrs. He left drs., Mary, wid. of James Brown, merchant, Elizabeth, wid. of James Lorton, and Gertrude, w. of Chas Dealson. Another dr., Catharine, m. Elijah Fountain. His eldest son was Isaac, b. Mar. 4, 1774. The late John Delamontanye, tailor, b. Feb. 16, 1778, was another son; issue, Matilda, Stanley, Mary-A., Vincent. Another was Vincent, b. Mar. 8, 1784, who at his d. Dec. 8, 1827, kept the Cold Spring Garden, cor. of Greenwich and Leroy Sts. His dr. Sarah-Ann m. Aris Bogart, and was the mo. of Mr. Vincent D. L. M. Bogart. His other chn. were Mary, who m. Richard D. Blauvelt; Susan, m. Wm. Cary; and George Fowler Delamontanye, who d. Mar. 12, 1857, in his 42d yr., issue Vincent, Sophia, George A., Mary J., Charles H., Maria L., and Clarence.

Peter Montanye, b. 1723, was a blacksmith, made freeman 1746, m. June 10, 1754, Catharine Vanderhoof, and acquired property. He d. June 20, 1798, at 281 Pearl St. He had chn. Ann, b. 1756, m. Thos. Parcells, coachmaker; Peter, 1759, not in fa.'s will, dated June 17, 1798; Catharine, 1761, m. John Van Varick, baker; Thomas, 1763, not in fa.'s will; Benjamin, 1766; John, 1768; Isaac, 1770; Elizabeth, 1774, who m. Wm. J. Waldron, grocer. Said John, master-cooper, inspector of provisions in 1805, d. a bachelor, 1823. His br. Isaac m. Mary Foskett, and d. July 1, 1805, his only ch. being John, of N. Y., cedar-cooper, b. Jan. 31, 1802, d. at Hoboken, Jan. 18, 1862. Benjamin, b. 1766, in 1798 china dealer at 281 Pearl St., d. Sept. 12, 1816, leaving by his w. Sarah, dr. of Peter Rushton Maverick, whom he m. May 10, 1792, chn. Charles-Kearney, Benjamin-Maverick, and Maria, who m. Andrew D. Veitch.

Benjamin Montanye, b. 1745, son of Thomas, was a blacksmith, and m. Elizabeth Norris, Apl. 14, 1768. Siding with his country at the Revolution, he left the city in 1776, as did most of the Montanyes, and retired up the Hudson, being employed as confidential messenger by the Provincial Convention. Once, sent by Washington with secret dispatches, he was taken by the enemy, and endured a cruel imprisonment in the Old Sugar House, at N. Y. He resumed his trade here at the close of the war, but soon after gave himself to the Baptist ministry, and in 1791 became pastor of the Oliver St. chh. He still worked at his forge, at 8 Prince St. In 1794 he removed to New Vernon, Orange Co., N. Y., where he founded a chh., and preached, beloved and revered, till his d., Dec. 29, 1825. Elder Montanye m. secondly Cornelia Cooper, an excellent woman, but his chn. were by his first w., being Thomas B., Benjamin, Rebecca, who m. Thos. Ustick; Nancy, who m. Saml King; and Elizabeth, who m. James Thompson, fa. of the late Dea. Benj. M. Thompson, of H. Thomas B. Montanye, b. in N. Y., Jan. 29, 1769, first joined the chh. under the care of Rev. John Gano (see p. 363), and in his 20th yr., namely, on Nov. 20, 1788, was ordained as pastor of the Baptist chh. at Warwick, N. Y., whence, in 1801, he removed to Southampton, Pa., where he ministered till his d., Sept. 27, 1829. He wrote for his epitaph, "The chief of sinners and the least of saints." By his w. Ann Edmonds, whom he m. May 20, 1788, he had eleven chn.; four—namely, Sarah-Ann, Eliza, Rebecca, and Thomas—still living. Benjamin, br. of Elder Thomas, was b. in N. Y. City in 1786, spent his life in Orange Co., was a man much respected, and at one time deputy sheriff. He m. Theodoria, dr. of Col. Samuel Clark, and d. at New Vernon, Apl. 19, 1848, æ. 62 yrs., having had thirteen chn., several of whom went west, the seventh son being the Hon. Isaac V. Montanye, of Goshen, N. Y., editor and proprietor of the *Independent Republican*.

C.

TOWN OFFICERS, 1660 TO 1710; WITH DATE OF APPOINTMENT

N.B.—Abbreviations: *assr.* for assessor; *ald.*, alderman; *asst.*, assistant alderman; *auth.*, authorized man; *col.*, collector; *com.*, commissioner of the town court; *con.*, constable; *clk.*, clerk; *vr.*, voorleser; *mag.*, magistrate; *overs.*, overseer; *scht.*, schout; *schn.*, schepen; *sur.*, surveyor of highways.

Benson, Johannes, sur., Sept. 29, 1710. Samson, con., Sept. 29, 1700; col., Sept. 29, 1704; assr., Sept. 29, 1708.
Bertholf, Guilliaem, clk. and vr., Mar. 6, 1690.
Bogert, John Louwe, overs., Oct. 29, 1675, Oct. 23, 1676.
Brevoort, Hendrick, col., Sept. 29, 1697. John Hend., overs., Oct. 28, 1678, Dec. 4, 1679, Dec., 1682; con., Nov. 2, 1686, Oct. 14, 1689; auth., Nov. 29, 1691; sur., Sept. 29, 1697.
Bussing, Arent Harm., schn., Aug. 23, 1673; overs., Oct. 23, 1676, Oct. 28, 1678, Dec. 4, 1679; con., Nov. 10, 1680; com., Dec. 18, 1683; con., 1690; sur., Sept. 29, 1694, Sept. 29, 1695; auth., Dec. 14, 1699; assr., Sept. 29, 1700.
Casier, Philip, schn., Nov. 16, 1662.
Claessen, Derick, schn., Nov. 16, 1662.
Cresson, Jaques, con., Dec. 7, 1669. Pierre, schn., Aug. 16, 1660.
Dolsen, Teunis, con., Sept. 29, 1697.
Delamater, Glaude, overs., June 12, 1666, Dec. 7, 1669, Dec. 3, 1672. Isaac, com., Nov. 2, 1686; con., Sept. 29, 1693; assr., Nov. 9, 1700; overs., Sept. 29, 1701, Sept. 29, 1702. John, overs., Dec., 1682; com., Jan. 28, 1685; con., Oct. 13, 1685; com., Nov. 1, 1687.
Demarest, David, overs., Aug. 6, 1667, Oct. 2, 1668, Feb. 7, 1671, Dec. 3, 1672; schn., Aug. 23, 1673; con., Dec. 8, 1674. John, con., June 1, 1670.
Dyckman, Cornelius, con., Sept. 28, 1698. Gerrit, col., Sept. 29, 1707; con., Sept. 29 1710. John, schn., Oct. 1, 1674; overs., Dec. 8, 1674; con., Oct. 29, 1675; overs., Oct. 23, 1677, Oct. 28, 1678, Nov. 10, 1680, Dec. 19, 1681; com., Dec. 18, 1683, Nov. 2, 1686; assr., Sept. 29, 1691; con., Sept. 29, 1693; assr., Sept. 29, 1699; sur., Sept. 29, 1708.
Gerritsen, Lubbert, overs., Dec. 3, 1672.
Harmanssen, Arent. See *Bussing*.
Holmes, George, con., Sept. 29, 1704.
Jansen, Cornelius. See *Kortright*. Lawrence, overs., Nov. 7, 1677, Oct. 28, 1678; com., Nov. 2, 1686, Oct. 14, 1689; con., Mar., 1691; sur., Sept. 29, 1694, Sept. 29, 1695; overs., Sept. 29, 1699, Sept. 29, 1700.
Journeay, Meynard, overs., Oct. 29, 1675.
Kiersen, John, assr., Sept. 29, 1695, Sept. 29, 1696, Sept. 29, 1697; col., Nov. 9, 1700; con., Sept. 29, 1701; assr., Sept. 29, 1706.
Kortright, Cornelius Jansen, con., Dec. 3, 1672; overs., Dec. 8, 1674, Dec. 19, 1681, Dec., 1682; com., Feb. 2, 1686, Nov. 1, 1687. Johannes Cornelissen, col., Sept. 29, 1698; con., Sept. 29, 1702; sur., Sept. 29, 1705. Lawrence Cornelissen, sur., Sept. 29, 1706; con., Oct. 1708.
Mabie, Caspar, con., Sept. 29, 1696.
Matthyssen, Nelis, overs., June 12, 1666.
Montanye, Abraham, con., Sept. 29, 1694; col., Sept. 29, 1702; sur., Sept. 29, 1704, Sept. 29, 1707. John, schn., Nov. 3, 1661; scht., Nov. 16,

1662, Nov. 17, 1663, retired June 17, 1665; clk., 1660–1672; vr., 1663–1670.

MYER, Adolph, schn., Oct. 1, 1674; overs., Dec. 8, 1674, Oct. 23, 1676, Oct. 23, 1677, Dec. 1682; con., Oct. 13, 1684, Oct. 14, 1687; auth., Nov. 29, 1691; asst., Sept. 29, 1693, Sept. 29, 1694; sur., Sept. 29, 1696, Sept. 29, 1697; auth., Dec. 14, 1699; overs., Sept. 29, 1701, Sept. 29, 1702; assr., Sept. 29, 1703; sur., Sept. 29, 1710. Johannes, col., Sept. 29, 1699; assr., Sept. 29, 1707; sur., Sept. 29, 1709; assr., Sept. 29, 1710.

NAGEL, Barent, sur., Sept. 29, 1705; con., Sept. 29, 1709. John, con., Oct. 23, 1677; com., Dec. 18, 1683, Feb. 2, 1686.

OBLENIS, Hendrick, con., Sept. 29, 1705; sur., Sept. 29, 1706, Sept. 29, 1708. Joost, overs., June 12, 1666, Aug. 6, 1667, Jan. 25, 1670, Dec. 3, 1672; schn., Aug. 23, 1673, Oct. 1, 1674; overs., Dec. 8, 1674, Oct. 29, 1675, Oct. 23, 1677, Dec. 4, 1679, Nov. 10, 1680; con., Dec. 19, 1681; com., Jan. 28, 1685. Peter, com., Oct. 14, 1689, 1690; con., Sept. 29, 1691; auth., Nov. 29, 1691; assr., Sept. 29, 1694; asst., Sept. 29, 1696; overs., Sept. 29, 1699, Sept. 29, 1700; col., Sept. 29, 1705; assr., Sept. 29, 1709.

ROELOFSEN, Peter, con., Oct. 2, 1668, Feb. 7, 1671.

SICKELS, Zacharias, con., Sept. 29, 1707.

SLOT, John Pietersen, scht. and schn., Aug. 16, 1660, Nov. 3, 1661; schn., Nov. 17, 1663, retired June 17, 1665.

TIBOUT, John, clk. and vr., Jan. 20, 1685 to 1690, Sept. 20, 1691 to 1697.

TIEBAUT, Marcus, col., Sept. 29, 1700, Sept. 29, 1703.

TOURNEUR, Daniel, schn., Aug. 16, 1660, Nov. 3, 1661, Nov. 17, 1663; mag., June 17, 1665; dep. shff., 1665–1670; overs., Feb. 7, 1671. Daniel, Jr., overs., Oct. 23, 1676, Oct. 23, 1677, Dec. 4, 1679, Nov. 10, 1680, Dec. 19, 1681; con., Dec. 18, 1683; col., Jan. 22, 1684; com., Feb. 2, 1686. Jacques, con., Sept. 29, 1692; overs., Sept. 29, 1699, Sept. 29, 1700. Thomas, assr., Sept. 29, 1692; ald., Sept. 29, 1696; assr., Sept. 29, 1704; col., Sept. 29, 1706; sur., Sept. 29, 1707; con., Sept. 29, 1708; col., Sept. 29, 1709.

VANDERVIN, Hendrick Jansen, vr., 1670; clk. and vr., 1672 to 1684.

VERMEULE, Adrian, clk. and vr., Sept. 29, 1699 to Feb. 1, 1708.

VERMILYE, Isaac, overs., June 12, 1666, Aug. 6, 1667. Johannes, court messenger, June 17, 1665; con., Aug. 6, 1667; overs., Dec. 7, 1669, Feb. 7, 1671; con., Dec. 4, 1679; overs., Dec. 19, 1681; con., Dec., 1682; assr., Oct. 13, 1684; com., Jan. 28, 1685, Nov. 1, 1687, Oct. 14, 1689.

VERVEELEN, Johannes, schn., Nov. 17, 1663; con., May 15, 1666; overs., Aug. 6, 1667, Oct. 2, 1668.

WALDRON, Barent, court mes., Sept. 23, 1673; assr., Sept. 29, 1698; sur., Sept. 29, 1702; col., Sept. 29, 1703. Johannes, sur., Nov. 9, 1700; overs., Sept. 29, 1701, Sept. 29, 1702; con., Sept. 29, 1703, sur., Sept. 29, 1704; assr., Sept. 29, 1705; con., Sept. 29, 1706; sur., Sept. 29, 1709. Resolved, con., June 17, 1665; overs., Oct. 2, 1668, Dec. 7, 1669, Feb. 7, 1671; scht. and schn., Aug. 23, 1673, Oct. 1, 1674; overs., Oct. 29, 1675; con., Oct. 23, 1676, Oct. 28, 1678, Nov. 10, 1680; assr., Dec. 10, 1683, Oct. 13, 1685. Samuel, auth., Nov. 29, 1691; assr., Sept. 29, 1693; sur., Sept. 29, 1696, Sept. 29, 1697; con., Sept. 29, 1699; auth., Dec. 14, 1699; assr., Sept. 29, 1702.

WOLTERS, Kier, overs., Oct. 2, 1668, Dec. 7, 1669.

D. Page 209.

LETTER: DR. MÓNTANYE TO STUYVESANT AND COUNCIL.

Honorable, Valiant and Worthy Lords.

My Lords, I have received here a letter of the 1st July last, and read the same with sorrow, not for the reproof, which I accept with thanks, but for my accounts which to me appear astonishing: because from the extract sent me by *Sieur* Jacob Sam the previous year, in October, I find myself credited upon the last of December A° 1660, for the sum of *f.* 96; and in the extract from the monthly pay book of the year 1661, I am debited for *f.* 1936 : 12; so that I the same cannot comprehend, since in my book of the year 1662, I find myself indebted for not more than *f.* 1159 : 5 : 8, whence I judge (under correction from my superiors), that a mistake must exist in the said reckoning: for of the two, either I was owing, at the end of the year 1660, more than *f.* 96:, or I am now not so much indebted as in my accounts stands. Further, in the year 1659, per balance of accounts from my book, I find myself to be indebted *f.* 432 : 13, to which added *f.* 1338 : 13 : 10, of the year 1660, makes the sum *f.* 1771 : 6 : 10, from which my wages deducted, to wit *f.* 900, I should remain indebted for *f.* 871 : 6 : 10, which yet added to *f.* 1159 : 5 : 8, being the whole that I for the year 1661, on my book sent off, was also indebted, makes *f.* 2030 : 12 : 2; now the wages of the year 1661 being deducted therefrom, I remain still indebted *f.* 1130 : 12 : 2, and not *f.* 1936 : 12 (but I refer me to the examination of *Sieur* Jacob Sam); which same excessive sum I behold with great heart grief, not that my conscience witnesses to me that I am fallen into the same by any *quis cingit ostio* that I may have practiced, having (without boasting), always kept my household in victuals and clothes as temperately as a common burgher here; but the excessive dearth of all things has driven me insensibly into such need and poverty, as that never in the 68 years that I have lived, so great distress have felt, finding myself destitute of all means to provide for my daily bread, and provisions for the winter; but my hope rests in those who until now have always helped me. It were well if that considering my support one should deem it to be sufficient; but those who have knowledge of the advantages of this place can well judge, that I, spending in bread, small beer and wood *f.* 800, have of necessity light money of the balance left to speak of.

I should to your Worthy Honors send a request, with an obligation in the form of a Note of the Hon. Lord Director Kieft, deceased, to me given; but the sudden departure of this yacht in haste, did not permit me, yet hope to do it the coming Monday with the other yacht.

In the meanwhile I remain, your Worthy Honors' humble and willing servant,

In Fort Orange, LA MONTAGNE.
18th August A°. 1662.

(Superscribed):

Honorable, Valiant and Worthy Lords, My Lords Petrus Stuyvesant Director, General and the Council of New Netherland.

E. Page 206.

JOCHEM PIETERS FLAT.

This large tract embraced three fourths of the grant made in 1639 to Jochem Pietersen Kuyter, and whence its name. It lay between the old Kingsbridge Road and Harlem River, and extended, say from the northern line of the old Church Farm and village plots of Heiser, Chesterman, etc., upward, including nearly all the late Myer Farm. The preceding pages may be consulted for its history prior to 1661, when it was divided into 22 lots, each 6½ *morgen*, or 13 a., as usually rated.

The earliest list of proprietors is that of 1670, given on p. 296, but we know, for the most part, who were the original owners. The subsequent titles, though difficult to trace, because of exchanges made from time to time (to group together lots having the same owner), and the vacating of three lots or numbers, as will further appear, have been clearly made out, it is believed; a work, which if it but adds a technical value to the modern title, is of real significance. It holds true (all modern legislation notwithstanding) that ordinarily every link carried backward into the "good old honest times," serves to improve the chain and strengthen confidence in the title. We believe our efforts to restore such lost links will also prove a material help to the modern conveyancer in his often perplexing work. To each of these lots on "Jochem Pieters" was originally attached a house lot in the village and a share of salt meadow. For many years these allotments were usually sold together; often a lot on Van Keulen's Hook being included. A knowledge of this fact is not without its value in tracing the title to the several parcels. It must also open to many a one a new source of pleasure, to discover the homes where the sterling characters treated of in these pages spent their years and energies, and which of these in the olden time tilled the soil he now occupies—reft indeed of its former rural charms, but invested by modern taste with other attractions no less endearing.

We name the owners of these lots in the order of the numbers, as on May 1, 1670; premising that No. 1 lay at the south end:

No.	1.	Daniel Tourneur.	No.	12.	Thomas Delavall.
"	2.	Laurens Jansen.	"	13.	Joost van Oblinus.
"	3.	Thomas Delavall.	"	14.	Glaude Delamater
"	4.	Lubbert Gerritsen.	"	15.	do.
"	5.	Pierre Cresson.	"	16.	Jan Nagel.
"	6.	Meynard Journee.	"	17.	Daniel Tourneur.
"	7.	David Demarest.	"	18.	Cornelis Jansen.
"	8.	Resolved Waldron.	"	19.	Thomas Delavall.
"	9.	Hendrick Karstens' heirs.	"	20.	do.
"	10.	Johannes Verveelen.	"	21.	do.
"	11.	Jean le Roy.	"	22.	do.

Lot No. 1, as it was originally laid out in 1658, belonged to John Montanye, who gave it up in 1661, for other land, when the upper part, with the lower part of No. 2, was taken to form No. 1, and to which Tourneur succeeded, as he had owned No. 2. See pp. 205, 206. Tourneur's chn. dividing up his property in 1690, this lot fell to his son Thomas, and passed in 1710 to Capt. Charles Congreve. He sold it, July 22, 1713, to John van Oblienis, and he, Aug. 12 ensuing, to Abm. Myer, whose son Abm., with his w. Mattie, conveyed the eastern part to Joh. De Witt (since Hon. D. P.

Ingraham's); and the western part, called the Pond Lot, containing 7 a. 4 r., to Joh. Sickels, by deed of Sept. 6, 1768, Sickels building a farm-house at the west end next the Kingsbridge Road, its site on 123d Street, south side, midway of 3d and 4th Aves. His son John S. succeeding by devise, this house became the home of *his* son-in-law, John Adriance, and the birthplace of the late Isaac Adriance, Esq., named p. 173. See Nos. 2, 3, 4.

No. 2. Nich. De Meyer owned this lot, and No. 18, in 1662; one of them bought that year from Simon Lucas. He sold both in 1669 to Cornelis and Laurens Jansen (see p. 288); the latter getting No. 2. From him descending to his son Albert Low, of Somerset Co., N. J., he released it to his br. Lawrence, Dec. 6, 1731. Lawrence sold to Isaac Myer, May 9, 1738, who gave it to his nephew Joh. Sickels. See p. 528.

No. 3. Simon de Ruine, called the Walloon, had this lot in 1662. He sold, Mar. 13, 1666, to Hussing and others (see p. 306), and they, Apl. 7 following, to Capt. Delavall. He exchanged it for No. 18, with Cornelis Jansen (Kortright), from whose wid., Metje Cornelis, it was gotten by Adolph Meyer, Apl. 6, 1697, in lieu of No. 10. Meyer's heirs conveyed No. 3 to Joh. Sickels, Nov. 15, 1748, when it is called 18 a. See No. 4.

No. 4. Hend. J. Vander Vin apparently owned this lot in 1662. Lubbert Gerritsen succeeded about 1664, at the sale of whose lands, July 5, 1674, it was bought by David Demarest, Sen. He sold it, Mar. 12, 1677, to Paulus Richard, and he, Aug. 1, 1677, to Adolph Meyer, to whose son Abm. the other heirs conveyed it Nov. 15, 1748. This lot had then received an addition of 6 a., as No. 3 had of 5 a.; caused as follows: The New Lots of Jochem Pieters, so called, were laid out, as we have seen, in 1677, beginning at Delavall's or Carteret's northern line. By mistake or otherwise in fixing this line, the "old lots," yet lying in common fence, were encroached upon full three lots: to remedy which, afterward, and give the Delavall heirs the quantity claimed by them in this tract, the town assigned to them the adjoining island, thence known as Carteret's Island, containing 12 a. of upland, and bargained with Dyckman and the Nagel heirs for 29 a. of the three lots which the latter owned here, and for which they took other land at Spuyten Duyvel. See p. 507. This arrangement could hardly have dated prior to 1690, nor later than 1700, but the Nagels retained a nominal possession of these lots for some years thereafter, and drew land on the *morgen rights* in 1712. In 1724 this flat was resurveyed, at the instance of Pipon and Gouverneur, claiming under Delavall. Nine lots due the claimants being set off to them at the upper end without regard to the old lines; and then the other lots to the several owners down to and including Zacharias Sickels, who held No. 5, there remained an excess of 11 a., which had already been ascertained, and sold by John Nagel, in 1722, to Abm. Myer; and of which 5 a. were added to No. 3, making it 18 a., and 6 a. to No. 4, making it 19 a. (See remark under No. 10.) Abm. Myer having set off from No. 4, about 2 a. at the west end on the Kingsbridge Road, as a building plot, and also reserving the river end, since in part the Coles property, sold the main portion of the lot to Joh. Sickels, Sept. 6, 1768. The 2 a. piece, mortgaged to Sickles by Abm. Myer, May 1, 1774, was purchased in 1815 by T. W. Van Norden. With these additions and exceptions noted, Joh. Sickels came to hold the Nos. 1 to 4; all which passed under his will of Feb. 12, 1781, proved Nov. 10, 1784, to his son John, known as John S. Sickels, remaining in his possession till his d., June 4, 1804, when it fell by devise to the heirs of his dr. Mary, Mrs. John Adriance. Thus the survey of 1724 affected the division lines of all the remaining lots yet to be described, as must be borne in mind by the inquirer after the original lines as they were prior to said survey, if he would fix these even approximately—for more than this can hardly be expected.

No. 5. Pierre Cresson, originally holding No. 6, exchanged in 1661 for

No. 5, in the way before shown. He sold to John Brevoort, May 23, 1677; he to his son-in-law, Zach. Sickels, Feb. 20, 1705, and he to Nich. Kortright, Jan. 15, 1729. See next Nos.

No. 6, owned by Michiel Muyden, was bought by Jaques Cresson. He sold, Dec. 4, 1669, to Meynard Journee, and he, Mar. 7, 1676, to John Nagel and John Delamater. These making a division of the Journee lands, July 14, 1677, Nagel took this lot or number, being one of those vacated by his heirs.

No. 7 was owned by John de Pre, who bought Simon Lane's allotment. De Pre sold, Apl. 7, 1662, to Wm. Montanye, who conveyed it to his br. John, and he, in 1665, to David Demarest. Demarest sold, Mar. 12, 1677, to Paulus Richard; he, July 31, 1677, to Joost van Oblinus, and he to his son Peter, Aug. 24, 1705. From the latter to Peter Waldron, and thence to Abm. Myer.

No. 8. Lubbert Gerritsen having bought the allotment of Matthys Boon, including this number, sold it, Nov. 22, 1662, to Jan Laurens Duyts. He sold to Resolved Waldron, who exchanged it for No. 12, with his son-in-law Nagel, whose heirs vacated it.

No. 9. Hendrick Karstens held this number, probably from 1662. At the sale of his estate, July 5, 1674, it was bought by his son Conrad Hendricks. He sold it, Aug. 16, 1678, to John Nagel, whose heirs vacated it with Nos. 6, 8. These three numbers were therefore dropped out, while the land embraced under them being assigned to the next owners in their order, left the requisite quantity to make up the nine lots for the Delavall heirs. We describe the remaining lots under the old numbers, which were in some cases retained.

No. 10 was owned successively by Do. Zyperus, Jurian Hanel (see his patent p. 526), and Johannes Verveelen. The latter sold to Adolph Meyer, Oct. 13, 1693, and on Apl. 6, 1697, he let Metje Cornelis have it for No. 3. Thus the Kortrights came to own Nos. 5 and 10, which two lots Nich. Kortright, the heir to a large part of Metje Cornelis' lands, sold in 1731 to Abm. Myer. The now-united Nos. 5, 7, 10 passed to Abraham's heirs, and became the famous 42 a. tract, or Lawrence Benson homestead. See p. 531. These three lots, computed at 6⅔ morgen each (and 2 a. to the morgen), made just 40 a., and with No. 4 adjoining, at first 13 a., but increased as before said to 19, made together 59 a., being so estimated in a mortgage for this tract, therein bounded north by *Aaron Bussing*, and south by *John Sickels*, given by Abm. Myer to St. George Talbot, June 7, 1766.

No. 11 was purchased from Jacob Elderts, June 1, 1663, by Jean le Roy, being part of an allotment Elderts had recently bought from David du Four. Le Roy sold, May 2, 1674, to Simeon Cornier; he, July 30, 1675, to Paulus Richard, and he, the same day, to David Demarest, jr. Demarest conveyed it back to Richard, Apl. 12, 1677, and he on the same date to Joost van Oblinus. Oblinus sold it, some twenty yrs. later, to Arent Bussing. See Nos. 12, 13.

No. 12 Capt. Delavall bought out of the estate of Jan Cogu. He exchanged with John Nagel for No. 16; Nagel exchanged with his fa.-in-law, Waldron, for No. 8. Waldron's wid. sold No. 12 to Arent Bussing, July 16, 1690, and Joh. Waldron confirmed the sale Apl. 5, 1697.

No. 13 was bought by Joost van Oblinus, Nov. 8, 1663, from Philip Casier's wid. and son-in-law Uzille; Casier having gotten it from Jean Gervoe. Oblinus conveyed it to Arent Bussing, Oct. 26, 1693. Bussing thus acquired Nos. 11, 12, 13, which passed in 1718 to his son Peter, and in 1737 to *his* son Aaron, under whose will (see p. 560), his executor, Adolph Myer, conveyed said tract, May 10, 1787, to John Adriance, who sold it, June 27, 1825, to Charles Henry Hall.

Nos. 14, 15. Jacques Cousseau, owning No. 15, Mar. 25, 1669, on that date bought 14, from John Sneden's estate. He sold both to Daniel Tourneur, and he directly to Delamater, whose patent of June 25, 1668, includes them. Delamater, about 1676, transferred 15 to Delavall, and shortly before his d. No. 14 also. See ensuing numbers, all which unite in Delavall.

No. 16, given by Jan Pietersen Slot to his son Peter, was sold by the latter, in 1665, to Resolved Waldron, who assigned it to John Nagel, by deed of June 2, 1670, Nagel afterward exchanging it with Delavall for No. 12.

No. 17. Tourneur bought, Feb. 1, 1667, from Dirck Claessen, potbaker, who having owned it five yrs. at least, was probably the original drawer. Tourneur sold it, about 1676, to Capt. Delavall.

No. 18. Nich. De Meyer, as before said, owned this and No. 2, in 1662, and sold them to the Jansens. No. 18, in the division, fell to Cornelis, who exchanged with Delavall for No. 3.

No. 19 was obtained by Delavall from Jaques Cresson, who bought it with No. 6, from Michiel Muyden.

Nos. 20, 21, 22, Delavall purchased, as would appear, two from Arent Moesman, and one from Valentine Claessen; in this order as to date, but their respective numbers we are not sure of. Claessen, we believe, bought Adam Dericksen's allotment. One of Moesman's had probably belonged to Philip Casier, and the other to Jean le Roy, who bought, 1662, of Philip Presto. In 1673, Delavall was the ostensible owner of nine lots here (see p. 344), of which he probably gave six to his son-in-law Carteret in 1676 (see p. 381), as in the subsequent division of Delavall's lands, Carteret's heirs got six, and Darvall's successors (see p. 424), three of these lots. The title to these nine lots involves largely the history of the Delavall lands hereafter given, App. 1. In an adjustment of their respective claims by Carteret's son-in-law, Philip Pipon, and Abm. Gouverneur, deriving from Darvall, Pipon took the six uppermost lots, and Gouverneur the three lower lots. By the survey of 1724, these nine lots were run out as each 6 morgen, the additional ⅔ of a morgen on each lot, making together 6 morgen, being put in Carteret's Island. It was this contraction of the nine lots that gave the 11 a. to lots Nos. 3, 4. On May 1, 2, 1725, by lease and release, Gouverneur and wife conveyed the "Three Lots," containing 18 morgen, to Joh. Myer, and on Feb. 11, 12, 1740–1, Simon Johnson, John Amboyneau, and James Faviere, as trustees of Elias Pipon, son of Philip, conveyed the "Six Lots" including an additional acre, probably for the road,* with nearly 8 a. of adjoining woodland (known as the Carteret Lot) and Carteret's Island, to Jacob Myer. This property descended to Jacob's gd.-chn. See p. 534. In the division of Joh. Myer's lands, in 1753, between his sons Jacob and John the latter took the Three Lots, together with the residue (called 5 a., see p. 533) of the Carteret Lot. From John Myer the title (terminating, see p. 534, in deeds from Gabriel Furman and Richard Harrison to Charles Henry Hall, in 1825 and 1826) forms one of Mr. Adriance's valuable series of printed abstracts.

* On laying out the New Lots in 1677, a road five rods broad was left "for the use of the land of Mr. De Lavall," along the north side of his lots. *Deed*, Zacharias Sickels to Samson Benson, Jan. 23, 1706.

F. Page 206.

VAN KEULEN'S HOOK.

THIS tract, known originally as the *Otterspoor*, but renamed from an early owner, Conrad van Keulen, of Amsterdam, included the range of farms to the north of the Mill Creek (108th Street): from the late Morris Randell farm, on Harlem River, westward to the Peter Benson or Mill farm. A line drawn from the foot of 125th Street westward to the 5th Avenue at 111th Street would nearly describe its northern boundary. Laid out in 1661, in 22 lots of equal breadth, all running to the river or creek, and designed to be three morgen each, the contents necessarily varied with the length, and this led, in 1676, to a new survey, by which most of the lines were contracted, and the lots equalized. The many transfers and exchanges occurring make it difficult to trace these lots by the numbers, but out of "confusion worse confounded," a result has been attained, which is here given with a reasonable assurance. See the names of the original grantees, p. 206.

Lot No. 1 passed from Du Four, with his other lands, to Jacob Elderts, and from him, June 1, 1663, to Jean le Roy. The latter sold out, May 2, 1674, to Simeon Cornier; he, July 26, 1675, to Paulus Richard; he, the same date, to David Demarest, Jr.; he again to Richard, and he to Joost Oblinus, on the same day, Apl. 12, 1677. Sold by Oblinus to John Delamater, it was bought of his heirs, in 1710, by Samuel Waldron, and annexed to the adjoining farm, late of his fa., Resolved Waldron.

No. 2 Resolved Waldron bought at the sale of Cogu's estate, in 1665. See No. 3.

No. 3 was sold by Gerritsen, with other lands, Nov. 22, 1662, to John Duyts; he sold these to Resolved Waldron, who bought himself a residence directly north of this lot, on the street, which ultimately formed the north-west corner of his farm. See pp. 294, 332. Waldron also secured the lower half of the adjoining lot, No. 4, giving him 2½ lots together. His son Samuel, who bought the farm Nov. 25, 1690, added, by sundry purchases, Lot No. 1, and all the upland and meadow lying between these lots and the street, including the old Haldron lot, which he bought of Kiersen, Jan. 1, 1701. We except, however, the small open space at the landing, kept till many yrs. later for public use, and on which stood Col. Lewis Morris's coach-house, the town having granted Morris, June 26, 1771, a plat twenty feet square whereon to place it. Samuel Waldron sold the farm to Capt. Congreve and John James, Mar. 23, 1711, and they, on Mar. 27 ensuing, to John Van Horn, who soon after conveyed it to Derick Benson. See pp. 484, 493, 494, 563. Benson d. in possession in 1751, and his only son John remained upon the property, for which he ultimately took a deed from Peter Lott, of N. Y., Nov. 2, 1758. John being an executor, with the wid. and Dr. Paterson, he probably joined with these in conveying to Lott, in order to get a lawful title. Benson built a new house on the farm proper; his old house stood on the north side of the street, on one of the old *erven* joining the river. He sold to John Bogert, Jr., Mar. 12, 1766. See p. 489. After his gd.-son, James Bogert, Jr., came to own the farm, in 1811, he took down the farm-house and built another; but this being burnt, Morris Randell bought the property in 1825, and erected on the old foundation a fine residence, still seen at the foot of 125th Street, south side.

No. 4. Do. Zyperus, Jurian Hanel, Johannes Verveelen, and his son-in-law Adolph Meyer, were the successive owners, Meyer getting it by the marriage contract with Maria Verveelen, though the patent was not transferred to him till Oct. 13, 1683. But it was then agreed that Verveelen should use this lot (*i.e.*, what remained of it) till his d. Meyer had sold John Dyckman, Nov. 9, 1673, a piece of the north end, and Dyckman appears to have leased for Verveelen's lifetime the rest of the half lot, with an acre in the rear left by the survey of 1676, making 2 *morgen*. This eventually returned to Meyer, after whose d. it was conveyed to Kierson for half of No. 9. Teunis Delamontanie got 3 a. of it, which he sold, in 1727, to Joh. Benson, who added in 1742 an acre adjoining, on which had stood the first Vermilye house. This 4 a. eventually passed to Benj. Benson, br. of Joh., from him to his son-in-law Lawrence Benson, and was conveyed, Sept. 4, 1797, to his dr. Susannah, w. of Dr. Philip Milledoler.

No. 5 Tourneur exchanged for No. 19, before or while John Montanye owned it, whose fa.-in-law, Isaac Vermilye, occupied a morgen at the upper end; see pp. 332, 547. His son Joh. adding an acre at the rear left vacant by the survey of 1676, his wid. sold in 1715 to John Delamater, who directly sold the house and 1 a. of the land to Humphrey Peto. Peto, in his will, proved July 20, 1742, says: "My house and lot of land in the township of Harlem, where I now live, I give and bequeath unto my nephew, Thomas Van Bremen, second son of my sister, Johanna Wickfield, now the wife of David Devoor." See p. 461. It was sold that yr. to Joh. Benson, as before noticed. Montanye sold the lower part of No. 5 to Demarest, he to Paulus Richard, and he to Laurens Jansen, Nov. 19, 1677, whence it rated as 2 *morgen*.

No. 6 was sold by Lucas, in 1662, to Nich. De Meyer; by him, in 1669, to the Jansens, and falling to Laurens' share, he built on the northern end, and lived there. It and the half of No. 5 descended, with his other lands, to his eldest son, Albert Low, who conveyed the whole, Dec. 8, 1731, to his br. Lawrence, from whom Maria Meyer bought this tract, May 22, 1732. She deeded it, Aug. 1, 1735, to her son Isaac, whence it passed by devise to his nephew, Joh. Sickels, who devised it to his dr. Mary, w. of Samson Benson. Benson and w. sold the same, Oct. 8, 1803, to their dr. Margaret, w. of Andrew McGown, and these, Oct. 31 ensuing, to John G. Bogert and Jacob Bradford, who made a division of the tract Mar. 15, 1809.

Nos. 7, 8, 9. Jan Pietersen Slot gave his son Peter one morgen off the west side of No. 9; the rest of the tract was included in his patent sold Joh. Verveelen. See p. 551. Verveelen sold this patent, Aug. 21, 1689, to his son-in-law Meyer, whose wid. acquired the one morgen of No. 9, now rated as a half lot. This had passed, in 1665, from Peter Slot to Resolved Waldron; from his wid., in 1690, to John Brevoort; from his son-in-law Sickels to John Kiersen, and to Mrs. Meyer. At her d. her chn. transferred the three lots to her gd.-son Benj. Benson, Nov. 15, 1748. Benson gave them to his son-in-law Lawrence Benson, who conveyed them to his dr. Susannah, w. of Rev. Philip Milledoler, Sept. 4, 1797, and to said Philip, Sept. 21, 1804.

No. 10 was sold by Casier's wid. and son-in-law, Uzille, to Joost Oblinus, Nov. 8, 1663. See Nos. 11 to 16.

No. 11 was sold by Gervoe to Philip Casier, who exchanged with Uzille for 16. Uzille and the wid. Casier conveyed it with No. 10 to Oblinus, who ab. 1688 sold these numbers to John Delamater.

No. 12 was sold by De Ruine, with his other lands, Mar. 13, 1666, to Hussing, etc., who sold out directly to Capt. Delavall. See p. 506. Delavall soon exchanged it for No. 21, with Glaude Delamater, whose son John sold it, with Nos. 10, 11, to Peter Oblienis, May 10, 1690.

No. 13 evidently passed from Adam Dericksen's wid. (m. to Necols Peterson), to Valentine Claessen, from him to Delavall, from him to Verveelen and Hussing, and from them to Joost Oblinus, who sold Nos. 13, 14, 15, to his son Peter, Aug. 24, 1705.

No. 14 Jaques Cresson sold with his other land, Dec. 4, 1669, to Meyndert

Journee, and he, Mar. 7, 1676, to John Nagel and John Delamater. The latter took this lot in a division made July 14, 1677, and sold the half, then the whole of it, to Cornelis Jansen, who conveyed it to Adolph Meyer, and he to Joost Oblinus, in exchange for 20. Joost to Peter as aforesaid.

No. 15, in the division of the De Meyer farm by the Jansens, fell to Cornelis, from whose wid., Metje Cornelis, Joost Oblinus obtained it, in exchange for No. 16, which see.

No. 16 Uzille exchanged for No. 11, with Casier, who sold it, Jan. 11, 1663, to Jacob Elderts, he to Delavall, and he to Joost Oblinus and John Brevoort as joint owners. Oblinus, getting the other half, exchanged this lot with Metje Cornelis for No. 15. His son Peter buying this lot also, thus came to own Nos. 10 to 16, which he ultimately conveyed to his nephew, Peter Waldron, Sept. 20, 1742, with the house, barn, and orchard, which occupied five of the out-gardens, lying north of the seven lots, and finally joined to them by the closing of the lower street. Waldron bought up the rest of these gardens (save Nos. 19, 20), and also an adjoining plot, once within the old village, by deed from the town, Mar. 11, 1747. See p. 565. This strip along the Church Lane, and the said seven lots, composed the late *John P. Waldron farm.*

No. 17 was sold by Derick Claessen to Daniel Tourneur, Feb. 1, 1667, and is described in his patent of Sept. 1, 1669, as "13 acres, or 6 morgen and 240 rod." It was equal to two of the other lots, and always carried a 6 morgen right.

No. 18 Tourneur bought from Cousseau. On the partition of Tourneur's lands in 1691, this and Lot 17 fell to his son Jacques, to whom Peter Bussing succeeded in 1726. They passed by devise to his son Aaron, whose dr. Mrs. Storm succeeded by deed from her fa.'s executors, Aug. 18, 1784, whence its title is well known. See pp. 499, 500. The two out-gardens, Nos. 19, 20, attached to these lots, contained the farm-house, the original home of the Bussings. See p. 256.

No. 19 passed with De Pre's property, in 1662, to William Montanye, from whom, or his br. John, Daniel Tourneur obtained it for No. 5. In 1691 it fell to Thomas Tourneur, and passed, in 1710, to John Dyckman, who drew land upon it in 1712. This lot was untaxed from 1715 to 1720. Doubt hangs around the after-history of this and the remaining lots; but more anon.

No. 20 was sold by Pierre Cresson, May 23, 1677, to John Brevoort, from whom, prior to 1700, as would appear, Joost Oblinus got it, and bartered with Adolph Meyer for No. 14. Mrs. Meyer drew land on it in 1712.

No. 21 Cousseau sold to Tourneur, and he to Glaude Delamater, who, prior to 1676, exchanged with Capt. Delavall for No. 12. But the last two persons being dead, Delamater's wid. claimed this lot, and on Jan. 4, 1690, sold it to her son-in-law, Arent Bussing, to whom Samuel Waldron, as successor to all the lands and rights of Glaude's eldest son, John Delamater, gave a quit-claim, Jan. 3, 1711, and it is named in his patentee deed, 1715.

No. 22, drawn by Jean le Roy, on the allotment gotten of Philip Presto, was sold to Arent Moesman, and by him to Capt. Delavall, who upon it built his grist-mill in 1667. See pp. 259–263.

Bussing's right to No. 21 was allowed, but it caused trouble among the lot-holders at this end, as there were more claimants than lots. To obviate the difficulty in part another lot, No. 23, was projected, for John Delavall, on the other side of his mill lot, which itself, on account of the mill, admitted of no substitution; and it seems indicated that the Dyckman and Bussing heirs gave up or sold out their rights, various small parcels of land being distributed to Peter Bussing and others in 1720, when this vexatious matter was finally arranged. This adjusted the number of lots existing to the number claimed. A "small strip of land lying west of the *lot* of Arent Bussing

(No. 21) and east of the *lots* of John Delavall," called 3 acres, a motion to sell which in 1691 was negatived, was added to Jacques Tourneur's lots. The two Delavall lots were purchased, Sept. 24, 25, 1747, by Benj. Benson, from Simon Johnson, assignee of Elias Pipon; and Benson, we believe, also succeeded to the Meyer lot, Nov. 15, 1748. The Kortrights claimed two lots here, but under the numbers 14, 15, before held by Cornelis Jansen, and on which Metje Cornelis and Marcus Tiebaut drew land in 1712. See p. 517. The heirs had divided one or both of these lots transversely into equal halves, but the whole came, in 1726, to wid. Grietie Kortright, who sold them, in 1730, to Derick Benson, from whose son John, Benj. Benson obtained them, half at a time, Dec. 30, 1755, and May 11, 1764. Thus the title to all the lots (we believe five in number) lying west of Jacques Tourneur, to whom Peter Bussing had succeeded, passed to Benj. Benson, and came to form part of the Benson farm, the remainder being taken from the Mill Camp, whose title we notice briefly. By the disuse of the mill, some years after the death of John Delavall, the privilege of using this land for mill purposes became void. On Oct. 23, 1738, the town granted a similar privilege to Samson Benson, owning the farm on the opposite side of the creek, who was authorized "to place a mill, with a dam, on the Mill Camp, wherever it may suit him best;" this right to revert to the town should the mill cease to run for two years. Benson built the mill on his said farm, but it was scarcely finished when he d., in 1740. His son Benjamin succeeding to the farm and mill, and buying several of the lots before mentioned, obtained from the town, by an award of May 30, 1753, and for the sum of 160*l*., a deed for the Mill Camp, by the following description: "Beginning at the fence of the said Benjamin Benson by the Mill Creek, and runs along his fence Northwardly to Harlem Road, about Thirty-one Chains, thence along said Road Twenty-three Chains and One-half,* which is Three Chains beyond a large Oak Tree near Van Bremen's House, thence South, Ten Degrees East, to the said Mill Creek, thence along the said Creek to the place where it began." Besides providing for a road to the mill, it enjoined "that no encroachments shall be made from the westernmost limits of this grant to Benjamin Benson, but that the small part of the Mill Camp which remains undisposed of, lying between his westernmost bounds and the Mill Creek, so far as the bridge, shall be and remain in common, free, and open for the benefit of all the freeholders and inhabitants, for their creatures feeding and going to salt."

During the Revolution the old mill on the south side of the creek was burnt, and after the war Benj. Benson built a new one on the Mill Camp farm, as also a substantial stone dwelling, which with the said farm and the creek itself he conveyed, Apl. 2, 1791, to his son Peter, whose son Benj. P. Benson, and dr., Mrs. Dr. Peter Van Arsdale, afterward shared it. In 1827, when the Harlem Canal was begun, the mill, a frame building three stories high, was taken down; but the dwelling stood till 1865. See p. 474.

* This course followed for a short distance the old road which bridged the little creek at 111th St., then took that laid out later, which, branching from the former, crossed the creek at 109th St. This last road cut off a gore from Van Keulen's Hook, of about 4 a., since known as the *Lanaw Benson* tract. It was sold by the town to Aaron Bussing, and confirmed to him by the award of May 30, 1753. The upper road being closed, joined it to Bussing's other land known as No. 1, 1st Division; but it was sold separately by his executor, Adolph Myer, to David Waldron, May 1, 1768, as 4 a. 19 r. Waldron sold it, June 6, 1793, to Lanaw Benson (colored woman), who conveyed it, all but ¾ of an acre of woodland at the east point, to John Rankin, Apl. 9, 1799.

G. Page 212.

MONTANYE'S FLAT.

This tract granted to Henry de Forest in 1636, and subsequently patented to Hudde and La Montagne, has a remarkably interesting history, for which reference must be had to the foregoing text, where both patents are recited (see pp. 144, 166), as also the circumstances which constrained the government to resume possession of these lands in 1662, and distribute them among the Harlem settlers. The Flat embraced the lands intersected by Harlem Lane, from the late Nutter farm to the Capt. John Kortright farm, both inclusive (109th Street to 124th Street); the whole bounded easterly by the creek, and westerly by the heights.

It is apparent that the Flat was originally laid out in lots of unequal quantity, to suit the requirements of those applying for land. See pp. 203-212. Original descriptions of nine of the lots name them as on "Montagne's Land," or "Montagne's Flat;" six as running "from the hills east to the kill," and one "from the kill to the hills west." The Flat was not so much as fenced in till 1673 (see p. 323), and the first house, after De Forest's, was not built till some years later. See pp. 398, 426. As in the other tracts, early exchanges among the owners broke up the order of the original numbers; and eventually there came to be ten lots, of nearly equal size, and rated as 6 morgen each. The lots first built upon by Tourneur and Delamater, began to be taxed in 1682, and all the rest in 1685, amounting to 54 morgen, Le Roy's lot, vacated, being excepted. This was added in 1725, making 60 morgen (120 a.), being 12 a. per lot; and even down to the Revolution they were never rated higher in the tax lists, though usually sold for 20 a. In further tracing these lots, we will refer to them as the 1st lot, 2d lot, etc., with regard to the actual order in which they lay, beginning at the south end of the Flat.

The 1st and 2d lots, described in De Meyer's patent of Jan. 29, 1664, as 80 rods broad and containing 12 morgen 360 rods, were bought, Sept. 25, 1669, by Cornelis and Laurens Jansen. Cornelis took them in a division of their lands, Feb. 6, 1675, and on Nov. 17, 1677, added Demarest's lot (the 3d lot, but originally No. 4); which is described in Demarest's patent of Mar. 3, 1671, as 26 rods broad, 160 rods long, and containing about 13 a., or 6 morgen 300 rods. These three lots, with drafts from the adjacent common land, descending to Lawrence Kortright, son of Cornelis Jansen, and to his son Lawrence, who on Apl. 5, 1760, conveyed it to Mrs. Sarah Nutter, became the well-known Nutter farm. See pp. 515-517. Here was the "Half-Way House," established in 1684 by Cornelis Jansen, and kept after his d. by his wid. Metje Cornelis. See p. 439. On Oct. 13, 1694, she was allowed pay "for entertaining his Excellency the Governor, on his return from Connecticut." She or her family, at one time or another, owned all of Montanye's Flat. After the tavern here was discontinued, the "Black Horse," below McGown's Pass (see p. 521), became the Half-Way House. It was kept during the Revolution by Richard Vandenburgh. The piece of the Nutter farm east of the lane (8 a.), sold by Valentine Nutter to Daniel McCormick, Nov. 8, 1806, was a part of the 3d lot; the adjoining pieces occupied by Nutter's son-in-law, Henry G. Livingston, and James Beekman, included parts of the 1st and 2d lots.

Daniel Tourneur, holding the 5th lot, by deed of Feb. 1, 1667 from Derick Claessen, and described in Tourneur's patent of Sept. 1, 1669, as No. 6, 21 rods broad, and containing about 13 a., or 6 morgen, 480 rods, also purchased the 6th lot, from Adolph Meyer, Jan. 28, 1673, described in Hanel's patent (see p. 526), as No. 7, 27 rods 44 feet broad, and containing 5 morgen 400 rods. This lot had come from Do. Zyperus. Daniel Tourneur, taking these two lots in his patrimony, bought the 4th lot in the range, Dec. 6, 1679, from Resolved Waldron (described as No. 5, and 30 rods broad), Waldron deriving title from Lubbert Gerritsen, to whom was originally allotted No. 3. In 1711, Tourneur's son Woodhull sold the three lots to Samson Benson, who sold them directly to Metje Cornelis. Their later history is to be traced through the Kortrights, Myers, and Bussings; see pp. 499, 500, 515, 516, 531. In the division of this farm made by John, Adolph, and Abraham Bussing, Apl. 6, 1787, each had an equal share of 19 a. 1 q. 13 r., Adolph taking most of the 4th lot. The highway parted the other two shares; that to the west fell to Abraham, and subsequently, after passing through several hands, was bought, Mar. 8, 1815, by David Wood, who had already purchased part of the adjoining Van Bramer tract, from Abm. Van Bramer, May 7, 1812.* These composed Mr. Wood's farm, which at his d., May 12, 1842, desc. to his wid., and chn. William G. Wood, M.D., etc.

The 7th lot was sold by De Ruine, Mar. 13, 1666, to Arent Bussing and others (see p. 505), as No. 8, being 16 rods broad, and containing 4 morgen 320 rods. Bussing, etc., sold, Apl. 7 ensuing, to Capt. Thomas Delavall, from whom it passed to his son-in-law Carteret, who sold it, Nov. 21, 1679, to Glaude Delamater. The latter exchanged it for another lot, with John Dyckman; Dyckman sold half to John Brevoort (which half passed to Zacharias Sickels), and later the other half to Sickels direct, who sold the lot, Jan. 15, 1729, to Nich. Kortright, from whom it passed in 1740 to his aunt Grietie Kortright, and from her sons to Benj. Benson, who owned the next lot, afterward, of Benjamin Vandewater. See pp. 516, 517.†

The 8th lot, in possession of John le Roy as late as 1668, is presumed to have been given up by him for his indebtedness to the town. See p. 404.

* The VAN BRAMER family (originally *Van Bremen*) came from Albany. Jacob, son of Abraham van Bremen and Maria Van Nestrand, m. in 1711 Johanna, dr. of Anna Wakefield, from Albany (see p. 401), and had sons, Abraham, of H., and Thomas, of Paramus, N. J. See p. 589. Abraham, to whom, in 1733, his step-fa., David Devoor, transferred an *erf*, which he soon sold to John Lewis, and was living some yrs. after near the bridge crossing the Mill Creek (I believe the place later of John Rankin), was fa. of Hendrick and Abraham, of Harlem Lane, the first a wheelwright and bachelor. These brs. divided the land bought of the Bussings in 1784; see p. 409. Hendrick, by his will of Jan. 14, 1809, left his residence on Harlem Lane to his nephew, Henry Van Bramer, whose br.-in-law, Tyler, afterward owned it. Abraham m. Abigail Brown, who survived him. She was a sr. of Abm. Bussing's w. Their chn. were Henry, d. unm., James, mariner, lost at sea, Abraham, Hester, who m. John Kimmel, and Susan, who m. Wm. Tyler.

† The VANDEWATERS and HOOGLANDS, of Harlem, had this origin: Cornelis Dircksen Hoogland, b. 1599, was living at Brooklyn in 1638, and for many yrs. kept the ferry. By his w., Aeltie Adriaens, he had a son, Derick, b. 1638, who m. Lysbeth, dr. of Joris Jansen Rapelje. From this union came, with other chn., Johannes, b. 1666, Adrian, 1670, and Aeltie, 1681, who m. Abm. Delamontaine. Johannes and Adrian removed to N.Y., where the latter, a respected merchant, was murdered by his own slave, Robin, in the negro outbreak, just after midnight, April 7, 1712; at which time Joris Marschalk, Henry Brasier, Augustus Grasset, and Adrian Beekman were also killed. See pp. 179, 244. Johannes Hoogland m. twice; in 1686, Anna Duyckinck, wid. of Peter Vandewater, from Amsterdam, in 1706, Jenneke Peel; and by the latter was fa. of Adrian, b. 1716, who lived on Bloomingdale Heights, owning half of the De Key Tract, purchased of Thomas De Key, in 1738, in company with Harman Vandewater. He d. in 1772, and his executors, Benj. and Wm. Hoogland, sold his lands to Nich. De Peyster, Dec. 7, 1785. Peter Vandewater's son Benjamin, b. 1677, was fa., we believe, to said Harman (see p. 504), whose son Benjamin, in 1751, succeeded to his lands, which, with what he had acquired on Harlem Lane, he sold to James W. De Peyster, Oct. 16, 1785. His w. was Mary, dr. of Adolph Meyer.

It is not included among his lands sold to Simeon Cornier, May 2, 1674, and *is omitted from the tax list down to 1724.* Sampson Benson then appears as the owner, and without doubt it descended to his son Benjamin aforesaid. From the latter the parts of the 7th and 8th lots, which lay to the west of Harlem Lane, passed, the first to Robert Hunter, the second to Benjamin Vandewater; the latter conveying his part, with his farm on the adjoining heights, to James W. De Peyster, Oct. 16, 1785. The remnants east of the Lane were sold to Adolph Myer, who conveyed the part of the 7th lot to John Dykman, except an acre sold to Hendrick Van Bramer on which his house was built, described on p. 398.

Two lots sold by Couseau to Tourneur, and by him to Glaude Delamater, are described in Delamater's patent of June 25, 1668, as situated "to the north of John Le Roy, to the south of Daniel Tourneur, an east line being run from the hills to the kill; it's in breadth 48, and in length 100 rod, and makes in all about 16 acres or 8 morgen." By adding to this the adjoining Tourneur lot (which Tourneur had given to his son-in-law Dyckman, who exchanged with Delamater for the 7th lot), Delamater came to be rated at 12 morgen. This being divided into halves, by his sons John and Isaac, formed the 9th and 10th lots, of which John took the lower one, and Isaac the upper. John's share passed, in 1710, to Samuel Waldron, and thence to his son Peter. Isaac's lot passed, Dec. 3, 1726, to his son John Delamater, who sold it to Aaron Kortright, Mar. 12, 1742. See its history continued, on pp. 516–519. The old Delamater homestead stood on the east side of the Lane. Capt. John Kortright built the large mansion which stood at a centre point in the block between 119th and 120th Streets, and 8th and 9th Aves.

H. Page 383.

THE HOORN'S HOOK FARMS.*

1. SAW-KILL FARM.

GEORGE ELPHINSTONE, the grantee of this tract, transferred his claim to Abraham Shotwell, to whom the patent was issued by Gov. Andros, Sept. 29, 1677. See pp. 382, 383. It grants a tract of land upon Manhattan Island, in breadth 51 rods, running from the East River north-west into the woods 120 rods, including the run of water formerly called the Saw Mill Creek, together with the pond; being bounded south-west by the land of John Bassett, and north-east by the land of Jacob Young, and containing 38½ acres.

Abm. Shotwell, with consent of his son John, sold the farm and improvements Nov. 6, 1679, to John Robinson, who, on Jan. 1, 1680, conveyed one half to John Lewin and Robt. Wolley, of London, for £60; and on Feb. 12, 1684, the other half to William Cox, for £160. See pp. 406, 409, 428.

Mr. Cox was drowned in July, 1689, in returning from Amboy, whither he had been sent by Leisler to proclaim the accession of William and Mary. On July 15, before taking his last fatal journey, he made his will, amply providing for his w. Sarah, and devising his share of the Saw-kill farm to her br. Henry Bradley. The latter, named in his br. Samuel Bradley's will, July 5, 1693, d. soon after, without issue, his estate falling to his said br. Samuel and sr. Sarah, late Mrs. Cox, who being left "a good rich widow,"

* The Dutch word *hoek*, or hook, is rendered "a nook, a corner, or an angle." In *Hexham's Groot Woordenboeck*, Rotterdam: 1653. In common usage, a neck of land bounded on three sides by streams or meadows; or where these limits were roads, or even surveyor's lines, was called a *hook*; see examples, pp. 512, 566. Hoorn's Hook, originally, was regarded as being bounded south by Marston's Creek, which emptied into the river near 89th Street.

had meanwhile m. John Oort, merchant, and now had her third hus., the noted Capt. Wm. Kidd. She m. Capt. Kidd by license of May 16, 1691. On June 1, 1695, Kidd and his br.-in-law Samuel Bradley (soon to sail for England, to prepare for that nefarious voyage in the *Adventure Galley*, from which Bradley returned only to be landed sick and dying on the island of St. Thomas, and Kidd to be arrested, sent to London, and executed for piracy), joined in conveying their half of the farm, etc., to Mrs. Kidd's fa., Capt. Samuel Bradley, for the term of his life. The reversion of the half farm falling to Mrs. Kidd by the d. of her hus. and br. Samuel, she obtained administration on the will of the latter, Apl. 13, 1703, and on Sept. 14 following, quit-claimed all her right and interest in the farm to her fa. Capt. Bradley. Before the yr. closed she m. Christopher Rousby. On Jan. 7, 1704, Bradley conveyed the said half farm to Rousby. But Rousby and w. doubting the sufficiency in the law of the patents to Shotwell and Cox, for the half farm and other their property, to assure them the legal possession (such at least was their plea), petitioned Gov. Cornbury, Mar. 23, 1704, to accept a deed of sale for their said property to her Majesty Queen Anne, and then to re-grant the same to them and their heirs forever. Obviously the true reason for this lay in the fact, as stated in a warrant of Aug. 4, 1701, for the seizure of Kidd's effects, that he had "been executed in England for piracy, whereby all his estate, both real and personal, is forfeited to his Majesty." With this request the governor complied; the deed to the Queen is dated Mar. 31, 1704, and Cornbury's patent to the petitioners, May 2, 1704. The Harlem freeholders, Apl. 15, 1703, had voted "Wolley and partner" a release of what part of their land lay within the town patent; and on Feb. 1, 1705, Rousby obtained from Charles Wolley, of N. Y., merchant, son and successor of "Robert Wolley, citizen and cloth-worker, of London," a deed for the other half of the Saw-kill farm.

From Rousby the farm passed to John Gurney, of N. Y., baker. Under Gurney's will, dated Sept. 23, 1708, his wid. Mary (Van Hosen) sold the farm, May 24, 1709, to Thomas Hook, Jr., of N. Y., gent., for £400. The parties to this sale were m. July 10, ensuing. Mr. Hook made his will Mar. 13, 1713, as he "designed to take a voyage for London." He was dec., May 29, 1723, the date his will was proved, but the farm stood in his name till 1730, and was then sold to John Devoor, who occupied it half a century. By will dated June 26, 1778, proved Oct. 2, 1780, Devoor gave 14 a. off the upper side of the farm to his son John, and the other 24½ a. to his dr. Aefie, w. of John Courtright. Courtright and w. sold their part, May 20, 22, 1786, to Isaac Gouverneur, and he on Sept. 9, 1791, to John Leary, Jr., whence it passed to David Dickson and Andrew Stockholm. These, loaning £3000 from the State Treasurer, Gerard Bancker, on a mortgage, July 30, 1793, put up near the river extensive cotton mills; employing workmen from Manchester, Eng. But this enterprise failed, and on Dec. 26, 1799, Dickson and Stockholm, for £4800, conveyed the property, now called 28 a., to Isaac Gouverneur. The latter d. intestate, the State foreclosed, and under a decree of Dec. 14, 1805, the premises were publicly sold Mar. 6, 1806, and bought by John Lawrence for $30,000, the deed to him being executed the same day by Pierre C. Van Wyck, master in chancery. Richard Riker and John Tom being partners in this purchase (the three were brs.-in-law), Lawrence, by deeds of Mar. 20, 1807, assigned portions of the premises to his said copartners. On July 21, 1807, Mr. Tom's executors reconveyed his share to Lawrence, who with Mr. Riker made a formal division June 21, 1811, the first having made his residence upon the upper, the other upon the lower part. For this purpose Mr. Lawrence had repaired the old house on his tract, while Mr. Riker built upon his part, now named *Arch-Brook*, a fine stone dwelling, occupied by him till his d. in 1841. His heirs divided the property into city lots.

John Devoor, Jr., mortgaged his 14 a. of this farm to Mangle Minthorne, Mar. 17, 1783; he assigned the mortgage to Anthony L. White, Nov. 25, 1786, and he, the same day, to Mary Ellis, "formerly of the Out Ward, now of the State of New Jersey, singlewoman." See next title.

II. THE BAKER FARM.

The patent to Jacob Young, dated May 1, 1677, grants a piece of land on Manhattan Island, in breadth by the riverside 43 rods, ranging thence north-west into the woods 120 rods; being bounded north-east by the Commons, or a certain run of water, and south-west by the land of George Elphinstone, and containing 32¼ acres. On Sept. 27, 1683, Young conveyed this land to William Holmes. See p. 423. The latter, b. in 1644, was a son of George Holmes of Turtle Bay, and m. in 1675 Elizabeth, dr. of Claes Wyp, of Albany. On Apl. 15, 1703, the town voted him a similar release as that to Wolley and partner. Holmes, by will made Sept. 18, 1705, gave his w. Elizabeth, the use of his farm, which at her d. was to be shared half by his son George, and half by his drs. Bregie, Jannetie, Judith, and Priscilla. Of these Jannetie m. 1712 Cornelius Mesurolle, and Judith m. 1718 Martin van Iveren; the other drs. d. unm. and intestate. George Holmes, b. 1678 (see his m. p. 492), came in possession of his patrimony prior to 1710, and by the d. of his unm. srs., and the purchase, Dec. 29, 1746, of Jannetie's interest, acquired ⅞ of the farm. Under his will, dated Sept. 13, 1743, his wid. Jenneke took the estate in fee, and after her d. Peter Anderson, with his w. Cornelia, only ch. and heiress of George and Jenneke Holmes, conveyed the farm, Mar. 30, 1756, to Abraham Lefferts, for £410. Lefferts devised it to his son Derick, and dr. Elizabeth, w. of Peter Clopper, and Clopper and w. sold their half to Derick, May 15, 1769, for £1400. Lefferts resided here till after the Revolution, and on June 25, 1788, conveyed the farm, 28 a., to Mary Ellis, for £3900, "in Spanish Milled Dollars."

Before Abm. Lefferts made his purchase, the remaining ⅛ of the farm, being a 4 a. strip on its southerly side, held by Martin and Judith van Iveren, had come to be owned by John Devoor, Jr., from whom it passed, by deed and mortgage of Feb. 15, 16, 1774, to David Provoost, and subsequently was purchased by Mary Ellis. On May 1, 1791, said Mary Ellis conveyed to John Baker, her farm called *Sans Souci*, 46 a., which included the 28, 4 and 14 a. tracts. The mortgages on the lesser pieces were assigned to Dr. Baker, who thus got title to this valuable property, which after his d. in 1796, and the expiration and surrender of certain life interests, enjoyed by the Delafields under the will of Dr. Baker, passed to the trustees of the New York Protestant Episcopal Public School.

III. THE MARSTON FARM.

The patent for this farm, dated Sept. 29, 1677, describes it as 44 rods in breadth by the water side, ranging in length north-west into the woods 120 rods; being bounded south-west by Jacob Young's land, and north-east and north-west by the Commons; and containing 30 a.

John Haignour, the patentee (see p. 428), sold the farm May 15, 1683, to Isaac Deschamps, he on Oct. 12, 1686, to John Spragge, and the latter, on Dec. 7, 1690, to Daniel Cox, of London, Doctor in Physic, and then principal proprietor of West Jersey. On Apl. 13, 1698, Dr. Cox, by his attorney Jeremiah Bass, Governor of N. J., and in consideration of £24, leased the farm to Thomas Codrington, of Raritan, for 99 yrs., at the yearly rent of one pepper-corn. On June 28, 1701, Dr. Cox conveyed the said farm in fee simple to his son Daniel Cox. Codrington must afterward have gotten a release of the fee. He also secured Nos. 1, 2, of the Hoorn's Hook lots, 16 a.; in exchange, one for No. 4, which he bought Sept. 4, 1700, from Israel Honeywell, who got it, Aug. 1, 1699, of Wm. Presker (see p. 572); the other for No. 3, obtained from Thos. Tourneur, or his heirs, Tourneur having gotten it, Mar. 13, 1689, from Joh. Verveelen. In 1704 the corporation leased him 60 a. of the commons, adjoining his farm, for 21 yrs., at 6 pence an acre per ann. Codrington set up a brewery, kept cattle and sheep, and owned half a dozen slaves. He left no ch. By will made Apl. 9, and proved Apl. 20, 1710, he gave £50 to each of his four srs.; £200 to his "cousin Frances Willett" (w. of Richard Willett; see p. 424), and his "farm at Harlem," etc., to his w. Margaret. See p. 396. Under her will, dated Sept. 2, proved Sept. 24, 1728, Martha, dr. of Richard Willett, and w. of Capt. Wm. Lawrence, should have taken the farm, as residuary legatee. But it paid quit rent for ten yrs. later as "the estate of Mr. Codrington." On July 24, 1738, "the Plantation of the late Capt. *Thomas Codrington*, containing about Thirty Acres of Land, besides two Out Lots of about Eight Acres each, with the Orchard and Dwelling House and Appurtenances; All in the Bounds of *Harlem*," was advertised in the *N. Y. Gazette*, to be sold at public vendue, on Sept. 2 ensuing, in the Exchange Market House. "The Title is good, and may be seen at the house of *John Chambers*, who is one of the persons impowered to sell the same."

The property was bought by John Brown. He exchanged parts of the Out Lots with Waldron (see p. 566), who built the "Hopper House," on No. 1. In 1749 the farm was purchased by Nathaniel Marston, of N. Y., merchant, and by his will, made Feb. 8, 1776, passed to his son Thomas, excepting the 8 a. gotten by Brown from Waldron, which Marston left to his son John, who sold it to Thomas, June 5, 1795. The *Prospect Farm*, as called, was sold in parcels by Thomas Marston, and formed the seats of Jones, Schermerhorn, etc.; but here we rest our notes, and with pleasure refer the inquirer for the later title to *Tuttle's Abstracts*.*

IV. THE WALDRON FARM.

This farm was made up of eight of the ten lots laid out in 1677 (see pp. 383, 384), with later additions. It is a mistake to deduce the title from Resolved Waldron, who never owned a foot of it. Peter van Oblienis had drawn lot No. 10 (see description, p. 406); his fa. bought No. 6, from Bogert, Dec. 9, 1679, and gave it to Peter (the deed passing Dec. 28, 1690); and Peter also acquired Nos. 7, 8, 9, from various parties to whom they had been transferred. See p. 460. Tourneur had exchanged No. 7 for No. 1, with Adolph Meyer; Oblienis agreed to give Meyer 300 gl. for it, and thereupon sold the five lots, with the improvements, May 10, 1690, to John Delamater. See pp. 503, 540. Delamater added three more lots, bought from Daniel Tourneur's heirs (see p. 544), and came to own Nos. 3 to 10, being 68 a. In the allotment of 1691 he secured an adjoining tract, described in his deed of May 21, 1701, from the town as "a piece of land lying in the Bay of Hellgate, extending from the north-west corner of the end of his lots to a white oak tree marked J. D. L. and J. L. D. To the river past a rock marked J. D. L. and

* NATHANIEL MARSTON was a son of Nathaniel, an original vestryman of Trinity chh., N. Y., named in its charter, 1697, and acting much of the time till 1731. His w. was Margaret, dr. of Abel Hardenbrook. Their son John m. and went to Jamaica, W. I. Their dr. Ann m. Ebenezer Grant. Nathaniel m. Mary, dr. of John Crook, and became wealthy. In 1731 he succeeded his fa. as vestryman, and in 1770 was made warden. He d. in his 75th yr., Oct. 21, 1778. His chn. were *Nathaniel*, whose dr. Mary m. Capt. Fred. Philipse; *Thomas*; *John*, mem. of the N. Y. Prov. Congress; *Margaret*, m. Hon. Philip Philipse and Rev. John Ogilvie; and *Frances*. Thomas m. 1759 Cornelia, dr. of Leonard Lispenard. He d. in N. Y., Jan. 11, 1814, in his 75th yr. For his portrait see *Stevens' Chamber of Commerce*. His eldest dr. m. Francis Bayard Winthrop.

J. L. B., and so onward by the strand till to the end of the meadow north of a rocky hill."

Samuel Waldron bought this farm in 1710, from the Delamater heirs (see p. 503), and on Dec. 20, 1712, obtained a patentee deed taking in the land westward to "the patent line." It is therein described as "ALL that tract of land commonly called or known as *Hoorn's Hook*, aforesaid, with all and singular the houses, house lots, lots of land, now in the possession of the said Samuel Waldron, as they are hereinafter named, expressed, bounded and numbered, that is to say; on the south, over against Hog Island, *a/s* Foucans Island, by the river of Harlem; on the south-west by the lot No. 2, now in the possession of Margaret Codrington, widow; on the north-west by the patent line of Harlem; on the north by a white oak stump upon the bounds of the lands now in the possession of Barent Waldron and John Benson; on the north-east by a rock marked on the north-east side thereof with the letters L. B., on the south-west by L. M.; and so goes down to the said river by several marked trees with the aforesaid letters, and runs on the north side of a rocky hill, and on the south side by a piece of meadow, and thence along the river to the said lot No. 2; including all points, meadows, and marshes within the bounds above mentioned; containing by estimation one hundred and fifteen acres, be the same more or less."

The farm remained intact during the life of Samuel Waldron. His son William, who came in possession in 1741, set off lots 3, 4, to his br. Benjamin (see pp. 563, 566), and, on Nov. 29, 1759, sold 21¼ a. at the southerly side of the farm to Jacob Leroy, (since the Com. Chauncey seat); but otherwise the farm underwent no material change, till divided by William's heirs, after his d. From that period dated the improvements, which the last few years have almost obliterated, that first associated with this fine property other notable names, such as Astor, Gracie, Prime and Rhinelander. It is not in our plan to extend these notes beyond this brief compendium of the early titles. *Tuttle's Abstracts* give full details as to the modern titles; and a volume only would suffice for the stirring reminiscences connected with the Hoorn's Hook farms.

I. Page 425.

THE DELAVALL LANDS.

THE considerable tracts of land at Harlem held by Capt. Thomas Delavall and his heirs have a history as little known as it is curious and interesting. For details regarding his purchases, the disposition he made of his lands, etc., the reader should consult the general history of the town.*

Capt. Delavall released, Aug. 8, 1676, to his son-in-law Capt. James Carteret and wife: "All that messuage, tenement and farm which the said Delavall formerly bought of one Moseman, situate lying and being in the township of Harlem, within or upon a certain island called or known by the name of Manhattan Island, in America; and all that water mill which the said Thomas Delavall built or caused to be built, situate, lying and being in and upon Manhattan Island aforesaid, together with all the land and meadows and pastures to the said mill belonging or adjoining, or therewithal usually held, used, occupied or enjoyed; and also all that island called Little Barnes Island, near adjoining to Manhattan Island, aforesaid; and all and singular houses," etc. See p. 381.

* See pp. 236, 259-262, 274, 322, 343, 344, 362, 373, 381, 384, 390, 396, 404, 418, 424, 425, 442, 446, 447, 450, 451, 456.

By his will, admitted to probate July 25, 1682, Capt. Delavall devised the lands he then owned at Harlem, together with Great Barnes Island, to his son-in-law William Darvall; he to pay certain moneys to Samuel Swynock, of London. See p. 424. On Nov. 24, 1684, William Darvall and wife, and John Delavall, son and heir of Capt. Thomas Delavall, of the *first part*; Joseph Benbrigge and others named, of London, creditors of said William Darvall, of the *second part*; and Samuel Swynock, of London, and Jacob Milborne, of New York, trustee for said Swynock, of the *third part*; joined in a deed, by which the parties of the first and second parts, for and in consideration of certain specified sums paid them by said Swynock, conveyed to said Swynock and Milborne, all those messuages, tenements, lands, etc. (those in Harlem, with Great Barnes Island, included), which were devised by said Thomas Delavall to said William Darvall: But nevertheless providing that if said Darvall should duly pay to said Samuel Swynock, the sum of £1647 : 6s., on Aug. 26, 1686, at his house in Pye Alley, Fanchurch Street, London; then said Swynock would reconvey all said premises to said Darvall.

Darvall failing to pay any part of the money due Swynock as aforesaid, John Delavall executed the release to Swynock and Milborne referred to on p. 446. On Aug. 9, 1687, Swynock conveyed to Milborne all the said lands at Harlem, with Great Barnes Island. Milborne sold the Island to Thomas Parcell. See pp. 425, 462.* Milborne, on losing his first w. Joanna, dr. of Samuel Edsall, m. Maria, dr. of Capt Jacob Leisler, and being involved with Leisler in the political tumults which brought both to the scaffold May 16, 1691, left beside his wid. an only son, Jacob. Upon these two, or the survivor of them, by an Act of Assembly of May 16, 1699, was settled the title to all the lands and tenements within the province of N. Y., of which the elder Milborne d. seized. On the day this act passed, the wid. m. Abraham Gouverneur; and Jacob Milborne, Jr., d. unm. some time after.

In the division of the Harlem common land made in 1691, there was laid out to the right of Capt. Delavall, lot No. 9, on Jochem Pieters Hills, containing 33⅓ *morgen*. See App. J. Other lots were laid out to Delavall's heirs, on the further division in 1712, according to the surveyor's certificate annexed:

"At the request and by the direction of Samuel Waldron, Zacharias Sickels and Johannes Meyer, persons authorized thereto by the owners of the undivided lands of New Harlem, in the City of New York, in an Instrument under their hands and seals dated the 19th May, 1711, I have surveyed and laid out these following parcels of land to the right of Capt. DELAVALL,

* THOMAS PARCELL was a son of John Parcell, otherwise "John Butcher," from Huntington Co., Eng., who early settled at Dutch Kills, L. I., d. in 1681, and left chn. Thomas, William, Henry, and Catharine; with an estate worth 6000 gl. Thomas, b. 1653, and bred a blacksmith, m. Christina Van Hattem. On removing to Great Barents Island he sold his lands at Dutch Kills to Bourgon Broucard and Hans Covert, June 21, 1690, for £287. Parcell built a grist-mill on the race at the upper side of his island. His son John bought the north half of the island, June 4, 1722, and on Mar. 29, 1723, Thomas and Christina sold the other half to their son-in-law, John Lanyon, of N. Y., innkeeper. Parcell d. prior to 1732, on Spectacle or Hart Island, which he then owned. He left chn. Nicholas, John, Henry, Hannah, m. successively Jeremiah Redding, John Lanyon, and Thomas Behena, and Eda, who m. Walter Dobbs. Nicholas m. a dr. of Hon. Rip Van Dam. Henry succeeded to Hart Island, and John, holding his half of Great Barent's or Parcell's Island till his d. in 1751, æ. 75 yrs., gave it to his son Thomas, one of nine chn. by his w. Leah, dr. of Joh. Van Alst. Thomas, who m. Deborah, dr. of Capt. Wm. Penfold, was drowned in Hellgate, Aug. 1, 1766, in the evening, in attempting to swim his horse over to his island. Behena succeeding to Lanyon's half of the island, it was mortgaged by his wid. in 1765, and eventually passed to Benj. Hildreth; Parcell's half passed to his kinsman John Wm. Penfold. *Valentine's Manual*, 1855, p. 495, gives other details regarding this property, now Ward's Island.

deceased, *viz.*: In the *1st Division*, No. 8, 16 a., 3 q., and 28 r., adjoining to the land of Mettie Cornelisse and the brook, the land now allotted to Samuel Waldron, and the highway; 1 a., 3 q. and 24 r. of land and meadow, lying on the other side of the highway, between the same and the mill creek, adjoining also to the land of the said Mettie; and also, 35 a. and 25 r., beginning at the top of the hill against the said Mettie's land, and runs thence northward along the land of Capt. De Key to the corner of the land now allotted to John V. Oblienis, thence along the same N. 79° E. to the land of Peter Van Oblienis, thence S. 31¼° E. to the highway, thence S. 45¾° W. to the land of Isaac Delamater, and then along the same with a crook to the upper end thereof until it even meets again with the land of the said John Van Oblienis, and from thence, along the fence and land of several people, with a crooked line, to the place where the same first began; in the *2d Division*, No. 16, 73 a., and 20 r. (with 2 a. allowance for the way which leads through the same to Harlem River), the same contains in breadth about four score rods, and runs from the highway between the land of Marcus Tiebout and John Dyckman, S. 53° E. to Harlem River; in the *3d Division*, No. 15, 18 a., 3 q. and 20 r., being in breadth 44 r., and runs from the middle line in said division, between the land of Isaac Delamater and Mary Meyer, S. 53° E. to said river; and, in the *4th Division*, No. 9, 32 a., 1 q. and 20 r., being in breadth 43½ r., and runs from the said highway between the land of Arent Bussing and John Nagel, N. 67° W. to Hudson's River; as appears by the several drafts of the same. Witness my hand, the 25th June, Anno Dni, 1712. PETER BERRIEN."

On Feb. 1, 1713, Peter van Oblienis, Johannes Waldron, etc., patentees of Harlem, confirmed to Abm. Gouverneur the several parcels of common land laid out to the right of Capt. Delavall. Gouverneur and w., on Feb. 13, 1720, obtained from Wm. Milborne, of Boston, N. E., baker, son and heir of Wm. Milborne, br. and heir of Jacob Milborne, Sen., dec., a release of all the estate, real and personal, of said Jacob Milborne, including all the lands he had or ought to have at Harlem.

Capt. James Carteret, son-in-law of Capt. Delavall, left a son George, who d. without issue, and a dr. Elizabeth, who was m. in the Island of Jersey, Nov. 11, 1699, to Philip Pipon, Esq., of Noiremont. On Aug. 11, 1705, Pipon and his w., then residing in London, empowered Thomas Newton, of Boston, N. E., to enter upon and take legal possession of all their lands, etc., upon Manhattan Island and Little Barnes Island, or elsewhere in America, whereof she, Elizabeth (or he, Philip, in her right) is seized, interested or entitled, as gd-dr. or heir of Thomas Delavall, dec., as dr. or heir of her fa. or mo., James Carteret, Esq., and Frances his w., or either of them, or as sr. or heir to George Carteret, Esq., also dec.; authorizing said Newton to lease said premises for a term not to exceed five years. What Judge Newton did in the case we know not.

Mrs. Pipon d. in Jersey, near Nov. 11, 1720, the date of her burial in the parish chh. of St. Brelade. Mr. Pipon, attended by one of his sons, now came to N. Y., "about his private affairs," arriving toward the close of 1721. For some years the Delavall lands had been partly in charge of Pipon's kinsman and agent, Richard Willett, of N. Y., merchant, (see p. 425), but had been mainly engrossed by Abm. Gouverneur, who, aspiring to four lots on Jochem Pieters and all the drafted lands, had, as we have seen, gotten a patentee deed, Feb. 1, 1713, and had disposed of about 150 a. to Peter van Oblienis, Isaac Delamater, and Johannes Myer.

Pipon, however, claimed the entire property; at least it stands in his name in the quit rent lists for 1722 and 1723. There was now an apparent agreement among the parties interested, to have the title to all the Delavall lands settled by the Supreme Court of the province. Pipon first brought suits against Samuel and Barent Waldron, evidently to test the validity of Capt. Carteret's sales mentioned pp. 404, 443, which lots were now held by these defendants.* The last named case was tried Nov. 27, 1723, and Barent Waldron's title sustained. In regard to the other lands, Pipon proceeded to eject Robert Crannell, Gouverneur's tenant, who thereupon brought his suit to regain possession. The cause was tried, with great array of evidence, on June 8 and 9, 1724; a verdict being rendered as follows: "The JURY do find that, as to a certain piece of ground known by the name of the Clover Wey, and as to the three southernmost lots of the Nine Lots, at the place called Jochem Pieters Flat, and as to one third part of the common lands that have been laid out in right of the estate of Thomas Delavall and John Delavall, deceased; the Defendant is *guilty*, and they do find for the Plaintiff sixpence costs and sixpence damages. And as to all the residue of the premises, they find the Defendant *not guilty*." The record adds: "It is agreed by Abraham Gouverneur, lessor of Robert Crannell in ejectment, and Philip Pipon, defendant, that the costs and charges in this cause may be equally paid between the parties."

This decision confirmed Pipon's title, except as to the Three Lots, and one third of the drafted lands, which went to Gouverneur. For the Clover Wey, consult the *Key to Titles*.

Pipon and Gouverneur now petitioned the Governor and Council, July 1, 1724, and representing that they were owners, Pipon of two thirds, and Gouverneur of one third, of certain Nine Lots, at Harlem, on Jochem Pieters Flat, and containing 60 *morgen* of land; and further that said lots having for some time laid unimproved, the bounds thereof could not be well ascertained except by a survey of all the tract called Jochem Pieters Flat, which contained about 66 *morgen* more, owned by several people of Harlem; prayed for a warrant to have said tract surveyed. This was granted, and the survey made, as already described in App. E.

On May 2, 1725, Abm. Gouverneur and Maria his w., for £235, released to Johannes Myer, their tract known as the Three Lots, being 18 *morgen*, bounded south by Peter Bussing, north by the Six Lots, east by Harlem River, and west by lands in possession of the heirs of James Carteret; and also an undivided third of lot No. 9, Jochem Pieters Hills, and of the Delavall lots in the 4 Divisions. This gave Myer 114 a., making good to him the quantity sold him by Gouverneur Mar. 25, 1720, though but in part the same lands. In this later deed Gouverneur particularly excepts and reserves

* I have not ascertained Capt. Carteret's ultimate history, nor where he died. "He certainly did not die in Jersey," says an able genealogist of that island, but, he adds, "most likely in Bedfordshire, England." His father left ample estates and seats at Hawnes, in that county. I should expect further traces of him at London. In the will of Sir George Carteret, dated Dec. 5th, 1678, occurs the following:

"And whereas I am desirous to make some provision for my son Captain James Carteret for his life, Therefore my mind and will is that the said Manor and premises [the Manor of Epworth, with Trestwood and Haxey, in Lincolnshire], be charged and chargeable with the payment of one annuity or yearly sum of one hundred pounds of lawful English money, to be paid and payable unto my said son and his assigns for and during his life, . . . in half yearly payments, namely every Lady day and Michaelmas day, the first payment to begin and to be made at such of the said days as shall first and next happen after my decease. . . . But this bequest of mine to my said son James Carteret, as aforesaid, is upon this condition, that he within two years next after my decease, shall convey or otherwise release unto my heirs at law, all such right, title, interest, claims and demand which he the said James Carteret hath or shall pretend to have, of, in and unto my lands and hereditaments in the said Island of Jersey. And in case my said son shall refuse to make such conveyance or release, as aforesaid, and shall not do the same, Then my will and meaning is that this bequest of mine, of the said yearly sum of one hundred pounds, limited to him for life, and charged upon the lands in manner as aforesaid, shall be void and of none effect, to all intents whatsoever."

all his right in any lands in Harlem "which now are held or claimed by the heirs or assigns of James Carteret and Frances his wife, deceased." What limit Gouverneur put to his claim, to which he so firmly adhered, is not apparent; only that it extended to all the drafted lands.*

Philip Pipon entailed upon his son James and his heirs male his estate in Jersey, and upon his son Elias and heirs male his property in America. Elias, being twenty four years of age, came hither to enjoy his possessions. He built upon Little Barent's Island, which he renamed Belle Isle, and m. Blanche, dr. of Mr. John Lafons. After several years, unable to support himself upon the scanty income derived from his mainly unproductive property, Pipon resolved to ask the colonial assembly to remove the entail and empower him to sell a part of his land, in order that he might improve the rest. Notice of his intentions was publicly read in the church at Harlem by the parish clerk, Van Harlingen, on three successive Sundays, beginning Sept. 27, 1730, and duly certified to the Governor and Council, Oct. 13; but Pipon's application to the Assembly was stayed by the adjournment of that body for a long interval. During this time the brothers Pipon exchanged releases, James conveying to Elias all his interest in the lands at Harlem and in Little Barent's Island by lease and release executed in the Island of Jersey, May 18, 19, 1732. Pipon's needs at length forced him to mortgage Belle Isle, for £432, to St. George Talbot, July 3, 1735. On Oct. 29, ensuing, he petitioned the Assembly for the proposed relief. A bill was introduced, read twice and committed, but nothing came of it. He was soon compelled to make an assignment to three principal creditors, Simon Johnson, John Auboyneau and James Faviere, in trust also for the rest; his wife joining with him.† These three, with Pipon, intending another appeal to the Assembly, gave notice as before by a poster upon the church door at Harlem. But a fatality seemed to attend their applications to the Assembly. A bill was brought in, but failed by a sudden dissolving of that body; another bill introduced at the next session, was agreed upon and ordered to be engrossed, though opposed by Gouverneur who alleged that he or his assigns were in lawful possession of part of said lands, "and claim a great part of the rest." This bill also failed, by an adjournment of the Assembly, Dec. 16, 1737, and no further attempt was made in that body.

Meanwhile Gouverneur d. By will, dated Sept. 12, 1739, and proved Oct. 8, 1740, he gave his estate to his w., with power to sell, or to devise to the chn.; named her sole executrix, but appointed to act after her dec., his drs. Jacoba, Elizabeth, and Maria, his nephew Nicholas Gouverneur, and friend Paul Richard. The trustees of Pipon and the wid. Maria Gouverneur now came to an agreement, in virtue of which she transferred all her right in the Six Lots and several other pieces of land in Harlem to said trustees, Johnson, Auboyneau, and Faviere, by lease and release of Feb. 9, 10, 1741; while they conveyed to her at the same time, the Three Lots, together with

* ABRAHAM GOUVERNEUR was the son of Nicholas and Machtelt (de Riemer) Gouverneur, and was b. in 1671, "upon the Single, near the Konings Pleyn," in Amsterdam. He took a zealous part for Leisler, though yet a minor, and was charged with having shot the parish clerk four days before Gov. Sloughter arrived. His fa. had been d. for yrs., his mo. being m. to Jasper Nessepott (Nesbitt), named p. 552. Gouverneur was afterward Recorder of N. Y., and mem. of the Assembly, and enjoyed considerable notoriety. He d. June 16, 1740. By Maria Leisler he had four chn. who reached maturity, viz., Nicholas, Jacoba, Elizabeth, and Maria, of whom the last m. Henry Myer, Jr., and Capt. Jasper Farmer. The son Nicholas d. Mar. 20, 1739, æ. 39 yrs., leaving issue Abraham, Esther, Barent, and Nicholas. *Bolton*, 1: 310, mistakes for desc. of Abm. Gouverneur, those of his br. Isaac.

† SIMON JOHNSON was the Recorder of N. Y. from 1747 to 1769; had previously served as Alderman and Assemblyman. He d. a year or two later.

half the woodlands, or commons before allotted to the right of Capt. Delavall. On Feb. 11, 12, 1741, the said trustees sold to Jacob Myer, of Harlem, the Six Lots aforesaid, with 7 a. 3 q. 37 r., of the adjoining Carteret woodlot, also Carteret's Island, containing 12 a. 13 r. of upland, and 10 a. 1 q. 31 r. of meadow; in all by survey 107 a. 15 r. By a separate writing, Johnson and Faviere also promised to warrant and defend the title, in proportion to Pipon's indebtedness to them.

The balance of Pipon's land stood in his name till 1743, when Simon Johnson succeeded.* The latter, on Sept. 12, 1747 (Pipon, Auboyneau, and Faviere were now all dead), sold to Jacob Myer, of Bergen Co., N. J., all his half of a lot at Round Meadow Hill; being the Delavall lot No. 15, 3d Division. On Sept. 25, 1747, he conveyed to said Jacob Myer all his half of the woodlot No. 16, 2d Div., and to Benjamin Benson the two lots on Van Keulen's Hook, near the Mill Camp. He also sold Lawrence Low his half of lot No. 9, of 1691, and his half of lot No. 9, 4th Div. Grietie Kortright bought parcels 1 and 2 of No. 6, 1st Div. (later added to the Nutter Farm); Harman Vandewater 17 a. of 3d parcel, and Adolph Myer, Jr., a remnant of the same, 4 a., being exclusive of a piece held by Peter Waldron (see p. 541). Johnson sold the balance of the Carteret woodlot, which joined upon the Three Lots, to Johannes Myer; and the two *erven* or village houselots to Derick Benson and John Lewis. And lastly, on Jan. 21, 1748, he released Belle Isle (Randell's Island), to St. George Talbot. See p. 534; also *Valentine's Manual*, 1855, p. 493. A deed from Jacobus Gouverneur, etc., chn., etc., of Maria Gouverneur, dec., to Johannes Myer, Apl. 30, 1748, conveying one half of a third of the Delavall common lands, a third having been before sold him by Abm. Gouverneur, perfected Myer's title to one half of said lands. Thus the estate of Capt. Delavall fell to many owners, originating as many separate titles. We only add that parcel 3 of No. 8, 1st Div., was subsequently included, mainly in the Molenaor and Capt. John Kortright farms; lot No. 16, 2d Div., extending along the Kingsbridge Road, between 179th and 185th streets, and thence to Harlem River, was afterward owned by Blasius Moore and others; lot No. 15, 3d Div., running from the Cut Line in that division to Harlem River, has since formed a part of Dyckman's Fort George Tract. See abstract by *Lockwood & Crosby*. Of No. 9, 4th Div., which ran from Kingsbridge Road to Hudson River, Myer took the upper, and Low the lower half; Myer's part passing to Adolph Myer, later to Wm. Molenaor, and Low's part to Gen. John Maunsell, being subsequently included in the large tract owned by Dr. Samuel Watkins, above Fort Washington.

* ELIAS PIPON succeeded his fa. in 1726. Whether he or a br. was the "young Mr. Pipon" who came out with the senior Pipon, but returned to Europe at the close of 1723, we know not. Mrs. Codrington, in her will dated Sept. 2, 1728, bequeaths "to Elias Pipon of the city of New York, Gent, £10, and my negro girl Betty." The records of the French Church *Du St. Esprit* contain the following:

A la Nouvelle York le 10 de Juin 1730, Baptesme. Aujourd'hui Mercredi après la priere, a été baptisé par moi L: Rou, ministre de cette Eglise, Jean Pipon, né à la Nouve York, le 28 de May dernier, fils d'Elie Pipon et de Blanche La Fonds, étant presenté au St. Bapteme par Mr. Jean La Fonds et Mademlle Charlotte Faviere ses parrain et marraine. L: Rou, Pasteur.
Jean Lafons. Elie Pipon.
Charlotte Fauviere.

Elias was b. in Jersey, in 1702. He d. in this country, having survived his w. Being sick and weak, he made his will, Aug. 30, 1744, leaving his estate to his four chn., John, Jane, Mary, and Elizabeth. It was proved Sept. 30, 1746. "John Pipon, Esq. of the Island of Jersey," d. at Cardiff, South Wales, Oct. 5, 1815. Mrs. Braithwaite (see p. 15) thinks he may have been the John b. May 28, 1730, as aforesaid.

J. Page 471.

DIVISION OF THE COMMON LANDS

Under the Dongan Patent.

I. *Division of* 1691.

At the date of the Dongan patent (see p. 465), the appropriated lands at Harlem were held principally under the three general allotments made in 1658, 1661, and 1677, of which a full history has been given. The patent conferred upon these proprietors, or properly such as were named therein, a joint interest in all the unappropriated or common lands. Four years having expired, the patentees agreed to make an allotment, and at a meeting held Nov. 29, 1691, chose Adolph Meyer, John Hendricks van Brevoort, Samuel Waldron, and Peter van Oblienis, "to consider and devise such measures as shall be most proper for the benefit and best interests of the town and inhabitants thereof." The following resolutions were then passed:

1. It is resolved that the land lying in the common woods, so much as may be found suitable for making good tillable land, shall be laid out and surveyed into lots, or parcels, whereof each inhabitant of this town shall draw a part as his property, every one according to his estate or proportion.

2. It is also resolved that the parcel of land lying at the end of the lots named Jochem Pieters shall be laid out, from the end of the old lots to the hill, and so again to the Clove of the Kill, behind the high hill in the hills; on condition that a good and sufficient King's or high way shall be left around the fencing of the same.

3. It is resolved to lay out a parcel of land situated and comprehended from Moertje Davids' Meadow eastward up Jochem Pieters Hills, and northerly so far as good tillable land shall be found. Provided, that the land of Barent Waldron being extended, the east side from the island according to the river, shall claim no further in than the King's way is now running.

4. It is also resolved to lay out a parcel of land at the southerly end of the Long Hill, so much as shall be found good tillable land.

5. It is also resolved to lay out a parcel of land at Spuyten Duyvel, between the high hills by the Round Meadow, on the other side of the swamp (*morass creupelbos*), so much as shall be found fit for tillage; on condition that there remain a good and sufficient King's way where shall be found best and most convenient.

6. The land lying at the end of the lots named Jochem Pieters shall be so estimated that one morgen shall go for two morgen upon any of the other parcels that shall be laid out. Also that the hills shall be fenced off from the corner of the land behind the high hill to the meadow of Daniel Tourneur at Montanye's Kill, for a sheep pasture—those having fences within this stretch to keep the same tight and in good order—with a draw-rail (*draei-hek*) at the road; and that a bridge shall be made there, beyond the stone bridge or thereabouts.

7. It is further resolved that when the said surveys shall take place, each inhabitant shall have the privilege to draw according to his right or apportionment, for the *erven* a third part; and then the rest shall be drawn according to the number of *morgen*.

The Authorized Men, with the aid of Adrian Appel, surveyor, made up a list of the freeholders, with the number of *erven* and *morgen* each one held, and on which lands could be drawn, and proceeded to survey and allot the designated tracts, as shown in the following schedule:

DIVISION OF 1691.—"*List of the drawn Lands, as they are measured out by the Surveyor, A. Appel, by lot, pursuant to order from the whole Community and Authorized Men of this Town.*"

Lot Numbers.	By whom drawn.	Erf Rights.	Morgen Rights.	Number of Morgen drawn.	Location of the Land.
1	Thomas Tourneur	1	9	7½	Behind the old lots of Jochem Pieters.
2	Daniel Tourneur, Jr., dec.	1	18	7½	do.
3	Johannes Waldron	1	16	7½	do.
4	Adolph Meyer	1	24	9⅓	do.
5	Johannes Vermilye	1	1½	6	On Jochem Pieters' Hills.
6	Jan Hendricks van Brevoort	1	26	14	do.
7	Jacques Tourneur	1	9	10	do.
8	Arent Harmans Bussing	1	13	12½	do.
9	Thomas Delavall, dec.	0	60	33⅓	do.
10	Metje Cornelis	1	31	20½	do.
11	Isaac Delamater	1	6	8⅓	do.
12	Barent Waldron	1	20	12	do.
13	Jan Tibout	1	0	5	do.
14	Jan Dyckman	0	18	20	do.
15	Lourens Jansen	1	11	11	do.
16	William Holmes	1	0	5	do.
17	William Haldron, dec.	1	0	5	do.
18	Samuel Waldron	1	7½	9½	do.
19	Joost van Oblinus	1	32	20½	On the Southern end of the Long Hill.
20	Pieter van Oblinus	1	9	10	By the Round Meadow.
21	Barent Waldron			*4	North of his *Erf*.
22	Metje Cornelis			*1½	Nigh Montanye's Flat.
23	Abraham Delamontanie	1	0	5	Between the Patent Line and King's Way.
24	Jan Dyckman	1	26	24½	North of the Round Meadow.
25	Jan Louwe Bogert	1	16	14	In the Bay of Hellgate.
26	Jan Delamater	1	9	10	do.

* Drawn upon rights given under Nos. 10 and 12.

In computing this allotment, 5 morgen, or 10 acres, were allowed for each *erf right*, and $\frac{333}{600}$ of a morgen, or 333 square Dutch rods, for each *morgen right*.* To avoid many fractional parts, where the quantity fell less than 100 rods short of a full morgen, it was counted as a morgen, while fractions of a morgen below 100 rods were thrown out. In addition to the tracts designated, the authorized men had disposed of some other parcels (the lots 21 to 26), which lay adjoining the farms of the persons to whom granted. The last was formally allowed and approved of by the freeholders, Dec. 11, as appears by the following document, of that date:

"Whereas on this day have assembled the community of New Harlem, and having from among themselves chosen and authorised Adolph Meyer, John Hendricks van Brevoort, Peter van Oblienis, and Samuel Waldron to lay out the available land, according to the surveyor's schedule hereunto annexed; So we undersigned promise to hold inviolate that which the four persons before named have caused to be measured and set off (*aangewezen*), to *Metje Cornelis*, *John Louwe Bogert*, *John Delamater*, *Abraham Delamontanie*, *Barent Waldron*, and *John Dyckman*. NOTA, All the lands that are unsuitable for tillage, shall bear half costs. And all those who have drawn the land behind the old land of Jochem Pieters shall be obligated to leave a convenient road for the town's use. The *erven* which have been drawn shall be required to contribute to town expenses. The path or road shall be taken from the newly drawn land. All this have we subscribed with our hands." [Signed by Adolph Meyer, Pieter van Ohliens, Joost van Oblinus, Jan Louwe Bogert, Arent Harmans, Jan Hendricks van Brevoort, Samuel Waldron, Johannes Waldron, Jan Delamater, Jan Dyckman, Metje Cornelis, Johannes Vermelje, Barent Waldron, Laurens Jansen, Isaac Delamater, Abraham Delamontanie, and Jan Tibout.]

During the years which expired before the title deeds for these lots were given, the town made several small grants and sales, hereafter noticed; and at a meeting held Nov. 2, 1699, "all the residents or proprietors of the town made a conveyance of the church, to the Reverend Consistory, upon condition that the proprietors who have helped build the church shall continue to hold their seats."† And on Dec. 14, following, Arent Bussing, Adolph Meyer, and Samuel Waldron were chosen as *Authorized-Men*, to act with the overseers, Laurens Jansen, Peter van Ohliens, and Jacques Tourneur, in giving the freeholders their deeds for the newly drawn lands. The six persons met Dec. 18, "to commence the business," and approved "the last survey, made by the surveyor, Adrian Appel." After fourteen days, allowed to hear

* The *erven* were only the original village plots so called, with such other house lots as had been granted or sold for that purpose by the town, for a price, usually 25 guilders; no other house lot was counted as an *erf*, or invested with the *erf right*. So the *morgen right* only attached to the lots on Jochem Pieters' Flat, Van Keulen's Hook, Montanye's Flat, the New Lots, Bogert's or Benson's Point, Gloudie's or Bussing's Point, and the Dyckman and Nagel lots, near Kingsbridge. This right never attached to the lands allotted under the Dongan patent. See last note on p. 529. This principle carried out with reference to any claims which the present Harlem proprietors may have upon such new lands as have been made by filling in the creeks and marshes, and never allotted to any one, must necessarily limit such claims to those holding the original *morgen* lands and *erven*!

† Donderdag den 2 Novemb: Anno 1699. N: Haarlem. Present, de Overziers Louwrens Jansen, Pieter Ohliens en Jacques Tourneur.

* * * * * * * * *

Oock is mede ten dage voornoemt, van alle de Inwoonders, off eygenaars, deses dorps, een opdragt gedaan van de Kerck, aan de eerwaarde Kerck-Raaden, onder conditie dat de eygenaars die de Kerck hebben helpen maaken sullen behouden haare vaste plaats.

* * * * * * * * *

Attesteert, datum ut supra.

Adr. Vermeule, Klerck.

objections, another meeting was held, Jan. 4, 1700, and no one having appeared to oppose the survey it was finally adopted. The inhabitants then subscribed another paper promising to pay their proportion of town charges, and agreeing to a *pro rata* distribution of the common lands. The meeting also voted a deed to Bastiaen Kortright for two pieces of meadow (see p. 297), "as soon as the purchase money shall be paid." The overseers and authorized-men met on Mar. 7, 1701, and gave the deeds referred to pp. 443, 512; also one to Adolph Meyer for "three feet of ground lying north of his house," and granted him in 1694. On May 2, deeds for all the newly drawn lands were ordered. These being prepared, were signed by the overseers and authorized-men Mar. 21, 1701. But to a brief notice of these lots:

Nos. 1 to 4, lying on the flats, and described as "behind the old lots of Jochem Pieters, by the high hill," were identical with the Lawrence, Molenaor, and Myer tracts, filling the space above the Samson A. Benson farm, to the junction of the roads. They were those which came under the rule making one morgen here equal to two in the other places. See references to these lots pp. 470, 471, 527, 529, 530, 534. Day's Tavern (pp. 471, 504) was on No. 4, on the line of 126th St., 200 feet west of 8th Ave.

Nos. 5 to 18 lay upon the heights above Manhattanville; the S. E. corner of No. 5 touching 133d St., say 100 feet west of 9th Ave., its S. W. corner the North River at 136th St. No. 18 reached up nearly to 162d St., at the Kingsbridge Road. The lots ran from the river within parallel lines, southeast, "according to the course of a pocket compass," and were 200 Dutch rods in length. Their breadth was as follows, Dutch measure: No. 5, 18 rods; No. 6, 42 rods; No. 7, 30 rods, 9 feet; No. 8, 36½ rods; No. 9, 100 rods; No. 10, 64 rods; No. 11, 25 rods; No. 12, 36 rods; No. 13, 15 rods; No. 14, 60 rods; No. 15, 33 rods; No. 16, 15 rods; No. 17, 15 rods; No. 18, 28½ rods.

No. 5, since owned by Schieffelin, may be traced by reference to pp. 548, 504, 517, 518. For Nos. 6 and 7, owned latterly by the Myer family, see pp. 496, 533, 534. No. 8, its lines crossing Bloomingdale Road at 139th and 141st Sts., passed from Arent Harmsing to his son Peter, and to his son Aaron, whose heirs sold it to John Myer, Nov. 6, 1790, and May 19, 1791. See pp. 498, 534. No. 9, extending (where intersected by the Bloomingdale Road) from 141st St. to 145th, is particularly referred to in App. I. In a resurvey it was called No. 6 (the Peter van Oblinus 100 a. tract taken as No. 1), was 20 chains 85 links broad, and ran from lot No. 16, 1st Div. (which lay between it and the highway), N. 38° W. to Hudson River, being in length on the south side 36 chains 43 links, and on the north side 37 chains 26 links. It was divided by Delavall's successors, first crosswise, afterward lengthwise, the upper half subsequently owned by Gen. John Maunsell, and later by Dr. Samuel Bradhurst; the lower half sold by Samuel Kelly to Jacob Schieffelin, Jan. 15, 1799. "Hamilton Grange," the former seat of Gen. Alex. Hamilton, occupied part of this lot.

No. 10, first in the range reaching to the highway, its N. line touching it at 148th St.,* was latterly owned by Dr. Bradhurst; the lower corner was included in Hamilton Grange. See pp. 515, 516, 520.

Nos. 11 to 13 were bought up by John Dyckman and the Nagel heirs. Dyckman had drawn No. 14, on his rights and those of John Nagel jointly, the latter 1 *erf*, 15 *morgen*, and Dyckman's, 1 *erf*, 3 *morgen*; the morgen rights being upon their lots on Jochem Pieters and Montanye's Flat. Each had a deed for his share of No. 14, Dyckman for 6½ morgen, and Nagel for 13½ morgen. Dyckman's patentee deed, of June 1, 1713, covers his undivided half, or 45 a., of Nos. 11 to 14. See further pp. 508, 509. Trinity Church Cemetery is on these lots; also "Minniesland," the seat of the late John J.

* That is the old Kingsbridge Road. The first move for extending the Bloomingdale Road through lots 5 to 10, was made in 1791.

Audubon. As this tract, when sold to John Watkins, in 1767 (it reaching nearly to 156th St. on Kingsbridge Road, and to 159th St., North River), contained about 112 a., we infer that it took in the Low lot, No. 15, 22 a. The lots in this range were resurveyed by Peter Berrien, and some surplus pieces were found and disposed of, forming the "Last Division." This survey is not well understood, yet it would appear that space was found between Lawrence Jansen and John Kiersen for two new lots (Nos. 16, 17), the last of these, containing 16 a., being allotted to John Dyckman (see p. 105), but subsequently added to Kiersen's tract. No. 16, extending upward to a line from Kingsbridge Road, 86 feet below 158th St., to the North River at 161st St., was sold by John Low, as 31 a., to John Watkins, enlarging Watkins' tract to 142½ a. This tract, embracing lots 11 to 16, being sold with other parcels, under a foreclosure by Gen. John Maunsell, to Charles Watkins, was reconveyed to Maunsell, Mar. 28, 1793. Two yrs. later Gen. Maunsell's wid. succeeded under his will, and devised her lands here, May 20, 1815, to her nephew, Dr. Samuel Watkins (son of said John), and her nieces, Lydia, w. of James Beekman, and Elizabeth, wid. of Robert H. Dunkin. These divided the 142½ a. into equal parts, under Nos. 1, 2, 3, and passed deeds Oct. 17, 1816; Mrs. Beekman taking No. 1 (the lower lot), Mrs. Dunkin No. 2, and Dr. Watkins No. 3. Dr. Watkins subsequently removed to Jefferson (since for him called Watkins), at the head of Seneca Lake.

The old Nos. 16 to 18, which completed this range of lots, and were bounded northerly by a line touching Kingsbridge Road, say 50 feet below 162d St., and the North River, midway of 164th and 165th Sts., formed a part of the Kiersen lands, which shortly before the Revolution came into possession of Col. Roger Morris. See pp. 512 to 514. This tract then contained 57 a., which included No. 17 Last Div. Col. Morris's estates being confiscated, because of his supporting the royal cause, his Harlem lands, called 115 a., were sold, July 9, 1784, by the Com. of Forfeiture, to John Berrien and Isaac Ledyard, and passed by several mesne conveyances, all of record, to William Kenyon, who sold this tract with others, Aug. 29, 1799, to Leonard Parkinson, Esq., of Kinnersley Castle, Herefordshire, Eng.* Col. Morris owned the Kiersen homestead, lying opposite, east of the road (see p. 513), and built the fine residence known as the Jumel House.† He enlarged this tract, which already included lot No. 6, 2d Div., by the purchase of No. 7, being 16 a., from John Bogert, and giving Morris 35 a. 1 q. 36 r., or 36 ½ a., as subse-

* William Kenyon, son of David Kenyon, of Liverpool, Eng., ironmonger, and of Dorothy Barnes, his w., was b. Feb. 2, 1753. At about twenty-one years of age he came to N. Y., where he was successful in business, and became an eminent shipping merchant. In 1779 he was admitted a member of the Chamber of Commerce. He was one of the governors of the N. Y. Hospital from 1795 to 1797. For some years he made his residence upon Hoorn's Hook, having purchased from Jos. Blackwell, May 4, 1799, 12 a. of land, since in the Prime tract; the house he is said to have built. He d. at Gloucester, Va., Nov. 29, 1826. Mr. Kenyon's parents were Quakers, and he adorned the same profession by an exemplary life. He was m. in N. Y. Apl. 8, 1778, to Abigail, dr. of Samuel Bowne. Their chn., save two who d. in inf., were Samuel, b. Mar 6, 1780, d. unm. Sept. 6, 1803; William-Barnes, b. Aug. 7, 1784, m. in 1815 (see p. 334), and d. at H., May 26, 1866, being fa. of Mr. Samuel B. Kenyon, etc.; and James, b. Aug. 20, 1791, who m. in 1813 (see same p.), and d. at H., Dec. 10, 1852, being the fa. of Mr. John S. Kenyon, etc.

† Col. Morris's 115 a. included, with his said homestead, and the 57 a. tract, the lots, Nos. 5, 2d Div., 8, 3d Div., and 7, 4th Div., besides salt meadows (see p. 333) not counted in the 115 a. The Dyckmans seem to have gotten the lot in 3d Div., in exchange for 8 a. of No. 17, 2d Div., before Sept. 25, 1793, when William Kenyon bought the Morris lands from Anthony J. Bleeker. Col. Morris d. in England in 1794; and it appearing that the Confiscation Act did not affect the rights of his children, it was not till 1828, after satisfaction had been made by the State, etc., that the persons who held the confiscated lands were quieted in their possession. See *Sabine's Loyalists*, ii. 104.

quently surveyed by Chas. Loss. This too passed through the same hands to Parkinson, who conveyed the said homestead-tract to Stephen Jumel, Apl. 28, 1810. Of Parkinson more anon. *Melbourne*, the rural seat of the late Shepherd Knapp, is on the 57 a. tract.

The remaining numbers, of the allotment of 1691, are sufficiently noticed as follows: No. 19, on p. 542; No. 20, on p. 297; No. 21, in note p. 529; No. 22, on p. 515; No. 23, on p. 521; No. 24, on p. 507; No. 25, on p. 491, and No. 26, on p. 597. We notice that these lots are described in the deeds, as *set off or designated* (*aangewesen*); but all the others, as *surveyed* (*gemeten*). This choice of terms was not without reason. These six lots lying adjacent to the farms or other lands of the grantees, and allotted, as we must conclude, under special arrangement between the latter and the town authorities, were taken as the tracts lay, consisting largely of heights, abrupt slopes or rocky land, not answering the description of "good and tillable," and allowing a margin in the measurement. Nos. 21, 22, 23 took in order (north to south) the small grants which conformed nearly to what was due on their rights, and Nos. 24, 25, 26, the principal grants; this explains the seeming want of order in the numbering. The reasons for the extraordinary grant to Dyckman and Nagel, at Spuyten Duyvel, have been given p. 507.* What interest gathers about this tract, whose title, in fact, reaches backward over two centuries to the closing days of Gov. Kieft's directorship; and whose history, in the times agone, recalls the most stirring incidents, whether of early Indian barbarity, or of civil contests for its ownership, or yet of British and Hessian sway, when the patriotic Dyckmans being fled, their home in ashes, and their fields a military camp, with breastworks and cannon frowning from every neighboring hill, this charming section of Manhattan was given over, for seven years, to the rude alarms of war! Pleasanter the anticipations of 1883, when on this very spot, now known as *Inwood*, visitors from every state and nation shall gather in friendly concourse at the WORLD'S FAIR.

II. THE FOUR DIVISIONS.

Under an act passed by the Governor, Council, and General Assembly, Oct. 30, 1708, entitled "An Act for the easier Partition of Lands in Joint Tenancy, or in Common," steps were taken by the Harlem freeholders, for a more complete division of their common lands.

This act allowed a majority of the resident owners to make a division, after giving public notice for three months previous, and required such division to be made by drawing of lots in the presence of at least three disinterested persons to be named by the dividers, and paid five shillings per day "for their trouble had in the making of said division." The surveys were to be made by a sworn surveyor, or any three neighbors, men of intelligence and integrity, to be chosen by the dividers; the lots after being laid out "as equally as possible in regard both to quantity and quality," must be numbered and then publicly drawn for; and in order to prevent dispute as to the costs of making the division, it provided that before any division was made, such part of the land as they should judge reasonable for defraying said costs, should be laid out and sold by the majority of the dividers, whose conveyance thereof should be good and effectual in the law.

* DYCKMAN and NAGEL, having, in 1677, gotten 74 a. at Spuyten Duyvel, or as subsequently estimated, 76 a. (see pp. 383, 386, 507), their rights upon these were arranged as follows: The 76 a. making 38 *morgen*, from this count 18 morgen were taken and the 2 house lots substituted, these being classed as *erven* and taking *erf rights*. This gave them 2 erven, 20 morgen (or 1 erf 10 morgen each), upon which they were entitled to draw land. The additional 6 morgen rights on which they drew here were partly on the Nagel lots on Jochem Pieters Flat, and partly on Dyckman's lot on Montanye's Flat, 3 morgen rights at each place. Thus they drew together upon equal rights at Spuyten Duyvel, viz., each on 1 erf 13 morgen right.

Pursuant to a Justice's warrant, issued May 9, 1711, and directed to Gerrit Dyckman, constable of Harlem, authorising a meeting for that purpose, the inhabitants and freeholders assembled on the 19th, and agreed that a division of the common land should be made forthwith; appointed Samuel Waldron, Zacharias Sickels, and Johannes Meyer to engage one or more surveyors to make a fair and equal division, and promised to defray the costs of the survey and all other charges attending such division, according to each one's proportion. A writing to this effect, dated at the town house, Harlem, May 19, 1711, was subscribed by Zacharias Sickels, Abram de Lamontanie, Samson Benson, Jan Kiersen, Metje Joirsen, Johannes Meyer, Charles Congreve, Marcus TieLaut, Laurens Cornelissen, Maria Meyer, Richard Willett, Pieter Oblienis, Samuel Waldron, Barent Waldron, Johannes Waldron, Abram Meyer, Jan Dyckman, Arent Bussing, Isaac Delamater, Gerrit Dyckman, Laurens Jansen, Jan Nagel, Derick Benson, Abraham Gouverneur, and Woodhull Tourneur.

The business was promptly undertaken, and so far as possible in the mode prescribed by the act of 1708. Peter Berrien, of Newtown, an experienced surveyor, was employed; and three disinterested persons, to wit, John Lawrence, Cornelius Luyster, and Edward Blagge, were chosen by the freeholders and inhabitants, "to see that a just and equal division be made of their undivided lands." No record remains of any sales of land, as provided for by the act, for meeting the necessary expenses; but it may be presumed that such sales took place, since a disregard of this provision might have caused dissatisfaction and impaired the legality of the entire proceedings, and because the records show that several tracts of the common land, not in the regular allotments, passed into private hands at about this date. These tracts consisted of 100 a. adjoining the North River and lot No. 5 of 1691 (now Manhattanville), which passed to Peter van Oblienis (see p. 541); 30 a. next to lot No. 1, of 1691, which passed to Lawrence Kortright, and since forming a part of the Samson A. Benson farm (see p. 487), and other parcels adjoining to the farms of Capt. Joh. Benson, Samuel Waldron, and John Kiersen, and which these persons secured. In making this division Peter van Oblienis figures prominently; no one did more to further the business, according to the wishes of the freeholders. Legal advisers held that whereas the Nicolls patentees had at no time during their joint tenancy made any lawful partition among themselves to alter said joint tenancy, the premises, on the decease of the other four patentees, became vested in the survivor, Joost van Oblinus, and at his death in 1706, in Peter, as his eldest son and heir. But nevertheless, it was a trust; not to inure to his peculiar benefit, but, on the contrary, held and to be used for the benefit of the whole body of freeholders who had rights in the land. The Nicolls patent constituted the freeholders and inhabitants a corporation, so far as was requisite to the ownership and enjoyment of their common lands, with the inevitable right of alienation. The patentees named therein received a trust, to be administered for and on behalf of all the freeholders in common. But these patentees, in such capacity, made no grants and gave no deeds. Interpreted by the usage which from the first obtained under the patent, we find the principle constantly recognised and acted upon, that the power to grant lands and give deeds resided in the body of freeholders, except when delegated by them to others. Hence such business was invariably done either in town meeting, or by the magistrates, or other persons chosen for that purpose. The act of 1708, therefore, conferred no new power upon the freeholders in this regard, only so far as to enable a majority who should be residents to act. And Peter van Oblienis, from the first favoring a pro-rata division of the common lands, is found, even after his father's decease, still acting under his former appointment, as one of the "trustees for the said town," in signing deeds. He subscribed, with the other freeholders, all preliminary agreements necessary for making the division of 1712, and admitted as grant ers with himself the heirs of the four other patentees, who also shared with him in the 60 a. of land voted by the freeholders, Mar. 20, 1712, to be laid out before the division should be made, to the only use and behoof of the heirs or assigns of the five original patentees, or to such person or persons as should be adjudged by counsel *proper to sign releases to the rest of the freeholders*. Oblienis' 100 a. being in his possession when Berrien laid out the other lots, leads us to regard it as a purchase; but that he arbitrarily appropriated it, on pretense of an exclusive fee in himself, is not to be supposed. Until the deed to Oblienis be found (for doubtless he had one from the freeholders, as authorised by the act and former usage), we shall hardly know more about the origin of this title. This tract, in the deed from Oblienis to Peter Waldron, referred to p. 541, is described as "Beginning at a stake near a rock, at the land of Margreta Cortright, thence north 37° west, along the said land 171 rods to Hudson's River, then along the said River 73 rods to a stake in the Meadow of Martje Davids aforesaid, thence along the said Meadow to a stake at the head of the Swamp above the said Meadow, thence to the highway or road, and so along the said highway to a certain chestnut tree marked and standing on the northwest side of the road, near the house of Johannes Meyer, and from thence along the land of said Meyer to the place where it at first began; containing by estimation one hundred acres of land." The convent and chapel of the Sacred Heart now occupy the north-east corner of this tract.

Peter van Oblienis, on his private rights (1 *erf* and 24 *morgen*,) was entitled to draw of the common land 81 a. 1 q. 4 r., including the 12 a., allowed him as a full patentee for signing deeds. This he sold to his br. Hendrick, who owned no erf or morgen rights. The latter was living on the farm given him by his fa. "upon the southern end of the Long Hill," (see p. 542,) his house standing at the intersection of 12th Ave. and 176th St., on the tract since Arden's. His 81 a. were laid out in one parcel, next above his farm, taking in Fort Washington heights. This with 6 a. named in the following vote of the town gave Hendrick 130 a. as rated, and which he held unchanged till his d. in 1745.

"At a town meeting, 27th March, 1712; Memorand; That it was then agreed by all the freeholders and inhabitants then met, that *Hendrick Oblenis* shall have laid out to his own use Six Rod, (in consideration of his share of the undivided land now surveyed,) from the southerly corner of his fence southerly, thence in a parallel line along the line of his lands, N. 67° W. to Hudson's River. The said Hendrick to leave a sufficient open road, with a swinging gate, up to the Long Hill; that is to say, from a certain brook where a bridge lies, where the old highway went.

Signed as evidence Cornelis Luyster.
John Lawrence."

The spring of 1712 found the work of the surveys essentially completed. The vacant lands to be disposed of were laid out in four general groups called the *Four Divisions*, in each of which every freeholder so entitled, drew a lot.

First Division embraced nearly all that remained of common land on and adjacent to Harlem plains. It numbered 21 lots, which of necessity lay considerably scattering, as we shall show. The 60 a. given as a consideration for signing deeds, were included in this division, except 6 a.*

* The 60 a. were awarded as follows: 12 to Peter Van Oblienis; 12 to Maria Meyer; 12 to the estate of Capt. Delavall; 6 to Jacques Tourneur; 6 to Woodhull Tourneur; 6 to Johannes Waldron, and 6 to Samuel Waldron. The distribution was thus confined to the sons or heirs of the five original patentees, and in no case extended beyond two representatives of any one patentee. At the same time any of the heirs or assigns of these patentees were "adjudged by counsel proper to sign releases to the rest of the freeholders." Hendrick van Oblienis signed patentee

SECOND DIVISION began above the lots on Jochem Pieters Hills, laid out in 1691, at the line heretofore designated, which ran from Kingsbridge Road, about 50 feet below 162d St., on a course N. 34° W. to Hudson River. Lots 1 to 5 were laid out on this (the west) side of the road, and extended up the same to Hendrick van Oblienis' line, which began at a point midway between 175th and 176th Sts., and ran thence to the Hudson, N. 67° W. Easterly of the road lay lots 6 to 20, beginning at the lower line, continued to Harlem River, and extending up to within a few feet of 194th St., at the highway, being bounded northerly by a line S. 53° E.

THIRD DIVISION beginning where the second ended, lay in two parallel tiers, separated by what was called the *Cut Line*, whose course was then N. 35° E.; and extended up to the farm of Bastiaen Kortright (see p. 297), and the Sherman's Creek meadows. It contained 16 lots, of which Nos. 1 to 13 lay between the highway and the Cut Line, and the remainder between the Cut Line and Harlem River.

FOURTH DIVISION, which also contained 18 lots, lay opposite the third, between the highway and the Hudson, and beginning upon Hendrick van Oblienis' northern line, which ran from a point on the highway about central between 165th and 166th Sts., N. 67° W. to the river, extended up to "the little bridge at John Dyckman's land," where the highway crossed Pieter Tuynier's Run; leaving a small gore of common land between lot 18 and Dyckman's line, which latter ran from the bridge N. N. W. to the "little Sand Bay," on the Hudson.

There was method in the divisions. These lands were to be kept chiefly as woodlands; but 3d Division occupying the slope and commanding heights then called the *Rondevlysberg*, or Round Meadow Hill, since known as Fort George, was planned for a future *dorp*, and indeed was often referred to as "the village." Lying so near to 4th Div., these were often joined in subsequent sales, as some had been in the original drawing. The 2d Div. bore a similar relation to the first, or to the homesteads, to which they were more especially the appendages. The whole planning was obviously the result of much study and wise forethought.

"The several Highways laid out in the new Divisions," were legalized by the following action:

"AT a town meeting held 22d March, 1711–12: It was then agreed by the freeholders of the said town—

1. That a sufficient wagon road be laid out and remain for the use of the owners of the lands laid out between the patent line and the line of Johannes Vermilye's land; the said wagon road to run across the *head* of each lot to the Round Meadow.

2. That a sufficient common wagon road be laid out and remain for the use of all the freeholders, over the lot of land laid out to John Dyckman in the 1st Division, No. 21, from the Queen's High Road, to the usual landing place on Harlem River.

3. That a sufficient common wagon road be and remain from the Queen's Road at Hendrick Oblienis's house, to the landing place on Harlem River over against Crab Island; as laid out in the *General Map* of the late undivided lands.

4. A road sufficient for wagons from the Round Meadow lying near Spuyten Duyvel, as near the middle line as conveniently may be, to the road laid out from the house of Hendrick Oblienis and the Queen's Road, to the landing place against Crab Island.

deeds, as did Barent Waldron, Samson Benson, and Capt. Congreve; Congreve and Benson, with Dyckman, holding parts of the Tourneur lands and rights, but none of the above, shared in the 60 a. Woodhull Tourneur, by heirship, took a share, though he had sold his lands, and then held neither erf nor morgen right, and was not even a resident. He signed deeds and was entitled to 6 a., as a half patentee, but probably sold his claim to Hendrick van Oblienis. See p. 611.

5. Another road for wagons etc., from the north end of the Long Hill, through the land of Hendrick Oblienis, to the Queen's Road.

6 Another road from Upbro's Hook, below the hill, to the land of John Kiersen, thence to the Queen's Road.*

7. A road from the Queen's Road along the fence of Barent Waldron, and along the meadow of Isaac Delamater.

8. A road from the Queen's Road, betwixt the houses of John Meyer and John Waldron, to the top of the hill, to the line of Peter Oblienis's land, and so along said line northward, and along the heads of the lots, to the land laid out to right of Capt. Delavall."

Messrs. Lawrence, Loysier and Illagge made a return, June 20, 1712, of the land due each person upon his *erf* and *morgen* rights, and of which we annex a copy; the apportionment being made upon the following basis, to wit: In 1*st Division*, 3 a. 1 q. 20 r. to each erf or house lot, and 2 q. 14 r. to each morgen; In 2*d Division*, 6 a. per house lot, and 1 a. 3 r. per morgen; In the 3*d Division*, 1 a. 2 q. 10 r. per house lot, and 1 q. 2 r. per morgen; In the 4*th Division*, 2 a. 2 q. 30 r. per house lot, and 1 q. 32 r. per morgen.

Peter Herrien, on June 25, signed certificates of the lands laid out for each person, similar in form to that given p. 599, and of these also, which give the quantities actually drawn, we append a summary. From these the deeds were prepared and executed; and in which the other lands of the grantee were included or not, at his option. These date all the way from 1712 to 1715. We would gladly learn the whereabouts of any of these *patentee deeds;* such as we have seen are engrossed on large sheets of vellum, and usually done by Capt. Congreve, then the town clerk.

The situation of the lots in 1st Division will be better understood by a brief description; as these lots lay in several detached groups, and some of the lots consisted of more than one piece. These lots usually overran by a few rods the quantity called for, owing to surplusage in the tracts divided. Lots 1 to 5 lay in one tract adjacent to the village.

No. 1, containing 24 a., ran from the end of the *Buyten Tuynen*, or Out Gardens, westerly, on the north side of the highway, to the Mill Creek. It was bought from Waldron by Samson Benson, and included in his patentee deed of Apl. 20, 1713.

No. 2, which Benson had drawn, lay next north, and butted easterly on the Kingsbridge Road, opposite the Church Farm.† He set off, probably at this end, to his br. Derick, a plot of 3 a. 1 q. 39 r., which Derick gave back under a later agreement; when Samson conveyed the two lots entire, in all 41 a. 1 q. 23 r., to his br. Joh. Benson, Feb. 19, 1724-5. Johannes sold the tract, Mar. 14, 1732-3, to Peter Bussing, it passing under his will of Feb. 19, 1733-4, proved July 27, 1737, to his son Aaron. In 1753, Aaron buying some strips next the roads, from the town, increased the contents to 45 a. 3 q. 22 r., as per Goerik's survey of May 5, 1787. On May 6, 1787, Bussing's executor sold this tract to Capt. Samson Benson, who near the close of his life had it laid off into several parcels, which by his will dated Apl. 28, 1823, he distributed among his heirs. St. Pauls Chh., (Catholic), stands on the

* TUBBY HOOK, a point of land on the North River side, at 206th St., is here referred to. It took its name from Peter Ubregt, a Brabanter. See p. 508. Ubregt, by a clipt pronunciation, became Upbro, and Ubby, or as the Dutch made it, *'t Ubby*, or Tubby Hook.

† On this corner where the roads met, Capt. Benson built a large tavern early in the present century—the site since within the "Harlem Park"—and which was conducted for some years by Capt. Marriner, who had previously kept the Ferry House (see p. 191), and who gained as great celebrity for the excellent table he set for his guests, as for his whale-boat exploits during the Revolution, which he was never tired of relating. He was an intelligent, well-educated man. See notice of him in *Thompson's Long Island*.

eastern part of said lot No. 1, 1st Div. See *Deduction of the Title of Peter Poillon*, etc., by Mr. Adriance.

No. 3, (23 a. 32 r.), lay above No. 2, extending from Kingsbridge Road westward to the meadows; its southern line running N. 86¼° W., its northern, N. 64 W. It was sold directly by Nagel to Abraham Myer, who in 1720 added 2 a. lying "in the hills," (Mount Morris), for which in 1747, he paid the town 16 shillings, and took a deed. The lot passed to Abm. Myer, Jr., thence to his kinsman Joh. De Witt, Jr., who sold it to Peter Benson, Apl. 9, 1759. See said *Poillon Title*, p. 30.

No. 4, (3 a. 1 q. 29 r.), lay next to No. 3, and was 5 rods broad; its lines parallel, and N. 64° W. It ran "almost to the meadow at the Mill Creek." Zach. Sickels took it in exchange for other land, as per his patentee deed mentioned p. 333, but sold it in 1722 to Abm. Myer, whence we believed it passed to Adolph Benson, owning No. 5, which lay next northerly.

No. 5, (25 a. 1 r.), included "the hills," or Mount Morris. Passing through several hands, to Adolph Benson, (see p. 437), it became a part of the Samson A. Benson farm. This exhausted the common land in this tract, except some 30 a. still reserved by the town, but subsequently sold to Adolph Benson, in 1747, for £50.

No. 6, (16 a. 1 q. 8 r.), embraced a strip of common land stretching along the Harlem patent line and the highway, from the northern end of the Horn's Hook or Waldron farm, (94th St.), up to lot No. 7, (the late McGown place, 102d St.), being bounded easterly by a crooked fence of Capt. John Benson. Samson Benson bought it May 4, 1721 (see p. 485), as an addition to his farm, but it is now mostly within Central Park.

No. 7 included the McGown plot referred to, laid out for 9 a. 3 q. 32 r., and also 2 a. 2 q. 12 r. lying opposite to it, west of the highway, and along the north side of the grant made Abram Delamontanie, in 1691; both pieces being now in Central Park. We have noticed this lot fully on pp. 490, 506, 510, 521. The venerable McGown house made a part of the late Stetson's, or rather Ryan and Radford's Hotel, destroyed by fire Jan. 2, 1551.

No. 8, alloted the heirs of Capt. Thos. Delavall, consisted of three parcels, two of these now in Central Park, the first containing 16 a. 3 q. 28 r., being bounded south by the small part of No. 7, east by the highway, west by the creek or run called the *fonteyn*, and north by the Metje Cornelis, or Nutter farm, to which it was afterward added. The second piece, (1 a. 3 q. 24 r.), lay opposite, across the highway; bounded south and east by the creeks, and north by Metje Cornelis' farm. Later the road to Harlem village was run over this piece; it is now mostly within Harlem Lake. The third and chief part of No. 8, (35 a. 25 r.), lay near the upper end of Harlem Lane, and was of very irregular shape; joining northwesterly to No. 9, of this division, northeasterly to Peter van Oblienis' 100 a. tract before noticed, southeasterly in part by the highway, and westerly upon Jacob De Key's land, or the Harlem patent line, along which it ran southerly, between said line and the Montanye Flat lots, to a point at the old Tourneur farm. The late Capt. John Korlright farm took in part of this parcel, other parts (one owned by Peter van Oblienis), were bought up by Adolph Myer, and included in the Molenaor 84 a. tract. See pp. 529, 530, and *App. I*.

Nos. 9, 10, 11, 12, 13, 14, all taking a course N. 70° E. and butting upon the land of Jacob De Key and the Oblienis 100 a. tract, formed a tier or wedge-like plot which reached to Moertje Davids' Fly. These lots also were subsequently included in the Molenaor 84 a. tract.

No. 15, (35 a. 32 r.) laid out to Maria and Joh. Myer, extended along the west side of Kingsbridge Road from 130th to 140th Sts., being bounded westerly (nearly on the line of 9th Ave.), by the Oblienis 100 a. tract, and lots 5 to 8, of 1691. It fell to Joh. Myer and his son Jacob. See p. 533.

No. 16 being in two pieces, the principal one, containing 9 a. 3 q. 14 r., stretched north from No. 15, between the end of lot 9 of 1691, and the highway, to 145th St., or the line of lot 10 of 1691. Joh. Myer bought this part, in 1722. See pp. 533, 534. A supplementary piece, (2 q. 23 r.), lay opposite, east of the road, at the south point of the triangular tract, since owned by Samuel Bradhurst, and probably not reaching above 145th St.

No. 17, (3 a. 1 q. 20 r.), lay next north, and was sold by Delamontanie to Barent Waldron, by the latter, Aug. 6, 1740, to John R. Myer, and called "4 a. more or less," and by John to Abm. Myer, July 21, 1743. It came to be included in the Bradhurst tract.

No. 18 lying next north, extended up between the highway and Bussing's Point Inlet to 150th St. It passed through the Low family (see *p.* 520), to John Maunsell, from him to Bradhurst.

No. 19 was sold by Congreve, Dec. 26, 1713, to Joh. Waldron, and by him to his son Samuel, Nov. 17, 1748. It passed to John Dykman, thence to John Watkins, (see p. 509), thence to John Maunsell, and from his wid. to Mrs. Beekman.*

No. 20 was sold by John Delamater to Joh. Waldron, in 1729, passed to John Dykman, thence to Lawrence Low, thence to his son John, thence to John Watkins (see pp. 509, 520), thence to John Maunsell. See No. 21.

No. 21, (12 a. 3 q. 7 r.,) making the last lot in 1st Div., extended up, on Kingsbridge Road, to 159th St., to the Kiersen or Jumel Homestead line. It passed to Gerrit Dyckman, to his son John, to Lawrence Low, to his son John, to John Watkins (see pp. 508, 509, 520), to John Maunsell, to his wid., and with No. 20, to Dr. Samuel Watkins.

We do not see an equal necessity for tracing the lots in the other three divisions, many references to which will be found in the foregoing pages. This may be done, usually, without much difficulty; care being taken to avoid the confusion which may arise in some cases from the re-plotting and re-numbering. This applies particularly to the lands purchased by Leonard Parkinson, who came to own (with the Roger Morris, or Jumel Homestead, and the 57 a. tract opposite), the lots 1 to 5, 2d Div., on the west of the highway, and on the east side, lots 8 to 11, inclusive, less the Wear portion of No. 8. He caused all these lands to be mapped by Chas. Loss, and divided up into 15 parcels, by new numbers, and which ignored all the original dividing lines. The Jumel Homestead alone remained unchanged, and this was called No. 8. From the 57 a. tract opposite, 48 a. 20 r. were set off as No. 1. This he sold Mar. 9, 1810, to Ebenezer Burrill. Above it, 37 a. 2 q. were laid off as No. 2, and sold, the same day, to R. C. Smith; later Dickey's. "Fanwood," the residence of the late Col. Monroe, is on this lot No. 2, as also the Deaf and Dumb Institution, the latter building being intersected by the line which before parted the 2d Div. from the Div. of

* CHARLES CONGREVE, Gent., arrived at N. Y., May 3, 1702, in the suit of Gov. Cornbury; the next year, as lieut., commanded a force sent to Albany, to guard the frontiers; in 1704, by Cornbury's order, reported to the Lords of Trade, upon the military resources of the province, and to the Venerable Society, upon the state of religion, and in 1706, being in England helped Oldmixon to facts for his *British Empire in America.* Capt. Congreve's zeal as a Churchman, with other circumstances, induces the belief that his clerkship at H. was not merely secular, but was designed for introducing the English liturgy. See p. 459. Here he acquired property, as noticed pp. 545, 563. His lands in the 4 Divisions were drawn on a 6 *morgen* 1 *rof* right, upon his lot on Jochem Pieters Flat, and its adjoining house-lot; except 16 a. "of first and second draft," gotten of Samuel Waldron. His lot in 2d Div. he sold, with his farm on Van Keulen's Hook, to John Van Horn, of N. Y., merchant; those in 1st, 3d, and 4th Div. to Joh. Waldron. Congreve was a frequent petitioner to the government for land, between 1702 and 1723, and received several grants. In 1736 he commanded at Oswego; in 1740, with his son-in-law, John Lindesay, went to Cherry Valley, but left on the breaking out of the French War in 1744; Mr. Lindesay, in whose favor Congreve had resigned his lieutenancy in the Independent Fusileers, going to take command at Oswego. And here we lose sight of Capt. Congreve. See *N. Y. Col. Hist.* vi. 707, note.

1691. Next came Nos. 3, 4, together 67 a. 2 q., sold the same date to John R. Murray. And next above this lay lot 5, (39 a. 1 q.), reaching to Arden's line, and sold the same day to Stephen Jumel, together with his lots 7, 9, 10, 11, 12, 13, 14, 15, which embraced the old lots 6 to 11, with the exception of Wear's part of No. 8; and also excepting parts of the old lots 10, 11, next the Kingsbridge Road, and a gore from No. 9, which made up his lot No. 6. This he sold on the same date to Gerardus Post, who conveyed it to Jumel, May 3, 1814. On Apl. 28, 1810, Parkinson also sold Jumel the Col. Morris Homestead. Thus Jumel came to own 39 a. west of Kingsbridge Road, (being the old lot 5, and most of 4), and 131 a. east of said road, the last stretching from 159th St. to midway of 174th and 175th Sts., excepting where separated by the 8 a. owned by Wear.*

As little common land remained within the patent lines after the division of 1712, except the tracts already named in connection with the farms to which they were finally attached, we will not extend these notes. It only remains to give the lists of the lands in the Four Divisions, *as awarded* upon the *erf* or house lot, and *morgen rights*; and an alphabetical "Summary," which shows the actual contents of the lots *as laid out*; the latter varying from the former in some cases, for reasons which are also noted.

FIRST DIVISION; 1712.

Nos.		H. L.	M. R.	Land Due.		
				A.	Q.	R.
1	John Waldron	1	22	16	1	8
2	Samson Benson	2	18	17	1	12
3	John Nagel	2	28	23	0	32
4	John Kiersen	1	0	3	1	20
5	Metje Cornelis	2	31	24	3	34
6	Barent Waldron	1	22	16	1	8
7	Samuel Waldron	3	16½	19	3	11
8	Thomas Delavall	2	60	42	0	0
9	John Van Oblienis	1	0	3	1	20
10	Isaac Delamater	1	6	6	3	24
11	Arent Bussing	1	21	15	2	34
12	John Benson	1	16	12	3	4
13	Jacques Tourneur	1	9	8	2	26
14	Marcus Tiebaut	½	3	3	1	32
15	Maria Meyer	2	28	23	0	32
16	Zacharias Sickels	1	12	10	1	28
17	Abraham Delamontanie	1	0	3	1	20
18	Lourens Jansen	1	11	9	3	14
19	Charles Congreve	1	6	6	3	24
20	Aeltie Vermilye	1	14	4	1	1
21	John Dyckman	1	16	12	3	4

* GEORGE WEAR, the sturdy blacksmith, we may thank him for holding on to this little 6 acre lot (the lower part of No. 8, 2d Div.), which he bought Nov. 7, 1809, from Ithamar Helly; although called 6¼ a., and all its boundaries reversed, with Benson, from whose lot it was taken, called *Bussing!* Because its transfer being clear to Helly through Wm. Molenaor and others, back to Capt. Joh. Benson, who drew it in 1712, it becomes an invaluable landmark in fixing the starting line of the 2d Division. Its lower line began at Kingsbridge Road, in the centre of 165th St., and nearly touched 164th St. at the bluff on Harlem River. But improvements going on must soon obliterate these old lines, save upon the maps.

Second Division.

No.		H. L.	M. R.	Land Due. A.	Q.	R.
1	Meije Cornelis............	2	31	43	2	13
2	Samuel Waldron..............	4	16½	40	3	9
3	John Kiersen.................	1	0	6	0	0
4	Lourens Jansen...............	1	11	17	0	33
5	Barent Waldron....	1	21	28	1	26
6	Aaltie Vermilye...............	1	1½	7	2	4
7	Charles Congreve.............	1	6	12	0	15
8	John Benson..................	1	16	22	1	8
9	John Nagel....................	2	28	40	2	4
10	Maria Meyer..................	2	28	40	2	4
11	John Van Oblienis............	1	0	6	0	0
12	Zacharias Sickels.............	1	12	18	0	36
13	John Waldron.................	1	22	28	1	26
14	Jacques Tourneur............	1	9	15	0	27
15	Marcus Tiebaut....	½	3	6	0	9
16	Thomas Delavall..............	2	60	73	0	20
17	John Dyckman................	1	16	22	1	8
18	Samson Benson...............	2	18	30	1	14
19	Isaac Delamater..............	1	6	12	0	18
20	Arent Bussing................	1	21	27	1	23

Third Division.

No.		H. L.	M. R.	Land Due. A.	Q.	R.
1	John Waldron..................	1	22	7	1	14
2	Jacques Tourneur..............	1	9	3	3	28
3	Aaltie Vermilye...............	1	1½	1	3	33
4	Samson Benson................	2	18	7	3	16
5	Lourens Janson................	1	11	4	1	32
6	Samuel Waldron...............	4	16½	10	2	13
7	Barent Waldron................	1	22	7	1	14
8	John Kiersen..................	2	12	6	1	4
9	Marcus Tiebaut	1½	3	3	0	21
10	John Dyckman.................	1	16	5	3	2
11	Charles Congreve........... .	1	6	3	0	22
12	John Nagel.....................	2	28	10	1	36
13	Arent Bussing.................	1	21	7	0	12
14	Isaac Delamater...............	1	6	3	0	22
15	Thomas Delavall..............	2	60	18	3	20
16	Maria Meyer...................	2	28	10	1	36
17	Meije Cornelis.................	2	31	11	1	2
18	John Benson...................	1	16	5	3	2

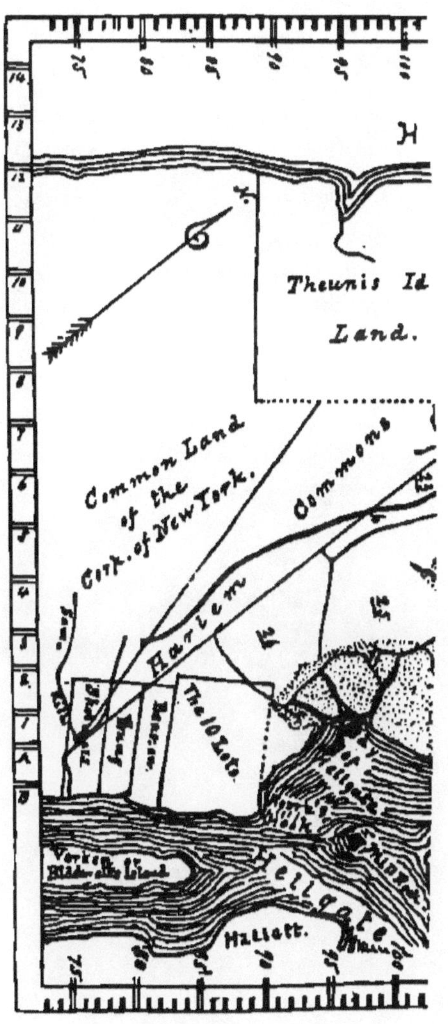
Theunis Id
Land.
Common Land
of the
City of New York.
Commons
Harlem
The 10 Lots
Hellgate
Hallett.

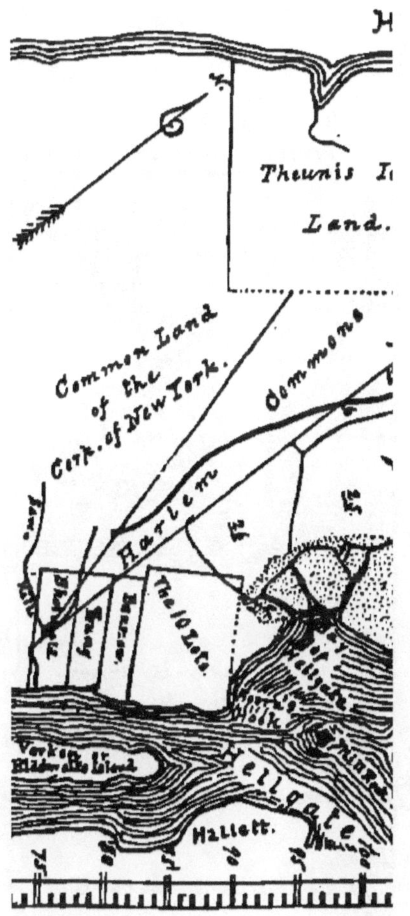

Theunis
Land.
Common Land
of the
Corp. of New York.
Commons
Harlem
The 10 Lots
Hellgate
Hallett.

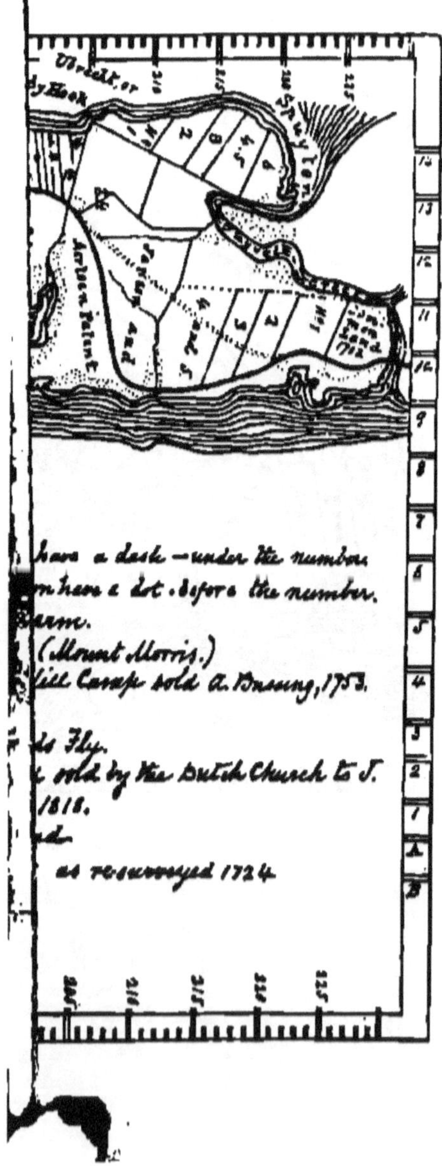

have a dash — under the number
n have a dot . before the number.
arm.
(Mount Morris.)
as resurveyed 1724

KEY TO TITLES.

N.B. Different designations are sometimes applied to the same tract. Consult also the Index, for the required parties, and under the head of *Names*.

INDEX.

—•••—

, For *Subjects*, see the General Contents. This Index is confined to *Names* chiefly, but excludes the historic names in the opening chapters, and, generally, those of the colonial governors, authors quoted, etc. Many towns and places referred to are also omitted. These excepted, no name is designedly left out; but such as are given in italics occurring very often, it is thought best to omit some of the references, but not to the exclusion of any pointing to their lands, unless found in the lists indexed under the word Names: hence these lists should be consulted for the proper names here italicized. One reference to each Genealogy (pp. [illegible] to 580) has been deemed sufficient, including all repetitions of these names occurring interchangeably; all others being duly indexed.

When a star follows a reference, consult the next page or two; when two stars, examine onward to the next reference.

Notice, that many references are abridged, thus: 105, 7, 10, for 105, 107, 110.

www.ingramcontent.com/pod-product-compliance
Lightning Source LLC
Chambersburg PA
CBHW021222300426
44111CB00007B/394

* 9 7 8 3 7 4 2 8 1 8 2 1 8 *